COMMERCIAL REPORTS

AREA STUDIES SERIES

EDITORIAL DIRECTOR   Professor J J O'Meara
RESEARCH UNIT DIRECTOR   T F Turley
ASSISTANT DIRECTOR   S Cashman

CHIEF EDITORIAL ADVISERS

P Ford
Professor Emeritus, Southampton University
Mrs G Ford

SPECIAL EDITORIAL CONSULTANT FOR
THE UNITED STATES PAPERS

H C Allen
Commonwealth Fund Professor of American History, University College, London
Director of the London University Institute of United States Studies

RESEARCH EDITORS
Johann A Norstedt
Marilyn Evers Norstedt

This Series is published with the active co-operation of
SOUTHAMPTON UNIVERSITY

IRISH UNIVERSITY PRESS AREA STUDIES SERIES

BRITISH PARLIAMENTARY PAPERS

UNITED STATES OF AMERICA

32

Embassy and consular
commercial reports
1887-88

IRISH UNIVERSITY PRESS
Shannon Ireland

PUBLISHER'S NOTE

The documents in this series are selected from the nineteenth century British House of Commons *sessional and command papers*. All of the original papers relating to the United States of America are included with the exception of two kinds of very brief and unimportant papers. Omitted are (1) random statistical trade returns which are included in the larger and complete yearly trade figures and (2) returns relating to postal services, which are irregularly presented, of tangential USA relevance, and easily available in other sources.

The original documents have been reproduced by photo-lithography and are unabridged even to the extent of retaining the first printers' imprints. Imperfections in the original printing are sometimes unavoidably reproduced.

Many papers in this reprint are enlargements from the original octavo format.

© 1971 Irish University Press Shannon Ireland
Microfilm, microfiche and other forms of micro-publishing
© *Irish University Microforms Shannon Ireland*

ISBN 0 7165 1532 6

Printed and published by
Irish University Press Shannon Ireland
DUBLIN   CORK   BELFAST   LONDON   NEW YORK
T M MacGlinchey *Publisher*   Robert Hogg *Printer*

Contents

IUP Page Number

For ease of reference IUP editors have assigned a continuous pagination which appears on the top outer margin of each page.

Commercial Reports

Commercial report no. 7 on Washington 1887 [in C.4998] LXXXI	11
Commercial report no. 10 on accession of the United States to the International Union for the Protection of Industrial Property 1887 [C.5044] LXXXI	19
Commercial report no. 11 on accession of the United States to the International Union for the Protection of Industrial Property 1887 [C.5046] LXXXI	23
F.O. annual series: report no. 20 on Newport News, 1885 1887 [in C.4923] LXXXVI	29
F.O. annual series no. 129: report no. 88 on Charleston, 1886 1887 [C.4923–11] LXXXVI	37
F.O. annual series no. 133: report no. 92 on New Orleans, 1886 1887 [C.4923–15] LXXXVI	47
F.O. annual series no. 135: report no. 94 on Baltimore, 1886 1887 [C.4923–17] LXXXVI	67
F.O. annual series no. 147: report no. 104 on Galveston, 1886 1887 [C.4923–27] LXXXVI	73
F.O. annual series no. 154: report no. 110 on Boston, 1886 1887 [C.4923–33] LXXXVI	85
F.O. annual series no. 185: report no. 136 on Savannah, 1886 1887 [C.4923–59] LXXXVI	93
F.O. annual series no. 186: report no. 137 on Wilmington, 1886 1887 [C.4923–60] LXXXVI	99
F.O. annual series no. 189: report no. 140 on Chicago, 1886 1887 [C.4923–63] LXXXVI	123
F.O. annual series no. 218: report no. 169 on Tennessee, 1886 1887 [C.4923–92] LXXXVI	155
F.O. annual series no. 227: report no. 177 on Philadelphia, 1885–86 1887 [C.4923–100] LXXXVI	163
F.O. annual series no. 233: report no. 182 on New York, 1886 1887 [C.4923–105] LXXXVI	191
F.O. annual series no. 237: report no. 186 on San Francisco, 1886 1887 [C.4923–109] LXXXVI	215
F.O. annual series no. 273: report no. 215 on Newport News, 1886 1887 [C.4923–138] LXXXVI	259
F.O. annual series no. 302: report no. 235 on the finances of the United States 1888 [C.5252–12] CIII	267
F.O. annual series no. 344: report no. 262 on Baltimore, 1887 1888 [C.5252–39] CIII	303
F.O. annual series no. 350: report no. 266 on Texas, 1887 1888 [C.5252–43] CIII	313

Continued

Contents

Continued

IUP Page Number

F.O. annual series no. 354: report no. 270 on New Orleans, Pensacola, Mobile, 1887
1888 [C.5252–47] CIII 321

F.O. annual series no. 375: report no. 289 on the finances of the United States, 1887
1888 [C.5252–66] CIII 349

F.O. annual series no. 383: report no. 296 on Charleston, 1887
1888 [C.5252–73] CIII 405

F.O. annual series no. 398: report no. 310 on the agriculture of Baltimore district
1888 [C.5252–87] CIII 415

F.O. annual series no. 399: report no. 311 on Savannah
1888 [C.5252–88] CIII 431

F.O. annual series no. 400: report no. 312 on Boston, 1887
1888 [C.5252–89] CIII 439

F.O. annual series no. 401: report no. 313 on San Francisco, 1887
1888 [C.5252–90] CIII 447

F.O. annual series no. 419: report no. 330 on Chicago, 1887
1888 [C.5252–107] CIII 455

F.O. annual series no. 432: report no. 340 on the agriculture of North Carolina, 1887
1888 [C.5252–117] CIII 487

F.O. annual series no. 448: report no. 356 on the agriculture of California, 1887
1888 [C.5252–133] CIII 495

F.O. annual series no. 456: report no. 362 on the agriculture of Colorado, 1887
1888 [C.5252–139] CIII 503

F.O. annual series no. 464: report no. 370 on New York, 1887
1888 [C.5252–147] CIII 515

F.O. annual series no. 469: report no. 375 on San Francisco, 1887
1888 [C.5252–152] CIII 541

F.O. annual series no. 489: report no. 392 on San Francisco, 1887
1888 [C.5252–169] CIII 573

F.O. annual series no. 497: report no. 398 on the agriculture of Massachusetts
1888 [C.5252–175] CIII 589

F.O. annual series no. 531: report no. 427 on the agriculture of South Carolina
1888 [C.5252–204] CIII 597

F.O. annual series no. 538: report no. 431 on the agriculture of New York, New Jersey, Connecticut, Rhode Island, Delaware
1888 [C.5252–208] CIII 605

As most commercial reports are extracted from larger papers, the reader should note that a particular report may lack a proper title page.

41

No. 9.

UNITED STATES.

WASHINGTON.

Sir Lionel West to the Marquis of Salisbury.

My Lord,   Washington, March 9, 1887.

WITH reference to the Foreign Office despatch, dated September 27 last, I have the honour to enclose a report which has been drawn up by Mr. Edwardes on the laws of the United States regulating the ownership in minerals and mining rents and royalties, which he has compiled with great care from reports received from Her Majesty's Consuls in this country.

I have, &c.
(Signed)   L. S. SACKVILLE WEST.

REPORT ON THE LAWS IN THE UNITED STATES REGULATING THE OWNERSHIP IN MINERALS AND MINING RENTS AND ROYALTIES.

The right of private ownership in minerals extracted from the soil is recognised in all the States and territories of the United States. All such minerals belong to the owner of the land.

All lands which have not been sold or disposed of to private individuals or corporations, or expressly ceded to any particular State, are held by the United States, but when once the land has been acquired in accordance with the provisions of the law, all rights pass without reserve to the grantee, and the right of the owner to minerals found thereon is absolute. Whenever any special donation of land by the Federal Government to a State is made, it is stipulated that, should any portion of such land be found to be mineral bearing, other lands of an agricultural nature should be selected by the State in lieu thereof.

The mining laws, as revised in 1872, provide that all valuable mineral deposits in lands belonging to the United States, both surveyed and unsurveyed, are declared to be free and open to exploration and purchase by citizens of the United States, and those who have declared their intention to become such, under regulations prescribed by law, and according to the local customs or rules of miners in the several mining districts, so far as are applicable and not inconsistent with the laws of the United States.

Mineral lands cannot be taken up for agricultural purposes, but if in course of time minerals should be found, unless fraud or misrepresentation be proved, the courts have, as a rule, held that the purchaser had acquired absolute title, and that the Government had parted with all its interest.

As regards the restriction against aliens, no mining claim can be located except by a United States citizen, or a person who has declared his intention of becoming so, but it has been held that where an alien and a citizen make a joint location of a mining claim, the deed to the two locators conveys perfect patent. Proof of citizenship may consist, in the case of an individual, of his own affidavit thereof; in the case of an association of persons unincorporated, of the affidavit of their authorised agent, made on his own knowledge, or upon information and belief; and in the case of a corporation organised under the laws of the United States, or of any State or territory thereof, by the filing of a certified copy of their charter or certificate of incorporation.

With regard to the customs or rules of miners in the several mining districts, the law above referred to directs that the miners of each mining district in the United States may make regulations not in conflict with the laws of the United States, or with the laws of the State or territory in which the district is situated, governing the location, manner of recording, amount of work necessary to hold possession of a mining claim subject to the following requirements. The location must be distinctly marked on the ground, so that its boundaries can be readily traced. All records of mining claims hereafter made shall contain the name or names of the locators, the date of the location, and such a description of the claim or claims located by reference to some natural object or permanent monument as will identify the claim. On each claim located after May 10, 1872, and until a patent has been issued therefore, not less than 100 dol. worth of labour shall be performed or improvements made during each year. On all claims located prior to that date 10 dol. worth of labour shall be performed or improvements made by June 10, 1874, and each year thereafter for each 100 feet in length along the vein until a patent has been issued therefore; but where such claims are held in common, such expenditure may be made upon any one claim, and upon a failure to comply with these conditions the claim or mine upon which such failure occurred shall be open to re-location in the same manner as if no location of the same had ever been made, provided that the original locators, their heirs, assigns, or legal representatives have not resumed work upon the claim after failure and before such location. Upon the failure of any one of the several co-owners to contribute his proportion of the expenditures required hereby, the co-owners who have performed the labour or made the improvements may, at the expiration of the year, give such delinquent co-owner personal notice in writing, or notice by publication in the newspaper published nearest the claim, for at least once a week for 90 days, and if at the expiration of 90 days after such notice such delinquent should fail or refuse to contribute his proportion of the expenditure required by law, his interest in the claim shall become the property of his co-owners who have made the required expenditures.

Taxation on mineral lands like that on other property is levied on their valuation, in accordance with the general appraisement laws; and corporations chartered for the purpose of working mines are taxed on the nominal value of shares issued. In a few States certain mines in process of development are exempt from taxation for a term varying from five to 10 years under certain conditions.

The only mines in the United States which are the property of the State Government are some salt mines in the State of New York. Any other salt mines which have been or may be discovered are the property of the owner of the land.

By one of the statutes of the State of New York, an exception to the above general law is made. By it the following mines are the property of the State in its right of sovereignty.

Gold and Silver Mines.

All mines of other metals upon lands owned by persons not citizens of the United States.

All mines of other metals upon lands owned by a citizen of the United States, the ore of which upon an average contains less than two equal third parts in value of copper, tin, iron, and lead, or any of those metals.

All mines, minerals, and fossils upon any lands belonging to the State, subject to certain provisions to encourage the discovery thereof.

The statute runs as follows:—

"The following mines are and shall be the property of the people of this State in their right of sovereignty.

"1. All mines of gold and silver discovered, or hereafter to be discovered, within this State.

"2. All mines of other metals discovered, or hereafter to be discovered, upon any lands owned by persons not being citizens of any of the United States.

"3. All mines of other metals discovered, or hereafter to be discovered, upon lands owned by a citizen of any of the United States, the ore of which upon an average shall contain less than two equal third parts in value of copper, tin, iron, and lead, or any of those metals.

"All mines and all minerals and fossils discovered, or hereafter to be discovered, upon any lands belonging to the people of this State are and shall be the property of the people, subject to the provisions hereinafter made to encourage the discovery thereof.

"All mines of whatever description other than mines of gold and silver discovered, or hereafter to be discovered, upon any lands owned by a citizen of any of the United States, the ore of which upon an average shall contain two equal third parts or more in value of copper, tin, iron, and lead, or any of those metals, shall belong to the owner of such land.

"Every person who shall make a discovery of any mine of gold and silver within this State, and the executors, administrators, or assigns of such person, shall be exempted from paying to the people of this State any part of the ore, produce, or profit of such mine for the term of 21 years, to be computed from the time of giving notice of such discovery in the manner hereinafter directed.

"No person discovering a mine of gold or silver within this State shall work the same until he give notice thereof by information in writing to the Secretary of this State, describing particularly therein the nature and situation of the mine; such notice shall be registered in a book to be kept by the Secretary for that purpose. After the expiration of the term above specified, the discoverer of the mine, or his representatives, shall be preferred in any contract for the working of such mines made with the Legislature, or under its authority. Nothing contained in this title shall affect any grants heretofore made by the Legislature to persons having discovered mines, nor be construed to give any person a right to enter on or break up the lands of any other person, or of the people of this State, or to work any mine in such lands, unless the consent in writing of the owner thereof, or of the Commissioners of the Land Office, when the lands belong to the people of this State, shall be previously obtained.

"In all cases in which a person or persons shall have discovered a mine or mines, and become entitled to work the same, pursuant to Title II., chap. 9, of the revised statutes, and such person or persons shall form a corporation pursuant to chapter 40 of the laws of 1848, and the several acts subsequent thereto and amendatory thereof, if the consent in writing to enter upon and break up the lands of any person in or

Title XI., chapter 9, Part I. of the revised statutes of New York of the interest of the State in mines.

upon whose lands the said mine or mines are found, shall be refused, or cannot be obtained by agreement or by reason of the infancy, or the absence of such person from the State, or other legal disability of the owners of said lands, the corporation so formed may enter upon and break up the lands of such person for the purpose of working such mine or mines in the manner hereafter provided, and the right and easement so to do shall be deemed granted for public use, and for the public purpose of obtaining minerals reserved to the State, and the said right and easement are hereby granted to the corporation so formed, on their filing, with the Commissioners of the Land Office, a full description of the location of such lands, and obtaining a grant thereof from the said Commissioners, who are hereby authorised to make such grant and file the terms thereof.

"The said company entitled to work such mines may file a petition in the Supreme Court of the State, setting forth the facts upon which they claim such right, and the reasons which prevent them entering upon the land necessary for their mining operations, and upon such petition the court may appoint three disinterested persons as Commissioners to examine into the matter, ascertain and fix the damages aforesaid, and report to the court. Notice of the filing of such petition shall be published in one of the papers printed in the county, or in each of the counties where the mine or mines are situated, and in the State paper, and a copy of such notice shall be served personally upon the owners of the land, or, if they are infants, upon the guardians, or, if lunatics or under any other legal disability, on the committee having charge of them and their property. And the publication of such notice in the State paper shall be deemed a sufficient notice to such owners as are residents in other States or in other countries, or are temporarily absent from the State, provided that when the actual residence of such absentees is known, or can be ascertained, a copy of such notice and petition shall be sent to them by mail. All the parties interested shall be entitled to hearing before such Commissioners, at such time or times as said Commissioners shall appoint. The report of the Commissioners shall state :—

" 1. The existence of the mine or mines proposed to be worked.

" 2. The names of the parties owning the land in which the mine or mines are situated, and the owners of the adjacent lands as far as they are affected by the application, and the nature and the value of their interest in the same, individually. A map of such lands for actual survey by meter and bounds shall accompany the report.

" 3. An estimate of the damages to such owners from the contemplated use and occupation of their lands.

" 4. Such other information as the court may direct.

"The report of the Commissioners shall be made within a reasonable time to be fixed by the court. An order shall be made in the discretion of the court, either denying the petition or granting it, and determining the quantity of land necessary for working the mine or mines, the damages to property by taking possession thereof, and the annual rent or the compensation to be paid to the owner, lessee, or occupant thereof, so long as the use and occupation shall continue, and, thereupon, the company in whose favour the order shall be made upon payment of the damages, and upon entering into an agreement to be approved by the court, to pay the annual rent or the compensation and damages thus determined, shall have the right to enter upon and occupy and use the land set apart by such order, so long as they, or their assignees, shall work the said mine or mines, and shall pay the said annual rent or compensation.

"If the parties owning the lands are infants, or otherwise incompetent to act, the court shall appoint guardians to take care of their interests, and shall direct how any damages assessed, or compensation or rents to become due, shall be paid and invested for their interest."

The foregoing statute is practically a dead letter, as no such mines as those referred to therein exist in the State, and it is doubtful whether, should an occasion occur to put it into force, the Federal Courts would uphold it.

No royalties are paid in any State or territory, either to the Federal Government or to the State Government.

The question of royalties on mine rents is entirely a matter of private contract between the miner and the landlord, and the terms of this arrangement are in no ways controlled by legislation, except that the general law provides that the lease is for more than one year; it must be in writing, and should be recorded.

The conditions of such a lease usually require a certain amount of development work, and the payment to the owner of the mine of a certain percentage on the value of the minerals extracted. The amount of this royalty varies according to the value of the minerals which the mine promises to yield—20 to 25 per cent. being the average amount.

The following is an ordinary form of lease, though special arrangements are often entered into with regard to sinking shafts, &c. The payment of royalties on ore extracted in sinking shafts is often withheld:—

"This indenture made this   between   of   lessor, and   of   lessee or tenant, witnesseth that the said lessor, for and in consideration of the royalties, covenants, and agreements hereinafter reserved, and by the said lessee to be paid, kept, and performed, hath granted, demised, and let, and by these presents doth grant, demise, and let unto the said lessee all the following described mine and mining property, situate in   mining district, county of   , State of   , to wit, the   together with the appurtenances to have and to hold unto the said lessee for the term of   from date hereof, expiring at noon on the day of   , unless sooner forfeited or determined through the violation of any covenant hereinafter against the said tenant reserved.

"And in consideration of such demise, the said lessee doth covenant and agree with said lessor as follows, to wit:

"To enter upon the said mine or premises and work the same mine fashion, in manner necessary to good and economical mining, so as to take out the greatest amount of ore possible, with due regard to the development and preservation of the same as a workable mine, and to the especial covenants hereinafter reserved.

"To work and mine said premises as aforesaid steadily and continuously from the date of this lease; and that any failure to work said premises, with at least two persons employed under ground for the total of 10 days, may be considered a violation of this covenant. To well and sufficiently timber said mine at any points where proper in accordance with good mining, and to repair all old timbering whenever it may become necessary.

"To allow said lessor and his agents from time to time to enter upon and into all parts of said mine for purposes of inspection.

"To not assign this lease or interest hereinafter, and to not sublet the said premises, or any part thereof, without the written assent of said lessor, and to not allow any person not in privity with the parties thereto to take or hold possession of said premises, or any part thereof, under any pretence whatever. To occupy and hold all cross or parallel lodes, spurs, or mineral deposits of any kind which may be discovered by the said lessee, or any person under him, in any manner within 75 feet of the centre line of said lode, as the property of said lessor, with privilege to said lessor of working the same as parcel of said demised premises.

"To keep at all times the drifts, shafts, tunnels, and other workings thoroughly drained and clear of loose rock and rubbish, unless prevented by extraordinary mining casualty.

"To do no underhand stopping, and to make all shafts seven feet long by four feet wide in the clear, and all drifts seven feet high by four feet wide in the clear.

"To deliver to said lessor, as royalty,   per cent. of all ore to be extracted from said premises of like assay to that retained by said lessee delivered at   as soon as mined, without deduction or charge whatever, except lessor's proportion of packing (provided always that no royalty shall be required upon ore extracted in sinking shafts).

"To deliver to said lessor said premises, with the appurtenances and all improvements in good order and condition, with all drifts, shafts, tunnels, and other passages thoroughly clear of loose rock and rubbish and drained, and the mine ready for immediate continued working (accidents not arising from negligence alone excusing), without demand or other notice on the said   at noon, or at any time previous upon demand for forfeiture.

"And, finally, that upon violation of any covenant or covenants hereinbefore reserved, the term of this lease shall, at the option of said lessor, expire, and the same and said premises, with the appurtenances, shall become forfeit to said lessor, and said lessor or his agent may thereupon, after demand of possession in writing, enter upon said premises, and dispossess all persons occupying the same, with or without force, and with or without process of law; or at the option of said lessor the said tenant, and all persons found in occupation, may be proceeded against as guilty of unlawful detainer.

"Each and every clause and covenant of this indenture shall extend to the heirs, executors, administrators, and lawful assigns of all parties thereto.

"In witness whereof, the said parties have hereunto set their hands and seals.   "(Signed)   ————————
              ————————"

In the State of South Carolina, however, there is a royalty collected by the agricultural bureau of the State, authorised by the State law, from the companies who mine or dredge phosphate rock in the navigable streams of the State. The present royalty is 1 dol. per ton on the crude phosphate rock, or 25 per cent. on the market value of the same.

This enactment runs as follows:—

"An Act to regulate the royalty on phosphate rocks and phosphatic deposits in the navigable streams in the State of South Carolina."

Section 1. Be it enacted by the Senate and House of Representatives of the State of South Carolina, now met and sitting in general assembly, and by authority of the same, that on and after the passage of this Act the royalty payable to the State on all phosphate rocks and phosphate deposits, dug or mined from the navigable streams of this State by any person, company, or corporation by virtue of any license, law, or charter, or other authority from this State, shall be estimated only upon the crude rock, and not upon rock after it has been steamed or dried.

An Act securing certain privileges to the Marine and River Phosphate

Mining and Manufacturing Company of South Carolina upon certain conditions.

Section 4. Nothing in this Act contained shall prevent the State from regulating the price of royalty to be paid by the said company on such terms as may be prescribed by Act of the General Assembly from time to time; provided that a less royalty than 1 dol. per ton upon the crude rock shall not be charged, nor a greater royalty than 25 per cent. of the market value of said crude phosphate rock.

COMMERCIAL. No. 10 (1887).
(UNITED STATES.)

ACCESSION OF THE UNITED STATES

TO THE

INTERNATIONAL UNION

FOR THE

PROTECTION OF INDUSTRIAL PROPERTY.

Presented to both Houses of Parliament by Command of Her Majesty.
May 1887.

PRINTED FOR HER MAJESTY'S STATIONERY OFFICE
BY HARRISON AND SONS, ST. MARTIN'S LANE,
PRINTERS IN ORDINARY TO HER MAJESTY.

And to be purchased, either directly or through any Bookseller, from
EYRE AND SPOTTISWOODE, EAST HARDING STREET, FLEET STREET, E.C., AND
32, ABINGDON STREET, WESTMINSTER, S.W.; OR
ADAM AND CHARLES BLACK, 6, NORTH BRIDGE, EDINBURGH; OR
HODGES, FIGGIS, AND CO., 104, GRAFTON STREET, DUBLIN.

[C.—5044.] *Price ½d.*

Accession of the United States to the International Union for the Protection of Industrial Property.

No. 1.

M. Vernet to the Marquis of Salisbury.—(Received April 20.)

My Lord,   25, Old Broad Street, April 19, 1887.

I HAVE the honour to hand your Lordship a Circular note from my Government with respect to the entry of the United States of America into the International Union for the Protection of Patents.

I have, &c.
(Signed)   H. VERNET,
Agent and Consul-General for Switzerland.

Inclosure in No. 1.

The President of the Swiss Confederation to the Marquis of Salisbury.

Excellence,   Berne, le 11 Avril, 1887.

NOUS avons l'honneur d'informer votre Excellence que le Sénat des États-Unis a ratifié la Convention du 20 Mars, 1883, pour la Protection de la Propriété Industrielle, et le Protocole adopté le 11 Mai, 1886, par la Conférence de Rome, et que le Gouvernement de ce pays a notifié à la Légation Suisse de Washington son intention d'accéder à l'Union pour la Protection de la Propriété Industrielle.

La date d'accession est fixée au 18 Mars, 1887, date de la notification adressée par le Gouvernement des États-Unis à la Légation Suisse. En ce qui concerne leur participation aux frais du Bureau International, les États-Unis sont rangés dans la première classe.

Nous croyons devoir attirer l'attention de votre Excellence sur la mention insérée au procès-verbal de la séance du 12 Mars, 1883, de la seconde Conférence de Paris (procès-verbaux, p. 37), et d'après laquelle le Gouvernement Fédéral Suisse est autorisé à accepter l'accession ultérieure des États-Unis sous la réserve formulée en ces termes au quatrième paragraphe du projet du Protocole de Clôture de 1880 :—

"Le Plénipotentiaire des États-Unis d'Amérique ayant déclaré qu'aux termes de la Constitution Fédérale le droit de légiférer en ce qui concerne les marques de fabrique ou de commerce est, dans une certaine mesure, réservé à chacun des États de l'Union Américaine, il est convenu que les dispositions de la Convention ne seront applicables que dans les limites des pouvoirs constitutionnels des Hautes Parties Contractantes."

En priant votre Excellence de vouloir bien prendre note de ce qui précède, nous saisissons, &c.

Au nom du Conseil Fédéral Suisse :
Le Président de la Confédération,
(Signé)   DROZ.
Le Chancelier de la Confédération,
(Signé)   RINGIER.

(Translation.)

Excellency,   Berne, April 11, 1887.

WE have the honour of informing your Excellency that the Senate of the United States has ratified the Convention of the 20th March, 1883, for the protection of industrial property, as well as the Protocol adopted the 11th May, 1886, by the Conference of Rome, and that the Government of the United States has notified to the Swiss Legation at Washington its intention of acceding to the Union for the Protection of Industrial Property.

The accession dates from the 18th March, 1887, the date of the notification addressed by the United States' Government to the Swiss Legation, and the United States will rank in the first class as far as regards their participation in the expenses of the International Office.

We think it right to draw your Excellency's attention to the condition inserted in the record of the sitting of the 12th March, 1883, of the second Conference of Paris (Records, p. 37), by which the Swiss Federal Government was authorized to accept the ulterior adhesion of the United States under the reserve drawn up in the following terms in the fourth paragraph of the draft of the final Protocol of 1880:—

"The Plenipotentiary of the United States of America having declared that, according to the terms of the Federal Constitution the right of legislating respecting manufacturing or commercial marks, is, to a certain degree, reserved to each of the States of the American Union, it is agreed that the stipulations of the Convention shall only be applicable within the limits of the constitutional powers of the High Contracting Parties."

In requesting your Excellency to be good enough to take note of the above communication, we avail ourselves, &c.

In the name of the Swiss Federal Council:
The President of the Confederation,
(Signed)   DROZ.
The Chancellor of the Confederation,
(Signed)   RINGIER.

No. 2.

The Marquis of Salisbury to M. Vernet.

Sir,   *Foreign Office, April* 22, 1887.

IN reply to your note of the 19th instant, I have the honour to transmit to you my reply to the communication in which the President of the Swiss Confederation announces the accession of the United States of America to the Union for the Protection of Industrial Property.*

I have, &c.
(Signed)   SALISBURY.

No. 3.

The Marquis of Salisbury to the President of the Swiss Confederation.

Sir,   *Foreign Office, April* 22, 1887.

I HAVE the honour to acknowledge the receipt of your Excellency's communication of the 11th instant, and to acquaint you that Her Majesty's Government have taken note with much satisfaction of the accession of the United States of America to the Union for the Protection of Industrial Property.

I have, &c.
(Signed)   SALISBURY.

---

* No. 3.

COMMERCIAL. No. 11 (1887).
(UNITED STATES.)

FURTHER CORRESPONDENCE relative to the Accession of the United States to the International Union for the Protection of Industrial Property.

[In continuation of "Commercial No. 10: 1887." United States.]

Presented to both Houses of Parliament by Command of Her Majesty. June 1887.

LONDON
PRINTED BY HARRISON AND SONS.

COMMERCIAL. No. 11 (1887).
(UNITED STATES.)

FURTHER CORRESPONDENCE

RELATIVE TO THE

ACCESSION OF THE UNITED STATES

TO THE

INTERNATIONAL UNION

FOR THE

PROTECTION OF INDUSTRIAL PROPERTY.

[In continuation of "Commercial No. 10 : 1887." United States.]

Presented to both Houses of Parliament by Command of Her Majesty.
June 1887.

PRINTED FOR HER MAJESTY'S STATIONERY OFFICE
BY HARRISON AND SONS, ST. MARTIN'S LANE,
PRINTERS IN ORDINARY TO HER MAJESTY.

And to be purchased, either directly or through any Bookseller, from
EYRE AND SPOTTISWOODE, EAST HARDING STREET, FLEET STREET, E.C., AND
32, ABINGDON STREET, WESTMINSTER, S.W.; OR
ADAM AND CHARLES BLACK, 6, NORTH BRIDGE, EDINBURGH; OR
HODGES, FIGGIS, AND Co., 104, GRAFTON STREET, DUBLIN.

[C.—5046.] *Price 1d.*

Further Correspondence relative to the Accession of the United States to the International Union for the Protection of Industrial Property.

[In continuation of "Commercial No. 10 (1887)." United States.]

No. 1.

M. Vernet to the Marquis of Salisbury.—(Received May 18.)

My Lord, 25, *Old Broad Street, London, May* 17, 1887.

I HAVE the honour to hand your Lordship a Circular note from my Government announcing that the date of the accession of the United States of America to the Union for the Protection of Industrial Property has not been definitely fixed, as stated in their note of the 11th April, but will be communicated shortly.

In requesting that your Lordship will be good enough to take note of the above, and to acknowledge to me the receipt of this communication, I have, &c.

(Signed) J. H. VERNET,
Agent and Consul-General for Switzerland.

Inclosure in No. 1.

The President of the Swiss Confederation to the Marquis of Salisbury.

Excellence, *Berne, le* 10 *Mai,* 1887.

EN se référant à la note que nous avons eu l'honneur de lui adresser en date du 11 Avril dernier pour l'informer de l'accession des États-Unis à la Convention du 20 Mars, 1883, pour la Protection de la Propriété Industrielle, nous avons l'honneur de faire savoir à votre Excellence que, ensuite de communications reçues de la Légation des États-Unis en Suisse, la date de l'accession de ce pays ne doit pas être fixée au 18 Mars, 1887, comme cela était indiqué dans la note susmentionnée, mais bien à une date ultérieure, que nous serons bientôt à même de communiquer à votre Excellence.

Nous saisissons, &c.
Au nom du Conseil Fédéral Suisse :
Le Président de la Confédération,
(Signé) DROZ.
Le Vice-Chancelier,
(Signé) SCHATZMAN.

(Translation.)

Your Excellency, *Berne, May* 10, 1887.

WITH reference to the note which we had the honour of addressing to you on the 11th April last, notifying the accession of the United States to the Convention of the 20th March, 1883, for the Protection of Industrial Property, we have the honour of informing your Excellency that, according to communications received from the United States' Legation in Switzerland, the accession of that country will not date from the 18th March, 1887, as stated in the above-mentioned note, but from a subsequent date which we shall shortly be in a position to communicate to your Excellency.

We avail, &c.
In the name of the Swiss Federal Council:
The President of the Confederation,
(Signed) DROZ.
The Vice-Chancellor,
(Signed) SCHATZMAN.

No. 2.

The Marquis of Salisbury to M. Vernet.

Sir,   *Foreign Office, May 23, 1887.*

I HAVE the honour to acknowledge the receipt of your note of the 17th instant inclosing a Circular note from the Swiss Government to the effect that the accession of the United States to the Convention for the Protection of Industrial Property will not date from the 18th March, as previously announced, but from a date to be subsequently fixed.

I have, &c.
(Signed) SALISBURY.

No. 3.

M. Vernet to the Marquis of Salisbury.—(Received June 7.)

My Lord,   *25, Old Broad Street, June 6, 1887.*

I HAVE the honour to hand your Lordship a Circular note from my Government to the effect that the accession of the United States of America to the Convention for the Protection of Industrial Property will date from the 30th May, 1887.

I have, &c.
(Signed) J. H. VERNET,
Agent and Consul-General for Switzerland.

Inclosure in No. 3.

The President of the Swiss Confederation to the Marquis of Salisbury.

Excellence,   *Berne, le 2 Juin, 1887.*

PAR notre note du 10 Mai dernier, nous avons informé votre Excellence que la date du 18 Mars, que nous lui avions indiquée le 11 Avril comme celle de l'accession des États-Unis d'Amérique à l'Union pour la Protection de la Propriété Industrielle, était inexacte.

Ensuite d'une notification que nous venons de recevoir de la Légation des États-Unis, nous avons l'honneur de faire savoir à votre Excellence que la date de l'accession de ce pays à l'Union a été fixée au 30 Mai, 1887.

Nous saisissons, &c.
Au nom du Conseil Fédéral Suisse:
Le Président de la Confédération,
(Signé) DROZ.
Le Chancelier de la Confédération,
(Signé) RINGIER.

(Translation.)

Your Excellency,   *Berne, June 2, 1887.*

IN our note of the 10th ultimo we informed your Excellency that the date of the 18th March, which we notified to you on the 11th April last as that of the accession of the United States of America to the Union for the Protection of Industrial Property, was inexact.

In accordance with a notification which we have now received from the United States' Legation, we have the honour to acquaint your Excellency that the date of the accession of that country to the Union has been fixed for the 30th May, 1887.

We avail, &c.
In the name of the Swiss Federal Council:
The President of the Confederation,
(Signed) DROZ.
The Chancellor of the Confederation,
(Signed) RINGIER.

No. 4.

The Marquis of Salisbury to M. Vernet.

Sir, *Foreign Office, June 8, 1887.*

I HAVE the honour to acknowledge the receipt of your note of the 6th instant, inclosing a Circular from your Government to the effect that the accession of the United States of America to the Union for the Protection of Industrial Property will date from the 30th May, 1887.

I have, &c.
(Signed) SALISBURY.

COMMERCIAL. No. 10 (1887).

(UNITED STATES.)

Accession of the United States to the International Union for the Protection of Industrial Property.

Presented to both Houses of Parliament by Command of Her Majesty. May 1887.

LONDON
PRINTED BY HARRISON AND SONS.

FOREIGN OFFICE.

ANNUAL SERIES, 1886.

Nº. 20.

DIPLOMATIC AND CONSULAR REPORTS ON TRADE AND FINANCE.

UNITED STATES.

REPORT FOR THE YEAR 1885
ON THE
TRADE OF NEWPORT NEWS.

REFERENCE TO PREVIOUS REPORT [C. 4525] Commercial No. 21, 1885.

Printed under the Superintendence of Her Majesty's Stationery Office.

By HARRISON AND SONS,
Printers in Ordinary to Her Majesty.

AND SOLD BY

Messrs. HANSARD and SON, 13, Great Queen Street, W.C., and 32, Abingdon Street, Westminster;
Messrs. EYRE and SPOTTISWOODE, East Harding Street, Fleet Street;
Messrs. ADAM and CHARLES BLACK, Edinburgh;
Messrs. ALEX. THOM and Co. (Limited), and Messrs. HODGES, FIGGIS, and Co., Dublin.

Price One Penny.

(1)

NEWPORT NEWS.

Acting-Consul Brancker to the Earl of Rosebery.

My Lord,   *Baltimore, U.S.A., July* 9, 1886.

I HAVE the honour to enclose a commercial report by Vice-Consul Warburton on the trade and commerce of Newport News.

I am, &c.,
(Signed)   J. S. BRANCKER.

Report by Vice-Consul Warburton on the Trade and Commerce of Newport News for the Year 1885.

For the year 1885 there is very little to report, and no improvement in the trade of this port; on the contrary an appreciable falling-off. The foreign imports and exports show a decrease from the preceding year, which is also the case with the British and other foreign tonnage entering for coaling purposes. This decrease is partly due to the general depression in trade which has pervaded the world, and to which the United States has formed no exception: partly also to the failure of the wheat crop, and the late movement of the cotton crop, as well as to the partial failure of cotton in 1884. A rival coaling port has also been established at Lamhert's Point, two miles from Norfolk, and about 10 from here, which has taken away about 40 steamers, which would doubtless have swelled the aggregate of steam tonnage entering the port for bunker coal. No improvement in trade.

All these causes may have been assisted by the intermittent conflict between labour and capital which has been growing during the past year, though it must be admitted that, in consequence of the strikes in the north, the two coaling stations inside of Hampton Roads have been benefited during a brief period. Labour and capital.

There has been an increase of 35 per cent. in the export of coal from Newport News over the previous year, represented by the following figures:— Coal.

	Tons.
1884	967,000
1885	1,298,000
Increase	331,000

This coal is, however, principally moved coastwise, although some cargoes have been shipped to Colon and other ports in the West Indies.

The price of bunker coal has been reduced from 15*s*. to 13*s*. 11½*d*. per ton f.o.b., while cargoes have sold for export at 10*s*. 5½*d*. f.o.b.

This does not appear to be a remunerative price, as the coal is carried over 400 miles, and costs from 4*s*. to 4*s*. 6*d*. delivered on the cars.

There has been great activity in the transport of freight coastwise, both eastward and westward, through the old Dominion Steamship Transport.

UNITED STATES.

Tobacco.

Company, which, with the Chesapeake and Ohio Railway, combines as to freights. A great deal of the eastward freight is for foreign export through New York agents: the quantity cannot be ascertained, as no official record is kept of coastwise freights in the custom-house, nor elsewhere of the destination of the merchandise.

In this way more than 13,000 hogsheads and 240 cases of tobacco have left this port in 1885, the majority being probably for foreign consumption.

Since the 1st of July the name "Chesapeake and Ohio" of the railway terminating at Newport News has been changed to "Newport News and Mississippi Valley," and includes the former line, with branches and leased lines terminating at Memphis on the great river.

Steam communication with United Kingdom.

The project of establishing a direct line of steamers between this port and the United Kingdom has remained in abeyance since the departure of the Union steamers in 1884. It is a question whether, at the time these vessels plied here, any direct line would have paid; but in any case, those steamers were totally unfit for the trade. With small carrying power they united a large expenditure of coal and a numerous crew. The "Arab," for instance, registered 2,044 tons, had 500 horse-power, and steamed 12 knots on a consumption of 35 tons of coal, or 10 knots on 30 tons, and had a crew of 63 men.

The "Nubian," registered 1,998 tons, with a crew of 48, had a speed of 10 knots on a consumption of 30 tons.

Besides her complement of coal, she carried but 2,048 tons of cargo, as follows:—

Articles.		Quantity.	Tons.
Wheat	Bushels	24,141	646
Oil-cake	Bags	1,300	163
Flour	Barrels	2,000	151
Oak	Plank	..	353
Cotton	Bales	1,729	595
Staves		1,011	30
Bark	Bags	206	10
Total			2,048

The "Lilburn Tower," in port at the same time, quite a different type of vessel, registered 1,891 tons, or 107 less than the "Nubian," but carried 3,147 tons, as follows:—

Articles.		Quantity.	Tons.
Staves		5,400	4
Bark	Bags	500	30
Walnut	Logs	15	11
Cotton	Bales	5,925	2,033
Oak plank	Feet	97,020	217
Cake	Bags	800	100
Cotton seed	"	1,090	127
Flour	Sacks	3,750	235
Cargo from Baltimore			350
Total			3,117

She had a speed of nine knots on a consumption of 18 tons of coal.

NEWPORT NEWS.

The above figures speak for themselves. The "Arab" and "Nubian," after their engagement here had terminated, transferred their services to Baltimore, and found the result even more unsatisfactory than at this port.

It seems probable that the immediate success of any line of freight steamers from this port to the United Kingdom will depend upon a freight combination with Baltimore and Norfolk—the former 160 miles and the latter 13 miles distant—although when the connections of the Newport News and Mississippi Valley Railway are completed, and its rolling stock increased (an increase which is rapidly taking place), there seems no reason to doubt that it will be fully competent to supply freight to a service of 1,000 to 1,500 tons register per week, with possibly limited passenger accommodation, which latter is, however, in my opinion an item that should not, for the present at least, be taken into consideration.

Railways.

The controllers of the port and railway are for obvious reasons very desirous that such a line should be established, but are, I think, quite decided not to entertain the idea of a subsidy or guaranty of anything but a sufficient supply of freight at market rates. I believe they are willing to arrange for an equitable division of the through rate obtainable between the road and the vessels, and to concede certain advantages, of which the following would be the principal:—

1. A preference to ports in the United Kingdom on all business which the steamship line can handle, whenever no unreasonable delay in transmission is incurred thereby.

2. Free wharfage while exchanging business, which may be represented as an advantage of one halfpenny a ton a day.

3. First-class coal on the most favourable terms; the present price to all steamers for bunker coal being, as before stated, 13s. 11½d. per ton, of 2,240 lbs. f.o.b.

4. The ordinary commission on passenger tickets over the Newport News and Mississippi Valley Railway.

RETURN of all Vessels at the Port of Newport News, United States of America, in 1885.

Shipping.

ENTERED.

Nationality.	Sailing.		Steam.		Total.	
	Number of Vessels.	Tons.	Number of Vessels.	Tons.	Number of Vessels.	Tons.
British	6	3,574	127	159,281	133	162,855
American	25	10,277	138	193,717	163	203,994
Spanish	...	...	10	14,067	10	14,067
German	2	1,205	3	4,194	5	5,399
Italian	4	2,140	...	...	4	2,140
Norwegian	1	339	1	1,223	2	1,562
Dutch	...	...	1	1,008	1	1,008
Total	38	16,535	280	373,490	318	391,025

(A)

UNITED STATES.

CLEARED.

Nationality.	Sailing. Number of Vessels.	Sailing. Tons.	Steam. Number of Vessels.	Steam. Tons.	Total. Number of Vessels.	Total. Tons.
British	6	3,574	128	159,324	133	162,784
American	18	7,035	139	206,517	157	213,552
Spanish	...	...	10	14,067	10	14,067
German	2	1,205	3	4,194	5	5,399
Italian	4	2,140	...	...	4	2,140
Norwegian	1	339	1	1,223	2	1,562
Dutch	...	...	1	1,008	1	1,008
Total	31	14,293	282	386,333	312	390,512

In the preceding table, only that portion of American shipping entered and cleared at the custom-house is shown. Vessels only are entered and cleared which contain dutiable freight in the former case, and in the latter carry freight to foreign countries: consequently all the purely coastwise tonnage is omitted. It is probable that this exceeds 250,000 tons each, entering and leaving the port, but no exact information is obtainable.

The aggregate of shipping visiting the port will probably amount to 600,000 tons register.

TABLE of British Shipping as compared with the Two previous Years.

Year.	Entered. Number.	Entered. Tonnage.	Cleared. Number.	Cleared. Tonnage.
1883	168	187,624	165	184,743
1884	150	163,612	154	168,585
1885	133	162,855	133	162,784

While during the first six months of 1886 no less than 99 British vessels, with 113,000 tons, entered the port, against an average during the past two years in that period of 77½ ships, of 92,000 tons.

Exports. The quantity and value of exports for 1885 was very much below that of the preceding year; both are shown below. It may be remarked, however, that for the first six months of the current year the exports have exactly doubled those of the entire year preceding it; a fact which is full of promise for the future of the port.

RETURN of the Principal Articles of Export from Newport News during the Year 1885 and 1884, excluding Coastwise Merchandise.

Articles.		1885. Quantity.	1885. Value.	1884. Quantity.	1884. Value.
			£		£
Coal	Tons	51,912	39,000	41,000	32,578
Wheat	Bushels	142,082	25,700	...	108,000
Flour	Barrels	33,016	38,500	...	94,000
Bacon and lard	Lbs.	538,264	10,070	...	13,635
Oak plank, &c.	Cubic feet	904,574	8,500	...	10,550
Corn	Bushels	533,850	55,000	...	...
Walnut logs	Number	3,226	13,400	...	9,750
Staves	,,	432,663	13,000	...	16,000
Cotton	Bales	10,419	103,000	30,491	325,460
Sundries		...	30,930	...	10,300
Whiskey		...	...	...	214,000
Total		...	347,000	...	844,273

The foregoing shows a considerable falling-off over 1884 in the export of cotton, wheat, and flour. The export of whiskey in that year was caused by the Federal Government requiring payment for the excise duty on bonded whiskey, which had been deferred, and is likely to be exceptional.

Climate. The winter of 1885–86 was unusually severe—more so than for nearly 30 years past—but though the James and Elizabeth rivers were frozen over, and the traffic to Richmond, Norfolk, and Baltimore was suspended on account of the ice, the channel to Newport News was unimpeded, and no delay was sustained by vessels entering or leaving the port.

Prospects, 1886. The promise of the year 1886 was good, and the performance so far has been better; while trade is reviving, and several commercial enterprises, among others a dry dock, are connected with the immediate future.

Indications are not wanting that the prosperity of this port, which has been somewhat retarded by various abnormal conditions, will receive an impetus during the next 12 months, which will raise it still higher in the scale of importance than it has already attained, especially in its relations to our mercantile marine.

Newport News, July 8, 1886.

(A)

FOREIGN OFFICE.
1887.
ANNUAL SERIES.

No. 88.

DIPLOMATIC AND CONSULAR REPORTS ON TRADE AND FINANCE.

UNITED STATES.

REPORT FOR THE YEAR 1886

ON THE

TRADE OF CHARLESTON.

REFERENCE TO PREVIOUS REPORT [C. 4737] Commercial No. 10, 1886.

Presented to both Houses of Parliament by Command of Her Majesty,
MARCH, 1887.

LONDON:
PRINTED FOR HER MAJESTY'S STATIONERY OFFICE,
BY HARRISON AND SONS, ST. MARTIN'S LANE,
PRINTERS IN ORDINARY TO HER MAJESTY.

And to be purchased, either directly or through any Bookseller, from
EYRE AND SPOTTISWOODE, EAST HARDING STREET, FLEET STREET, E.C., and
32, ABINGDON STREET, WESTMINSTER, S.W.; or
ADAM AND CHARLES BLACK, NORTH BRIDGE, EDINBURGH; or
HODGES, FIGGIS, & Co., 104, GRAFTON STREET, DUBLIN.

1887.

[C.—4923—11.] *Price 1d.*

New Series of Reports.

Reports of the Annual Series have been issued from Her Majesty's Diplomatic and Consular Officers at the following places, and may be obtained from the sources indicated on the title-page:—

No.		Price
1.	Varna	1d.
2.	Florence	1d.
3.	Tangier	1d.
4.	Loanda	1d.
5.	Teneriffe	1d.
6.	Manila	1d.
7.	Batavia	1d.
8.	Beyrout	1d.
9.	St. Michael's	1d.
10.	Cuba	1d.
11.	Tunis	4d.
12.	Canton	1d.
13.	Newchwang	1d.
14.	Shanghai	1d.
15.	Tientsin	1d.
16.	Vienna	1d.
17.	Corfu	1d.
18.	Hakodate	1d.
19.	Hiogo	1d.
20.	Newport News	1d.
21.	Stockholm	1d.
22.	Christiania	1d.
23.	Antwerp	1d.
24.	Salonica	1d.
25.	Tonga	1d.
26.	Batoum	1d.
27.	Costa Rica	1d.
28.	Mexico	4d.
29.	Bushire	1d.
30.	Erzeroum	1d.
31.	Bilbao	1d.
32.	Rio Grande do Sul	1d.
33.	Piræus	1d.
34.	Sandakan	1d.
35.	Stockholm	1d.
36.	Tahiti	1d.
37.	Syra	1d.
38.	Kanagawa	2d.
39.	Nagasaki	1d.
40.	Chefoo	1d.
41.	Pekin	1d.
42.	Ciudad Bolivar	1d.
43.	Puerto Cabello	1d.
44.	Réunion	1d.
45.	Sarawak	1d.
46.	Würtemberg	1d.
47.	Tokyo	1d.
48.	Amsterdam	1d.
49.	Lisbon	1d.
50.	Königsberg	2d.
51.	Cagliari	1d.
52.	Frankfort	1d.
53.	Bogota	1d.
54.	Kharput	1d.
55.	Trieste	1d.
56.	Crete	1d.
57.	Berne	3d.
58.	Rotterdam	1d.
59.	Düsseldorf	4d.
60.	Mozambique	5d.
61.	Hanyang	1d.
62.	Stockholm	1d.
63.	Paris	1d.
64.	Tunis	1d.
65.	The Hague	2d.
66.	Italy	2d.
67.	Smyrna	2d.
68.	Fiume	1d.
69.	Tabreez	1d.
70.	Philippopolis	1d.
71.	Rome	1d.
72.	Vienna	1d.
73.	St. Petersburg	2d.
74.	Ichang	1d.
75.	Salonica	1d.
76.	Brussels	2d.
77.	Alexandria	1d.
78.	Patras	1d.
79.	Maranham	1d.
80.	Taganrog	2d.
81.	Jeddah	1d.
82.	Suakin	1d.
83.	Colonia	1d.
84.	Suez	1d.
85.	Paris	1d.
86.	Brest	1d.
87.	Puerto Plata	1d.

No. 88.

Reference to previous Report [C. 4737], Commercial No. 10, 1886.

UNITED STATES.

CHARLESTON.

Consul Cridland to the Marquis of Salisbury.

My Lord,   British Consulate, Charleston, February 12, 1887.

I HAVE the honour to enclose herewith a report of the trade and commerce of Charleston for the past year, and of the productions and internal resources of the State of South Carolina during that same period.

I have, &c.
(Signed)   FREDERICK J. CRIDLAND.

Report of Consul Cridland on the Trade and Commerce of Charleston and the Productions of the State of South Carolina for the Year 1886.

The principal articles of trade at Charleston are cotton, rice, turpentine, rosin, phosphate rock (crude and ground), fertilisers, lumber, and cotton goods manufactured in South Carolina. The decline in the receipts of cotton last year was very small compared with 1885, while there was a large increase in the receipts of naval stores and phosphate rock; also an increase in the production of local manufactures as compared with the previous years. [Cotton. Naval stores. Phosphate.]

The exports to foreign countries decreased last year, while the imports from foreign ports to the port of Charleston increased. [Imports and exports.]

With reference to British shipping visiting Charleston, though the number of steam and sailing vessels was larger in 1885 by nine ships in all, the tonnage of 1886 exceeded that of 1885 by nearly 1,000 tons. It is probable that a much larger number of steamships would seek Charleston as a port of loading if there was a greater depth of water on the bar. It is hoped that the work on the jetties will progress this year, the United States Congress having appropriated money for that purpose, and much is expected if the work is ever completed. At present it is doubtful if vessels drawing over 16 feet can cross the bar except at very high tides. [British shipping. The jetties of Charleston. Depth of water on bar.]

With reference to the imports and exports for the past year, compared with 1885 and 1884, there seems to be a considerable improvement in the former, but a decided falling-off in the exports, as will be seen in the Annex B. and C. herewith.

The area planted in cotton in South Carolina in 1885 was 1,722,107 acres, and the yield 590,910 bales of 450 lbs. each, while in 1886 the acreage was 1,630,856, yielding about 530,102 bales of 450 lbs. The decrease in production is probably due in a great measure to a most unprecedented drought in the autumn of last year, no rain having fallen in this State for over 60 days. [Area in cotton for 1885 and 1886.]

UNITED STATES.

Rice planted: production. From all I can hear rice-planting in South Carolina last year proved very unprofitable, owing to the low price obtained for the article, brought about by the low rate of duty on cleaned rice imported being 2¼ c. per lb. The area planted in South Carolina was in 1885 78,086 acres, and the crop 82,431,850 lbs. The area in 1886 was 80,504 acres, and the crop 69,625,922 lbs.

Land cultivated and in forest. In South Carolina there are 19,308,800 acres; of this, 9,000,000 acres are new forest, and 4,500,000 acres under cultivation.

The productions of the soil are as follows:—

Productions of the soil.

QUANTITY Produced in 1886.

Article.		Quantity.	Acres.	Average per Acre.	Value.
					£ s. d.
Indian corn	Bushels	13,925,168	1,484,851	9·2	2,030,753 10 10
Wheat	,,	1,161,097	192,746	6·1	266,084 11 8
Rye	,,	32,000	8,285	3·8	6,666 13 4
Oats	,,	3,700,000	311,406	9·0	539,693 10 10
Barley	,,	18,000	1,212	15·2	3,750 0 0
Potatoes	,,	471,532	4,413	60·0	488,852 14 2
Hay	Tons	42,300	3,000	1·30	118,087 10 0
Cotton	Bales	530,102	1,630,856	·30	4,224,250 4 2
Rice	Lbs.	69,625,922	...	20 bushels.	308,239 11 8
Tobacco	,,	465,309	3·27	...	14,542 1 8
Sorghum	...	...	...	...	60,165 16 8
Fodder	...	...	...	...	772,985 8 4
Peas	...	...	...	...	135,201 0 10
Sugar cane	...	...	...	...	39,582 5 10
Orchard and garden products	...	...	...	...	191,637 5 10
Value. Total	...	...	...	...	9,200,492 5 10

Value of farm products per acre. The gross value per acre of the principal crops in South Carolina for the year 1886 was as follows:—

Article.	Currency.	Sterling.
	Dol. c.	£ s. d.
Irish potatoes	88 68	18 9 6
Tobacco	84 39	17 11 8
Sugar cane	64 77	13 9 10
Sweet potatoes	47 54	9 18 1
Sorghum	29 26	6 2 0
Rice	18 37	3 16 6
Cotton	12 43	2 11 9
Oats	8 31	1 14 7
Wheat	6 32	1 7 7
Indian corn	6 56	1 7 4
Peas	4 55	0 19 0

Phosphate rock.

PHOSPHATE ROCK.

The phosphate rock deposits of the State of South Carolina form her most important and valuable mining interest. The rock is found in the streams and ore land. The stream or river rock occurs at the bottom of various streams and rivers, and is raised by hand with tongs or by powerful steam dredges, which furnish the bulk of the supply. A royalty of 1 dol. per ton of crude rock is paid to the State on all rock mined in the navigable streams of the State, all such mining being **Royalty.** done under licence from the State. This royalty, amounting in 1886 to 196,089 dol., formed an important part of the revenue. The land rock deposits are the property of individuals or companies, and pay no royalty to the State. The rock occurs at various depths, 10 feet being the limit of economical excavations, and is obtained entirely by surface mining. The economic excavation and utilisation of river rock dates fom about the year 1870; of land rock 1867. The production of land rock has increased from 18,000 tons in 1868-70 to 294,000 tons; in 1886 of river rock from 1,989 tons to 191,174 tons. The total amount of land rock produced from 1868 to 1886, inclusive, has been 1,991,000 tons; of river rock 1,592,256 tons, or a total production of 3,583,256 tons, which, at an average selling price of 6 dol. per ton, gives 21,499,536 dol. as the value of the product of this industry. *Quantity of rock mined.*

The most important industry in comparatively recent establishments in South Carolina is the manufacture of commercial fertilisers. There were no factories of this kind in the State in 1860. The growth of the business since then is fully shown by the following statement:— *Fertilisers.*

Year.	Establishments.	Capital.	Product.
		Dollars.	Dollars.
1870	2	350,000	425,000
1885-86	14	3,900,000	3,574,300

This industry sprang into existence a very short time after the discovery of the agricultural value of the phosphate rock, which exists in such abundance on the coast and in the rivers of the State.

The shipments of fertilisers from South Carolina were in 1885 150,000 tons, and in 1886 196,814 tons. Those shipments represent about the annual production of the South Carolina companies, exclusive of the fertilisers manufactured by the cotton seed oil mills. *Fertilisers shipped.*

The trade terms for the various kinds of commercial manures are fertilisers, guanos, acid phosphates, and dissolved bone, or acidulated rock. The fertilisers, or complete manures, contain phosphoric acid, obtained by treating ground phosphate rock with sulphuric acid; ammonia in the form of dried blood, fish scrap, cotton, seed, meal, &c., and potash, usually obtained by adding the requisite percentage of kainite, or German potash salts. The acid phosphate is composed of phosphate, rock, sulphuric acid, and potash; the dissolved bone, or acidulated rock, of phosphate rock and acid. The phosphate rock is obtained in the locality of the factories, the ammoniating material usually from the Western States, and the cotton seed oil mills in the State; the potash is imported direct from Germany, and the sulphur from Spain and Sicily. *Trade terms of manures.*

The discovery of phosphate rock, and the manufacture of commercial fertilisers from this product, has worked a revolution in southern agriculture. By the use of these artificial stimulants worn-out and waste lands have been brought back into cultivation, and made to yield almost as abundantly as when they were first cultivated. The astonishing increase in the cotton production of the South is due more to the use of commercial fertilisers than to any other one cause. It forces the crop to maturity much earlier than formerly, and its use has enabled farmers to produce cotton at the foot of the mountains, thus bringing an area into cultivation that had not previously been planted in this crop. Grain of all kinds is benefited by its judicious application, and it has been used in Louisiana and Florida on orange trees and on sugar cane with most satisfactory results. *Use of phosphates. Advantageous use of phosphates on cotton lands. Also for grain.*

(129)

UNITED STATES.

LUMBER MILLS.

Lumber mills. The statements given concerning the lumber mills in South Carolina in 1886 are based on a very careful enumeration and upon correct estimates. If these are true, this industry leads all others in South Carolina in value of annual production. With few exceptions the mills are cutting pine and cypress timber, making boards, mast timber, shingles, and staves. The timber is exported to foreign countries, and the other classes of lumber are consumed in home and domestic markets.

The following comparative table shows the condition of this industry in 1860 and in 1885-86:—

Capital invested.

Year.	Number of Establishments.	Capital.	Value of Products.
		Dollars.	Dollars.
1860	360	1,140,616	1,124,440
1885-86	813	3,256,870	6,236,677

TAR AND TURPENTINE.

Tar and turpentine. Rosin. It appears that in 1880 South Carolina was the second State in the South in the production of turpentine and rosin, the product then being by the census report 4,593,000 gallons of turpentine and 333,940 gallons of rosin. This industry has grown with the lumber business, and is one of the chief industries of the lower and middle sections of the State. The following comparison will show the condition of business at the two periods :—

Year.	Number of Establishments.	Capital.	Value of Products.
		Dollars.	Dollars.
1880	95	932,270	1,096,974
1885-86	291	1,454,800	2,912,271

Manufactories and value of goods, products, &c. The value of manufactured products in 1880 was in South Carolina 16,738,008 dol., and at the present time the value of such products is 29,951,551 dol., an increase of 13,213,543 dol., or nearly 80 per cent. in six years, or about 13½ per cent. annually. The condition and character of these industries is shown by the following tables :—

Industries, 1885-86.	Mills, &c.	Hands.	Capital.	Product.
			Dollars.	Dollars.
Cotton mills	29	4,889	5,092,000	5,638,648
Fertiliser mills	14	1,154	2,900,500	3,574,300
Cotton seed oil mills ..	6	190	232,700	371,500
Lumber mills	813	6,598	3,256,870	6,236,677
Flour, grist, and rice mills	1,608	4,402	4,030,850	5,849,200
Turpentine stills	291	6,991	1,455,800	2,912,271
Foundries and machine ..	44	974	643,330	899,500
Printing and publishing ..	14	242	132,700	299,520
Other manufactories ..	423	7,938	2,584,220	4,169,935
Total	3,242	33,378	20,238,970	29,951,551

Equal in sterling, 6,239,791*l.* 13*s.* 4*d.*

CHARLESTON.

The bulk of the product of the South Carolina mills goes by rail to New York, Philadelphia, Baltimore, and Charleston, and a large part of the goods shipped to these ports is exported to China, South America, and other foreign countries. There are also shipments of considerable importance by many of the mills to the North-Western States. A part of the goods go to the New England States, and are there bleached and exported. The business of the mills is chiefly conducted through agents. The cotton used in the manufacture of the goods is bought almost entirely from the planters in the vicinity of the mills. None of the mills are ever prevented from running by extremes of heat or cold. The manufacturers can compete successfully with the mills of other sections, because they get their raw material near by. Again, living near the mills is cheap, and labour is cheaper than in other sections. Some of the mills in South Carolina are also exempt from taxation either by the county or State. Some of the manufacturers are of the opinion that the Southern mills could not compete with foreign factories, without a continuance of the protection afforded by the tariff laws of the United States. *[Markets for manufactured goods produced in South Carolina. Cheap labour mills exempt from taxes. Competition.]*

Farm labour is reported more efficient during 1886 than for some years. The system of tenant farming prevails largely throughout the State of South Carolina, and is generally unsatisfactory to both landowners and tenants. The negro renters are without the means of making their crops without a resort to credit for supplies, which are usually obtained at prices that leave little margin for profit on the crop. The result is careless cultivation, poor crops, and constant depreciation of the value of the land. The relations existing between the employers and labourers are reported as harmonious and pleasant. *[Labour.]*

The depression in foreign freights continued during last year, and it would seem impossible for vessels to run and make any profit, and yet there is very little sign of improvement. *[Freights.]*

The ruling rates of cotton freights for 1884–85 left a small margin; the rates for 1885–86 left none. For instance, steamers carried cotton to Liverpool at 2 dol. 70 c. per bale; deduct 1 dol. 21 c. for compressing, stevedore, and insurance at press, and there was left 1 dol. 49 c. to pay port charges, wages, coal, and expenses at Liverpool. The same state of things exists in reference to sailing vessels, and what is said about cotton freights applies equally to phosphate rock, naval stores, lumber, &c. *[Cotton freights by steamships.]*

The report in reference to the health of the city of Charleston for 1886 gives the rate of mortality among the white population as 17·64, and among the negroes 38·49 per 1,000. *[Health and number of deaths.]*

The credit of the State of South Carolina, and of the city of Charleston and its banks, seems to be in a very excellent condition, the bonds and stocks being constantly in demand, and sold daily by the stockbrokers. *[State credit: city and banks credit.]*

The report of the Agricultural Department at Washington for the past year gives the following as a correct return of the live stock in South Carolina in 1885:—

UNITED STATES.

Live stock in South Carolina.

	Number.	Average Price.	Value.
		Dol. c.	Dollars.
Horses	62,789	95 18	5,917,055
Mules	71,119	101 21	7,126,702
Cows	141,896	18 50	2,625,076
Oxen	216,880	10 96	2,377,005
Sheep	112,935	1 76	207,048
Hogs	567,181	4 14	2,348,129
Total	1,172,800	..	20,601,015

Reference to tariff of United States.

As long as the present United States tariff laws remain in force it would be very hard to tell what goods, wares, or merchandise could be imported here with profit from England.

Cotton growing in India; the advantage of using phosphates.

It might be profitable for the cotton growers in India to be made aware of the advantages of using South Carolina phosphates in the cultivation of cotton, its advantages in that respect having been already set forth in this report.

A.—RETURN of all Shipping at the Port of Charleston in the Year 1886.

ENTERED.

Nationality.	Sailing.		Steam.		Total.	
	Number of Vessels.	Tons.	Number of Vessels.	Tons.	Number of Vessels.	Tons.
British	25	14,072	52	53,760	77	67,832
American	325	137,818	145	199,573	470	337,391
German, Danish, Italian, Austrian, and French	59	14,538	7	8,472	66	23,010
Norwegian, Swedish, and Russian	60	25,483	1	1,244	61	26,727
Total	469	191,911	205	263,049	674	454,960

Total for the year preceding (no correct report published).

CLEARED.

Nationality.	Sailing.		Steam.		Total.	
	Number of Vessels.	Tons.	Number of Vessels.	Tons.	Number of Vessels.	Tons.
British	33	18,568	50	52,574	83	71,142
American	324	136,763	146	201,114	470	337,877
German, Danish, French, Italian, and Austrian ...	59	12,730	8	9,867	67	22,597
Norwegian, Swedish, and Russian	59	25,424	1	1,244	60	26,668
Total	475	193,485	205	264,799	680	458,284

Total for the year preceding (no correct report published).

CHARLESTON.

B.—Return of Principal Articles of Export from Charleston during the Year 1886.

Articles.		1886. Quantity.	1886. Value in Sterling. £ s. d.	1885. Quantity.	1885. Value in Sterling. £ s. d.
Cotton, uplands	Bales	495,547	4,645,728 0 0	498,360	4,572,125 0 0
Cotton, sea islands	Bags	9,621	240,525 0 0	13,679	341,975 0 0
Rice	Barrels	70,017	233,390 0 0	97,966	326,761 13 4
Turpentine	Casks	62,854	183,324 3 4	44,099	128,622 1 8
Rosin	Barrels	273,309	99,643 15 0	218,979	80,877 10 0
Phosphate rock, crude	Tons	255,660	266,312 10 0	219,901	297,782 10 0
,, ,, ground	,,	15,511	29,083 2 6	21,640	45,083 6 8
Lumber and cross ties	Feet	27,615,705	108,333 6 8	30,033,961	112,500 10 0
Cotton goods, domestics	Bales	46,725	486,718 15 0	44,004	458,374 0 0
Fertilisers	Tons	141,287	573,978 6 8	158,136	642,427 10 0
Fruits and vegetables		...	182,291 13 4	...	203,125 0 0
Total		...	7,049,328 12 6	...	7,209,654 0 8

Return of Principal Articles of Import to Charleston during the Year 1886.

Articles.	Value. 1886. £	Value. 1885. £
The principal articles imported are cotton, iron ties, salt, beer, fruit, brimstone, and kainite	148,180	103,060

Table showing the Total Value of all Articles Exported from Charleston and Imported to Charleston from and to Foreign Countries during the Years 1886-85.

	1886. £ s. d.	1885. £ s. d.
Exports	3,695,852 15 2	3,913,134 15 10
Imports	148,180 3 2	103,060 8 4

The statistics of trade published in this city do not show the total value of articles exported to each country, but only the total value of the exports to foreign countries and the total value of the imports from foreign countries, consequently it is impossible to give the same in detail as desired.

LONDON:
Printed for Her Majesty's Stationery Office,
By HARRISON AND SONS,
Printers in Ordinary to Her Majesty.
(Wt. 7730   75   3 | 87 — H & S   129)

FOREIGN OFFICE.
1887.
ANNUAL SERIES.

No. 92.

DIPLOMATIC AND CONSULAR REPORTS ON TRADE AND FINANCE.

UNITED STATES.

REPORT FOR THE YEAR 1886
ON THE
TRADE OF THE CONSULAR DISTRICT OF NEW ORLEANS.

REFERENCE TO PREVIOUS REPORT [C. 4654] Commercial No. 5, 1886

Presented to both Houses of Parliament by Command of Her Majesty,
MARCH, 1887

LONDON:
PRINTED FOR HER MAJESTY'S STATIONERY OFFICE,
BY HARRISON AND SONS, ST. MARTIN'S LANE,
PRINTERS IN ORDINARY TO HER MAJESTY.

And to be purchased, either directly or through any Bookseller, from
EYRE AND SPOTTISWOODE, EAST HARDING STREET, FLEET STREET, E.C., and
32, ABINGDON STREET, WESTMINSTER, S.W.; or
ADAM AND CHARLES BLACK, NORTH BRIDGE, EDINBURGH; or
HODGES, FIGGIS, & Co., 104, GRAFTON STREET, DUBLIN.

1887.

[C.—4923—15.] *Price 9d.*

New Series of Reports.

Reports of the Annual Series have been issued from Her Majesty's Diplomatic and Consular Officers at the following places, and may be obtained from the sources indicated on the title-page:—

No.		Price.
1. Varna		1d.
2. Florence		1d.
3. Tangier		1d.
4. Loanda		1d.
5. Teneriffe		1d.
6. Manila		1d.
7. Batavia		1d.
8. Beyrout		1d.
9. St. Michael's		1d.
10. Cuba		1d.
11. Tunis		4d.
12. Canton		1d.
13. Newchwang		1d.
14. Shanghai		1d.
15. Tientsin		1d.
16. Vienna		1d.
17. Corfu		1d.
18. Hakodate		1d.
19. Hiogo		1d.
20. Newport News		1d.
21. Stockholm		1d.
22. Christiania		1d.
23. Antwerp		1d.
24. Salonica		1d.
25. Tonga		1d.
26. Batoum		1d.
27. Costa Rica		1d.
28. Mexico		4d.
29. Bushire		1d.
30. Erzeroum		1d.
31. Bilbao		1d.
32. Rio Grande do Sul		1d.
33. Piræus		1d.
34. Sandakan		1d.
35. Stockholm		1d.
36. Tahiti		1d.
37. Syra		1d.
38. Kanagawa		2d.
39. Nagasaki		1d.
40. Chefoo		1d.
41. Pekin		1d.
42. Ciudad Bolivar		1d.
43. Puerto Cabello		1d.
44. Réunion		1d
45. Sarawak		1d.
46. Würtemberg		1d.

No.		Price.
47. Tokyo		1d.
48. Amsterdam		1d.
49. Lisbon		1d.
50. Königsberg		2d.
51. Cagliari		1d.
52. Frankfort		1d.
53. Bogota		1d.
54. Kharput		1d.
55. Trieste		1d.
56. Crete		1d.
57. Berne		3d.
58. Rotterdam		1d.
59. Düsseldorf		4d.
60. Mozambique		5d.
61. Hanyang		1d.
62. Stockholm		1d.
63. Paris		1d.
64. Tunis		1d.
65. The Hague		2d.
66. Italy		2d.
67. Smyrna		2d.
68. Fiume		1d.
69. Tabreez		1d.
70. Philippopolis		1d.
71. Rome		1d.
72. Vienna		1d.
73. St. Petersburg		2d.
74. Ichang		1d.
75. Salonica		1d.
76. Brussels		2d.
77. Alexandria		1d.
78. Patras		1d.
79. Maranham		1d.
80. Taganrog		2d.
81. Jeddah		1d.
82. Suakin		1d.
83. Colonia		1d.
84. Suez		1d.
85. Paris		1d.
86. Brest		1d.
87. Puerto Plata		1d.
88. Charleston		1d.
89. Tripoli		1d.
90. Saigon		1d.
91. Cherbourg		1d.

No. 92.

Reference to previous Report [C. 4654], Commercial No. 5, 1886

UNITED STATES.

NEW ORLEANS.

Report by Consul de Fonblanque on the Trade and Commerce of New Orleans for the Year 1886.

AGRICULTURE.

I HAVE little to report under this head which would be of practical use to the British farmer, although the endeavours that are being made to increase and diversify the yield of the land are of great local importance. Two experimental farms and a department in the State University at Baton Rouge have been organised, and are doing good work in this respect, and a State agricultural society is being formed. It is to be hoped that reform in the matters mentioned in my last report, notably in the administration of justice for the suppression of thefts of stock and depredations upon crops, and a better system of credit, will also receive attention. An agricultural convention will be held at Lake Charles towards the end of February, at which these questions will doubtless be discussed. I will here quote some experiments made in growing oats at the Kenner Farm, under the direction of Professor Stubbs, as they may be interesting to the scientific agriculturist as a study in comparative husbandry. *[Practical farming. Required reforms. Experimental farming: oats.]*

The object of these experiments, as well as those upon the State experiment station, was primarily to test the economy of growing oats at home as a food crop for stock, in preference to the prevailing custom of importing annually large quantities at great cost. With this end in view we have striven to decide two questions, viz.: 1st. Best time to sow? 2nd. Manurial requirements of our soils for growing oats? A third question might have been propounded, viz.: Which is the best seed? But the experience of Southern cultivators has been so unanimous in favour of the rust-proof varieties that this question was eliminated this year. Perhaps hereafter it will be worthy of trial to decide the best time to plant a series of experiments; covering planting in every month from October to March was proposed. Accordingly plats were planted on October 27th, November 17th, January 30th, and February 2nd. Pressure of other business prevented planting in December, and the cold and wet weather prohibited an earlier planting in January. The intense cold of January 8th to 13th killed completely the oats sown in November, while those sown in October were unhurt—a valuable suggestion to those intending hereafter to make fall planting. Those sown in October had attained a greater root development than those sown in November, and hence were enabled to withstand a greater severity of cold. *[Object of experiment. Sowing. Results of planting in point of time.]*

Manurial Requirements.—To test this question cotton seed, meal, acid phosphate, and kainite were used respectively to furnish nitrogen, *[Manures.]*

(133)

UNITED STATES.

phosphoric acid, and potash. These substances were used in different quantities and combinations, which will be fully explained under each plat.

The cotton seed meal used contained 7 per cent. nitrogen, 3 per cent. phosphoric acid, and 2 per cent. potash. The acid phosphate had 15 per cent. of available phosphoric acid; there was 12 per cent. of potash in the kainite.

Plat No. 1. Need of potash.

Object.—To test the proportions of cotton seed meal to acid phosphate best adapted to oats, and incidentally the need of potash to the soil which was alluvial in character, consisting of a mixture of sandy and black land, the latter predominating; badly drained and in poor tilth. The plat was about two arpents from the front level, and was about one arpent in depth. Culture of the previous year, old stubble (bad stand), filled in with corn.

Preparation of the soil.

Preparation of Soil.—Land broken with two-horse plough, October 23rd; harrowed on 26th; manures distributed broadcast, and red-rust proof (Texas) seed sown at the rate of 2½ bushels per acre, both lightly ploughed in with one-horse ploughs, October 27th. This, on account of prevailing drought, was preferred to harrowing in, the usual course adopted in covering oats. The land was left flat with the exception of water drains between the plats.

Nos. 1 and 3, upon the east side, and No. 12 upon the west side, were injured by water standing upon them during the continuous rains of March. As soon as discovered, open drains for relief were constituted; but these plats never fully recovered from this temporary injury.

Results.

The oats came up quickly and gave an excellent stand. The cold of January, which killed other plats, injured this one very little, beyond turning the bottom leaves yellow, and this damage was quickly repaired by a few days of subsequent sunshine.

This plat was cut May 20th and 21st with a cradle, seed in dough state, stalks just turning yellow, cured and weighed on the 22nd.

Cost of manures.

The present prices in New Orleans are, for cotton seed meal, 18 dol. per ton; acid phosphate, 15 per cent., 18 dol. per ton; kainite, 12 per cent., 15 dol. per ton.

Plat No. 12. Oats.

Sugar Experiment Station, Kenner, Louisiana.

Results.

No. of Experiment	Fertilisers. Kind.	Amount per Acre. Lbs.	Cost per Acre. Dol. c.	Weight of Oats in Sheaf. Lbs.	Bushels of Oats.
1*	Cotton seed meal	270	4 86	6,137	67¾
	Acid phosphate	270			
2	Cotton seed meal	270	6 80	6,673	73 21/32
	Acid phosphate	270			
	Kainite	270			
3	Cotton seed meal	360	4 86	5,564	64 17/32
	Acid phosphate	180			
4	Cotton seed meal	360	6 80	6,127	67 29/32
	Acid phosphate	180			
	Kainite	270			
5*	Cotton seed meal	405	4 86	4,991	55 3/32
	Acid phosphate	135			
6	Cotton seed meal	405	6 80	5,409	62 11/32
	Acid phosphate	135			
	Kainite	270			
7	Cotton seed meal	300	2 70	6,095	59 20/32
8	Acid phosphate	150	1 35	5,405	57 30/32
9	Kainite	150	1 12	5,014	51 6/32
10	Nothing	...	...	5,041	51
11	Cotton seed meal	300	4 05	8,135	103 6/32
	Acid phosphate	150			
12*	Cotton seed meal	300	5 17	5,837	70 4/32
	Acid phosphate	150			
	Kainite	150			

* Damaged by water standing on plats.

As before remarked, the defective drainage of a portion of this plat prevents accurate comparisons and deductions. Nos. 1, 3, and 5, occupying the eastern length of the plat, had a slight declivity running entirely through each experiment, which, after the continuous rains of March, held water several days before discovery. Again, there were also found slight depressions in Nos. 5 and 12, which greatly injured these experiments. The rest of the field appeared to be well-drained, especially Nos. 7, 8, 9, 10, and 11.

These can be compared with each other, but it is manifestly wrong to compare them with the rest of the field. Omitting the others and taking these we have the following:—

	Lbs. of Sheaved Oats.	Bushels of Oats.
Nothing	5,041	51
Kainite	5,014	$51\frac{6}{32}$
Acid phosphate	5,405	$57\frac{30}{32}$
Cotton seed meal	6,095	$59\frac{20}{32}$
Cotton seed meal } Acid phosphate	8,135	$103\frac{6}{32}$

From the above we find that kainite alone has given no increase. **Results of fertilisers.** Acid phosphate is accountable for 364 lbs. sheaved oats; nearly seven bushels of grain. Cotton seed meal increases the yield of sheaved oats 1,054 lbs., and the grain $8\frac{2}{3}$ bushels; while acid phosphate and cotton seed meal combined have given the enormous yield of 8,135 lbs. (over four tons) of sheaved oats and 103 bushels of grain.

Ten years ago the farmer sowed every rod he could plough with **Old practice.** cotton, and bought all his provisions—even the corn and hay for his mules—from the city.

If an Act now before Congress for repealing the import duty on **Sugar.** sugar and giving American manufacturers a bonus upon its production be passed, we shall probably see a revolution in this industry. The business of growing cane will be divorced from that of making sugar. Central sugar houses (advocated years ago in these pages) will be **Central factories.** established, and as a natural consequence the country will be opened up by passable roads to the general benefit. Upon the subject it is worthy of remark that the climate in the cane-growing districts has undergone a change in the last decade. Frosts, fatal to standing crops and stubble, appear to come earlier and be more severe. A cold wave in January **Change of climate.** played havoc—much more than was admitted at the time—in this respect, and almost totally destroyed the orange trees. Should this continue the manufacturer of sugar will, perhaps, have to earn his bounty from other staples than that afforded by the cane.

A considerable quantity of the rice crop (excellent in quality) was **Rice.** destroyed by floods; but as the total output was more than double that of previous years, enough remained for the general profit.

The culture and decortication of ramie has not yet emerged from **Ramie.** the field of discussion, and experiments are on too small a scale to prove anything definite.

IMMIGRATION.

As inducements to immigration in these States are mainly directed **Warning to immigrants.** to farmers, the observations I have to make on this head may properly come in here. I have before me several pamphlets (which I understand

(133)

are circulated in the United Kingdom) containing highly-coloured accounts of the beauty and richness of the land, and promising easy and quick prosperity to those who would come and possess it. As Florida has been added to my Consular district, I think it my duty to state that the warnings contained in my previous reports apply equally to that State.

Alabama iron.

The rapidly expanding iron-works of North Alabama might provide steady work and good wages. I hope to add a report from the Vice-Consul at Mobile on this subject.

Exports and Imports.

Exports and imports.

As this report is the first wholly compiled under the new instructions, I beg to repeat the reasons given in its predecessors why the returns I am able to make are not strictly reliable. The manifesto of British ships are not produced to me, and according to custom-house showing every export from a British port (home or colonial) would figure as British. But large quantities of foreign goods come in transit in our ships. Thus given: wines, spirits, hardware, dry goods, &c., from France, Germany, Spain, and Belgium, viâ a British port, would all appear as of British origin.

Official statistics misleading.

Imports from British ports, value.

According to customs showing the value of all imports from British ports during the year ended December 31, 1886, it was 2,370,615 dol., and the exports 43,116,025 dol. In this connection I may note that of 372 British ships entered in 1886, 212 came in ballast.

Exports in value.

Table showing the Total Value of all Articles Exported from and Imported to New Orleans from and to Foreign Countries during the Year 1886.

Country.	Exports.	Imports.
	Dollars.	Dollars.
British and colonial	43,116,025	2,370,615
Spanish	26,690	2,016,069
Italian	375,141	1,878,963
German	185,806	11,099,940
French	538,077	18,407,643
Belgium	32,365	908,076
Total to all ports	80,809,765	8,760,115

Note.—Large quantities of European goods are brought here through jobbers in New York.

I am unable to obtain the material for making up the quality and value of the various exports and imports in detail.

British trade.

As British trade and the means which may be suggested for its development should form the principal object of these reports, I beg to refer to the observations made in my last upon the possibilities of pushing British trade in this district. These were written before I had seen Mr. Kenric B. Murray's letter to Lord Rosebery, dated June 10th, 1886, in which he stated "that the London Council of Commerce has been led to believe, from circumstances which have come under its notice, that there exists in the minds of British merchants engaged in various branches of foreign trade an opinion that Her Majesty's . . . Consular officers abroad have not, as a rule, been prepared to give their assistance in the promotion and development of British commercial

Consular assistance.

interests." I think that there is rather a disinclination on the part of the British merchant to make use of his Consul.

During the 15 years that I have been in charge of this post (New Orleans) I have received certainly not more than 20 letters on commercial subjects, and half of these related to shipping. I answered all, to the best of my ability, and added that there was no necessity for the apology for troubling me, which my correspondents invariably offered, for that I considered it part of my day's work to give the information required. *Not asked by merchants.*

When the "World's Cotton Centennial Exposition" was in course of preparation, I did not receive an application for information or advice from any British manufacturer. The observations and advice given in my last general report were reproduced (being knowledge) with favourable comments in Martineau and Smith's "Trade Journal," in the "Manchester Guardian," and in the "London Times." It is probable that the subject was taken up in other journals, but so far as I am aware with no result whatever. I might, perhaps, be justified in taking this as conclusive evidence that I am wrong, and that there is no opening in this district for British goods worth attention. I must, however, show a little British obstinacy on my side, and persist. I have facts to support my views, whilst those who ignore them are blinded by a combination of qualities which have been summed up by a colleague into one word, which most accurately defines them. The British merchant, spoiled by a long career of prosperity, is not quick to make changes in his modes of conducting business, or to accept the new methods of others. It would seem that he has not yet fully realised that Her Majesty's Consuls are no longer allowed to trade, and that they have become his allies instead of his competitors. In Mr. Helyar's report upon the Depression of Trade in the United States, he writes that French and Germans are supplanting the British in New Orleans, "the latter not meeting American requirements." This is undoubtedly true, but not all the truth. In several of the few articles of import left to us, our merchants err in not "putting them up" in a handy and saleable manner to meet American requirements, but in all others they do not seek to find out what is required. If there has been a British commercial traveller in New Orleans during the last 15 years I have not seen or heard of him. Latterly I have received by post a number of illustrated trade magazines and price lists. These are of no use. I can hardly get our men of business to accept them. What they require to see is the thing itself. Let me offer an example. Some friends of mine in an extensive line of trade, finding that the transport of their samples (owing to diversity and bulk) was very expensive, had them photographed on a large scale from all points of view, and provided their "drummer" with a book of these illustrations. Their business immediately fell of. Buyers accustomed to see and handle the thing itself could not understand, or would not trust, its asserted likeness, and the old system had to be re-adopted. The increase in late years at home, both in number and artistic excellence of illustrated advertisements, shows that the trade is alive to the importance of bringing its wares more closely to the senses of possible purchasers than can be done by descriptive letterpress. Here a further advance is required. The thing itself must be shown. In many, indeed most, cases with regard to the goods I have in mind, it is impossible to present their merits properly on paper. The portrait of a merino undershirt, or a bolt of linen, proves nothing in their favour. You can say in print, or otherwise, that the former is soft and light, or stout and warm (as the case may be), or that the latter is *Information not applied for.* *No result from former observations.* *The merchants' mistakes.* *His obstinacy.* *Price lists useless.* *Illustration of sample.* *Samples prevail.*

(133)

UNITED STATES.

Vague advertisements.

fine or strong, but the storekeeper wants you to do to him what he has to do to his customers, *i.e.*, let them know by the ordeal of touch that they actually have the qualities he claims for them. The success of the "Comptoir Industriel Belge" is due to its possession of samples, and the carefully prepared estimates it has ready of the costs of freight, duty, and all other expenses attending importation, so that the foreign producers may not only know at what rates they can sell, but (what is of equal importance) how much their competitors here could cut down to meet opposition.

Nine advertisements out of 10 in our trade journals end with such phrases as "special terms for shippers on application," or "send for price list postage free," leaving an ordinary purchaser entirely in the dark, and involving the delay of a month before he can obtain enlightenment.

Assistance again proposed.

If the British manufacturer had considered my observations on this subject worth attention (and I call the success of the Belgians as a witness that they were), and had applied to me, I could have pointed out a means whereby goods could have been presented to this market, and sold by sample at no greater expense than commission of a commercial traveller at home. To the articles already enumerated in past reports as capable of being profitably exported, I have now to add the following:—Bobinet for mosquito bars (an absolute necessity for rich and poor alike), Nottingham lace in curtains, borderings and trimmings; all sorts of hosiery (especially linen, muslin, and cambric handkerchiefs), towellings, and light Bradford woollens, in pieces for dress wear such as nuns' veiling.

Articles suitable for this market.

Iron ware.

A trade could also be done in iron work, as the following incident will show:— A large brewery required additional cellarage, the roofs of which were to be constructed with wrought-iron girders. These were imported from Belgium, duty paid, for 2,500 dol. less than the estimate furnished from Pittsburg in a contract of 15,000 dol.

Belgium cheaper than Pittsburg.

Cotton ties.

Cotton ties are as indispensable for the export of cotton as bread is for the life of those who work the crop. Multiply any estimated cotton crop by five, and you have the number of "ties" that must be bought and sold. Last summer some New Orleans dealers had a conference with manufacturers at Sheffield respecting a direct importation by the consumers of these ties, and everything was settled but the terms of credit. Sheffield wanted its money as soon as the goods were on board ship. New Orleans wanted credit until they were delivered. Upon this rock they split, but within 24 hours a German firm stepped in, accepted the discarded terms, and secured the contract!

Sheffield's old-fashioned terms.

Houses in the business part of the city are built on the ground, which carries water in all seasons within three feet of the surface. The lower floors are planked, and this flooring, however prepared, will not last more than four years. Here is a chance for encaustic tiling, and the Belgians (as usual) are pushing it. Their tiles are unnecessarily thick, very heavy, and so hard that a sharp fracture of one will cut glass. They are not by any means as artistic or effective as those I have seen at home, and considerably more expensive. Paying equal duty and freight per ton, I should think that Staffordshire or Lambeth could easily obtain command of the market in these articles.

Encaustic tiles.

Slate and granite.

It has been demonstrated that slate in slabs and granite in blocks can be shipped from Antwerp to this port and sold here, duty paid, for less than the same articles can be obtained from Vermont or Massachusetts.

Roofing slate.

I have been able to give a firm at Portmadoc, North Wales, information respecting prices for roofing slates, which may lead to business. There is an opening also for window glass, shipped direct by sea to avoid breakage caused by reapeated handling on railways. With little difficulty and no deviation from my proper duties as a Consul, I could assist our manufacturers to establish an agency in the city: in the first place to ascertan what goods and classes of goods can favourably compete with native productions and imports from other continental countries, and in the next to sell them by sample direct to the retailer. There is no room in the present state of competition for the commission merchant or the jobber, or any other class of middleman. Advantage should be taken of the existing labour troubles which threaten production in all quarters and in every particular. *Window glass. Agency proposed. Direct sales*

Careful observation will, I think, prove that although American industry has expanded in a wonderful manner during the last quarter of a century, and especially in the past 10 years, the quality of the goods produced has not improved. They are showy, handily "put up," ingenious, but in the struggle for sudden wealth, economies have been introduced for which durability is sacrificed. This is especially the case with all textile fabrics that I see here. *Decadence of American goods.*

SHIPPING.

RETURN of all Shipping at the Port of New Orleans in the Year 1886.

ENTERED.

Nationality.	Sailing. Number of Vessels.	Sailing. Tons.	Steam. Number of Vessels.	Steam. Tons.	Total. Number of Vessels.	Total. Tons.
British	57	46,965	315	397,590	372	441,554
American	92	37,710	316	402,223	408	439,933
Spanish	...	...	...	...	59	82,429
Italian	...	...	...	...	72	35,514
French	...	...	...	...	17	34,491
Austrian	...	...	...	...	12	9,430
Swedish and Norwegian	...	...	...	...	9	5,771
German	...	...	...	...	21	26,345
Total	...	...	...	...	970	1,078,467

CLEARED.

Nationality.	Sailing. Number of Vessels.	Sailing. Tons.	Steam. Number of Vessels.	Steam. Tons.	Total. Number of Vessels.	Total. Tons.
British	75	67,076	307	390,113	382	457,189
American	71	34,856	301	391,874	372	426,730
Spanish	...	...	...	...	58	80,251
Italian	...	...	...	...	82	38,301
German	...	...	...	...	24	28,880
French	...	...	...	...	17	34,491
Austrian	...	...	...	...	8	5,726
Swedish and Norwegian	...	...	...	...	8	5,231
Total	...	...	...	...	951	1,076,799

The returns with which my foreign colleagues have favonred me do not discriminate between sail and steam. Another year I hope to be able to supply this deficiency: compared with last year there is an increase in British shipping entered of 41 vessels and of 68,987 tons, and is the best showing since 1879, and in point of tonnage is the highest on record. *Increase of British shipping.*

UNITED STATES.

Quarantine.

Removal of, from Ship Island.

Quarantine.—In a previous report I pointed out certain objections to Ship Island as a quarantine station. Owing to an outbreak of yellow fever at Biloxi, on the main land, only 12 miles distant, to which (as it is said) the crews of infected ships had access, the United States station at this point will probably be transferred to some safer locality. The stringent but at the same time reasonable and discriminating action of the present Board of Health of the State of Louisiana are worthy of all support and approbation.

Coals to Liverpool.

What may (at least for the present) be termed a commercial eccentricity occurred on the 15th January last, when the s.s. "Carn Marth" sailed with 2,000 tons of Virginia coal for Liverpool. to be used by the gasworks of that city. This coal is said to produce a 6,000 candle power of gas per ton, and I am told that the freight paid was barely 5s. a ton.

Labour.

Labour.—The movement for a general reduction in the price of labour, which promised favourable results in the month of December, 1887, has subsided, and New Orleans will not yet resign her position as the most expensive port in America.

Seamen.

Discipline of Seamen.—On this head I have to report with pleasure that in 1886 there were only two complaints calling for Consular action against seamen, and not one well-founded case of ill-usage by master or officers.

MOBILE.

Mr. Vice-Consul Barnwell reports as follows:—

Cotton: receipts of. Prices.

Commercial year commencing September 1, 1885, and ending August 31, 1886. Receipt 248,526 bales, valued at 10,713,955 dol., against 236,871 bales, valued at 11,663,528 dol. Receipts of the year preceding: tonnage price per bale, 43 dol. $\frac{11}{100}$ c., average price per lb. 8 dol. 59 c., against 49 dol. 24 c. per bale, and 9 dol. 91 c. per lb. the year preceding.

Timber.

Another year has passed in one of the most important branches of the pitch pine trade. In timber, one of the leading articles of export in this port, a large business was transacted, but not quite as large as last year, and not entirely satisfactory to all connected with it, especially the latter half of it.

Exports of, to United Kingdom.

The timber markets of the United Kingdom, which are the leading markets of the world, and where the greater part of the timber from this port is shipped, have, as well as others, felt the general depression of trade, and this, together with the heavy arrivals of timber that shippers from this side continued to force on an unwilling market, caused these markets to go from bad to worse, and prices to steadily decline, until there was very little profit left to the shippers. Although neither sawn nor hewn timber has brought shippers very satisfactory returns, yet the leading merchants in this market have no doubt done fairly well, as cargoes in many cases were sold previous to shipment, and not forced on declining markets.

Sawn timber.

In sawn timber, which is fast taking the place of hewn, a larger trade was done the past year than in any previous year, and the mills manufactured sawn timber cheaper than ever before, and while there has been but little profit to the shippers, the mills generally show a balance more or less in their favour. The demand for hewn is becoming less every year, but there will always be a demand for hewn timber of special size, as shippers cannot get as long sticks of sawn as of hewn, and producers will experience little difficulty in obtaining contracts for such at paying prices.

At the present time it is almost impossible to give any prediction as to the future, as any depression or advance in the coal and iron trade of Europe causes a corresponding advance or decline in the timber trade of this country; but we hope and expect to see an improving trade the coming season, as there is generally a revival in trade, and Mobile is one of the cheapest ports in the gulf for vessels. *Future prospects.*

The shipments compared with last year show a decrease of 150,000 cubic feet which was entirely hewn, as the exports of sawn show an increase of 200,000 cubic feet, while hewn exhibits a decrease of about 350,000 cubic feet. *Exports of timber.*

The shipments to the United Kingdom of Great Britain and Ireland were 860,000 cubic feet of hewn and 1,670,000 cubic feet of sawn, against 1,300,000 cubic feet of hewn and 1,500,000 cubic feet of sawn last year.

The value of the exports were less than last year: total shipments, hewn and sawn, 2,973,206 cubic feet, value 336,780 dol. 27 c., against 3,122,749 cubic feet, total value 370,878 dol. 99 c. last year.

The naval store trade continues to be an important branch of business in this section, and in sections tributary to Mobile are many stills in operation, situated on the Mobile and Ohio and Mobile and Montgomery railways, the Bigbee, Alabama, and Mobile rivers, and on the eastern shore in Baldwin county. *Naval stores.*

Receipts: rosin 175,817 barrels, turpentine 38,733 barrels, total value 1,034,682 dol. 75 c., against rosin 200,688 barrels, turpentine 41,718 barrels, total value 1,027,166 dol. the year preceding. Shipments: rosin, foreign, 36,864 barrels, value 67,862 dol. 32 c., against 61,617 barrels, value 115,335 dol. 60 c. the year preceding. *Rosin and turpentine.*

Annex A.—RETURN of all Shipping at the Port of Mobile in the Year 1886.

CLEARED.

Nationality.	Sailing. Number of Vessels.	Sailing. Tons.	Steam. Number of Vessels.	Steam. Tons.	Total. Number of Vessels.	Total. Tons.
British	45	30,210	5	4,784	50	34,994
American	34	8,945	...	...	34	8,945
Italian	6	2,850	...	...	6	2,850
Russian	8	4,154	...	...	8	4,154
French	1	470	...	...	1	470
Swedish	13	7,538	...	...	13	7,538
Honduras	3	120	...	...	3	120
German	10	6,433	...	...	10	6,433
Norwegian	25	16,799	...	...	25	16,799
Austrian	2	1,547	...	...	2	1,547
Spanish	1	385	...	...	1	385
Total	148	79,451	5	4,784	153	84,235
,, for the year preceding	...	...	...	...	182	105,358

UNITED STATES.

Entered.

Nationality.	Sailing. Number of Vessels.	Sailing. Tons.	Steam. Number of Vessels.	Steam. Tons.	Total. Number of Vessels.	Total. Tons.
British	41	26,011	4	3,632	45	29,643
American	32	8,526	...	...	32	8,526
Swedish	12	6,265	...	...	12	6,265
Italian	2	1,075	...	...	2	1,075
Spanish	2	887	...	...	2	887
German	5	4,042	...	...	5	4,042
Austrian	2	1,547	...	...	2	1,547
Honduras	3	120	...	...	3	120
Russian	7	3,636	...	...	7	3,636
Norwegian	19	11,619	...	...	19	11,619
Total	125	63,728	4	3,632	129	67,360
,, for the year preceding	...	...	...	...	173	101,512

Annex B.—RETURN of Principal Articles of Import to Mobile during the Years 1885–86 and 1884–85.

Articles.		1885 and 1886. Quantity.	1885 and 1886. Value. £ s. d.	1884 and 1885. Quantity.	1884 and 1885. Value. £ s. d.
Bagging	Pieces	30,366	...	24,630	...
Iron ties	Bundles	54,417	...	52,125	...
Bacon	Hogsheads	15,140	...	12,518	...
Cotton	Bales	248,526	2,232,074 2 9	236,871	2,429,901 13 6
Coffee	Sacks	19,270	...	21,002	...
Corn	,,	371,480	...	234,801	...
Flour	Barrels	122,517	...	107,643	...
Fertilisers	Sacks	137,769	...	90,972	...
Hay	Bales	43,182	...	33,346	...
Lard	Tierces	2,727	...	3,276	...
Molasses	Barrels	3,146	...	4,619	...
Oats	Sacks	92,330	...	77,103	...
Potatoes	Barrels	20,534	...	20,303	...
Pork	,,	2,055	...	1,127	...
Rice	,,	4,833	...	3,357	...
Salt	Sacks	27,019	...	30,349	...
Sugar	Barrels	15,986	...	13,928	...
Tobacco	Boxes	25,277	...	21,994	...
Whiskey	Barrels	5,773	...	6,604	...
Soap	Boxes	24,414	...	25,080	...
Various articles from foreign countries to June 30, 1886 and 1885		...	14,465 4 2	...	26,884 11 8

Value £ sterling, 4 dol. 80 c.

I cannot enumerate articles imported from foreign countries, nor give the value of above-enumerated articles, with exception of cotton.

RETURN of Principal Articles of Export from Mobile during the Years 1885–86 and 1884–85.

Articles.		1885 and 1886. Quantity.	1885 and 1886. Value. £ s. d.	1884 and 1885. Quantity.	1884 and 1885. Value. £ s. d.
Cotton	Bales	255,796	2,297,367 15 8	246,976	2,533,562 19 4
Timber	Cubic feet	2,973,206	70,162 11 0	3,122,749	77,266 9 1
Lumber	Feet	21,435,453	53,771 6 11	22,265,804	56,523 11 8
Rosin	Barrels	36,864	14,137 19 8	61,617	24,028 5 0
Staves		79,956	1,968 6 8	107,884	2,772 8 4
Shingles		345,950	302 5 10	745,000	628 0 5
Coal	Tons	200	145 16 8	1,497	996 7 9
Merchandise		...	2,139 16 3	...	3,249 9 4
Total		...	2,439,995 18 8	...	2,699,027 10 11

Value £ sterling, 4 dol. 80 c.

Annex C.—TABLE showing the Total Value of all Articles Exported from Mobile and Imported to Mobile from and to Foreign Countries during the Years 1885-86 and 1884-85.

EXPORTS.

	£	s.	d.
1885-86	550,769	2	4
1884-85	597,197	10	4

IMPORTS TO JUNE 30.

	£	s.	d.
1886	14,465	4	2
1885	26,884	11	8

Value £ sterling, 4 dol. 80 c.

I have no means of dividing the above as to countries, except as regards cotton included in above—

	£	s.	d.
Great Britain, 1885-86	425,854	19	0
,, 1884-85	442,441	18	4
Bremen	7,180	16	8

Since the last report of F. J. Cridland, Esq., Her Britannic Majesty's Consul at Mobile, published in 1885, on the Resources of the State of Alabama, there has been an unparalleled stride in her onward march of progress. *Advance of trade in Alabama.*

Years ago, away back in the forties, when the Mobile and Ohio Railroad was in its infancy, the pioneer engineer of the road, Captain Childs, made this remark to one of its originators: "You Alabamians little dream of the wealth Alabama buries in her bosom, or of the fortunes she has in store for those who will unearth her hidden treasures of iron, coal, and limestones, which will crown her the Queen State of the Union." *Trade 40 years ago.*

Forty years have elapsed, and his prophecy is working towards fulfilment, for not only her own people, but the eyes of capitalists from all sections are piercing into her secrets, greedily seeking to devour her riches, and all this is due to the development of the great natural advantages and wonderful mineral wealth of the State.

Coal has been termed the source of power, iron the source of strength, and these two minerals with the limestones (marble is nothing more than a durable limestone, and is found extensive in quantity, of the finest and most durable quality, and in all varieties of colour, particularly in the Cahaba quarries: pure white in one ledge, almost touching it is another ledge black as jet, near by quantities of pale pink, then again a ledge called cabio, showing every hue of the rainbow weaving in and out and through in perplexing and tangled skein) form a triumvirate power of wealth that no goldfields can equal, still less excel. *Coal. Marble.*

The mountain region of Alabama is the southern terminus of the great Opalachin coalfield (the basin of the Ohio). It once formed here in Alabama one great connected coalfield, covering one-fourth the surface area of the State, but now consists of three more or less distinct fields of an area of 8,860 square miles, cut up by long, narrow valleys, which hold inexhaustible beds of limestone, and of red and brown iron ores. In 1849 they were named by Professor Juomey *Coalfields.*

from the rivers that drain them. The Warrior, the Cahaba, and the Coosa fields are all fertile in coal, and two of them comprise the thickest coal measures in the United States.

In the heart of this region are located the cities of Anniston, Sheffield, Tuscaloosa, and Florence, grouped around at short distances, and threatening, in the race of prosperity and wealth, to rival Birmingham, truly called the Magic City, from its sudden and unheard-of rise and progress. In 1871 her population was from 700 to 1,000; to-day Birmingham proclaims it will double itself in five years, and from the causes that now make it 40,000 there seems no reason to doubt the truth of the prediction. In November, 1880, the first furnace was erected; to-day she counts 23 factories and foundries, and 12 furnaces in full blast, with 14 more building; the capital of the latter aggregate 6,000,000. This, with an indefinite number of other enterprises, have made her what she is, and promise to make of her not only a magic city, but the centre city of the South.

Birmingham, Alabama.

Its progress.

That the great source of Alabama's prosperity rests upon the intelligent direction of her agriculture begins to be an acknowledged fact. At the close of the war planters and farmers found themselves without capital, with their labour system demoralised, their implements and machinery destroyed, and nothing left them but their fields. Since then they have accomplished wonders; and with a reduced cost of farming, a gradual escape from the credit system, a cultivation by small farms instead of large plantations, they are entering a new era of progress full of promise for the future; and it is these new ideas, these new systems in conformity with the new necessities, occasions, and opportunities which, above all things, the South requires. Agricultural lands in all parts of Alabama are exceedingly cheap. Why? There is more land than money. Alabama's great want is more people to cultivate the land, more capital and better-directed labour, and this want is yearly better supplied by the tide of immigration which is turning southward instead of all westward as heretofore.

Agriculture.

Improved farming.

If Alabama lands are cheap, her soil is very fertile and very varied, consisting of rich bottom lands of alluvial formation, of sandy lands that yield large crops by the use of fertilisers manufactured at home, and of red lands: these are considered the most desirable, as they are least affected by excessive rain or drought.

Land.

The products from these lands are abundant, and of superior quality. There is a great diversification of crops. Cotton, the great staple, jute, ramie, corn, oats, rye, barley, wheat, peas, rice, potatoes, millet, clover, sugar-cane, tobacco, fruits of every kind, peaches, apples, pears, figs, melons, pomegranates, grapes, especially from which a most delicious wine is made, the cultivation of all which is constantly increasing and introducing new trades. Fruit exportation and vegetable shipments are looming up extensively, and promise to be sources of very lucrative and productive traffic.

Crops.

Central Alabama is also well adapted to stock-raising, and has already many fine farms of blooded cattle, vast areas of pine land, and grasses and vegetation furnish abundant pasturage for cattle, sheep, and hogs.

Stock-raising.

The perennial winter pasture grass, white and yellow clover, and the vetch; the summer grass, the bermuda, which grows on the same sod with the vetch, the one in no way interfering with the other, thus affording from the same enclosure perpetual pasturage of a most valuable and nutritious nature.

Fodder.

Then add to all these natural advantages for agriculture the delightful climate of Alabama, where the labourer may work in the open air through all seasons, and cattle will thrive unsheltered and almost unfed

Climate.

NEW ORLEANS.

all the year round; and there is presented a mass of attractions that no other State in the Union can surpass.

Finances of Alabama for the Year ending 30th September, 1886.

The total debt of the State of Alabama amounts to 9,193,900 dols.

DESCRIPTION OF BONDS.

Bonds.	Amount.	Interest per Annum.
	Dollars.	Per cent.
Class A.	6,747,900	4
„ B.	539,000	5
„ C.	953,000	4
„ Sixes	954,000	6

Annual interest 392,226 dols., which is punctually paid half-yearly.

The receipt of taxes for the fiscal year ending 30th September, 1886, exclusive of the amount received and paid out for the public schools in the several counties, 888,724 dols. 23 c.; the disbursements 818,366 dols. 70 c. Balance of cash in the State Treasury, at the end of the past year, 269,538 dols. 3 c.

Mobile during the past year has nothing to complain of; business as a general thing has been satisfactory. Industrial affairs have much improved, and give employment to a large number of the labouring class. There is now established a regular line of steamers from and to Liverpool, which will enable us to export double the amount of cotton; the agent of the line feels much encouraged, and gives promise of an increase of steam tonnage in the future.

For particulars in regard to Mobile Bay and harbour improvements, I must respectfully call attention to the following tabular statement:—

CONDITION of Dredged Channel, Mobile Harbour, on the 31st day of December, 1886.

Locality.	Dredged 1881 and 1884.			Examined, 1885 and 1886.	
	Length.	Width.	Depth.	Min. Top.	Min. Central.
	Miles.	Feet.	Feet.	Width.	Depth.
Initial point in Mobile River to Upper Gap obstructions	·72	145	19·20	200	20·23
Upper Gap obstructions to Chester No. 2	·19	245	18·19	300	20 21
Chester No. 2 to Lower Gap obstructions	·87	155	18·19	190	19·20
Lower Gap obstructions to 149 Gr. S. Chester No. 4	1·02	145	18·19	180	18·19
1,408 Chester No. 4 to 2,155 Gr. S. Chester No. 8.	2·51	145	18·19	180	18·19
2,155 Gr. S. Chester No. 8. to Chester No. 12	1·64	105	18 19	140	18·19
Chester No. 12 to 1,632 Gr. S. Chester No. 16	2·14	145	18·19	180	18·19
1,632 Gr. S. Chester No. 16 to Chester No. 30	7·01	105	18·19	140	17·18½
Chester No. 30 to Chester No 50 (south entrance)	10·35	185	18·19	200	17·18½
Total length	26.45	...	...	...	...

PENSACOLA.

Mr. Vice-Consul Howe reports as follows:—

The tables will show that the trade of Pensacola for the past year was beyond the business of the previous year in the export of the chief

UNITED STATES.

staple of the place, consisting of pitch-pine wood, prepared and manufactured as hewn and sawn timber, lumber, &c.

Exports. The decrease in the total value of exports for the year 1886, when compared with the preceding year, as shown by the tables, must be accounted for by the explanation that a lesser quantity of cotton was shipped through this port during the past year.

Imports. Only the articles usually referred to in these reports have been brought in from foreign countries direct during the past year; mostly fertilisers and salt from the United Kingdom. All chief articles of food and clothing are brought here from the northern and western markets of the United States, and from some of the larger southern markets, by railroad. Also, agricultural implements, machinery, hardware, railroad iron, fertilisers, and such things are brought here from the western and northern ports of the United States by railroad and by sailing vessels. It may be considered that in dry goods and other things English products and manufactures form a good part of the value received from the northern ports of the United States, and viâ those ports from England on direct order.

English products and manufactures.

British shipping. When it is stated that the number of British vessels arriving and loading at the port of Pensacola for the nine years preceding the past year averaged 111 vessels per year, of the usual average tonnage—about or not less than 800 tons each vessel—it will be noticeable in this report that during the year just past there was quite a falling-off in the arrival of British vessels; and, in explaining the reason therefore, it may be stated, as I have been informed, that British owners refused to entertain the low offers of freight ruling, whenever they could place their vessels otherwise than at this port.

General remarks. New life appears to have been awakened and continuing with many projects in view for the advancement of Pensacola, and the extension of her export trade, particularly in new and well laid down lines; and, advancing as the place has been in the main for some years past, it is expected that it will, at no distant day, be doubly prosperous, which expectation no doubt will be realised, many things being in favour of the place to this end. In view of British interests in connection with the export trade of Pensacola—much British capital being used in the trade, not only in direct business but by controlling shipments hence—the prosperity of the port must always be a source of pleasant interest to those referred to in the United Kingdom so concerned.

Regular steam line. It is the opinion here that with direct, regular steam communication between Pensacola and Liverpool, or some principal port in the United Kingdom, Brazil, and other ports, a brisk import business would be established between this and other southern and western markets direct with the United Kingdom and Brazil and other ports. I am informed that such direct, regular steam communication by an expected arrangement in England is contemplated, to work particularly in connection with the Pensacola and Memphis railroad, now about to be built, which new road, it is said, will add largely to the exportation of cotton from this port in the near future.

RETURN of all Shipping at the Port of Pensacola in the Year 1886.

ENTERED.

Nationality.	Sailing. Number of Vessels.	Sailing. Tons.	Steam. Number of Vessels.	Steam. Tons.	Total. Number of Vessels.	Total. Tons.
British	49	36,679	4	4,326	53	41,005
American	139	64,368	...	...	139	64,368
Swedish and Norwegian	118	87,876	...	...	118	87,876
Italian	93	59,785	...	...	93	59,785
Russian	36	23,231	...	...	36	23,231
Austrian	13	9,296	...	...	13	9,296
Netherlands	4	3,373	...	...	4	3,373
German	2	1,625	...	...	2	1,625
Other countries	8	3,393	...	...	8	3,393
Total	462	289,626	4	4,326	466	293,952
,, for the year preceding	445	277,381	8	9,477	453	286,858

CLEARED.

Nationality.	Sailing. Number of Vessels.	Sailing. Tons.	Steam. Number of Vessels.	Steam. Tons.	Total. Number of Vessels.	Total. Tons.
British	57	43,812	4	4,326	61	48,138
American	135	71,299	...	...	135	71,299
Swedish and Norwegian	121	89,577	...	...	121	89,577
Italian	102	64,902	...	...	102	64,902
Russian	33	20,513	...	...	33	20,513
Austrian	13	9,592	...	...	13	9,592
Netherlands	6	4,844	...	...	6	4,844
German	5	3,802	...	...	5	3,802
Other countries	7	2,220	...	...	7	2,220
Total	479	310,561	4	4,326	483	314,887
,, for the year preceding	481	293,771	8	9,477	489	303,248

RETURN of Principal Articles of Export from Pensacola during the Year 1886.

Articles.	1886. Quantity.	1886. Value. £ s. d.	1885. Quantity.	1885. Value. £ s. d.
Pitch pine lumber	108,125,487	270,313 14 4	100,950,573	252,376 8 7
Sawn pitch pine timber	8,317,683	190,613 11 4	7,556,522	173,170 5 11
Hewn ,, ,,	935,078	19,480 15 10	2,055,609	42,825 3 9
Cotton	1,475	14,596 7 1	12,787	133,197 18 4
Pig iron	...	...	2,083	8,679 3 4
Rosin	4,434	1,154 13 9	...	...
Other articles	...	2,019 7 2	...	930 4 2
Total	...	498,178 9 6	...	611,179 4 1

(133)

16 UNITED STATES.

RETURN of Principal Articles of Import to Pensacola during the Year 1886.

Articles.	1886.		1885.	
	Quantity.	Value.	Quantity.	Value.
		£ s. d.		£ s. d.
Chief articles* ..	..	..	..	..
Other ,, ..	..	8,629 10 0	..	26,189 11 8
Total ..	..	8,629 10 0	..	26,189 11 8

The following, as regards the above table of exports, is descriptive of the values, quantities, weights, and measures; the conversion of money into sterling being at the rate of 4 dol. 80 c. per £ :—Lumber at average of 12 dol. (2l. 10s.) per 1,000 superficial feet; sawn timber at average of 11 c. (5½d.) per cubic foot; hewn timber at average of 10 c. (5d.) per cubic foot; cotton at average of 9½ c. (4¾d.) per lb., in bales of 500 lbs. average weight each bale; pig iron, in tons, at 20 dol. (4l. 3s. 4d.) per ton; rosin, in barrels, at 1 dol. 25 c (5s. 2½d.) per barrel.

TABLE showing the Total Value of all Articles Exported from Pensacola and Imported to Pensacola from and to Foreign Countries during the Years 1885 and 1886.

Country.	Exports.		Imports.	
	1886.	1885.	1886.	1885.
	£ s. d.	£ s. d.	£ s. d.	£ s. d.
United Kingdom	167,800 16 2	233,410 4 2	7,117 0 0	25,658 6 8
Italy	49,496 11 10	19,368 15 0	...	...
Argentine Republic	34,010 12 11	35,172 10 0	...	...
Netherlands	32,912 13 10	17,898 19 2	...	...
Spain and colonies	24,405 16 10	20,406 0 10	...	...
France	23,430 16 4	36,970 8 4	...	...
Uruguay	16,878 1 9	21,884 3 4	...	...
Germany	16,676 16 7	4,430 8 4	...	...
United States of Colombia	12,647 14 2	20,221 17 6	...	...
Belgium	11,393 9 6	12,707 5 10	...	...
Brazil	8,430 17 11	...	...	...
Portugal	2,527 10 8	4,966 17 6	...	...
Other countries	2,257 13 11	7,459 11 8	1,512 10 0	531 5 0
Total	402,869 12 5	434,897 1 8	8,629 10 0	26,189 11 8

TABLE showing the Total Value of all Articles Exported from Pensacola to Ports in the United States during the Years 1885 and 1886.

		£ s. d.
1886	.. ..	95,308 17 1
1885	.. ..	176,282 2 5

* As regards the above table of imports, the quantities and values of the chief articles of trade cannot be positively ascertained. Breadstuffs, groceries, hardware, and such-like goods are received from the large northern, southern, and western markets of the United States. In a recent publication, "Facts about Florida," it is stated that "the coastwise imports of fertilisers, steel rails, ice, &c., exceeded 2,000,000 dol. for the year ended July 1, 1886."

LONDON:
Printed for Her Majesty's Stationery Office,
By HARRISON AND SONS,
Printers in Ordinary to Her Majesty.
(Wt. 7730 75 3 | 87--H & S 133)

FOREIGN OFFICE.
1887.
ANNUAL SERIES.

Nº. 94.

DIPLOMATIC AND CONSULAR REPORTS ON TRADE AND FINANCE.

UNITED STATES.

REPORT FOR THE YEAR 1886
ON THE
TRADE OF BALTIMORE.

REFERENCE TO PREVIOUS REPORT [C. 4654] Commercial No. 5, 1886.

Presented to both Houses of Parliament by Command of Her Majesty,
MARCH, 1887.

LONDON:
PRINTED FOR HER MAJESTY'S STATIONERY OFFICE,
BY HARRISON AND SONS, ST. MARTIN'S LANE,
PRINTERS IN ORDINARY TO HER MAJESTY.

And to be purchased, either directly or through any Bookseller, from
EYRE AND SPOTTISWOODE, EAST HARDING STREET, FLEET STREET, E.C., and
32, ABINGDON STREET, WESTMINSTER, S.W.; or
ADAM AND CHARLES BLACK, NORTH BRIDGE, EDINBURGH; or
HODGES, FIGGIS, & Co., 104, GRAFTON STREET, DUBLIN.

1887.

[C—4923—17.]   Price 1d.

New Series of Reports.

Reports of the Annual Series have been issued from Her Majesty's Diplomatic and Consular Officers at the following places, and may be obtained from the sources indicated on the title-page:—

No.		Price.
1. Varna		1d.
2. Florence		1d.
3. Tangier		1d.
4. Loanda		1d.
5. Teneriffe		1d.
6. Manila		1d.
7. Batavia		1d.
8. Beyrout		1d.
9. St. Michael's		1d.
10. Cuba		1d.
11. Tunis		4d.
12. Canton		1d.
13. Newchwang		1d.
14. Shanghai		1d.
15. Tientsin		1d.
16. Vienna		1d.
17. Corfu		1d.
18. Hakodate		1d.
19. Hiogo		1d.
20. Newport News		1d.
21. Stockholm		1d.
22. Christiania		1d.
23. Antwerp		1d.
24. Salonica		1d.
25. Tonga		1d.
26. Batoum		1d.
27. Costa Rica		1d.
28. Mexico		4d.
29. Bushire		1d.
30. Erzeroum		1d.
31. Bilbao		1d.
32. Rio Grande do Sul		1d.
33. Piræus		1d.
34. Sandakan		1d.
35. Stockholm		1d.
36. Tahiti		1d.
37. Syra		1d.
38. Kanagawa		2d.
39. Nagasaki		1d.
40. Chefoo		1d.
41. Pekin		1d.
42. Ciudad Bolivar		1d.
43. Puerto Cabello		1d.
44. Réunion		1d.
45. Sarawak		1d.
46. Würtemberg		1d.
47. Tokyo		1d.

No.		Price.
48. Amsterdam		1d.
49. Lisbon		1d.
50. Königsberg		2d.
51. Cagliari		1d.
52. Frankfort		1d.
53. Bogota		1d.
54. Kharput		1d.
55. Trieste		1d.
56. Crete		1d.
57. Berne		3d.
58. Rotterdam		1d.
59. Düsseldorf		4d.
60. Mozambique		5d.
61. Hanyang		1d.
62. Stockholm		1d.
63. Paris		1d.
64. Tunis		1d.
65. The Hague		2d.
66. Italy		2d.
67. Smyrna		2d.
68. Fiume		1d.
69. Tabreez		1d.
70. Philippopolis		1d.
71. Rome		1d.
72. Vienna		1d.
73. St Petersburg		2d.
74. Ichang		1d.
75. Salonica		1d.
76. Brussels		2d.
77. Alexandria		1d.
78. Patras		1d.
79. Maranham		1d.
80. Taganrog		2d.
81. Jeddah		1d
82. Suakin		1d.
83. Colonia		1d.
84. Suez		1d.
85. Paris		1d.
86. Brest		1d.
87. Puerto Plata		1d.
88. Charleston		1d.
89. Tripoli		1d.
90. Saigon		1d.
91. Cherbourg		1d.
92. New Orleans		2d.
93. Galatz		1d.

No. 94.

Reference to previous Report [C. 4654], Commercial No. 5, 1886.

UNITED STATES.

BALTIMORE.

Consul Donohoe to the Marquis of Salisbury.

My Lord,   Baltimore, U.S.A., February 7, 1887.

I HAVE the honour to enclose my annual report upon the trade and commerce of the port of Baltimore for the year 1886.

I have, &c.
(Signed)   DENIS DONOHOE.

Report by Consul Donohoe on the Trade and Commerce of Baltimore for the Year 1886.

SHIPPING AND NAVIGATION.

There has been a very considerable increase in the number of British steamers at this port during the year. The principal improvement in the business of the port has been during the last six months of the year, as the shipment of grain has been quite lively. Many of the steamers coming here for grain arrive in ballast from United States ports, where they have landed their cargoes; and many others bring direct cargoes of iron ore from the Mediterranean. *Increase of shipping. Increase of grain trade.*

The following table shows the movement of shipping at this port, without including the coasting trade in American vessels; and the return as to these vessels represents the entries and clearances to and from foreign ports only.

RETURN of all Shipping at the Port of Baltimore in the Year 1886.

ENTERED.

Nationality.	Sailing. Number of Vessels.	Sailing. Tons.	Steam. Number of Vessels.	Steam. Tons.	Total. Number of Vessels.	Total. Tons.
British	46	24,656	476	614,113	522	638,769
American	127	49,139	5	1,702	132	50,841
German	20	20,257	35	89,265	55	109,522
Italian	33	20,126	...	...	33	20,126
Spanish	...	...	16	37,798	16	37,798
Norwegian	16	11,011	1	1,166	17	12,177
Total	242	125,189	533	744,044	775	869,233
„ for 1885	...	...	...	...	642	656,153

(135)

UNITED STATES.

Cleared.

Nationality.	Sailing. Number of Vessels.	Sailing. Tons.	Steam. Number of Vessels.	Steam. Tons.	Total. Number of Vessels.	Total. Tons.
British	51	27,485	469	602,561	520	630,046
American	159	56,315	6	1,936	165	58,251
German	20	20,298	35	89,265	55	109,563
Italian	30	17,885	...	...	30	17,885
Spanish	...	...	15	35,113	15	35,113
Norwegian ...	15	10,544	1	1,166	16	11,710
Total	275	132,527	526	730,041	801	862,568
,, for 1885 ...	...	...	...	...	661	670,098

Trade and Commerce.

I annex a table showing the principal articles of export and import at this port during the past two years.

Return of the Principal Articles of Export from Baltimore during the Years 1885 and 1886, calculated at 5 dol. to the £1 sterling.

Articles.		1886. Quantity.	1886. Value.	1885. Quantity.	1885. Value.
Wheat ...	Bushels ...	10,104,354		4,537,922	
Maize ...	,, ...	13,965,342		13,528,857	
Flour ...	Barrels ...	1,642,286		1,051,262	
Cotton ...	Bales ...	180,540		107,028	
Petroleum	Gallons ...	15,880,612	Total value of exports, 9,587,110*l*. sterling.	11,847,556	Total value of exports, 6,977,259*l*. sterling.
Tobacco	Hogsheads	49,367		37,630	
Bacon ...	Lbs. ...	15,267,859		11,299,277	
Lard ...	,, ...	17,625,706		15,838,524	
Quercitron bark	Bags ...	48,042		58,042	
Coal ...	Tons ...	65,500		71,527	
Rosin ...	Barrels ...	32,801		38,490	
Live cattle	Head ...	12,458		17,897	

Imports.

Articles.		1886. Quantity.	1886. Value.	1885. Quantity.	1885. Value.
Coffee ...	Bags ...	325,984		501,527	
Tin plates	Boxes ...	618,715		455,902	
Iron ore	Tons ...	359,314		78,822	
Pig iron	,, ...	55,572		6,178	
Salt ...	Sacks ...	235,113	Total value of imports, 2,358,941*l*. sterling.	354,653	Total value of imports, 2,275,180*l*. sterling.
,, ...	Bushels ...	72,517		103,564	
Chemicals	Packages ...	31,004		30,623	
Brimstone	Tons ...	14,590		14,796	
Nitrate of soda	Bags ...	27,672		13,412	
Guano ...	Tons ...	9,820		11,423	
Lemons	Boxes ...	11,914		14,526	
Oranges	,, ...	57,502		20,122	
Bananas	Bunches ...	302,657		187,557	

Grain. Wheat and maize. The stock of grain on hand in the elevators on the 31st December, 1886, was 850,375 bushels of wheat and 650,723 bushels of maize. Though the increase in the shipment of maize has been but small, there has been a very considerable increase in the quantity of wheat sent abroad.

The export of flour from this port is increasing every year, and, of the 1,642,286 barrels exported in 1886, 1,234,910 barrels went to the United Kingdom. *Flour.*

A great deal of the flour exported from here comes from the West, the production of Baltimore mills during the year being 540,567 barrels. To Brazil there was exported from this port 305,898 barrels.

The export of bacon and lard is increasing at this port. *Bacon and lard.*

In all the articles given in the table of exports, with the exception of bark, coal, rosin, and live cattle, there is a marked increase. *Increase of exports.*

The falling-off in the Rio coffee trade at this port is very marked; and the importation of sugar at this port, which used to be quite extensive, and in which many small sailing vessels were employed, has now ceased entirely, there not being a single refinery within this district. *Imports. Coffee. Sugar.*

The receipt of tin plates from Great Britain has increased considerably, as also of iron ore from Mediterranean ports. *Tin plates. Iron ore.*

Dry goods are not imported here to any great extent, as the jobbing houses usually make their purchases in the New York market. *Dry goods.*

Population and Industries.

The railway workshops have been fully employed during the year, and have had but little trouble with their hands. The two principal ones employ much labour, both on new work and in the repairing of engines and cars. *Railways.*

The three factories for cotton duck and twine have been doing a steady business during the year, with every prospect of an improvement in 1887. They employ from 600 up to 1,200 hands in each establishment. *Cotton duck.*

The iron industry has been rather depressed, but there are signs of improvement. There are nine charcoal furnaces in this city and neighbourhood, which are capable of turning out about 30,000 tons a year. *Iron industry.*

The census returns give as the population of Maryland 852,137 natives and 82,806 foreigners; of the latter, 1,169 are given as Bohemians, 45,481 Germans, 8,813 British, and 21,865 Irish. *Population.*

The number of immigrants landing at this port during the year was 22,566, of whom 11,564 were males and 11,102 females. In 1885 there were only 8,285 in all. Most of the immigrants are booked through to the Western States. *Immigration.*

Taking the population of Baltimore as 400,000, the deaths have been 8,339, and births 7,694, during the year. *Vital statistics.*

LONDON:
Printed for Her Majesty's Stationery Office,
By HARRISON AND SONS,
Printers in Ordinary to Her Majesty.
(Wt. 7730   75   3 | 87—H & S   135)

FOREIGN OFFICE.
1887.
ANNUAL SERIES.

No. 104.

DIPLOMATIC AND CONSULAR REPORTS ON TRADE AND FINANCE.

UNITED STATES.

REPORT FOR THE YEAR 1886
ON THE
TRADE OF GALVESTON, TEXAS.

REFERENCE TO PREVIOUS REPORT [C. 4761] Commercial No. 12, 1886.

Presented to both Houses of Parliament by Command of Her Majesty,
APRIL, 1887.

LONDON:
PRINTED FOR HER MAJESTY'S STATIONERY OFFICE,
BY HARRISON AND SONS, ST. MARTIN'S LANE,
PRINTERS IN ORDINARY TO HER MAJESTY.

And to be purchased, either directly or through any Bookseller, from
EYRE AND SPOTTISWOODE, EAST HARDING STREET, FLEET STREET, E.C., and
32, ABINGDON STREET, WESTMINSTER, S.W.; or
ADAM AND CHARLES BLACK, NORTH BRIDGE, EDINBURGH; or
HODGES, FIGGIS, & Co., 104, GRAFTON STREET, DUBLIN.

1887.

[C.—4923—27.] *Price 1d.*

New Series of Reports.

Reports of the Annual Series have been issued from Her Majesty's Diplomatic and Consular Officers at the following places, and may be obtained from the sources indicated on the title-page:—

No.		Price	No.		Price
1.	Varna	1d.	53.	Bogota	1d.
2.	Florence	1d.	54.	Kharput	1d.
3.	Tangier	1d.	55.	Trieste	1d.
4.	Loanda	1d.	56.	Crete	1d.
5.	Teneriffe	1d.	57.	Berne	3d.
6.	Manila	1d.	58.	Rotterdam	1d.
7.	Batavia	1d.	59.	Düsseldorf	4d.
8.	Beyrout	1d.	60.	Mozambique	5d.
9.	St. Michael's	1d.	61.	Hanyang	1d.
10.	Cuba	1d.	62.	Stockholm	1d.
11.	Tunis	4d.	63.	Paris	1d.
12.	Canton	1d.	64.	Tunis	1d.
13.	Newchwang	1d.	65.	The Hague	2d.
14.	Shanghai	1d.	66.	Italy	2d.
15.	Tientsin	1d.	67.	Smyrna	2d.
16.	Vienna	1d.	68.	Fiume	1d.
17.	Corfu	1d.	69.	Tabreez	1d.
18.	Hakodate	1d.	70.	Philippopolis	1d.
19.	Hiogo	1d.	71.	Rome	1d.
20.	Newport News	1d.	72.	Vienna	1d.
21.	Stockholm	1d.	73.	St. Petersburg	2d.
22.	Christiania	1d.	74.	Ichang	1d.
23.	Antwerp	1d.	75.	Salonica	1d.
24.	Salonica	1d.	76.	Brussels	2d.
25.	Tonga	1d.	77.	Alexandria	1d.
26.	Batoum	1d.	78.	Patras	1d.
27.	Costa Rica	1d.	79.	Maranham	1d.
28.	Mexico	4d.	80.	Taganrog	2d.
29.	Bushire	1d.	81.	Jeddah	1d.
30.	Erzeroum	1d.	82.	Suakin	1d.
31.	Bilbao	1d.	83.	Colonia	1d.
32.	Rio Grande do Sul	1d.	84.	Suez	1d.
33.	Piræus	1d.	85.	Paris	1d.
34.	Sandakan	1d.	86.	Brest	1d.
35.	Stockholm	1d.	87.	Puerto Plata	1d.
36.	Tahiti	1d.	88.	Charleston	1d.
37.	Syra	1d.	89.	Tripoli	1d.
38.	Kanagawa	2d.	90.	Saigon	1d.
39.	Nagasaki	1d.	91.	Cherbourg	1d.
40.	Chefoo	1d.	92.	New Orleans	2d.
41.	Pekin	1d.	93.	Galatz	1d.
42.	Ciudad Bolivar	1d.	94.	Baltimore	1d.
43.	Puerto Cabello	1d.	95.	Tokio	4d.
44.	Réunion	1d.	96.	Havre	3d.
45.	Sarawak	1d.	97.	Barcelona	3d.
46.	Würtemberg	1d.	98.	Volo	1d.
47.	Tokyo	1d.	99.	Damascus	1d.
48.	Amsterdam	1d.	100.	Paris	1d.
49.	Lisbon	1d.	101.	Bordeaux	2d.
50.	Königsberg	2d.	102.	Serajevo	1d.
51.	Cagliari	1d.	103.	Manila	1d
52.	Frankfort	1d.			

No. 104.

Reference to previous Report [C. 4761], Commercial No. 12, 1886.

UNITED STATES.

GALVESTON.

My Lord, *British Consulate, Galveston, February* 22, 1887.

I HAVE the honour to enclose commercial report for the year 1886 for the State of Texas.

I have, &c.
(Signed) WALTER T. LYALL.

Report by Consul W. T. Lyall on the Trade and Commerce of Texas for the Year 1886

The past year has been characterised by some sinister occurrences.

Strikes. At the close of 1885 determined and aggressive strikes of working men, chiefly navvies, dock labourers, and railway employés set in all over the lines of traffic, and continued, accompanied in some instances by affrays and open violence, until the close of the winter season.

Climate. At the commencement of the past year the severest frost ever experienced in Texas took place, freezing the water in the bay, and completely destroying all sub-tropical vegetation.

At the end of May a severe storm from the N.E. and N.W. damaged the wharves, coasting craft, fishing boats, &c., to a considerable extent, and caused some loss of life.

At the end of August another severe gale took place, coming from the S.E., sinking and damaging coasting vessels as before, destroying the town of Indianola, 70 miles to the S.W. on the Gulf of Mexico, and submerging the east end of the city of Galveston to a depth of four or five feet. Many cottages and small wooden shanties were wrecked and floated away, the ornamental trees and shrubs which had survived the frost were destroyed, and a deposit of foul-smelling mud and débris was spread over the east end of the town, causing fevers of a typhoidal type.

Towards the middle of October a storm approaching a cyclone in violence set in. This was a whirlwind which travelled up the coast of Florida from the S.E., and centred about 60 miles east of Galveston, at Sabine Pass, a small port on the Gulf of Mexico, which was totally destroyed, many lives lost, and hundreds of cattle drowned by the inundation which it produced. It caused an inundation in Galveston, but not to such an extent as in the previous storm, because the wind, which veered round the compass in the course of 24 hours from S.E. to S.W., blew with its greatest fury from the N.W., which had the effect of checking the inroad of the water from the Gulf of Mexico.

In spite of these drawbacks Galveston is, to use a local expression

(147)

UNITED STATES.

"still doing business at the old stand," and the State of Texas, whose great resources and possible developments I have described in previous reports, is extending its commercial enterprises, and improving its relations both with neighbouring States and with Europe.

Wharves, &c. The wharves are being largely extended, the construction of a solid seawall to protect the city against future inundations is seriously considered, and the commencement of strong stone breakwaters to deepen the entrance of the harbour, and permit vessels to complete their lading at the wharves, has been definitely decided upon; also the construction without delay by the Wharf Company of substantial "ways," by means of which vessels up to 1,000 tons burden can be expeditiously docked, cleaned, and repaired.

New buildings, most of them of superior design, have replaced those destroyed in the great fire, whose traces are now almost entirely obliterated; and an aqueduct is talked of, which will furnish the town with an abundant supply of fresh water, instead of as at present depending on the rainfall.

Communication with interior. As regards the interior of the State, the Santa Fé Railway is being actively and energetically extended in two directions—the first branch towards Mexico, the other through the Indian territory towards Arkansas city.

In fact, every branch of export and commercial enterprise, from cotton and oilcake the oldest to fresh beef the latest idea, may be said to exhibit a fairly progressive aspect.

Cotton crop. The Texas cotton crop has this year reached the important figure of 1,300,000 bales, of which 162,286 bales have already (February 15) been exported to England by Galveston alone (and 78,170 bales to foreign ports) by British vessels. The bulk of the crop of cotton has gone to New York and New Orleans, either by railway direct from the plantations, or by the Mullory and Morgan lines of coasting steamers. A small quantity has been exported to the Mexican ports of Matamoras and Vera Cruz.

Imports from Great Britain. The import trade from Great Britain exhibits, as usual, a "hiatus"; the few vessels that arrive with cargo contain principally coal, while an insignificant trade is done in cement and salt. The strangling of imports by prohibitive and protective duties continues, and with it the steady impoverishment of the non-manufacturing States.

Protective duties. The average duty now imposed on European imports is an *ad valorem* of nearly 50 per cent. Consequently, a New York merchant who purchases 100 dol. worth of British goods must, after paying the above sum for them, pay nearly 50 dol. more to the New York customhouse before he can get them. The Texan wholesale dealer who purchases from the New York merchant will have to pay 150 dol., plus the New York merchant's profit, so that the goods before they reach the consumer will have cost 170 dol. to 175 dol. at least. Previous to the Civil War the duty on foreign imports or tariff averaged 18 per cent., and the whole expense of the entire Administration did not exceed 60,000,000 dol. In 1884 President Blaine's Administration expended 244,000,000 dol. 48,000,000 dol. of this money was set down as interest on the national debt, leaving a balance of 196,000,000 dol., of which 121,000,000 dol. was raised by internal revenue, which sum alone, it is asserted, was amply sufficient to have defrayed the whole expense of the Administration, paid the interest of the national debt, and left a surplus of 12,000,000 dol., without any necessity for raising one halfpenny by import duties. Yet in that year the United States Government collected 195,000,000 dol. from foreign imports alone, and altogether, in fact, plus sales of public lands and internal revenue, 325,000,000 dol., amounting to a poll tax of over 6 dol. a head for every man, woman, and child, white or black, in the Southern and Western States, which is about seven times the average cost, *per capita*, of the local or "States" government of those territories; at any rate it is so as regards Texas. It is complained that the present tariff not only deprives the Southern American consumer of a cheap purchasing market, but enables the Northern manufacturers to combine and fix exorbitant prices just below the cost of imports.

According to a *résumé* lately made by an influential Western journal, the "protected steel manufacturers" have realised during the past year 67 per cent. profit on their united capital of 21,000,000 dol. The price of steel rails in America is 34 to 35 dol. per ton. Steel rails, &c.

In England the price is 18 dol. 50 c. per ton, and the import duty is 17 dol. per ton. If there were no duty 25 dol. per ton would pay for imported English rails in New York. Therefore, the protected American manufacturers having turned out and sold 1,700,000 tons of rail during 1886, have pocketed a "bonus" of 17,000,000 dol. clear and above the natural cost of English rails landed in New York.

The natural price of English rails in New York (minus duty) being 25 dol. per ton, it follows that the British manufacturer, even if rails were duty free, would be handicapped by a natural protective duty of 6 dol. 50 c. per ton in favour of the American rail producer, and it is by no means certain that the American manufacturers do not actually make a profit out of this natural duty.

The amount of wages paid by the combined American ironmasters to their working men in 1886 is asserted to be 5,000,000 dol. Assuming the total output to be as above, *i.e.*, 1,700,000 tons, the cost of production is therefore under 3 dol. per ton, but say 3 dol. 50 c., in which case the natural protection of 6 dol. 50 c. per ton cost of transport would pay the wages cost, and leave a profit of 3 dol. per ton, which on 1,700,000 tons would be 5,100,000 dol. Wages.

According to the American manufacturers' statement the total cost of the raw material and wages combined was 41,757,277 dol., and the total value produced was 55,805,210 dol.; deduct 41,757,277 dol., and 14,047,933 dol. remains total profit.

Agricultural produce, excepting sugar and rice, is scarcely if at all protected; the above two staples, however, are protected, the first by an import duty of 53 per cent., and the second of 104 per cent. *ad valorem*. Agricultural produce (imports).

The United States sugar crop of 1884 was 142,000 tons, which is about the average, while the total consumption was 908,000 tons. The value of the imported sugar was 98,000,000 dol.; thus the American consumers paid 47,000,000 dol. above what their sugar, if duty free, would have cost them.

The farmer gets starvation prices for his hides, but has to pay as much as ever for the machine-made harness, boots, shoes, &c., made from them at the factories "up north," and so with everything; while the rates for transport and commission are the same as when all farm produce was at double present figures. This is because the price of food staples in this country no longer regulates that of other articles, the farmer being compelled to take what he can get for his produce, while the manufacturers, thanks to the protected tariff which keeps away competition and gives them a monopoly, can combine to keep up prices and to limit production. Farming.

A uniform scale of prices is adopted by them and rigidly adhered to, and they will combine, if necessary, even to prevent the establishment of competing factories in their own country. A Western American

(147)

farmer knows the prices of wheat in the world's markets by reading the London and Liverpool quotations; but the Birmingham, Sheffield, and Manchester quotations, for hardware, cloth, leather goods, and the like indispensables, are of no use to him. The American food staple producer has to compete with food producers all over the world, but the American manufacturer, whose goods the food stapler must purchase to produce his staples, have no outside competitors to fear, and can keep up prices.

"Rings" and "corners."

Following on the heels of the customs protective tariff are the private rings and corners, virtual monopolies, and all more or less prejudicial to producers, especially to agriculturists. Cotton seed oil is a great export staple of Texas and other cotton-growing States, from which it is sent to Europe, chiefly to Italy, where it is refined, bottled. and sold all over the world as olive oil, for which it really forms a wholesome substitute.

Cotton seed.

Cotton seed was, therefore, not long ago a profitable article to the cotton farmer, but a syndicate has lately been formed, under the name of the American Oil Mill Company, which has bought up nearly every oil mill in Texas, and is now said to control nearly every oil mill in the Southern States. They have, in consequence, already run down the price of seed from 7 dol. 50 c., the normal figure, to 5 dol. per ton, while they have run up the price of oil from $28\frac{1}{2}$ c. ($1s.$ $2\frac{1}{2}d.$) to 40 c., or $1s.$ $7\frac{1}{2}d.$

Having purchased the mills they close down such of them as are not convenient for their operations, and thereby lessen the rates of labour and expenditure, while they contrive to break down such opposition mills as hold out for a time by paying high prices for oil seed.

Cattle combinations.

Then there is the Chicago cattle combination. This syndicate has, it is affirmed, so managed to control the cattle market that both purchase and sale are at its mercy. While reducing prices to the grazier by from 10 dol. to 15 dol. per head, the consumer is paying about the same retail prices for beef as formerly, while the competition of local butchers all over the country, as far as the Atlantic seaboard, has been completely broken down. The ranche men and cattle owners are consequently meditating a combination on their side to stop all shipments of cattle to the Chicago market, thus compelling the syndicate either to advance prices or forcing purchasers to purchase from cattle producers, avoiding also the exorbitant charges for care, yardage, and feed, which alone, at present, amount to 1 dol. per head, an important item. Then there are the railroad combinations, or "poolings," as they are termed, by which rates of freight and transport of merchandise are regulated and raised at pleasure of the "operators."

Coal.

Towards the end of last year (1886) four coal-carrying lines—the Hocking Valley railroad, the Wheeling and Lake Erie, the Toledo and Ohio Central, and the North Texan division of the Pennsylvanian—combined to make a rise of 60 per cent. in coal, in conjunction with the coal mineowners.

They advanced the rates of freight on coal 25 per cent., informing the mineowners that they must put up prices 30 per cent. all round at once, and 30 per cent. more later on; and that they must also restrict their output of coal, so as not to overstock the market, for that they would only carry a certain amount, and no more, having already fixed the amount of coal which they estimated the market would stand.

Land. Cattle ranching.

In the early days of the republic most of the land in Texas was given away to the pioneers, or sold at nominal prices, and the best lands, situated in Central and Eastern Texas, have all been expropriated.

The price of vacant land in Western Texas, not worth in reality more than 25 c. (1s.) to 1 dol., or 4s. per acre, has been run up by speculators and agencies to 2 dol. 50 c., or 10s. per acre, at which rate the State or public lands are usually quoted. This figure, though it may seem moderate to an immigrant from Europe, is actually, when the quality of the article is considered, dear enough, there being thousands of square miles for sale in those counties which will barely support a cow per 40 acres, and are quite useless for agricultural purposes. This is the sort of land which is frequently purchased by the "unposted" immigrant. To sustain a small herd of 100 cattle will require 4,000 acres of this sort of land, which at 2 dol. 50 c. per acre will cost 10,000 dol., or 2,000l. Fictitious land values.

Ten acres of the very best land in the country will not feed more than one cow, and that only during favourable seasons.

Of tolerably good land 15 acres per head of cattle will be required, but this, even at 2 dol. per acre, costs 30 dol., and the average market value of a cow is 8 dol. to 10 dol. only.

Experienced local stockmen and cattle owners will never purchase these lands at present prices, knowing that they are not worth one-quarter of the figure demanded for them. They will file a pre-emption claim to them, or lease them for a nominal figure, to secure the pasture, and when this is eaten up will move elsewhere.

Western Texas, where alone large tracts of unappropriated land at present exist, is actually only fit for stock-raising purposes; farming does not pay there, on account not only of the poor quality of the land, but of the scarcity of water and the extremely limited rainfall. It is a stock-raising country, and nothing more.

It is calculated that, with good management, these western prairies are capable of sustaining 3,000,000 horned cattle, 1,000,000 horses, and 4,000,000 or 5,000,000 sheep, and if the land could be sold for what it is worth, i.e., at 1s. to 1 dol. per acre, it would soon find purchasers, but not at present prices, unless fresh arrivals can be deluded into buying.

This country is dry nearly all the year round, and though in favourable seasons enough sorghum, millet, lucerne, &c., could be raised to tide the cattle over the droughts, it will never, unless artificially irrigated at great expense, repay cultivation. Need of irrigation.

The drawback to cattle-raising in Texas is chiefly the lawlessness prevailing in most cattle districts. Although many cases are not published, the local papers teem with instances of cattle and horse theft, fence cutting to facilitate the same—miles of iron fencing being destroyed: there is also considerable terrorising and intimidation to suppress evidence. These outrages are often accompanied by killing and wounding of cattle men, with whom fights often occur. The law seems to be a dead letter. This is not surprising when, by a calculation published last year, apparently from official sources, it was computed that over 4,000 convicted felons, many of them murderers and homicides, were at large throughout the State of Texas. These were the escaped convicts, and the estimate will afford some idea of the total number of criminals, including those acquitted for lack of evidence and those who are "wanted," but have not been caught, especially as the entire population does not exceed 2,750,000. Though cases of wholesale prison-breaking are common enough, it must not be supposed that this whole 4,000 have escaped from Texan gaols; probably one-half, at least, are immigrants, Texas having long been a "refugium peccatorum" for the outlaws, desperadoes, and "tough citizens" of the adjoining States, as is also the Indian territory lying immediately to the north of it. Lawlessness.

UNITED STATES.

Militia

According to an estimate lately compiled in the United States' Adjutant-General's Office, there are not more than 1,700 militia in the whole State, which is considerably larger than France, and as there are certainly not more than 300 policemen, it follows that the escaped convicts alone are just double the number of the available force of the States Government, to say nothing of the undetected, unarrested, &c., who must "figure up" to at least thrice as many again. These facts, joined to the inefficiency of the courts and the shortcomings of the jury system, demonstrate the necessity of Lynch law; which institution, joined to the power of money, freely expended by law-enforcing private associations, alone keeps the formidable phalanx of rascality in check.

Lynch law.

It also demonstrates the known determination of the industrious, law-abiding citizens to at least enforce order and avenge heinous crimes, if they cannot enforce the laws. Lynching is steadily on the increase; there have been more cases than ever during the past year. Five or six ruffians per week have at times been lynched. Lynch law has been described as a net, which catches small fish, but which big ones break through, and this it to some extent is; nevertheless, under present conditions there would be no living safely in some countries without it. The knowledge that it impends is a good *in terrorem* where reckless evil-doers abound: just as the knowledge that a great percentage of brave and patriotic citizens would, should any serious revolutionary crisis arise, certainly turn out rifle in hand to maintain order, acts as a powerful deterrent from attempting the plunder on a large scale, which the anarchists of the great cities are perpetually contemplating.

Predatory adventurers.

Another cattle run calamity is a tribe of predatory adventurers who have for some years infested Western Texas, where they live by extorting black mail from ranche owners, which is effected as follows: The land is, as already stated, unfit for agricultural purposes, nevertheless these fellows will enter claims and take up land professedly to cultivate. After "entering," or "homesteading," as it is called, a small tract, they will build a hut or "dug out" in the bank of some ravine, near a waterhole which the ranchman's cattle frequent to drink; they will then plough and sow an acre or two of maize or oats; they know this crop will never come, even if undisturbed, to maturity, and that the cattle, as soon as it has got three or four inches high, will get at it (or if they do not the fellows themselves will drive them in), thereby affording them an excellent grievance against the cattle men; they accordingly spend their time in riding from one ranche to another all the summer, and claiming damage for injuries inflicted on their "crops," underlying which demand is the unexpressed but implied threat that if their claims are refused they will, on the first opportunity, burn the grass, and thereby entail great loss. These men are the *bêtes noires* of cattle owners: to detect them in the act of firing the grass, whereby the pastures may be destroyed for miles, is next to impossible; they are thoroughly acquainted with the country, well mounted and armed, and dangerous men to threaten or bully. Many of them have been employed all their lives in entering claims to Government lands in half-a-dozen other States, selling them and squandering the proceeds If one of these fellows takes up a section of land in the middle of a run, he must either be supported by the ranche owners or killed off.

The above and, in fact, all the marauding classes of the population usually permanently retain lawyers in the county towns to defend them when they get into difficulties. One able practitioner (the more impudent, of course, the better) will enable a whole community of rascals to carry on their malpractices with comparative impunity. It is understood that whenever any one of the "community" has 10 or 15 dollars to spare he is to hand it over to the lawyer, and that the latter, whenever a "client" is indicted for any atrocity up to murder, is to set to work to defend him.

The first thing to be done is to get the culprit released on bail, for which responsible persons are required by the authorities. I have been informed on good authority that honest, hard-working farmers possessed of considerable means, but having the misfortune to live in the neighbourhood of these bad characters, are often cajoled or intimidated into giving bond for men whom they are perfectly aware habitually live by cattle theft.

At the trial the jury, themselves often ignorant and improvident petty landowners or squatters, are powerfully appealed to by the "counsel" for the accused, who holds up the prosecuting cattle owners as "mean grasping tyrants, actuated by the basest motives;" "men who do not want poor people to live," "who would like to depopulate the entire country in order to pasture their cattle," &c., and consequently if there is the least flaw in the evidence will acquit the prisoners.

In a case tried here a few months ago, six notorious fellows, who had made a practice of killing cattle for years for the sale of the meat and hides, were tried; the jury, unwilling to convict, but seeing no loophole, as the evidence was clear and conclusive, brought in a verdict of "unauthorised skinning of cattle," and the thieves were discharged. It was at this trial, I believe, that the counsel for the accused told the judge that "his clients were" as honest men as he (the judge) was. *Farming, fruit-growing, &c.*

Northern and Central Texas contains the best farming and orchard land in the State, with a good rainfall, in consequence of the proximity of the hills and forests of the Indian territory; there are also numerous creeks and rivers.

Eastern Texas is in great part covered with pine forests; there is a fair rainfall, and the soil, though sandy, is fertile. The drawback to farming more or less throughout the State, but especially in South-Western Texas, is the prevalence of long spells of dry weather, which, since the felling and clearing of large tracts of forest in the interior, are undoubtedly on the increase. Texas is in about the same degree of latitude as Algeria, Syria, Southern Persia, &c., and the climate will, eventually I believe, become, at any rate in the south and west, much what it at present is in the above countries, afflicted with dry, hot summers, little or no rainfall, and agriculture entirely dependent on artificial irrigation. Irrigation has hardly been attempted as yet in Texas, though at least half its area is practically unfit for cultivation without it. *Climate, &c.*

Another climatic defect is the "northers"—cold, piercing winds, of the nature of the "mistral," which suddenly descend during the cold months from the Rocky Mountains, often causing serious destruction both to vegetation and to live stock. These "northers" will kill off all but the very hardiest sub-tropical vegetation, so that although the mean temperature of the climate, for the year round, is very much higher than that of European and Asiatic countries, where the orange, lemon, date, pomegranate, fig, citron, &c., perennially flourish, these fruits can hardly be grown in Texas, the trees being continually killed off by frosts. On the other hand, the heat is too great for the fruits of temperate climates (except far to the north), such as the vine, apple, pear, &c., which is an unsatisfactory condition of things. *North winds.*

In January, 1886, a "norther" set in, which in a few hours sank the temperature 45 degrees. The bay, long before morning, was a sheet of solid ice for many miles. Fishermen were frost-bitten in their boats, and in two or three instances actually frozen to death. This frost killed every sub-tropical tree or shrub, orange, lemon, oleander, date, palm tree, &c., in and around Galveston, and temporarily ruined the entire orange industry in Florida for four or five degrees to the southward. Cattle died of cold in thousands all over the country.

Southern and Eastern Texas have this year (Feb., 1887) suffered from a prolonged draught, no rain to speak of having fallen for nearly two months, and were it not for heavy dews, fogs, and mists, which have set in occasionally, every blade of grass would have been burnt up.

Extremes of climate. The climate of Texas is perpetually in extremes, either of heat or cold, damp or dryness, *i.e.*, the climate of South and East Texas. In the north and west the climate, though dry and hot in summer, is as healthy or healthier than in most parts of the world. These are the stock-raising districts above-mentioned, which is the best occupation for an intending settler to follow, there being less drudgery and dependence in it than in farming. Men who can shoot and ride well, who do not mind "roughing it," and do not give themselves airs, will always be popular and respected, and if they have the sense to keep away from gambling dens and variety theatres will never run any serious danger. Nine-tenths of the fatal affrays and "difficulties" occur in these establishments, patronised and supported as they are by local desperadoes, and men who enter with the avowed intention "to have a spree" and "shoot the town up," and commence by drinking until they feel reckless.

Stock-raising qualities required for.

Prospects of success depend upon capital and character. A young man who goes in for ranching will find that perseverance in rounding up cattle, riding and breaking in of mustangs, practice with firearms, and shooting from horseback, &c., will in a few years make him hardy, daring, and self-reliant, as well as a successful man. If he does not think himself equal to the acquirement of the above accomplishments he had better stay in England. Every European country is numerously represented in Texas, and there is, of course, a large negro and coloured population to boot.

All things considered, it is surprising that in the absence of troops and police the population is as orderly as it actually is.

LONDON:
Printed for Her Majesty's Stationery Office,
By HARRISON AND SONS,
Printers in Ordinary to Her Majesty.
(Wt. 7730   75   3 | 87—H & S   147)

FOREIGN OFFICE.
1887.
ANNUAL SERIES.

N° 110.
DIPLOMATIC AND CONSULAR REPORTS ON TRADE AND FINANCE.

UNITED STATES.

REPORT FOR THE YEAR 1886
ON THE
TRADE OF BOSTON.

REFERENCE TO PREVIOUS REPORT [C. 4657] Commercial No. 6, 1886.

Presented to both Houses of Parliament by Command of Her Majesty,
APRIL, 1887.

LONDON:
PRINTED FOR HER MAJESTY'S STATIONERY OFFICE,
BY HARRISON AND SONS, ST. MARTIN'S LANE,
PRINTERS IN ORDINARY TO HER MAJESTY.

And to be purchased, either directly or through any Bookseller, from
EYRE AND SPOTTISWOODE, EAST HARDING STREET, FLEET STREET, E.C., and
32, ABINGDON STREET, WESTMINSTER, S.W.; or
ADAM AND CHARLES BLACK, NORTH BRIDGE, EDINBURGH; or
HODGES, FIGGIS, & Co., 104, GRAFTON STREET, DUBLIN.

1887.

[C.—4923—33.] *Price 1d.*

New Series of Reports.

Reports of the Annual Series have been issued from Her Majesty's Diplomatic and Consular Officers at the following places, and may be obtained from the sources indicated on the title-page:—

No.		Price.	No.		Price.
1.	Varna	1d.	56.	Crete	1d.
2.	Florence	1d.	57.	Berne	3d.
3.	Tangier	1d.	58.	Rotterdam	1d.
4.	Loanda	1d.	59.	Düsseldorf	4d.
5.	Teneriffe	1d.	60.	Mozambique	5d.
6.	Manila	1d.	61.	Hanyang	1d.
7.	Batavia	1d.	62.	Stockholm	1d.
8.	Beyrout	1d.	63.	Paris	1d.
9.	St. Michael's	1d.	64.	Tunis	1d.
10.	Cuba	1d.	65.	The Hague	2d.
11.	Tunis	4d.	66.	Italy	2d.
12.	Canton	1d.	67.	Smyrna	2d.
13.	Newchwang	1d.	68.	Fiume	1d.
14.	Shanghai	1d.	69.	Tabreez	1d.
15.	Tientsin	1d.	70.	Philippopolis	1d.
16.	Vienna	1d.	71.	Rome	1d.
17.	Corfu	1d.	72.	Vienna	1d.
18.	Hakodate	1d.	73.	St. Petersburg	2d.
19.	Hiogo	1d.	74.	Ichang	1d.
20.	Newport News	1d.	75.	Salonica	1d.
21.	Stockholm	1d.	76.	Brussels	2d.
22.	Christiania	1d.	77.	Alexandria	1d.
23.	Antwerp	1d.	78.	Patras	1d.
24.	Salonica	1d.	79.	Maranham	1d.
25.	Tonga	1d.	80.	Taganrog	2d.
26.	Batoum	1d.	81.	Jeddah	1d.
27.	Costa Rica	1d.	82.	Suakin	1d.
28.	Mexico	4d.	83.	Colonia	1d.
29.	Bushire	1d.	84.	Suez	1d.
30.	Erzeroum	1d.	85.	Paris	1d.
31.	Bilbao	1d.	86.	Brest	1d.
32.	Rio Grande do Sul	1d.	87.	Puerto Plata	1d.
33.	Piræus	1d.	88.	Charleston	1d.
34.	Sandakan	1d.	89.	Tripoli	1d.
35.	Stockholm	1d.	90.	Saigon	1d.
36.	Tahiti	1d.	91.	Cherbourg	1d.
37.	Syra	1d.	92.	New Orleans	2d.
38.	Kanagawa	2d.	93.	Galatz	1d.
39.	Nagasaki	1d.	94.	Baltimore	1d.
40.	Chefoo	1d.	95.	Tokio	4d.
41.	Pekin	1d.	96.	Havre	3d.
42.	Ciudad Bolivar	1d.	97.	Barcelona	3d.
43.	Puerto Cabello	1d.	98.	Volo	1d.
44.	Réunion	1d.	99.	Damascus	1d.
45.	Sarawak	1d.	100.	Paris	1d.
46.	Würtemberg	1d.	101.	Bordeaux	2d.
47.	Tokyo	1d.	102.	Serajevo	1d.
48.	Amsterdam	1d.	103.	Manila	1d.
49.	Lisbon	1d.	104.	Galveston	1d.
50.	Königsberg	2d.	105.	Aleppo	1d.
51.	Cagliari	1d.	106.	Rio de Janeiro	1d.
52.	Frankfort	1d.	107.	Truxillo	1d.
53.	Bogota	1d.	108.	St. Petersburg	3d.
54.	Kharput	1d.	109.	Leghorn	1d.
55.	Trieste	1d.			

No. 110.

Reference to previous Report [C. 4657], Commercial No 6, 1886.

UNITED STATES.

BOSTON.

Consul Henderson to the Marquis of Salisbury.

My Lord,   Boston, *February* 28, 1887.

I HAVE the honour to enclose a report on the Trade and Commerce of Boston and the Boston Consular District for the year 1886.

I have, &c.
(Signed)   C. A. HENDERSON.

Report by Consul Henderson on the Trade and Commerce of Boston and the Boston Consular District for the Year 1886.

Statistics for Massachusetts. According to official statistics for 1886, real and personal property in Massachusetts amounts to 369,500,000*l.*,* being an increase † of 13,000,000*l.*, and deposits in savings banks amount to 58,240,000*l.*, or an increase of 3,249,000*l.* Persons liable to poll tax have increased by 14,743, and the number of dwelling houses by 7,766.

Foreign trade of Boston. The value of foreign imports at Boston was 12,347,000*l.*, an increase of rather more than 1,600,000*l.*, and that of foreign exports was 11,506,000*l.*, or an increase of over 600,000*l.*

Maritime trade. Arrivals of vessels at Boston in the foreign trade, as stated in the custom-house returns, were: American 555, of 254,697 tons, a decrease of 14,918 tons; British 1,949, of 892,897 tons, an increase of 90,491 tons; other nationalities 143, of 110,930 tons, an increase of 40,973 tons: making a total of 2,647 vessels and 1,258,524 tons, and an increase of 177 vessels and 116,546 tons. The actual arrivals of British vessels, as entered at the Consulate, were 1,989, of 901,530 net register tons, namely, 405 steamers, of 679,046 tons, and 1,584 sailing vessels, of 222,484 tons.

Maritime freights were maintained at uniform rates, and a slight advance on some articles.

Domestic trade and industries. Although prices continued to rule low, and numerous and prolonged strikes and some heavy failures and defalcations had the momentary effect of arresting business development and the revival of confidence, railway traffic and earnings increased, the stock market regained its former stability, capital circulated more freely, and a progressive though gradual gain was perceptible in the volume of domestic trade and industry, which are now in a sound and improving condition, not only in Boston, but throughout this Consular district.

* Sterling amounts are given at the rate of 4*s.* to the dollar.
† Statements of increase and decrease in quantities and values are by comparison with those of the year immediately preceding.

(154)

UNITED STATES.

Mercantile failures.

Failures in Boston were more numerous, and the liabilities of insolvent firms, amounting to 1,864,000*l.*, increased by 989,000*l.* In the remainder of this Consular district, which comprises other parts of Massachusetts and the States of Vermont, New Hampshire, and Maine, the liabilities of insolvent firms amounted to 1,262,000*l.*, or an increase of 243,000*l.* The number of firms in business increased meanwhile from 73,783 to 76,786.

REVIEW OF BOSTON TRADES AND INDUSTRIES.

Wool, woollens, and clothing.

Notwithstanding large receipts of wool in 1885, the stock at the beginning of the year was small. Owing, however, to a fall in foreign markets early in the year, to uncertainty regarding possible changes in the import duties on wool, and to strikes and failures in woollen mills, prices continued low during the first six months, but were somewhat better, with very slight fluctuation, during the remainder of the year.

Receipts of native wool decreased by 64,650 bags, but in imports of foreign wool there was an increase of 22,320 bales. Of this latter, however, a portion was re-exported, prices abroad having risen above those of the home market.

Woollen factories were on the whole fairly busy, but, with the exception of flannel, worsted, and blanket mills, made little or no profit.

Clothing trade.

Clothiers, though not effecting large winter sales, owing to a mild season, did a tolerably profitable year's business.

Cotton.

The attempt a few years since to establish a large cotton market in Boston was not successful, manufacturers in this and adjoining States having found it more to their advantage to obtain their supplies directly from the south. On such sales as were effected here prices ranged between $4\frac{13}{50}d.$ per lb., to which they fell in March, and $4\frac{59}{100}d.$, which they touched in August, and closed with the year at $4\frac{41}{100}d.$

Cotton goods.

The cotton goods market was exceedingly active, and production could barely keep pace with demand for home consumption and a somewhat improved export trade. Without much improvement in prices, both manufacturers and merchants made a profit on their largely increased sales.

Iron, steel, and other metals.

A small advance in the price of iron at the close of the year 1885, but principally the well-founded conviction that a large supply would soon be required to meet the wants of consumers, led to a considerable increase in production early in the year. But though the demand confirmed the prediction, and sales were active from the beginning, prices did not materially improve until the autumn. Since then they rose steadily, and at the close of the year, when American pig iron was quoted at 4*l.* 6*s.*, Scotch pig at 4*l.* 12*s.*, and steel rails at 7*l.* 12*s.* per ton, the market was firm, with an upward tendency. Copper and pig tin followed pretty much the same course as iron, but pig lead was lower at the end than early in the year.

Hides and leather.

Receipts of hides show a large increase, and prices were high at the beginning of the year; but in consequence of a suspension of work in tanneries, occasioned by strikes, and a considerable fall in leather, they soon declined, and did not recover, the leather market itself, notwithstanding the reduced production, continuing low throughout the year.

Boots and shoes.

Business in the boot and shoe trade was remarkably brisk, and sales showed an increase of 200,000 cases; but active competition, low prices, and extensive strikes (resulting in an advance in wages), not only rendered the year's transactions generally unprofitable, but led to heavy failures

Flour experienced a sensible and oats a slight decline in price, but the former partially recovered towards the close of the year, due to a demand for both flour and wheat for exportation. Maize, on the other hand, rose and maintained a higher price. Flour opened with the year at 13*s.* (1*l.* 3*s.* 6*d.*), according to quality, and fell to 10*s.* (1*l.* 1*s.* 6*d.*) per barrel; oats opened at 1*s.* 7*d.*, and fell to 1*s.* 6*d.* per bushel; and maize rose from 1*s.* 11*d.* to 2*s.* 1*d.* per bushel. *Flour and grain.*

In consequence of large imports of beet sugar in competition with raw West Indian sugar, prices were unprecedentedly low, and the year was an unprofitable one for domestic refiners. Raw sugar declined from 1*l.* 5*s.* 9*d.* to 1*l.* 1*s.* 3*d.*, and refined from 1*l.* 11*s.* 1*d.* to 1*l.* 6*s.* per cwt. *Sugar.*

The year was an unprosperous and unfortunate one for New England fishermen, owing to their exclusion from Canadian waters, the smallness of the catch elsewhere, the low price of fish, and the loss of 26 vessels and 137 men. The total catch of mackerel, 82,900 barrels, shows a decrease of 248,000 barrels, and that of cod, 823,000 quintals, a decrease of nearly 80,000 quintals. In Boston, which is the principal market for fish, the price of mackerel and herring improved somewhat after the month of June, but that of cod continued low and entirely unremunerative to fishermen. *Fisheries and fish trade.*

Canadian mackerel imported at Boston amounted to 53,216 barrels, an increase of 11,607 barrels. Canadian competition, whilst injurious to native fishermen by increasing the supply and keeping down prices, is, on the other hand, of advantage to fish merchants, who are benefited by a large supply wherever it may come from, and a low purchasing price, which enables them to sell cheap, and thus increase the demand and the volume of their sales at as much profit for a given quantity as when prices are high.

A general strike at the beginning of the year in the building trade (though ultimately unsuccessful in its double object of procuring an increase of wages and a reduction in working hours) caused the suspension or abandonment of many building projects in this city and its vicinity. It is estimated, nevertheless, that about 3,000,000*l.* were invested in erecting and improving stores and dwelling-houses, in order to meet an increasing demand for both. *Building operations in Boston.*

Foreign exchange opened high in January, bankers' sight bills being 4 dol. 90 c. per £, but they fell successively to 4 dol. 88 c. by July, 4 dol. 84 c. by September, and 4 dol. 82 c. by the early part of December, when some gold was imported, and a reactionary movement set in and continued without intermission. *Foreign exchange.*

It may not be without interest to mention here that in the prosecution of inquiries as to the practicability of steps being taken to promote and increase trade with the United Kingdom, it has been found to be the opinion of merchants here, most experienced and most directly interested in this trade, that the existing system is the most efficient and the most conducive to permanently sound and profitable business relations that can be devised. The system referred to, and followed by large importing houses as the result of long experience in their respective trades, is this: Having carefully studied the wants of the home market, the prevailing tastes and fashions of the moment, and the prices at which certain articles can compete with domestic manufactures, each importer sends to Europe periodically (and occasionally to other parts of the world) a competent representative, generally a member of the firm, who visits the manufacturing establishments in his line of business, not only in Great Britain but on the Continent, and who, after a full and careful inspection, decides for himself where he can obtain the best adapted goods, or have his orders most satisfactorily executed at the *System of trade with foreign countries.*

lowest cost. By this method alone can importing merchants succeed in supplying themselves with the most desirable and most profitable selections, and in securing themselves against close and active competition, whilst manufacturers are relieved from the alternative of publicly exhibiting abroad, by means of travelling agents or sample rooms, either inappropriate or new and popular goods, with the chance of the former being unsaleable, and the latter being closely imitated before they themselves can take advantage of a favourable market; and they moreover reap the benefit of effecting large sales directly to a limited number of customers of established credit, in lieu of selling abroad, at greater risk and expense in collecting debts, to small dealers whose commercial standing it is more difficult to ascertain, and whose liability may be more easily evaded.

The importer is thus enabled, by his thorough acquaintance with the condition of the market, to keep it supplied to its fullest capacity with the goods which are most sought after, and to exclude those which would only lead to loss and disappointment, whilst the success of the manufacturer is only made dependent, as it would be under any other system, on his ability to compete with rival establishments at home and abroad.

At the same time that this system is assumed to be most conducive to the prosperity and development of the foreign trade of Boston, as of other large commercial centres in the United States, exporting merchants and manufacturers here have come to the conclusion that it is not equally applicable to all countries, and they find it expedient to send representatives or establish agencies in various parts of the world, and to avail themselves of the reliable information acquired through them, to ascertain the precise class of goods that are in demand at any particular place, and to judge whether they can be produced and exported at a profit. In this way, in addition to frequent shipments elsewhere, a well-established and growing export trade (supplemented to a certain extent by imports) has for many years been carried on with Australia, the principal articles of export, besides many of minor importance, being: Machinery, locomotives, sewing machines, stoves and ranges, agricultural implements, hardware, including all kinds of tools, railway cars, carriages, carts, musical instruments, manufactures of wood, oils, and tobacco.

Some of these goods are such as are not produced in the United Kingdom, but it is admitted that others continue to sell readily, though not able to compete in price with those of British manufacture, owing to greater attention having been paid to their adaptation, in quality and make, to the requirements of the markets to which they are exported.

It may be added that in the course of conversation with the gentlemen referred to, it was incidentally suggested that Consular reports and other similar official publications, however valuable they may be for statistical purposes, are rarely if ever available as a guide to business men in their commercial operations, for whilst the information they convey cannot be otherwise than incomplete in the requisite technical details of each particular branch of trade, and therefore not safe to be acted upon by itself, the delay necessarily incurred in transmission, printing, and distribution entails the result of its being forestalled by the direct and ready information communicated by telegraph or letter to such as rely upon their own correspondents to avert any loss of time in anticipating the action of other competitors.

BOSTON.

Annex A.—RETURN of all Shipping in the Foreign Trade* at Ports in the Boston Consular District in the Fiscal Year ended June 30, 1886.

ENTERED.

| Nationality. | Sailing. || Steam. || Total. ||
	Number of Vessels.	Tons.	Number of Vessels.	Tons.	Number of Vessels.	Tons.
Foreign†	3,556	461,546	555	784,022	4,111	1,245,568
American	814	240,234	383	256,044	1,197	496,278
Total fiscal year 1886	4,370	701,780	938	1,040,066	5,308	1,741,846
,, ,, ,, 1885	3,956	641,223	93	1,014,373	4,894	1,655,596

CLEARED.

| Nationality. | Sailing. || Steam. || Total. ||
	Number of Vessels	Tons.	Number of Vessels.	Tons.	Number of Vessels.	Tons.
Foreign†	3,499	443,339	466	647,957	3,965	1,091,296
American	1,241	328,611	384	256,591	1,625	585,202
Total fiscal year 1886	4,740	771,950	850	904,548	5,590	1,676,498
,, ,, ,, 1885	4,253	696,263	857	896,707	5,113	1,592,170

Annex B.—RETURN of Principal Articles of Export from and Imports to Ports in the Boston Consular District during the Fiscal Year ended June 30, 1886.

EXPORTS.

| Articles. | Value. ||
	1886.	1885.
	£	£
Meat and dairy products	2,887,437	3,471,758
Horned cattle	818,143	1,107,409
Corn, flour, and other breadstuffs	2,632,982	3,455,338
Raw cotton	1,972,883	1,611,616
Cotton manufactures	243,365	218,003
Tobacco in leaf and manufactured	545,769	501,335
Iron, steel, and manufactures of	285,090	294,441
Sugar and molasses	130,600	244,159
All other domestic merchandise	2,177,693	2,589,435
Coin and bullion	6,604	15,340
Foreign merchandise re-exported	233,767	178,071
Total	11,934,333	13,686,905

* Statistics cannot be obtained in regard to the coasting trade.
† The nationality of foreign vessels can only be ascertained in the aggregate for the whole of the United States.

UNITED STATES.

IMPORTS.

Articles.	Value. 1886.	Value. 1885.
	£	£
Sugar and molasses	2,609,885	2,605,182
Wool	1,512,043	1,472,721
Woollen goods	767,148	675,834
Hides, goat, fur skins, and furs	1,222,393	1,061,085
Chemicals, drugs, and dyes	817,591	856,447
Iron ore, iron, steel, and manufactures of	960,518	840,680
Flax, hemp, and jute	515,583	783,719
Cotton goods	345,399	311,488
Fish	286,314	460,228
All other merchandise	4,636,918	3,402,394
Coin and bullion	59,924	33,808
Total	13,733,716	12,503,586

Annex C.—TABLE showing the Value of all Articles Exported from and Imported to Ports in the Boston Consular District during the Fiscal Years ended June 30, 1886 and 1885.

Country.	Exports. 1886.	Exports. 1885.	Imports. 1886.	Imports. 1885.
	£	£	£	£
United Kingdom and colonies	10,758,772	12,190,872	7,648,477	6,733,662
Spain and colonies	91,685	162,636	1,338,417	2,173,355
France and colonies	159,518	124,220	676,587	628,419
Argentine Republic	104,542	89,753	606,346	626,903
Germany	14,786	7,723	535,349	626,167
Brazil	3,584	6,806	218,880	304,322
Italy	18,980	18,721	230,385	268,296
Netherlands and colonies	51,814	62,339	149,520	211,540
Belgium	99,422	112,224	194,063	147,703
Sweden and Norway	4,095	12,077	171,861	189,599
Chili	116,483	120,277	38,253	32,078
Turkey	11,439	23,577	79,503	102,905
All other countries	499,213	755,680	1,846,069	458,637
Total	11,934,333	13,686,905	13,733,716	12,503,586

LONDON:
Printed for Her Majesty's Stationery Office,
By HARRISON AND SONS,
Printers in Ordinary to Her Majesty.
(Wt. 7730   75   4 | 87—H & S   154)

FOREIGN OFFICE.
1887.
ANNUAL SERIES.

No. 136.
DIPLOMATIC AND CONSULAR REPORTS ON TRADE AND FINANCE.

UNITED STATES.

REPORT FOR THE YEAR 1886
ON THE
TRADE OF SAVANNAH.

REFERENCE TO PREVIOUS REPORT [C. 3593], Commercial No. 18, 1883.

Presented to both Houses of Parliament by Command of Her Majesty,
MAY, 1887.

LONDON:
PRINTED FOR HER MAJESTY'S STATIONERY OFFICE,
BY HARRISON AND SONS, ST. MARTIN'S LANE,
PRINTERS IN ORDINARY TO HER MAJESTY.

And to be purchased, either directly or through any Bookseller, from
EYRE AND SPOTTISWOODE, EAST HARDING STREET, FLEET STREET, E.C., and
32, ABINGDON STREET, WESTMINSTER, S.W.; or
ADAM AND CHARLES BLACK, NORTH BRIDGE, EDINBURGH; or
HODGES, FIGGIS, & Co., 104, GRAFTON STREET, DUBLIN.

1887.

[C.—4923—59.] *Price 1d.*

New Series of Reports.

Reports of the Annual Series have been issued from Her Majesty's Diplomatic and Consular Officers at the following places, and may be obtained from the sources indicated on the title-page:—

No.		Price.
8.	Beyrout	1d.
9.	St. Michael's	1d.
10.	Cuba	1d.
11.	Tunis	4d.
12.	Canton	1d.
13.	Newchwang	1d.
14.	Shanghai	1d.
15.	Tientsin	1d.
16.	Vienna	1d.
17.	Corfu	1d.
18.	Hakodate	1d.
19.	Hiogo	1d.
20.	Newport News	1d.
21.	Stockholm	1d.
22.	Christiania	1d.
23.	Antwerp	1d.
24.	Salonica	1d.
25.	Tonga	1d.
26.	Batoum	1d.
27.	Costa Rica	1d.
28.	Mexico	4d.
29.	Bushire	1d.
30.	Erzeroum	1d.
31.	Bilbao	1d.
32.	Rio Grande do Sul	1d.
33.	Piræus	1d.
34.	Sandakan	1d.
35.	Stockholm	1d.
36.	Tahiti	1d.
37.	Syra	1d.
38.	Kanagawa	2d.
39.	Nagasaki	1d.
40.	Chefoo	1d.
41.	Pekin	1d.
42.	Ciudad Bolivar	1d.
43.	Puerto Cabello	1d.
44.	Réunion	1d.
45.	Sarawak	1d.
46.	Würtemberg	1d.
47.	Tokyo	1d.
48.	Amsterdam	1d.
49.	Lisbon	1d.
50.	Königsberg	2d.
51.	Cagliari	1d.
52.	Frankfort	1d.
53.	Bogota	1d.
54.	Kharput	1d.
55.	Trieste	1d.
56.	Crete	1d.
57.	Berne	3d.
58.	Rotterdam	1d.
59.	Düsseldorf	4d.
60.	Mozambique	5d.
61.	Hanyang	1d.
62.	Stockholm	1d.
63.	Paris	1d.
64.	Tunis	1d.
65.	The Hague	2d.
66.	Italy	2d.
67.	Smyrna	2d.
68.	Fiume	1d.
69.	Tabreez	1d.
70.	Philippopolis	1d.
71.	Rome	1d.
72.	Vienna	1d.
73.	St. Petersburg	2d.
74.	Ichang	1d.
75.	Salonica	1d.
76.	Brussels	2d.
77.	Alexandria	1d.
78.	Patras	1d.
79.	Maranham	1d.
80.	Taganrog	2d.
81.	Jeddah	1d.
82.	Suakin	1d.
83.	Colonia	1d.
84.	Suez	1d.
85.	Paris	1d.
86.	Brest	1d.
87.	Puerto Plata	1d.
88.	Charleston	1d.
89.	Tripoli	1d.
90.	Saigon	1d.
91.	Cherbourg	1d.
92.	New Orleans	2d.
93.	Galatz	1d.
94.	Baltimore	1d.
95.	Tokio	4d.
96.	Havre	3d.
97.	Barcelona	3d.
98.	Volo	1d.
99.	Damascus	1d.
100.	Paris	1d.
101.	Bordeaux	2d.
102.	Serajevo	1d.
103.	Manila	1d.
104.	Galveston	1d.
105.	Aleppo	1d.
106.	Rio de Janeiro	1d.
107.	Truxillo	1d.
108.	St. Petersburg	3d.
109.	Leghorn	1d.
110.	Boston	1d.
111.	Buenos Ayres	3d.
112.	Kewkiang	1d.
113.	Teheran	2d.
114.	Beyrout	1d.
115.	Odessa	5d.
116.	Carthagena	1d.
117.	Santo Domingo	1d.
118.	Mollendo	1d.
119.	Guayaquil	1d.
120.	Valparaiso	1d.
121.	San José	1d.
122.	Pakhoi	1d.
123.	Hyogo	1d.
124.	Tamsui	1d.
125.	Malaga	1d.
126.	Marseilles	1d.
127.	Boulogne	2d.
128.	Warsaw	1d.
129.	Monte Video	1d.
130.	Christiania	4d.
131.	Gothenburg	2d.
132.	Kiungchow	1d.
133.	Amoy	1d.
134.	Genoa	1d.
135.	Trebizond	1d.

No. 136.

Reference to previous Report [*C.* 3593], *Commercial No.* 18, 1883.

UNITED STATES.

SAVANNAH.

Consul Cridland to the Marquis of Salisbury.

My Lord,   *Charleston, March* 28, 1887.

I HAVE the honour to enclose herewith a report of the Trade and Commerce of the Port of Savannah for the past year, furnished by Mr. Vice-Consul Robertson.

I have, &c.
(Signed)   FREDERICK J. CRIDLAND.

Report by Vice-Consul Robertson on the Trade and Commerce of the Port of Savannah for the Year 1886.

The trade and commerce of the port of Savannah for the year 1886 shows a continuance of the prosperity and activity which has marked it for some years, and which has helped to make it the second port of importance in the Southern States of America.

As the annexed returns will show, the quantities and value of both imports and exports for 1886 compare most favourably with those of the preceding year, and there is every indication of a still further increase for 1887.

Means of communication. The Central Railroad, one of the leading roads of the State, with its terminus at this port, has in course of construction a new line which will very materially benefit the trade of Savannah, embracing, as it will, a large area of the cotton-growing district at present out of the line of railways connecting with this port.

The work of improving the Savannah river, so as to enable ships of heavier tonnage to come up to the city to load, is still being carried on. The appropriations, however, granted by Congress for this purpose are very inadequate to ensure a speedy and lasting improvement.

A committee was appointed by the Savannah Board of Trade to impress upon the proper authorities the necessity of increasing the appropriations for 1886, but unfortunately they met with only partial success.

The general health of the port during the year has been good. Many cases of malarial fever have occurred, and must necessarily occur, from the fact of Savannah being low lying and partly surrounded by swamps.

A local law which compels the crews of all vessels to sleep on shore—from the 1st of April until the end of September—has done much towards preventing sickness among the seamen.

Imports. Fertilisers. Of the various articles of import entered at this port but two are brought from Great Britain, viz., fertilisers and salt.

(185)

UNITED STATES.

Salt.

The former is steadily increasing in both quantity and value, and will doubtless in a few years be a valuable article of importation.

This article is usually carried more as a ballast than as a cargo. Ships arriving in ballast have to discharge some miles down the river, whereas with salt they can come right up to the city and discharge, thereby saving expense to the ship.

Exports. Cotton.

The increase in the quantity of cotton brought to Savannah for export, although not particularly large, is still sufficient to prove that the port is holding its own against the very keen competition which is everywhere being felt. The increase for 1886 is due more to the exceptionally favourable season for the cultivation and gathering of the cotton than to any very large increase in the area of the cotton fields.

Cotton seed.

This is quite a new article of exportation from this port. Previously all the cotton seed brought to Savannah was taken and used by the Savannah oil mills, which in the early part of the year under review were burnt down, and have not nor are they intended to be rebuilt.

Spirits of Turpentine.

Savannah is the principal port in the United States for the exportation of this article of commerce, and, from the very extensive pine forests which are annually being brought into use for this purpose, there is little reason to doubt that the trade will go on improving.

RETURN of all Shipping at the Port of Savannah in the Year 1886.

ENTERED.

Nationality.	Sailing. Number of Vessels.	Sailing. Tons.	Steam. Number of Vessels.	Steam. Tons.	Total. Number of Vessels.	Total. Tons.
British	31	16,188	76	93,538	107	109,726
American	17	6,985	234	445,536	251	452,521
Norwegian	132	72,040	...	...	132	72,040
German	20	11,251	1	1,794	21	13,045
Other countries	35	18,003	1	1,822	36	19,825
Total	235	124,467	312	542,690	547	667,157

CLEARED.

Nationality.	Sailing. Number of Vessels.	Sailing. Tons.	Steam. Number of Vessels.	Steam. Tons.	Total. Number of Vessels.	Total. Tons.
British	41	24,858	62	87,321	103	112,179
American	6	977	329	448,737	335	449,714
Norwegian	118	59,920	...	...	118	59,920
German	24	14,023	1	1,794	25	15,817
Other countries	39	20,269	1	1,822	40	22,091
Total	228	120,047	393	539,674	621	659,721

SAVANNAH.

Return of Principal Articles of Export and Import from Savannah during the Years 1886-85.

Export.

Articles.		1886. Quantity.	1886. Value.	1885. Quantity.	1885. Value.
			£		£
Cotton	Lbs.	211,872,323	3,700,101	166,137,736	3,231,063
Cotton seed	,,	1,341,018	2,384	...	...
Lumber and timber	Feet	17,727,340	48,386	21,129,470	67,549
Spirits of turpentine	Galls.	3,498,244	229,302	2,800,838	183,402
All other articles	...	...	139,461	...	95,826
		...	4,119,634	...	3,577,840

Import.

Articles.		1886. Quantity.	1886. Value.	1885. Quantity.	1885. Value.
			£		£
Fertilisers	Tons	25,940	45,714	17,471	41,182
Coffee	Lbs.	1,211,714	43,900	295,558	16,072
Salt	,,	14,550,153	3,053	15,664,498	2,606
Cigars	...	255,000	1,223	275,000	1,804
Mollases	Galls.	29,321	829	76,322	1,968
All other articles	...	...	5,134	...	10,194
		...	99,853	...	74,826

Table showing the Total Value of all Articles Exported from Savannah and Imported to Savannah from and to Foreign Countries during the Years 1885-86.

Country.	Exports. 1886.	Exports. 1885.	Imports. 1886.	Imports. 1885.
	£	£	£	£
Great Britain	2,067,339	..	40,943	..
Germany	836,667	..	10,571	..
Spain	229,804	..	23,314	..
Russia	282,814	..	..	..
Netherlands	199,848	..	..	..
Belgium	172,080	..	..	..
Brazil	..	..	23,911	..
Other countries	331,082	..	1,114	..
Total	4,119,634	3,577,840	99,853	74,826

LONDON:
Printed for Her Majesty's Stationery Office,
By HARRISON AND SONS,
Printers in Ordinary to Her Majesty.
(Wt. 7730 75 5 | 87—H & S 185)

FOREIGN OFFICE.
1887.
ANNUAL SERIES.

No. 137.
DIPLOMATIC AND CONSULAR REPORTS ON TRADE AND FINANCE.

UNITED STATES.

REPORT FOR THE YEAR 1886
ON THE
TRADE OF WILMINGTON.

REFERENCE TO PREVIOUS REPORTS [C. 4737], Commercial No. 10, 1886, and [C. 3781], Commercial No. 32, 1883.

Presented to both Houses of Parliament by Command of Her Majesty,
MAY, 1887.

LONDON:
PRINTED FOR HER MAJESTY'S STATIONERY OFFICE,
BY HARRISON AND SONS, ST. MARTIN'S LANE,
PRINTERS IN ORDINARY TO HER MAJESTY.

And to be purchased, either directly or through any Bookseller, from
EYRE AND SPOTTISWOODE, EAST HARDING STREET, FLEET STREET, E.C., and
32, ABINGDON STREET, WESTMINSTER, S.W.; or
ADAM AND CHARLES BLACK, NORTH BRIDGE, EDINBURGH; or
HODGES, FIGGIS, & Co., 104, GRAFTON STREET, DUBLIN.

1887.

[C.—4923—60.]   *Price 2d.*

New Series of Reports.

Reports of the Annual Series have been issued from Her Majesty's Diplomatic and Consular Officers at the following places, and may be obtained from the sources indicated on the title-page:—

No.		Price.	No.		Price.
23.	Antwerp	1d.	80.	Taganrog	2d.
24.	Salonica	1d.	81.	Jeddah	1d.
25.	Tonga	1d.	82.	Suakin	1d.
26.	Batoum	1d.	83.	Colonia	1d.
27.	Costa Rica	1d.	84.	Suez	1d.
28.	Mexico	4d.	85.	Paris	1d.
29.	Bushire	1d.	86.	Brest	1d.
30.	Erzeroum	1d.	87.	Puerto Plata	1d.
31.	Bilbao	1d.	88.	Charleston	1d.
32.	Rio Grande do Sul	1d.	89.	Tripoli	1d.
33.	Piræus	1d.	90.	Saigon	1d.
34.	Sandakan	1d.	91.	Cherbourg	1d.
35.	Stockholm	1d.	92.	New Orleans	2d.
36.	Tahiti	1d.	93.	Galatz	1d.
37.	Syra	1d.	94.	Baltimore	1d.
38.	Kanagawa	2d.	95.	Tokio	4d.
39.	Nagasaki	1d.	96.	Havre	3d.
40.	Chefoo	1d.	97.	Barcelona	3d.
41.	Pekin	1d.	98.	Volo	1d.
42.	Ciudad Bolivar	1d.	99.	Damascus	1d.
43.	Puerto Cabello	1d.	100.	Paris	1d.
44.	Réunion	1d.	101.	Bordeaux	2d.
45.	Sarawak	1d.	102.	Serajevo	1d.
46.	Würtemberg	1d.	103.	Manila	1d.
47.	Tokyo	1d.	104.	Galveston	1d.
48.	Amsterdam	1d.	105.	Aleppo	1d.
49.	Lisbon	1d.	106.	Rio de Janeiro	1d.
50.	Königsberg	2d.	107.	Truxillo	1d.
51.	Cagliari	1d.	108.	St. Petersburg	3d.
52.	Frankfort	1d.	109.	Leghorn	1d.
53.	Bogota	1d.	110.	Boston	1d.
54.	Kharput	1d.	111.	Buenos Ayres	3d.
55.	Trieste	1d.	112.	Kewkiang	1d.
56.	Crete	1d.	113.	Teheran	2d.
57.	Berne	3d.	114.	Beyrout	1d.
58.	Rotterdam	1d.	115.	Odessa	5d.
59.	Düsseldorf	4d.	116.	Carthagena	1d.
60.	Mozambique	5d.	117.	Santo Domingo	1d.
61.	Hanyang	1d.	118.	Mollendo	1d.
62.	Stockholm	1d.	119.	Guayaquil	1d.
63.	Paris	1d.	120.	Valparaiso	1d.
64.	Tunis	1d.	121.	San José	1d.
65.	The Hague	2d.	122.	Pakhoi	1d.
66.	Italy	2d.	123.	Hyogo	1d.
67.	Smyrna	2d.	124.	Tamsui	1d.
68.	Fiume	1d.	125.	Malaga	1d.
69.	Tabreez	1d.	126.	Marseilles	1d.
70.	Philippopolis	1d.	127.	Boulogne	2d.
71.	Rome	1d.	128.	Warsaw	1d.
72.	Vienna	1d.	129.	Monte Video	1d.
73.	St. Petersburg	2d.	130.	Christiania	4d.
74.	Ichang	1d.	131.	Gothenburg	2d.
75.	Salonica	1d.	132.	Kiungchow	1d.
76.	Brussels	2d.	133.	Amoy	1d.
77.	Alexandria	1d.	134.	Genoa	1d.
78.	Patras	1d.	135.	Trebizond	1d.
79.	Maranham	1d.	136.	Savannah	1d.

No. 137.

Reference to previous Report [C. 4737], *Commercial No.* 10 1886, *and* [C. 3781], *Commercial No.* 32, 1883.

UNITED STATES.

WILMINGTON.

Consul Cridland to the Marquis of Salisbury.

My Lord,
British Consulate,
Charleston, March 12th, 1887.

I HAVE the honour to report to your Lordship that in the early part of this year I called upon Mr. Vice Consul Sprunt, of Wilmington, North Carolina, for a Report of the Commerce of that Port for the past year, which I have now the honour to enclose.

I have, &c.
(Signed) FREDERICK J. CRIDLAND.

Report of Vice-Consul James Sprunt on the Trade and Commerce of Wilmington for the year 1886.

In my Report of 1883, I made extended reference to the River and Bar improvement work, which was making satisfactory progress at that time. The success of these operations, under the direction of the General Government, has since then been fully assured. A short review of the history of this undertaking may be useful in order to show the results. The improvement of the Cape Fear River below Wilmington has been under the consideration, either of the State of North Carolina or of the United States, since 1821. Prior to 1761, the Cape Fear River was reported as allowing vessels of 14 feet draft to pass over its main bar at low water, and to enter the river by the same route as they follow to-day.

Navigation.

In 1761, however, during a violent equinoctial storm of four days' duration, the wind and sea made a breach, reported at first as 13 feet deep at high water, and later as not over 2 feet 5 inches deep at low water, and nearly a half mile wide, through the sand banks into the Cape Fear River, about 8 miles above its former bar entrance, at a place called the "Haulover."

This breach cutting off about six miles of the river's length, gradually increased in importance so as to form a new mouth to the river, deepening from 6 feet at low water in 1797 to 10 feet at low water in 1839, and received the name of the "New Inlet." The effect of this new mouth upon the river was to diminish the depth of water upon the main bar entrance from 15 feet in 1797 to 9 feet in 1839.

Prior to the opening of New Inlet, and even until 1839, Baldhead Channel was the natural and main entrance to the river. From 1839

(186)

to 1872, both the Rip and New Inlet were the main entrances, and the use of Baldhead was discontinued. Since 1872, and the closure of New Inlet, Baldhead has again become the main Channel, and has been gradually regaining its former depths.

In 1821, the date of the first detailed survey of the river, vessels of over 10 feet draft were obliged to lighten their cargoes 14 miles below Wilmington; 10 feet draft at high water, and 7 feet 5 inches draft at low water, being all that could be carried from the point of lighterage up to Wilmington.

From 1822 to 1829, the State of North Carolina attempted to improve the channel between New Inlet and Wilmington, by dike closures of the minor channels, by jetty contraction of the main channel way, and also by dredging across the shoals. A small amount of money, supposed to have been from £12,000 to £16,000, was spent in this way with moderately good results.

In 1829, when the U.S. Government assumed active charge of the improvements, the river had three bar entrances with least depth about as follows:—9 feet at Baldhead channel, 9 feet at the Rip channel (both near the old river mouth), and 10 feet at the New Inlet channel. The total amount of appropriations by the General Government for closing of New Inlet and for other necessary work, has reached about 2,300,000 dollars or £460,000. The method of closing New Inlet, a project resulting in great success, has been fully described in a former report (Blue Book of 1883).* Since that time the dam is being extended about two miles further down the stream, dredging is greatly assisting the tidal currents, and a continuous channel of 270 feet width and 16 feet depth at low water, is being made from the ocean bar to Wilmington; this channel will be marked by guide piles and range targets. The New Inlet dam is being extended from Zekes Island southward to Smith's Island, and this extension will be raised to mean tidal level.

The average rise of tide is 4 feet 5 inches at the bar, and 2 feet 5 inches at Wilmington, so that vessels loaded to 17 feet draft can now readily go from Wilmington to the ocean in a single tide.

The Engineers are confident that a depth of 20 feet at low water is only a question of time, under the present system of improvement. The immediate effects of this highly successful work have here been most gratifying in the largely increased commerce of Wilmington, notwithstanding the general stagnation in trade.

Exports.

From the tables appended it will be seen that the total exports of 1886 exceed those of 1885 to the value of £360,440 sterling. There has also been a large increase in British tonnage employed, especially in steam vessels. During 1885 there were entered in Wilmington eight British steamers, in 1886 this number was increased to 21 steamers.

Difficult points in the navigation of the Cape Fear River, notably on the shoals nine miles below Wilmington, and in the "cut" about 20 miles below Wilmington, are being improved or removed by dredges now at work, and the shoal in the river off the Champion Cotton Press at Wilmington, which caused much annoyance to ship masters this season, will be removed by dredging during the summer months of the present year, an appropriation having been made by the Government for that purpose.

I am indebted for much of the foregoing information with direct reference to the river and bar improvement, to Captain W. H. Bixby

* No. 32 Commercial, 1883, C. 3781.

Corps of Engineers, United States Army, under whose skilful direction the work is being carried on.

For nearly a century, and until four years ago, Wilmington was the principal market for turpentine, tar, spirits of turpentine, rosin, and pitch in America. *Turpentine and cotton.*

The trade in these articles, notably the lower grades of rosin, tar, and pitch, is still held here, but the virgin pine trees of South Carolina, Georgia, and Florida attracted many North Carolinians to those states where the production of spirits, turpentine and fine rosins is now carried on.

The receipts at Wilmington of spirits of turpentine for the year 1886, 62,494 casks, compare favorably with those of 1885, 63,513 casks, there being a decrease of only 1019 casks.

Several years ago, in consequence of reckless over-production in Georgia, the supply of spirits of turpentine largely exceeded the demand, and the result was the total failure of many small operators (who had no financial support), and a much lower range of values.

During the past two years, however, this surplus product has been gradually absorbed by a steady healthy demand for consumption, and the visible supply to-day in the United Kingdom is about 20,000 casks less than it was at this time a year ago. The receipts at the American markets have almost ceased for this season, which closes in March, and the preparations for next season's supply are more guarded than was the case in former years. An attempt has been made by the distillers in Georgia and Florida to form a protective association, in order to control the supply, regulate the skilled labour, reduce the cost of marketing the crop in railway freights, factors' charges, &c., and generally to co-operate for each others good.

This scheme promises well, but must yet be regarded as a doubtful experiment.

The receipts of rosin at Wilmington, 1885, were 350,031 barrels; in 1886 they were reduced to 312,647 barrels, which is owing more to the low prices current for the common grades, of which Wilmington supplies nearly the entire demands, than to a scarcity of material, as many old trees which yield crude turpentine suitable for this product were abandoned. *Rosin.*

The trade in fine rosin, especially in Georgia, has been much hampered by a practice among unprincipled dealers of "horning" the grades.

By this term is meant the fraudulent changing of class marks from low grades to higher ones—the "raising" of H rosin to IK by adding two horns, sic, IK; cutting off the last stroke of the grade M and changing it to an N, &c.

This abominable method is still a shame and a reproach to the American trade, especially in Savannah, where it is most practised.

In a recent circular issued by the Co-operative Association already referred to, the following paragraph with reference to this evil appears, which is much to the credit of this society of distillers:—

Our Position on the "Horning" Question.—The Association has resolved to break up the nefarious practice of "horning" rosin, and does not propose to be "bluffed" or turned aside from its honest resolution in the matter. There is no doubt of the fact that a gigantic swindle has been flourishing right here in our midst for several years, and it is a lasting reproach to the leading Naval Stores Factors of Savannah that they have tolerated the practice, if some of them, indeed, have not "winked" at it. A system of doing business, under which hundreds of thousands of barrels of rosin have been foisted upon

(186)

distant consumers at from one to three grades above its original inspection and return rendered to the innocent producer in the country calls for the condemnation of all honest men, and must be effectually stamped out of existence at this, the leading naval stores port of the world, where it should never have been allowed to exist for a single moment. The practice of "horning" has been appropriately styled " a moral cancer, fastened on the naval stores trade." It is our duty now, in view of recent events, to refresh the minds of the producers, and the public generally, on the somewhat remarkable position taken by the Savannah Board of Trade, on May 7th, 1885, on this dishonest practice of "horning" rosin, which then came up for their official consideration and action. The vote shows that "horning" was (practically) sustained by twenty-one (21) to eleven (11)! Of the naval stores element in the Board of Trade it appears that eleven voted against horning and nine voted in its favor! The worst feature of the case is that of these nine votes cast (practically) in favor of the practice, five are shown to have been by factors.

We hope to push our investigation into the matter with such success that "the horner and his little hatchet" will soon be a thing of the past.

There is a large demand for fine rosins in America, especially in the western and south-western states. The production of tar in North Carolina has been much reduced during the past year, the receipts for 1885 being 80,722 barrels at Wilmington, and for 1886 only 63,120 barrels. This decrease is attributed to the great falling off in the demand for export to the United Kingdom, which was formerly large, but which during the past two years has almost ceased. The North Carolina tar was used for smearing of sheep, but principally for distillation in Great Britain, but the demand for its products has diminished, and the dealers now give preference to Stockholm or Archangel tar, because of late years the American article was very carelessly prepared for market. The barrels were of thin unseasoned staves, irregular in shape and size, and the tar mixed with water and sand. These objections have since been overcome by more careful inspection at Wilmington, by regulating the size by weight, and by stringent rules with reference to sand.

Cotton.

The receipts of cotton at Wilmington are largely in excess of former years, being 137,357 bales for 1886 as compared with 90,624 bales in 1885. This increase is the direct result of the river and bar improvements enabling exporters to employ steamers instead of sailing vessels, which were formerly the only means of export, and to compete successfully with Norfolk, which has hitherto controlled the greater part of the North Carolina crop. The crop has been remarkably clean and bright, although such is generally the character of Wilmington shipments; but the yield has been much below an average of former years throughout the State, and the season is practically over a month earlier than usual.

Attempts have been made in this vicinity to improve the staples of our uplands with fairly good results, and cases of false, fraudulent, or water-packed bales are less frequent than formerly.

Population of North Carolina.

The following statement shows the population of the State of North Carolina classified as white and coloured, and also the number of males of 21 years of age and over foreign white, native white and coloured, according to the United States census of 1880:—

WILMINGTON.

	Number.
White population	867,242
Coloured population	532,508
Total	1,399,750

Males of 21 years of age and over—

Foreign white	2,095
Native white	187,637
Coloured	105,018
Total	294,750

The number of acres of land in farms in North Carolina, according to the census of 1880, were as follows:—

	Acres.
Improved	6,481,191
Unimproved	15,882,367

The principal of the bonded debt recognised in the Act of March 4, 1879, and authorised to be exchanged, was as follows:— *State debt*

	Dollars.
Bonds issued before May 20, 1861, the last date of which is April 1, 1861, 40 per cent.	5,477,400
Bonds issued during and since the late war, by authority of Acts passed prior thereto, and subsequently renewed and registered certificates held by the State Board of Education, 25 per cent.	3,261,045
Bonds issued in pursuance of the funding Acts of March 10, 1866, and August 20, 1868, 15 per cent.	3,888,600
Total recognised debt	12,627,045

Bonds have been surrendered and exchanged as follows:—

	Dollars.
Class 1 at 40 per cent.	4,865,900
„ 2 „ 25 „	2,525,045
„ 3 „ 15 „	3,116,100
Total amount bonds exchanged.	

New four per cent. bonds have been issued as follows:—

	Dollars.	c.
For bonds at 40 per cent.	1,946,360	0
„ „ 25 „	631,261	25
„ „ 15 „	467,415	0
Total amount of new bonds issued	3,045,036	25

The old fundable bonds not surrendered are as follows:—

	Dollars.
Redeemable at 40 per cent.	611,500
„ „ 25 „	736,000
„ „ 15 „	772,500
Total amount old bonds outstanding	2,120,000

The estimated resources for the year 1888 and 1889, or probable income therefrom:—

UNITED STATES.

	Dollars.	c.
The valuation of real and personal property as appears from the returns to the auditor, is 202,000,000 dol. A tax of 23 c. on every 100 dollars' value of property, deducting commissions of sheriffs, will raise	441,370	0
Taxes collectable by sheriffs	35,000	0
„ „ „ on incomes	28,000	0
„ on drummers	81,300	0
Revenue from other sources	35,000	0
	620,670	0
Balance to credit November 30, 1886	172,327	6
	792,997	6

The estimated expenses for 1887 and 1888:—

	Dollars.
For support of the Government, including the Legislature, Executive and Judicial Departments, and other special appropriations to asylums, schools, university, &c.	269,750
Charitable and penal institutions	313,900
Interest on four per cent. bonds	114,000
	697,650

The receipts and disbursements of the Educational Fund, as embraced in the foregoing report, are as follows:—

RECEIPTS.

	Dollars	c.
Entries of vacant lands	6,121	58
Corporation tax on railroad companies	650	00
Interest on 4 per cent. State bonds	7,940	00
Expense account (amount refunded)	91	21
Total receipts	14,802	79
Balance on hand November 30, 1884	20,981	58
Grand total	35,784	37

DISBURSEMENTS.

	Dollars	c.
Public schools	801	60
Survey swamp lands	9,313	24
Expense account	421	15
Railroad corporation tax refunded	25	00
Fees of attorney and allowance by court in case of State Board of Education v. D. S. Bible and S. T. Canon	2,000	00
Total disbursements	12,560	99
Balance	23,223	38
Grand total	35,784	37

The receipts for the two fiscal years contain special funds, not constituting a part of the ordinary revenue. They are stated as follows:—

	Dollars.
Tax on fertilizers for the benefit of Agricultural Department	81,500
Sale of useless arms appropriated to benefit of State Guard	2,000
Sale of lot in city of Raleigh	50
Dividends on State stock in the N.C.R.R. Company, received under amended decree of the United States Circuit Court in the Swasey suit, and applied to the payment of the interest on new six per cent. bonds	269,310
Total	353,860

The expenditures embrace special subjects, the payment of which is not provided for from the ordinary resources.

	Dollars	c.
Agricultural Department	82,500	00
Interest on 6 per cent. renewal bonds	279,435	00
Executive mansion	2,068	36
Investment in 4 per cent. bonds	247,815	98
Total	611,819	34

Hence the expenditures, provided for from the ordinary revenue, were as follows:—

	Dollars	c.
Year ending November 30, 1885	675,746	26
,, ,, 1886	680,572	97

The receipts and disbursements of the public fund, which include all of a general or special nature, not connected with the Educational Fund, as shown in the foregoing report, are as follows:—

RECEIPTS.

	Dollars.	c.
Public taxes for general purposes	554,495	47
Special taxes for interest on 4 per cent. bonds	60,262	82
Sales of useless arms	2,000	00
License tax on banks	975	00
Tax on bank stock	11,089	45
,, corporations	1,050	00
,, itinerant practitioners, &c.	930	00
Dividends from N.C.R.R.	269,310	00
Dividends on special stock N.C.R.R.	168	00
Tax on drummers' licenses	168,100	00
,, express companies	955	20
,, on telegraph companies	956	31
,, licensed halls	1,450	00
Fees from officers	6,378	20
Tax on insurance companies	22,185	55
,, receipts of N.C.R.R.	16,815	02
,, seals	960	58
,, sewing machines	3,800	00
,, sleeping cars	1,000	00
Stationery, furnished counties	655	90
Sales, Supreme Court reports	3,321	29
Tax on fertilizers	82,500	00
Miscellaneous sources	2,107	96
Public printing charged	2,865	90
Conscience fund	46	00
Total receipts	1,214,378	65
Balance on hand November 30, 1884	926,086	98
Grand total	2,140,465	63

DISBURSEMENTS.

	Dollars	c.
Department State Government	47,270	52
Agricultural societies	2,450	00
Agricultural department	82,500	00
Appropriation, disabled soldiers	8,190	00
Contingent expenses	43,155	92
Conveying convicts to penitentiary	19,230	69
Executive mansion	2,068	36
General assembly	58,286	71
Insane asylum, Raleigh	105,500	00
,, ,, Morganton	86,525	00
,, ,, ,, construction and furnishing	85,000	00
,, ,, Goldsboro'	50,000	00
Institution: deaf, dumb and blind	82,000	00
Interest on 4 per cent. State debt	224,638	00
,, ,, 6 ,, ,, ,,	279,435	00
Investment in 4 per cent. State bonds	247,815	98
Judiciary	87,024	03
Normal schools	16,000	00
Oxford orphan asylum	20,000	00
Penitentiary	257,132	59
Pension to confederate soldiers, &c.	41,430	75
Public printing	36,866	29
Quarantine regulations	2,781	70
Settling State taxes	1,696	92
State Board of Health	4,000	00
,, guard	13,207	14
,, library	1,359	44
University of North Carolina	51,250	00
Miscellaneous	10,313	53
Total disbursements	1,968,138	57
Balance	172,327	06
Grand total	2,140,465	63

The biennial report of the treasurer of the State of North Carolina for the two fiscal years ending November 30, 1886, shows the following summary statement of receipts and disbursements of both years and the balance to the credit of the educational and public funds at the close of each year:—

WILMINGTON.

	Dollars.	c.	Dollars.	c.
Balance of educational fund, November 30, 1884	..	..	20,981	58
,, ,, public fund, November 30, 1884	..	..	926,086	98
Total	..	..	947,068	56
Receipts of educational fund year ending November 30, 1885	7,176	54		
Receipts of public fund year ending November 30, 1885	378,957	62		
Total receipts for fiscal year..	..	..	386,134	16
Amount of resources for the fiscal year	..	..	1,333,202	72
Disbursements of educational fund year ending November 30, 1885	5,195	14		
Disbursements of public fund year ending November 30, 1885	795,486	26		
Total receipts for fiscal year..	..	..	800,681	40
Balance November 30, 1885..	..	..	532,521	32
This balance as follows—				
Educational fund	22,962	98		
Public fund	509,558	34		
Receipts of educational fund year ending November 30, 1886	7,626	25		
Receipts of public fund year ending November 30, 1886	835,421	03		
Total receipts for fiscal year..	..	..	843,047	28
Amount of resources for the fiscal year	..	..	1,375,568	60
Disbursements of educational fund year ending November 30, 1886	7,365	85		
Disbursements of public fund year ending November 30, 1886	1,172,652	31		
Total disbursements for fiscal year..	..	..	1,180,018	16
Balance November 30, 1886..	..	..	195,550	44
This balance is made up as follows—				
Educational fund	23,223	38		
Public fund	106,402	84		
Four per cent. interest fund	65,924	22		
Total	195,550	44		

There has been no time in the history of North Carolina when so **Minerals.** much attention has been directed to her mineral wealth as at present. The enquiries from abroad are numerous and of such a character to require the Agricultural Department, under whose auspices exhibits of minerals were made at New Orleans and Boston, to give the subject more attention than heretofore. It is estimated that the Museum at Raleigh is visited daily by twenty or more persons in quest of information and inspection of specimens of minerals. The display at this Museum is certainly a very large and creditable one, and is well worth seeing. The people of North Carolina themselves are surprised at the quantity and quality of the ores which are found mingling with the soil of all our hills and valleys. Indications are that the mining operations will be largely augmented at an early day, and that the rich treasures of the "Old North State" will ere long make her the leading state in the south.

Iron is found in considerable quantities in 30 counties in the **Iron ores.** State. The iron regions of Granville, Chatham, Guilford, and Stokes County, lying to the north of the centre of the state, in convenient distance of the coal fields. The deposits of Gaston, Lincoln, and Catawba Counties lying to the west of the centre on the southern border, with beds like those of Big Ore Bank and Yellow Ridge reported to run to a thickness of 16, 18, and even 40 feet. In the north-west corner of the state, in Ashe, Caldwell, and Mitchell Counties, the famous Cranbury deposit, in fabulous thickness and entire freedom from phosphorus and sulphur In Cherokee County, in the extreme south-west corner of the state, deposits of limonite ore, reported of great thickness. The ores of Chatham County show 58 per cent. metallic iron; those of Cherokee County 60 per cent. of metallic iron. In Davidson County the per cent. of metallic iron averages 37; in Gaston County from 52 to 67 per cent. metallic iron; in Guilford County 55 per cent. metallic iron; in Mitchell County 65 per cent. metallic iron; in Stokes County 65 per cent. metallic iron; and in Watanga County 67 per cent. metallic iron. In Nash and Duplin Counties the limonite ores give 42·73 per cent. of iron. The hematites of Granville and Halifax Counties show 63·76 per cent. of iron. Some of the mines were worked during the Revolutionary War, and many worked more or less ever since. Several new lines of railway are now in course of construction, which will open up many of the mines which have laid dormant for so many years for want of transportation facilities.

Copper ores. Copper ores are found in many localities in the State. The principal deposits are in Puson, Granville, Guilford, Cabarrus, Mecklenburg, Ashe, and Alleghany Counties. Messrs. Clayton and Co. have 600 men at work at Ore Knob Copper Works in Ashe County. Average of ores 20 per cent. copper.

The Conrad Hill Mine in Davidson County is successfully worked by 130 men. Copper assays 5 to 30 per cent.

Gold. There are two coal districts in the State, mainly in Stokes and Chatham Counties, the first being called the Dan River district and the latter the Deep River district. The area of the Deep River district is estimated at 300 square miles, and the analysis is—

	Miles.
Volatile matter	31·30
Fixed Carbon	64·40
Ash	4·30

These mines were worked for several years, and very successfully. The coal was transported by rail to Fayetteville, N.C., and thence by water to Wilmington, N.C., which necessitated such an expense for handling that the operators could not compete with other markets, hence they discontinued to work them. But now that the Cape Fear and Yndkin Valley Railroad is to be extended to Wilmington, putting the coal fields in direct communication with all the world, they will be opened again, and no doubt prove a great success.

Gold ores Gold is widely distributed through the State, it being found in twenty-nine counties in workable quantities. It is generally alloyed with silver, it being pure gold on one side and silver on the other. It is estimated that over 30,000,000 dols. in gold have been taken from North Carolina mines. The mining interests in Cabarrus County are very extensive. The discovery of gold in this county was in 1799, and in 1803 the largest nugget, twenty-eight (28) pounds, was found. In Caldwell County gold is found widely distributed, but only worked to a very slight extent. The "Shuford Mine" in Catawba County pays well under a hydraulic treatment. Dividson County is the seat of the greatest mining activity in the state. In Gaston County gold is found disseminated through a bed of bluish limestone.

No regular mining operations are conducted in Guilford Country, although considerable labour has been expended in opening up different properties. Nine mines are worked in Mecklenburg County, and fifty odd localities have been opened; three reduction works have been erected. Mining is extensively carried on in Rowan County by the Gold Hill Mining Co., Howard Gold and Copper Co., North Carolina Mining and Reduction Co., Rowan Mining and Milling Co., Holmes and Co., Union Mining Co., and others. Several mines are being worked in Rutherford, Stancy, Union, Lincoln, and other counties in the state.

Silver is found in Guilford, Cabarrus, Mecklenburg, Pusin, and Granville Counties.

Silver.

Mr. Harma, of United States Assay Office, Charlotte, N.C., reports production of North Carolina in precious metals as follows:—

	Dollars.
The production for 1885 was	125,866·17
Unreported production	15,000·00
Shipped, and not included in above	6,900·00
Total	147,766,17

	Number.
Number of men regularly employed	698
Men employed at intervals	100
Number of stamps	459
Chilian and other mills	17
Smelting works	1
Reduction works	1
Chlornidim works	3

Tin Ore.—Tinstone has been found at King's Mountain, appears abundant, and contains from 45 to 75 per cent. of metallic tin.

Albite.—Found in large quantities in Macon, Madison, Mitchell, and Yancey Counties.

Agalmatolite.—Soapstone found in large quantities in Chatham and Montgomery Counties. An article of trade on a considerable scale for many years, it being used in the manufacture of paper, soaps, cosmetics, pencils, &c.

Asbestos.—The short staple asbestos is found in Macon and Madison Counties. The long staple is found in large quantities in Mitchell County.

Barite.—Very pure is found in Cabanus, Gaston, and Madison Counties.

Chromite.—Found in Jackson, Madison, and Yancey Counties.

Corundum.—Found in Clay, Haywood, Ireden, and Yancey Counties.

Fire Clay.—Found in Gaston County of a very superior quality.

Garnets.—Found in Burke, Madison, Mitchell, and Macon Counties. Some of these crystals weigh 15 to 20 lbs. They are ground to make a cutting and polishing powder, for which there is good demand.

Graphite.—Found in Wake, Stokes, Puson, Yancey, Catâwba, and Burke Counties. There is a very extensive deposit at the Hepborn mine, four miles west of Raleigh.

Kaolin.—Found all over the state. The largest beds near Gumsbon in Guilford County.

Manganese.—Found in large quantities in Aslu, Lincoln, Suny, and Madison Counties.

Mica.—This mineral is found in large quantities and of excellent quality. The largest mines are in Clay, Yancey, and Mitchell Counties. The aggregate product of these mines has been about 300,000 lbs., worth over 500,000 dol. This region is yielding more mica than any other in the world.

Pyrite.—Suitable for making sulphuric acid; is abundant through the gold and copper belt.

Limestone.—Found in several counties; the best is found in Gaston and Pender Counties.

Millstone, Grindstone, and Whetstone.—Are found in Moone, Anson, Chatham, and Swain Counties.

Talc.—Is found in Aslu, Burke, and Cherokee Counties.

Railway commission.

The General Assembly of North Carolina of 1886–1887 had some important measures before it, but none the people were more interested in than that providing for the creation of a Railroad Commission.

The petitions presented from all sections of the State very forcibly made known to the legislators the wishes of the people, and a joint committee was appointed to take into consideration any and all measures which would be introduced referring to the railroads and people. The Committee met from day to day and patiently listened to all the arguments made by learned attorneys on the part of corporations, and by business men for the people. Having fully considered the question in all its bearings, they reported a Bill to be entitled an Act to establish a Railroad Commission. The provisions of the Bill were not silent on essential matters in the problem of railway government, or very pronounced on non-essential features, yet it provided a remedy that would have proved acceptable to the people and protected railroads. It was not antagonistic to the railroads, and it was supposed that the railroad companies would not antagonise the Bill proposed; but this surmise was not well founded. As soon as these measures of reconciliation were announced, the three trunk lines and their affiliations in and out of the State combined for the purpose of defeating any legislation of any character whatever. It was shown that Railroad Commissions had been for years and were now in successful and satisfactory operation in 26 different states in the United States, and that it was a necessity in this State, but it all availed nothing, the legislature adjourning giving to the railroads all they asked and leaving the people unprotected. This all-inclusive combination of railroad managers and legislators cannot expect to be regarded with favor by the public. In so far as they attain the object, the producers and consumers of the State will be compelled to give the transportation companies a larger proportion than before of the annual wealth product. The slight advance in rates which were issued by all lines in the State on February 17, 1887, will transfer thousands from the pockets of the people to the treasuries of the railroads, that is if these rates are rigidly maintained. Certainty and steadiness in railroad charges is of advantage to all business men, and this cannot now be guaranteed. The arguments against a great combination like the Associated Lines of Virginia and the Carolinas are of a general nature. The railroads seem bound to come under some permanent form of centralised administration. They tend more and more to consolidation into a system. Ordinary principles of competition and of supply and demand seem not to operate with any success in the railroad world. They claim self-preservation forces them to combine, to divide business, and to regulate charges. In doing this they claim they are not intentional conspirators against the public, and they all argue that under the pooling system, or whatever other name they choose to call it, that they can serve the public more satisfactorily. Unfortunately some roads cannot protect themselves and have to go into the through traffic arrangements. Returns must be earned for a larger amount of capital, and rates are reduced more slowly than if fewer roads did the whole of a constantly expanding business. The companies insist upon fixing charges at such rates as to pay an income, not on the actual value of their properties, but upon the fictitious values represented by their inflated issue of stock and bonds. This the people object to, and look upon pooling systems as an attempt to force value into millions of excessive securities. The effect of the combination of the trunk lines in North Carolina caused the people to ask for the enactment of a railroad commission law. Sentiment everywhere condemns the combination known as the Associated Lines of Virginia and the Carolinas and their pooling system. The people do not forget that railroads have a public character, that they exist by virtue of public franchises, and that pooling, or by whatever term it may be known, is a virtual denial of this public character. It has a tyrannical and monopolistic aspect that the people cannot view without apprehension and strong dislike. Two years hence a railroad commission will certainly be established.

The following table shows the increase in cotton factories in North Carolina:—

Year.	Number of factories.	Number of Looms.	Number of Spindles.	Capital Invested.	Cotton Consumed.	Cost of Cotton.	Operatives Employed.	Wages Paid Operatives.
1870	33	618	39,897	1,030,900	9,170	495,180	1,255	166,915
1880	49	1,790	92,385	2,855,800	27,642	1,125,984	3,270	438,603
1886	80	4,519	200,333	6,350,100	67,685	1,395,530	5,340	715,560

These factories are located in the following Counties:—

	Number.
Alamance	14
Alexander	2
Bertie	1
Cabarrus	2
Caldwell	2
Cleveland	2
Catawba	3
Craven	1
Cumberland	6
Durham	1
Forsythe	1
Guilford	2
Iredell	2
Johnston	1
Lincoln	1
Mecklenburg	1
Montgomery	2
Nash	2
New Hanover	1
Pasquotank	1
Randolph	10
Richmond	7
Rockingham	1
Surry	4
Wilson	1
Franklin	1
Gaston	8
Total	80

UNITED STATES.

Fertilizers.

Commissioner Montford McGehu in his report to the General Assembly of North Carolina for the years of 1885-86, says in regard to fertilizers, "Of late the trade in fertilizers has been remarkably free from any attempts of the evasion of the law or irregularities of any kind. The vigorous enforcement of the law against offenders, and the exercise of a constant vigilance through the Inspector, has resulted in placing the manufacture and trade in fertilizers generally in the hands of men as much distinguished by the spirit of honor in their transactions as in any other branch of business whatsoever." He states that the number of brands of fertilizers for which licences were issued, were for 1885-86 eighty-two, and the number for 1883-84, eighty-three. In referring to the Geological Survey, which is a co-operative department with this department, he says, "The field of industrial requirements is yearly extending, and there are few substances in the earth's crust which are not now turned to account in the multifarious industries of civilized life;" and recommends that the survey be continued so that the nature, geological position, and abundance of the substances may be of use to mankind, and converted into objects of utility and ornament. In respect to phosphate rock, he remarks, "According to the estimate made by the State chemist of the yield of 124 acres only of the phosphate land actually explored (in Pender and New Hanover Counties), there exists enough phosphate rock to make all the super-phosphates sold in North Carolina in one year." Reference is made to the explorations in Deep River section to ascertain the quantity between Farmville and Tyson, and the available tonnage is reported as 6,050,000 tons.

The experimental farm at Raleigh, N.C., under control of this department, has cost, including purchase-money and improvements from December, 1885, to December, 1886, 3,854 dol. 89 c. As to immigration, he says, "Immigration comes mostly from the Northern States." The character of the immigrant is desirable, as they are farmers with means to settle comfortably, or thoroughly trained mechanics. Hundreds of this class have been established in various parts of the State, and there is yet room for more, for as the Commissioner says, "In its soils, its mines, its minerals, its water-powers, North Carolina holds out inducements unsurpassed." As to the culture of grapes, the Commissioner says, "It is extending every year, while peaches, on account of their perishable nature, are diminishing." In rendering the account of this department from December, 1884, to December, 1886, it shows the

	Dollars.
Receipts to be	8,974,692
Disbursements	8,399,363
Balance	575,329

which certainly shows that the agricultural department has been well managed. The revenue is derived from the tax imposed on fertilizers, and the amount expended is for fairs, industrial schools, promotion of growth of grapes and fruits, &c., &c.

The last census of North Carolina gives the following:—Farms, 157,609: 22,363,558 acres. Improved, 6,481,191; unimproved, 15,882,367; average size, 142 acres; value of farms, 135,793,602 dol.; of farming implements, 6,078,476 dol.; live stock, 22,414,659 dol.; cost of fertilizers per year, 2,111,767 dol.; products, 51,729,611 dol. The principal vegetable productions:—Barley, 2,421 bushels; buckwheat, 44,686 bushels; corn, 28,019,839 bushels; oats, 3,838,068 bushels; rye, 285,160 bushels; wheat, 3,397,393 bushels; potatoes,

Irish, 722,773 bushels, sweet, 4,576,148 bushels. Hay, 93,711 tons; rice, 5,609,191 pounds; cotton, 389,598 bales; wool, 917,756 lbs; milk, 446,798 gals.; butter, 7,212,507 lbs.; cheese, 57,380 lbs.; orchard products, 903,513 dol.

Live stock: horses, 133,686; mules, 81,871; oxen, 50,188; milch cows, 232,133; other cattle, 375,105; sheep, 461,638; hogs, 1,453,541.

The foregoing figures clearly indicate the adaptability of the soil of the State for the production of almost everything. The intelligent farmers are yearly giving more attention to the science of chemistry, adopting the most improved farm utensils and machinery, and are listing farming among the sciences. They are putting their farms in order by draining them, fencing them well, improving the dwellings and out-houses, taking pains with their teams and stock, experimenting with different fertilizers, studying character of the soils and the diversity and rotation of crops. A new era has dawned, and advance is now the watchword of the farmers of North Carolina.

The increase in this industry in the last ten years has been twofold. In 1870 the number of factories was 108, the number now is 218, and are distributed as follows:— *Tobacco factories.*

	Tobacco Factories.	Cigar Factories.		Tobacco Factories.	Cigar Factories.
In Alamance	6	1	In Mecklenburg..	..	3
Buncombe	4	..	Mc Dowell	1	..
Caldwell	1	..	New Hanover	..	2
Caswell	3	1	Orange	2	..
Catawba	5	2	Puson	1	2
Cleveland	5	2	Rockingham	23	1
Craven	..	1	Rutherford	1	..
Davie	7	..	Rowan	6	1
Davidson	3	1	Stokes	8	..
Durham	10	4	Surry	22	..
Forsythe	41	2	Vance	4	..
Granville	5	..	Wake	2	1
Guilford	9	2	Wilkes	4	..
Hertford	1	0	Wilson	..	1
Iredell	7	1	Yadkin	9	..

During the year 1886, Blackwell's Durham Bull Tobacco Manufacturing Company declared a dividend of 25 per cent. on the 1,000,000 dol. capital stock. The company is empowered by the State Legislature to increase its stock to 2,000,000 dol., and make the shares 25 dol. each.

In North Carolina, 1877, there were but few schools, few school- *Public* houses, no system, no interest in public education, no anything that *schools.* could serve as an index to the progress made during the last ten years in the line of making our public schools meet the demands upon them.

The last census figures shows that there were in North Carolina—

	Number.
Public schools for white	4,015
,, ,, colored	2,146
	6,161
Public school teachers, white	4,291
,, ,, ,, colored	1,975
	6,266
Average daily attendance, white	102,254
,, ,, ,, colored	62,316
	164,570

(186)

UNITED STATES.

Value school property, 248,015 dol.; revenue, 553,464 dol.

In 1884 there was expended for public schools, 580,311 dol. 6 c.; in 1885, 632,004 dol. 38 c.; in 1886, 670,671 dol. 79 c. This increase has not been made by any increase in the rate of taxation. It is due in part to special levies in some counties, and in part to the careful attention of county officers to the enforcement of the law. The increase in attendance in 1885 over the previous year was 14,723; in 1886, 17,181 over 1885, a total for the two years of 21,904. The whites increased in the two years 17,111, and colored increase was 4,793. There are double the number of school-houses than there were 20 years ago, presided over by carefully selected competent teachers. The system is supplied with twice the amount of funds of former days. The school-houses are more comfortably and conveniently arranged, and the text-books uniform.

Private schools and colleges.

In the past ten years private schools in the State of North Carolina have been augmented two-fold, whose teachers are continually learning and adopting the improved methods of teaching. The provision for higher education is ample schools for both sexes are numerous in every section of the State. The principal institutions for education are of the highest order. At the head of these is the University of the State located at Chapel Hill. This institution was established in pursuance of the Constitution, and is maintained in part by annual appropriations. Science and learning in their widest range are there taught by professors eminent in their several branches. Second only to the University are the denominational colleges of the State, each having a corps of learned professors and tutors.

Marls and phosphates.

Marl, which is classified as greensand, eocene and miocene, abounds in 25 counties in the eastern portion of the State. The greensand is found between the Neuse River and Cape Fear, it comes to the surface along the banks of the Cape Fear, on Black and South Rivers, on the Neuse River at Kinston, along the Contentuca and Moccasin, and at a few points on the Tar River. The marls of the eocene formation are found overlaying the preceding, when the two occur together. They are composed of comminuted shells, corals, and marine exuviæ. Analysed are found to contain 90 to 95 per cent. of carbonate of lime. The miocene are known as shell or blue marls. They are found in beds scattered over a wide territory, and are more extensively used and much better known. These marls are not only valuable for the lime they contain, but also for the phosphoric acid. Phosphatic marls are found in New Hanover and Pender Counties, also the phosphatic rock in Sampson, Duplin, and Onslow Counties, which when analysed gave 45 per cent. of phosphate of lime.

Precious stones.

Emeralds.—Found in Alexander County, are very rich, and highly prized.

Hiddenites.—Found in Alexander County, N.C., which are transparent spodumene, colored green by chromium oxide, and are only found in North Carolina. The value is same as price of diamonds, and it is now considered the richest of gems.

Spodumene.—Found only in North Carolina and Brazil. Very rare gem; color, pale yellow to greenish yellow.

Beryl.—Found in Yancey, Alexander, Rutherford, Madison, and Mitchell Counties, of green, yellow, blue and colorless crystals.

Rutile.—Found in Alexander County, which are like black diamonds in lustre and color.

"Arrows of Love" Stones.—Found in Alexander, Burke, and Catawba Counties, are clear quartz mixed with crystals of rutile, of red, brown, and yellow color.

Garnets.—Found in Alexander County, are of various shades of deep red.

Citrine Topaz.—Found in Burke County, are of a beautiful golden yellow color.

Smoky Topaz.—Found in Alexander County, are perfectly transparent and clear chocolate brown color.

Kyanite.—Found in Yancey County, of a sky blue color.

Dolomite (carbonate of lime and magnesia), very rare; Apatite (phosphate of lime), transparent and colorless; Calcite (carbonate of lime), gray crystals; Siderite (carbonate of iron), brown crystals; Torbenite (hydrated phosphate of uranium and copper), dark green crystals, are found in Alexander and Mitchell Counties.

Phosphoranite.—Found in Mitchell County, a lemon yellow color.

Gahnite.—Found in Mitchell County.

Columbite.—Found in Yancey County.

Samarskite.—Found in Mitchell County.

Gummite.—Found in Alexander County, very rare in color, orange red to lemon yellow, with a velvet black core of uraninite.

Tourmaline.—Found in Catawba, Burke, and Gaston Counties, color black and brown.

Milanite (garnets).—Found in Mitchell, Yancey, and Burke Counties. Fine specimens of stones, quartz, &c., have been found in Iredell, Alexander, Cherokee, Davidson, Mecklenburg.

From the opening of the Asylum in 1856, to January, 1887, the admissions have numbered 1,818. Of these, 1,005 were males, and 813 females. Of this number, 486 have been discharged as cured, 258 improved, 333 unimproved, and 293 have died. There are now in the Asylum 248 inmates, 125 are males and 123 are females. During the last two years 17 have been discharged cured, 36 discharged improved, 28 discharged unimproved, and 28 have died. During the year 1886 the percentage of cures upon admission has been 17 per cent. The expenses of the Asylum for 1886 was 48,874½ dol. a per capita for furnishing everything of 188 dol. per year, or 51½ c. per day. The appropriation was 51,000 dol. *Insane asylum at Raleigh, New York.*

There are now in operation in North Carolina 13 woolen mills, with 131 looms and 4,466 spindles. These mills are in the following Counties:—

Buncombe	1
Caldwell	1
Catawba	1
Forsythe	2
Guilford	1
Lincoln	1
Richmond	1
Rockingham	1
Rowan	1
Surry	3
Total	13

There is in the State manufacturing establishments, of various kinds, 3,802; capital, 13,045,639 dol.; employés, 18,109; wages, 2,740,768 dol.; materials used, 13,090,937 dol., and product, 20,095,037 dol.

There has been established at the Southern Pines in North Carolina a sanatorium, with the finest prospects of success. The spot was selected by Professor Kerr, late state geologist, as one which offered unequalled conditions of health. The deep sand with its dry atmosphere, the pure water and the mild air brought health to the seeker. Two years ago it was a wild wood; now it is laid off into streets, has a large hotel and some twenty-five cottages.

UNITED STATES.

Fisheries.

Eastern North Carolina abounds in fish, oysters, turtles, &c., and a large and increasing business affords employment to thousands, who depend almost exclusively on this pursuit for a living. In former years the large seines were dragged with windlasses drawn by horses and mules. Now the fisheries are being operated on improved plans, the seines are laid out and drawn in by steam, and as a consequence, five hauls of a seine can be made now in the same time that three were formerly made. Shad and herring fisheries are the most extensive. The largest seines are 2,500 yards in length, about one mile and a half. From end to end of hauling ropes, when the seine is out, the distance is nearly four miles. From 50 to 100,000 herrings, and often twice that number are frequently taken at a single haul of a large seine in a good season. Shad and rock are also taken in large quantities. Besides these, among the commercial fishes, are mullet, blue fish, Spanish mackerel, chub, perch sturgeon, minhaden, trout, spats, hogfish, croakers, &c. To give an idea of the immensity of this business the following summary represents the statistical review of the fisheries in the *Albermarle Section* alone, for 1885:—

	Number.	Quantity.	Value.
		Lbs.	Dollars.
Persons employed	5,274	..	..
Fishing vessels	95	..	..
„ boats	2,714	..	..
Capital dependent on industry	..	..	506,561
Sea product	..	11,357,300	
„ „	..	..	280,745
River product	..	20,892,188	
„ „	..	..	546,950
Total value of products	..	..	827,695

The fisheries of Pamlico section is only second to those of the Albermarle, only a partial attempt has been made to give full statistics, and we can furnish such as seem official. There were caught in 1885—

	Number.	Value.
		Dollars.
Spanish Mackerel—about	200,000	60,000
Pompano „	50,000	15,000
Blue Fish „	1,500,000	300,000
Mullet „	3,368,000	160,000
Spotted Sea Trout „	180,000	36,000
Spat „	520,000	52,000
Pig fish and Snap fin „	400,000	32,000
Weak Fish „	170,000	40,000
Sheepshead „	80,000	16,000
Flounder „	40,000	5,000
Croaker „	350,000	17,000
Black Fish „	125,000	12,000
Whiting „	150,000	12,000
Red Dunn „	175,000	10,000
Black Dunn „	150,000	12,000
Sailors' Chine „	70,000	7,000
Striped Bass „	770,000	10,000
Shad „	3,221,263	329,569
Herring „	15,520,000	142,784
		1,288,353

WILMINGTON.

There is the greatest abundance of material for all purposes in North Carolina. Granite and gneiss throughout the whole State are the commonest rocks, except in the coast region. The State yields every variety and style of granite. White, gray, red, and white with rich dark green spots, which is highly polished very readily. Sandstones, red and gray, are availed in various localities. Shell limestone furnishes a very fair building material in the eastern portion of the State, while the crystalline limestones and marbles of the west supply ornamental building stone of great variety and beauty. There are numerous beds of marble of various colors: white, pink, black, gray, drab, and mottled. It receives a very fine polish, and the only reason they have not ever acquired a high value is on account of the present difficulties of transportation. There are several fine beds of serpentine in the State, found in Wake and Caldwell Counties. Slate is found in Swain County.

Building stones.

Silk culture can be profitably pursued in North Carolina. The mulberry, which supplies the food of the silkworm, is indigenous, and attains its fullest development without any cultivation. The climate suits the business, and silk culture is no longer a matter of experiment, as silk grown in this State has been put to the test, and has been found equal to the best French and Italian silks.

Silk culture.

Annex A.—RETURN of all the Shipping at the Port of Wilmington, North Carolina, in the Year 1886 (over 100 tons each).

ENTERED.

1886. Nationality.	Sailing. Number of Vessels.	Tons.	Steam. Number of Vessels.	Tons.	Total. Number of Vessels.	Tons.
British	24	8,075	21	33,129	45	41,204
Scandinavian	74	29,431	...	...	74	29,431
German	51	20,667	...	...	51	20,667
Italian	2	717	...	...	2	717
Dutch	3	647	...	...	3	647
Austrian	1	434	...	...	1	434
Russian	1	319	...	...	1	319
Total foreign	156	60,290	21	33,129	177	93,419
,, American	171	47,747	53	46,183	224	93,930
Grand Total	327	108,037	74	79,312	401	187,349

CLEARED.

1886. Nationality.	Sailing. Number of Vessels.	Tons.	Steam. Number of Vessels.	Tons.	Total. Number of Vessels.	Tons.
British	24	9,148	18	27,932	44	37,080
Scandinavian	69	26,704	...	...	69	26,704
German	41	16,604	...	...	41	16,604
Italian	2	717	...	...	2	717
Dutch	3	647	...	...	3	647
Austrian	1	434	...	...	1	434
Russian	1	319	...	...	1	319
Portuguese	1	228	...	...	1	228
Total foreign	144	54,801	18	27,932	162	82,733
,, American	175	49,069	53	46,183	228	95,252
Grand Total	319	103,870	71	74,155	390	177,985

UNITED STATES.

TOTAL return of all the Shipping at the Port of Wilmington in the Year 1885.

		Sailing.		Steam.		Total.	
		Number of Vessels.	Tons.	Number of Vessels.	Tons.	Number of Vessels.	Tons.
Entered	Foreign	143	54,244	8	8,027	151	62,271
	American	178	49,597	54	46,706	232	96,303
Cleared	Foreign	272	77,400	8	8,027	280	85,427
	American	186	54,405	54	46,706	240	101,211

Annex B.—RETURN of Principal Articles of Export from Wilmington, North Carolina, during the Years 1886–85.

FOREIGN.

Articles.		1886.		1885.	
		Quantity.	Value.	Quantity.	Value.
			£		£
Cotton	Bales	109,360	984,240	66,502	598,518
Spirits of Turpentine	Casks	41,738	145,714	47,277	165,331
Rosin	Barrels	30,284	75,150	286,943	71,600
Tar	,,	8,570	2,140	26,549	7,625
Crude Turpentine	,,	...	...	768	230
Lumber	Feet	11,731,389	198,000	12,553,347	201,500

DOMESTIC.

Articles.		1886.	1886.
		Quantity.	Quantity.
Cotton	Bales	25,152	27,746
Spirits of Turpentine	Casks	20,946	19,326
Rosin	Barrels	29,313	27,781
Tar	,,	55,637	34,720
Crude Turpentine	,,	24,409	38,267
Lumber	Feet	27,780,852	23,403,482

RETURN of Principal Articles of Import to Wilmington, North Carolina, during the Years 1886–85.

Articles.		1886.		1885.	
		Quantity.	Value.	Quantity.	Value.
			£		£
Earthenware	Crates	217	959	41	175
Salt	Tons	4,240	2,878	4,024	2,420
Guano and Phospates	,,	1,676	11,884	1,450	3,623
Kainit	,,	13,235	19,018	9,755	13,038
Molasses	Hhds. and Tierces	634	3,605	1,237	4,195
Miscellaneous		...	1,531	...	910

WILMINGTON.

Annex C.—TABLE showing the Total Value of all Articles Exported from Wilmington, and imported to Wilmington from and to Foreign Countries during the Years 1886 and 1885.

Countries.	Exports. 1886.	Exports. 1885.	Imports. 1886.	Imports. 1885.
	£	£	£	£
Great Britain	888,079	671,873	5,041	5,618
Ireland	12,028	7,123	..	..
Germany	126,414	120,650	19,018	13,038
Belgium	25,028	11,617	..	..
Russia	14,480	3,316	..	..
West Indies	24,153	27,985	3,602	4,196
Austria	..	1,708	..	..
Miscellaneous	..	..	1,531	911
South America	13,181	13,109	..	..
Holland	..	14,483	..	..
Mexico	..	360	..	..
Nova Scotia	..	529	..	..
Spain	10,300	..	..	..
France	53,850	..	10,682	600
Italy	21,100	..	..	..
Africa	686	..	..	..
U. S. Columbia	919	..	..	..
Total	1,190,218	872,753	39,874	24,363

RETURN of Principal Articles received at Wilmington, N.C. during the Years 1886-85.

Articles.		1886. Quantity.	1886. Value.	1885. Quantity.	1885. Value.
			£		£
Cotton	Bales	137,357	1,166,856	90,624	770,304
Spirits of turpentine	Casks	62,494	218,730	63,513	222,296
Rosin	Barrels	312,647	62,000	350,031	70,100
Tar	,,	63,120	16,200	80,722	20,150
Crude turpentine	,,	23,959	7,000	38,674	11,100

UNITED STATES.

Table showing destination of Exports to Foreign Countries from Wilmington, North Carolina, for the Years 1886-85.

Countries.	1886.						1885.					
	Cotton.	Spirits, Turpentine.	Rosin.	Tar.	Crude Turpentine.	Lumber.	Cotton.	Spirits, Turpentine.	Rosin.	Tar.	Crude Turpentine.	Lumber.
	Bales.	Casks.	Barrels.	Barrels.	Barrels.	Feet.	Bales.	Casks.	Barrels.	Barrels.	Barrels.	Feet.
Great Britain	85,357	36,429	179,941	8,549	..	294,439	54,288	41,001	185,445	25,770	748	..
Continent	24,003	5,305	121,458	..	..	907,974	12,214	5,940	99,886	..	..	961,435
West Indies	..	4	104	21	..	6,673,980	..	6	6	54	..	8,976,529
South America	..	..	681	..	..	3,719,968	..	260	1,486	..	..	2,502,629
Africa	..	..	..	..	..	135,028	..	..	..	..	..	..
Mexico	..	..	..	..	..	..	..	70	120	725	20	112,754
Halifax, N.S.	..	..	..	..	..	..	..	..	..	..	..	..
Total	109,360	41,738	302,184	8,570	..	11,731,389	66,502	47,277	286,943	26,549	768	12,553,347

Wt. 7730 75 5 | 87—H & S 186)

FOREIGN OFFICE.
1887.
ANNUAL SERIES.

No. 140.
DIPLOMATIC AND CONSULAR REPORTS ON TRADE AND FINANCE.

UNITED STATES.

REPORT FOR THE YEAR 1886
ON THE
TRADE OF THE CONSULAR DISTRICT OF CHICAGO.

REFERENCE TO PREVIOUS REPORT [C. 4526], Commercial No. 22, 1885.

Presented to both Houses of Parliament by Command of Her Majesty,
MAY, 1887.

LONDON:
PRINTED FOR HER MAJESTY'S STATIONERY OFFICE,
BY HARRISON AND SONS, ST. MARTIN'S LANE,
PRINTERS IN ORDINARY TO HER MAJESTY.

And to be purchased, either directly or through any Bookseller, from
EYRE AND SPOTTISWOODE, EAST HARDING STREET, FLEET STREET, E.C., and
32, ABINGDON STREET, WESTMINSTER, S.W.; or
ADAM AND CHARLES BLACK, NORTH BRIDGE, EDINBURGH; or
HODGES, FIGGIS, & Co., 104, GRAFTON STREET, DUBLIN.

1887.

[C.—4923—63.]   *Price 2d.*

New Series of Reports.

Reports of the Annual Series have been issued from Her Majesty's Diplomatic and Consular Officers at the following places, and may be obtained from the sources indicated on the title-page:—

No.		Price.	No.		Price.
14.	Shanghai	1d.	77.	Alexandria	1d.
15.	Tientsin	1d.	78.	Patras	1d.
16.	Vienna	1d.	79.	Maranham	1d.
17.	Corfu	1d.	80.	Taganrog	2d.
18.	Hakodate	1d.	81.	Jeddah	1d.
19.	Hiogo	1d.	82.	Suakin	1d.
20.	Newport News	1d.	83.	Colonia	1d.
21.	Stockholm	1d.	84.	Suez	1d.
22.	Christiania	1d.	85.	Paris	1d.
23.	Antwerp	1d.	86.	Brest	1d.
24.	Salonica	1d.	87.	Puerto Plata	1d.
25.	Tonga	1d.	88.	Charleston	1d.
26.	Batoum	1d.	89.	Tripoli	1d.
27.	Costa Rica	1d.	90.	Saigon	1d.
28.	Mexico	4d.	91.	Cherbourg	1d.
29.	Bushire	1d.	92.	New Orleans	2d.
30.	Erzeroum	1d.	93.	Galatz	1d.
31.	Bilbao	1d.	94.	Baltimore	1d.
32.	Rio Grande do Sul	1d.	95.	Tokio	4d.
33.	Piræus	1d.	96.	Havre	3d.
34.	Sandakan	1d.	97.	Barcelona	3d.
35.	Stockholm	1d.	98.	Volo	1d.
36.	Tahiti	1d.	99.	Damascus	1d.
37.	Syra	1d.	100.	Paris	1d.
38.	Kanagawa	2d.	101.	Bordeaux	2d.
39.	Nagasaki	1d.	102.	Serajevo	1d.
40.	Chefoo	1d.	103.	Manila	1d.
41.	Pekin	1d.	104.	Galveston	1d.
42.	Ciudad Bolivar	1d.	105.	Aleppo	1d.
43.	Puerto Cabello	1d.	106.	Rio de Janeiro	1d.
44.	Réunion	1d.	107.	Truxillo	1d.
45.	Sarawak	1d.	108.	St. Petersburg	3d.
46.	Würtemberg	1d.	109.	Leghorn	1d.
47.	Tokyo	1d.	110.	Boston	1d.
48.	Amsterdam	1d.	111.	Buenos Ayres	3d.
49.	Lisbon	1d.	112.	Kewkiang	1d.
50.	Königsberg	2d.	113.	Teheran	2d.
51.	Cagliari	1d.	114.	Beyrout	1d.
52.	Frankfort	1d.	115.	Odessa	5d.
53.	Bogota	1d.	116.	Carthagena	1d.
54.	Kharput	1d.	117.	Santo Domingo	1d.
55.	Trieste	1d.	118.	Mollendo	1d.
56.	Crete	1d.	119.	Guayaquil	1d.
57.	Berne	3d.	120.	Valparaiso	1d.
58.	Rotterdam	1d.	121.	San José	1d.
59.	Düsseldorf	4d.	122.	Pakhoi	1d.
60.	Mozambique	5d.	123.	Hyogo	1d.
61.	Hanyang	1d.	124.	Tamsui	1d.
62.	Stockholm	1d.	125.	Malaga	1d.
63.	Paris	1d.	126.	Marseilles	1d.
64.	Tunis	1d.	127.	Boulogne	2d.
65.	The Hague	2d.	128.	Warsaw	1d.
66.	Italy	2d.	129.	Monte Video	1d.
67.	Smyrna	2d.	130.	Christiania	4d.
68.	Fiume	1d.	131.	Gothenburg	2d.
69.	Tabreez	1d.	132.	Kiungchow	1d.
70.	Philippopolis	1d.	133.	Amoy	1d.
71.	Rome	1d.	134.	Genoa	1d.
72.	Vienna	1d.	135.	Trebizond	1d.
73.	St Petersburg	2d.	136.	Savannah	1d.
74.	Ichang	1d.	137.	Wilmington	2d.
75.	Salonica	1d.	138.	Bolivar	3d.
76.	Brussels	2d.	139.	Wenchow	1d.

No. 140.

Reference to previous Report [C. 4526], Commercial No. 22, 1885

UNITED STATES.

CHICAGO.

Consul Hayes Sadler to the Marquis of Salisbury.

My Lord, British Consulate, Chicago, March 19, 1887.

I HAVE the honour to transmit herewith a report on the Trade and Commerce of Chicago during the year 1886, in which I have included extracts from the report of the British Vice-Consul at Denver.

A report from the British Vice-Consul at St. Paul is also enclosed.

I have, &c.
(Signed) T. HAYES SADLER.

Report of Consul Hayes Sadler on the Trade and Commerce of Chicago during the Year 1886.

INTRODUCTION.

Progress of the district.

The vast territory extending from Lake Michigan to the Rocky Mountains, which at the commencement of the century was almost entirely unknown, has shewn of late years the most rapid development, while the advancement of civilisation has been no less remarkable.

The progress of cultivation and mining enterprise have opened out the rich resources of the land; agricultural and grazing farms extend over those prairie States which, even a few years ago, were only partially improved and scantily inhabited; vast herds range over the arid region of the north-west, where only the pioneer and hunter had explored; railroads, aided by large grants of State land, have stretched in almost every direction, and are still opening out fresh country, affording easy transportation to the eastern markets, for the increasing quantities of grain, cattle and mineral; important cities and towns have sprung up as centres for the increasing population and trade, and manufactures and commercial transactions of great magnitude have followed in their train. This district now supplies the greater bulk of the grain and cattle produce, which is yearly exported from the country; and with large tracts of land, yet unoccupied, much yet unsurveyed, ready for the ever-arriving immigrant, a vast field for enterprise and capital still remains.

Growth of Chicago.

The wonderful growth of this city has mainly resulted from its situation at the head, and the most southern point of the series of inland seas dividing the United States from Canada, through which the various products of the west can be distributed, and its increasing wants can be supplied. It is well placed to receive from the western producer, and to forward to the consumer in the east, to form a chief market for the rich agricultural and farm produce of the prairies which surround it, as well as for the mineral and cattle growing districts beyond. With a vast network of railways on every side, in the midst of inexhaustible resources of coal, it now chiefly provides the West with the varied merchandise it requires, while its industries and manufactures largely furnish the supplies which increased wealth and civilisation demand. Rival and younger cities are constantly growing up, and rapidly developing manufacturing and commercial enterprise, but there appears to be room for all, and there is little sign but of progressive prosperity for the trade of this city.

Population. When Chicago was incorporated in 1837 the population numbered 4,179; at the census of 1880 it amounted to 503,185, and is now estimated at 750,000, exclusive of the townships of Lake View, Jefferson, Cicero, Lake and Hyde Park, which are calculated to contain nearly 150,000 inhabitants, and are merely an extension of the city limits. The 899,454 square miles comprised in the states of Illinois, Wisconsin, Minnesota, Iowa, Nebraska, Kansas, and Colorado, and the territories of Wyoming, Dakota, and Montana contained in 1850 less than 1,500,000 inhabitants; the population increased from 5,799,437 in 1870, to 8,436,706 in 1880, and is still increasing at fully the same rapid rate.

Temperature and climate. The mean temperature of Chicago is 48° Fahrenheit, but the climate is subject to very violent changes, a difference of 30° and 35° often occuring in a few hours. These sudden changes are trying to the new comer, and in winter the thermometer falls not unfrequently to 10° and even 20° below zero, the cold being intensified by strong winds from the north and west; otherwise the climate is healthy. The average rain-fall is about 40 inches.

AGRICULTURE.

Agriculture in general. The foundation of the prosperity of this district is the wealth of its agricultural product, which has assumed such marvellous proportions, and is yearly extending over a fresh area of virgin land. Corn, wheat, and oats form the chief crops; barley, rye, and buckwheat are also largely grown, the latter almost exclusively for home consumption.

The year 1886 was one of medium productiveness; there was less corn grown and more wheat; an increase of acreage under corn and wheat, and a slight decrease under oats. The continued drought in the summer more especially affected the crops in the territories of Montana and Wyoming, the western parts of Dakota, and of the States of Nebraska and Kansas, and the eastern portion of Colorado.

Though that region is rich in grasses, on which cattle can feed all the year round, irrigation is very generally necessary for the cultivation of the soil, on account of the very slight rainfall; and, though much has been done by ditch and canal corporations, as well as by private enterprise, the cost is beyond the means of the small holder. If, however, there has been partial failure, it has been compensated by abundance elsewhere; the harvest was gathered in excellent condition and stored in depôt, or put on the market at an unusually early period, in dry and perfect weather. The extension of railway communication and improvement in country roads have added greatly to the speed with which crops can be brought to market, and farmers are anxious to realise early, not only as holding back offers little chance of a better price, but also on account of the prevailing system of cash payments for mercantile purchases. The constantly extending use of agricultural machinery likewise enables the crops to be early prepared for market, and consequently the whole crop is soon in view for the calculation of the capitalist, and a premium is often paid for future delivery.

The yield of wheat in this district was 184,289,000 bushels, or 12½ bushels per acre, against 154,079,000 bushels at 11⅓ bushels per acre, in 1885. After Minnesota, which produced nearly 43,000,000 bushels, the State of Iowa grows the most wheat, the yield in 1886 having been 32,500,000. The produce of corn was 706,757,000 bushels, or 160,000,000 less than in the preceding year, and the yield 24⅔ against 32⅓ bushels per acre. The States of Illinois and Iowa, which out of their large extent of rich soil, contain scarcely ten square miles of sterile land, produced respectively 210,000,000 and 199,000,000 bushels of corn. There were 331,190,000 bushels of oats grown in this district, or nearly the same quantity as in 1885, at 30¾ bushels per acre, of which the State of Illinois produced 103,000,000. The farm price of wheat averaged 5d. a bushel less than in 1885, while corn and oats slightly increased in value. *Yield of crops.*

Experimental work is systematically carried on at various agricultural colleges and State universities in almost every part of this district, which are supported by appropriations from State funds, and in some of these establishments, though for the most part but lately organised, good work has been done with a view to benefit the farmer. One of the Government stations for the purpose of conducting agricultural experiments on an improved system, is now established in the State of Wisconsin, and its publications are eagerly read. *Experimental farming establishments.*

Cattle.

Next in importance to the cultivation of the land are the cattle industries, and here the same marvellous progress has been made, not only in the raising of stock, but in all farm produce. Great attention is paid to the breeding of cattle, the favourite classes being Holstein-Friesland, Shorthorn, Hereford, Devon, and Polled Angus, and a considerable number are yearly imported for the purpose of improving the breed. There are numerous stock growers associations, some of great magnitude; that of Wyoming, which was established 15 years ago, now represents 2,000,000 cattle, besides horses and sheep, with real estate and plant worth 20,000,000l. sterling, and its object is to assist in detecting theft, to inspect cattle, return strays, and prevent disease. State and county fairs and cattle shows have done much to encourage farmers and stimulate production of the higher grades of animals. In the same manner the breed of horses has greatly improved, and there are numerous establishments in this district where the different classes of draught-horse, the Clydesdale, Percheron, and others of known imported stock are bred and offered for sale. *Cattle industries.*

There are now fine powerful horses to be met with in most parts of the country. A considerable percentage of the swine raised is also of imported breed, Poland, China and Berkshire being specially cultivated; and some attention is paid to the breeding of sheep.

The improvement of all farm produce attracts much attention. In the States of Illinois, Wisconsin, and Iowa, alone there are 900 large cheese factories, and butter and all dairy productions are prepared with greater care and in large quantities for the ever-increasing market. *Farm produce.*

The Oleo-margarine Bill has proved of benefit to dairy farmers who are encouraged by the prospects of the future. The markets, however, ruled low in the early part of the year, cheese fetching as low as 4d. per lb., and butter 7d. per lb., but on account of the summer drought they gradually rose, and in December were respectively 6d. and 12d. per lb.

(189)

Stock grazing.

The summer season of 1886 was not propitious for the grazing of cattle from the absence of rain; in the arid region, which appears to be fully if not over-stocked, many of the streams were dry, and grass was burnt up, more especially in Montana, where large herds were in search of food and water. Cattle have also suffered much from the extreme severity of the winter in those parts, as they cannot scratch the snow in the same manner as horses, or go the same distance in search of water.

Cattle disease.

With the remarkable development and the free movement from place to place of the flocks and herds of this district, various diseases have made their appearance or have spread to a serious extent in some parts. The most dreaded of these, pleuro-pneumonia, which broke out at Chicago in the autumn, has luckily been confined to the limits of this city and suburbs, though there can be no assurance that the germs may not have spread westward, and the neighbouring States prohibited the entry of all cattle from the State of Illinois, except with a satisfactory bill of health, at great loss to cattle growers. Whatever may have been the cause of this outbreak of pleuro-pneumonia, which caused so much alarm, it can scarcely be doubted that the condition in which the animals were kept at the distilleries where it broke out, was not conducive to health; they were chiefly milch cows kept in large sheds or stables, with no exercise for months, fed on distillery slops, and with little regard to cleanliness.

Hog cholera.

Though there has been no widespread disease, hog cholera has continued to be prevalent in some parts. In Illinois the loss amounted to 11 per cent. of the whole number in the State, in Kansas 9 per cent., and in Iowa and Nebraska 7 per cent.; in the other States the mortality was less. The greatest variety of views are reported as to the cause of disease or the reason of exemption, and though much knowledge from careful study has been obtained no definite mode leading to its extinction has been arrived at. Half the loss is in young pigs, which are not marketable, while hogs are sent early to market, partly through fear of disease, and partly as they gain little after a certain age. The losses in the important business of swine breeding are remarkable when the excellence and cheapness of the corn they are fed on, and the general infusion of fresh blood are taken into consideration; perhaps the proper care of swine may scarcely have kept pace with the rate at which they have multiplied.

TRADE AND COMMERCE.

Trade and commerce in general.

The general character of trade and commerce in 1886, except for a few drawbacks, has been progressive and satisfactory. The situation of affairs, and the condition of the continent of Europe and other parts of the world, have always a sensitive effect on business transactions here, and last year proved of much benefit to trade; canned meats and other food were in active requirement, and the sales of wheat and flour were stimulated by greater deficiencies in Europe, as well as by purchases in France in anticipation of an augmentation of duty, which was supposed would be placed on cereals. Manufactures and industries are fast creeping westward, and there are now many cities fast rising in population and trade. The provision and packing business is rapidly developing where the necessary supplies are nearer, and whence the transportation of product is less costly than that of live stock. Among these cities may be specially mentioned Kansas City and Omaha. The former has already become the business centre of a large surrounding district, and contains a population of nearly 150,000, and Omaha, which 20 years ago was little more than a river landing-place, has risen in population from 30,000 in 1880 to about 80,000. The Union Stock yards in the latter city now own 350 acres of land, and some of the large stock merchants of Chicago have established branch or auxiliary houses there. At a wonderful concentration of railways to all parts, its situation well fits it for a stock market. Its manufacturing trade is growing fast, and the smelting and refining works last year turned out to the value of 2,625,000*l.* sterling. Des Moines, which has now a population of 40,000, Dubuque, Sioux City, Cedar Rapids, and many other cities might be mentioned, which are rapidly rising in importance.

Excluding speculative business as well as transactions in real estate, the trade of Chicago is estimated at 206,000,000*l.* sterling in 1886, against 198,000,000*l.* sterling in 1885, or an increase of 4 per cent. Of this amount 30 per cent. may be put down to the produce trade, 38 per cent. to wholesale, and 32 per cent. to manufacturing trade. It is the highest figure yet reached, except in the three years 1881–83, when speculative excitement was followed by depression. The trades which show the greatest increase in volume, according to degree, are groceries, iron manufactures, and dry goods, the only falling off having been in receipts of cereals, and in hay packing. Iron manufactures show the greatest increase in price, while wheat and live stock declined in value. Merchants have done a large business and goods are cheaper, from the growing principle of small and quick profits and from increased competition.

General trade of Chicago.

Movement of Produce.

The movement of produce in Chicago has somewhat retrograded, though the main product of the West still passes through the hands of merchants here, for the route by which it is transported depends on the condition of the freight market, which has been somewhat discriminative against this city; it is hoped, however, that this apparent discrimination, which has reduced the eastward shipments from Chicago, will be rectified by the passing of the Inter-State Commerce Bill.

Movement of produce.

Railroad freights from Chicago to the coast have, in general, ruled on the basis of 1*s.* per 100 lbs. for grain, and 1*s.* 2½*d.* for provisions to New York. In December they rose to 1*s.* 1½*d.* and 1*s.* 5*d.* at which they remain. Notwithstanding fluctuations Lake freights have been better than on many preceding years, the demand for vessels in the iron trade having caused a rise in grain freights. The average rate from Chicago to Buffalo was 2*d.* for wheat, and slightly less for corn, to Georgian ports 70 per cent. of above rates, and to Kingston, Oswego, and Ogdensburg, about one and a half the rate to Buffalo. Vessels up to 3,000 tons trade on the Lakes, which are closed for about five of the winter months.

Freights.

Shipping.

The shipping at the ports of Chicago and Milwaukee is given in Annex A.

Shipping.

Exports and Imports.

Annex B is a return of the principal articles of export and import entered in the Customs of Chicago, and Annex C shows the value of all articles exported to and imported from foreign countries, during the years 1885–86.

Exports and imports.

The actual exports from this city are but imperfectly represented in these returns, the greater part of the products being shipped to the seaboard, either viâ Huron or Detroit, or direct by rail and entering in the Customs Returns of seaboard ports.

Exports.

(189)

Imports.	In the same manner the imports included in the returns do not represent a third of the real volume of imported goods, duty being chiefly paid at New York, Philadelphia, and other Atlantic ports. The Custom House here also keeps no record of the country from which each separate class of merchandise is imported, which renders it impossible to report the amount of the different goods entered from Great Britain.
Steel and iron.	Manufactures of steel and iron from foreign countries cannot, as a general rule, compete with the home product, especially as regards heavy goods, on account of the high rate of duty.
Cutlery.	There is, however, a constant demand for razors, cutlery, needles, and other fine goods from Great Britain.
Steel rails.	Whatever steel rails may have been imported from England on account of the late unusual demand in this district would probably have paid duty at New York, and if for Kansas and west of that part at New Orleans, but with a duty of 3*l*. 10*s*., it is only when the demand exceeds what local mills can deliver at a required time that there would be any call for English rails. The present price of steel rails here is 7*l*. 12*s*. 7*d*. per ton; and of pig iron, charcoal, 4*l*. 19*s*., soft fluid 4*l*. 10*s*. 2*d*., and wheel, 6*l*. 18*s*. d.
Caustic soda. Tin.	The imports of caustic soda and tin plates show a falling off, larger shipments of the latter to this city having been paid for at the seaboard on account of regulations here with regard to precise payment according to weight.
Dry goods and clothing.	The chief increase in imports is in dry goods and clothing of all kinds, which in some measure may be accounted for by an increased proportion of shipments having been sent on in bond. English and Scotch cloth are in demand for those who can pay for a superior article, being of better quality than that of American manufacture. Linen, cotton, and dress goods from Ireland, Manchester, and Bradford, and jute goods from Scotland are largely imported, and haberdashery, underclothing, and articles of ladies' dress are in great demand.
Lumber.	On account of the heavy duty but little lumber is imported from Canada.
Exports and imports at Milwaukee.	The exports at the port of Milwaukee amounted to the value of 3,917*l*. against 31,271*l*. in 1885, and the imports to 130,771*l*. against 92,403*l*. in 1885. Much the same remarks apply as to Chicago.

Grain and Stock Market.

Receipts of wheat and flour.	The receipts of wheat and flour at Chicago have been less than in 1885, and the tendency in that direction, though this city practically controls the market and furnishes much of the capital required, may be accounted for by the increasing importance of the mills of Minneapolis and the greater shipment of cereals from that city and the port of Duluth. The flour market here has been especially active, but large sales for export were shipped direct from the mill to the coast without entering Chicago. The receipts of wheat in round numbers were 16·77 million bushels, about 2·8 less than in 1885, and nearly 9·5 less than in 1884. The shipments amounted to 15·75 million. The receipts of flour were 4·14 million, about 1·2 million less than in the preceding year, and the shipments to 3·77 million. Wheat was at its highest price at the commencement of the year, No. 2 Spring fetching 3*s*. 4½*d*. a bushel, but gradually fell as the probability of war in Europe subsided, and it was seen that the quantity in hand, with the prospect of a good harvest, would be enough to meet requirements, the lowest price being 2*s*. 11*d*.

in October. From that time, owing to renewed fear of war, there was a recovery to 3s. 1d. in December; the average price for the year was 3s. 1½d. against 3s. 5½d. in 1885.

The market for corn was fairly steady, and there was a good demand for shipping, the average price having been 1s. 6d. per bushel. The receipts amounted to 62·5 million bushels, nearly equal to those of the previous year. {Receipts of corn.}

The quantity of oats received amounted to nearly 40 million bushels, or a gain of 2·5 million, at an average market price of 1s. 1½d. per bushel. Barley fetched 2s. 5d., and rye 2s. 3d. a bushel. The receipts of barley, which was of excellent quality, showed an increase of 2·5 million bushels, while only half the quantity of rye was received compared with the preceding year. {Receipts of oats and other grain.}

The stock of grain in Chicago at the close of the year, in round numbers, was 13·5 million bushels of wheat and 4·75 million of corn, making with rye, oats, and barley, a total of 19·2 million bushels. {Stock of grain.}

Large quantities of flax seed are received here, the amount having been nearly the same as in 1885, or about 6·5 million bushels, the market price closing at 4s.; clover seeds closed low at about 19s. a bushel. The receipts of grass seed were 30·755 tons at about 7s. a bushel. {Seeds.}

Many circumstances had a depressing effect on the stock market, and prices were low throughout. Cheapness of grain and greater facility of transport had for some time lowered the selling price, but in 1886 the trade had to contend with a formidable strike at the stock yards, and the outbreak of pleuro-pneumonia at Chicago, together with general shortness of pasture, all which combined to prejudice the confidence of cattle buyers. An advance in the rate of railway freight eastward early in the year also tended to lower the market here. Shipping grades were as low as 14s., but improved to 21s. per 100 lbs. The receipts of cattle were 1,9*3,900, a small advance on the preceding year, and the shipments amounted to 704,645. {Stock market. Cattle.}

The importance of Chicago as a horse market is yearly increasing; 27,599 horses were received at the yards in 1886, against 19,356 in 1885, which was a large advance on any previous year, some of them being for shipment. {Horses.}

Owing to the strike at the stock yards, the receipts of hogs fell off by about 220,000, and amounted to 6,718,761, 2,000,000 of which were shipped. The demand is now greater than the supply, and prices have risen with a prospect of the rise continuing for the present, from apparent scarcity. The receipts of sheep at Chicago was rather over 1,000,000—about the same as last year—and prices ranged low. {Hogs and sheep.}

Trades and Industries.

The pre-eminence of Chicago over other cities in the live stock and provision trade is marked not only in volume but in the perfect arrangement and complete system for its prosecution. In the winter season there are generally from 22,000 to 25,000 hands employed in receiving, preparing, packing, and shipping the provisions, but this winter some houses have been working short. The trade in fresh beef is increasing, and the number of cattle slaughtered for the dressed beef, canning and packing trade is believed to have exceeded that of 1885, which amounted to 1,334,775. The business of hog packing, like every branch of the provision trade, was much affected by the strike, which told to the profit of packing houses in the west, and shows a considerable falling-off, the supply of hogs also having lately been short. The house of Armour and Co., the largest in the packing trade, whose {Provision trade.}

business, exclusive of Board of Trade transactions, exceeds 10,000,000*l.* sterling a year, last year opened extensive glue works covering 8 acres, and are now doing a large business in glue, brewers' isinglass, gelatine, oils, greases, and fertilizers, besides refined lard and butterine.

Railroad building.
One of the most striking features of the year has been the great extension given to the construction of railways in the whole of this district. In Kansas alone 1,520 miles were constructed in 1886, chiefly in the latter half of the year, owing to the strikes, and the State has now 6,060 miles in operation. Many new lines have also been built in Iowa, Minnesota, and Dakota, and railroad building promises to be equally active this year, extensive preparations being made for constructing fresh lines. The State of Illinois has now the large number of 9,441 miles of railway in operation, and the State of Iowa 7,907 miles. Taking them altogether, however, the lines in Illinois do not pay more than $1\frac{9}{10}$ per cent, on the capital. Out of the 58 corporations only 11 pay dividends, and 12 of the smaller lines, being unable to work at a profit or pay expenses, are in the hands of receivers, which is not generally a satisfactory arrangement. There is a tendency for the larger and paying companies to absorb branch railways as feeders to their main line.

Steel and iron manufactures.
Consequent on this extension of railway building, the demand for steel rails has been unusually great, and has created much activity in all branches of the iron trade. There are now rail manufactories in most of the Western States, and iron work of every description, rolled, cast, and wrought, is actively carried on. Iron and steel industries indeed are bound to increase round these great coal and iron districts, and the more the country is opened out, the more important will all industries become. The State of Illinois, though the iron found is not commercially important, has the advantage of inexhaustible supplies of coal, and is surrounded by the rich iron districts of neighbouring States. The furnaces and rolling mills of Chicago, South Chicago, and Joliet have become very extensive, and yearly increase their output. According to statistics of the Iron and Steel Association, the production of ingots of Bessemer steel in this State was 535,692 net tons against 366,659 in 1885, and of these 436,075 tons were converted into rails in 1886 against 308,242 in the preceding year. The six rolling mills of Chicago are in full work, and have contracts to last them through the summer. The output of these in 1886 is reckoned at a value of 2,500,000*l.* sterling. The 40 foundries and 58 machine works of this city turned out respectively to the value of about 1,750,000*l.* and 1,250,000*l.* sterling, and the four car-wheel works to the value of 940,000*l.* The production of pig-iron has been 750,000 tons handled in this city at an all-round price of 3*l.* 16*s.* 11*d.* per ton, and prices have been rising throughout the year. The total iron and steel manufactures of Chicago in 1886 are valued at 9,650,000*l.* There are about 21,000 men engaged, and wages have risen nearly 15 per cent. at the rolling mills.

Iron and wood manufactures.
The railway car manufactories, as well as those of waggons and carriages and agricultural implements, have been exceedingly active, the output of the latter being valued at 2,999,999*l.* sterling. Planing mills, furniture manufactories, and all wood-work establishments show also a large increase in the year, but these, as well as the iron and steel trade, are by no means confined to Chicago, and are rapidly developing in other cities of this district.

Wholesale trade.
The chief feature in the wholesale trade is the general cheapening of merchandise, which makes it appear, when judged by money value, that it has not increased in volume in the manner it really has

Almost every description of goods, owing to improvement in manufacture, increased competition, or facility of transport, is much reduced in price. The practice of many of the leading stores is now to keep a more varied assortment of goods, and there is a general tendency to extend operations into more departments of trade, so as to supply customers with other classes of merchandise than that of their regular business. The sales in the dry goods trade at Chicago are estimated to have amounted last year to 13,000,000l., or an increase of 10 per cent. It is chiefly in the hands of a few leading merchants, one of whom in the jobbing dry goods business is said to have effected sales to the value of 6,000,000l. In the grocery business the sales are estimated to have increased 20 per cent. in value, and nearly 40 per cent. in volume, having amounted to about 12,000,000l. The value of sales in the clothing trade are reckoned at 4,500,000l., books and paper 6,500,000l., and jewellery and clocks at 2,500,000l. The boot and shoe trade is growing in importance, the best material being at hand and tanneries on the spot. Chicago is now a great fruit market, not only for the large local product, but for green and dried fruits of every variety from the South and California. The value of the lumber trade is calculated at 8,000,000l. The wool clip of the West is greatly controlled by merchants here. A large business is done in hides and tallow, and in almost every branch of wholesale trade in this city the increase has been considerable.

Notwithstanding labour troubles, the building trade, from the immense demand of a prosperous and steadily augmenting population, has been extremely active, fine public and business blocks, besides handsome residences, continually springing up throughout this district. New buildings, to the number of 3,369, with every modern improvement, were erected in Chicago in 1886 at a cost of more than 5,000,000l., with a frontage of 21 miles in length. In this trade bricklayers gain about 3s. an hour for pressed brick facing, and 1s. 8d. for other work, and carpenters and painters from 10s. to 12s. a day. *Building trade.*

The value of real estate, as far as regards desirable residence and office property, has greatly increased, and there are many districts in the adjoining townships where frontage has increased 100 per cent. in the last 18 months; the building lots vary in size from 50 feet by 150 feet to larger blocks, and in a good situation frontage fetches 25l. a foot, though higher prices are often given, while business frontage in the city fetches an enormous price. Handsome mansions and pretty villa residences continue to be constructed, and stretch many miles, while in the city some magnificent business blocks have been built during the year. Rents show no signs of failing, and as servants' wages are very high, the cost of living is by no means reasonable. *Real estate.*

The aggregate bank clearings in this city amounted to over 538,000,000l., or an increase in the year of 12 per cent., and the Board of Trade clearings to about 20,750,000l. Capital has found ample means of employment, and large sums have been invested in railroads and real estate. The prevailing rates for money were 6 to 7 per cent. for call and time; in the summer months they were lower, and in December they rose to 7 and 8 per cent., partly owing to large loans on wheat to other cities in the neighbourhood, and to the demand caused by accumulation of grain in this city, and partly to larger demands for currency in the North west, as well as for the increasing number and importance of packing establishments outside of Chicago. The banks of St. Paul, Minneapolis, Omaha, Kansas City, and other cities keep large reserves in Chicago banks. *Banks and rates.*

UNITED STATES.

MINES.

Mining industries.

The various mines of this district have been in constant work; fresh ones have been discovered and opened, and the mineral wealth of Colorado, Montana, and Dakota is constantly passing eastward. The value of the metal products of Montana in 1886 is estimated as follows: gold, 712,000*l*.; silver, 1,980,000*l*.; copper, 1,650,000*l*., and lead, 256,000*l*. The discovery of tin in the Black Hills of Dakota is attracting much attention, supply of that mineral being dependent on importation. The mining industries of Wyoming are commencing to develop, though as yet there are no manufactures, and lubricating oil springs have been lately discovered of very high quality, while petroleum exists over a vast extent of that territory. Valuable discoveries of iron, making the best Bessemer steel, have lately been made in the Gogebic range in the north of the State of Wisconsin, some 60 miles east of Ashland, and about 40 mines have commenced work. A large amount of capital has already been invested, and the discovery of these mines has had a direct influence on the prosperity of Milwaukee, where they are greatly owned. Within a few days, at the close of the year, four new companies, with an aggregate capital of 1,000,000*l*., are said to have been organised. Miners have been in great request, at from 7*s*. to 10*s*. a day, and the cost of living is low. One village, near the centre of these mines, has now 3,000 inhabitants, whereas some 18 months ago there was not a building on the range, and railways are pushing in that direction. Other discoveries have been made east of the Gogebic range, on the borders of Michigan.

Discoveries.

Coal industries of Illinois.

Though there are some valuable lead and zinc mines, coal is the chief mining industry of the State of Illinois and employs 26,000 men. The output of coal in this State was 9,500,000 tons in 1886. The controversy between mine operators and miners seems to rest for solution on the question of payment for all coal sold, the prevailing system here being that screened coal only is paid for and not what passes below the screen.

LABOUR TROUBLES.

Strikes and labour troubles, so frequently alluded to in this report, have been the chief drawback to the otherwise smooth current of industrial operations, and the record has been heavy. In the spring the employment of capital was much interrupted in different trades in numerous parts of the country, and in some instances riots occurred necessitating employment of the military to prevent destruction of property. In Chicago the eight hours movement for ten hours' pay took a serious form, and was renewed at the stock yards in the autumn, the commencement of the winter season, the busiest time in the packing trade, and materially affected the receipts of cattle and the provision business. The packers finding it impossible to compete with other rising cities in the trade, all of them working on the ten hours system, refused the demands of the men, and had they not been firm the existence of the live-stock and packing trade in this city would have been imperilled. After some weeks, when violence and intimidation were resorted to, and the presence of two regiments of Militia was found necessary to protect the lives of those willing to work, the labourers surrendered unconditionally, seeing their places rapidly being filled by new hands; but the money losses were heavy, and it is hoped a check has been given to these labour disturbances. There seems little reason for this strike at the stock yards as the wages paid here from the gutters, ham-trimmers and choppers, to the labourer, average about 13s. a day, or at least 2s. 6d. a day higher than the rate in packing establishments at other cities. The attention of State legislatures has been very generally called to this question of labour and capital in this district, with a view to some solution of the difficulty. State laws are liberal and in many instances specially designed to protect the working man, but accumulation of capital seems to be driving individual effort to a certain degree from many fields of industry and any spark of discontent is eagerly fanned by the professional agitator.

CIVILIZATION.

With all the rapid development of this new country, civilization and education have advanced in no less a rapid manner. Grants of public land, some of which have become extremely valuable, were made to each State for educational purposes, and two sections in each township are allotted for public instruction. The States have willingly responded in the appreciation of the benefits of education by a large yearly expenditure, and the proportion of attendance at schools is numerically high. School-houses for all classes, colleges, churches of different denominations, hospitals and asylums for every description of sufferer, besides private establishments are numerous and are being constantly erected in the district as necessity arises. Luxury and comfort are carried to a high pitch among the wealthier classes, much taste and elegance is shown in decorative art and architecture, and every modern invention and appliance quickly pass into general use. Nor is this civilization confined to the older cities, but has stretched far into the West, where little remains of that wildness so characteristic of life but a few years ago.

IMMIGRATION.

The great flow of population which is constantly spreading over this region is chiefly formed of United States citizens, though it is considerably swelled by foreign immigrants. The cultivators of the soil and purchasers of public land are almost entirely composed of the former element, while immigrants come chiefly from the rural districts of Europe, knowing nothing but agricultural work, and are thrown unexpectedly upon city life, having no means whatever to purchase land or cultivate farms. The United States citizen who migrates, as a rule knows what he is going for, whereas for the most part the immigrant arrives in search of he knows not what. Attracted by the stories he has heard of the high rate of wages and fortunes made, the foreign immigrant seems to think he has nothing to do but to come here and immediately get highly remunerative employment, but he is very generally doomed to disappointment. The man unsuccessful elsewhere, can find no certainty of success here. In the manufacturing and commercial centres the supply of labour appears generally to exceed the demand, and this is especially applicable to Chicago, which is the centre of attraction to so many immigrants, who have often to wait long before getting any employment, and consequently fall into great poverty. The number of applicants for relief, or to be sent home, is great; charitable resources are strained, and as far as this city is concerned, however thriving it may be and undoubtedly is, the annual number of persons arriving in search of work cannot be absorbed even by the ever-increasing labour demand. For the skilled mechanic or educated workman it may be easier to find employment but, as a rule, skilled labour is performed by the native born and unskilled by the foreign citizen. An immigrant should have some special qualification, some special trade, if he resolves to come out here, or friends who can at once place him in a position to gain a livelihood, or means sufficient to enable him to wait, as otherwise, being driven by force of circumstances to the towns, he has to learn before he can get work to pay him, and there is no longer the same need of the new comer, however ignorant he might be, as long as he had hands to work. In more distant parts of the country and at the mines there may still be demand for unskilled labour, and there is a fair prospect of work to be had in the spring, but many poor immigrants cannot penetrate so far, and fall into the lowest grade of work, at the farthest city which their funds enable them to reach. In fact, employers of labour can get all the men they want who know their work.

It is a common practice for the more successful immigrant from Great Britain to naturalise at an early period after his arrival, especially among miners. In Montana, where the mining population is largely composed of labourers from Cornwall, Scotland, and other mining districts of Great Britain, this practice has been very general. They find it their interest to become United States citizens, on account of the vote and local importance it gives them; they seem to feel greater security with regard to any property they may obtain, and have likewise the advantage denied to the foreigner of a right to purchase public lands.

Public Lands.

How acquired. All land in this district, which has not been already sold to private persons or granted to any State or Territory for educational or other purposes, or to any railway company, is vested in the United States Government, and can be purchased by any citizen of the United States, or foreigner who has declared intention of becoming such, of the age of 21 years, under the terms of the Homestead, Pre-emption, and Timber Culture Laws, or those relating to Timber and Stone, Saline, and Desert Lands, or the Mining Act. These laws vary in mode of procedure and terms under which the land can be acquired, but the principle is that no one shall have a right to enter on more than 160 acres of public domain, and that all persons shall reside on, cultivate, and improve the land, and unless the conditions relating thereto are complied with, no final proof or title can be obtained, the right to the land being forfeited.

Mineral lands. Mineral lands are not subject to pre-emption or homestead entry; the Mining Act differs in this respect, that the right being first acquired by possession, it can be lost by discontinuance of possession, the possessory title is conditional on compliance with local rules and the performance of annual labour, and the limit of claim that can be located is 1,500 feet by 300 feet. The mode of perfecting title also differs, but once a patent to the land is granted the proprietor has whole right in the minerals found thereon. The Mining Act does not apply to the States of Wisconsin, Minnesota, and Kansas, where mineral bearing land is subject to disposal as agricultural land.

Homestead Laws. No entry can be filed under the Homestead Act for more than 160 acres, but a person may acquire in addition 160 acres by pre-emption, if adjoining the homestead. Before patent can be obtained there must be a residence of five years, and the price to be paid to Government is 5s. or 10s. per acre, according to situation. The homestead is by the Act exempt from seizure for debt contracted prior to patent, and the different States have extended this exemption to a varying value or proportion of the land, and to personal effects to a certain limit for debt contracted at any time, for the purpose of protecting settlers. In the Territories of Dakota, Wyoming, and Montana, 64 acres of desert land, that is such as cannot be cultivated without irrigation, can be acquired by one person.

A very large quantity of land has been taken up during the year, especially in the State of Kansas, which is fast filling up, and has increased 271,124 in population in the last two years. The aggregate land entries of all classes, including sales, during the fiscal year ended June 30, 1886, in the State of Kansas were 55,051, and the area disposed of amounted to 5,836,824 acres, which includes 20,688 entries and 3,224,214 acres under the Homestead Laws, and 12,825 entries and 1,920,802 acres under the Timber Culture Act. The aggregate entries in Nebraska amounted to 36,257, and the area disposed of to 3,551,518 acres, including 10,269 entries and 1,590,410 acres under the Homestead, and 6,234 entries and 969,706 acres under the Timber Culture Laws. In the North of Nebraska, near Dakota and the Sioux reservations, there is rich land which is fast being taken up; indeed a great deal of the western part of what used to be called the arid region of this district extending west of the 100th meridian to the Rocky Mountains, is found to contain rich land, which can be cultivated without irrigation. In Montana and Wyoming land is in comparison but slowly taken up. The total number of entries under the Homestead Laws in this district since the passing of the Act in 1862, up to June 30, 1886, have been 472,980, comprising 64,132,317 acres; not much more than one-third of these entries have been finally patented, as there is no limit of time in taking out a title, and many persons, having complied with the law, rely on their possessory rights, and in some few cases land has been relinquished or forfeited. There is now practically no public land available in Illinois and Iowa, and but little agricultural land in Wisconsin.

<small>Land entered.</small>

In Montana and the North-west there is much country unsurveyed, where cattle range undisturbed, but will all be subject to location. In Montana only 18,142,855 out of 92,016,640 acres have been surveyed, while more than half Dakota, and nearly one-fourth of Wyoming, remain as yet unsurveyed.

<small>Land unsurveyed.</small>

Besides the public domain there are school and college lands still to be disposed of, which were originally granted to the different States and Territories by the Central Government, and can be acquired by any purchaser at very varying prices, and a considerable extent of railway land grants is still unsold.

<small>School and railroad lands.</small>

Extracts from the Report of Mr. Vice-Consul Pearce on the Trade and Commerce of Denver during the Year 1886.

Mr. Vice-Consul Pearce reports that "it is only within the last four years that Denver has been made a port of entry and even now by far the largest bulk of the goods which reach Colorado pass through the Customs at other points, viz., New York, Boston, Philadelphia, and New Orleans, and find their way to the customers either direct from these parts, or through large business houses; so that in reality the returns from the Denver Custom House only represent a small proportion of what is imported into Colorado from foreign countries. The value of the imports of British goods through the Denver Custom House in 1886 was 3,201*l*.

<small>Exports and imports. Imports.</small>

"The exports from Colorado to Europe may be said to be nil. 15 years ago Colorado exported a large quantity of silver ore and metallurgical products for treatment, principally to Swansea and

<small>Exports.</small>

Germany, but for the last 10 years improvements have been made in methods of extracting the metals (silver, gold, lead, and copper) from their ores, so that at present the mines are independent of European skill; and, notwithstanding the increased cost of labour and fuel, the local metallurgist is able to compete favourably with European establishments. This is, perhaps, owing in a great measure to the heavy cost of freight to the Atlantic coast; but something may be said for the improved facilities which force of circumstances has driven the smelters to adopt.

Industries.

"Mining and its kindred branches may be said to form the principal industry in Colorado. The metals of greatest importance are silver, gold, lead, and copper. The following figures will indicate approximately the value of these metals produced in Colorado during the year 1886:—

						£
Silver	..	..	..	..	..	3,290,184
Gold	..	..	..	..	..	1,017,580
Lead	..	..	..	..	..	1,024,660
Copper	..	..	..	..	..	26,514
Total	..	..	..	..	..	5,358,938

"The gross output of these metals, however, from Colorado is considerably larger than the above figures show, owing to the fact that Colorado, from its railroad facilities, and from the abundance of good fuel, is now a large centre for smelting; and in addition to the product from its own State, it draws supplies of ore from other States and Territories, the principal being Montana, Idaho, Utah, Nevada, California, Arizona, New Mexico, and even Old Mexico.

Agriculture.

"Owing to the very limited rainfall in Colorado (average for 12 years 14·97 inches), agriculture is practically dependent on, and limited by artificial irrigation. In those parts of the State which have been the longest settled, viz., immediately east of the Rocky Mountains, nearly the whole of the available water has been utilised for the purpose of irrigation, and in an unusually dry season, such as 1886, the supply falls short of the requirements.

Cost of irrigation.

"The average charge for irrigating water supplied to agriculturists by the Corporations or persons owning ditches, varies from 6s. to 10s. per acre per annum, and one cubic foot of water is considered sufficient to irrigate 55 acres of land. The State hardly produces sufficient agricultural products for its own consumption.

Cattle.

"Of late years there has been a marked improvement in the quality and character of the range stock by the importation of thoroughbred cattle from the United Kingdom, such as Shorthorns, Herefords, Polled-Angus, &c.

Public health.

"Colorado has of recent years attained a very wide reputation as a health resort for persons suffering from pulmonary affections, and a large portion of the present population, including very many from Europe, have come here on account of the special advantages offered by the altitude and extreme dryness of the atmosphere to those suffering from consumption and asthma."

CHICAGO.

Annex A.—Return of Shipping at the Port of Chicago in the Year 1886.

Entered.

Nationality.	Sailing. Number of Vessels.	Sailing. Tons.	Steam. Number of Vessels.	Steam. Tons.	Total. Number of Vessels.	Total. Tons.
British	55	20,739	51	22,467	106	43,206
American	6,560	1,635,592	4,491	2,247,520	11,051	3,883,112
Total	6,615	1,656,331	4,542	2,269,987	11,157	3,926,318
,, for the preceding year	6,262	1,595,470	4,482	2,058,466	10,744	3,653,936

Cleared.

Nationality.	Sailing. Number of Vessels.	Sailing. Tons.	Steam. Number of Vessels.	Steam. Tons.	Total. Number of Vessels.	Total. Tons.
British	52	19,403	51	22,376	103	41,779
American	6,583	1,644,831	4,529	2,264,152	11,112	3,908,983
Total	6,635	1,664,234	4,580	2,286,528	11,215	3,950,762
,, for the preceding year	6,285	1,608,607	4,513	2,043,679	10,798	3,652,286

Return of Shipping at the Port of Milwaukee in the Year 1886.

Entered.

Nationality.	Sailing. Number of Vessels.	Sailing. Tons.	Steam. Number of Vessels.	Steam. Tons.	Total. Number of Vessels.	Total. Tons.
British	2	536	4	2,315	6	2,851
American	2,710	519,143	2,620	1,894,938	5,330	2,414,081
Total	2,712	519,679	2,624	1,897,253	5,336	2,416,932
,, for the preceding year	2,502	468,147	2,311	1,686,238	4,813	2,154,385

Cleared.

Nationality.	Sailing. Number of Vessels.	Sailing. Tons.	Steam. Number of Vessels.	Steam. Tons.	Total. Number of Vessels.	Total. Tons.
British	2	536	4	2,315	6	2,851
American	2,753	538,230	2,585	1,924,031	5,338	3,462,261
Total	2,755	538,766	2,589	1,926,346	5,344	2,465,112
,, for the preceding year	2,554	473,114	2,281	1,651,384	4,825	2,124,498

UNITED STATES.

Annex B.—RETURN of Principal Articles of Export from Chicago during the Years 1885 and 1886.

Articles.		1886. Quantity.	1886. Value.	1885. Quantity.	1885. Value.
			£		£
Wheat	Bushels	1,092,909	177,310	764,591	130,815
Corn	,,	2,396,221	193,889	2,158,993	207,889
Oats	,,	2,016	127	31,199	1,587
Flour	Barrels	1,170	776	16	19
Corn meal	,,	1,000	523	1,140	689
Pork	,,	12,127	25,555	1,547	3,028
Lard	Lbs.	59,370	875	6,250	118
Cured meats	,,	62,534	984	7,352	124
Other articles		...	1,648	...	979
Total		...	401,687	...	345,248

RETURN of Principal Articles of Import to Chicago during the Years 1885 and 1886.

Articles.	1886. Quantity.	1886. Value.	1885. Quantity.	1885. Value.
		£		£
Free goods	..	527,979	..	360,418
Earthen and Glassware	..	71,162	..	57,107
Caustic soda	10,782,486	46,003	12,254,440	59,444
Cigar and tobacco manufacture	..	69,677	..	78,034
Dry goods, all kinds	..	946,143	..	795,297
Leather, manufacture of	..	44,896	..	21,458
Musical instruments	..	40,804	..	30,892
Salt	..	23,503	..	25,521
Tin plates	32,290,414	211,429	44,516,312	296,599
Wine and liquors	..	41,961	..	48,148
Other articles	..	279,345	..	252,934
Total	..	2,302,902	..	2,025,852

NOTE.—Values converted at the rate of 4 dol. 85 c. per £ sterling.

Annex C.—TABLE showing the Total Value of all Articles Exported from and Imported to Chicago from and to Foreign Countries during the Years 1885 and 1886.

Country.	Exports. 1886.	Exports. 1885.	Imports. 1886.	Imports. 1885.
	£	£	£	£
Great Britain	..	..	947,196	948,429
British Colonies and Possessions	401,687	345,248	71,037	41,151
Germany	..	..	304,667	245,300
France	..	..	315,105	293,562
Austria	..	..	23,189	15,446
Sweden	..	..	23,675	17,074
Switzerland	..	..	88,914	69,529
Japan	..	..	337,528	233,598
China	..	..	54,963	32,632
Cuba	..	..	90,758	97,112
Other countries	..	..	45,870	32,019
Total	401,687	345,248	2,302,902	2,025,852

NOTE.—Values converted at the rate of 4 dol. 85 c. per £ sterling.

Report on the Trade and Commerce of St. Paul for the Year 1886.

I may safely say that the many-sided growth of St. Paul in the last twelve months, is one that has never been surpassed in the history of marvellous development in the western world. The old St. Paul, whose reputation as a wonder of progress travelled far and wide, is fairly eclipsed by the new St. Paul. There are gathered here not less than 135,000, possibly nearer 150,000 ambitious and enterprising people, and adjoining St. Paul lies the city of Minneapolis with an equal population. Directly tributary to St. Paul there are now upwards of 8,200 miles of railway, this indicating merely the amount of road which fetches and carries for St. Paul primarily, every mile of which is utilized in building up her local trade. Over these roads there were transported in 1886 more than 2,755,000 tons of St. Paul freight. Through the union depôt there passed in the same time a total of more than 5,000,000 passengers, an average of about 15,000 for every day in the year. Within the year there has been invested in business buildings and residences the sum of 9,658,692 dol., which is now considered the usual increase upon the yearly building. The jobbing trade, the corner stone of St. Paul's commercial interests, has taken another leap and raised its volume to nearly 100,000,000 dol. There has been more additions to the manufacturing business of the city, more new enterprises located here, and a greater diversity in the commodities produced than was ever known in any previous year. On street improvements alone the city has expended 1,300,000 dol., exclusive of bridges costing half a million dollars. The customs house receipts, showing 136,213 dol. as against 83,272 dol. in 1883, evidence the growth of a direct importing business which is rapidly becoming a distinctive feature of the city's commerce. The reflection of this progress has been felt in an increase of property values which leaves them still below those of other cities equalling St. Paul in population

Progress of St. Paul generally

and falling behind her in growth; and the appreciation of this by capitalists appears in a total of real estate transactions for the year of 31,000,000 dol.

The opening of 1887 finds every industry in St. Paul in a more flourishing condition, and with more solid promise of future increase than it ever boasted heretofore. Her merchants are besieged with orders, her manufactories are running to their full capacity, her city sought by representative business men and by capitalists from every part of the country. By every argument that can be drawn from the past, by every present material condition, by the certain promise of her situation and surroundings, by every proof which has been tried in the experience of American city growth, I am assured that the era of prosperity now upon her is to witness changes more astounding and more satisfying to her citizens than those which have already made St Paul the wonder of every state in the Union.

Imports. The increase of receipts at the St. Paul custom house from duties has been 60 per cent. over those of 1885. The comparative table for 1885 and 1886 reads as follows:—

Months.	1886.		1885.	
	Dol.	c.	Dol.	c.
January	17,789	04	6,133	75
February	10,460	71	5,955	72
March	11,568	10	4,628	61
April	7,740	38	3,624	88
May	11,321	88	3,158	93
June	..	..	4,285	93
July	14,066	88	5,403	25
August	14,550	12	12,068	32
September	9,877	22	10,137	25
October	11,056	83	7,991	22
November	10,523	80	12,377	67
December	8,213	57	6,233	35
Total	136,213	57	83,272	87

Wholesale trade. Progress, development, success, all these are relative terms. They are to be measured not by absolute standards, but by the rapidity of movement from the small to the great. Long before St. Paul had achieved the commercial reputation which she now enjoys—when, indeed, she was but the thriving and ambitious capital of a new border state—the wholesale trade was the foundation of her prosperity. Now, in the larger dreams that visit her, and the more magnificent future that lies ahead, it is still the jobbing business which stands at the head of her industries. Her supremacy as the trade centre of the North-west has never been questioned by any rival. With the proportions which that business has reached to-day, it is clear that she is to be for all time to come the one great jobbing centre west of Chicago and north of St. Louis. And yet this element, too, of her success is of but recent growth. To the outside public, even to all of her own citizens save the little band of those who can call themselves "old settles," it seems almost impossible that the average lifetime of a single generation is not too short to span the period since the first rude and feeble beginnings of the wholesale business were made in St. Paul. It was in 1857 that Mr. Auerbach engaged in the dry goods trade in St. Paul with D. J. Justice, who was then conducting on Third Street a retail dry goods business of not more than 25,000 dol. per annum.

Occasionally a small country merchant would lay in his little stock of supplies by purchases from their stock. He was furnished with what he needed out of the retail stock, and a purchase of from 50 dol. to 100 dol. was a heavy transaction. In 1858 Mr. Forepaugh came into the concern, which next year crept up to a total of about 100,000 dol. pretty evenly divided between retail and wholesale transactions. The war of the rebellion brought the business boom of 1861 and 1862, and in the latter year the change to a business exclusively wholesale was made. In 1863 the total had grown to about 250,000 dol. at war prices, equivalent to some 75,000 dol. to-day. But this was regarded at the time as something colossal, and St. Paul began to put on the airs of a metropolis. After 1865, by which time Messrs. Beaupré and Gotzian had also fully established their businesses, St. Paul had acquired quite a reputation as a wholesale centre for merchandise of all kinds. New lines of goods were added to the stock, and from that time to this there has been a regular and healthy progression.

In 1878 the Lindeke Brothers, who for ten years had been conducting a retail dry goods establishment here, organized under the present firm name of Lindekes, Warner and Schurmeier, and also entered the wholesale field. At first they occupied a store 33 feet wide and three stories high on Third Street. From that the work grew until it crowds its present quarters, in a building 100 by 130, and containing six stories, and aggregates a total of about 3,000,000 dol. per annum in sales. And meantime the older firm had become, through various changes, the present house of Auerbach, Finch and Van Slyck, occupying the most spacious quarters in the north-west devoted to this purpose, and selling every week far more goods than were disposed of in an entire year when it first ventured upon the uncertain sea of wholesaling. In 1861 Mr. Gotzian began to do a small jobbing business in boots and shoes. By 1866 the wholesale portion of his trade had grown so far that the retail branch had to be abandoned. In 1863 both wholesale and retail transactions had amounted to 100,000 dol. When, in 1871, a change was made to the present location of the firm, C. Gotzian and Co., on lower Third Street, the total had reached from 300,000 to 400,000 dol. per year. Mr. Beaupré started in the grocery business in 1856, and began immediately to sell at wholesale. It was up-hill work. The firm originally was Temple and Beaupré, and its business in 1861 had grown to 250,000 dol., more than ten times what it was at the beginning. Then, as in the case of all branches of trade, the war came to stimulate natural growth. For the years during and after this the increase was steady, though new firms were, at the same time, coming in to divide the business which was being created faster than it could be handled. The present firm of Beaupré, Keogh and Co., occupies a building 100 by 130 feet, and six stories in height, and presses upon its accomodations. The business of this single house runs well into the millions in 1886. At the start its working force consisted of two partners, a porter and a bookkeeper. Now, exclusive of the firm, it has upwards of eighty men in its employ. These are three prominent and typical examples which show how the trade of St. Paul has been developed. And the oldest part of the business was organized only 30 years ago. The territory from which this business was to be drawn originally included the valley of the St. Croix River as far as Taylor's Falls, the Minnesota River Valley, as far as then settled, and the portion of the Mississippi River valley adjacent to St. Paul. If anyone ask the explanation of the marvel why a city has grown up here within the memory of man, why the shanty of the trader has been removed to

(189)

make way for the costly business block, and why transactions which a few years ago were great when they ran well into the thousands would now be poor if they did not crowd into the millions, the answer is that this little basin of operations has been expanded until the field supplied by the wholesale trade of St. Paul stretches straight 2,000 miles to the westward, with less than one acre in a hundred yet under cultivation. Where the business field was limited to a little basin of river bottoms, the jobbing interests of St. Paul now have for their own a territory more magnificent in area and resources than yields homage to any other city. Where the most distant order emanated from a Minnesota merchant a few score of miles distant, last week an order was filled for 3,500 dol. worth of as inexpensive an article as candles, and these were to be shipped to a point 1,800 miles from St. Paul. These sharp and effective contrasts, which might be multiplied indefinitely, bring home to the comprehension what the jobbing business of St. Paul has really become and what it yet may be. In the year 1870 the jobbing sales amounted to about 10,000,000 dol.; by 1881 they had risen to 46,550,000 dol. At this time, and from this time onward, the history of its progress interlocks with and is explained by the history of north-western railway developments. Every iron way laid down was an inlet and an outlet for new branches of trade. Every foot of track added to mileage meant so many new customers. Every immigrant of the thousands who were annually pouring in upon these fields in numbers that taxed the resources of transportation, was another factor to build up and multiply trade. Every year since then has seen its increment, and that annual increase, as is natural in a country where civilization is rising constantly towards higher standards, grows greater and greater. By 1882, when the last era of business prosperity was at its height, the wholesale business had risen to more than 66,600,000 dol. The time of depression checked slightly but did not stop its advance. Year by year the total rose to 72,000,000 dol. in 1883, to 74,829,000 in 1884, and to 81,596,000 in 1885. The increase had been over 75 per cent. in four years. For 1886 the statistics are not yet compiled with accuracy sufficient to give them standing here. But it is no secret that the past year has been the busiest and most successful in the experience of the St. Paul jobbers, and data already gathered indicate a grand total not much short of 100,000,000 dol. The concentration here of a network of railways such as few cities in the country can boast of has multiplied facilities and customers, and given rates that put this city upon a more favourable footing than any of its competitors. Her mart is now a recognized source of supply for that vast reach of country which stretches from the neutral district of Wisconsin to the shores of the Pacific Ocean, and shares the honours with St. Louis and Kansas City on the south, while it draws to itself most of the commerce of the Canadian North-west. The little 25,000 dol. start in the dry goods trade had expanded last year into an aggregate of 9,000,000, and an increase of 85,000 dol. in a year of heavily falling prices; the grocery business has become a trade of 11,275,000 dol., growing at the rate of nearly 3,000,000 dol. a year; the shanty in which boots and shoes were sold has been replaced by a group of great firms, doing a business of nearly 4,000,000 dol. annually.

Cattle shipments.

The total number of cattle received during the year at the Union Stock Yards was	..	..	..	116,000
Of Montana cattle	..	..	..	80,000
Total number of sheep ..	..	..	..	110,000
,, ,, hogs ..	..	..	..	41,000
,, ,, horses	..	..	..	15,000

Later on in this report I will speak of the increase of the live stock industry in St. Paul.

The following table shows the total shipments and receipts, in railroads, of the several railroads entering in St. Paul.

General shipments and receipts.

	Received.	Shipped.
Agricultural implements	380	591
Barley	434	..
Brick and stone	5,943	..
Corn	704	..
Cattle and horses	1,127	..
Coal	17,918	..
Castings and machinery	945	628
Flour	2,728	3,474
Feed	1,188	..
Hay	1,350	..
Lumber	16,525	8,938
Lime and cement	2,073	..
Merchandise	22,843	34,845
Oats	1,609	..
Pig and other iron	432	..
Railroad material	10,428	7,331
Wheat	3,729	2,702
Wood	10,376	..
Miscellaneous	11,891	16,002
Total	112,613	74,413

St. Paul stands in one particular in an equal footing with any city in the country, and that is in the size, scope and ability of her banking institutions. The first two particulars, size and extent, are to be taken, of course, relatively, but in the third, that of stability, the St. Paul banks are second to none the world over. As early as 1853 the business of private banking had been begun. At this early date the capital invested was slight indeed, and some idea of the enormous growth of the business may be obtained from this:—A well-known citizen who has been interested in the banking business for over a quarter of a century, said a few weeks ago that the total amount of capital in the early banks was not over 100,000 dol., while his estimate of the capital and surplus at the present time was over 7,000,000 dol. About 1862 the private banks began giving way to state and national institutions, based upon stable financial foundations. Since that time the growth in business has kept even pace with the city. About 1880 the banks of St. Paul received a fresh impetus. The capital was increased, men of large means took new or increased their old stock, business began to grow largely in volume, and now the highest point in the history of St. Paul has been reached, while the outlook is the most promising the city has ever had. Even within the past two years the growth in banking has been very marked. Below will be found a table taken from the current report of Public Examiner Knox, showing this increase. It pertains to the state at large, and it should be noted that St. Paul plays a most prominent part in the increase shown:—

Banks.

(189)

	Totals.	Increase since 1884.
Number of banks	237	21
Capital stock (173 banks)	20,149,100 dol.	3,855,001 dol.
Surplus fund (103 banks)	3,195,836 „	885,692 „
Individual deposits (100 banks)	34,992,873 „	7,652,924 „
Loans and discounts (101 banks)	46,406,270 „	8,564,724 „

I believe St. Paul has the largest banking capital of any city in the United States in proportion to its size. The following are the totals of the business of the thirteen banks of St. Paul:—

	Dollars.
Capital	6,540,000
Surplus and undivided profits	2,144,210
Deposits	16,436,647
Loans	19,131,238
Exchange	148,768,864
Circulation	450,000

Oleomargarine.

Ex-governor Hubbard's message to the State Legislature last January contains the following in reference to the State Dairy Commission.

"The dairy interests of the state were at one time threatened with irreparable injury by the competition of oleagineous products which were being generally introduced into our markets. As a measure of protection to this important and rapidly growing industry of our people, the legislature of 1885 enacted a new law probibiting 'the sale or manufacture of unhealthy or adulterated dairy products.' A commissioner and an assistant authorised by the law were appointed to enforce its provisions. The very interesting report of the commissioner will advise you of his proceedings and experience in the discharge of his duties. As was expected, he encountered the energetic opposition of manufacturers and dealers in the fraudulent product, who attacked the law in the courts, and by every possible device sought to defeat its execution. The commissioner and his able assistant, however, were indefatigable and persistent, and as a result of their efforts the base fabrications sold as pure dairy products are substantially expelled from the state. It is estimated that the import of oleomargarine for the past year has been not to exceed 300,000 lbs., while for the year preceding it was fully 4,000,000 lbs.; and as a consequence, the genuine product of the dairy has sold at from three to five cents per lb. better prices."

The effect that the manufacture and sale of oleomargarine, butterine and other imitations of butter has had is difficult to arrive at, as authorities differ. There has recently been a most unusual, I may say, phenominal development of butter-making throughout the North-west, owing to the introduction of the creamery system. The effect of this was the immediate and very material reduction of prices of poor quality butter, and of better qualities also, but to a less extent. The manufacture of oleomargarine being inaugurated at the same time, renders it hard to say what proportion of the reduction is due to these two causes respectively. From the data before me I think that fully 45 per cent. of the price reduction of common farmers' butter may be attributed to the introduction of oleomargarine, and perhaps 25 per cent. of the decline in prices of first class creamery and dairy butter. So far as the amount of butter sold is concerned, the introduction of oleomargarine seems not to have had any very considerable influence in Minnesota. Good butter commands ready sale in her markets, so far as I can learn, but at lower prices than formerly. It may be more difficult to sell poor butter, as I am informed that among lumbermen, miners, and railroad building gangs, good "oleo" is preferred to poor butter, and it is, no doubt, used in the lower class hotels to a considerable extent; but it is also true that much more butter or its substitute is used in such instances than formerly, because the price is less.

In both Iowa and Wisconsin the butter industry has suffered worse from competition with oleomargarine than in this state, because more men are employed in such labour as I have mentioned there than here; and both states have more common hotels and boarding houses than Minnesota has. I am persuaded that Iowa uses twice as much oleomargarine as Minnesota, and Wisconsin half as much more, in proportion to the respective populations; and no doubt 75 per cent. of the decline in price of common butter in Iowa, and 60 per cent. in Wisconsin is due to the bogus article, and in these states the sales of common butter are considerably diminished for the same reason. Good butter is but little more affected in those markets, from this cause, than in Minnesota, say from 30 to 35 per cent. of its reduction in price is due to this cause.

The worst of the tallow used in the manufacture of the neutral oil which is the basis of the oleomargarine is from cattle fed upon the plains of the far west. As these cattle are mostly grazed upon government land, the cost to their producers is small as compared to the expense of maintaining cattle upon the more expensive lands of dairy districts. This makes the competition unequal, and the dairyman is driven to the wall.

Minnesota makes 30,000,000 lbs. of marketable butter per year. Three years ago this butter would average 20 c. per lb. in the markets. So rapid has been the growth of the imitation butter business, that last year butter hardly averaged 14 c. per lb.

The palm for phenominal municipal development, so long accorded *Population.* Chicago, has by common unprejudiced consent been transferred to this city; statistics proving that St. Paul's growth since 1881 has been in greater ratio than that which any other American city has ever enjoyed in an equal period of its history. Both the "City Directory" publishers and the commercial agencies are authority for the statement that no previous year in St. Paul's history has added more than half or two-thirds as many persons to the population as has 1886. It is stated authoritatively that the forthcoming "City Directory" will contain not less than 57,000 names—indicating a population of at least 150,000. When it is considered that the "City Directory" of 1880 contained 16,399 names, and that the known population for that year by United States census was 41,498, it will be seen that the official estimate upon known number of names in the directory must be very nearly correct. It can be held as unquestionable, therefore, that St. Paul starts in upon the year 1887 with a population of 150,000 within its corporate limits—presenting the unparalleled record of over 300 per cent. increase within 6 years; a record that Chicago never reached and maintained for a like period.

From the directory publishers it is learned that the number of new *Increase of business concerns* in the city exceeds the number of those of 1885 by *business concerns.* about 1,800. Of the concerns established in 1886, the largest relative increase over preceding years was in the line of manufactures. It may occur to the reader that the actual establishment of 1,800 new firms in a city like St. Paul might possibly be overdoing the thing, and prepare the way for competition that would prove disastrous to business interests. This would undoubtedly be the result but for the fact that the general population of the city increased during 1886 in even greater proportion than did the business houses. The business man would naturally inquire, "If 1,800 new concerns opened up in St. Paul during 1886, how many hundred failures, and how many millions liability did you have?" Bradstreet's Commercial Agency reports that there were of large and small concerns embarrassed during the year just 20, and not one of account enough to reach 27,000 dol. liabilities, while 14 out of the 20 showed less than 5,000 dols. liabilities each. The total liabilities of the 20 concerns did not amount to quite 190,000 dol. It may be mentioned *en passant*, that the total liabilities did not exceed the actual assets by more than 35,000 dol.

Manufactures. Perhaps no better indication of the prominence which the manufacturing interests of St. Paul have assured can be given than are shown by the statistics of their growth in the past. Tabulated they are as follows :—

Year.	Number of Establishments.	Number of Employés.	Value of Products.
			Dol.
1870	88	985	1,611,378
1874	216	2,155	3,953,000
1878	223	3,117	6,150,900
1880	667	6,778	12,212,148
1881	792	8,937	16,071,535
1882	794	12,267	22,390,589
1884	843	15,725	26,662,000
1885	864	17,581	29,437,000

The statistics for 1886 are not yet tabulated, but, so far as examined they indicate a large increase over the preceding year in all the above items. The data at hand indicate that this increase will be from 15 to 20 per cent.

Live stock industries. Foremost among the new industries of St. Paul must be placed that of live stock, and the innumerable specialties that grow out of it. That St. Paul possesses peculiar advantages for handling, slaughtering, packing, and shipping cattle and hogs is now universally admitted. The magnitude that this industry is to assume here in the near future is but faintly realized even by those who have given considerable attention to the current discussion of the subject. Several hundred acres of ground on the Mississippi River, some four miles below the city, have been set apart for this business. Three corporations, with an aggregate capital of 3,250,000 dol. have been already organized for active operations. An expenditure of about three quarters of a million dollars has been incurred in building and other improvements preparatory to active operations this spring. Forty thousand tons of ice have been housed preparatory to packing operations, and every movement in the different operations is on a most extensive scale. These facts are indicative of the enterprise and energy of those who are pushing the work. A dissatisfaction with the methods and prices in marketing live stock at more eastern markets, led the North-Western cattle growers to fall in readily with the proposition to establish this stock-handling plant at St. Paul. It would save them shrinkage on beef and freight on long hauls. Therefore, when A. B. Stickney of

St. Paul, and his colleagues of the chamber of commerce, appeared before the stock growers' convention at Miles City, Montana, in June, 1886, and presented the St. Paul Union Stockyards proposition, it met with unreserved favour, and the cattlemen sent a representative committee to assist in selecting the site chosen. With exceptional sagacity and forethought, a comprehensive system for handling the live stock and its products has been co-ordinated and arranged from the ranges of Montana and the farm of Minnesota and adjacent territories to the seaboard, and even to the market places on the other side of the ocean. The cumbersome and expensive system of lightering in New York harbour has been avoided, and the economy effected in the transportation of cattle between St. Paul and New York amounts to not less than 15 dols. per car load. Under the operation of such a far-sighted and wisely-adjusted plan, and favoured by the peculiar advantages which the yards afford for drainage, pure water, and ice, the live-stock interest may be expected to grow to immense proportions, and, indeed, to overwhelm any other class of industries here. The owners of the immense herds of Minnesota, Dakota, Montana, and Washington Territory, not to speak of other adjacent districts, will feel a direct and positive benefit from the establishment of such a market here. Minnesota and Montana alone have cattle to the value of 100,000,000 dols. for the most favourable market, and with the facilities afforded by this stockyards' enterprise, St. Paul is destined to receive and hold the cattle business of the North-West, and to handle all other kinds of live stock as well.

New manufactories. The advent of the Bohn Manufacturing Company, and the erection of its immense wood-working plant during the year, is an event of no ordinary importance. This Company, with a capital of 250,000 dols., employs from 250 to 400 skilled hands. Besides this, established here are the Waterous Engine Company of Winnipeg, with a capital of 100,000 dol.; the Warner and Hough Machinery Company, capital 50,000 dol.; the Holland and Thompson Brass Works, capital 75,000 dol.; the Devane Foundry Company, capital 20,000 dol.; the Edison Electric Light and Power Company, capital 200,000 dol.; and a large undertakers' manufacturing establishment, capital 100,000 dol., with numerous other concerns of less note. The aggregate capital represented by these additions to the city's productive industries amounts to more than 4,000,000 dol. In connection with these facts it should be stated that the additions acquired during the year have been secured as a result of a careful examination in each case of the merits of different localities, and St. Paul has been selected on account of its intrinsic advantages as a manufacturing and distributing centre over other competing points.

Iron industries. The proximity of St. Paul to the wonderful iron ranges of Minnesota and Wisconsin, the low rates of transportation growing out of the sharp competition of rival lines, and the favourable conditions of the fuel question, all conspire to favour the establishment here of the various branches of the iron industry. Whether the organization of smelting works be yet practicable or not, certain it is that the promotion of secondary industries that result from the reduction of ores is a living issue, and steps are being taken to enlarge the class of manufactories. The production of engines, boilers, mill machinery, and railway supplies, and lathe and forge work generally will soon be entered upon. Rolling mills will doubtless soon follow. The necessities of the railway interests centreing here will compel the establishment of car works in the near future.

Mineral resources. The mineral wealth of a country, unless it consists in deposits of the precious metals, is frequently the last of its resources to be developed. It seems probable that the North-West is now entering upon a period when those resources will figure largely in the account of its prosperity and wealth. While the product of the superior region in copper had furnished the public with the knowledge that the mines of the North-West were not to be omitted in making out a list of its assets, it is only of recent date that evidence has been at hand to prove that the more homely, but more useful, and, in a practical sense, the more valuable metal, iron, is probably distributed throughout this section in quantities that may give a new impetus, if not a new direction to its future. The iron mines of Northern Minnesota now enjoy an established reputation. Their product is ore of the highest grade, and it is annually increasing in quantity and value. But recent developments in Wisconsin go to show that this deposit is not a local eccentricity, but simply the first tapping of a store of wealth which underlies great areas of the North-West. A short time ago mines were opened in Wisconsin, whose prospective value created quite a furore. Now great and valuable deposits in the western part of the state have been brought to light, whose richness contains at least a promise of what would be fairly a revolution in the industries of this section. Time is necessary in every such case to show whether ore exists in paying quantities; whether a given outcropping is merely the end of a vein, or the beginning of untold wealth. But it appears to be true that the quality of this West Wisconsin ore is all that it has been represented. When men from Pittsburgh, who are familiar with the iron industry, and men in St. Louis equally well versed, declare that this deposit of ore is worth from eleven to twelve dollars per ton, the question of quality may be considered settled. The question of quantity remains the only debateable point. If these iron mines show a sufficient depth of ore to make them profitably workable, then the North-West is about to enjoy a development unprecedented even in its history. It will help to understand the importance of this to St. Paul, to learn that the new fields are but sixty-three miles distant by railway from here. As to extent, the mines at Tower, the discoveries in the Gogebic region, and these latest discoveries when viewed as parts of a whole, would indicate the existence in the North-West of mineral beds of great richness and wide distribution.

Logs and lumber. The several surveyors-general of logs report the following statistics respecting the lumber interest of the State:—

Timber.	1885.	1886.
Feet of logs scaled	663,402,860	581,636,266
„ lumber manufactured	656,051,060	623,976,780

Public health. Through the agency of the 1,060 local boards of health, prompt information is received by the State Board of the presence of any epidemic of infectious disease in any quarter among men and animals, and equally prompt measures are applied for its isolation and suppression. The Board has adopted elaborate precautionary measures to protect the herds of the State against pleuro-pneumonia, which recently developed to an alarming extent among cattle in states to the south and east of here. The danger of a spread of the infection to Minnesota is regarded as remote, but in the event of its appearance here most energetic measures for its quarantine and extirpation have been prepared.

CHICAGO.

Railways. St. Paul and Minneapolis constitute, in fact, one railroad centre, as they constitute, in fact, one city. Both are the focus of a system of railroad communication more extensive and commanding than that of any city of the west. Every railroad which enters the one city pays of necessity tribute to the other, and becomes a part of the common system of both. St. Paul and Minneapolis are the centre of seventeen trunk lines of railway, radiating to every point of the compass, and supporting extensive systems of lateral ramifications which penetrate every part of the North-West. They are under the control of ten distinct railroad corporations, of which six have their terminal headquarters in St. Paul and three in Minneapolis. This entire system of railways centering here extend over between 8,100 and 8,200 miles of lines, allowing for the additional construction now in progress. It is no longer a question how St. Paul may secure new lines, but a question on the part of all the great roads out of Chicago east and south, of how best and quickest they may reach St. Paul. The recent advent of the Chicago, Burlington and Northern, the Wisconsin Central, and the Minnesota and North-Western railroads tells the story of the year in the line of St. Paul's development as a railway centre. No less than eleven new passenger depôts have been built during the past year within the city limits on suburban lines. Without an exception, the business of the various railways centering here shows very rapid increase, notwithstanding the competition of new lines.

Comparative progress. Statistics are so much more convincing than mere assertion or theory, that the reader will be interested in the succinct statements concerning St. Paul's past development which follow:—

		1880.	1886.
Population	..	41,498	150,000
Customs receipts ..	Dollars ..	16,788	136,213
Wholesale trade ..	„ ..	36,000,000	90,000,000
Number of manufacturing establishments	..	542	1,000
Value of products of manufacturing establishments ..	Dollars ..	11,000,000	45,000,000
Capital of St. Paul banks	„ ..	3,000,000	8,594,210
Number of new business firms started ..	..	201	1,800
Number of new buildings	..	981	4,000
Cost of new buildings ..	Dollars ..	2,671,000	10,500,000
Real estate sales ..	„ ..	3,500,000	31,000,000
Aggregate post office business ..	„ ..	81,299	4,289,102

Attention is called particularly to the figures of the post office business. They are official, and tell beyond controversy the story of St. Paul's growth far more explicitly than any amount of argument could do. The increase in aggregate business from 81,299 dol. in 1880 to 4,289,102 dol. in 1886 is proof enough. Then, again, the official figures of customs receipts that have increased from 16,788 dol. in 1880 to 136,213 in 1886 mean a corresponding increase in manufactures and wholesale trade. The increase in real estate transactions from 3,500,000 dol. in 1880 to over 30,000,000 in 1886 is in reality not so indicative of development as are the figures of the customs house and post office.

Public works The six years covering the period between the opening of 1880 and the close of 1886 mark the era in which St. Paul as a city has paid close attention to the matter of her public works. In 1873 the first work of the present system of sewers was commenced by Captain

James Starkey, and 1·78 miles of sewers completed. From that time to 1880 only a total of 8·87 miles of sewers were constructed. In 1880, through the increase of area of the city, the necessity for more sewers was felt, and the work commenced that culminated in the record of 1886. In the table following the total sewer work of St. Paul is shown.

Year.	Miles.
Up to 1880	8·87
1880	2·12
1881	2·63
1882	4·28
1883	7·41
1884	4·50
1885	8·00
1886	12·00
Total	49·81

St. Paul now has 50 miles of sewers for her 38 square miles of area, and the work planned for 1887 contemplates adding 15 miles more to this. The total cost of this sewer work to date has been close upon 1,000,000 dol. In 1882 the expense of sewer work for the year was 89,000 dol.; in 1886, it was about 250,000 dol. There are now about 225 miles of graded streets in St. Paul, with plans arranged for adding 50 miles more in 1887. This street grading represents such engineering feats as the Seventh Street "fill," costing 139,000 dol., requiring 250,000 cubic yards of earth, creating a bank roadway 80 feet high, and requiring over a year to complete. As a rule such obstacles as bluffs, ravines, and rock have caused unusual expense in street gradings in St. Paul. The present system of waterworks was planted by a private corporation. In 1880 the city purchased the plant for 510,000 dol. The city has now a visible water supply of 40,000,000 gallons per day, though the present daily consumption is not over 5,000,000 gallons. The present system has cost the city 2,154,032·49 dol. to date, and there are 85 miles of water mains in the city. The bridge work during 1885 and 1886 has been very heavy, involving (with 1884) an expenditure of nearly 500,000dol. This includes the new Robert Street bridge across the Mississippi River, costing 191,000 dol. and just completed. Of all the six years since 1880, 1886 is the most noted as having had more work accomplished, and that to a value of 1,370,444 dol. The record for 1886 shows:—

	Dollars.
Total cost of public works	1,370,444
Cost street-grading	599,295
,, ,, paving	143,026
,, sidewalks	98,414
,, sewers	250,000
,, engineering department	126,425
,, bridge work in 1886	270,578

Ownership of real estate.

The legislature at its biennial session this year passed a law, which, if proved constitutional, will affect many British holders of Minnesota real estate. It reads as follows:—

AN ACT to restrict the ownership of real estate in the State of Minnesota to American citizens, and those who have lawfully declared their intentions to become such, and so-forth, and to limit the quantity of land which corporations may acquire, hold, or own.

Be it enacted by the Legislature of the State of Minnesota:

Section 1. That it shall be unlawful for any person or persons, not citizens of the United States, or who have not lawfully declared their intentions to become such citizens, or for any corporations, not created by or under the laws of the United States or of some state or territory of the United States, to hereafter acquire, hold, or own real estate so hereafter acquired, or any interest therein in this state except such as may be acquired by devise or inheritance, or in good faith in the ordinary course of justice in the collection of debts hereafter created.

Provided, That the prohibition of this section shall not apply in such cases as the right to hold lands in the United States is secured by existing treaties to the citizens or subjects of foreign countries, which rights shall continue to exist so long as such treaties are in force.

Provided further, That the provision of this section shall not apply to actual settlers upon farms of not more than 160 acres of land who may settle thereon at any time before January 1st, 1889.

Provided further, That none of the provisions of this Act shall be construed to apply to lands acquired, held, or obtained in good faith by due process of law in the collection of debts or the foreclosure of mortgages.

Section 2. That no corporation or association, more than 20 per centum of the stock of which is, or may be owned by any person or persons, corporation or corporations, association or associations, not citizens of the United States, shall hereafter acquire, or shall hold or own any real estate hereafter in this state.

Section 3. That no corporation other than those organised for the construction or operation of railways, canals, or turnpikes, shall acquire, hold, or own over 5,000 acres of land, so hereafter acquired in this state; and no railroad, canal, or turnpike corporation shall hereafter acquire, hold, or own lands so hereafter acquired in this state other than as may be necessary for the proper operation of its railroad, canal, or turnpike, except such lands as may have been granted to it by Act of Congress or of the Legislature of the state.

Section 4. That all property acquired, held, or owned in violation of the provisions of this Act shall be forfeited to this state, and it shall be the duty of the Attorney-General of the state to enforce every such forfeiture by due process of law.

Section 5. This Act shall take effect and be in force from and after the first day of July, A.D. 1887.

This Act was approved by the Governor, March 2nd, 1887. I have not yet secured legal opinion as to its constitutionality, but in my own opinion it conflicts with the constitution of the United States.

LONDON:
Printed for Her Majesty's Stationery Office,
By HARRISON AND SONS,
Printers in Ordinary to Her Majesty.
(Wt. 7730   75   5 | 87—H & S   189)

FOREIGN OFFICE.
1887.
ANNUAL SERIES.

No. 169.
DIPLOMATIC AND CONSULAR REPORTS ON TRADE AND FINANCE.

UNITED STATES.

REPORT FOR THE YEAR 1886
ON THE
TRADE OF TENNESSEE IN THE CONSULAR DISTRICT OF CHARLESTON.

REFERENCE TO PREVIOUS REPORT, Annual Series No. 88.

Presented to both Houses of Parliament by Command of Her Majesty,
JUNE, 1887.

LONDON:
PRINTED FOR HER MAJESTY'S STATIONERY OFFICE,
BY HARRISON AND SONS, ST. MARTIN'S LANE,
PRINTERS IN ORDINARY TO HER MAJESTY.

And to be purchased, either directly or through any Bookseller, from
EYRE AND SPOTTISWOODE, EAST HARDING STREET, FLEET STREET, E.C., and
32, ABINGDON STREET, WESTMINSTER, S.W.; or
ADAM AND CHARLES BLACK, NORTH BRIDGE, EDINBURGH; or
HODGES, FIGGIS, & Co., 104, GRAFTON STREET, DUBLIN.

1887.

[C.—4923—92.]   *Price 1d.*

New Series of Reports.

Reports of the Annual Series have been issued from Her Majesty's Diplomatic and Consular Officers at the following places, and may be obtained from the sources indicated on the title-page:—

No.		Price.	No.		Price.
47.	Tokyo	1d.	108.	St. Petersburg	3d.
48.	Amsterdam	1d.	109.	Leghorn	1d.
49.	Lisbon	1d.	110.	Boston	1d.
50.	Königsberg	2d.	111.	Buenos Ayres	3d.
51.	Cagliari	1d.	112.	Kewkiang	1d.
52.	Frankfort	1d.	113.	Teheran	2d.
53.	Bogota	1d.	114.	Beyrout	1d.
54.	Kharput	1d.	115.	Odessa	5d.
55.	Trieste	1d.	116.	Carthagena	1d.
56.	Crete	1d.	117.	Santo Domingo	1d.
57.	Berne	3d.	118.	Mollendo	1d.
58.	Rotterdam	1d.	119.	Guayaquil	1d.
59.	Düsseldorf	4d.	120.	Valparaiso	1d.
60.	Mozambique	5d.	121.	San José	1d.
61.	Hanyang	1d.	122.	Pakhoi	1d.
62.	Stockholm	1d.	123.	Hyogo	1d.
63.	Paris	1d.	124.	Tamsui	1d.
64.	Tunis	1d.	125.	Malaga	1d.
65.	The Hague	2d.	126.	Marseilles	1d.
66.	Italy	2d.	127.	Boulogne	2d.
67.	Smyrna	2d.	128.	Warsaw	1d.
68.	Fiume	1d.	129.	Monte Video	1d.
69.	Tabreez	1d.	130.	Christiania	4d.
70.	Philippopolis	1d.	131.	Göthenburg	2d.
71.	Rome	1d.	132.	Kiungchow	1d.
72.	Vienna	1d.	133.	Amoy	1d.
73.	St. Petersburg	2d.	134.	Genoa	1d.
74.	Ichang	1d.	135.	Trebizond	1d.
75.	Salonica	1d.	136.	Savannah	1d.
76.	Brussels	2d.	137.	Wilmington	2d.
77.	Alexandria	1d.	138.	Bolivar	3d.
78.	Patras	1d.	139.	Wênchow	1d.
79.	Maranham	1d.	140.	Chicago	2d.
80.	Taganrog	2d.	141.	Fiume	1d.
81.	Jeddah	1d.	142.	Port Saïd	1d.
82.	Suakin	1d.	143.	Java	1d.
83.	Colonia	1d.	144.	Puerto Cabello	1d.
84.	Suez	1d.	145.	Coquimbo	1d.
85.	Paris	1d.	146.	Vera Cruz	2d.
86.	Brest	1d.	147.	Bengazi	1d.
87.	Puerto Plata	1d.	148.	Canary Islands	1d.
88.	Charleston	1d.	149.	Rome	1d.
89.	Tripoli	1d.	150.	Madeira	1d.
90.	Saigon	1d.	151.	Tahiti	1d.
91.	Cherbourg	1d.	152.	Corunna	1d.
92.	New Orleans	2d.	153.	Vienna	1d.
93.	Galatz	1d.	154.	Cagliari	1d.
94.	Baltimore	1d.	155.	St. Petersburg	2d.
95.	Tokio	4d.	156.	Taiwan	1d.
96.	Havre	3d.	157.	Foochow	1d.
97.	Barcelona	3d.	158.	Tonga	1d.
98.	Volo	1d.	159.	Wuhu	1d.
99.	Damascus	1d.	160.	Lisbon	1d.
100.	Paris	1d.	161.	Ning-po	1d.
101.	Bordeaux	2d.	162.	Cadiz	2d.
102.	Serajevo	1d.	163.	Bilbao	1d.
103.	Manila	1d.	164.	Jaffa	1d.
104.	Galveston	1d	165.	Van	1d.
105.	Aleppo	1d.	166.	Bushire	1d.
106.	Rio de Janeiro	1d.	167.	Riga	1d.
107.	Truxillo	1d.	168.	Santos	1d.

No. 169.

Reference to previous Report, Annual Series, No. 88.

UNITED STATES.

CHARLESTON.

Consul Cridland to the Marquis of Salisbury.

My Lord,   *Charleston, April* 21, 1887.

I HAVE the honour to enclose herewith a report of the trade, commerce, productions, and internal resources of the State of Tennessee for the past year.

I have, &c.
(Signed)   FREDERICK J. CRIDLAND.

Report on the Trade and Commerce and Productions of the State of Tennessee for the Year 1886.

The State of Tennessee, as now settled and developed, lies between latitudes 35° and 36°30′ north, rhomboidal in shape, having an extreme length of 432 miles and width 109 miles, with an area of 41,750 square miles or 26,720,000 acres. The population of the State is now over 1,600,000; 1,180,000 whites and 420,000 blacks. *Situation, area, and population.*

The principal productions of Tennessee are Indian corn, wheat, oats, cotton, tobacco, potatoes, pea-nuts, hay, flax, hemp, rice, and fruit. *Productions.*

The indigenous timbers include nearly all the varieties, poplar, ash, white, red, black, and chestnut oak, beech, birch, cedar, cypress, cotton-wood, elm, hickory, sugar maple, yellow and white pine, and walnut, many of which are in great demand for home consumption and shipment. The forest area in the State is 11,000,000 acres, and the farm area 8,500,000. *Woods.*

FARMS Cultivated.

Number of farms.

Years.	Number.	Area in Acres.	Value.
			Dollars.
1860	82,368	6,795,337	271,358,985
1870	118,141	6,843,218	218,743,747
1880	165,650	8,496,556	206,749,837

(218)

UNITED STATES.

Crops.

Crops Cultivated.

Articles.		1884. Acres.	1884. Production.	1883. Acres.	1883. Production.
Indian corn	Bushels	3,245,082	65,723,000	3,212,952	64,259,000
Wheat	„	1,336,230	9,320,000	1,323,000	7,408,800
Oats	„	568.895	7,680,000	586,490	6,997,700
Cotton	Bales	815,678	313,807	807,602	310,700
Tobacco	Pounds	45,048	31.392,000	40,221	28,538,602
Potatoes	Bushels	38,551	2,390,000	38,169	2,404,647
Pea-nuts	„	..	1,250,000	..	800,000
Hay	Tons	181,097	217,316	188,341	244,843

The above are the latest statistics that can be obtained in a complete form in reference to Tennessee.

Live stock in Tennessee.

Live Stock.

Cattle.	1885. Number.	1885. Value.	1884. Number.	1884. Value.
Horses	288,604	18,966,758	282,945	19,862,739
Mules and asses	187,208	13,046,443	183,537	14,018,556
Milk cows	326,417	6,528,340	320,017	7,523,600
Oxen	475,406	6,386,604	466,084	7,471,327
Sheep	603,780	967,255	635,558	1,137,649
Swine	2,122,646	6,788,222	2,021,568	8,126,703

Value of railroads to agriculture.

The foregoing tables, compiled by the Chief of the Bureau of Statistics at Washington, show the aggregate agricultural productions for a series of years, and their values. It is noticeable that upon the introduction of railroad transportation, by which the range of markets was greatly extended, the aggregate values of the products of the farm were a little more than doubled between 1850 and 1860; and the production of wheat increased more than 300 per cent., owing to increased transportation facilities.

Values doubled.

Indian corn and its valuable uses.

It may perhaps surprise Europeans that such vast quantities of Indian corn are produced in the Western States of America; but when they become aware of the numerous uses to which Indian corn, or maize, is put to, they will probably be astonished that in the South of Europe, where so much corn is produced, the people have never yet discovered how many nutritious articles of food it does afford.

Indian corn a certain crop.

In the first place, it is the most certain crop; requires the least amount of labour in its culture, and comes to maturity in the shortest time. The pith of the matured stalk of the corn is esculent and nutritious, and the stalk itself compressed between rollers furnishes what is known as "corn stalk molasses." This grain requires also the least care and trouble in preserving it. The machinery for converting it into food is also exceedingly simple and cheap. As soon as the ear is fully formed it may be roasted or boiled, and forms thus an excellent and nourishing diet. At a later period, it may be grated and furnishes

Boiled corn.

in this form the sweetest bread. The grain boiled in a variety of modes either whole or broken in a mortar, or roasted in the ashes, is well relished. — Corn bread.

If the grain is to be converted into meal, a simple tub-mill answers the purpose best, as the meal least perfectly ground is always preferred. A bolting-cloth is not needed, as it diminishes the sweetness and value of the flour. — Corn meal.

Boiled in water it forms the dish called hominy, eaten with milk, honey, molasses, butter or gravy. Mixed with cold water it is at once ready for the cook. — Corn hominy.

Covered with hot ashes, the preparation is called "ash cake," placed upon a piece of board, and set near the coals, it forms the "johnny cake," or managed in the same way upon a helveless hoe, it forms the "hoe cake"; put in an oven and covered over with a heated lid, it is called in a large mass a "pone" or "loaf." It has the further advantage over all other flour, that it requires in its preparation so few culinary utensils, and neither sugar, yeast, eggs, spices, soda, potash, &c., to qualify or perfect the bread. To all this it may be added that it is not only cheap and well-tasted, but it is unquestionably the most wholesome and nutritive food. Some of the largest and healthiest people in the world have lived upon it exclusively. — Corn cake.

The "Statistician" says that without Indian corn the Western States would still be a wilderness.

In recent years considerable attention has been given throughout the State to the cultivation for shipment of fruit and vegetables, the climate and soil of Tennessee apparently being well-adapted to the same, and a ready market being found for the production. There is hardly a vegetable that could be named that is not produced in large quantities all over the State; and, among the fruit, strawberries, raspberries, grapes, blackberries, apples, pears, plums, and peaches, come to perfection, several millions of dollars worth being exported every year to markets outside the State. — Fruit and vegetables. Export of fruit.

The tobacco crop of Tennessee—which is annually increasing—is almost wholly shipped out of the State for consumption, 90 per cent. of it going to Europe, the remaining 10 per cent. being consumed in the State. — Tobacco.

The chief minerals found in Tennessee are coal, iron, copper, zinc, lead and manganese. Marble, millstone grit, hydraulic rock, barytes and fire-clay are also abundant, and petroleum has also been discovered in several localities, but thus far for the want of cheap transportation has not been developed. Gold, in paying quantities, is found in East Tennessee. Coal and iron ore—magnetic and red—and brown hematite are found throughout the State, and their good qualities are generally known and being rapidly developed; and iron is now made at a cost of from 12 dol. to 16 dol. (2l. 10s. to 3l. 6s. 8d.) per ton. The production of iron in 1885 was 326,040 tons, and was exported to the north and west. From this iron a very fine quality of steel is made. — Minerals. Coals, iron, &c. Petroleum. Gold. Coal and iron. Cost of making iron. Production.

The coal of Tennessee is considered excellent for all purposes, is free from sulphur or slate, and out-cropping on hill slopes or mountain sides the mines are well situated for entry by drifts, and are easily drained and ventilated and cheaply worked. — Coal.

The out-put of coal in 1884 was 1,000,000 tons, and coke 219,700 tons; in 1885 it was 1,100,000 tons, and coke 268,400 tons. The production of the mines at present is consumed in the State. — Out-put.

Copper is found in Tennessee, the mines having been worked since 1850. Some 6,000,000 dol. capital is employed in its production, and, in 1880, 153,880 lbs. was produced and shipped. — Copper.

Zinc is also found, and, in 1884, 17,415 tons was produced. — Zinc.

Manganese is found in considerable quantities, and being used in — Manganese.

UNITED STATES.

the manufacture of steel the mines have been worked a good deal, and it promises to become one of the most useful and valuable of the Tennessee minerals.

Manufacturing. Manufacturing since 1875 shows a vast increase. Each succeeding year witnesses the penetration of the coal fields by new entries, the opening of new beds of iron ore, the erection of new iron furnaces, coke ovens increased in numbers, the construction of iron foundries of all descriptions, the erection of additional furniture and lumbering establishments, the building and enlarging of cotton and woollen factories. Last year witnessed the erection of a very extensive fruit and vegetable canning establishment at Nashville, the capital of the State, the first built in the South, which is doing an immense business and finding ready sale in Tennessee and other States for its products. Besides the manufacture of iron and steel before referred to, those of cotton and wool, ploughs and waggons, cotton-seed oil and cake, fertilizers, furniture, tin and sheet-iron ware, stove and other foundries, grist and flour mills, show great activity and progress.

Labour. Labour is plentiful and regular at reasonable prices; no stoppages by reason of extremes of heat or cold occur.

The following statement exhibits the aggregate of all branches of manufacture in the years named:—

Number of manufacturing establishments.

Years.	Number of Establishments.	Capital Invested.	Value of Products.
		Dollars.	Dollars.
1850	2,887	6,527,729	9,725,608
1860	2,572	14,426,261	17,987,225
1870	5,317	15,595,295	34,362,636
1880	4,326	20,092,845	37,074,886
1885	4,425	40,763,650	75,216,211

The extraordinary number of establishments in 1870 is due to the fact that sorghum mills and evaporators were included in the census of that year and in none of the others.

Cotton manufacturing. Cotton manufacturing has very much increased in Tennessee since 1880, and this increase is due in a great measure to the saving of long hauls of raw material supplied by home markets and the reliability of labour. The product consists of drills, shirtings, sheetings, carpet warps, yarns, rope, twine, and batting; 78 per cent. of the production being shipped out of the State. **Production, capital, &c.** In 1885, 2,258,190 dol. was invested in cotton factories, 1,447,409 dol. worth of material was used, and the production was 2,719,768 dol.

Wool industry. The woollen industry also shows a healthy growth, the raw material used being the production of the sheep farms in the State; the value of annual production in one factory alone having increased from 20,000 dol. in 1881 to 200,000 dol. in 1885.

Cotton-seed oil. One of the articles exported from Tennessee to foreign countries is cotton-seed oil. There are now 15 mills in the State, producing from 2,000,000 gallons to 3,000,000 gallons of oil annually, employing a capital of 1,250,000 dol. **Export of oil to Europe.** The production depends on the extent of the cotton crop, and the price fluctuates accordingly. One-half of the oil and oil cake is exported to Europe, and the other half to neighbouring States.

Summary. The State of Tennessee produces in excess of her own wants and requirements all the products of the farm and orchard, including butter, poultry, eggs, horses, mules, asses, sheep, and hogs; coal, lime, marble, lumber, iron, cotton, wool, tobacco, cotton-seed oil, &c., but she is dependent on other States and countries for the finer cotton and woollen fabrics, white goods, hardware, cutlery, boots, shoes, chemicals, machinery, sugar, salt, coffee, tea, glass, queen's-ware, paints, rice, &c.; and in all probability, even with the high rates of duty of the United States' tariff, if British manufacturers would send agents to Nashville, Memphis, Chattanooga, and other towns in the State with samples of English goods, they might obtain orders for the same, and find the undertaking quite profitable. *Suggestion to British manufacturers.*

Tennessee having no ports from which a direct trade is carried on with the outward world, no tables can be rendered as annexes to this report. *No ports. No annexes.*

Its exports go direct from Memphis to New Orleans, or by railroad to the Atlantic ports. The most valuable article exported is cotton, and the statement here rendered shows the quantity shipped from Memphis during the past two years, its value, &c.:— *Exports of cotton.*

Year.	Quantity.	Average Weight.	Average Price.	Total Value.	Freight.
	Bales.	Per Bale.	Per lb.	Dollars.	Cents.
1883–84	450,077	493	10·33	22,917,920	63 to 67
1884–85	430,127	493$\frac{59}{100}$	10·10	21,441,831	62 67

LONDON:
Printed for Her Majesty's Stationery Office,
By HARRISON AND SONS,
Printers in Ordinary to Her Majesty.
(Wt. 7730 75 6 | 87—H & S 218)

FOREIGN OFFICE.
1887.
ANNUAL SERIES.

No. 177.

DIPLOMATIC AND CONSULAR REPORTS ON TRADE AND FINANCE.

UNITED STATES.

REPORT FOR THE YEARS 1885-86
ON THE
TRADE OF THE CONSULAR DISTRICT OF PHILADELPHIA.

REFERENCE TO PREVIOUS REPORT [C. 4240], Commercial No. 41, 1884.

Presented to both Houses of Parliament by Command of Her Majesty,
JUNE, 1887.

LONDON:
PRINTED FOR HER MAJESTY'S STATIONERY OFFICE,
BY HARRISON AND SONS, ST. MARTIN'S LANE,
PRINTERS IN ORDINARY TO HER MAJESTY.

And to be purchased, either directly or through any Bookseller, from
EYRE AND SPOTTISWOODE, EAST HARDING STREET, FLEET STREET, E.C., and
32, ABINGDON STREET, WESTMINSTER, S.W.; or
ADAM AND CHARLES BLACK, NORTH BRIDGE, EDINBURGH; or
HODGES, FIGGIS & Co., 104, GRAFTON STREET, DUBLIN.

1887.

[C.—4923—100.]   *Price 2d.*

New Series of Reports.

Reports of the Annual Series have been issued from Her Majesty's Diplomatic and Consular Officers at the following places, and may be obtained from the sources indicated on the title-page:—

No.		Price.	No.		Price.
51.	Cagliari	1d.	114.	Beyrout	1d.
52.	Frankfort	1d.	115.	Odessa	5d.
53.	Bogota	1d.	116.	Carthegena	1d.
54.	Kharput	1d.	117.	Santo Domingo	1d.
55.	Trieste	1d.	118.	Mollendo	1d.
56.	Crete	1d.	119.	Guayaquil	1d.
57.	Berne	3d.	120.	Valparaiso	1d.
58.	Rotterdam	1d.	121.	San José	1d.
59.	Düsseldorf	4d.	122.	Pakhoi	1d.
60.	Mozambique	5d.	123.	Hyogo	1d.
61.	Hanyang	1d.	124.	Tamsui	1d.
62.	Stockholm	1d.	125.	Malaga	1d.
63.	Paris	1d.	126.	Marseilles	1d.
64.	Tunis	1d.	127.	Boulogne	2d.
65.	The Hague	2d.	128.	Warsaw	1d.
66.	Italy	2d.	129.	Monte Video	1d.
67.	Smyrna	2d.	130.	Christiania	4d.
68.	Fiume	1d.	131.	Gothenburg	2d.
69.	Tabreez	1d.	132.	Kiungchow	1d.
70.	Philippopolis	1d.	133.	Amoy	1d.
71.	Rome	1d.	134.	Genoa	1d.
72.	Vienna	1d.	135.	Trebizond	1d.
73.	St. Petersburg	2d.	136.	Savannah	1d.
74.	Ichang	1d.	137.	Wilmington	2d.
75.	Salonica	1d.	138.	Bolivar	3d.
76.	Brussels	2d.	139.	Wênchow	1d.
77.	Alexandria	1d.	140.	Chicago	2d.
78.	Patras	1d.	141.	Fiume	1d.
79.	Maranham	1d.	142.	Port Said	1d.
80.	Taganrog	2d.	143.	Java	1d.
81.	Jeddah	1d.	144.	Puerto Cabello	1d.
82.	Suakin	1d.	145.	Coquimbo	1d.
83.	Colonia	1d.	146.	Vera Cruz	2d.
84.	Suez	1d.	147.	Bengazi	1d.
85.	Paris	1d.	148.	Canary Islands	1d.
86.	Brest	1d.	149.	Rome	1d.
87.	Puerto Plata	1d.	150.	Madeira	1d.
88.	Charleston	1d.	151.	Tahiti	1d.
89.	Tripoli	1d.	152.	Corunna	1d.
90.	Saigon	1d.	153.	Vienna	1d.
91.	Cherbourg	1d.	154.	Cagliari	1d.
92.	New Orleans	2d.	155.	St. Petersburg	2d.
93.	Galatz	1d.	156.	Taiwan	1d.
94.	Baltimore	1d.	157.	Foochow	1d.
95.	Tokio	4d.	158.	Tonga	1d.
96.	Havre	3d.	159.	Wuhu	1d.
97.	Barcelona	3d.	160.	Lisbon	1d.
98.	Volo	1d.	161.	Ning-Po	1d.
99.	Damascus	1d.	162.	Cadiz	2d.
100.	Paris	1d.	163.	Bilbao	1d.
101.	Bordeaux	2d.	164.	Jaffa	1d.
102.	Serajevo	1d.	165.	Van	1d.
103.	Manila	1d.	166.	Bushire	1d.
104.	Galveston	1d.	167.	Riga	1d.
105.	Aleppo	1d.	168.	Santos	1d.
106.	Rio de Janeiro	1d.	169.	Charleston	1d.
107.	Truxillo	1d.	170.	Newchwang	1d.
108.	St. Petersburg	3d.	171.	Amsterdam	1d.
109.	Leghorn	1d.	172.	Ajaccio	1d.
110.	Boston	1d.	173.	Chinkiang	2d.
111.	Buenos Ayres	3d.	174.	Naples	3d.
112.	Kewkiang	1d.	175.	Smyrna	1d.
113.	Teheran	2d.	176.	Belgrade	1d.

No. 177.

Reference to previous Report [*C.* 4240], *Commercial No.* 41, 1884.

UNITED STATES.

PHILADELPHIA.

Consul Clipperton to the Marquis of Salisbury.

My Lord, *Philadelphia, March* 31, 1887.

I HAVE the honour to enclose to your Lordship a report on the trade, commerce, and manufactures of the Consular district of Pennsylvania, Ohio, Indiana, and Michigan for the years 1885 and 1886.

I have, &c.
(Signed) ROBT. CHAS. CLIPPERTON.

Report by Consul Clipperton on the Trade, Commerce, and Manufactures of the Consular District of Pennsylvania, Ohio, Indiana, and Michigan for the Years 1885 *and* 1886.

PENNSYLVANIA, &C.

The vast resources of this favoured continent continue to develop, and this Consular district has had its full share of increased prosperity in shipping, internal commerce, and manufactures. The whole Union now contains a population of nearly 60,000,000, and, according to the statistical tables of Mr. Edward Atkinson, the national growth of the country has been enormous. This writer reports a yield of 3,014,063,984 bushels of grain in 1885, or twice as much as was raised 15 years ago; hay 48,470,460 tons, or double that of 10 years ago; and cotton under free labour 6,550,215 bales, over three times as much as was ever raised by slave labour. The iron production has more than doubled in 15 years, and the present efforts to develop the iron yield of the Southern States will greatly enhance this increase. The means of transportation have grown beyond all precedent, as in 1865 there were 33,908 miles of railroad, while now the rails cover 128,967 miles, moving from 1881 to 1885 the enormous amount of 1,597,058,562 tons of freight an average distance of 111 miles, at a cost of 412,570,000*l.*, and that within the last four years the payments for railway traffic by the business community have been reduced $2\frac{1}{5}$ c. per ton per mile, saving thereby 765,674,632*l.* Fire insurance has quintupled in the last 20 years, and life insurance has quadrupled. In the state of Massachusetts alone saving bank deposits were 55,000,000*l.*—four times what they were 20 years ago. Since the year 1860 the population has doubled, and is now claimed to be 60,000,000.

Of this vast wealth this Consular district has enjoyed its full share of increased foreign shipping, internal commerce, manufactures, and mineral developments. Since the last commercial report from this Consulate, four States have withdrawn from its jurisdiction in order to form the Consular district of Chicago; but notwithstanding this reduction in the number of States, the district is still the largest in point of area, population, manufactures, and productions. A short review of the general character and resources of the States now composing the district becomes therefore desirable.

Pennsylvania. This State, viewed as a whole for its soil, climate, and industrial and mineral resources, ranks as the second in the Union, and is properly designated the "Keystone State," lying as it does midway between the eastern and western portions of the continent. The condition of its working classes, rural and urban, is unequalled for steady employment, wages, and home comforts by any other of the United States, and as a great railway centre it is equalled by none. Harrisburgh, with a population of 30,760 in 1880, is its capital; and Philadelphia, with a population claimed to be 1,000,000, the chief port. This beautiful city has important Government Navy yards, besides private shipbuilding yards. It is a great depot for grain, petroleum, the trade in sugar and molasses, and the growing fruit trade with Jamaica and other West India islands, as well as a large iron trade with Cuba. It ranks first in manufactures and fourth in commerce; its universities and colleges of law, medicine, and science, its schools of art, public libraries, and system of public school education are famous; and its streets are filled with telegraph, telephone, and electric light wires overhead, and their surface covered with tramways in every direction, with one cable road through the heart of the city. Pittsburgh, with a population of 170,000, is the great iron-producing district; while Reading, with a population of 45,000, the coal-shipping centre, and the other cities of lesser degree are devoted to petroleum, textiles, and inland trade. The population of the State is 4,282,891 (in 1880), and the industries are coal, iron, petroleum, and manufactures.

Ohio. Next in importance and the chief Western State is Ohio, with its 39,964 square miles, or 25,576,960 acres, and a population of 3,198,062 in 1880. Columbus is the capital, population 51,647; and Cincinnati the chief shipping point, population 255,139. Its coal beds cover upwards of 10,000 square miles, and iron ore abounds; some petroleum and wells of salt abound; the soil is most fertile, producing crops for a number of years without manure; agriculture and manufacture are the chief products; cattle of a high grade, and hogs are raised for distribution throughout the Western States to improve the breed; timber is abundant, and is chiefly hickory, walnut, sugar maple, ash, oak, and poplar. Labour is chiefly farming and mechanical, performed mostly by Germans, Irish, English, Scotch, and a few French: the Germans work on farms, the Irish on railways, and the English, Scotch, and Welsh in coal and other mines. Products: wheat 36,396,119 bushels, price per bushel 90 c.; corn (maize) 87,897,813 bushels, price per bushel 45 c.; meadow productions in value 5,912,400*l.*; live stock 4,000,000*l.*; dairy products 2,123,420*l.*; forest products 1,900,000*l.*; wool 1,178,000*l.*; oats 24,621,347 bushels, price per bushel 30 c.; potatoes 9,450,025 bushels, price per bushel 35 c.; orchard products 1,444,250*l.*; vineyard products 500,000*l.*; tobacco 551,231*l.*; barley 109,990*l.*; maple products 123,552*l.*; sorghum products 40,300*l.*; rye 454,981 bushels, price per bushel 60 c.; honey 1,731,095 lbs., price 16 c. per lb.; buckwheat, sweet potatoes, flax, and broom corn are received in lesser quantities.

Indiana. Indiana is a great corn (maize) producing State, with a population of

1,978,301 (in 1880), consisting of 33,809 square miles. Public debt 1,201,321*l.*; abundant with timber and prairie lands; labour principally agriculture, but mechanical, coal mining, railway, and mill work prevail; number of mines 208; capital invested in mining 400,000*l.*; number of miners 6,406; output of coal 3,000,000 tons. The labourers are chiefly Irish and German, with the native American population; the Irish exceed in numbers, and are distributed on farms and railways. Indianapolis is the capital town, situated on the White river, with a population of 75,056, with manufacturing industries, and a very large inland trade; wages, cost of living, and prices of live stock vary but little with those quoted for Ohio.

Michigan. This State has profited by the increment of immigration. In 1830 its population was under 32,000. In 1880 it numbered 1,636,937. It has an area of 56,423 square miles, or 35,995,520 acres. It is divided into two great peninsulas by the Lakes Michigan and Huron—the northern mountainous and wooded, the southern portion of rich prairie, studded with oak and watered by many rivers; the latter favoured by a mild climate, while the upper regions are cold and bleak. The principal products are wheat and Indian corn (maize). Rich mines of copper and iron prevail in the upper regions. The chief town is Detroit, on Lake Michigan, opposite the Canadian frontier. Wild lands are easily purchased but not easily rented. Improved farms bring good prices, ranging according to situation and improvements. Unimproved lands can be bought at very low rates, higher prices ranging only when the land is cleared, fenced, or well wooded. The prices of small improved farms for rent depends upon the nature of the arrangement, whether stock, seed, and implements are supplied or not by the owner, and are after taken on shares. The soil is clay, loam, and sand, with beech, maple, oak, ash, cedar, pine, and hemlock as forest products. Labour, skilled and unskilled, finds a good market, and the agricultural and forest work is chiefly done by German, Irish, and Swiss, with some English and Scotch—Germans and Irishmen prevailing. Immigration has a vast field in this State, as land is abundant, and railways render a ready market accessible. Mining also offers an opening for industrial occupation. Cattle are higher in price than in the other Western States.

Wages in the Western States. The average rates of wages in the States of Ohio, Indiana, and Michigan, as well as the other Western States, are quoted as follows:—

	Per day.
	Dol. c.
Blacksmiths	2 25
Bricklayers	3 00
Cabinetmakers	2 00
Carpenters	2 50
Coopers	1 50
Plasterers	3 00
Painters	2 25
Shoemakers	2 00
Stonecutters	2 50
Tailors	2 13
Tinsmiths	2 25
Wheelwrights	2 25

The wages given for farm labour average as follows:—

Experienced hands, in summer, 17 dol. per month, with board.
    "   "   winter, 28 "   "   without board.
Ordinary hands, in summer, 1 dol. 50 c. per month, with board.
    "   "   "   2 dol.   "   without board.
Common labourers at other than farm work, 1 dol. 40 c. per day.
Female servants, 2 dol. 50 c. per week.

(227)

UNITED STATES.

Where the labour is engaged without board it averages about 50 c. per day higher, and in the case of farm hands about 10 dol. per month higher than the above rates. Farm hands are largely engaged by the day, especially in the spring and summer seasons.

In the mines the average wages are :—

	Per day.
	Dol. c.
For labourers	1 65
miners	1 85

Shipping and navigation.

The American merchant marine continues to decline, and for the past two years propositions have from time to time been made to Congress for subsidies in various forms—one of which by the Philadelphia maritime exchange is for the payment of 33 c. per ton register for every 1,000 miles sailed by American vessels in the foreign trade, and another for the right to have ships built in foreign shipyards. All these propositions have met with little encouragement. The foreign trade in American vessels at the port of Philadelphia shows entrances for 1885, number 437, with a tonnage of 213,783 ; clearances number 287, tonnage 160,123 ; and in 1886 entrances, number 421, tonnage 202,782 ; clearances, number 256, tonnage 148,150. The foreign trade in vessels of all nations, except American, in 1885 figures as follows :—Entrances, number of vessels 850, and tonnage 863,602 ; clearances, vessels 788, tonnage 795,238 ; for 1886 the entrances were 961, and the tonnage 1,005,330 ; clearances, 727, with a tonnage of 743,005. The American coasting trade for 1885 was carried on in 4,728 vessels of all classes, from steamers to small schooners ; and in 1886 the number was 4,529. This trade is not open to foreign flags.

Trade in British ships at the port of Philadelphia.

The British commercial marine trading with this port has steadily increased, with slight variation from year to year. The foreign trade under the American flag does not improve. The Italian and Norwegian flags hold their own. In 1858 the number of British ships that entered the port was 79, and the tonnage 14,044 ; in 1870 the entrances were 308, with a tonnage of 112,557 ; in 1880 entrances were 485, and the tonnage was 541,018 ; in 1883 entrances 375, tonnage 387,554 ; in 1885 entrances 455, tonnage 616,883 ; and in 1886 the entrances figure 589, with a tonnage of 690,309. The trade in British steamships has largely increased. The entrances in 1877 were 32, with a tonnage of 82,038 ; in 1880 159 steamers, tonnage 468,714 ; in 1883 there were 174 steamers, tonnage 261,538 ; in 1885 259 steamers, tonnage 436,092 ; and in 1886 421 steamers, tonnage 570,342.

PHILADELPHIA.

Shipping of all Nations at Philadelphia.

	Number of Ships.	Tonnage.
American in 1885	437	213,031
,, ,, 1886	421	202,782
Austrian in 1885	20	14,831
,, ,, 1886	6	3,887
British in 1885	455	616,883
,, ,, 1886	589	690,309
Belgian in 1885	13	40,535
,, ,, 1886	13	46,294
German in 1885	105	97,239
,, ,, 1886	99	110,682
Italian in 1885	111	69,550
,, ,, 1886	82	53,890
Norwegian in 1885	129	92,669
,, ,, 1886	118	100,192
Russian in 1885	7	6,432
,, ,, 1886	10	8,812
Swedish in 1885	14	10,094
,, ,, 1886	12	10,559
Portuguese in 1885	1	237
,, ,, 1886	..	..
Danish in 1885	5	1,542
,, ,, 1886	..	..
Dutch in 1885	6	7,648
,, ,, 1886	10	13,096
Spanish in 1885	5	2,063
,, ,, 1886	22	25,555
French in 1885	1	301
,, ,, 1886	..	..

The above figures are the entrances. Clearances to foreign ports represent a much smaller number, because many vessels enter this port from other countries, discharge their cargoes, and depart for other American ports to load for Europe, thereby not being included in the official tables of the foreign trade.

Imports and exports. The exports from the whole United States in 1885 were 137,649,960*l.*, and in 1886 they were 142,659,934*l.* The imports in 1885 were 117,573,735*l.*, and in 1886 they were 132,683,442*l.* The balance of exports over imports in 1885 was 20,076,225*l.*, while in 1886 it fell off to 9,974,491*l.* It is claimed that this showing is due to the growth of imports, more or less caused by the labour strikes in the early part of the year, when supplies to fulfil contracts had to be bought at once. The imports and exports at Philadelphia in 1885 were:—Imports, 33,365,242 dol.; exports, 37,281,739 dol. In 1886 they were: imports, 37,997,005 dol.; exports, 33,607,386 dol; and the duties paid into the United States' custom-house were 13,915,553 dol. 66 c. in 1885, and 16,303,918 dol. 77 c. in 1886. American ships carried 3,352,627 dol. worth of the imports, the remainder being carried in foreign ships, England having by great odds the bulk of the trade, and receiving the exports together with Scotland and Ireland 17,534,719 dol. in corn, oats, wheat, provisions, and illuminating oils chiefly.

Iron shipbuilding. Iron shipbuilding in the United States commenced in the year 1868, and the largest number built was in the year 1882, when 43 steamers were constructed, with a tonnage of 40,097; the greater

(227)

number of them were built on the River Delaware, within this Consular district.

The United States Government yards at Philadelphia have some work going on in the completion of ships of war, but it is not of a character to demand special mention.

There is one good basin dock at Philadelphia, capable of receiving the largest ships, belonging to the Messrs. Cramp, and it is in almost constant use for repairs of craft of all sizes.

The Messrs. Cramp and Sons are about to lay the keel of a Government steel cruiser of 1,700 tons, to be armed with six 6-inch rifles, five Hotchkiss cannon, and one Gatling gun; to show a speed of 16 knots an hour. Two other steamers are being constructed—one for the trade between Tampa and Havana, and the other for the Metropolitan line plying between New York and Boston. The former is 291 feet in length, 35 feet beam, and 20 feet 9 inches in depth; has a triple expansion engine of 1,800 horse-power, and a speed of 14 or 15 knots per hour. She will carry 110 first class and about 75 second class passengers; will be lighted with electricity, and fitted up with all the latest improvements. The latter will be 288 feet 6 inches long, 31 feet deep, with a gross tonnage of 2,625, and 2,000 horse-power.

The Harlan and Hollingsworth Shipbuilding Company have just launched a steamer for the Albany Day Line from New York, 300 feet long, 40 feet beam, and 12½ feet deep. Other yards, one at Wilmington, one at Kensington, one at Chester, and one at Camden, have all been engaged on iron and steel vessels of more or less dimensions, and, as a rule, shipbuilding on the Delaware has been prosperous.

The basin dock of the Messrs. Cramp has been constantly engaged, and its capacity is for vessels 425 feet long, 22 feet deep, and on 3 feet of keel block. In connection with this dock is a marine railway of 1,000 tons capacity.

Wages of seamen.—No advances are allowed by the American Shipping Act of 1882, but the law is impracticable and inoperative, as seamen cannot leave port without paying their boarding-house accounts and obtaining a necessary kit. The money is paid in an underhand manner, and charged up against the future earnings of the seaman. The law is based on the principles of the British Merchant Act of 1881, seamen's wages having varied but slightly within recent years. During the American Rebellion (1861 to 1865) they ran as high as 50 dol., while now they are as follows:—

	Per Month.	
To United Kingdom and Continent north of Bayonne	30 dol.	with 40 dol. advance
To Continent south of Bayonne to Gibraltar	20 „	30 „
To the Mediterranean	18 „	30 „
Around Cape Horn or Cape Good of Hope	18 „	50 „

Mates receive 35 dol. to 45 dol. per month; second mates, 25 dol. to 35 dol.; cook and steward, 30 dol. to 40 dol.; ordinary seamen, 5 dol. per month less than A.B.'s. American shipmasters, on coast and foreign, 60 dol. to 120 dol.; average 75 dol. to 80 dol. Coasters, on half share of gross freight, pay all wages and provisions and half of all other expenses and port charges. Owners keep vessels in repair.

The American Shipping Act of 1882, which was taken from the British Act of 1881, making radical changes as to advances and imprisonment for desertion, has given rise to many illegal methods of shipping sailors, and the danger of conniving at such methods, practised at divers Atlantic ports, from time to time come to the surface. Two recent decisions at the Consular court at Shanghai illustrate the practice. In one case the master of a British barque was summoned by a Japanese seaman to show cause why the contract of hiring and service made between them should not be rescinded. Others had applied for similar summonses, but it was arranged that the decision in the first should govern all, as the circumstances were identical. The judge had power under the Act of 1881, if the contract had been entered into under circumstances which appeared to him to be unfair, to cancel it upon equitable terms. The plaintiff proved that he went to the British Consulate in America to be shipped, and his wages were to be 11 dol. or 12 dol. per month, with no advance to be paid, as that is not allowed by the American law. On arrival at Shanghai he discovered that the articles specified that he was to work for 78 days at the rate of 1s. a month, receiving thereafter 2l. 5s. per month. The Japanese seaman had received no advance, never agreed to the 1s. a month stipulation, and desired to be discharged and paid the wages he laboured for. The device of the 1s. a month is the accustomed and palpable evasion of the United States law forbidding the payment of advances to seamen, and the boarding-house keepers doubtless pocketed the complainant's proper wages for the 78 days mentioned in the articles. The master of the vessel pointed out that the articles had endorsed upon them a memorandum signed by the British Consul that the men named therein had signed the articles and fully understood them. This official endorsement, the defendant urged, exonerated him from all responsibility. The judge, however, refused to accept the Consular certificate as final, and proceeded to open the case to further testimony. It was then developed that although the men were told they would be finally discharged in New York, where the voyage was to terminate, the articles mentioned England instead; and to this, also, they strenuously objected. Ultimately the judge held that it was desirable, in the interest of all parties, that the contract should be cancelled, and ordered the seamen to be paid 2l. 5s. per month during the whole period from the signing of the articles until the discharge. The master, who really seems to have been the victim of this evasion of the American Shipping Act, was indignant with the termination of the case, and, it is said, threatened to appeal to the courts in England. The other decision was almost similar, except that the Complainant was an European and the Consular officer not a prominent feature in the defendant's case. The court was satisfied that the master had not complied with the regulation requiring him to explain the articles to the crew, and as the men emphatically denied agreeing to serve for 1s. a month they were all discharged with full wages.

While it is quite true that seamen are not permitted to ship in the American ports without paying for their kit and their boarding bills, it should be borne in mind by master mariners that the only safe course for them to pursue is to take the seaman's personal acknowledgment, over his signature, that his debts were paid by the master, and are to be charged up against him at the end of the voyage. This may be construed by a court of justice in America to be a manifest intent to evade the law, but it is equally manifest that seamen for long voyages cannot be got without their boarding bills being paid and a necessary outfit provided.

Immigration. Emigration to the United States has increased during the 11 months ending November 30, 1886; the number landed were 365,577, or an average of a little more than 1,000 per day, being an increase of 50,000 over the preceding year. England, Wales, Scotland, and Ireland contributed 120,564, being an increase of nearly 20,000. The

UNITED STATES.

German immigration has fallen off 23,000, while the emigration from Austria, Hungary, and Bohemia increased from 24,297 to 37,822; from Russia, 19,195 to 30,197; Italy, from 14,527 to 27,631; and from Sweden, Norway, and Denmark, from 36,572 to 50,373. In the small contributions from France and other countries of Europe there has been little change.

The commissioners of immigration continue to execute the rules respecting the landing of paupers, stowaways, and all passengers presenting an appearance of inability to earn a livelihood in the country, and the ships bringing them out are not permitted to allow them to land, being ordered to return them whence they came.

Demurrage and lay-day scale at Philadelphia. As approved by the Philadelphia maritime exchange on June 6, 1882, and in absence of any special agreement to the contrary, to be understood as governing all grain and petroleum charters made in Philadelphia, to be known as the Philadelphia demurrage and lay-day scale, to take effect July 1, 1882.

For Sailing Vessels loading Grain for Foreign Ports.

For Vessels Registering.	Lay-day for Vessels loading Grain.
From 200 to 250 tons	21 days to load and discharge.
„ 251 300 „	22 „ „ „
„ 301 350 „	23 „ „ „
„ 351 400 „	24 „ „ „
„ 401 450 „	25 „ „ „
„ 451 500 „	26 „ „ „
„ 501 550 „	27 „ „ „
„ 551 600 „	28 „ „ „
„ 601 650 „	29 „ „ „
„ 651 700 „	30 „ „ „
„ 701 800 „	31 „ „ „
„ 801 900 „	32 „ „ „
„ 901 1,000 „	33 „ „ „
„ 1,001 1,100 „	34 „ „ „
„ 1,101 1,200 „	35 „ „ „
„ 1,201 1,300 „	36 „ „ „
„ 1,301 1,400 „	37 „ „ „
„ 1,401 1,500 „	38 „ „ „
„ 1,501 1,600 „	39 „ „ „
„ 1,601 1,700 „	40 „ „ „
„ 1,701 1,800 „	40 „ „ „

For Vessels loading Petroleum for Foreign Ports.

Lay-days.

Vessels of 2,000 to 2,500 barrels capacity to have 10 lay-days.
„ 2,501 3,000 „ „ „ 12 „
„ 3,001 4,000 „ „ „ 14 „
„ 4,001 5,000 „ „ „ 15 „
„ 5,001 6,000 „ „ „ 17 „
„ 6,001 7,000 „ „ „ 20 „
„ 7,001 8,000 „ „ „ 22 „
„ 8,001 2,000 „ „ „ 25 „

Customary despatch for discharging.

Demurrage Scale.—The demurrage on sea-going vessels shall be as follows, viz.:—

For vessels of 200 tons or under, 12 c. per ton.
For vessels over 200 tons and not exceeding 500 tons, 24 dol. for the first 200 tons and 8 c. per ton for each ton additional.

PHILADELPHIA.

For vessels over 500 tons and not exceeding 900 tons, 48 dol. for the first 500 tons and 6 c. per ton for each ton additional.

For vessels over 900 tons 72 dol. for the first 900 tons and 5 c. per ton for each additional ton.

STEAMERS WHEN LOADING GRAIN.

LAY-DAY and Demurrage Scale for Loading and Discharging.

When capacity guaranted is:—

Quarters		Days		Demurrage
6,500 / 7,000	quarters 10 per cent.,	12 days, Sundays excepted,		30*l.* demurrage.
7,500 / 8,000	„	13 „	„	35*l.* „
8,500 / 9,000	„	14 „	,	40*l.* „
9,500 / 10,000	„	15 ,	„	45*l.* „
10,500 / 11,000	„	16 „	„	45*l.* „
11,500 / 12,000	„	17 „	„	50*l.* „
12,500 / 13,000	„	18 „	„	50*l.* „
14,000	„	19 „	„	60*l.* „

Case Petroleum Cargoes.—In absence of any fixed scale of lay-days for loading case petroleum at Philadelphia, it is customary to use the barrel-oil scale; and taking cases at five to the barrel, on the present scale, makes an arrangement satisfactory alike to vessel and shipper.

RATES of Pilotage for Delaware River and Bay.

Feet.	State of Pennsylvania Rates. Act of June 8, 1881.				State of Delaware Rates. Act of April 5, 1881.	
	Inward. If spoken east of five fathom Bank Lightship or north of Hereford Inlet Lighthouse or south of Fenwick's Island Light.	Inward. If spoken inside of five fathom Lightship and outside of line drawn from Cape May Light to Cape Henlopen Light.	Inward. If not spoken until inside of line drawn from Cape May Light to Cape Henlopen Light.	Outward.	Inward.	Outward.
	Dol. c.	Dol. c.	Dol. c.	Dol. c.	Dol. c.	Dol. c.
12	49 37	44 88	40 39	36 00	44 88	44 88
14	64 06	58 24	52 42	42 00	58 24	58 24
15½	70 93	64 48	58 03	46 50	69 75	69 75
17	77 79	70 72	63 65	51 00	76 50	76 50
18	82 37	74 88	67 39	54 00	81 00	81 00
19	86 94	79 04	71 14	57 00	95 00	95 00
20	91 52	83 20	74 88	60 00	100 00	100 00
21	96 10	87 36	78 62	63 00	115 50	115 50
22	100 67	91 52	82 37	66 00	121 00	121 00
23	105 25	95 68	86 11	69 00	126 50	126 50
24	109 82	99 84	89 86	72 00	132 00	132 00
25	114 40	104 00	93 60	75 00	137 50	137 50
26	118 98	108 16	97 34	78 00	143 00	143 00
26½	121 26	110 24	99 22	79 50	145 75	145 75
27	123 55	112 32	101 09	81 00	148 50	148 50

Note.—An extra rate of 10 dol. is charged under the law of the State of Delaware for winter pilotage between November 1 and April 1.

During the past year trade has gradually increased in firmness, and **Trade and commerce.**

appears to be at the present writing on a better basis than it was one year ago. Substantial evidence of this is shown by the enlarged business in wheat at this and other shipping ports. The receipts of wheat have increased from 4,140,012 bushels in 1885 to a total of 6,289,611 bushels in 1886. This improvement is a fair percentage of the exportation of wheat from the country at large, which can approximately be said to have doubled what it was in 1885. The change for the better is due to less favourable crop conditions in other countries, and to the comparative cheapness of grain throughout the world. The prices averaged lower in this country than they did in 1885, although a little higher than in 1884. The inspection system in this port and the range of prices in this market, especially for the higher grades of wheat, have compared favourably with that of other markets and the high reputation of Philadelphia cargoes in European markets has been unimpaired throughout the year. The exports of corn (maize), an inconsiderable percentage of the total yield, show a market falling-off, and Philadelphia has her full share of the general shrinkage of business in this cereal by a decline from 6,115,051 bushels cleared from the docks in 1885 to a total of less than 2,000,000 bushels in 1886. This decline is relatively greater here than at other ports, being confined, however, to the export trade; the local business being about the same as in recent years past. The changes in other cereals are comparatively unimportant. The chief feature is that the grain trade does not keep pace with the growth of other commercial interests of the port, nor does it equal the facilities of the port for foreign shipments. Philadelphia's geographical position and terminal facilities should swell the grain shipments to triple their present bulk. The receipts of flour have declined from 1,369,732 barrels in 1885 to 931,758 barrels in 1886. This decline is of slight significance as to any indication of decline in the flour trade. The following statement shows the exports of wheat and corn from the Atlantic ports in divers years, with the percentages from each port:—

Exports of Wheat and Corn for the Years 1875, 1880, 1885, and 1886.

Ports.	Montreal. Bushels.	Per cent.	Portland. Bushels.	Per cent.	Boston. Bushels.	Per cent.	New York. Bushels.	Per cent.	Philadelphia. Bushels.	Per cent.	Baltimore. Bushels.	Per cent.	New Orleans. Bushels.	Per cent.	Total.
1875.	... ...	... ...	... ...	... ...	... ...	... ...	25,733,447 W. 12,425,177 C.	... ...	3,909,878 W. 4,532,038 C.	... ...	2,106,734 W. 6,566,744 C.	... ...	... ...	... ...	... ...
Total exports	8,300,300	12·4	550,789	0·8	2,316,375	3·4	38,158,624	56·9	7,441,916	11·4	8,673,478	12·9	1,475,640	2·2	67,107,122
1880.	8,221,895 W. 7,065,745 C.	5·6 8·2	1,041,375 W. 1,329,811 C.	0·9 1·5	11,263,798 W. 3,275,665 C.	7·6 3·8	74,863,083 W. 34,646,089 C.	50·5 40·1	11,312,590 W. 16,579,644 C.	7·7 19·2	34,923,152 W. 14,604,364 C.	23·6 16·9	5,505,020 W. 8,855,579 C.	4·1 10·3	147,130,913 W. 86,356,897 C.
Total exports	15,287,640	6·5	2,371,186	1·0	14,539,463	6·3	109,509,172	46·9	27,892,234	11·9	49,527,516	26·2	14,360,599	6·2	233,487,810
1885.	3,372,160 W. 1,945,898 C.	10·5 3·2	854,538 W. 458,581 C.	2·6 0·7	1,680,022 W. 3,778,823 C.	5·2 6·2	17,111,294 W. 27,214,189 C.	53·7 44·8	3,532,192 W. 5,929,244 C.	11·1 9·7	4,581,261 W. 14,048,287 C.	14·4 23·1	678,283 W. 7,302,910 C.	2·1 12·0	31,809,750 W. 60,677,927 C.
Total exports	5,318,058	5·7	1,313,119	1·4	5,458,845	5·9	44,325,483	47·9	9,461,436	10·1	18,629,548	20·1	7,981,193	8·6	92,487,677
1886.	5,885,662 W. 3,910,209 C.	... ...	960,882 W. 411,555 C.	... ...	2,376,298 W. 3,025,673 C.	... ...	32,090,610 W. 20,996,705 C.	... ...	6,079,146 W. 1,857,353 C.	... ...	10,475,395 W. 13,188,229 C.	... ...	1,041,141 W. 7,896,339 C.	... ...	... ...
Total exports	9,795,871	...	1,372,437	...	5,401,971	...	53,087,315	...	7,936,499	...	23,613,624	...	8,937,480	...	110,145,294

UNITED STATES.

The sugar and molasses trade.

The importations of sugar at Philadelphia were :—

	Hogsheads.	Tierces.	Boxes.	Bags.	Tons.
1875	50,016	15,250	..	23,969	34,306
1880	79,494	..	653	2,058	48,096
1885	99,285	..	1,210	475,551	112,615
1886	83,383	..	No return	742,057	112,927

The importations of molasses were :—

	Hogsheads.	Gallons.
1875	108,467	14,097,092
1880	97,306	12,985,830
1885	114,023	15,514,455

The total consumption of sugar in the United States amounted to 1,367,503 tons in 1886 and 1,254,116 tons in 1885. The State of Louisiana crop was 127,958 tons, the Texas and other Southern States and domestic molasses sugar 77,425 tons for the year 1886. The prices of sugar in 1885 were—highest $5\frac{9}{16}$ c., lowest $4\frac{9}{16}$ c., average 5·02 c., and average in bond 3·06 c. In 1886 they were—highest $5\frac{9}{16}$ c., lowest $4\frac{9}{16}$ c., average 4·88 c., and average in bond $2\frac{92}{100}$ c. Average price for 42 years $4\frac{705}{1000}$ c.

RECEIPTS of Produce.

	1885.	1886.
Flour	1,369,732	1,171,758
Wheat	4,140,012	6,643,100
Corn	8,175,610	3,998,881
Oats	4,003,920	3,866,000
Rye	48,000	45,000
Barley	16,343	1,489,100
Clover seed	16,343	12,175
Flax seed	198,127	222,918
Timothy seed	15,714	11,827
Lard	68,239	65,688
Butter	240,805	176,759
High wines	40,684	39,437
Whiskey	39,079	52,042
Eggs	256,087	229,202
Wool	293,921	178,170
Cotton	129,875	136,896
Dressed hogs	44,649	52,775

NUMBER of Cattle Received and Sold in Philadelphia.

	Hogs.	Sheep.
1885	326,456	616,573
1886	333,849	583,579

PHILADELPHIA.

The wool market was smaller in volume than in 1885, owing largely to a shortage of the domestic clip, and the marketing of a larger quantity in the west. Philadelphia's sales showed a falling-off of 19,000,000 lbs., while the receipts were 25,000,000 dol. less than in 1885. The prices, however, advanced 10 to 15 per cent., which rendered the trade prosperous to those engaged in it. Manufacturers find it difficult to get enhanced prices for their products proportionate to the rise in wool, still the prospects continue favourable to trade in the raw material for the year 1887.

The Merchants' Fund. This organisation for the relief of indigent and aged merchants, who have encountered misfortunes in trade, is in a prosperous condition, and continues to increase its resources by donations and bequests. Its invested funds run well towards 100,000*l.* sterling, and the silent, publicly unknown amount of continuous assistance rendered to merchants formerly in affluence, who have been ruined in their declining years, ranks it as one of the most interesting private charities in the city. The past year has recorded the death of three useful members—John Welsh, John D. Taylor, and Christian J. Hoffman. Mr. Welsh was a few years ago United States Minister to the Court of St. James's, Mr. Taylor was a merchant and railway officer of great influence, and Mr. Hoffman a successful merchant in the grain trade, who devoted much of his time and ability to the interests of the Merchants' Fund. Another death, that of George L. Oliver, originally from London, who left a large residuary estate to the fund, was also announced. No greater misfortune can be experienced than that of families suddenly falling from affluence to abject poverty, and this fund was organised to have the drop as gentle as possible.

The iron and steel trade. The pig-iron production continues to increase in the United States, amounting to 6,366,688 net tons in 1886, while for 1885 the production in net tons was 4,529,869, showing the increase for 1886 to be over 40 per cent. In Pennsylvania the output in 1886 was 283,859 tons, while the State of Tennessee produced a total of 200,526 tons, and Virginia a total production of 200,526 tons. The iron and steel industries have been especially active throughout the year 1886, and the production of pig iron, Bessemer steel and steel rails, open-hearth steel, structural steel and iron, and some other products has largely exceeded that of any previous year. For the whole country the production has been as follows:—

Products.	1885.	1886.
	Gross Tons.	Gross Tons.
Pig-iron	4,044,526	5,600,000
Bessemer steel ingots	1,519,430	2,000,000
Bessemer steel rails	959,471	1,500,000
Open-hearth steel	133,375	200,000

Iron ore was produced in 1886 to the extent of, say, 10,000,000 tons, and the importation 1,000,000 tons. The stock of pig-iron in this country at the close of the year 1886 was probably no larger than at the close of 1885, when they amounted to 371,885 tons, which was a very small surplus when the pig-iron wants of the country are considered.

During 1886 this country built over 7,000 miles of new railroad, against 3,131 miles reported for 1885. This great increase in railroad building in 1886 contributed largely to the improvements of the iron and steel industries.

UNITED STATES.

The general business outlook for 1887 is at the present writing very favourable, and for the iron and steel industries it is especially so.

Railroad building promises to be even more active in 1887 than in 1886.

The present price for pig-iron and steel rails have only recently been established, and in the case of steel rails large contracts for delivery in 1887 have been made at 34 dol. (7l. 0s. 6d.) to 35 dol. (7l. 5s. 5d.).

The importations of iron and steel during 1886 have been very heavy and much in excess of those of 1885. In 1886 there were about 400,000 tons of pig-iron, about 75,000 tons of old iron, over 100,000 tons of steel blooms and billets, nearly 250,000 tons of tin plates, fully 125,000 tons of wire rods, and about 50,000 tons of steel rails. Total importations of iron and steel in the United States for the year 1886 were at least 1,000,000 tons.

Bessemer steel production. Great as was the increase in the production of American pig-iron during the year 1886, the relative increase in the Bessemer steel output was still greater. The production of Bessemer steel ingots in the United States for the year 1886 was 2,541,493 net tons, showing an increase of 839,731 net tons over the production of 1,701,762 net tons in 1885. The year 1885 largely exceeded that of any previous year, and the production of 1886 was 49 per cent. larger than that of 1885.

Bessemer steel rails produced in 1886:—

	Net tons.
Pennsylvania	1,097,943
Illinois	430,975
All other States	220,981
Total	1,749,899

It is 20 years since Bessemer steel was first made in this country as a commercial product, and now the production of steel in the United States exceeds that of the mother country, the growth having been marvellous. In 1867 the total product was 2,277 gross tons, while now the production is over 2,500,000 tons open-hearth steel.

The production of open-hearth steel in 1886 in the United States was 245,606 net tons, or 219,291 gross tons,* an increase of 64 per cent. upon the production of 1885, which was 149,381 net tons. The production of 1886 was the largest on record. There were six new plants located in Pennsylvania, one in Ohio, and two in Indiana. The States of New Hampshire, Massachusetts, New York, New Jersey, Illinois, and California have open-hearth plants, and the total number in operation in the whole country is 31 old and eight new plants above referred to. Pennsylvania's share of the production was over 70 per cent. of the whole. The quantity of open-hearth casting was not materially larger than in previous years, and was relatively very small. The quantity of open-hearth steel rails produced in 1886 by open-hearth works was also very small, amounting to only 5,255 net tons, which were made in Pennsylvania and California. Of the whole quantity, 2,518 net tons were steel rails. The open-hearth branch of the steel industry has made slow progress during the 18 years which have elapsed since the first American open-hearth steel in this country at Trenton, New Jersey, in 1868. During the last year, however, the manufacture of open-hearth steel in this country received a very decided impetus, and the prospects are that it will continue throughout 1887.

* Gross ton weighs 2,240 lbs., net ton 2,000.

PHILADELPHIA.

New process for hardening and tempering steel.

A drill made by this process penetrated in 40 minutes a steel safe plate warranted to resist any burglar drill for 12 hours. A penknife tempered by the same process cut the stem of a steel key readily, and with the same blade the inventor shaved the hairs from his arm. It is claimed that this tempering process is conducted without expense or skilled labour. The same inventor has also a process for converting iron into steel at small expense, and claims to make steel so elastic and hard as to turn a ball fired from the heaviest gun ever constructed. The invention is a secret, is being patented, and a company forming to introduce it. These extraordinary claims have yet to be proven to the satisfaction of the trade.

Railways.

The railway mileage of the States composing this Consular district is as follows:—

	Miles.
Pennsylvania	7,817
Ohio	7,403
Indiana	5,700
Michigan	5,468
Total for the United States	56,122
In 1885 it was	53,592

The railways sold under foreclosure and transferred to new ownership throughout the United States were 45 in number, of 7,687 mileage, funded debt 34,300,000*l*., and capital stock 75,000,000*l*. Receiverships in 1886 were appointed for 13 roads, with a mileage of 1,799 miles, funded debt of 79,846,200*l*., and capital stock of 6,223,060*l*.

The inter-State commerce law, recently passed by Congress, will make great changes in railway traffic and passenger travel from State to State; freights and passenger fares will be regulated on a permanent and equable basis, the issuing of free passes prohibited, and "pools" and combinations illegal. Radical changes are to go into effect, and it remains to be seen whether the law will be a public benefit or a hamper to the channels of trade.

Coal.

The production of bituminous coal in the United States is double that of anthracite, but it is distributed over a large number of States and territories. The mining of anthracite coal maintains a moderate but continuous increase from year to year, while that of bituminous varies greatly, due chiefly to the different methods of mining and marketing. Bituminous coal, common in so many States and territories, is mined as wanted, generally for industrial purposes.

The production of bituminous coal in this Consular district is—

	1886.	1885.
	Tons.	Tons.
Pennsylvania	29,000,000	25,000,000
Ohio	9,000,000	6,750,000
Indiana	3,000,000	1,300,000
Michigan	150,000	150,000
	41,150,000	34,200,000
All other States and territories	33,340,000	31,408,246
Grand total	74,490,000	65,608,246

The marked increase in production is found in the States of Pennsylvania and Indiana—the former with a gain for 1886 over 1885 of 4,000,000 tons, and the latter of 1,700,000 tons. Pennsylvania's

UNITED STATES.

gain is striking when it is considered that the increased production and extended use of natural gas as an industrial and illuminating fuel are so marked.

The total annual production of bituminous coal in the United States as compared with anthracite, in long tons (2,282 lbs.), is reported as follows:—

	Bituminous.	Anthracite.	Total.
	Tons.	Tons.	Tons.
1880	37,138,000	24,400,000	62,588,000
1882	51,523,000	31,550,000	83,073,000
1884	60,000,000	33,319,000	93,319,000
1885	58,300,000	34,258,000	92,558,000
1886	66,200,000	34,814,000	101,014,000

The bituminous coal is quoted in long tons in order to permit addition with totals of anthracite coal produced. The latter are made to include the total quantities of coal mined and used in the years noted, instead of the aggregate "shipped," as has been customary.

Anthracite coal.

The product of the anthracite mines in Pennsylvania for the year 1886 was 32,136,000 tons, while for the year 1885 it was 31,623,529 tons. The trade has been very brisk, and at the present writing it may be said as unprecedented so far as the wholesale trade is concerned. The production of the year 1886 was the largest on record. The coal tonnage for the year 1886 by the Pennsylvania railroad, Belvidere division, was 1,702,158 tons, while in 1885 it was 1,740,527 tons; by the same company over main line and branches anthracite and semi-bituminous 11,373,272 tons, with a tonnage of 3,520,630 in coke; by the Lehigh Valley railroad 6,621,852 tons for 1886 and in 1885 it was 6,251,593 tons; by the Philadelphia and Reading railroad 13,047,610 tons in 1886, and for 1885 it was 12,540,214 tons; and by the Huntingdon and Broad Top Mountains 651,969 tons for 1886. The Cumberland Valley coal trade shows a production of 2,446,765 tons for the year 1886.

Petroleum.

There was a marked increase in the production of petroleum in the year 1886, yet a steady decline in all the old reliable districts; a large increase in field operations, a material increase in domestic and foreign consumption, and necessarily a larger export of crude as well as refined oil than has ever been recorded in the history of the trade.

In production the average daily runs were as follows:—

In 1882	..	..	..	..	..	..	87,094
1883	..	..	..	..	..	..	66,811
1884	..	..	..	..	..	..	64,472

In 1885 they fell to 58,156 barrels; a falling-off within that period of nearly 30,000 barrels. In 1886 the average daily run for the year was 68,358 barrels.

In consequence of five new pools being successfully struck in the early part of the year, unusual activity was shown in drilling for both natural gas and coal oil. New territory was bored, generally ending in absolute failure. At Lima, Ohio, 4,000 barrels per day have been produced, but the quality is poor, worth only about 35 c. (1s. 6d.) per barrel. This oil resembles the Canada product, coming through the same sandstone, and having even a worse odour than the Canada product. It is used almost entirely as fuel, and for this purpose it is being utilised.

The grave features of the American oil production is that the Old Bradford (Pennsylvania) district, long regarded as the mainstay of the industry, where the production in one day, August 31, 1881, reached 81,000 barrels, has touched its highest output, as it now flows only 25,000 barrels per day. The Alleghany (Pennsylvania) district, showing in 1882 24,000 barrels per day, now figures but 5,000 barrels per day. These two districts have been the chief producers, and their rapid decline causes apprehension, and seems to foreshadow a further general decrease in the production so far as the present available sources of supply are concerned. In 1885 the runs produced 21,163,847 gallons, a daily average of 57,983 gallons. In 1886 they increased to 25,914,312, or a daily average of 68,258 gallons. The consumption of this important staple continues on the increase: as an illuminator it is unsurpassed by any other oil, and its fields of usefulness continue to expand. The domestic consumption was at least 8 per cent. greater in 1886 than it was in 1885. The exports for the year 1886 show an increase of 5 per cent. Russian oil is said to be a competitor, but for illuminating purposes the Pennsylvania product is without competition. The exports from this district show an increase in 1886 over the previous year, especially to the East Indies, India and Siam, and South America; but the shipment to China and Japan have fallen off. Holland, Norway, and Sweden have increased their consumption, while Great Britain, Germany, Denmark, and Austria have decreased.

PRICES of Petroleum.

Average Prices in—	Per Barrel.
	Dollars.
1863	3·15
1865	6·59
1870	3·84
1874	1·15
1879	·85$\frac{7}{8}$
1882	·78$\frac{1}{2}$
1885	·88$\frac{03}{100}$
1886	·71$\frac{37}{100}$

Exports from all ports in the United States to Great Britain, Germany, Norway and Sweden, Russia and Finland, Denmark, Belgium, Holland, Spain, Portugal and Azores, Gibraltar and Malta, Italy, Austria, Greece, Turkey in Europe, Turkey in Asia, Arabia, India and Siam, China and Japan, East Indies, Africa, Australia, New Zealand, Sandwich Islands, South America, Central America, Mexico, British North American colonies, Cuba, British West Indies, and British Guiana, &c., show a total of—

	Refined Gallons.	Crude Gallons.
1886	339,835,154	46,246,278
1885	314,088,132	48,599,038
1884	312,914,992	61,982,099

For the seven months ending January 31, 1887, the value of the exports from the United States of mineral oils fell off 580,000*l*., com-

UNITED STATES.

Natural gas.

pared with the same period ending in 1886, while the quantity had increased from 342,935,649 gallons to 356,643,367 gallons.

The use of natural gas for illuminating and manfacturing purposes continues to expand. Iron, glass, and steel-making industries in certain sections have adopted its use, as if the supply were to continue indefinitely. The results show great economy in one of the important items of manufacturing expense and a large impetus to industrial activity in the gas-favoured regions of Pennsylvania. For Pittsburgh, especially, the discovery has been a most timely and beneficial one, for without it the iron industries would have seriously felt the competition of the Southern States of Georgia and Alabama. In domestic use, not only illuminating but all cooking is done by it. Its great danger lies in the fact that it is odourless, leaks in pipes (possible at all times), and cannot be discovered by the sense of smell. Many explosions and loss of life have resulted in consequence. Otherwise, for domestic use, it is without a peer—no smoke, no dust, intense heat obtained in a minute and tempered down in a second. Should the supply give out, the skill of man will surely follow nature in this particular, and some gaseous material will be brought forth as a substitute for coal and gas, both in manufacturing and domestic use, and become the staple for fuel, as it is now for artificial light.

Agriculture.

In Pennsylvania the agricultural balance sheet for 1885 and 1886 is quite unfavourable to the farmer, and the investment of floating capital, as a means of profit, in farm lands are not enticing. Prices have been low, and in many districts the crops have been below the average. The margin between the market prices and the cost of the crop has been small. The calculation as an average over several years past shows that a bushel of wheat cannot be produced (summarising the whole State), after paying interest upon capital, taxes, and other fixed rates, in Pennsylvania, for less than 85 c. (3s. $6\frac{1}{2}d$.), and the greater portion of the year's crop was sold for 90 to 95 c. This becomes a losing investment for the Pennsylvania farmer. The Western States, with their lower-priced lands and railway facilities to the seaboard, are, doubtless, the main cause. The product of Pennsylvania land, costing 20l. an acre, commands very little more at the points of shipment to markets, both domestic and foreign, than the product of western land at 5l. per acre.

Wheat.—The maximum of this crop is 30 bushels per acre, yet the average for the whole State is little, if any, over 9 bushels per acre. For 1885 the wheat crop is recorded as equal to 13,500,000 bushels, produced from 1,500,000 acres, or at the average rate of 9 bushels to the acre. The future out-look for this crop is not encouraging. The foreign market is being cut off by the product of India, where the cost of producing a bushel of wheat is considerably lower than it is in the United States, and it is not far in the future when the wheat of the Western States of America will be placed in the same position as to wheat from India, as the Eastern States now are as to wheat from the West.

The corn (maize) crop in 1885 was about 5 per cent. less than the average of the past 10 years in Pennsylvania, taking the average as 40,750,000 bushels; the yield for 1885 being 38,750,000 bushels on an acreage of 1,275,000 bushels, being an average yield of $33\frac{1}{3}$ bushels to the acre.

The oat crop in Pennsylvania is but slightly below the corn crop in acreage, showing 1,150,000 acres, with a yield of 29 bushels per acre, equal to 33,350,000 bushels for 1885, which is about 400,000 bushels below the average of the past 10 years. A dry season was the chief cause of this falling-off, the crop being considerably below the standard in weight and quality.

Potatoes in Pennsylvania have also fallen off in the yield, due to divers local causes and mutations of the season, yielding not more than 75 per cent. of the average crop for the past 10 years.

Ohio is the most important agricultural State in the Union, her wheat and corn crop averaging larger per acre than any other State. In 1884 the wheat crop was 36,396,119 bushels, an average of 14·4 bushels to the acre, and in 1886 it was 40,566,868 bushels, equal to 15·2 bushels per acre. The corn crop in 1885 was 112,192,744 bushels, an average of 39 bushels per acre. The number of horses and cattle in the State assessed for taxation in 1885 were: Horses 724,975, value 44,501,695 dol. (8,900,000*l*.); cattle 1,625,573, value 5,900,000*l*.; mules 24,302, value 301,000*l*.; sheep 4,928,332, value 1,869,160*l*.; hogs 1,603,261, value 990,000*l*. Wine products in 1885, 439,610 gallons; acres of vineyards, 17,292; sorghum in acres, 12,119; products, sugar, 3,496 lbs.; syrup, 1,113,140 gallons; maple in pounds of sugar, 1,967,467; in gallons of syrup, 801,610; and number of trees tapped, 3,046,561. In the year 1885 the number of hogs dying from disease was 174,114, valued at 23,245*l*.; sheep 176,748, value 66,430*l*.; cattle 21,618, value 92,161*l*.; horses 13,184, value 197,266*l*. The wool product was 22,081,552 lbs., and the number of milch cows in the State 595,524. The total number of acres under cultivation 20,431,440, and the number lying waste 444,843 acres. Of butter product, 51,769,819 lbs.; milk, 14,605,551 gallons; tobacco, 33,113,822 lbs.; cheese, 18,867,363 lbs.; potatoes, 10,214,343 bushels; flax, in pounds of fibre, 3,309,743; clover seed, 100,967 bushels; clover hay, 442,027 tons; meadow hay, 2,266,925 tons; barley, 351,616 bushels; oats, 26,599,264 bushels, averaging 29·28 per acre; buckwheat 308,431 bushels; and rye, 579,082 bushels.

Michigan. Agriculture in the State of Michigan, as per last returns, has a cultivation of 36,443,346 acres, the number of acres in farms being 14,852,226, or nearly 40 per cent. of the total land area of the State. The total number of farms returned is 159,605. The area in wheat is 1,709,535 acres, and the average yield of winter wheat per acre is 15 bushels, and of spring wheat 13 bushels. In corn (maize) there are 919,656 acres, with a yield of 32,461,452 bushels; oats were produced on 650,928 acres, with a yield of 21,324,130 bushels, averaging per acre $32\frac{3}{4}$ bushels. In barley there were 46,200 acres, yielding 849,757 bushels, averaging $18\frac{1}{2}$ bushels per acre. Hay was reaped from 1,035,033 acres, giving 1,422,928 tons, an average of $1\frac{1}{3}$ tons per acre. Sheep sheared numbered 2,724,789, yielding 15,337,249 lbs. of wool, or $5\frac{64}{100}$ per head.

Oleo-margarine. Most of the States have passed laws either prohibiting the manufacture of or regulating the marketing of oleomargarine. Doubtless the manufacture of the product will increase, but the laws will protect the public from dishonest dealers, substituting the product for genuine butter, and prevent the manufacturers using unhealthy and deleterious compounds in their processes of manufacture.

Pleuro-pneumonia. The alarming spread of this cattle disease, especially in the States of New York, Ohio, Kentucky, Illinois, and others, has attracted universal attention to the means of suppressing it in the respective districts where it has already gained more or less of a foothold. The Governor of Indiana issued a proclamation prohibiting the importation of cattle from other States except under stringent regulations. A disease broke out in certain districts of that State last year, which was at first pronounced pleuro-pneumonia, but subsequent examinations declared it to be "verminous bronchitis," known among cattle-breeders as "hoose," which principally affects young cattle, and that it is curable and not contagious.

UNITED STATES.

Many States of the Union have enacted laws bearing upon the subject, and forbidding importation from adjoining States within their borders; but the results, although largely useful, have not been satisfactory, and the only sure hope for extirpation of all contagious diseases among cattle in this country is a general law applying to all the States and territories. The committee of the Cattle Growers' Association of the United States introduced a Bill in Congress appropriating 200,000*l.* for the suppression of this disease throughout the Union, and appealed to the country at large to aid in its passage, alleging that the only proper course now to take is to rid the entire country of a disease which the various States, individually, have signally failed to keep from invading their borders from time to time. At the rate pleuro-pneumonia is at present extending from State to State, westward and southward, the existence of the cattle-growing industry is threatened with annihilation. The local quarantines between the several States have proved practically of little avail, and by interfering with the inter-State traffic have in a measure paralysed the cattle trade, and the system is shown to be ruinous alike to the breeder, feeder, and shipper. The Bill was strongly supported by all interested and fully acquainted with the necessity of its passage. In the United States there are over 45,000,000 head of cattle, valued at 240,000,000*l.*, an industry well deserving the fostering care of the National Government. Still by local prejudices and faction jealousies the Bill was not passed, and, until another Congress at least, no national aid is to be given to the suppression of pleuro-pneumonia in the United States.

An experiment is being tried in Chicago, under the auspices of Dr. J. W. Gadsden, M.R.C.V.S., of this city—a veterinary surgeon well known in London—to prove that the disease pleuro-pneumonia can only be communicated by actual contact with living diseased animals. After the "Shufeldt distilleries," where the disease ravaged a few months ago, had been thoroughly fumigated and cleaned out, and all neighbouring cattle removed from the adjacent premises, 894 western steers, direct from the plains, where, as yet, no pleuro-pneumonia exists, were driven in to remain for three months. Should Dr. Gadsden be successful in this highly interesting test case, he will have done the cattle interests in this country a great and invaluable service by proving that the only sure system of stamping out the disease is to slaughter every animal found to be affected with it.

Up to the present writing no symptoms of disease have appeared, and the three months having expired, it only remains for examination of the lungs when the animals are slaughtered for market to prove the doctor's case, which, if no trace of the disease can be found, will have been effectually done.

Laws. A Bill defining the rights, powers, and liabilities of married women has been introduced into the Pennsylvania Legislature, and doubtless will become law. It aims at radical changes in the law touching the rights of married persons, especially married women, relieving them of the trammels—sometimes called disabilities or privileges—which, while all right in primitive times, are now obstacles in the way of business and the protection of personal rights. The Bill permits married women to deal with their property, make deeds and contracts, and sue and be sued without joining their husbands, and without resorting to the courts to be declared *femme sole* traders. This accords with the law in England, New York, Connecticut, and other States: real estate, being now treated as a commodity, is bought and sold with almost as much frequency as stocks. It is alleged to be a hindrance upon trade to require that a man's wife should have to sign a transfer, and be called before a magistrate to declare that she signed without compulsion. On the other hand, the law that a married woman's deed without the signature of her husband is void, although the fact that she is married is not known, has served its purpose and ought to be changed. It is positively dishonest to declare such a deed invalid, and let her keep the property and the money too.

A married woman's earnings during her marriage under the present law belong to her husband, and his creditors may take them all away from her. An instance occurred in Washington of a coloured woman escaping the loss of her home by foreclosure for the husband's debts, by pleading that she and her husband were slaves when they were married; and as marriage between slaves was illegal before the abolition of slavery, the marriage ceremony between them was null and void. She saved her property at the expense of her children, who thus were declared illegitimate. Such a law should be changed. The new law will give the husband the same interest in his wife's estate after her death as she has in his: at present he has a greater.

Strikes during the present winter have been rife throughout the country, and have done incalculable injury to the channels of trade and to the strikers themselves. In many sections distress to the verge of starvation has visited large communities of working people. At this present writing (January, 1887) 40,000 steamship workers in New York went off the docks at the dictate of the Unions of the Knights of Labour, to which they belong, thus forcing an almost entire suspension of the marine commerce of that metropolis. All ocean vessels were delayed. A fleet of ships are stopped from sailing, some because they have no coal and others because they have no cargo. In all districts this first month of the year is marked by a serious struggle between employer and employed. Such a strike as the coal handlers would be a grave event at any time, but coming at a season of the year when fuel is a prime necessity it has an added weight. It has assumed formidable proportions, also, having involved other working men, either by sympathy or necessity, in different branches of labour. Ocean steamers have been stopped, factories and mines shut down, and suffering, through lack of fuel, brought to many homes. With 50,000 working men idle, some solution must be arrived at before any great length of time. Thus far these strikes have been attended with little or no violence. A number of innocent Poles were attacked at Hoboken, New Jersey, in a cowardly manner, but the influence and entire power of the community are averse to such outrages. The coal companies, however, are not entirely blameless, having never shown an unwillingness to take advantage of people's needs, or to enforce their rights to the utmost limit. The statements put forth by the companies are disingenuous, in representing that the men earn, by hourly wages, fair wages, because it is well known that the labour is not continuous, many weeks throughout the year being spent without labour. Strikes are now prevailing at New York, Pensacola. In Philadelphia the ingrain carpet trade is threatened with a strike of 6,000 hands and a pay roll of 50,000 dol. a week, the average wages reaching 8 dol. per week. The weavers demand an advance of $\frac{1}{2}$ c. per yard; their present pay averages $5\frac{1}{4}$ c. per yard. The manufacturers claim that their trades cannot stand this claim for higher wages, as their New England competitors in the trades pay less rates, and that the price of raw material has gone up at least 10 per cent., woollen yarns being fully that much higher than they were last year. The present strike of the longshoremen in New York seems to be a mystery, not only to the public, but to most of the strikers themselves. The ringleaders know the object of the strike, but the workers only know that they have been ordered out, and that personally each man has no grievance. The employers have been paying full wages, and the employés have been fully satisfied. Other districts of labour are seriously affected, either by assessment for the support of the strikers or by orders to " go out." Such a system cannot and should not last long. The labour meetings have gone too far. The doctrine that " we propose that our organisation shall go to that point where it will dominate all the institutions of the country" will prove fatal to all organised strikes in the United States. To terrorise and subjugate capital, to dominate over Government, religion, and law will never succeed with the people of the Anglo-Saxon race. The strikes, so numerous throughout different sections of the country in the past year, have been failures to the strikers, and the physical resistance to the employment of outside labour—in many instances ending in bloodshed—has so alarmed capital that special officers are employed to protect property and the lives of new workmen. This phase in American labour strikes is known as the "Pinkerton soldiery:" it is an unlimited and dangerous force, supported by capital, well paid and well armed, and is called forth by the alleged reason that the governors, sheriffs, and mayors have political causes for not using the militia, police, and posse to suppress disorder and to protect property. All efforts by labour to dictate on what bases commercial and manufacturing companies and other employers shall conduct their business, or, failing in that, to reduce law to lawlessness or to disorder, government to anarchy, and society to chaos, must surely fail, as capital, unlimited in its powers for self-preservation, can call out these Pinkerton men with their revolvers and muskets.

The best estimates given present the number of men on strike during January, 1887, at 78,000, as compared with 47,200 in January, 1886: 9,900 have struck since January 31, 1887, making the comparison 87,900 men on strike since January 1, 1887. In addition to these figures 16,300 workers in factories, mills, and elsewhere are idle in consequence of the scarcity of coal, or because of lack of work caused by strikes of others.

Textiles.

The various channels of trade among the textiles at Philadelphia have been prosperous during the year 1886. The labour agitations had a depressing effect in the early part of the year for a time. A period of confidence and increased demand followed, continuing over the year up to the present writing. Failures became less frequent, credit on a sounder basis, and payments more regularly met. The retail traders report the largest Christmas business known for years. Some uncertainties existed in the early part of the year on account of the rapid devolopment of the labour movement, which seemed to threaten almost a revolution. The outlook for the year 1887 is likely to continue in this current of prosperity for the retail dealers in textiles; and, unless serious and long-continued labour agitations arise to frighten off capital from contemplated enterprises, the general trade will be very large. The hosiery and "notion" dealers have had a steady trade, regular, and in some grades higher prices. The demand for "Jerseys" increased enormously during the year 1886, and seven-eights of all made in the United States are from Philadelphia looms. There is absolutely no surplus to be carried over to 1887, as accumulated stocks were taken up before the demands, occasioned by the strikes in the early part of the year, commenced. Failures in this line of trade have also been less frequent and for smaller amounts than for many years back. There were marked advances in the prices of underwear, chiefly due, perhaps, to the strikes in New York; and the sharp advance in the price of wool in Europe had the effect of adding to the rise of all woollen goods in America. The market for knit goods was short for some portion of the year owing to the strikes, but it soon rallied to a healthy condition. The rapid strides made in the iron trade seem to have revived all textile productions, and all districts tributary to Philadelphia felt, and continue to feel, its influence. Carpets, especially the tapestries, have glutted the market and suffered a reduction of 2½ to 4 per cent. in price. What is known as body Brussels and ingrain carpets, however, have been in constant demand, and have advanced on an average of about 3 per cent. All stocks became exhausted towards the close of 1886, and manufacturers are now running to fill positive orders.

The one question in the metropolis of Philadelphia is " protection." With it prosperity abounds; without it mills would necessarily succumb to English superiority and stability. The woollens, tapestries, and cloths—productions that have grown to fabulous dimensions—are built on the skill and industry of Bradford, Leeds, and Manchester emigration; an emigration that has developed the factories in this district, enhanced the capital, and flooded the market with cheap but good productions. In the line of stockings, for instance, not only large factories but small tenement houses in the factory districts of Philadelphia run machines for their production. Women and children in their humble homes turn out, with the improved and cheap machinery, millions of pairs of cotton and woollen stockings, an output requiring little skill and trifling labour. The production is sold cheap, and an improvident people recklessly consume it. Again, it is to be marked that in a home market of 60,000,000 of people variety and cheapness are great factors. This is especially exemplified in the case of carpets, rugs, and tapestries. These productions, by emigrated English skill and labour, are bright in colours, fresh in designs, and sufficiently under price, compared with the imported article, to attract the popular eye and monopolise the national market. Rugs in imitation of the finest Smyrnas are put out for a few shillings, and the homes of working men are adorned with them. Tapestry hangings are taking the place of swinging doors between rooms in ordinary houses, while carpets and oilcloths are purchased by housekeepers, not because they are durable, but because they are novel and fresh.

The wealthy classes of this country take the English productions, because the higher grades of them are superior in texture, durability, and colour. Having fought the battle of life they are not fond of change. Hence these grades of textile manufactures, especially cloths for men's clothing, are not so materially interfered with.

The productions of silk fringes, chenille curtains, table covers, &c., are growing into vast proportions and are attractive in designs. A grade of worsted dress goods for women's wear, called "Henriettas," is being manufactured in great bulk, and reserved for the dyes until the season opens, when the dyeing in a number of popular tints, reported from Paris and London, is done as the orders of the wholesale trade demand. This dyeing is finished within 10 or 12 days, thus forestalling the shipment of the English manufactures of similar material, and commanding the market before the Manchester goods could arrive.

The importation of English machinery for all textile manufactures has rather fallen off than otherwise during the past year. The best English machines are imitated by the American machinists, and sold at a slightly lower price than the imported. Notwithstanding the mill-owners would, in many instances, prefer to pay the higher price for the English machinery, they, as upholders of a protective tariff for their own products, must reciprocate with the machine manufacturers of the country.

Some cloths have been and continue to be purchased in England "in the gray," dyed here, and placed on the market as American products. To what extent this new feature may extend it is impossible to predict.

LONDON:
Printed for Her Majesty's Stationery Office,
By HARRISON AND SONS,
Printers in Ordinary to Her Majesty.
(Wt. 7730   75   6 | 87—H & S   227)

FOREIGN OFFICE.
1887.
ANNUAL SERIES.

Nº 182.
DIPLOMATIC AND CONSULAR REPORTS ON TRADE AND FINANCE.

UNITED STATES.

REPORT FOR THE YEAR 1886
ON THE
TRADE OF NEW YORK.

REFERENCE TO PREVIOUS REPORT [C. 4737], Commercial No. 10, 1886.

Presented to both Houses of Parliament by Command of Her Majesty,

JUNE, 1887.

LONDON:
PRINTED FOR HER MAJESTY'S STATIONERY OFFICE,
BY HARRISON AND SONS, ST. MARTIN'S LANE,
PRINTERS IN ORDINARY TO HER MAJESTY.

And to be purchased, either directly or through any Bookseller, from
EYRE AND SPOTTISWOODE, EAST HARDING STREET, FLEET STREET, E.C., and
32, ABINGDON STREET, WESTMINSTER, S.W.; or
ADAM AND CHARLES BLACK, NORTH BRIDGE, EDINBURGH; or
HODGES, FIGGIS & Co., 104, GRAFTON STREET, DUBLIN.

1887.

[C.—4923.—105.] *Price 2d.*

New Series of Reports.

Reports of the Annual Series have been issued from Her Majesty's Diplomatic and Consular Officers at the following places, and may be obtained from the sources indicated on the title-page:—

No.		Price.	No.		Price.
56.	Crete	1d.	119.	Guayaquil	1d.
57.	Berne	3d.	120.	Valparaiso	1d.
58.	Rotterdam	1d.	121.	San José	1d.
59.	Düsseldorf	4d.	122.	Pakhoi	1d.
60.	Mozambique	5d.	123.	Hyogo	1d.
61.	Hanyang	1d.	124.	Tamsui	1d.
62.	Stockholm	1d.	125.	Malaga	1d.
63.	Paris	1d.	126.	Marseilles	1d.
64.	Tunis	1d.	127.	Boulogne	2d.
65.	The Hague	2d.	128.	Warsaw	1d.
66.	Italy	2d.	129.	Monte Video	1d.
67.	Smyrna	2d.	130.	Christiania	4d.
68.	Fiume	1d.	131.	Gothenburg	2d.
69.	Tabreez	1d.	132.	Kiungchow	1d.
70.	Philippopolis	1d.	133.	Amoy	1d.
71.	Rome	1d.	134.	Genoa	1d.
72.	Vienna	1d.	135.	Trebizond	1d.
73.	St. Petersburg	2d.	136.	Savannah	1d.
74.	Ichang	1d.	137.	Wilmington	2d.
75.	Salonica	1d.	138.	Bolivar	3d.
76.	Brussels	2d.	139.	Wênchow	1d.
77.	Alexandria	1d.	140.	Chicago	2d.
78.	Patras	1d.	141.	Fiume	1d.
79.	Maranham	1d.	142.	Port Said	1d.
80.	Taganrog	2d.	143.	Java	1d.
81.	Jeddah	1d.	144.	Puerto Cabello	1d.
82.	Suakin	1d.	145.	Coquimbo	1d.
83.	Colonia	1d.	146.	Vera Cruz	2d.
84.	Suez	1d.	147.	Bengazi	1d.
85.	Paris	1d.	148.	Canary Islands	1d.
86.	Brest	1d.	149.	Rome	1d.
87.	Puerto Plata	1d.	150.	Madeira	1d.
88.	Charleston	1d.	151.	Tahiti	1d.
89.	Tripoli	1d.	152.	Corunna	1d.
90.	Saigon	1d.	153.	Vienna	1d.
91.	Cherbourg	1d.	154.	Cagliari	1d.
92.	New Orleans	2d.	155.	St. Petersburg	2d.
93.	Galatz	1d.	156.	Taiwan	1d.
94.	Baltimore	1d.	157.	Foochow	1d.
95.	Tokio	4d.	158.	Tonga	1d.
96.	Havre	3d.	159.	Wuhu	1d.
97.	Barcelona	3d.	160.	Lisbon	1d.
98.	Volo	1d.	161.	Ning-po	1d.
99.	Damascus	1d.	162.	Cadiz	2d.
100.	Paris	1d.	163.	Bilbao	1d.
101.	Bordeaux	2d.	164.	Jaffa	1d.
102.	Serajevo	1d.	165.	Van	1d.
103.	Manila	1d.	166.	Bushire	1d.
104.	Galveston	1d.	167.	Riga	1d.
105.	Aleppo	1d.	168.	Santos	1d.
106.	Rio de Janeiro	1d.	169.	Charleston	1d.
107.	Truxillo	1d.	170.	Newchwang	1d.
108.	St. Petersburg	3d.	171.	Amsterdam	1d.
109.	Leghorn	1d.	172.	Ajaccio	1d.
110.	Boston	1d.	173.	Chinkiang	2d.
111.	Buenos Ayres	3d.	174.	Naples	3d.
112.	Kewkiang	1d.	175.	Smyrna	1d.
113.	Teheran	2d.	176.	Belgrade	1d.
114.	Beyrout	1d.	177.	Philadelphia	2d.
115.	Odessa	5d.	178.	Stockholm	2d.
116.	Carthagena	1d.	179.	Pernambuco	1d.
117.	Santo Domingo	1d.	180.	Frankfort-on-Main	1d.
118.	Mollendo	1d.	181.	Mogador	2d.

No. 182.

Reference to previous Report [C. 4737], *Commercial No.* 10, 1886.

UNITED STATES.

NEW YORK.

Consul-General Booker to the Marquis of Salisbury.

My Lord,　　　　　　　　　　　　　　　　New York, April 9, 1887

I HAVE the honour to transmit, herewith, my annual report upon the trade of New York, with some information in regard to other parts of my district.

I have, &c.
(Signed)　　WM. LANE BOOKER.

Report by Consul-General Booker on the Trade, Navigation, and Commerce of New York for the Year 1886.

The year 1886 has been, generally, a prosperous one. It opened with a fairly active demand for goods of all descriptions, but the trade was held in check during the first few months by serious labour troubles; with the settlement of these there was confidence in the future, and a greatly increased demand sprung up. Textile mills and other industrial works, which had not for a long time been worked to their full capacity, increased very considerably their outputs to meet a demand not only sufficient to take all the product, but to reduce the large accumulated stocks on hand to a reasonable limit; the same applies to articles of import, the stocks of which became reduced in the face of increased receipts. Had there been no offset to the improved outlook by labour complications, it is very probable that a speculative spirit would have got headway, which would have caused trade operations of every character to have gone beyond legitimate bounds, and resulted in a reaction; as matters now are we may reasonably look for a continuance of prosperity for some time.

The clearing-house returns of this city show an increase of 20 per cent. in the year, and taking from these what may be regarded as stock transactions, the increased commercial operations will, it is estimated, reach 25 per cent.

Railroads have been kept fully employed, and the earnings show a wonderful recovery from the depression of 1885 and 1884. The stock market has been greatly affected by strikes, but many railroad shares, especially the lower-priced ones, have materially advanced, whilst most of those paying dividends command higher prices than at the end of 1885.

In the first half of 1886 there was an abundant supply of money; on call, it was freely offered at 1 to 2 per cent., but with the demand for moving the crops in the west, activity in railroad building in the west and south, and the increase of speculative business at the

General report on trade.

Exchanges, rates for money advanced materially. From August to November there was a demand which kept rates at 5 to 6 per cent., with occasional spurts to 7, 8, and 10 per cent., and in the middle of December there was a stringency in the loan market, when call loans were made at 10 per cent. and upwards; rates subsequently became easier, and remained so till the end of the year. Commercial paper in the first quarter ranged from 3 to 5 per cent., in the second and during July from 3½ to 5½ per cent., and from August to the end of December 5 to 6½ per cent.

Bank returns. The condition of the associated banks (63) of the city at different periods of the year is shown in the following table:—

ASSOCIATED Banks of New York City.

1886. Week ending	Average Amount of				
	Loans and Discount.	Specie.	Legal Tenders.	Net deposits other than U.S.A.	Circulation.
	£	£	£	£	£
January 2 ..	70,0[illegible],420	18,482,545	5,934,490	77,653,615	2,055,830
April 3 ..	72,060,160	16,162,715	5,405,665	76,392,630	1,642,765
July 3 ..	73,283,200	13,283,680	8,423,420	77,746,750	1,610,850
October 2	70,080,315	15,261,075	3,825,440	71,431,800	1,681,875
December 31	70,799,625	17,039,930	3,990,400	74,009,335	1,629,770

The annual report of the superintendent of the State banks department states that the increase in the year (fiscal, ended October 1) in the aggregate resources of the banks was 2,385,726*l.*; in loans and discounts, 2,600,326; in deposits, 2,812,914*l.*; and in surplus and undivided profits, 223,400*l.*

Sterling exchange. The following gives the rates of bankers' sterling exchange during the year:—

	Sixty days.	Sight.
January—Highest	4·88	4·90
„ Lowest	4·86	4·89
February—Highest	4·88½	4·90
„ Lowest	4·87½	4·89½
March—Highest	4·88½	4·89½
„ Lowest	4·87	4·90
April—Highest	4·87½	4·89½
„ Lowest	4·86½	4·88½
May—Highest	4·88	4·89½
„ Lowest	4·87	4·88½
June—Highest	4·88	4·90
„ Lowest	4·87¼	4·89½
July—Highest	4·88½	4·90
„ Lowest	4·85½	4·87
August—Highest	4·85½	4·87
„ Lowest	4·81½	4·84
September—Highest	4·83	4·86
„ Lowest	4·82	4·85
October—Highest	4·83	4·86
„ Lowest	4·81½	4·84
November—Highest	4·82	4·85½
„ Lowest	4·81½	4·84½
December—Highest	4·81½	4·85
„ Lowest	4·80	4·84

NEW YORK.

The failures, as exhibited in the following table, taken from Dun's Commercial Agency, show the liability in the States of my district to be very much below those of 1885, with the exception of Connecticut, where they are in excess about 10 per cent., but the amount involved is inconsiderable. New York city shows a reduction of about 16½ per cent., and the whole State 20 per cent.

Failures in district.

	Number of Failures.		Amount of Liabilities.	
	1886.	1885.	1886. £	1885. £
New York city and Brooklyn	528	506	3,416,838	4,094,249
New York State (outside of cities of New York and Brooklyn)	621	677	} 1,174,040	} 1,647,865
Connecticut	132	176	393,130	353,185
New Jersey	111	122	128,292	195,628
Rhode Island	92	126	149,597	257,209
Delaware	25	23	36,392	40,220

The import returns in Annex B. show an increase in merchandise receipts of nearly 12,000,000*l.* over those of 1885, of which about 3,100,000*l.* comes under the heading of dry goods, and 4,450,000*l.* consists of specie. The dutiable merchandise entered for consumption and withdrawn from bonded warehouses in 1886 exceeds that of the previous year by about 5,075,000*l.*, equal to $9\frac{23}{100}$ per cent. This may be regarded as an indication of the increased consumption in the past year.

Annex B. Imports generally.

The imports from Great Britain in Annex C. show an increase of nearly 3,000,000*l.* over 1885, but are 1,000,000*l.* short of 1884.

Annex C. Imports from Great Britain.

The export returns in Annex B. show an increase of about 2,360,000*l.*, but if the specie be excluded there is a decrease of about 2,560,000*l.* The principal articles showing a decrease are fresh and salt meats, butter, cheese, flour, Indian corn, and refined sugar, and those showing an increase are wheat and cotton. The decrease in refined sugar is due partially to a reduction in the drawback on the raw importation allowed by Government; this only came into force on November 1. The old drawback amounted practically to a bonus of about 1*s.* to 1*s.* 3*d.* per cwt.

Annex B. Exports generally.

Amongst the minor exports may be mentioned agricultural implements, carriages and horse-cars, steam-engines, clocks, and tools of various descriptions.

The exports to Great Britain in Annex C. show a falling-off of about 5,800,000*l.*

Annex C. Exports to Great Britain.

REPORT ON DRY GOODS.

Cottons.—It is well known that importations into this country from England of all the heavier and coarser descriptions of cotton goods have long since ceased, and the markets here are supplied entirely with goods of American manufacture. This applies not only to the goods known as sheetings, shirtings, drillings, Osnaburgs, and similar classes, but also to the finer and lighter descriptions, such as plain and rolled jaconets, both dyed and printed, and to most descriptions of

Dry goods. Cottons.

ginghams, printed lawns, and similar fabrics, of which the consumption is enormous, and which used to be imported in large quantities from Lancashire and Glasgow. This is also the case with printed calicoes, or the goods known in the American market as prints, the production of which has reached very large dimensions, and now includes a better, finer, and more expensive class of fabrics than formerly, great improvements being also visible in the taste, style, colourings, and work of these productions. During the last few years, also, cotton manufactures have received a great impetus in some of the cotton-producing States, especially Georgia and South Carolina. The mills in these States have taken up the manufacture of the lower and coarser counts of yarns and cloths, which have been made by them with considerable success, and which are, to the extent of their production, taking the place of similar fabrics formerly made exclusively in the northern mills. This fact, with other influences, has had the effect of stimulating the newer and better-equipped factories of Massachusetts, Rhode Island, and Connecticut to turn their attention more largely to the finer and lighter fabrics, which had, up to a more recent period, been imported entirely from England in the form of jaconets, cambrics, nainsooks, and muslins, a branch of the trade known as the white goods trade, in which many large houses are engaged on both sides of the Atlantic. The progress which has been made not only in the manufacture of these goods by the New England mills, but the improvement in the processes of bleaching and finishing, as well as dyeing and printing, has been remarkable, so much so as to attract the attention of all interested in the trade. Great care is given to the putting up and finish of the goods, the same taste and originality being displayed in this respect as was the case in previous years with bleached shirtings and similar fabrics. Great efforts are being made by leading American manufacturers and merchants to extend the sale of these goods in foreign markets, and it is maintained that wherever they are introduced they meet at once with favour by reason of the perfection and, above all, the purity of the fabrics. Still, notwithstanding all these facts, and the heavy duties levied upon English manufactures, important quantities of the finer and lighter goods are continually imported, and it is in these, as well as in the finest counts of yarns, that the spinners and manufacturers of Lancashire yet display special strength, and as against these neither the French and Germans appear to be able seriously to compete.

Worsteds and Woollens.—In the worsted, or what is known popularly as the dress goods trade, the large production of American manufactures of goods with cotton warps has interfered materially with the importation of that class of fabrics from the Bradford district, while the fashion for soft or all-wool fabrics has, for some years, almost entirely superseded the trade in the bright or lustre goods known as mohairs and alpacas. In the place of these the Yorkshire all-wool goods made to compete with the French, and to which Yorkshire manufacturers have largely directed their attention, have been introduced, and have met with no little favour, especially in the finer grades and in blacks, although it must be said that the great supplies of all-wool goods, such as cashmeres and merinos, particularly in colours, are still drawn chiefly from France, though Germany has made great efforts recently in this direction, and not without success. In worsted coatings a large business has been done by Yorkshire makers, while in the finer class of woollens for men's wear the English goods are still held in much favour, although the wants of the great bulk of the population are supplied by American manufacturers. In these classes of goods other countries only compete to a moderate extent

Laces and Hosiery.—In laces the French goods from Calais and other points interfere greatly with the productions of Nottingham, while in hosiery the same district has to meet a close, continual, and very formidable competition from the manufactories of Chemnitz and the neighbouring districts in Saxony.

Laces and hosiery.

Linens.—As regards the linen trade, manufacturers of the North of Ireland and of Fifeshire still hold the pre-eminence, and although it is supposed here that little money has been made in the manufacture of these goods, they have as yet nearly the entire possession of the markets of the United States.

Linens.

Silks.—The importations of silk manufactures have been largely in excess of 1885, the increase being mainly in satins, plushes, and velvets. The only import which has shown a falling-off has been that of crapes.

Silks.

The New York canals were open for 215 days, the longest period since 1882. The report of the superintendent shows that 5,293,982 tons passed through against 4,731,784 in 1885. The arrivals of grain and flour at Buffalo by the lakes in 1886 amounted to the equivalent of 93,034,953 of the former; this was 50 per cent. advance on the receipts in 1885. Of these receipts 45,407,534 bushels were sent to New York by canal. The freights were better than for many years, wheat averaging from Buffalo to New York 6·5 cents. per bushel, equal to about 10s. per ton of 2,240 lbs. The report earnestly recommends that the locks on the Erie Canal should be lengthened. No tolls are now charged on the canals.

Canals.

The rates of transportation by the railroads of the State were maintained throughout the year at a higher point than for some years. The through rate from Chicago to New York was 25 c. per 100 lbs. (22s. 6d. per ton of 2,240 lbs.) for grain, and 30 c. (27s.) for provisions until the close of the year, when there was an advance of 5 c. per 100 lbs.; this is stated to have been the first instance of rates being maintained when brought into competition with water communication by the opening of canal navigation. About 1,100,000 tons were sent westward from this city.

Railroad rates.

A bridge is in course of construction at Poughkeepsie, about midway between this city and Albany, which will faciliate greatly the traffic between the New England States and the West and South. The bridge is to have three cantilever spans of 548 feet each, and two connection spans of 525 feet. The bottom of the trusses will be 130 feet above high water, and the track on the top 212 feet. From the track to the foot of the cribs at the river bed will be a distance of 365 feet of a continuous structure, in which it is estimated that not less than 40,000 tons of steel and 40,000 yards of stone will be used.

Bridge at Poughkeepsie

The bridge is to have two railroad tracks, and to be of sufficient strength to support two trains, each drawn by two 85-ton locomotives, a moving load of 3,000 lbs. to the lineal foot on each track; any road will have the right to connect with these tracks.

This will be the only bridge between this city and Albany.

The following table shows the total grain shipments by sail and steam from this port to Great Britain and the Continent in 1886, the number of vessels, nationality, &c.:—

Carrying of grain.

(233)

UNITED STATES.

Nationality.	Number of Vessels.	Bushels.	Percentage.
American	..	..	..
British	743	32,929,266	62·72
Belgian	76	4,661,930	8·88
German	183	4,580,278	8·72
French	55	2,405,612	4·58
Italian	61	2,192,882	4·18
Spanish	33	1,724,362	3·28
Dutch	51	1,522,609	2·90
Danish	27	1,062,889	2·03
Austrian	24	772,037	1·48
Portuguese	19	441,991	0·84
Swedish and Norwegian	7	209,517	0·39
Total	1,279	52,503,373	100·00

Of the above ships 1,181 were under steam and 98 under sail.

Labour.

LABOUR MARKET.

There has been no very material change in wages in my district during the year, but the tendency has been upwards, and in the cotton and woollen mills an advance of about 5 per cent. has been established. The most serious thing in connection with labour has been the numerous strikes. The Commissioner of the Bureau of Labour Statistics of this State, in his report to the Legislature, not yet published for general distribution, presents a table of 1,900 strikes in this State, alone for the year ending 31st October against 222 in 1885. He regards the result of the struggle as, on the whole, beneficial to the working men, but his figures do not bear this out. He estimates the loss in wages alone at 2,858,191 dols. (589,318*l*.). Of the 1,900 strikes, reports of the facts were obtained in reference to 1,238, of which 723, or a little more than one-half, were successful. The Commissioner gives, as an offset to the great loss of wages, a gain to those directly engaged in the strikes of 937,079 dols. (193,212*l*.); and the Commissioner states, in explanation of his view of the result of the struggle between employers and employés having been beneficial to the latter, that non-union men have been benefited to an equal extent with the unionists, but this cannot be more than an assumption, and there are no figures to support it. In regard to the loss to employers by the strikes, the Commissioner remarks that the definite statement of only 58 firms puts it at 3,000,000 dols. (618,000*l*.) : a critic on this statement very properly suggests that if employers sustained such heavy losses from the strikers by failure to fulfil contracts, diversion of business, unavoidable expenses, &c., it is certain that their ability to employ men and pay wages was seriously impaired, and this must add to the losses of workmen.

In regard to shorter hours of labour (eight hours having been proposed by the Knights of Labour to take effect on the 1st May last), the Commissioner says :—" As predicted in the last report of this Bureau, a very general movement was made on the first day of May last, looking to the reduction of the hours of labour from 10 to eight per day. The organisations of New York and Brooklyn seem to have acted more in concert than those of other cities in the State, and were by far more successful, having won a majority of the cases when demands were made. It is true that while a large percentage of all engaged in the movement asked for a reduction of two hours per day, very many of the organisations did it with a view to compromising on nine hours as a day's work."

The State Legislature of New York passed an Act, which was approved in May last, providing for the amicable adjustment of disputes between employers and employés by local boards of arbitration, and for the creation of a State Board of Arbitration: the local board to be composed of two members of the labour organisation, of which the parties concerned are members, and if not members of any, by two arbitrators designated by a majority of the parties concerned, the employers to designate two other arbitrators, and the four to designate the fifth, who shall be the chairman of the board. The decision to be a settlement of the matter referred, unless an appeal be taken to the State board. When the local board shall have rendered its decision its power shall cease, unless there may be in existence at the time other disputes between the same class of persons before-mentioned, and in such case such person may submit their differences to said board, as if it were originally created for the settlement of such other dispute or disputes. The State board of arbitration to be composed of three salaried officers, appointed by the Government with the consent of the Senate, each of whom shall hold the office for the term of one year. One of the said arbitrators must be selected from the party which at the last general election cast the greatest number of votes for Governor of the State, one from the party which cast the next greatest number for Governor, and the third from a bonâ fide labour organisation of the State. The local board of arbitration has proved useless, and it became apparent at once on the passage of the Act that parties to disputes preferred to solicit the mediation of the State board, but the State board had only the right under the Act to act on appeals from the decision of local boards. The secretary of the board informs me that in several cases the State board, through some of its members, have endeavoured by mediation to effect a settlement of labour difficulties, and their efforts in this direction were attended with good results. All the actions of the State board have been outside the strict letter, but in accordance with the spirit and object of the law. The experience of the board demonstrated clearly that its powers were too limited to enable it to accomplish all that was expected of it; therefore, in its report to the Legislature, changes in the law were recommended, and an Act has passed both branches of the Legislature, amending the former one so as to make the board one of both mediation and arbitration. It vests it with powers of original jurisdiction and action in all cases of grievances and disputes between employers and employés that may come to its knowledge, so as to be able to initiate and supervise any means of settlement that shall, in its judgment, seem best adapted to the end in view, and may be more agreeable to the parties at issue, whether it be direct reference to and decision by the board, or a local board, or other agency, and that in all such cases, whether arbitration follows or not, it shall have warrant as a body, or through one of its members, or its secretary, to make investigation, take testimony, &c.

Labour boards of arbitration.

"Bradstreet," a reliable authority, gives a list of the more important strikes of the year, from which I extract those in my Consular district.

Strikes.

In January.—10,000 cigar-makers were on strike in this city in connection with wages for from four to six weeks, and failed.

6,000 employés in glove factories at Gloversville, New York, for new wages scale were out three weeks, ending in a compromise.

2,000 street railway employés were out for 10 hours for shorter hours, and had their demand acceded to.

1,000 in various textile mills in Rhode Island, out for an average of two weeks for higher wages, were partially successful.

In February.—1,900 moulders in Troy, New York, out for five months for higher wages failed.

2,000 employés in silk mills in Paterson, New Jersey (few days) for higher wages failed.

In March.—7,000 employés in knitting mills in Cohoes and vicinity in this State, out for one month for higher wages, ending in a compromise.

600 in rubber works in Paterson, New Jersey, out for a few days for higher wages were successful.

1,000 employés in Russell Manufacturing Company in Middletown, Connecticut, for higher wages, ending in a compromise.

1,000 in a cotton mill in Baltic, Connecticut, out for one month in connection with fines, ending in a compromise.

10,000 cloak and silk makers in this city, out for two weeks in regard to hours of labour, ending in a failure.

In April.—12,000 street railway employés in this city out for one day succeeded.

1,000 street railway employés in this city, out for one month through Knights of Labour interference, failed.

400 employés in jute mills in this city, mill management, failed.

2,500 employés in Brooklyn sugar refineries, out for one month for higher wages, failed.

3,000 painters in New York city in regard to hours of labour succeeded.

500 ironfounders in Brooklyn, foundry management, compromised.

1,500 warehousemen in New York city for higher wages compromised.

1,000 employés in sewing-machine factory for higher wages compromised.

In May.—35,000 persons in New York city for shorter hours, out for three weeks, few succeeded.

1,200 in Newark, New Jersey, for shorter hours, out for three weeks, failed.

2,600 tanners for higher wages, out for one month, compromised.

In June.—15,000 laundry employés, lock-out in Troy, New York, against strike for more wages by 200, succeeded.

400 builders for shorter hours in Rochester, New York, failed.

In July.—2,000 cigar makers in New York city for trade unionism, out for one month, succeeded.

In August.—400 employés in foundries, locking out 5,000 in Paterson, New Jersey, for higher wages, failed.

1,050 street-car employés, for hours and trips, in New York city, out for two days, compromised.

1,000 coal boatmen in New York and Amboy for higher rates, out for two weeks, succeeded.

In September.—400 pressmen in New York city, for higher wages, were partly successful.

3,000 builders' employés in Albany, New York, against non-unionists, out for one week, failed.

In October.—20,000 knitting mills' employés, lock-out in Cohoes and Amsterdam, New York, for right to discharge, practically broken.

In November.—None in this district.

In December.—1,900 street-car employés in Brooklyn, trades' union recognition, out for one day, succeeded.

The Commissioner of the Bureau of Labour Statistics of Connecticut has lately presented to the Legislature a report for the year ending November 30, and I give the following extracts therefrom :— *Labour statistics of the State of Connecticut.*

"*Employment of Women and Children.*—Of some 70,000 hands, whose sex and age are specified in our returns, there are 20,000 women and a little less than 3,000 children. The latter figure is undoubtedly too small in proportion to the whole number. On the other hand, the United States census figures on this same subject are pretty certainly too large. It seems likely that about 5,000 children under 15 are employed in Connecticut establishments.

"Monthly payment is most frequent with children, somewhat less so with women, and least frequent with men.

"The average proportion of women employed increases with the size of the factory. In the smaller establishments less than a quarter of the hands are women; in the larger ones nearly one-third. On the other hand, the number of children reported reaches a maximum in mills employing between 100 and 200 hands, and then diminishes. This seems to make it probable that most of the smaller mills employing children made either no returns, or inadequate ones.

"The employment of women reaches by far the largest proportion in the manufacture of wearing apparel, where they are nearly twice as numerous as the men; also in the silk mills, where about the same proportion holds good. In other textile mills, especially in the wool manufacture, the men outnumber the women.

"The employment of children reaches the largest proportions in textile industry, which gives employment to nearly twice as many children as all other factory industries put together. The proportion of children, and in particular of young children, is much largest in the cotton mills, where it reaches nearly 12 per cent. of the whole number employed. The general percentage of children in all textile industries is a little less than nine.

"The greater part of the children employed in the production of textile goods and wearing apparel are engaged in tending machinery; in other lines of industry, such employment is the exception. Most establishments, either in metal or in miscellaneous manufacture, represent children as engaged in cleaning and packing, in helping adult labourers, or simply in occasional odd jobs about the shops. The result of this difference is, that the direct competition of child labour is hardly felt in many of these lines, and the system is seen at its best instead of at its worst.

"The employment of women in metal establishments is for the most part on lines similar to that of children—cleaning, finishing, assorting, or packing. There are, however, a great many establishments, especially in the brass manufacture, where the work of tending machinery is largely done by women. The number employed in the administrative force of all lines of industry is also considerable.

"Returns giving the wages of about 3,000 women in the city of New Haven, where they are perhaps employed in a greater variety of lines than anywhere else in the State, show an average weekly wage of a trifle over $6\frac{1}{2}$ dol. The lowest average wages are found in the manufacture of wearing apparel. Wages under 6 dol. are exceptional.

"Returns concerning the employment of children in four mill towns in the eastern part of the State show a scale of wages running down from about 1 dol. a day for hands over 18 years of age, to 35 c. to 40 c. for the youngest hands; in exceptional cases still lower. The average wages were higher, and the work a little steadier in woollen mills than in cotton mills for children of the same age.

UNITED STATES.

Hours of labour.

"Of 65,627 hands in the larger establishments of the State, 3,345, or about 5 per cent., were employed 54 hours or less; 14,647, or a little over 22 per cent., from 55 to 59 hours; 37,033, or considerably over 56 per cent., were employed either 59½ or 60 hours, that is to say, 10 hours a day; while the remainder, 10,602, or 16 per cent., had an average working week of more than 60 hours.

"Nearly all the cases of steady employment for more than 10 hours daily in the factories of the State were found in the textile industry, although there were many other establishments reporting more or less overtime. The longest hours reported in work of any kind were among the barbers—92 hours weekly. Several outdoor employments, with exceptionally long hours—for instance, street-car drivers—made no report.

"Some of the mineral industries, like lime-burning, report very long, though usually somewhat irregular hours. The paper mills run for exceedingly long hours, though with such relays that comparatively few of the hands work over 10 hours daily. The regular working time of the bakers sometimes has been 12 hours a day, and this is considerably less than it was a few years ago.

"On the other hand, the cigar makers work but eight hours a day, a decided reduction in recent years, the last stage of which was accomplished in May of this year (1886). This was the only trade where the attempt to secure an eight-hour day, which was to have been widely undertaken, was actually carried into effect. A number of other trades report slight reductions in recent years.

"Of establishments paying weekly, only 1 per cent. run over 60 hours a week; of those paying fortnightly 7 per cent.; of those paying monthly 32 per cent. Or to put the same result in another form: of 20,812 hands employed less than 10 hours a day, 6,279, or 30 per cent., were paid monthly; of 33,870 hands employed 10 hours a day, 12,349, or 36½ per cent., were paid monthly; while of 10,465 hands employed regularly more than 10 hours a day, 9,425, or fully 90 per cent. were paid monthy.

"12 per cent. of the men, 25 per cent. of the women, and 34½ per cent. of the children are employed more than 10 hours daily. On the other hand, 30 per cent. of the men, 28 per cent. of the women, and only 11 per cent. of the children are employed less than 10 hours daily.

Wages of men.

The average wage in textile mills is 1 dol. 26 c. per day, and the average annual earnings 345 dol. (71*l.*).

Strikes.

During the preparation of this report there has been a strike amongst the longshoremen, and others connected with shipping and the coal trade, which has caused great inconvenience to all interested. At one time it was estimated that there were on strike, connected with the shipping trade, 15,500 longshoremen, 1,000 boatmen, 5,000 grain handlers, 1,500 coal handlers, 6,000 grain ceilers and weighers, 400 bag sewers, and 10,000 railroad freight-handlers, brakemen, and coal-passers. The strike is now at an end, and the union men are willing to return to work on the old terms, but a great number find themselves unable to get employment, as employers are not disposed to discharge hands, at all capable, whose services they have been able to secure during the strike. Although there were no riots, assaults were committed upon the new men, and various means were adopted by their employers to protect them, either by having them taken from their work in towboats, or finding accommodation for them on their premises.

The strike originated against the "Old Dominion Line" running between this port and Norfolk, Virginia; at the latter point, the men engaged in loading and discharging their ships struck, refusing to work on Sundays, but on others being sent from here, they resumed work, and the substitutes were brought back and given employment at rather lower wages than union men were getting, when the line, and all engaged in handling freight brought by it, were "boycotted" by order of District Assembly 49 of the Knights of Labour. About the same time a reduction in the wages of some coal-passers at Jersey city, from 22½ c. to 20 c. per hour, was made, when there was a general strike of coal-handlers. The other strikes were not from any personal grievance, but at the instance of Assembly No. 49, to strengthen the position taken against the Dominion Line and the employers of the coal-passers. The strike probably would not have been continued long under the firm stand taken by the employers, but it culminated at once on the refusal of the brewers and others in no way connected with the shipping and coal trades to respond to an order to quit work. The result has been a most serious loss to the men, who failed to get the assistance they expected from the Order, and many of whom are now in enforced instead of voluntary idleness.

AGRICULTURE.

Agriculture.

In agriculture there is little to report, except that the hop crop of this State, which in 1885 amounted to 158,000 bales, of 180 lbs. each, did not much exceed 10,000 bales in 1886, and most of the hops were of very inferior quality. Lice and honey-dew sapped the life of the plant, and the leaves shrivelled up and turned black. In Rhode Island, Delaware, Connecticut, and New Jersey there are no hop vines of any consequence.

The grain crops of the States mentioned were about an average.

IMMIGRATION.

Immigration.

There were 321,814 immigrants landed at this port in 1886, and they were of the following nationalities:—

	Immigrants.
England	46,215
Ireland	36,415
Scotland	12,277
Wales	1,043
Germany	73,099
Austria	15,772
Hungary	18,135
Sweden	21,905
Norway	10,443
Denmark	8,001
Netherlands	3,323
Belgium	1,704
Switzerland	5,531
France	4,998
Italy	29,312
Roumania	2,461
Malta	36
Greece	96
Spain	438
Portugal	17
Armenia	32
Russia	23,987
Bohemia	4,222
Luxemburg	257
Turkey in Europe	173
China	8
Japan	27
British East Indies	27

UNITED STATES.

	Immigrants.
Egypt	10
Arabia	8
Canada	1,185
West Indies	237
Mexico	3
Central America	165
South America	95
Australia	3
New Zealand	5
Iceland	149
Total	321,814

During the past year 997 immigrants were returned to Europe through the agency of the Emigration Board. Of this number 70 were insane, 20 were idiots, 1 blind, 88 were enceinte, 8 were convicts, 18 were cripples, 355 suffered from diseases which prevented them from earning a livelihood, and 437 were without means of support. At the Labour Bureau attached to Castle Garden 8,435 males and 5,912 females found employment during 1886. Of the male immigrants, 6,894 were hired for agricultural and common labour. The average wages paid to farm hands was 12 dol. per month and board; to female house servants, 9 dol. per month and board.

PRISONS.

Prisons.

The superintendent of the State prisons of this State, in his annual report to the Legislature, says that the transactions of the prisons during the last year are without precedent, and the embarrassments which perplexed the superintendent and the warden of the prison at Auburn in the preceding year, arising from their inability to put a large body of prisoners at work, have been continued during the whole of 1886. This situation is the result of want of action on the part of the Legislature to meet the grave exigency which, it was fully informed during the session, existed in the State prisons. The prisoners numbered in the three State prisons 3,155 on the 1st September, an increase of 194 over 1885. These are divided as follows:—

	Prisoners.
At Sing Sing	1,532
Auburn	1,084
Clinton	539

The receipts exceeded expenditures by 744*l*. The earnings and expenditures were distributed as follows:—

	£
Sing Sing earnings	49,860
,, expenditures	34,396
Auburn earnings	9,084
,, expenditures	25,667
Clinton earnings	18,866
,, expenditures	17,003

The great deficit at Auburn was caused by non-employment of prisoners.

The prison physician and the prison chaplain at Auburn testify to the evil moral and physical effects of the close confinement resulting from lack of employment for prisoners. Many have fallen into a condition bordering on insanity, and 43 have been sent to the asylum for insane convicts.

NEW YORK.

STATE FINANCES.

At the close of the fiscal year (September 30) the total funded debt of this State was 1,921,403*l.*, classified as follows:—

	£
Indian annuities	25,275
Canal debt	1,710,728
Niagara reservation bonds	185,400
	1,921,403
Aggregate sinking fund	1,040,520
	880,883

The tax rate for the fiscal year is 2·95 per mille.

NEW YORK CITY FINANCES.

The total funded debt of the city of New York on January 1, 1887, amounted to 25,952,445*l.*, against which there is a sinking fund on hand of 8,488,325*l.*

Valuation and tax rates for the past five years are given in the following table:—

Year.	Real Estate.	Personal.	City Tax.
	£	£	Per cent.
1886	248,011,860	44,707,606	2·29
1885	240,699,285	41,750,816	2·40
1884	230,670,888	45,018,570	2·25
1883	222,300,918	40,694,578	2·29
1882	213,251,986	40,854,151	2·25

VITAL Statistics, New York City, 1886.

Births	31,319
Marriages	37,351
Deaths	12,216

The causes of death were principally as follows:—

Zymotic diseases	9,660
Consumption	5,477
Pneumonia	3,657
Diarrhœal diseases	3,494
Diphtheria	1,727
Bronchitis	1,701
Heart disease	1,894
Diseases of brain and nervous system	3,156
Bright's disease	2,216
Apoplexy	762
Cancer	780
By violence	1,463
Small-pox	31
Typhus fever	14
Typhoid fever	325
Cerebro-spinal-meningitis	223
Measles	668
Croup	968
Whooping-cough	575

UNITED STATES.

Annex A.—RETURN of all Shipping at the Port of New York in the Year 1886.

ENTERED.

Country.	Sailing. Number of Vessels.	Sailing. Tons.	Steam. Number of Vessels.	Steam. Tons.	Total. Number of Vessels.	Total. Tons.
Great Britain	1,408	701,651	1,354	2,300,946	2,762	3,002,597
United States	1,466	674,360	241	371,381	1,707	1,045,741
Germany	218	34,694	231	532,686	449	567,380
France	2	732	90	264,600	92	265,332
Sweden and Norway	302	189,052	58	28,246	360	217,298
Belgium	...	...	88	243,936	88	243,936
Italy	191	115,746	22	34,166	213	149,912
Mexico	6	924	...	...	6	924
Netherlands	14	12,306	45	90,270	59	102,576
Austria	64	39,488	...	...	64	39,488
Spain	34	9,792	86	113,702	120	123,494
Denmark	14	3,682	34	65,348	48	69,030
Other European countries	33	17,952	2	1,876	35	19,828
South America	1	1,391	...	...	1	1,391
Central America	3	537	...	...	3	537
Other countries	...	...	...	...	...	...
Total	3,756	1,802,307	2,251	4,047,157	6,007	5,849,464
„ for the year preceding	3,728	1,795,404	2,239	3,913,465	5,967	5,708,869

CLEARED.

Country.	Sailing. Number of Vessels.	Sailing. Tons.	Steam. Number of Vessels.	Steam. Tons.	Total. Number of Vessels.	Total. Tons.
Great Britain	1,480	737,782	1,347	2,288,339	2,827	3,026,121
United States	941	433,078	233	359,206	1,174	792,284
Germany	205	187,294	231	532,894	436	720,188
France	4	1,465	93	273,507	97	274,972
Sweden and Norway	289	181,153	60	29,250	349	210,403
Belgium	...	...	90	249,498	90	249,498
Italy	178	108,018	23	35,727	201	143,745
Mexico	4	616	...	...	4	616
Netherlands	16	14,079	51	102,320	67	116,399
Austria	62	38,285	...	...	62	38,285
Spain	32	9,227	76	99,368	108	108,595
Denmark	12	3,161	25	48,069	37	51,230
Other European countries	32	17,415	2	1,876	34	19,291
South America	1	1,391	...	...	1	1,391
Central America	3	537	...	...	3	537
Other countries	...	...	...	...	...	...
Total	3,259	1,733,501	2,231	4,020,054	5,490	5,753,555
„ for the year preceding	3,274	1,614,993	2,025	3,647,187	5,299	5,262,180

Annex B.—RETURN of Principal Articles of Import to New York during the Years 1886-85.

Articles.		1886. Quantity.	1886. Value.	1885. Quantity.	1885. Value.
			£		£
Cocoa	Bags	74,596	299,891	58,550	232,063
Coffee	Cwts.	3,786,933	7,155,173	3,770,147	6,818,077
China, glass, and earthenware	Packages		1,591,779	...	1,441,059
Cotton	Bales	8,420	89,915	...	114,825
Dry goods—					
Manufactures of cotton	...	...	4,648,728	...	4,330,565
,, ,, flax	...	...	3,183,793	...	3,068,904
,, ,, silk	...	...	7,142,501	...	5,968,834
,, ,, wool	...	...	6,428,724	...	5,349,832
,, ,, miscellaneous	...	...	2,362,168	...	1,993,589
Fancy goods	...	...	179,770	...	214,810
Furs	Packages	23,305	1,105,667	17,524	916,381
Fruits	...	...	2,940,232	...	3,071,909
Hair	...	...	372,474		315,935
Hemp	Bales	339,990	994,870	...	1,151,348
Hides, dressed	Number	7,424	969,116	7,323	1,063,460
,, undressed	,,	19,449,213	4,011,446	16,417,827	3,382,173
Hops	...	...	488,848	...	...
India rubber	...	...	2,642,811	...	1,975,938
Jewellery, watches, and precious stones		...	2,082,797	...	1,489,517
Jute and jute butts	...	...	456,831	...	459,644
Linseed	Packages	83,219	56,356	476,381	378,707
Molasses	Gallons	...	278,341	...	275,681
Paper stock	...	...	446,960	...	786,410
Metals—					
Cutlery	...	...	330,383	...	276,704
Iron, pig	Tons	95,816	222,490	86,821	340,237
,, spiegel	,,	102,124	471,949	...	...
,, other	...	...	446,430	...	390,912
Metal goods	...	...	322,990	...	390,719
Steel	...	...	849,380	...	542,070
Tin plates	Boxes	2,099,876	1,613,376	2,010,869	1,657,664
,, slabs	Tons	12,240	1,256,927	9,873	869,299
Soda, ash	...	...	290,946	...	323,671
,, caustic	...	...	167,094	...	150,830
Spices	...	...	510,373	...	518,031
Stationery and books	...	...	922,655	...	857,913
Sugar	Tons	849,870	10,335,201	797,269	10,090,505
Specie and bullion	...	...	7,991,090	...	3,527,802
Tea	Packages	1,367,920	2,412,010	1,214,925	2,493,263
Tobacco and cigars	...	...	1,635,110	...	1,869,006
Wines, spirits, &c.	...	...	1,741,390	...	1,655,327
Wood	...	...	1,307,026	...	1,551,637
Wool	Lbs.	63,607,927	1,595,520	44,729,255	1,008,772
Other articles	...	...	13,165,055	...	12,265,293
Total			97,536,486		85,579,316

UNITED STATES.

Annex B.—RETURN of Principal Articles of Export from New York during the Years 1886-85.

Articles.		1886. Quantity.	1886. Value.	1885. Quantity.	1885. Value.
			£		£
Agricultural implements	...	...	397,142	...	...
Bacon and hams	Lbs.	259,300,838	4,196,542	264,380,796	4,605,963
Beef, fresh	,,	52,541,703	1,032,421	71,347,035	1,429,090
Butter	,,	11,904,885	359,228	14,542,382	466,390
Cattle, live	Number	53,117	975,466	60,607	1,158,408
Cotton, domestic	Packages	207,285	2,317,906	198,150	2,282,914
,, raw	Bales	939,369	8,820,886	739,981	7,866,755
Cheese	Lbs.	74,524,037	1,343,595	79,607,405	1,357,357
Flour	Barrels	3,466,840	3,046,846	3,705,029	3,603,366
Indian corn	Bushels	20,504,141	2,104,676	26,259,228	2,963,988
Lard	Lbs.	250,334,625	3,482,870	214,809,076	3,260,886
Oilcake and meal	...	...	789,385	...	...
Pork and beef (salt)	Lbs.	59,354,315	724,699	70,077,624	960,564
Petroleum, refined	Gallons	341,665,783	5,708,513	313,980,239	5,787,453
,, crude	,,	42,127,133	598,975	49,496,978	764,796
,, lubricating	,,	13,160,266	254,249	11,836,668	501,455
Sewing machines	...	...	411,310	...	...
Sugar	Cwts.	1,452,315	2,138,431	2,224,027	3,249,379
Specie and bullion	...	...	9,837,013	21	4,955,286
Tallow	Lbs.	25,024,416	248,570	24,810,942	318,072
Wheat	Bushels	31,267,839	5,770,904	16,286,200	3,170,564
Other articles	...	...	20,867,660	...	24,306,430
Total	...	...	75,427,287	...	73,009,116

Annex C.—TABLE showing the Total Value of all Articles Exported from and Imported to New York from and to Foreign Countries during the Years 1886-85.

Country.	Exports. 1886.	Exports. 1885.	Imports.* 1886.	Imports.* 1885.
	£	£	£	£
Great Britain	29,739,216	35,523,364	20,914,192	18,005,175
British possessions	4,414,691	4,723,489	6,209,516	5,209,317
Germany	6,004,875	6,798,438	13,147,638	12,148,906
France and possessions	3,781,752	3,950,853	11,266,408	11,263,707
Belgium	3,196,287	3,135,388	1,248,767	1,185,110
Spain and possessions	3,003,798	2,903,372	8,817,506	9,201,130
Netherlands and possessions	2,761,568	2,898,456	2,136,778	2,251,120
United States of Columbia	965,720	1,339,044	809,553	351,343
Central America States	300,855	..	610,514	610,562
Italy	1,168,905	1,321,104	2,896,677	2,619,000
Brazil	924,495	757,175	7,309,586	6,963,706
China	1,227,350	688,752	2,489,152	2,027,758
Denmark	698,467	687,638	110,102	71,084
Venezuela	542,215	636,406	1,334,612	1,227,208
Portugal	750,725	618,024	298,908	220,290
Argentine Republic	857,015	600,632	306,558	326,746
Mexico	533,764	586,212	1,138,756	1,062,559
Hayti	491,866	578,563	374,946	377,220
Sweden and Norway	467,085	509,562	328,725	283,270
Japan	268,167	311,387	867,136	745,313
Chili	247,363	210,098	232,153	30,570
St. Domingo	198,025	193,351	296,648	314,680
Uruguay	223,982	174,933	708,987	553,600
Austria	25,692	104,364	1,319,473	1,196,545
Russia	64,158	38,730	687,093	599,013
Switzerland	10,262	..	2,738,965	..
Other countries	606,827	3,719,781	1,487,976	6,734,384
Total	63,475,125	73,009,116	90,117,225	85,579,316

UNITED STATES.

Annex D.—RETURN of the Number of Seamen who have been Engaged, Discharged, Left Behind, Reported Dead or Deserted, or who have been Relieved at the British Consulate-General, New York, and showing the Total Number of British and Foreign Sailors who were Engaged, Discharged, &c., from British Ships, with the Amount of Wages paid at the Consulate to Seamen on Discharge from their Ships, and from Hospital or Gaol; and also showing the Number of New Agreements entered into during the Year 1886.

Seamen.											Wages.			Agreements.
Engaged.	Discharged.	Left Behind.			Died.			Deserted.	Relieved.	Nationality.		Total Number of Seamen.	Paid on Discharge from Vessels.	Paid on Discharge from Hospital or Gaol.	Total Wages Paid.	Number Opened.
		In Gaol.	In Hospital.	Total.	At Sea.	On Shore.	Total.			British.	Foreign.					
11,614	6,862	12	158	170	55	16	71	5,114	372	15,561	8,642	24,203	Dollars c. 320,075 15	Dollars c. 4,202 47	Dollars c. 324,277 62	277

PROVIDENCE.

Mr. Vice-Consul Stockwell reports as follows :—

During 1886 there has been a general improvement in business. The jewellery business, one of our greater industries (about 160 establishments), shows an increase in volume of 25 per cent. The cotton and woollen industries have been successful—the former more than the latter, perhaps. The conflicts between capital and labour, with one or two exceptions, have not been long continued. Wages are generally unchanged. An organisation of manufacturing capitalists has been formed "to fight" the Knights of Labour. It is believed that, at the present time, this organisation is helping a "boycotted" company to hold out against the demands of the strikers. It is true, doubtless, in this State at least, that labour has only interfered with itself to its own injury, and to the injury of capital.

The number of arrivals, coastwise and foreign, at the port of Providence was 4,552, bringing the following merchandise, the foreign lumber and crude manufactures thereof coming from Canada :—

Marginal notes: General report on trade. Labour. Arrivals and principal imports.

Articles.		Quantity.
Lumber	Feet	8,195,000
Shingles	„	2,877,000
Laths	„	13,715,000
Pickets	Pieces	10,480
Piling	„	1,000
Wood (pulp)	Cords	575
Salt	Lbs.	6,529,295
Logwood	Tons	2,448
Brimstone	„	1,185
Potatoes	Bushels	33,311
Coal, foreign	Tons	966
„ domestic	„	1,037,000
Starch	Casks	646
Wool, foreign	Lbs.	26,776
„ domestic	Bales	35,397
„ „	Socks	39,036
Cotton „	Bales	225,140
Lumber „	Feet	57,632,715
Flour „	Barrels	277,661
Corn ,	Bushels	1,949,000
Oats „	„	1,217,000
Liquors	Barrels	68,528

The above are importations direct. Foreign importations received under the Act providing for bonded cars and boats, 460,041 dol. Amount of duties collected, 141,445 dol. Tonnage dues, 344 dol. 52 c. Customs fees, 866 dol. 79 c. Tonnage of the port: Sail, 16,314 tons; steam, 19,167 tons.

Exports were very small, aggregating in value only 1,866 dol. Vessels clearing at this port cannot obtain cargoes enough for ballast, and are obliged to take earth. A good part of a bluff fronting the harbour has been carried away as ballast; and yet there is a fine harbour—a good roadstead easy of access. Vessels chartered to bring foreign merchandise discharge at Boston, because they cannot get return cargoes here The port charges are less than at other ports and are as follows for a vessel of 500 tons, American or foreign pilotage.

Marginal note: Exports small.

UNITED STATES.

	Dol.	c.
Pilotage, compulsory (14 feet)	35	00
Health officer, if needed	2	50
Towage, if needed	8	00
Entry fee	2	50
Surveyor's fee	3	00
Port warden	2	50
Discharging cargo	125	00
Tonnage dues	150	00
Hospital „ (7)	2	80

Cotton.

The charge for wharfage is ½ c. per ton, except when discharging or receiving cargo, then wharfage is free.

The price of cotton during the year ranged from 10 to $9\frac{3}{8}$ c., and sales amounted to 133,392 bales, which does not include shipments direct from the south to manufacturers.

The price of print cloths has ranged from $3\frac{1}{8}$ to $3\frac{1}{4}$ c. for 64,464 squares, and the bales amounted to 2,139,800 pieces. The price of 56 by 60 square fluctuated between $2\frac{3}{4}$ and $3\frac{1}{16}$ c.

Population.

POPULATION.

Providence, 1885	118,070
Newport „	19,566
Whole State	304,284
Gain since 1880	18,292
Total vote, gubernatorial, 1886	26,875
„ „ presidential, 1884	32,771
Area, State, square miles	10,531

The 250th anniversary of the founding of Rhode Island and Providence Plantation was celebrated on June 23 and 24, 1886.

Railroad terminal facilities.

The question of greatest importance to the commerce of Providence is that of terminal facilities for railways. A Commission was appointed three years ago to report a plan, but its suggestions were of too costly a character and were rejected; since then nothing has been done. The difficulty lies in the land approaches to the city.

Annex A.—RETURN of all Vessels Entered from and Cleared for a Foreign Port during the Year 1886.

ENTERED.

Nationality.	Sailing. Number of Vessels.	Sailing. Tons.	Steam. Number of Vessels.	Steam. Tons.	Total. Number of Vessels.	Total. Tons.
British	57	6,883	1	626	58	7,509
American	25	5,444	...	...	25	5,444
Italian	2	983	...	...	2	983
Australian	1	691	...	...	1	691
Total	85	14,001	1	626	86	14,627
„ for the year preceding	88	13,688	...	...	89	14,731

NEW YORK.

Cleared.

Nationality.	Sailing. Number of Vessels.	Sailing. Tons.	Steam. Number of Vessels.	Steam. Tons.	Total. Number of Vessels.	Total. Tons.
British	55	6,546	1	626	56	7,172
American	7	1,970	...	...	7	1,970
Total	62	8,516	1	626	63	9,142
,, for the year preceding	37	4,894	...	...	45	6,226

Annex B.—Return of Principal Articles of Export from Providence during the Years 1886-85.

Articles.	1886. Quantity.	1886. Value.	1885. Quantity.	1885. Value.
	Tons.	£		£
Coke	659	339	..	884
Coal	36	35	..	..
Miscellaneous	..	11	..	..
Total	..	385	..	884

Return of Principal Articles of Import into Providence during the Years 1886-85.

Articles.	Value.	Value.
	£	£
Dry goods	49,985	42,112
Chemicals	21,504	13,711
Metals, and manufactures of	10,340	18,555
All other	25,330	29,473
Total	107,159	103,851

UNITED STATES.

Annex C.—TABLE showing the Total Value of all Articles Exported from Providence and Imported into Providence from and to Foreign Countries during the Years 1886-85.

Country.	Exports.		Imports.	
	1886.	1885.	1886.	1885.
	£	£	£	£
Nova Scotia	35	..	..	..
Cuba	339	..	..	..
Turk Island	..	116	..	..
Prince Edward Island	..	64	..	..
England	..	..	40,385	49,567
Germany	..	..	13,808	17,494
France	..	..	9,252	6,463
Austria	..	..	3,691	..
Other countries	..	..	40,023	30,100
Total	374	180	107,159	103,624

LONDON:

Printed for Her Majesty's Stationery Office,

By HARRISON AND SONS,

Printers in Ordinary to Her Majesty.

(Wt. 7730　75　6 | 87—H & S　233)

FOREIGN OFFICE.
1887.
ANNUAL SERIES.

No. 186.
DIPLOMATIC AND CONSULAR REPORTS ON TRADE AND FINANCE.

UNITED STATES.

REPORT FOR THE YEAR 1886
ON THE
TRADE OF THE CONSULAR DISTRICT OF SAN FRANCISCO.

REFERENCE TO PREVIOUS REPORTS [C. 4737], Commercial No. 10, 1886, and [C. 4761], Commercial No. 12, 1886.

Presented to both Houses of Parliament by Command of Her Majesty,
JUNE, 1887.

LONDON:
PRINTED FOR HER MAJESTY'S STATIONERY OFFICE,
BY HARRISON AND SONS, ST. MARTIN'S LANE,
PRINTERS IN ORDINARY TO HER MAJESTY.

And to be purchased, either directly or through any Bookseller, from
EYRE AND SPOTTISWOODE, EAST HARDING STREET, FLEET STREET, E.C., and
32, ABINGDON STREET, WESTMINSTER, S.W.; or
ADAM AND CHARLES BLACK, NORTH BRIDGE, EDINBURGH; or
HODGES, FIGGIS, & Co., 104, GRAFTON STREET, DUBLIN.

1887.

[C.—4923—109.] *Price 6d.*

New Series of Reports.

Reports of the Annual Series have been issued from Her Majesty's Diplomatic and Consular Officers at the following places, and may be obtained from the sources indicated on the title-page:—

No.		Price.	No.		Price.
60.	Mozambique	5d.	123.	Hyogo	1d.
61.	Hanyang	1d.	124.	Tamsui	1d.
62.	Stockholm	1d.	125.	Malaga	1d.
63.	Paris	1d.	126.	Marseilles	1d.
64.	Tunis	1d.	127.	Boulogne	2d.
65.	The Hague	2d.	128.	Warsaw	1d.
66.	Italy	2d.	129.	Monte Video	1d.
67.	Smyrna	2d.	130.	Christiania	4d.
68.	Fiume	1d.	131.	Gothenburg	2d.
69.	Tabreez	1d.	132.	Kiungchow	1d.
70.	Philippopolis	1d.	133.	Amoy	1d.
71.	Rome	1d.	134.	Genoa	1d.
72.	Vienna	1d.	135.	Trebizond	1d.
73.	St. Petersburg	2d.	136.	Savannah	1d.
74.	Ichang	1d.	137.	Wilmington	2d.
75.	Salonica	1d.	138.	Bolivar	3d.
76.	Brussels	2d.	139.	Wênchow	1d.
77.	Alexandria	1d.	140.	Chicago	2d.
78.	Patras	1d.	141.	Fiume	1d.
79.	Maranham	1d.	142.	Port Saïd	1d.
80.	Taganrog	2d.	143.	Java	1d.
81.	Jeddah	1d.	144.	Puerto Cabello	1d.
82.	Suakin	1d.	145.	Coquimbo	1d.
83.	Colonia	1d.	146.	Vera Cruz	2d.
84.	Suez	1d.	147.	Bengazi	1d.
85.	Paris	1d.	148.	Canary Islands	1d.
86.	Brest	1d.	149.	Rome	1d.
87.	Puerto Plata	1d.	150.	Madeira	1d.
88.	Charleston	1d.	151.	Tahiti	1d.
89.	Tripoli	1d.	152.	Corunna	1d.
90.	Saigon	1d.	153.	Vienna	1d.
91.	Cherbourg	1d.	154.	Cagliari	1d.
92.	New Orleans	2d.	155.	St. Petersburg	2d.
93.	Galatz	1d.	156.	Taiwan	1d.
94.	Baltimore	1d.	157.	Foochow	1d.
95.	Tokio	4d.	158.	Tonga	1d.
96.	Havre	3d.	159.	Wuhu	1d.
97.	Barcelona	3d.	160.	Lisbon	1d.
98.	Volo	1d.	161.	Ning-po	1d.
99.	Damascus	1d.	162.	Cadiz	2d.
100.	Paris	1d.	163.	Bilbao	1d.
101.	Bordeaux	2d.	164.	Jaffa	1d.
102.	Serajevo	1d.	165.	Van	1d.
103.	Manila	1d.	166.	Bushire	1d.
104.	Galveston	1d.	167.	Riga	1d.
105.	Aleppo	1d.	168.	Santos	1d.
106.	Rio de Janeiro	1d.	169.	Charleston	1d.
107.	Truxillo	1d.	170.	Newchwang	1d.
108.	St. Petersburg	3d.	171.	Amsterdam	1d.
109.	Leghorn	1d.	172.	Ajaccio	1d.
110.	Boston	1d.	173.	Chinkiang	2d.
111.	Buenos Ayres	2d.	174.	Naples	3d.
112.	Kewkiang	1d.	175.	Smyrna	1d.
113.	Teheran	2d.	176.	Belgrade	1d.
114.	Beyrout	1d.	177.	Philadelphia	2d.
115.	Odessa	5d.	178.	Stockholm	2d.
116.	Carthagena	1d.	179.	Pernambuco	1d.
117.	Santo Domingo	1d.	180.	Frankfort-on-Main	1d.
118.	Mollendo	1d.	181.	Mogador	2d.
119.	Guayaquil	1d.	182.	New York	2d.
120.	Valparaiso	1d.	183.	Swatow	1d.
121.	San José	1d.	184.	Berlin	1d.
122.	Pakhoi	1d.	185.	Philippopolis	1d.

No. 186.

Reference to previous Report [C. 4737], Commercial No. 10, 1886, and [C. 4761], Commercial No. 12, 1886.

UNITED STATES.

SAN FRANCISCO.

Acting-Consul Mason to the Marquis of Salisbury.

My Lord,   *San Francisco, April* 16, 1887.

I HAVE the honour to enclose my commercial report on the trade of San Francisco for the year 1886.

I regret to say that the preparation of this report has been delayed owing to a serious attack of illness, from which I am slowly recovering.

I have also the honour to transmit reports on the trade of Portland and Astoria, Oregon, Port Townsend, Washington, and Los Angeles, San Diego, and Wilmington, California, for the year 1886.

                                       I have, &c.
                       (Signed)   CHAS. MASON.

Report on the Trade and Commerce of California for 1886.

General remarks. It was mentioned in Mr. Consul Stanley's report for 1885 that California had emerged from depression into a measure of prosperity, and I have now to report that the year 1886 was characterised by the general prosperity of almost all the leading industries throughout the State.

Increased prosperity.

Increased immigration. I cannot find that any strictly accurate statistics are kept of the immigration into the State; but from such as are obtainable, as well as from the large general expansion in the demand which has been experienced for many and varied descriptions of commodities, there is no doubt that the State has acquired a large increase of population during the past year.

Causes of increased immigration. This immigration is the result of two causes, and it is significant, that so far as the first is concerned, it only became operative about four years ago, and then to a much smaller extent than exists to-day.

1st. The completion of rival transcontinental railroads.

2nd. The advertising of the varied resources of this coast, and particularly of this State, which has been undertaken primarily in the interests of these railroads.

Increased transcontinental railroad facilities. Previous to 1883, the only through railroad connections between this State and Coast, and the great centres of population in the Eastern States and Europe, were the roads under the control of the Central Pacific system, now known as the Southern Pacific Company. In that year, the Northern Pacific Railroad Company completed their through connection from the East to Portland, Oregon.

It was stated in last year's report that a through transcontinental

(237)

2   UNITED STATES.

road, having its terminus at San Diego, had been completed. This road forms part of the Atchison, Topeka, and Santa Fé system, which a short time previously had acquired running powers over the Southern Pacific road, from a point where it joins their system in Southern California into San Francisco.

During last summer the completion of the Canadian-Pacific Railroad into Port Moody, British Columbia, made the fourth transcontinental connection between the Atlantic and Pacific coasts.

Immigrants arriving viâ Canadian-Pacific Railroad.

I mention this last road, as it is found that not a few immigrants have reached this State by means of it, and the coast steamers which run in connection with it.

We have thus within the past few years acquired three great transcontinental systems of railroads upon this coast, in addition to that of the Central Pacific system, which had previously held a complete monopoly of the through traffic.

Railroad competition causing low fares and freights, and the result thereof.

These roads have entered into competition with each other for public patronage, and while fares and freights over those within United States territory have been regulated in a measure by what are known as "pool" arrangements; these in their observance have not lessened competition for public favours, and by reason of breaches of their conditions, and open ruptures, this coast has, for the first time in its experience, had the benefits resulting from free competition in railroad fares and freights.

The presence of these competing roads—I confine my remarks now to those having their terminus on the Pacific Coast of the United States—is characterised by all the signs of rivalry; each is advertising their system and the resources of this coast, and each is fortifying their through system by the building of branch roads upon the coast itself.

Activity in branch railroad building in this State.

The result is that within California new branch roads are either projected, or are in course of being built, to very many points which have not heretofore possessed railroad communication. In fact, railroad building within the State was never so active as at present.

Perhaps the most important roads being built are two under the control of the Southern Pacific Company.

Railway communication between Oregon and California nearly completed.

Important branch line through southern part of State.

One will complete the Oregon and California road, and give through railroad communication between San Francisco and Portland, Oregon. It is expected that this will be completed during the ensuing summer, and that it will enable San Francisco merchants and manufacturers to regain trade which they lost to eastern competitors on completion of the Northern Pacific Railroad into Portland. The other will connect San Francisco with the fertile coast counties as far south as Santa Barbara, where it strikes inland, rejoining the Southern Pacific Overland system to the north of Los Angeles. The entire length is little short of 400 miles.

I have mentioned the railroads as having primarily conduced to the comparatively large immigration which the State has experienced, and may here state that this immigration is for the most part composed of a very desirable class.

Class of immigrants arriving.

It is largely of people from the Eastern and Middle States, and possessed of some small amount of capital.

For the most part they have had some agricultural experience, and are found to purchase small tracts of land and adopt a purely agricultural life.

Grain crop generally abundant.

With the single exception of wheat, the grain crops of the State in 1886 were, generally speaking, abundant. The wheat crop in many important sections proved a great disappointment, resulting, no doubt, from an excess of moisture during the months of sowing.

SAN FRANCISCO.

The surplus of wheat available for exportation from the crop of 1886 is estimated at about 715,000 tons (of 2,240 lbs.). *Surplus of wheat for exportation.*

The actual exports of wheat and flour from July 1 to December 31, 1886, have been together equal to 447,000 tons of wheat, and the estimated surplus remaining on hand on the latter date was therefore about 268,000 tons. *Exports of wheat.*

Farmers sold freely of their wheat during the autumn months, preferring to accept current prices rather than incur the expenses of holding over to a later period. *Farmers free sellers.*

From the best information I can gather, I believe that as a class they improved their condition during the year.

In the last years' report, it was mentioned that they were exercising all the various economies of improved farming machinery, &c.; and there remains no doubt that wheat and other cereal crops are now being produced in this State at a cost for labour, &c., far below what was conceived as possible some years ago. *Continued economies in garnering crops.*

A very large saving of the labour of harvesting has been accomplished in the pretty general use during the past year of a combined machine, which cuts, threshes, and bags the grain. I am informed that the success of this machine is assured, and that it accomplishes a large economy.

The wheat of the State has been almost exclusively shipped to Europe; and mainly, as usual, to the United Kingdom, the deficiency there of the harvest having caused a ready demand for it. *Bulk of wheat still shipped to Europe.*

The average monthly price of No. 1 Californian wheat from the opening of the season on July 1 to December 31, 1886, was as follows:— *Average monthly price of wheat at San Francisco.*

I quote free on board ship at San Francisco, and per quarter of 500 lbs.

	Dol.	c.		£	s.	d.
July	6	25	equal to	1	5	0
August	6	65	„	1	6	6
September	6	75	„	1	7	0
October	6	75	„	1	7	0
November	7	05	„	1	8	2
December	7	50	„	1	10	0

The average price in Liverpool was as follows, likewise per quarter of 500 lbs.:— *Average price of wheat in Liverpool.*

	£	s.	d.
July	1	13	
August	1	14	3
September	1	14	9
October	1	13	9
November	1	15	3
December	1	18	0

The margin between the San Francisco and Liverpool quotations represents freight, insurance, commission, and charges.

The flour millers in this State do not now find, to any extent, a profitable market for their manufacture in Europe; but they have an increasing demand within the bounds of the State itself, and for export to the Pacific Islands and China. *Flour trade.*

The milling capacity of the State did not increase during 1886. A very large mill is now, however, approaching completion, and will probably start work some time this year if our new wheat crop proves a good one, as it now promises. This is the new Starr and Company's mill at Wheatport, which will be of an estimated daily capacity of 8,000 barrels, being probably the largest flouring mill in the world.

Outlook for next crop good.

At the close of 1886, an insufficient quantity of rain had fallen in many important wheat-growing sections of the State, and a reduced acreage had been seeded. The rainfall has since been ample, and the deficient acreage is made good. At present the outlook is for an average wheat crop.

Wine.

The vintage of the past year, though not so large as that of 1885, was most satisfactory, and the quality of the wine produced has shown great improvement upon that of late years. The weather was very favourable for the growth of the vines and maturing the fruit, and the vineyards were, to a great extent, free from many of the pests and accidents to which they are more or less liable. The total production is estimated at from 18,000,000 to 19,000,000 gallons. Annex B. shows that 757,600 gallons were exported; this was sent by sea. About 4,500,000 gallons were sent by rail to New York.

Grape grafting; increased attention thereto.

Each year shows increased attention to the value of grafting foreign cuttings on the Missouri grape, those of the Bordeaux and Sauterne type being especially selected for the purpose.

It is estimated that there are 180,000 acres of bearing vines in California.

Successful raisin cultivation.

The raisin grape is now extensively cultivated in many of the more southerly counties, and raisins are likely to become a large product of the State. In some districts the quality of the raisins packed has been quite equal to the imported European varieties.

Fruit-growing, drying, &c.

Fruit-raising has made rapid strides throughout the entire State, north as well as south.

California has been distinguished as a wheat-growing State, but in many of the counties the wheat fields lessen each year, and the area of orchards and vineyards increases. Other counties, notably those of Fresno, Tulare, Merced, and San Joaquin, are coming to the front as fruit-producing districts, owing to the successful introduction of irrigation. The southerly counties are likewise producing very largely now of citrus fruits, much of the crop being shipped east to good markets. To the immigrant, with more or less means, the attractions of fruit-farming are great, and very many have been successful in their investment in this branch of industry. It is more than probable that the time is coming when California may be the chief fruit and wine-producing State of the Union.

Product of dried fruits &c.

I give below the product for the past year of dried fruits, honey, and bees'-wax:—

Articles.		Quantity.
Raisins	20-lb. boxes	702,000
Honey, extracted	Lbs.	6,000,000
Honeycomb	,,	800,000
Bees'-wax	,,	80,000
French prunes	,,	2,000,000
German ,,	,,	125,000
Apples, sun-dried	,,	300,000
Peaches ,,	,,	750,000
Plums ,,	,,	500,000
Pears ,,	,,	50,000
Grapes ,,	,,	175,000
Apricots ,,	,,	150,000
Nectarines ,,	,,	30,000
Figs ,,	,,	150,000
Apples, evaporated	,,	500,000
Apricots, evaporated and sun-dried, bleached	,,	450,000
Peaches, evaporated, peeled	,,	100,000
,, ,, unpeeled	,,	200,000
Plums, evaporated	,,	85,000
Nectarines, evaporated	,,	25,000
Walnuts	,,	750,000
Almonds	,,	600,000
Pea-nuts	,,	275,000

There was shipped besides from this State to points east of the Missouri river, over 16,000 tons of green fruit.

Green fruit shipped East.

At the date of the last report it was mentioned that the shipping interests on this coast were in an especially depressed condition; and, so far as what is known as the foreign service is concerned, this condition is not changed for the better. By the foreign service is meant chiefly the service of carrying wheat and other produce to Europe. The average monthly rates of freight ruling for this service during 1886, were as follows:—

Shipping interests on Pacific Coast.

	Per Ton. £ s. d.
January	1 10 0
February	1 11 3
March	1 12 6
April	1 13 9
May	1 13 9
June	1 15 0
July	1 14 0
August	1 12 6
September	1 11 3
October	1 10 0
November	1 7 6
December	1 10 0

Monthly rates of freight to Europe, and tonnage chartered.

There were chartered during 1886 for this European service:— 520,574 tons register of shipping, of which 341,209 tons register were British, and 179,365 tons register of other nationalities, chiefly American.

It is quite certain that the rates of freight which shipowners received for this service, must have been again quite unremunerative.

Rates of freight unremunerative.

On the other hand, the coast shipping trade during 1886 experienced a great revival of business. The increase of immigration, and the railroad building, which has been already referred to, have created a very large demand for timber and coal all along the coast; and the

Coast shipping trade good.

comparatively large fleet of coasting vessels, now owned in San Francisco and on the coast, have been employed to their utmost capacity at rates of freight highly remunerative to their owners. The condition of the coast shipping trade has not been better in ten years than it was during the most part of 1886.

Iron shipbuilding. — Mention was made in last year's report of the inauguration of iron shipbuilding on this coast, by the Union Iron Works Company having their large works at the "Potrero," on the south side of the Bay of San Francisco.

This company, which has long held a reputation for the manufacture of all descriptions of large machinery, has lately added all the appliances necessary for iron shipbuilding, and has already built a number of small steamers for coasting business.

They are now constructing a steel steamer of 1,000 tons register with triple expansion engines, &c., for the Canadian Pacific Railroad; and have contracted with the United States Government for the construction of a steel cruiser of 4,000 tons register, to carry eight large rifled guns, besides other smaller armament. The contract price of this vessel is 1,000,000 dol.

The shipbuilding department of the works is provided with permanent scaffolding over the launching ways; overhead are travelling cranes and hoisting shears, with a capacity to lift 120 tons in a single piece.

Dock accommodation. — Adjoining the shipbuilding ways, the company is just completing the construction of a hydraulic-lift dock of a sufficient size to accommodate ships of the largest dimensions, which may require repairs. I consider this an important addition to the shipbuilding facilities of the port.

Good demand for labour. — In the city of San Francisco, and generally on the coast, workmen of all classes were well employed during the past year.

San Francisco growing. — The city itself continues to grow in population, and the number of substantial houses and business buildings which have lately been erected, point to an increase of wealth and prosperity.

Exports generally. — The statistics given in Annex B. show a fair increase in the export trade of San Francisco compared with that of 1885.

Wheat. — Wheat as usual heads the list of exports; the yield was the best since 1880, the quality good, and the prices to the producer on the whole satisfactory. The flour-milling business has been rather under the average in extent, and its profits less than in ordinary years. The

Flour. — exports of flour were about 1,250,000 barrels, one half of which was sent to Europe, and the other to ports in the North and South Pacific; Sydney, New South Wales, taking an unusually large proportion. Attention is called in Annex B. to the increased value of exports to France, these exports consisted mainly of wheat and flour.

Salmon. — The salmon pack for this coast was as large as that of 1885, and the prices much better.

Imports generally. — The import returns in Annex B. show, in the aggregate, a considerable improvement over those of 1885. This is especially noticeable in raw silk, tea, tin-plates, and cement.

Tin plates. — These all come from Great Britain; the requirements of the fish, fruit and vegetable canneries, resulted in an increased demand for the article.

Cement. — The importation is steadily on the increase. There is likely to be a continued demand for cement; negotiations are now on foot for the sale of one or more of the City "Horse Car" tram lines to a company who will convert them into cable lines. The road-bed for the cable will be laid with cement, and large quantities required for the purpose.

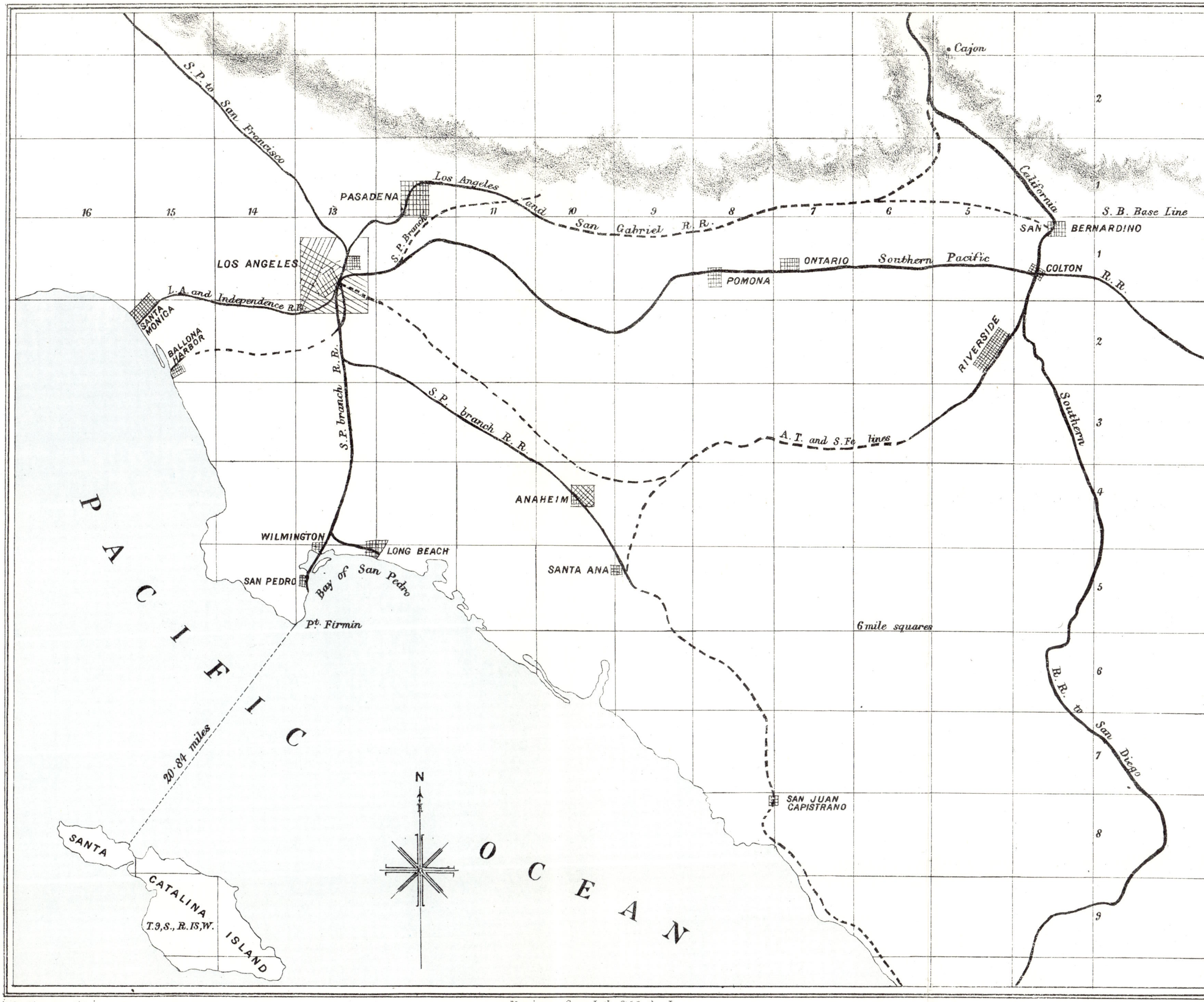

(1075.6/87. 126-67.)

Harrison & Sons Lith. St Martins Lane.

SAN FRANCISCO.

The importations of coal, salt, scrap and pig-iron, are well maintained, though the prices have not been remunerative.

The following table has been compiled by Mr. John Valentine, vice president and general manager of Wells, Fargo and Company. *Precious metals.*

"The following is the annual product of gold, silver, copper and lead, in the States west of the Missouri river, excluding British Columbia and Mexico":—

Year.	Gold.	Silver.	Copper.	Lead.	Total.
	£	£	£	£	£
1886	5,912,285	10,427,370	1,855,351	1,837,038	20 032,044
1885	5,277,000	8,903,000	1,568,000	1,713,000	17,461,000

Of this result the States of California, Nevada and Oregon, and the territories of Washington, Idaho, Utah, and Arizona, comprising this Consular district, contributed 9,439,338*l*.

The production of quicksilver in this State is gradually falling off, *Quicksilver.* owing to a decreased demand at lessening prices. The number of flasks produced in 1885 was 32,080; in 1886, 29,900. Almost all the quicksilver exported goes to Mexico.

Gold mining in this State has prospered throughout the year, and *Gold mining* the output from some of the mines of the celebrated Comstock Lode *prosperous.* in the State of Nevada is again on the increase.

The passenger arrivals and departures by sea and rail at and from *Immigration.* San Francisco in 1885 and 1886 were as follows:—

Year.	By Rail. Arrived.	By Rail. Departed.	By Sea. Arrived.	By Sea. Departed.	Totals. Arrived.	Totals. Departed
1886	77,519	53.982	20.201	22,193	97,720	76,175
1885	56,957	35,924	22,498	22,160	79,455	58,084

The above figures are those furnished by the Southern Pacific system, and of course are exclusive of the many who came by the Atlantic and Pacific and Northern Pacific lines.

The arrivals and departures by sea, from different countries, were as follows in 1886:—

Country.	Arrived.	Departed.
China and Japan	10.208	13,366
Panama	3,295	3,152
British Columbia	2,628	1,973
Australia and Hawaiian Islands	3,590	3,118
Mexico	339	475
Other countries	141	109
Totals	20,201	22,193

Since the completion of the Northern Pacific and Canadian Pacific railroads, there has been a large immigration from the Eastern States to

UNITED STATES.

the States and Territories north and east of us, and this will in time largely stimulate the demand for California products.

Government land being settled upon, and estimated amount remaining.

The California Immigration Association claims to have been instrumental in settling about 3,000,000 of the 5,000,000 acres filed upon and entered during the past five years. It is estimated that there remain about 13,000,000 acres of land, mostly remote, suitable for agricultural purposes. The total amount of remaining land is estimated at 38,000,000 acres, including 10,000,000 acres for the areas of the lakes, bays, rivers, landsteep, rocky or otherwise unproductive. The remainder is timber land.

Extract from report of the President of the California Immigration Association.

The annual report of Arthur R. Briggs, President of the Association, says:—"The year just closed is in striking contrast with that of 1880 or 1881, when depression existed in almost every branch of industry. Now there is activity and growth in all directions. Within a few years thousands of new homes have been established on Government land that for years before was regarded as valueless for general agricultural purposes; large private holdings have been subdivided and improved; new railroads have been built and projected and new towns have been established. As illustrative of the growth of the State, it may be mentioned that 71 post-offices have been established in less than a year.

"The point has now been reached in our experience which presents new and important factors in the work. Each year the average of desirable Government land near railroad communication grows less. Locations which a few years ago were thought remote, are now, in matter of distance, regarded as quite desirable. There is still much Government land in the State suitable for agricultural purposes, but it is not situated near railroads or towns. It is generally in sparsely settled districts. The more distant from railroad communication, the greater the difficulty in effecting settlement. While a considerable portion of newcomers are willing to go inland 30 or 50 miles, others, with perhaps more money, are desirous of securing houses in well-settled portions of the State, where they can have school, church, and social privileges. This class desire to purchase improved farms or lands unimproved near railroad towns. There is almost daily inquiry at the office in respect to lands thus situated. I call your attention to this feature of immigration, because I deem it worthy of your careful consideration. The people who come to the States to purchase improved lands comprise a most desirable immigration."

Population.

The population of the State, exclusive of Chinese, is estimated at rather over 1,000,000. San Francisco has a population of 350,000. I am informed by the Chinese Consul-General that it is estimated there are 50,000 Chinese in this State, and that the Chinese population of the United States, and who are mainly centred on this coast, has decreased over 30,000 since May 1882, when the present Restriction Act went into effect.

Labour.

The demand for labour in 1886 showed a great improvement on the previous year. Although a great many skilled artisans and others came into the State, most of them found remunerative employment, and there were probably fewer unemployed men in San Francisco than there have been for several years. The tendency of wages has been to decline, and there is hardly a doubt but that in time they will fall to the rates paid in the Eastern States; last year they remained about steady. There was a brisk demand for mechanics of all descriptions for the southern part of the State, still there was no particular dearth of men. White men were engaged in the place of Chinamen to a certain extent at lumbering and in logging camps; but Chinese are still

SAN FRANCISCO.

principally employed in vineyards and on fruit farms, as they are willing to accept lower wages.

The following table gives the remuneration of men paid by the day, and their hours of labour:— *Tables of wages.*

	Hours.	Rate of Wages.			Average.
		s.		s.	s.
Blacksmiths	10	12	to	14	12
Bricklayers	9	10	„	22	20
Cabinet-makers	10	10	„	14	12
Carpenters	9	10	„	16	14
Gardeners	10	10	„	16	12
Iron Workers	10	7	„	14	12
Miners (coal)	..	8	„	11	10
„ (gold)	..	10	„	12	12
Moulders (iron)	10	13	„	14	13
Painters (house)	9	8	„	12	12
Pattern-makers	9	13	„	16	14
Plasterers	8	16	„	20	20
Plumbers	9	14	„	16	12
Wheelwrights	10	9	„	20	12
Whiteners	9	10	„	14	12

The undermentioned receive weekly wages:—

	Hours.	Rate of Wages.		Average.
		£ s. d.	£ s. d.	£ s. d.
Bakers	10	1 10 0 to	4 8 0	2 8 0
Barbers	..	2 8 0	4 4 0	3 6 0
Bookbinders	10	3 0 0	4 16 0	3 12 0
Coopers	10	3 12 0	4 4 0	3 0 0
Drayman	11	2 8 0	3 0 0	3 0 0
Locksmiths	10	2 8 0	3 0 0	2 8 0
Silversmiths	10	3 0 0	5 0 0	3 12 0
Tailors	10	2 8 0	4 0 0	3 0 0

Those mentioned below are paid by the month:—

	Hours.	Rate of Wages.		Average.
		£ s. d.	£ s. d.	£ s. d.
Book-keepers	9	8 0 0 to	40 0 0	..
Brewers	12	10 0 0	18 0 0	12 0 0
Butchers	12	10 0 0	25 0 0	16 0 0
Chemists	8	8 0 0	30 0 0	15 0 0
Cooks (female)	..	4 0 0	8 0 0	6 0 0
Servants (women and girls)	..	3 0 0	6 0 0	5 0 0
Steamship men	..	5 0 0	14 0 0	..

UNITED STATES.

Seamen engaged, &c.

The following table shows the entries made at this Consulate regarding seamen during the years 1885-86:—

Years.	Engaged.	Discharged.	Deserted.	Sent to Hospital.	Reported Dead.
1886	2,720	861	1,966	34	31
1885	2,461	1,031	1,474	36	58

City finances.

The financial condition of the city and county of San Francisco on the 1st day of October, 1886, was as follows:—

	£
Funded debt, at 6 per cent. and 7 per cent. interest..	466,071
Less sinking fund on hand	185,079
Net funded debt	280,992

The value of property owned by the city and county amounted to 3,404,600*l*.

The valuation of property for city and county and State purposes (taxes) for 1886-1887 was:—

	£
Assessed value of real estate and improvements ..	35,081,829
Assessed value of personal property	10,948,372
Total	46,030,201

The rate of taxation for city and county purposes was equal to 4*s*. 0½*d*. per 20*l*., and for State purposes 2*s*. 3*d*. per 20*l*. The taxes levied amounted to 723,132*l*.

NOTE.—The values are reduced to sterling at the rate of 5 dol. to the £. The current value of the £ sterling is 4 dol. 84 c.

Annex A.—RETURN of all Shipping at the Port of San Francisco in the Year 1886.

ENTERED.

Nationality.	Sailing. Number of Vessels.	Sailing. Tons.	Steam. Number of Vessels.	Steam. Tons.	Total. Number of Vessels.	Total. Tons.
British	255	362,823	55	80,237	310	443,060
American, from foreign countries	281	188,066	167	234,634	448	422,700
American, from Atlantic ports of Union	29	52,323	...	...	29	52,323
Hawaiian	4	1,570	12	20,562	16	22,132
German	14	17,381	5	1,840	19	19,221
French	...	...	2	1,106	2	1,106
Others	11	8,282	3	3,119	14	11,401
Total	594	630,445	244	341,498	838	971,943
" for the year preceding	575	578,885	223	368,043	798	946,928

SAN FRANCISCO

Cleared.

Nationality.	Sailing. Number of Vessels.	Sailing. Tons.	Steam. Number of Vessels.	Steam. Tons.	Total. Number of Vessels.	Total. Tons.
British	250	353,568	53	80,882	303	434,450
American, for foreign countries	288	264,421	168	232,801	456	497,222
American, for Atlantic ports of the Union	9	11,557	...	...	9	11,557
Hawaiian	7	2,453	15	22,950	22	25,403
German	16	18,717	5	1,840	21	20,557
French	...	...	2	1,106	2	1,106
Others	11	7,400	5	2,685	16	10,085
Total	581	658,116	248	342,264	829	1,000,380
,, for the year preceding	575	553,829	228	367,591	803	921,420

The entries and clearances of American ships do not include the coasting trade or whaling and fishing voyages.

Annex B.—Return of Principal Articles of Export from San Francisco during the Years 1885-86.

Articles.		1886. Quantity.	1886. Value.	1885. Quantity.	1885. Value.
			£		£
Wheat and flour	Tons	850,425	5,121,800	777,000	4,216,000
Tinned salmon	Cases	181,300	183,000	180,900	165,000
Lead	Lbs.	10,611,700	103,000	9,845,800	85,350
Tinned fruit and vegetables	Cases	98,700	86,300	121,000	110,000
Borax	Lbs.	7,934,000	80,000	7,506,000	89,000
Wine	Gallons	757,600	74,700	1,201,100	125,600
Timber	Feet	15,352,600	59,000	19,266,000	90,000
Quicksilver	Flasks	7,000	46,000	16,000	92,000
Leather	Rolls	4,100	46,000	4,120	48,600
Other articles	...	...	2,178,500	...	2,360,450
Total	...	...	7,978,300	...	7,382,000

Return of Principal Articles of Import to San Francisco during the Years 1885-86.

Articles.		1886. Quantity.	1886. Value.	1885. Quantity.	1885. Value.
			£		£
Raw silk	Lbs.	4,455,700	2,546,700	2,690,000	1,748,000
Sugar	Tons	101,451	2,095,700	76,500	1,644,000
Coffee	Lbs.	20,432,190	358,000	22,600,000	420,000
Coals	Tons	548,000	340,600	568,400	348,000
Tea	Lbs.	8,949,800	260,400	17,000,000	214,000
Rice	Tons	24,340	205,600	19,300	210,000
Tin-plates	Boxes	152,450	104,950	119,000	83,800
Cement	Barrels	159,000	33,130	66,400	18,000
Scrap-iron	Tons	14,903	30,770	9,600	19,000
Pig-iron	,,	14,200	21,000	11,120	20,000
Other articles	...	...	1,919,650	...	2,375,200
Total	...	...	7,916,500	...	7,100,000

Annex C.—TABLE showing the Total Value of all Articles Exported from San Francisco and Imported to San Francisco from and to Foreign Countries during the Years 1885–86.

Country.	Exports. 1886.	Exports. 1885.	Imports. 1886.	Imports. 1885.
	£	£	£	£
Great Britain	4,095,300	4,185,000	589,470	630,000
China	749,150	740,000	1,225,090	1,200,000
Hawaiian Islands	655,470	500,000	2,140,550	1,800,000
France	533,880	51,800	287,750	300,000
Australia	281,040	272,000	264,880	180,000
Canada	267,450	250,000	192,450	250,000
Mexico	228,050	288,230	58,940	54,730
Central America	146,600	140,000	382,550	460,000
Belgium	122,930	3,600	52,600	62,000
Japan	117,760	121,000	2,042,480	1,300,000
Germany	22,700	14,000	156,150	161,000
Spanish Possessions	3,560	3,000	121,350	108,000
India	750	500	243,250	240,030
Domestic ports and other countries	753,660	812,870	158,990	254,270
Total	7,978,300	7,382,000	7,916,500	7,100,000

PORTLAND OREGON.

Mr. Vice-Consul Laidlaw reports as follows:—

Trade generally. In every branch of business the trade of this district shows a large increase over that of 1885. In all sections of Oregon and Washington Territory tributary to this port the harvests were large, but market prices were low throughout the entire year. From present appearances, business has recovered from the depression that has existed during the past two years, and the general impression is that next year will show a wonderful development of trade. **Tonnage.** The proportion of British tonnage employed in the foreign trade, was 82 per cent. of the whole; about the same proportion as last year.

Imports. Although, as usual, only a small proportion of this trade was done, direct imports being principally received by steamer from San Francisco, and by sail and rail from the Eastern States, yet the annexed tables show a considerable increase in direct foreign trade as compared with last year. **Teas in transit.** They also show a new feature viz., the import of teas in transit by rail for Eastern States and Canada.

Coals. The values of imports by indirect routes cannot be estimated with any degree of accuracy. Prices of coals have again been very low, and nearly all those brought from Australia have been either free of freight, or at a merely nominal rate. The receipts were 20,801 tons domestic, 7,961 tons from British Columbia, 13,518 tons from Australia, 7,350 tons from Great Britain. Market prices of Australian coal ranged from 16s. to 20s. per ton for Sydney, 20s. to 24s. for Newcastle, New South Wales, and of Scotch and English from 24s. to 26s. **Salt. Tin-plates.** The total imports of salt, including direct imports from Liverpool as given in Annex B., were 14,356,000 pounds. Although the consumption of tin-plate was even smaller than last year, yet this is always a large trade and likely to remain so, until American manufacturers succeed in producing a good article to compete. This is one of the few articles which can yet be imported from Great Britain with profit to the manufacturer, in spite of the tariff. Market prices averaged about 20s. per box B.V. for grades of coke, and other grades and charcoal in proportion

Rice. The total imports of rice of all grades were 6,726,000 pounds, including direct imports from Hong-Kong as per Annex B. There was a large increase in imports of tea, and the transit trade has also been Tea. large as the tables show. Imports of pig-iron were trifling, and stocks Pig-iron. at close of the year are reduced. The Oregon Iron and Steel Company, produced none during the year, while in 1885 this company produced 4,137 tons.

Perhaps the largest indirect imports are of jute bags and bagging Jute bags and from Calcutta viâ San Francisco, receipts exceeding 6,000,000 yards and bagging. bags. Market prices were very low, averaging only about 2¾d. for standard 22 by 26 purlap grain-bags. Of wool-packs imports were probably about 50,000. The imports of cement are shown in the Cement. tables. Market prices were fair, averaging 14s. per barrel, and the demand was good. Receipts of American were trifling.

There was an increase of 17 per cent. in the total value of exports to foreign countries, and by sail and rail to the Eastern States and Exports coastwise. The Oregon Pacific Railroad, which has been extended some generally. 15 miles during the year to Albany (the capital of Linn County) has diverted some trade, viâ Yaquina Bay, to San Francisco. The tables annexed to this report give the foreign shipments in detail. Shipments of produce by sail and rail to the Eastern States and exports coast- Coastwise wise are valued at 1,778,845*l*., against a valuation of 1,674,680*l*. in 1885. and rail

Of the total shipments of wheat, 9 per cent. was shipped to San shipments. Francisco and Puget Sound, and in like manner 23 per cent. of the Breadstuffs. flour was exported. These proportions were 30 per cent. and 45 per cent. respectively last year. The wheat crops of Eastern Oregon and Washington Territory were lighter than those of the previous year.

During the cereal year ended July 31, the following were the receipts at this port from the sections of country tributary thereto; those from the districts east of the Cascades Mountains being more than double of those of 1885.

Year.	Willamette Valley.		Eastern Oregon and Washington Territory.	
	Wheat.	Flour.	Wheat.	Flour.
	Quarters.	Sacks.	Quarters.	Sacks.
1885-1886	281,672	150,221	968,050	96,675
1884-1885	361,422	135,949	438,674	103,442
Aug.-Dec., 1886	199,040	78,015	465.589	33.705
Aug.-Dec., 1885	154,376	54,098	677,064	56,525

The total shipments of breadstuffs, both foreign and coastwise, were 983,870 quarters of wheat valued at 1,209,785*l*., and 423,985 sacks of flour valued at 441,935*l*.

The average market prices of wool during the year were about Wool. 19½ c. or 9¼d. per pound for Valley, and 17½ c. or 8½d. per pound for wool grown east of the Cascades Mountains. The quality from both sections was average. Receipts and shipments at this port were as follows :—

	Receipts.	Shipments.
	Lbs.	Lbs.
During 1886	13,541,226	13,227,105
„ 1885	12,481,962	11,558,427

Valley wools shrink from about 50 per cent. in washing, and other wools 62 per cent. The consumption of Oregon woollen mills was about 1,500,000 pounds.

Hops. During the past year, 7,098,445 lbs. of hops were received here, and 6,520,036 lbs. were shipped viâ San Francisco and Atlantic ports. In 1885, receipts were 5,210,837 lbs., and shipments were 5,561,381 lbs. The average value of Oregon hops during the year was about $22\frac{1}{2}$ c. or $10\frac{3}{4}d$. per pound.

Timber. The timber trade revived a little during the year, and some business has been done with interior States by way of the Union Pacific Railroad. Foreign exports from this district were small, as given in the tables

Salmon. Unless destined for the Eastern States, nearly all the shipments of salmon are made at Astoria. The product of the packing establishments on the Columbia River during 1886, was about 560,000 cases of 4 dozen, each 1 lb. cans, or equivalent in other sizes; and the shipments by railway from this district were 280,870 cases. Of British Columbia salmon in transit for Canada, 16,256 cases passed through, but in future this transit trade will go by the Canadian Pacific Railway.

Money market. Exchange. Throughout the year, market has been easy and money plentiful for all legitimate enterprises. Legal rate of interest is 8 per cent. per annum, but 10 per cent. may be collected by agreement. Exchange on London fluctuated very much during the year, but has generally been high. Sixty days' bills on London varied from 4 dol. $79\frac{1}{2}$ c. to 4 dol. 88 c. per £ sterling for bank; and from 4 dol. $78\frac{1}{2}$ c. to 4 dol. 87 c. per £ sterling for mercantile.

Shipping and navigation. British tonnage. There has been a large increase in the amount of tonnage trading to this port rendered necessary by the constantly increasing exports of grain. Larger ships are now frequenting the Colombia River. The following comparison shews the increase in British tonnage:—

	Ships Entered.	Registered Tons.
During 1884	61	60,878
„ 1885	113	111,101
„ 1886	121	130,941

Tonnage engagements. The engagements of tonnage during the last two years (exclusive of coasting voyages) have been as under:—

	Registered Tons.	
	1886.	1885.
Grain and flour cargoes	146,824	105,026
Salmon, and assorted cargoes	5,873	6,288
Timber cargoes	3,136	2,885
Miscellaneous cargoes	2,961	803
Total	158,794	115,002

SAN FRANCISCO.

Rates of freight were lower even than last year, yet they were comparatively higher than those ruling at other Pacific Coast ports. The average rates for the year were 39s. 6d. iron vessels, and 35s. 1d. wooden vessels to a port in the United Kingdom. The highest rates paid were 45s. and 37s. 6d., and the lowest 37s. 6d. and 30s. for iron and wood, respectively. *Rates of freight.*

The steam tonnage employed in the coasting trade has not increased, and the freight carried to and from San Francisco by the allied lines was:— *Steam tonnage.*

	From San Francisco.	To San Francisco.
	Tons.	Tons.
During 1886	87,090	78,400
„ 1885	75,863	132,260

Seamen's wages have averaged 6l. per month for able seamen in cases where no bonus has been paid. *Sailors.*

There has been a change in the United States Shipping Acts, legalising the payment of an allotment of 10 dol. per month for periods varying according to the length of the voyage "for bonâ fide board and clothing to enable the seamen to go to sea." I do not think that these enactments do much good, as crimps simply insist upon the payment of a stipulated sum per man as blood-money, before they will permit seamen to leave their houses, and reduce the rate of wages accordingly. Perhaps in no port of the United States is the need of a Consular Convention more apparent than here, where the practice of the United States Admiralty Court is to take jurisdiction of the most trivial cases occurring on board of British ships. As a consequence of this, the discipline of British crews in port is very hard to maintain. Certain attorneys take advantage of the known aversion of British owners to incur legal expenses, and compel masters to make private settlements with deserting seamen in order to avoid threatened delay and expense in litigation. As a rule, very little of the money so collected goes into the pockets of the seamen. In nine cases out of ten, these suits are instigated by boarding-house crimps. *Allotment notes and crimps.* *Practice of United States' Admiralty Court.*

The number and changes in crews of British ships entering this port during the year have been:— *Changes in crews.*

Total Number of Crews.	Deserted.	Discharged.	Engaged.	Reported Dead.	Percentage of Desertion.	Hospital Permits.
2,202	316	91	232	3	14·35	13

RIVER AND HARBOUR IMPROVEMENTS.

Congress of 1885 appropriated 75,000 dol. for work on the channels of the Columbia and Willamette rivers between Portland and the sea, the object being to maintain a permanent ship channel of 20 feet depth at low water. Some progress was made with the dyke at St. Helen's Bar on the Columbia below Portland; and while these permanent improvements are going on they are usually supplemented by resorting to propeller-sluicing for temporary improvement. A channel 1,500 feet *River bars and channels.*

long, 200 feet wide, and 20 feet deep at low water, was thus maintained through the bar at St. Helen's with great benefit to navigation.

22,000 dol. was also appropriated for clearing out the upper reaches of the Columbia, Willamette, and Snake rivers, navigable for river steamers and tributary to this port.

Mouth of the Columbia. For the permanent improvement of the Columbia river 187,500 dol. was appropriated. As yet, this great work has barely commenced, only 1,020 feet of the jetty, which is to be 4½ miles in length, having been constructed. When completed, the engineers expect to maintain a straight channel across the bar of 30 feet depth at mean low water. At present, the bar channel carries 22 feet at mean low water, and 29 feet at mean high tide. The crossing is straight, short, and well buoyed.

Pilotage. By competition with pilots of Washington Territory, rates have been reduced from the legal rate of 8 dol. per foot, up to 12 feet, and 10 dol. per foot for any excess to half or less of these rates.

Towage. There is also strong competition for bar towage, which has caused a reduction of fully 20 per cent. from tariff rates.

Agriculture. Crops generally. Crops were generally good and were got in in fine condition, but, owing to low market prices for produce, farming has not been profitable during the year.

Wheat. The wheat harvest of Oregon west of the Cascade, was rather larger than last year, while on the contrary Eastern Oregon and Washington Territory were deficient about 40 per cent.

Oats. The oat crop was less than last year. Receipts here were 284,467 centals, while in 1885 they were 444,892 centals. Eastern Oregon sent very little to market.

Hops. This was a very profitable crop. Growers received very good prices, and contracted largely before picking at figures ranging from 8½d. to 13¼d. per lb. for Oregon. Washington Territory hops generally sell higher. Receipts here were 7,098,455 lbs., against 5,210,837 lbs. last year.

Fruit culture. Since the transcontinental railroads opened the markets of the middle and western States, this branch of agriculture has largely developed, the climate being eminently suitable for the growth of all the larger fruits. Fruit culture is now quite a profitable branch of agriculture. The yield of apples, pears, plums, cherries, and other fruits was much greater than last year.

Sheep and cattle. The losses of sheep and cattle on the ranges have been light during the year, the demand and prices have been good and the business profitable. Official reports give the number of animals in the State of Oregon as: sheep, 2,600,000; milch cows, 75,000; oxen and other cattle, 643,000; horses, 167,000; hogs, 230,000; and mules, 3,155.

Population and industries. Immigration Arrivals at this port by sea during 1886 were 13,484, and departures 10,598. There has been a large immigration by rail into Oregon and Washington Territory, but statistics are unobtainable.

Manufactures. About 2,800 hands were employed in Portland in various manufacturing enterprises, and the estimated value of manufactured produce is 1,084,700l.

Reduction works. Reduction works, for the treatment and smelting of ores, have been built here during the year at a cost of 10,000l. This is likely to prove the beginning of a large business.

Mining. Mines being rapidly developed. In all the mining districts of this State, and those parts of Washington Territory and Idaho tributary to this district, mining is being rapidly developed, and prospects are that as capital is turned into this channel the mines of the north-west will take a high place in the scale of production. In 1886 Oregon, Washington, and Northern

Idaho produced in gold 1,500,000 dol., or 300,000*l*.; while the product of 1885 was 1,100,000 dol., or 220,000*l*. Many believe that the Cœur D'Alène district of North Idaho will eventually prove to be the richest mining district of this coast. The following comparison shows the increase during the year :—

Gold yield.

	1886.	1885.
	£	£
Cœur D'Alène	120,000	60,000
Oregon	160,000	140,000
Washington Territory	20,000	10,000

As Oregon possesses rich prospects of the base metals and coal, it is safe to presume that ere long capital will be forthcoming to develop them.

Base metals.

At the Cascades of the Columbia, the United States Government has been engaged for some years in the construction of a canal and locks to permit of continuous navigation of the river, and for the continuation of this work 187,500 dol. was appropriated, and the work is going slowly forward. When this work is completed, estimated to cost the sum of 2,000,000 dol., or 400,000*l*., the Columbia will be open for a distance of 200 miles from its mouth; and a project is also under consideration to overcome the rapids at the Dalles, either by ship, railway, or canal, and so enable light-draught steamers to navigate the Snake and Columbia rivers for a further aggregate distance of 350 miles. All the trade of this district is tributary to Portland.

Public works. Canal.

A fine drawbridge of wood and iron has been nearly completed during the year, connecting Portland and East Portland. The draw is wide enough to permit of the passage of any vessel. A fine iron railway bridge is also about to be commenced.

Bridges.

Large machine-shops, round-houses, and other railway terminal works are being built in and around Portland. These are of brick and iron, solid and substantial structures, estimated to cost 150,000*l*.

Terminal works.

There has been no railroad construction in my district proper, but throughout Oregon and Washington Territory, many miles have been added to the existing roads during the year. Already, three overland lines centre here, and more are projected. The Oregon and California Railroad, in which British and German capital is largely interested, having virtually passed into the control of the Southern Pacific Railroad Company of California, will now be pushed rapidly to a junction with the California and Oregon road.

Railways.

The traffic over the lines of the Oregon Railway and Navigation Company, which includes all through traffic of the Northern Pacific and Union Pacific Railways, and that of the Oregon and California is given below, and compared with that of the previous year.

Railway traffic.

	Forwarded.		Received.	
	1886.	1885.	1886.	1885.
	Tons.	Tons.	Tons.	Tons.
Oregon Rail. and Navigation	213,115	157,836	325,519	312,978
„ and Cal., east side	33,352	20,154	89,307	75,318
„ „ west side	12,234	7,310	56,359	55,695

City finances and taxation. Debt. Revenue. Expenditure.	At the close of the year, the bonded debt of this city was 100,000 dol., or 20,000*l*., bearing interest at 6 per cent. The total revenue was 279,930 dol., or 55,986*l*., and the expenditure was 242,726 dol., or 48,545*l*.
Water bonds.	During the year the city bought the waterworks, hitherto owned by a private corporation, and water bonds were issued to the extent of 500,000 dol., or 100,000*l*., bearing interest at the rate of 5 per cent. per annum. These bonds sold at an average premium of 7·86 per cent.
Taxation.	The State, county, and city tax rates were as under:—

	Per cent.
State tax	0·205
„ school tax	0·400
County tax	0·630
City tax	1·000
School district tax	0·500
Total	2·735

The city tax levy for 1887 is 1 per cent. Property is, however only taxed in this State to about half its value.

Remarks. City property.	Values of city property have advanced during the year, and the sales have been much larger. There is a good demand for city lots at improving prices.
City improvements.	During the year, from 80 to 100 dwellings, many of them quite handsome, have been constructed, which cost together about 63,400*l*. About 9,800*l*. was spent on wharves, and on brick and wooden business buildings, about 71,000*l*.
Labour.	There has been a good demand for labourers during the year, and able-bodied men, willing to work, had generally little difficulty in finding employment; the demand for skilled labour was not, however, all that could be desired, but prospects are improving.

Note.—The values given in this report are reduced to sterling at the rate of 5 dol. to the pound. The custom-house standard for duties is at the rate of 4·8665 dol. to the pound.

Annex A.—RETURN of all Shipping at the Port of Portland, Oregon, in the Year 1886.

ENTERED.

Nationality.	Sailing.		Steam.		Total.	
	Number of Vessels.	Tons.	Number of Vessels.	Tons.	Number of Vessels.	Tons.
British	121	130,941	...	...	121	130,941
United States—						
Foreign	10	12,469	...	...	...	...
Atlantic	2	2,967	...	...	...	...
Coasting	8	4,373	117	234,202	137	254,011
German	3	2,645	...	...	3	2,645
Total	144	153,395	117	234,202	261	387,597
„ for the year preceding	...	...	...	...	298	399,701

SAN FRANCISCO.

CLEARED.

Nationality.	Sailing. Number of Vessels.	Sailing. Tons.	Steam. Number of Vessels.	Steam. Tons.	Total. Number of Vessels.	Total. Tons.
British	134	142,182	...	...	134	142,182
United States—						
Foreign	12	16,218	...	...	...	...
Coastwise	6	1,347	116	231,543	134	249,108
German	3	2,645	...	...	3	2,645
Norwegian	1	901	...	...	1	901
Total	156	163,293	116	231,543	272	394,836
„ for the year preceding	...	...	...	...	279	386,003

Annex B.—RETURN of Principal Articles of Export from Portland and Oregon during the Years 1886 and 1885.

Articles.		1886. Quantity.	1886. Value.	1885. Quantity.	1885. Value.
			£		£
Wheat	Quarters	895,489	1,106,374	628,958	791,900
Wheat flour	Sacks	324,579	339,559	175,796	198,172
Timber	Mil. feet	3,310	7,017	2,375	5,698
Salmon in tins	...	...	...	...	2,390
Other articles	...	...	2,514	...	3,430
Tea in transit	Lbs.	465,121	13,508	...	...
Total exports (foreign)	...	...	1,468,972	...	1,001,590

RETURN of Principal Articles of Import to Portland and Oregon during the Years 1886 and 1885.

Articles.		1886. Quantity.	1886. Value.	1885. Quantity.	1885. Value.
			£		£
Coals	Tons	24,931	13,900	28,328	17,294
Tin and terne plates	Lbs.	1,339,976	8,377	787,995	5,090
Tea	,,	270,990	8,179	...	...
Earthenware and glass	...	...	5,820	...	2,084
Rice	Lbs.	1,534,401	5,760	3,316,336	11,390
Salt	,,	6,441,212	4,689	6,764,019	4,572
Cement	Barrels	19,347	3,995	...	...
Soda and chemicals	Lbs.	...	2,742	720,919	1,887
Hemp	Tons	80	1,399	...	...
Beer, porter and ale	Gallons	7,156	1,364	5,467	1,001
Oils	,,	19,170	1,151	49,160	3,296
Pig iron	Tons	347	820	226	571
Wines and liquors	...	...	1,090	...	1,320
All other articles	...	...	12,251	...	12,405
Tea in transit for Canada	Lbs.	465,121	13,508	...	...
Tea in transit for Eastern States	,,	2,413,981	78,019	...	...
Total	...	...	163,064	...	60,910

NOTE.—The above returns do not include exports or imports coastwise or by rail, with the exception of articles exported in bond.

Annex C.—TABLE showing the Total Value of all Articles Exported from Portland and Imported to Portland, Oregon, from and to Foreign Countries during the Years 1886-85.

Country.	Exports. 1886.	Exports. 1885.	Imports. 1886.	Imports. 1885.
	£	£	£	£
Great Britain	1,411,227	973,315	33,779	23,429
Belgium	27,725	..	..	..
British Columbia	6,982	6,655	5,977	7,252
China	1,812	595	12,271	18,015
Japan	..	..	99,005	..
Australia	..	..	7,349	9,029
Uruguay	4,540	..	..	..
Canada, transit	13,508	..	..	..
Denmark	..	17,300	..	..
Other countries	3,178	3,725	4,683	3,185
Total	1,468,972	1,001,590	163,064	60,910

ASTORIA, OREGON.

Mr. Vice-Consul Cherry reports as follows:—

General business for 1886. General business has shown a marked and steady improvement, and a permanent improvement in the town and vicinity may be noted.

Imports. Show a lower volume, owing to the fact of the cannery supplies being received by rail and coasting steamers from San Francisco.

Tin plates. The retail price of plates varied but little from the year before.

Salt. The same can be said of F. F. Liverpool.

Twine. This article seems to be more and more manufactured in the United States, and the whole amount used comes by rail, and averages the same price as last year, viz., 3s. 9d.

Block tin. Still arrives altogether from San Francisco, being imported thence from Australia.

Coals. A larger quantity, all from Australia, was imported, mostly to meet the increased demand for steam and gas purposes, and partly through the closing up of the Puget Sound collieries.

Exports. The reason of the very slight differences in the total exports is that the amount of salmon canned (the most valuable product) is being more and more consumed in the United States, and consequently does not figure in the export trade; however, the larger export of bread-stuffs more than make up for this deficiency.

Canned salmon. The total number of cases exported is 156,187, against 229,426 of the previous year.

Wheat and flour. There is a large increase of the export of bread-stuffs, more than double the quantity of last year.

Lumber. A large increase can be noted, one vessel going to China, the rest to South America.

Manufacturing and industry. Better prices for the two staples manufactured in this district, viz.: lumber and canning salmon, and consequently the promise of further investments in these two industries may be noted.

Lumbering. As before stated, the district of this Vice-Consulate is almost one continuous forest, intersected by numerous bays and rivers. Facilities for bringing logs from some distance from water have been improved upon, both for the use of mills lying within the limits of this Vice-Consulate and some that lay beyond.

Deep-sea fishing has received a slight impetus by the putting on of a steam trawler by the citizens of this place, and so far has been a very profitable venture; and, as the facilities of taking the fish to market increase, so will opening for small capital improve. *Fishing interests.*

A well-organised association of fishermen, finding that the price hitherto paid, viz., 2s. for each salmon, was too small, determined to fix the price at a more remunerative figure for themselves, with the final result of securing 3s. per fish. Notwithstanding this large increase of price, and the loss of one-third of the fishing season before the price was finally adjusted, nearly the same quantity of canned salmon was put up as was in the season of 1885. *Salmon fishing.*

For 1886 has been unusually profitable, the decrease in stocks in the United Kingdom, and a larger and growing demand in the United States, made very much firmer prices, which ranged from 16s. to 22s. 6d. per case of 4 dozen 1 lb. tins. *Canning salmon.*

The total pack of the Columbia River Canneries for 1886 was 520,000 cases, of which 60,000 cases were put up after the 31st of July when the "spring run" ceases; these Fall fish are of a greatly inferior quality, and some of the Fall canned fish was unfit for food. But the large price, after three or four years of depressed prices, was too great a temptation for the more unscrupulous of the packers to resist. These Fall fish have, however, been put up under different brands to that of the packers' regular label.

Besides the catch of the Columbia River proper, there are the results of the packing of fish in Gray's Harbour, Shoalwater Bay to the north, and Tillamook Bay to the south; nearly all of which comes directly to this port to be forwarded either by sail, steamer, or rail. The total amount aggregates 75,000 cases.

An increase in numbers of vessels and total tonnage will again be found as compared with 1885; a still larger class of vessels coming here. The very low rates of freight prevailing making it unremunerative for vessels of a small tonnage to come here. The proportion of tonnage is still very greatly in favour of vessels under the British flag. The fluctuations have not been so marked as last year, but the average rate has been lower, viz., about 40s. to the United Kingdom. *Shipping.*

Freights.

The work on the Cascade Locks, 150 miles up the river from this port, have been greatly delayed by some differences in the Government officials, as has also the improvement of the mouth of the river. The latter is exceedingly disappointing, as not only delaying a much needed work, but making it additionally costly by the wear of storms on unfinished work. *Internal improvements by Government.*

The want of better means of communication by rail is still unrelieved. A number of propositions have been made, but all of them so far falling through. *Railway.*

Owing to the more remunerative price for fish, and consequent better paid labour, the agitations of 1885 continuing till the spring of 1886, have died down. *Labour.*

General business promises very well indeed for the coming year. Larger orders for cannery supplies, and machinery for lumber manufacture have been sent forward. The last year saw the first attempt to light this port by the electric light, and which is now successfully in operation. However, it is the arc light that is in use. *General business.*

Owing to the large extent of forest country in this district, there is but a limited field for the usual agricultural immigrant. Conse- *Immigration.*

quently but a small portion of the immigration flowing into Oregon and Washington Territory, finds its way to the limits of this Consular district. The growing importance of the lumber industry is drawing the attention of lumber men to this section.

Health. The health of the district has remained as perfectly good, as has been hitherto noted.

Annex A.—RETURN of all Shipping at the Port of Astoria, Oregon, United States, during the Year 1886.

ENTERED.

Nationality.	Sailing. Number of Vessels.	Sailing. Tons.	Steam. Number of Vessels.	Steam. Tons.	Total. Number of Vessels.	Total. Tons.
British	126	134,637	...	...	126	134,637
American	17	20,643	4	2,422	21	23,065
German	4	3,845	...	...	4	3,845
Norwegian	1	1,100	...	...	1	1,100
Total	148	160,225	4	2,422	152	162,647
,, for the preceding year	...	...	...	...	122	123,149

CLEARED.

Nationality.	Sailing. Number of Vessels.	Sailing. Tons.	Steam. Number of Vessels.	Steam. Tons.	Total. Number of Vessels.	Total. Tons.
British	141	148,930	...	...	141	148,930
American	16	19,321	17	15,136	33	34,457
German	5	4,011	...	...	5	4,011
Norwegian	1	1,100	...	...	1	1,100
Total	163	173,362	17	15,136	180	188,498
,, for the preceding year	...	...	...	...	109	108,816

Annex B.—RETURN of Principal Articles of Export from Astoria, Oregon, United States, during the Year 1886.

Articles.		1886. Quantity.	1886. Values in £ Sterling.	1885. Quantity.	1885. Values in £ Sterling.
Preserved salmon	Cases	156,187	155,265	222,594	229,426
Wheat	Bushels	814,264	121,762	395,843	60,836
Flour	Barrels	26,991	20,248	13,525	13,088
Lumber	Metrical feet	2,346	4,973	558	1,232
Sundries	...	...	2,804	...	85
Total	...	...	305,052	...	304,667

SAN FRANCISCO.

Return of Principal Articles of Import for 1885-1886.

Articles.			1886.		1885.	
			Quantity.	Value in £ Sterling.	Quantity.	Value in £ Sterling.
Tin plates	Boxes		45,704	30,795	32,800	25,889
Salt	Tons		85	110	200	260
Coals	,,		4,228	2,635	1,297	1,420
Sundries			...	400	...	...
Total			...	33,940	...	27,569

Annex C.—Table showing the Total Value of all Articles Exported from Astoria, Oregon, and Imported to Astoria, Oregon, from and to Foreign Countries during the Years 1886 and 1885.

Country.	Exports.		Imports.	
	1886.	1885.	1886.	1885.
	£	£	£	£
Great Britain	273,200	303,359	30,954	26,105
British colonies	168	77	2,779	266
Other countries	31,851	1,232	..	1,198
Total..	305,219	304,668	33,733	27,569

WILMINGTON AND LOS ANGELES.

Mr. Vice-Consul Mortimer reports as follows:—

In the introductory remarks to my reports for 1884 and 1885, I commented on the rapid progress of this district in business, wealth, and population, and stated that there was every indication that the prosperity of the people was permanent. I must again chronicle a very marked increase in material wealth and population.

Introductory remarks.

In 1880 the population of this city was about 11,000; in the past year it has increased from 40,000 to about 50,000. Buildings have been erected of an aggregate value of 800,000*l*.; an increase of 550,000*l*. on the operations of 1885.

Three cities have been incorporated in this (Los Angeles) county in the past year, Pasadina, Santa Aña, and Santa Monica. In Pasadina upwards of 1,100,000*l*. has been expended in building operations during 1886. Vacant land there, that was sold for 300*l*. per acre three years ago, is now selling for 20,000*l*. per acre. The books of the county recorder show that upwards of 13,300 transfers of real property, situated in this city and county, were made during 1886. The value of the property so transferred exceeded 5,600,000*l*., an increase on the operations of 1885 of about 150 per cent.

The main cause of the remarkable prosperity of this district is the fact, that it is now recognised that this climate is the best in North America for those suffering from consumption, and kindred diseases. In this report, attention is drawn to many matters of local interest for the following reasons:—1st. There are upwards of 8,000 British-born persons resident in this district. 2nd. I have information that large numbers of British subjects contemplate coming to reside here. 3rd. A very large amount of British capital has been invested here, one

Climate.

UNITED STATES.

Trade and commerce. company alone—the L. J. Rose Company, Limited—has recently invested 200,000*l.* here. There are some indications that the prosperity of the past will receive some check. Reference is made below to the facts and circumstances which militate in favour of and against this view.

Chief exports. The chief exports from this district are wine, grain, oranges, and other fruits.

Product of wine. The vintage of 1886 was exceptionally good. The product of this district will be between 5,000,000 and 6,000,000 gallons. The low price of our really good wines here is due to the competition created by the quantity of "bogus" adulterated stuff made and sold as California wines. It is stated on good authority, that in New York, two firms alone manufacture, and sell as Californian wine, 15,000 gallons a month of some spurious compound. The spurious wines are made of

Spurious wines. glucose acids, and various colouring matters and flavouring extracts. The Wine-growers' Association, at a recent meeting, passed a series of resolutions, of which the following are two:—Resolved: "That cheap grain alcohol is the foundation of "bogus" and imitation wines, and that any general reduction in the tax on such alcohol would materially increase the present difficulties of wine-growers, and would tend to demoralise and bring into disrepute all trade in alcoholic and fermented beverages."

Resolved: "That the existing law taxing spurious wines should be so amended as to afford ample protection to the people against imposition."

Sanguine people here think that the wine product of this State will, in a few years, equal that of France. In my report for 1885, I drew attention to a combination of the wine-makers to reduce the price of grapes to 2*l.* per ton. One result of this combination has been, that in

Co-operative wineries. various places the grape-growers have combined, and constructed co-operative wineries. I am unable to say whether they have succeeded in making a good quality of wine. The best wines are made by such old-established firms as L. J. Rose and Co.—now an English company—E. J. Baldwin, and the San Gabriel Wine Company.

Oranges. About 2,300 car loads (23,000 tons) of oranges will be marketed from this district this season. The orange-growers' union so regulates shipments to the cities of the Eastern States that an over supply is not sent to any point.

Imports. Principal imports. The principal imports from the United Kingdom to the port (Wilmington) are shown in Annex B. The imports to this city by way of New York and New Orleans, are not shown, as I cannot get the returns from the Transcontinental Railway.

Portland cement. Very large quantities of Portland cement are used here annually in the construction of side walks, sewer pipes, and pipes for irrigation. It is imported by way of San Francisco; the railway freight to Los Angeles (482 miles) increases the cost to the consumer here by about 32*s.* per ton. I am informed on the best authority that the Southern Pacific Railway discourage direct importations to this port in order that they may get the freight on the long haul from San Francisco (482 miles), instead of the short haul from Wilmington (24 miles.)

Coal It will be seen (Annex B.) that the imports of coal have largely increased in the past year. The retail price here is from 3*l.* to 4*l.* per ton; wholesale 2*l.* 10*s.* per ton. Taking the average rates of freight from Australia for the past three years, Australian coal can be laid down at the port for 1*l.* 10*s.* per ton (inclusive 3*s.* per ton duty.) From these figures it will be seen that the profit of the importer must be very considerable.

42 British ships entered the port of Wilmington in 1886 (see Annex A.) This is a marked increase on the number (13) for 1885. Shipping and navigation.

Mr. A. R. Street, C.E., has prepared for me, and I have appended hereto a map of this vicinity, showing the harbour of Wilmington (San Pedro), and a new harbour, Ballona, now being improved and made capable of receiving foreign-going ships. In the past 15 years the Government has expended 140,000*l.* in improving Wilmington Harbour. In so far as foreign-going shipping is concerned, this expenditure has been almost barren of result. Foreign-going ships have still to anchor in the outer harbour, and discharge and receive cargo in lighters. They are entirely unprotected from the south-east wind, as shown on map herewith. Recently two large foreign-going American ships were driven ashore and wrecked during a gale from the south-east. Harbour. Ballona harbour.

Ballona Harbour is at present private property; it is a small lake into which the sea has just been admitted. The owners state that they intend expending 50,000*l.* in making a sufficiently deep channel to admit foreign-going ships. They are constructing a railway from the harbour to Los Angeles, 14 miles: should they succeed in getting ships alongside their docks, the harbour will be superior to Wilmington. The entrance is protected from the south-eastern gales by the Palos Verdes Hills. Large appropriations have recently been made by Congress for the further improvement of Wilmington Harbour. Unless, however, the channel be deepened sufficiently to admit ships to the docks in the inner harbour, it can only be described as an unsafe open roadstead for foreign-going shipping. Improvement of Wilmington harbour.

Formerly Los Angeles county was known as the "Cow County," owing to the number of live stock; now it is essentially a fruit-producing district, viticulture and orange-growing being now the chief industries. Agriculture.

The Cottony Cushion scale, commonly called the "White scale," is doing great damage to the orange groves. Many of the orchards have been cut down, and many others now badly infected will have to be treated in the same way. Nothing has as yet been discovered that will kill the pest without injuring the tree, and sufficiently inexpensive to admit of common use. Spraying the trees has been found ineffectual, owing to the fact that the liquid used did not reach every part of the tree. It is now stated that Mr. J. W. Wolfskill, the owner of the oldest orchard in this district, is about to patent an apparatus for applying a gas to orange and other trees, which it is claimed will kill all scale bugs without injuring the tree. A tent is constructed over the tree, and the gas is generated in the tent. Many are of opinion that the destruction worked by the white scale bug and other pests is due to the fact that, fertilisers not having been used, the soil is becoming impoverished. The fact that the 250 acre orange grove of Mr. A. B. Chapman, at San Gabriel, which for some years has been fertilised, is free of scale bugs and other pests, seems to indicate that the true remedy is good husbandry. White scale.

Up to the present time the viticulturists have been exempt from destructive pests in this district. The *Phylloxera* is doing some damage to the vineyards in the northern part of the State, about 400 miles from here. Irrigation, which is extensively and necessarily practised here, is supposed to be the cause of our immunity from this pest. Mr. L. J. Rose, an officer of the State Board of Viticulture, states that there has never been a failure of the grape crop in Southern California. So Viticulture. No failure of grape crop.

UNITED STATES.

many new vineyards are being planted it is difficult to get reliable statistics of the acreage in vines. 40,000 acres in bearing is, I think, a fair estimate for this district. The quality of the wine made here is steadily improving.

Cold storage. The market for good qualities of fruit is practically unlimited. Every description of fruit and vegetable are now prepared for transportation to the cities of the Eastern States. They are reduced to a low temperature in artificially-cooled rooms, and are transported in cars kept at a low temperature. By these means Southern California strawberries and other delicate fruits are delivered in New York in perfect preservation.

Value of land. The value of land in this city and vicinity has increased marvellously in the past three years. Farming lands have doubled, and in many cases trebled, in price, and in city property the increase is even more marked. A house and lot that the writer thought of purchasing in 1881 for 2,700 dol., was sold recently for 20,000 dol.

Government lands. There are about 7,000,000 acres of Government lands open for settlement in this district. About 90 per cent. of these lands are mountainous or desert, not fit for cultivation.

Crystallization of fruit. A large business is being built up by Messrs. Barnard and Benedict, of this city, in the crystallization of fruit. Their product is, I think, equal in quality to that made in the South of France. At present only one firm is engaged in the business, and a market is found for these goods on this continent. The price of good fruit is so low here—from a farthing to one halfpenny per pound—that it is probable that manufacturers here could compete with those of the South of France for the English market.

Population and industries. There are hundreds, and of some nationalities thousands, of representatives of every European state resident here. Fully one-third of the population are of foreign birth. Newspapers are published here in five different languages.

List of factories. The following list of factories is taken from the "Los Angeles Daily Times" of January 1, 1887:—

"The manufactures of Los Angeles county pertain principally to the working up of the natural products of the county.

"Wine and brandy making, from the vast quantities of grapes produced here, form one of the principal industries.

"Raisin making is also well established, and furnishes a most lucrative business. The raisin product of Los Angeles county for 1886 is placed at 200,000 boxes.

"The canning, drying, dessicating and candying of fruits, to transform them into commercial products, form still other branches of industry, which are on a most flourishing basis.

"Two extensive milling establishments are located in Los Angeles, which supply from home-grown wheat about all the flour required for home consumption and quantities for export.

"Iron and brass foundries and machine shops of large capacity supply the requirements of the country in this particular.

"Petroleum is refined to some extent at the Newhall works.

"The Southern Pacific Railway Company has at this place large shops where cars and engines are repaired, and even some construction is undertaken.

"A dozen planing mills and wood manufacturing establishments are constantly busy.

"The manufacture of pipe—cement and iron—is a very extensive business here, owing to the large quantities required for irrigation, drainage, &c.

"The manufacture of the cruder sorts of pottery and of tiling is successfully carried on.

"Brea is manufactured for paving and roofing purposes.

"Wagon and carriage making has a fair representation, although vast numbers of vehicles are imported from the East.

"A firm of practical men of means from Chicago are about to begin the manufacture of pressed and moulded brick and terra-cotta on a large scale, a suitable clay having been found for the purpose.

"Bricks to supply the local demand are made here.

"Ice is an article of manufacture, by a patent process, there being two factories in Los Angeles.

"Two large breweries are in operation in the city and find plenty to do.

"Cooperage is also a well-patronised branch of industry, as an adjunct to the manufacture of wines and brandies.

"Furniture and cabinet making are carried on to a considerable extent, the native California redwood being largely employed.

"There are also manufactories of soda-water, ice-cream, vinegar, pickles and relishes, patent fence, woven-wire mattresses, baking-powder, spices and extracts, candies, boxes (paper and wood) blank books, and a large number of others, incident to a thriving, active, and money-getting population.

"As natural facilities become better known, markets widen, and technical skill becomes available, manufactures will largely increase. The possibility of a cheap and abundant fuel-supply in the petroleum, which is to be piped to Los Angeles, makes it probable that very extensive manufactories, reduction works, &c., may some day find a place here."

The following list of companies incorporated here in the year 1886 is taken from the "Los Angeles Herald." It will be observed that the aggregate capital stock exceeds 5,000,000*l.* This list does not include a number of English companies doing business, but not registered here :—

UNITED STATES.

Name of Incorporation.	Capital Stock.
	Dollars.
San Bernardino and San Diego Railroad Company	3,000,000
Pasadena Manufacturing Company	500,000
Palmdale Irrigating Company	100,000
Santa Monica Mission	..
Raymond Improvement Company	200,000
Tustin Land and Improvement Company	25,000
City Railway Company of Pasadena	50,000
Los Angeles Development Company	500,000
Zion Evangelist Lutheran Church of Pasadena	..
East Side Bank	50,000
The Bank of Orange	100,000
Orange Investment Company	40,000
Anglo-Nevada Assurance Corporation	2,000,000
Alhambra Hotel and Improvement Company	41,000
Abstract and Title Insurance Company of Los Angeles	100,000
San Bernardino and Los Angeles Railroad Company	1,500,000
Troy Laundry Machinery Company, Limited	100,000
Pasadena Gas and Electric Light Company	50,000
The Azusa Land and Water Company	500,000
Emanuel Methodist Church of Pasadena	..
East Side Water Company	250,000
Rubio Cañon Land and Water Company	185,000
Sierra Madre Vintage Company	100,000
Grace M. E. Church	..
Pasadena Street Railroad Company	50,000
Fairview Land and Water Company	60,000
San Gabriel Valley Bank	33,750
Mill Creek Lumber Company	200,000
E. C. Niedt Soap and Chemical Manufacturing Company	75,000
Los Angeles Printing Company	24,000
American Live Stock and Land Company	100,000
Temple Street Cable Railroad Company	100,000
The Congregational Church of Vernon	..
Athletic Base Ball Club	460
Pasadena Building and Loan Association	250,000
Los Angeles Young Ladies' College	..
Exchange Block Company of Pasadena	..
California Telephone Company	100,000
Sierra Madre Library Association	..
Ballona Harbour Improvement Company	800,000
Colton Terrace Land and Water Company	100,000
Crystal Springs Land and Water Company	1,240,000
Consumers' Gaslight, Heat, and Power Company	200,000
Hermitage Water Company	100,000
Edgemount Church of Christ	..
Times-Mirror Company	60,000
Santa Aña and Newport Railroad Company	100,000
Victor Marble Company	500,000
Los Angeles Ostrich Farm Railroad Company	60,000
Los Angeles Electric Railway Company	300,000
Southern California Blue Gravel Mining Company	650,000
Grape and Wine Growers' Association	2,500
Southern California Land Company	300,000
Santa Aña Investment Company	60,000
Baker Iron Works	75,000
Glendale Reservoir and Pipe Association	5,230
Santa Aña Hotel and Land Company	50,000
American Colony Water Company	20,000
All Saints' Church, Pasadena	..
Pomona Wine Company	15,000
Christian Church, Orange	..
Los Angeles Land Bureau	100,000
Capital Milling Company	150,000

Name of Incorporation.	Capital Stock.
	Dollars.
Santa Aña Gas Company	50,000
San Dimas Land and Water Company	60,000
The Azusa Irrigating Company	60,000
Florence M. E. Church	
Citizens' Water Company	1,000,000
Charity Street Cable Railway	250,000
Fulton Wells M. E. Church	
Providence Land, Water, and Development Company	500,000
Christian Church, Santa Aña	
Woman's Christian Temperance Union	
East Los Angeles Baptist Church	
Guadalupe Mill and Mining Company	50,000
Los Angeles Humane Company	
Ogilby Gold Mining Company	500,000
Los Angeles and Santa Monica Railroad Company	300,000
Pasadena Fruit and Crystallizing Company	20,000
Southern California Conference M. E. Church	
Y. M. C. A. of Pasadena	
Glendale Reservoir and Pipe Association	1,950
Pomona Bank	50,000
Main Street M. E. Church	
Mexican Oil and Gas Company	2,000,000
Los Angeles Planing Mill Company	24,000
Christian Science Union	
Downey Wine and Fruit Company	10,000
Ranchito Company	50,000
Irrigation Company of Pomona	245,000
First Universalist Church of Santa Aña	
Paradise and Los Angeles Gold and Silver Mining Land and Water Company	100,000
Evening Express Company	100,000
Pipe and Reservoir of Childs Tract, San Rafael	1,237
Vista Bonita M. E. Church	
Salt River Land and Water Company	300,000
Sierra Madre College, Pasadena	
Monrovia Land and Water Company	200,000
Stearn's Manufacturing Company	50,000
Azusa Wine and Fruit Company	20,000
St. Vincent Hotel Company	200,000
Baker Iron Works	75,000
Cambria Mill and Mining Company	250,000
Los Angeles University	
Lake Hemet Company	2,000,000
First Christian Church of Santa Aña	
The Clydesdale	2,500
Southern California Investment Company	2,50,000
Hemet Gold Mining Campany	240,000
Emanuel M. E. Church of Pasadena	
Salem M. E. Church, Lamanda Park	
The Azusa Land and Water Company	500,000
Oak Knoll Water Company	100,000

Rate of wages. The attempt to "boycott" the employers of Chinese labour, referred to in my report for 1886, failed. Skilled mechanics receive from 8s. to 1l. per day. The wages paid to mechanics have declined a little, and it is probable that in time the rates here will be uniform with those in the Eastern States.

Oil. Flowing wells of oil. A number of oil wells have been sunk in this county in the past year. Flowing wells have been discovered at Puente, 25 miles east of Los Angeles. The output of this district is about 800 barrels per day.

UNITED STATES.

Petroleum is used for fuel in a number of factories here owing to the high price of coal.

Tramways, cable and electric roads.
There are upwards of 26 miles of street railroads—horse, cable, and electric—in operation in this city. They carried upwards of 4,000,000 passengers in the past year. Franchises have been granted for the construction of about 12 miles more in this city, and work has been begun on some of these new roads.

Public works.
In view of the large number of British ships now coming yearly to Wilmington, I have thought it necessary to attach a map to this report to illustrate how completely foreign-going shipping is unprotected while at anchor in the harbour. On this map I have had traced the various railroads entering Los Angeles. The dotted lines indicate railways constructed during the year 1886, or now being constructed. The Atlantic and Pacific, Atchison, Topeka and Santa Fé, and California Southern, are working together as a transcontinental railway in opposition to the Southern Pacific Railway. I will refer to the three first-named lines as the Atlantic and Pacific. The Atlantic and Pacific obtained an entrance to Los Angeles in 1886 by acquiring a right of way over the Southern Pacific Railway from Colton. They are now constructing two lines to Los Angeles from their main line in San Bernardino county. One to connect at Duarte with the Los Angeles and San Gabriel Valley Railway, which line they have purchased, and the other by way of Riverside and Santa Aña. Both these lines are shown on map herewith, they are being pushed to completion as rapidly as possible. It is stated that the Atlantic and Pacific are interested in the Ballona Harbour project (referred to herein), and in the railway from Ballona to Los Angeles, now in process of construction. The advantage to this district of a railway to the Eastern States in competition with the Southern Pacific cannot be over-estimated. Last season, the fruit shippers in the Sacramento Valley paid 120*l*. per car load to Chicago, while the Los Angeles fruit shippers paid only 60*l*. The difference in favour of Los Angeles being due to the competition of the Atlantic and Pacific Railway.

Competition between railways.

New railways being constructed.

Advantage of competing lines of railway.

Railway to Santa Barbara.
A railway is being constructed by the Southern Pacific from Newhall to Santa Barbara, 70 miles.

A short line is being constructed from Los Angeles to an ostrich farm about 6 miles north of the city.

Los Angeles has now got two transcontinental lines, four local lines, and three local lines in course of construction.

General remarks.
Emigration.
Of the British subjects resident here, the Canadians, who are numerous, are the most successful; they adapt themselves more readily to the ways and habits of the people. Many Englishmen who have come here have been unsuccessful, owing to the unpractical character of the education they had received. Many, too, have been ruined owing to their having relied on the false representations of interested parties in London. The Antelope Valley, the poorest part of this district, is full of English and Scotch families, many of whom have not now means to get away. At the invitation of the Southern Pacific Railway, I visited the Valley in May last, and found that the bulk of the land is an alkali desert; where the land is good, the water is from 200 to 300 feet from the surface. Many of the residents in the Antelope Valley had arranged to settle there, by the advice of railroad agents in London, before leaving their homes in the old country.

Deluded emigrants.

Financial. ate of interest.
As stated in my previous reports, there is a good opening here for a mortgage company. The current rate of interest on the best first mortgage security is 10 per cent. nett. A higher rate is reserved to

cover taxes; the nett interest to the mortgage is, as stated, 10 per cent.

Thoroughbred racehorses.
I am advised that there is an excellent opening here for parties wishing to make a business of raising thoroughbred racehorses. Those engaged in the business here have achieved most satisfactory results, horses raised here having of late defeated the celebrated thoroughbreds of Kentucky. Owing to the mildness and equability of the climate, live stock generally are raised with less difficulty than in any other part of the country; they can feed in the fields all the year round.

Capital wanted.
There are a great many industries here in which more capital could profitably be invested.

Clothing.
Clothing is expensive here, and of inferior quality. The writer recently imported a suit from a firm in London, for which was paid (inclusive of duty, carriage, and insurance) 8*l*. This suit was superior in make and texture to a similar one purchased here for 13*l*. The difference between these figures would indicate that a profitable trade in custom-made clothing might be started by some enterprising London tailor.

Climate.
The prosperity of this district is due to its magnificent climate. Probably seven-tenths of those who have become residents here in the last 10 years came in delicate health, or in company with some sick relative or friend. The heat in summer is not enervating, and near the coast is not oppressive. The "Los Angeles Herald," commenting on the climate, recently said, "The railroad companies have all established general agencies in Los Angeles, and reduced their clerical forces in Florida. Mentone, Nice, Cannes, and other European climatic resorts, also *feel keenly the inroads made by our advancement*. Therefore, we can well look for and anticipate attacks from these 'fallen empires.'" Much as I doubt the accuracy of the paragraph I have italicised, I am satisfied that it ought to be, and some day will be, true; first, because this climate is for consumptives superior to that of the places named; and secondly, because (the bulk of those who suffer from consumption being dependent on their own exertions for a living) there is a fair chance here for an intelligent man to make a comfortable living, when renewed health admits of his engaging in some occupation. For full information about this climate, I beg to refer to my report on this district for the year 1884.* For further general information about this district, I beg to refer to my reports for 1884 and 1885.†

NOTE.—In this report dollars have been converted into pounds at the rate of 5 dol. per £.

Annex A.—RETURN of all Shipping at the Port of Wilmington (San Pedro), California, in the Year 1886.

ENTERED.

Nationality.	Sailing. Number of Vessels.	Sailing. Tons.	Steam. Number of Vessels.	Steam. Tons.	Total. Number of Vessels.	Total. Tons.
British	42	61,685	...	...	42	61,685
American	6	7,178	...	...	6	7,178
Other countries	2	1,359	...	...	2	1,359
Total	50	72,222	...	...	50	70,222
„ for the year preceding	28	44,113	...	...	28	44,113

* See No. 20 Commercial, 1885 (C. 4524).—*Ed.*
† See No. 10 Commercial, 1886 (C. 4737).—*Ed.*

UNITED STATES.

CLEARED.

Nationality.	Sailing.		Steam.		Total.	
	Number of Vessels.	Tons.	Number of Vessels.	Tons.	Number of Vessels.	Tons.
British	45	65,600	...	...	45	65,600
American	9	11,016	...	...	9	11,016
Other countries	2	1,359	...	...	2	1,359
Total	56	77,975	...	...	56	77,975
,, for the year preceding	25	33,477	...	...	25	33,477

NOTE.—This return does not include 507 sailing and steam coasting vessels, aggregate tonnage about 280,000 tons.

Annex B.—RETURN of the Principal Articles of Export from Wilmington, California, during the Years 1886-85.

Articles.	1886.		1885.	
	Value.	Quantity.	Value.	Quantity.
	£	Tons.	£	Tons.
Wheat	30,342	5,776	18,400	3,066
Canned fruits	..	..	..	47
Honey	184	9	4,288	268
Total	30,526	5,785	22,688	3,381

NOTE.—The transcontinental railways cannot furnish the statistics called for in this return for the city of Los Angeles.

RETURN of the Principal Articles of Import to Wilmington, California, during the Years 1885-86.

Articles.		1886.		1885.	
		Value.	Quantity.	Value.	Quantity.
		£		£	
Coal	Tons	155,124	77,562	96,526	48,263
Pig iron	,,	226	106	191	75
Cement	Barrels	...	...	...	...
Salt	Tons	193	185	283	249
Caustic soda	,,	177	28	849	184
Tin plate	,,	...	...	749	36
Sulphur	,,	115	11	...	...
Total	...	155,835	77,892	98,598	48,807

NOTE.—The transcontinental railways cannot furnish the statistics called for in this return for the city of Los Angeles.

ANNEX C.—Table showing the Total Value of all Articles Exported from Wilmington and Los Angeles, and Imported to Wilmington and Los Angeles, from and to Foreign Countries during the Years 1885-86.

Country.	Exports. 1886.	Exports. 1885.	Imports. 1886.	Imports. 1885.
	£	£	£	£
Great Britain	30,526	22,688	155,835	98,598
Total	30,526	22,688	155,835	98,598

NOTE.—The above returns do not include exports or imports coastwise or by rail, with the exception of articles exported in bond.

SAN DIEGO.

Vice-Consul Winchester reports as follows:—

The year 1886 has been marked by rapid growth and development in San Diego and the district of which it is the distributing centre.

Shipping. Arrivals of British ships have been 4 vessels, 3,932 tons; departures, 3 vessels, 2,589 tons. In 1884, arrivals and departures were *nil*.

Imports. The imports, of British origin, have consisted exclusively of coal from England, Australia, and British Columbia. There have been no cargo exports in British ships.

Coal. The coal business has outgrown existing facilities for discharge and ballasting, and vessels have recently been subject to detention. New wharves are, however, rapidly approaching completion; machinery is contracted for capable of discharging over 200 tons per diem; a powerful tug and large ballast-lighters are in course of construction, and arrangements are made for delivery of sand ballast alongside ship, at a cost of 40 to 60 cents per ton. As the port expenses are light, supplies cheap, extra sailors easily procurable, and the harbour is safe under all conditions of wind and weather, there seems to be no reason why, in the near future, this port should not be preferred by shipowners to any other on the coast, which does not regularly offer return cargo.

There is evidence of its growing importance in the fact that, at the date of this writing, there are nine British ships named as *en route* or loading for this port; and at least 13,000 tons of cargo are known to be under contract for delivery here, for which no charters are as yet reported. Of the cargoes expected, 10,000 tons will consist of steel rails, six vessels will bring coal, and four or five miscellaneous cargo, principally cement. The demand for coal is large and growing, railroad companies being the chief buyers. As a rule, ships are chartered and loaded in execution of positive orders. The consignment of cargoes for sale is not advisable.

Railroads. Many railroad extensions are in progress in this district, the most important being a branch giving direct communication with Los Angeles, avoiding the long circuit and heavy grades of the present route. This is to be open for traffic in June, when merchandise can be discharged here from ship direct into railroad car, and delivered in Los Angeles at as cheap a rate as if landed at San Pedro and forwarded thence. The latter place is described as the "harbour" of Los Angeles, but its harbour is only available for coasting vessels of light draught. Large vessels have to lie at anchor in the open roadstead, and discharge into lighters which are towed into the harbour, and there unloaded into cars. This process involves extra cost, occasional losses in transhipment, and injury to merchandise through excessive handling. Should storms arise from the south-east—to which this coast is liable in the winter months—ships have to slip their cables and sail to a safe distance from land. Recently, two large American vessels were caught by a gale unprepared and driven on shore. From San Diego to Los Angeles will be about 132 miles by the new route. From San Pedro the distance is only 25 miles; but the advantages of shipping through San Diego are considered fully to compensate for the increased length of railway haul; and the general cargoes expected here are intended, to a large extent, for the Los Angeles district. The principal article of import at San Pedro is coal for the Southern Pacific Railroad system. As that company is said to be locating a branch to this place, it is believed that ultimately some of their importations will be distributed through this port.

In view of the requirements of shipping, a company has been organised to build a dry dock and ships-ways, calculated to receive for examination and repair vessels up to 1,500 tons. *Docks.*

A line of steamships is projected to trade to Mexican ports, under contract with, and assisted by subsidy from, the Mexican Government. The ultimate establishment of lines of steamships sailing to Australia, China, and Japan, is spoken of as part of the plans of the powerful railroad companies which are now identified with this place.

In rapid development San Diego has lately shared with other districts in Southern California, but, in the rate at which development has progressed, it has outstripped them all. Population (now 12,000) has doubled within the year. Buildings have been erected of a substantial and costly class. Tram-roads and electric lighting have been introduced, wharves built, a ferry established, streets graded, a thorough system of sewerage planned and being pushed to completion; and costly schemes are in course of rapid execution for the storage of winter rainfall, and making it available for the irrigation of country lands and the use of the city. Progress in the settlement and improvement of country lands, is almost as rapid as the development of the city. The climate is of great equability, free from extremes of heat and cold, and attracts many settlers of means, especially from those States where winters are of great severity. These build homes, and generally engage in farming or fruit culture, and, where reasonable judgment is displayed, the pecuniary results are satisfactory. The raisin, grape, and olive appear to be the fruits for which the district is especially adapted, though oranges, peaches, apricots, apples, and pears are successfully grown. In one valley (the "El Cajou") up to 1885, 300 acres had been planted in raisin grapes. In 1886, 1,400 acres; and in 1887 (up to April), a further 3,000 acres have been planted. This is but one out of many valleys adapted to this industry. The local trade of San Diego is being benefited by the opening to colonisation of large tracts of land in Lower California—a State of Mexico adjoining the county of San Diego and commencing at a distance of 15 miles from the city. Many settlers are entering upon these lands for farming and fruit-growing, and mining enterprises are being developed. Large tracts are being sold to individuals and syndicates. *Population. Land. Fruit.*

The attention of British capitalists and emigrants has been drawn to to this enterprise, but investments should be preceeded by careful investigation, as land-titles in Mexico have not the same security as in the United States, and there are climatic and other drawbacks existing in this district.

(237)

UNITED STATES.

Annex A.—RETURN of all Shipping at the Port of San Diego in the Year 1886, omitting Small Coasters trading to Lower California (Mexico).

ENTERED.

| Nationality. | Sailing. || Steam. || Total. ||
	Number of Vessels.	Tons.	Number of Vessels.	Tons.	Number of Vessels.	Tons.
British	4	3,932	...	...	4	3,932
American (U.S.)	5	6,713	...	...	5	6,713
Other countries	2	1,473	1	101	3	1,574
Total	11	12,118	1	101	12	12,219
,, for the year preceding	...	...	...	...	...	64,771

CLEARED.

| Nationality. | Sailing. || Steam. || Total. ||
	Number of Vessels.	Tons.	Number of Vessels.	Tons.	Number of Vessels.	Tons.
British	1	758	...	...	1	758
American (U.S.)	2	1,425	...	...	2	1,425
Other countries	...	...	1	80	1	80
Total	3	2,183	1	80	4	2,263
,, for the year preceding	...	...	...	...	...	...

Annex B.—RETURN of Principal Articles of Export from San Diego during the Years 1885-86.

| Articles. | Value. ||
	1886.	1885.
	£	£
No direct foreign exports, other than to Lower California (Mexico). These consist of live stock, lumber, &c., not classified	15,671	16,985
Total	15,671	16,985

SAN FRANCISCO.

RETURN of Principal Articles of Import to San Diego during the Years 1885-86.

Articles.	1886. Quantity.	1886. Value.	1885. Quantity.	1885. Value.
Coal	Tons. 16,141	£ 10,860	Tons. 7,211	£ 4,554
Sundries from Lower California (Mexico), not classified..	..	16,312	..	No returns.
Total	16,141	27,172	7,211	4,554

Annex C.—TABLE showing the Total Value of all Articles Exported from and Imported to San Diego during the Years 1885-86.

Country.	Exports. 1886.	Exports. 1885.	Imports. 1886.	Imports. 1885.
	£	£	£	£
Great Britain	..	..	502	..
British Possessions	..	..	10,358	4,554
Lower California (Mexico)	15,671	16,985	16,312	No returns.
Total	15,671	16,985	27,172	4,554

PORT TOWNSEND.

Vice-Consul Alexander reports as follows:—

The statistical matter contained in the several annexes has, by the courtesy of the Collector of Customs at this port, been taken from the official records in the Custom-house; and apart from these tables I have not much data to present to you differing greatly from that embraced in my report for the year 1885.

Commerce. Trade and commerce did not improve with the rapidity it was generally expected would follow the depression in business last year, although a little more activity has been perceptible lately. To get a better idea, however, of the commerce of this district, I would respectfully refer to Annex A., from which it will be noticed that, although the number of vessels which have entered and cleared during the present year, as compared with last year, is smaller, there is a greater increase in tonnage, showing that vessels of greater burthen are seeking freights from this quarter.

Exports and imports. A marked falling-off in the exports and imports from and to this port will also be noticed by referring to Annexes B. and C., and comparing this year with last, the decrease may be attributed to the facts that last year a shipment of wheat was made to Europe, and two very valuable tea cargoes were sent here from Japan, as an experiment, to test the facilities and despatch of the new route viâ the Northern Pacific Railway as compared with the Canadian Pacific Railway, to the New York markets; and, as no cargoes of tea this year have arrived for transportation viâ the Northern Pacific Railway, and at least twelve cargoes have been forwarded viâ the Canadian Pacific Railway, we must infer that the latter has the preference, and has been proved to be the most expeditious and cheapest route.

I am pleased to be able to report that a commencement has just been made in what I think will be of great value to British commercial interests, and lead to the opening-up and development of direct trade between Great Britain and this district: our cargo, arriving unfortunately too late to be included in the appended tables, consisting of general merchandise, principally pig iron, Portland cement and salt, has been discharged, and three more cargoes of rails for the railroads are on the way direct to this port; the undeveloped state of the country and the paucity of the population in this district will, for the present, make it a difficult matter to find markets for any large consignments of general merchandise from England, and the high rate of duty chargeable on imported goods, all but debars them from this country.

I venture to hope that upon the completion of the Cascade Division of the Northern Pacific Railroad, which it is expected will be this autumn, British vessels will obtain wheat charters from this district direct to Europe.

It is worthy of note that one shipment of assorted lumber was made in a British vessel direct to London as a specimen cargo; the lumber was selected pieces from the different mills, and was the best shipment of clear timber that has ever left the Sound. To another British vessel, the "Knight of St. Michael," belongs the honour of carrying the largest cargo of lumber which has ever left these waters for a foreign port; this ship was built as a carrier, her measurement is 2,230 tons, and she took 1,777,000 feet of lumber on a draught of 21 feet, of which amount 1,050,000 feet was stowed in the lower hold.

Coal and lumber. The coal and lumber trade from Puget Sound to foreign and coastwise ports, has steadily increased during the past year. The aggregate tonnage engaged was about 518,400.

In the lumber trade, there has been a small decrease in the coastwise shipping compared with that of last year, but the coastwise coal trade has more than made up for that deficiency.

There were 212 cargoes of coal carried in American vessels from the Sound to coastwise ports, principally to San Francisco, amounting to 454,280 tons, and valued at 326,719*l.*, chiefly shipped from Seattle and Tacoma; it being in the vicinity of these two towns where the most important coal-fields are worked, lines of railroad connecting the mines with the wharves. *Freight.* The freight-money received for transportation, averaging 9*s.* per ton, amounted to 196,031*l.* No shipments of coal have ever been made to foreign countries from this district.

There were 284 cargoes of lumber carried in American vessels to coastwise ports, amounting to 142,000,000 feet, and valued at 387,958*l.*; the freight-money received for transportation, averaged 1*l.* 4*s.* per 1,000 feet. amounting to 145,895*l.* These shipments were made from the various milling ports on the Sound, chiefly in vessels owned by the mill companies, which being return cargoes of general merchandise for their respective ports from San Francisco.

Three cargoes of timber, principally spars, were shipped from this district round Cape Horn to Eastern American ports, and are included in the above statement,

Grain, &c. Large shipments of oats, potatoes, fruits, and other produce of the surrounding country have been made by steamers to San Francisco, the value of the grain and produce being estimated at 61,645*l.*

SAN FRANCISCO.

The output and export of hops from Washington Territory for the past year amounted to 22,000 bales, averaging 180 lbs. to the bale and valued at 2s. per lb.; these shipments were made, viâ the railroads, to New York markets chiefly. **Hops.**

All the wool shipments from this section are made viâ steamer to San Francisco, and viâ the railroads to Eastern markets, and it is extremely difficult to obtain accurate figures of the quantity shipped, as no official records are kept. **Wool.**

Large quantities of cattle, horses, and sheep have been sent to Eastern markets, principally from Eastern Washington Territory, but no official records of the number have been kept: the quality of each is improving by the farmers purchasing better blood, particularly in the case of the two former. Inducements are now held out for the breeding and raising of a better quality of animal, as such command higher prices, by the recent introduction of "fairs," as our agricultural shows are called in this country, which gives the producer an excellent opportunity, not only to learn the points of the various favourite breeds, but to dispose of his own stock to purchasers: it is to be regretted that this Territory is so far, and transportation so costly from England, as good animals for breeding purposes are eagerly sought after, and high prices are given for often very inferior animals. **Cattle, stock, &c.**

The country has been exceptionally free from infectious and contagious diseases, and no cases have been reported among the cattle and stock generally during the year. **Disease.**

The weather has been unusually severe all over the Territory this winter, but stock have wintered well, and very few losses are recorded, the cases occurring principally in Eastern Washington. Stockmen are now taking the precaution to guard against the winters by providing shelter and food for their herds. **Climate.**

There appears to be little scope at present for the extension of British commerce in this district; but upon the better development of the country, the increase of population, and the introduction of manufacturing industries, it is reasonable to hope that Great Britain will not be behindhand in securing her share of trade in this part of the world.

Annex A.—RETURN of all Shipping at the Port Townsend for the Year ending March 31, 1887.

ENTERED.

Nationalities.	Sailing. Number of Vessels.	Sailing. Tons.	Steam. Number of Vessels.	Steam. Tons.	Total. Number of Vessels.	Total. Tons.
British	55	43,615	23	2,430	78	46,045
United States of America	183	125,771	646	280,693	829	406,464
Norwegian	25	20,981	...	...	25	20,981
Chilian	10	7,381	...	...	10	7,381
German	8	5,453	...	...	8	5,453
Swedish	7	5,405	...	...	7	5,405
Bolivian	2	1,136	...	...	2	1,136
Belgian	1	865	...	...	1	865
Italian	1	823	...	...	1	823
Nicaraguan	1	609	...	...	1	609
French	1	413	...	...	1	413
Hawaiian Islands	1	382	...	...	1	382
Total	295	212,834	669	283,123	964	495,957
,, for year 1885	217	120,075	869	371,941	1,044	492,01

UNITED STATES.

The following statement shows the receipts from the several objects of Internal Taxation in the United States during the fiscal years 1886 and 1887:—

Objects of taxation.	Receipts during Fiscal year ended June 30. 1886. Dol. c.	Receipts during Fiscal year ended June 30. 1887. Dol. c.	Increase. Dol. c.	Decrease. Dol. c.
Spirits—				
Spirits distilled from apples, peaches, and grapes	1,400,394 48	1,090,379 07	...	310,015 41
Spirits distilled from materials other than apples, peaches, and grapes	62,365,825 13	59,551,972 59	...	2,813,852 54
Rectifiers (special tax)	178,650 17	176,600 12	...	2,050 05
Retail liquor-dealers (special tax)	4,714,735 18	4,587,268 21	...	127,466 97
Wholesale liquor-dealers (special tax)	418,406 24	416,304 66	...	2,101 58
Manufacturers of stills (special tax)	1,102 90	860 86	...	242 04
Stills and worms manufactured (special tax)	3,000 00	2,860 00	...	140 00
Stamps for distilled spirits intended for export	10,151 90	3,076 20	...	7,075 70
Total	69,092,266 00	65,829,321 71	...	3,262,944 29
Tobacco—				
Cigars and cheroots	10,532,804 05	11,364,916 33	832,112 28	...
Cigarettes	655,569 55	792,379 60	136,710 05	...
Snuff	493,283 80	524,942 26	31,658 46	...
Tobacco, chewing and smoking	14,834,095 42	15,995,019 46	1,160,924 04	...
Dealers in leaf-tobacco (special tax)	53,875 63	51,891 14	...	1,984 49
Dealers in manufactured tobacco (special tax)	1,208,529 17	1,245,412 65	36,883 48	...
Manufacturers of tobacco (special tax)	5,575 85	5,563 75	...	12 10
Manufacturers of cigars (special tax)	108,695 45	113,340 00	4,644 55	...
Peddlers of tobacco (special tax)	14,933 61	14,701 94	...	231 67
Total	27,907,362 53	30,108,067 13	2,200,704 60	...
Fermented liquors—				
Ale, beer, läger-beer, porter and other similar fermented liquors	19,157,612 87	21,387,411 79	2,229,798 92	...
Brewers (special tax)	186,928 89	187,352 24	423 35	...
Retail dealers in malt liquors (special tax)	169,502 56	177,148 13	7,645 57	...
Wholesale dealers in malt liquors (special tax)	162,686 97	170,275 33	7,588 36	...
Total	19,676,731 29	21,922,187 49	2,245,456 20	...
Oleomargarine—				
Oleomargarine, domestic and imported	...	435,924 04	445,924 04	...
Manufacturers of oleomargarine (special tax)	...	31,700 00	31,700 00	...
Retail dealers in oleomargarine (special tax)	...	154,924 00	154,924 00	...
Wholesale dealers in oleomargarine (special tax)	...	101,400 00	101,400 00	...
Total	...	723,748 04	723,948 04	...
Banks and bankers, not National—				
Bank circulation other than National, and banks, bankers, and other parties liable on amount of any person, State bank, or State banking association, or of any town, city or municipal corporation, paid out by them	...	4,288 37	4,288 37	...
Total	...	4,288 37	4,288 37	...
Miscellaneous—				
Collections not otherwise provided for	32,087 17	29,283 49	...	2,803 68
Penalties	194,422 45	220,204 83	25,782 38	...
Total	226,509 62	249,488 32	22,978 70	...
Aggregate receipts	116,902,869 44	118,837,301 06	934,431 62	...

Annex C.—TABLE showing the Total Value of all Articles Exported from Port Townsend and Imported to Port Townsend from and to Foreign Countries during the Years 1885 and 1886.

Country.	Exports. 1886.	Exports. 1885.	Imports. 1886.	Imports. 1885.
	£	£	£	£
Great Britain	1,717	39,449	..	..
British Columbia	159,494	239,086	81,942	40,410
British possessions in Australia	114,275	98,675	136	5
Chili	35,380	38,986	..	6
Hawaiian Islands	30,980	27,867	18	300
China	8,906	2,673	1,430	1,391
Peru	8,882	5,563	..	34
Mexico	6,734	123	..	..
Argentine Republic	4,268	2,182	..	..
Uruguay	2,785	5,845	..	..
New Caledonia	2,154	982	..	..
Brazil	1,772	..	..	..
Japan	..	..	4	83,543
Total	377,347	471,486	83,530	125,679

LONDON:
Printed for Her Majesty's Stationery Office,
By HARRISON AND SONS,
Printers in Ordinary to Her Majesty.
(Wt. 7730   75   6 | 87—H & S   237)

FOREIGN OFFICE.
1887.
ANNUAL SERIES.

No. 215.

DIPLOMATIC AND CONSULAR REPORTS ON TRADE AND FINANCE.

UNITED STATES.

REPORT FOR THE YEAR 1886
ON THE
VICE-CONSULAR DISTRICT OF NEWPORT NEWS.

REFERENCE TO PREVIOUS REPORT, Annual Series No. 20.

Presented to both Houses of Parliament by Command of Her Majesty,
AUGUST, 1887.

LONDON:
PRINTED FOR HER MAJESTY'S STATIONERY OFFICE,
BY HARRISON AND SONS, ST. MARTIN'S LANE,
PRINTERS IN ORDINARY TO HER MAJESTY.

And to be purchased, either directly or through any Bookseller, from
EYRE AND SPOTTISWOODE, EAST HARDING STREET, FLEET STREET, E.C., and
32, ABINGDON STREET, WESTMINSTER, S.W.; or
ADAM AND CHARLES BLACK, NORTH BRIDGE, EDINBURGH; or
HODGES, FIGGIS, & Co., 104, GRAFTON STREET, DUBLIN.

1887.

[C.—4923—138.] *Price 1d.*

New Series of Reports.

REPORTS of the Annual Series have been issued from Her Majesty's Diplomatic and Consular Officers at the following places, and may be obtained from the sources indicated on the title-page:—

No.		Price.	No.		Price.
89.	Tripoli	1d.	152.	Corunna	1d.
90.	Saigon	1d.	153.	Vienna	1d.
91.	Cherbourg	1d.	154.	Cagliari	1d.
92.	New Orleans	2d.	155.	St. Petersburg	2d.
93.	Galatz	1d.	156.	Taiwan	1d.
94.	Baltimore	1d.	157.	Foochow	1d.
95.	Tokio	4d.	158.	Tonga	1d.
96.	Havre	3d.	159.	Wuhu	1d.
97.	Barcelona	3d.	160.	Lisbon	1d.
98.	Volo	1d.	161.	Ning-po	1d.
99.	Damascus	1d.	162.	Cadiz	2d.
100.	Paris	1d.	163.	Bilbao	1d.
101.	Bordeaux	2d.	164.	Jaffa	1d.
102.	Serajevo	1d.	165.	Van	1d.
103.	Manila	1d.	166.	Bushire	1d.
104.	Galveston	1d.	167.	Riga	1d.
105.	Aleppo	1d.	168.	Santos	1d.
106.	Rio de Janeiro	1d.	169.	Charleston	1d.
107.	Truxillo	1d.	170.	Newchwang	1d.
108.	St. Petersburg	3d.	171.	Amsterdam	1d.
109.	Leghorn	1d.	172.	Ajaccio	1d.
110.	Boston	1d.	173.	Chinkiang	2d.
111.	Buenos Ayres	3d.	174.	Naples	3d.
112.	Kewkiang	1d.	175.	Smyrna	1d.
113.	Teheran	2d.	176.	Belgrade	1d.
114.	Beyrout	1d.	177.	Philadelphia	2d.
115.	Odessa	5d.	178.	Stockholm	2d.
116.	Carthagena	1d.	179.	Pernambuco	1d.
117.	Santo Domingo	1d.	180.	Frankfort-on-Main	1d.
118.	Mollendo	1d.	181.	Mogador	2d.
119.	Guayaquil	1d.	182.	New York	2d.
120.	Valparaiso	1d.	183.	Swatow	1d.
121.	San José	1d.	184.	Berlin	1d.
122.	Pakhoi	1d.	185.	Philippopolis	1d.
123.	Hyogo	1d.	186.	San Francisco	6d.
124.	Tamsui	1d.	187.	Lisbon	1d.
125.	Malaga	1d.	188.	Lisbon	2d.
126.	Marseilles	1d.	189.	Nice	2d.
127.	Boulogne	2d.	190.	Tientsin	1d.
128.	Warsaw	1d.	191.	Hankow	1d.
129.	Monte Video	1d.	192.	Erzeroum	1d.
130.	Christiania	4d.	193.	Syra	1d.
131.	Gothenburg	2d.	194.	Athens	3d.
132.	Kiungchow	1d.	195.	Vienna	2d.
133.	Amoy	1d.	196.	Alexandria	1d.
134.	Genoa	1d.	197.	Constantinople	1d.
135.	Trebizond	1d.	198.	Hakodate	1d.
136.	Savannah	1d.	199.	Shanghai	2d.
137.	Wilmington	2d.	200.	Tokyo	2d.
138.	Bolivar	3d.	201.	Tamatave	1d.
139.	Wênchow	1d.	202.	Mexico	1d.
140.	Chicago	2d.	203.	Chefoo	1d.
141.	Fiume	1d.	204.	Nagasaki	5d.
142.	Port Saïd	1d.	205.	Cuba	1d.
143.	Java	1d.	206.	Tunis	1d.
144.	Puerto Cabello	1d.	207.	Réunion	1d.
145.	Coquimbo	1d.	208.	Hyogo	2d.
146.	Vera Cruz	2d.	209.	Tangier	1d.
147.	Bengazi	1d.	210.	Antwerp	1d.
148.	Canary Islands	1d.	211.	Stettin	1d.
149.	Rome	1d.	212.	Ezeroum	1d.
150.	Madeira	1d.	213.	Rotterdam	1d.
151.	Tahiti	1d.	214.	Nantes	2d.

No. 215.

Reference to previous Report, Annual Series No. 20.

UNITED STATES.

NEWPORT NEWS.

Consul Segrave to the Marquis of Salisbury.

My Lord, Baltimore, *July* 25, 1887.

I HAVE the honour herewith to transmit, in original, a trade report for 1886, from the British Vice-Consul at Newport News.

I have, &c.
(Signed)   W. F. SEGRAVE.

Report by Vice-Consul Warburton on the Trade and Commerce of Newport News for the Year 1886.

For 1886, there has been a considerable increase over former years in British shipping frequenting this port, and also in the imports and exports; amounting in the case of British shipping to nearly 34 per cent. in imports to 400 per cent., and in exports to 383 per cent. over the preceding year. *Increase in shipping; imports and exports.*

Very little of this is due to the direct line of steamers plying to Liverpool, which only commenced to run in December, and a considerable increase may be looked for from that cause in the current year, as is indicated by the fact that up to April 30, there has been an export of 400,000*l.* against one of 360,000*l.* in 1886, for the same period, which has scarcely touched the export of tobacco at all. *Direct line of steamers between Liverpool and Newport News.*

The "Huntingdon line," as it is called, comprises at present four vessels, of which two belong to the Ducal Line, and two are hired by that line at a cost, it is said, of 7*s.* per gross ton per month, the Ducal Line steamers receiving 10*s.* The latter are the "Duke of Westminster," 2,426 tons, and "Duke of Buckingham," 2,020 tons register, while the "Florida" and "City of Manchester" are, respectively 2,040 and 2,089 tons. For purely carrying purposes the latter are undoubtedly the better, being more economical in construction, manning, and consumption of coal, while they carry larger freights per ton register. In fact, they are much better adapted to this trade than the Ducal boats, in the selection of which little judgment has been exercised; for, while they are too expensive as carriers, they have little passenger accommodation: the "Duke of Westminster" carrying 50, and the "Duke of Buckingham" no first-class passengers, or, at most, half-a-dozen. If it is seriously intended to establish a passenger trade, different vessels must be employed. The passage averages about 18 days, and the service is supposed to be fortnightly, but this rate is not attained. The vessels are all well manned and officered. Although but a few emigrants have been landed here, complaints have already been made at the British *Length of passage. Emigrants.*

(273)

Legation at Washington, by men who have been induced by false pretences, or promises, to make use of the line, and who have been put to considerable expense in reaching their proper destinations.

The Huntingdon Line is principally managed by the Newport News and Mississippi Valley Company, which has absorbed the Chesapeake and Ohio Railway, and several others.

Mismanagement. The officials of that Company have had no experience of shipping, and this among other things militated against the financial success of the line.

Want of a cotton-press. The want of a cotton-press is shown in the fact that while the "Florida" carried from Norfolk 9,724 bales, she could only take 7,982 bales from this port. As the average freight of a bale of cotton is 2 dol., or 8s. 4d., this deficiency entails a loss on 1,742 bales of 3,484 dol., or 725l. per trip, where cotton is the only cargo; or, as recompressing costs about 10d. per bale, a net loss of about 650l. The bales are now compressed inland, and expand considerably on their journey to the port. Unquestionably, if the export of cotton becomes considerable, it will be necessary to recompress the bales. It is questionable whether it would not be economical to carry the bales in their country-pressed condition from the interior, and compress them only at the port. A loss in land freight would of course be sustained, because fewer bales could be carried per car, but, as the railway and steamship line are practically one, the saving which would accrue in ocean freight as well as on inland pressing, would more than compensate, and I am inclined to believe that the latter alone would compensate fully for any such loss.

Combinations of land and ocean carriers unsuccessful.
May serve to divert trade. I believe it is an established fact that, in this country, every combination of railway and shipping to Europe has hitherto proceeded unsatisfactorily, and has resulted in a loss. Whether this venture will prove an exception remains to be seen. The principal service it will perform for this port is to divert the flow of trade into a new channel, and make the route known to importers and exporters; a result which in itself is worth a considerable amount of otherwise unprofitable expenditure.

Articles of import.
Articles of export. The principal articles of import so far are salt, soda-ash, rails and steel blooms. Of export, cotton which comes from Memphis and the district of which it is the centre, wheat, corn, tobacco, lard, flour, bacon and lumber, the latter principally black walnut, white oak, poplar and staves. Coal for ships' use has ceased to be recorded as an export in the customs, and about 30,000 tons have been exported principally to the West Indies, Colon, &c., as cargo. One cargo of about 150 oxen has been shipped from here, and from the central situation of the port, and its proximity to the grazing grounds of Kentucky, Virginia, Tennessee, and more Western States, this is likely to prove a very important item of export in the future.

Dry dock. A dry dock is now in course of construction, and will be completed in about a year's time. It will cost about 125,000l., be 650 feet long, and 100 wide at the floor. Vessels visiting the port about the expiration of their classification, or when required to be examined under Lloyds' rules, will probably make use of the dock, which they can do without discharging cargo.

A few casualties may also swell the list of its customers, and there is a probability of its proving an attraction to the port.

Population.
Material progress satisfactory. The population has considerably increased within the last few months, and may be estimated at about 1,700, although there is no accurate means of determining the number. Altogether, the material progress of Newport News has, during the last six months, been more satisfactory than at any period of its five years' existence.

I wish I could report its condition as satisfactory in all other respects. *Unhealthiness of the port.*

During the past year there has been a great deal of sickness—the usual malarial fever, and over 100 cases of scarlet fever, or scarlatina, which is a large proportion for a population of 1,200 to 1,500.

The cause of sickness is partly the unhealthiness of the climate, its sudden changes, and extremes of heat and cold. But, in a great measure, also the prevalence of swamps and marshy ground, as well as the total absence of drainage and sanitary precautions. *Causes.*

There is not even an hospital of any kind.

The mortality from "accidents," which is the term used indiscriminately for mishaps caused by reckless driving over the level crossings, and on the unfenced railway tracks, and by the negligence of the monopoly companies has been considerable; and, unfortunately, redress for the families of the killed or injured is difficult, if not impossible, to obtain. *Frequency of violent deaths. Negligence of the monopolists.*

The monopoly of the Companies is most complete. They own or control all the means of exit and entrance, the land, the telegraph, and the administration of justice.

The greater number of houses in Newport News are built and owned by the Old Dominion Land Company who rent them to their officials and to those of the railroad, the latter being by far the most numerous, and constituting the majority of the white population. From all these who occupy houses belonging to the former Company, their rent is deducted from their wages without their assent and handed over to the landlord.

The Sunday laws are very strict in the State, and, while enforced as regards private individuals, they are evaded as regards the Companies.

I have considered it advisable to state these facts, because emigrants are induced to ship for Newport News by glowing accounts of the place, its prosperity and its advantages as a field for labour and capital; whereas, under the condition of affairs prevailing, I know few places less desirable.

Where private enterprise is strangled or overshadowed by an all-pervading monopoly, and where the administration of justice, as well as other conditions of the place are unsatisfactory, there is no field for honest independent labour, much less for capital, and especially such small capital as is usually at the disposal of emigrants. Where every article of food is 25 per cent. dearer than at any eastern port, where bread is $2\frac{1}{2}d.$ per lb., milk $8d.$ per quart, tea, of the worst quality, $3s.$ per lb., potatoes $1d.$, and lodging even dearer in proportion, with the addition of bad water, and very little of it, the small earnings of an emigrant soon melt away while he is hopelessly looking for work. *Newport News no field for emigrants.*

I append tables showing the amount of shipping British and foreign, exports, &c. Imports amount to only 25,000$l.$

UNITED STATES.

Exports.

RETURN of Quantity and Value of Exports from Newport News to Foreign Ports for 1886, and the two preceding Years.

Articles.		1886.		1885.		1884.	
		Quantity.	Value.	Quantity.	Value.	Quantity.	Value.
			£		£		£
Coal	Tons	73,570	50,000	51,912	39,000	41,000	32,578
Wheat	Bushels	1,686,006	265,000	142,082	25,700	...	108,000
Flour	Barrels	...	56,063	83,016	38,500	...	94,000
Bacon	Lbs.	...	4,200	538,264	10,070	...	13,635
Lard	,,	...	12,000	...	...	...	...
Corn	Bushels	1,004,572	290,000	533,850	55,000	...	...
Walnut	Logs	...	...	3,226	13,400	...	9,750
Staves	Pieces	...	53,000	432,663	13,000	...	16,000
Lumber	Feet	...	...	904,574	8,500	...	10,550
Cotton	Bales	56,715	591,000	10,419	103,000	30,491	325,460
Whiskey	Gallons	...	...	...	...	...	214,000
Sundries	...	...	22,000	...	30,930	...	10,300
Total	...	...	1,263,263	...	347,000	...	844,273

RETURN of all Vessels Clearing the Port in 1886; Coastwise American vessels excluded.

Nationality.	Sailing.		Steam.		Total.	
	Number of Vessels.	Tons.	Number of Vessels.	Tons.	Number of Vessels.	Tons.
British	9	6,486	190	208,802	199	217,282
American	9	4,272	13	26,128	22	30,400
German	1	191	5	6,381	6	6,572
Spanish	...	...	9	14,509	9	14,509
Italian	6	3,399	...	...	6	3,399
Norwegian	3	1,687	1	389	4	2,076
Portuguese	3	1,004	...	...	3	1,004
Austrian	1	560	...	...	1	560
Russian	1	452	...	...	1	452
French	...	...	1	953	1	953
Total	33	17,851	216	257,162	252	275,013

It is difficult to ascertain the purely Coastwise tonnage of vessels carrying the United States' flag. I estimate it at 400,000 tons, including all vessels which touch at the port.

NUMBER and Tonnage of British Vessels.

Year.	Entered.		Cleared.	
	No.	Tonnage.	No.	Tonnage.
1884	150	163,612	154	168,585
1885	133	162,855	133	162,784
1886	200	217,282	199	215,288

RETURN of all Vessels Entering the Port in 1886; Coastwise American vessels excluded.

Nationality.	Sailing. Number of Vessels.	Sailing. Tons.	Steam. Number of Vessels.	Steam. Tons.	Total. Number of Vessels.	Total. Tons.
British	9	6,486	191	210,796	200	217,282
American	7	3,185	12	23,933	19	27,118
German	1	191	5	6,381	6	6,572
Spanish	...	...	8	12,723	8	12,723
Italian	6	3,399	...	...	6	3,399
Norwegian	3	1,687	1	389	4	2,076
Portuguese	3	1,004	...	...	3	1,004
Austrian	1	560	...	...	1	560
Russian	1	452	...	...	1	452
French	...	...	1	953	1	953
Total	31	16,964	218	255,175	260	273,139

LONDON:
Printed for Her Majesty's Stationery Office,
By HARRISON AND SONS,
Printers in Ordinary to Her Majesty.
(Wt. 7730   75   8 | 87--H & S   273)

FOREIGN OFFICE.
1887.
ANNUAL SERIES.

No. 235.
DIPLOMATIC AND CONSULAR REPORTS ON TRADE AND FINANCE.

UNITED STATES.

REPORT FOR THE YEAR ENDED JUNE 30, 1886,
ON THE
FINANCES OF THE UNITED STATES.

REFERENCE TO PREVIOUS REPORT [C. 3669], Commercial No. 24, 1883.

Issued during the Recess and Presented to both Houses of Parliament by Command of Her Majesty.

LONDON:
PRINTED FOR HER MAJESTY'S STATIONERY OFFICE,
BY HARRISON AND SONS, ST. MARTIN'S LANE,
PRINTERS IN ORDINARY TO HER MAJESTY.

And to be purchased, either directly or through any Bookseller, from
EYRE AND SPOTTISWOODE, EAST HARDING STREET, FLEET STREET, E.C., and 32, ABINGDON STREET, WESTMINSTER, S.W.; or
ADAM AND CHARLES BLACK, 6, NORTH BRIDGE, EDINBURGH; or
HODGES, FIGGIS, & Co., 104, GRAFTON STREET, DUBLIN.

1887.

[C.—5252—12.]   *Price Threepence.*

New Series of Reports.

Reports of the Annual Series have been issued from Her Majesty's Diplomatic and Consular Officers at the following places, and may be obtained from the sources indicated on the title-page:—

No.		Price.	No.		Price.
113.	Teheran	2d.	174.	Naples..	3d.
114.	Beyrout	1d.	175.	Smyrna	1d.
115.	Odessa	5d.	176.	Belgrade	1d.
116.	Carthagena	1d.	177.	Philadelphia..	2d.
117.	Santo Domingo	1d.	178.	Stockholm	2d.
118.	Mollendo	1d.	179.	Pernambuco	1d.
119.	Guayaquil	1d.	180.	Frankfort-on-Main	1d.
120.	Valparaiso	1d.	181.	Mogador	2d.
121.	San José	1d.	182.	New York	2d
122.	Pakhoi	1d.	183.	Swatow	1d.
123.	Hyogo..	1d.	184.	Berlin..	1d.
124.	Tamsui	1d.	185.	Philippopolis..	1d.
125.	Malaga	1d.	186.	San Francisco	6d.
126.	Marseilles	1d.	187.	Lisbon..	1d.
127.	Boulogne	2d.	188.	Lisbon..	2d.
128.	Warsaw	1d.	189.	Nice ..	2d.
129.	Monte Video ..	1d.	190.	Tientsin	1d.
130.	Christiania	4d.	191.	Hankow	1d.
131.	Gothenburg	2d.	192.	Erzeroum	1d.
132.	Kiungchow	1d.	193.	Syra ..	1d.
133.	Amoy ..	1d.	194.	Athens	3d.
134.	Genoa ..	1d.	195.	Vienna	2d.
135.	Trebizond	1d.	196.	Alexandria	1d.
136.	Savannah	1d.	197.	Constantinople	1d.
137.	Wilmington	2d.	198.	Hakodate	1d.
138.	Bolivar	3d.	199.	Shanghai	2d.
139.	Wênchow	1d.	200.	Tokyo..	2d.
140.	Chicago	2d.	201.	Tamatave	1d.
141.	Fiume..	1d.	202.	Mexico	1d.
142.	Port Saïd	1d.	203.	Chefoo..	1d.
143.	Java ..	1d.	204.	Nagasaki	5d.
144.	Puerto Cabello	1d.	205.	Cuba ..	1d.
145.	Coquimbo	1d.	206.	Tunis ..	1d.
146.	Vera Cruz	2d.	207.	Réunion	1d.
147.	Bengazi	1d.	208.	Hyogo..	2d.
148.	Canary Islands	1d.	209.	Tangier	1d.
149.	Rome ..	1d.	210.	Antwerp	1d.
150.	Madeira	1d.	211.	Stettin..	1d.
151.	Tahiti ..	1d.	212.	Erzeroum	1d.
152.	Corunna	1d.	213.	Rotterdam	1d.
153.	Vienna	1d.	214.	Nantes..	2d.
154.	Cagliari	1d.	215.	Newport News	1d.
155.	St. Petersburg	2d.	216.	Rio Grande do Sul	1d.
156.	Taiwan	1d.	217.	Rio de Janeiro	1d.
157.	Foochow	1d.	218.	Corea ..	1d.
158.	Tonga ..	1d.	219.	Kanagawa	1d.
159.	Wuhu ..	1d.	220.	Wurtemburg ..	1d.
160.	Lisbon..	1d.	221.	Tahiti ..	1d.
161.	Ning-po	1d.	222.	Bangkok	1d.
162.	Cadiz ..	2d.	223.	St. Petersburg	2d.
163.	Bilbao..	1d.	224.	Canton	1d.
164.	Jaffa ..	1d.	225.	Erzeroum	1d.
165.	Van ..	1d.	226.	Rio de Janeiro	1d.
166.	Bushire	1d.	227.	Valparaiso	1d.
167.	Riga ..	1d.	228.	St. Thomas	1d.
168.	Santos..	1d.	229.	Stockholm	1d.
169.	Charleston	1d.	230.	Nyassa..	1d.
170.	Newchwang	1d.	231.	Buenos Ayres .	1d.
171.	Amsterdam	1d.	232.	The Hague	1d.
172.	Ajaccio	1d.	233.	Trieste..	1d.
173.	Chinkiang	2d.	234.	Vienna	1d

No. 235.

Reference to previous Report [C. 3669], *Commercial No.* 24, 1883.

UNITED STATES.

WASHINGTON.

Sir L. Sackville West to the Marquis of Salisbury.

My Lord,   Washington, *July* 15, 1887.

I HAVE the honour to transmit to your Lordship herewith a despatch from Mr. Edwardes, Secretary of H.M. Legation, enclosing a report on the finances of the United States for the year 1886.

    I have, &c.
    (Signed)   L. S. SACKVILLE WEST.

Mr. Edwardes to Sir L. Sackville West.

Sir,   Washington, *July* 15, 1886.   Report.

I HAVE the honour to transmit herewith a report on the finances of the United States for the fiscal year ended June 30, 1886.

The information and details given is taken from the annual report of the Secretary of the Treasury, and from reports issued by the different departments under his charge.

    I have, &c.
    (Signed)   H. G. EDWARDES.

Report on the Finances of the United States for 1886.

The net receipts of the United States during the twelve months ended June 30, 1886, amounted to 336,439,727 dol. 6 c. (70,091,609*l.*);* the net expenditures were 242,483,138 dol. 50 c. (50,517,320*l.*). The receipts were 12,749,020 dol. 68 c. (2,656,045*l.*) greater, and the expenditures were 17,743,796 dol. 61 c. (3,696,624*l.*) less than the year ending June 30, 1885; making an increase in the net receipts for the year over those of 1885, of 30,492,817 dol. 29 c. (6,352,670*l.*). The excess of revenue over expenditure was 93,956,588 dol. 56 c. (19,574,289*l.*). Receipts and expenditures

  * The United States' dollar is calculated at 50 pence.

UNITED STATES.

The following statement contains the details:—

RECEIPTS.

	1885.	1886.	Increase.	Decrease.
	Dol. c.	Dol. c.	Dol. c.	Dol. c.
Revenue from customs	181,471,939 34	192,905,023 44	11,433,084 10	...
Internal revenue	112,498,725 54	116,805,936 48	4,307,210 94	...
Sale of public lands	5,705,986 44	5,630,999 34	...	74,987 10
Miscellaneous sources	24,014,055 06	21,097,767 80	...	2,916,287 36
Total	323,690,706 38	336,439,727 06	15,740,295 04	2,991,274 36
Net increase	...	...	12,749,020 68	...

EXPENDITURES.

	1885.	1886.	Increase.	Decrease.
	Dol. c.	Dol. c.	Dol. c.	Dol. c.
Expenditure on account of: Civil and miscellaneous—				
Customs, lighthouses, public buildings, &c.	27,125,972 67	24,165,246 36	...	2,960,726 31
Internal revenue	4,550,623 21	4,113,319 90	...	437,303 31
Interior civil (land patents, &c.)	8,979,266 36	7,306,224 44	...	1,673,041 92
Treasury proper (legislative, executive, and other civil)	36,854,109 05	33,323,749 66	...	3,530,359 39
Diplomatic (foreign relations)	5,439,609 11	1,332,320 88	...	4,107,288 23
Judiciary, and quarterly salaries	4,544,677 98	3,926,068 61	...	618,609 37
War department	42,670,578 47	34,324,152 74	...	8,346,425 73
Navy department	16,021,079 67	13,907,887 74	...	2,113,191 93
Interior department (Indians and pensions)	62,654,762 12	69,504,022 20	6,849,260 08	...
Interest on public debt	51,386,256 47	50,580,145 97	...	806,110 50
Total	260,226,935 11	242,483,138 50	6,849,260 08	24,593,056 69
Net decrease	...	...	...	17,743,796 61
Surplus available for reduction of debt	63,463,771 27	93,956,588 56	30,492,817 29	...

The receipts on account of the post-office department not included in the above statement, amounted to 52,997,135 dol. 26 c. (11,041,069*l.*), an increase of 5,687,399 dol. 91 c. over those of the preceding year. The expenditures increased from 50,326,314 dol. 50 c. in 1883, to 50,682,585 dol. 72 c. in 1886; or 356,271 dol. 22 c. Of the amounts received and expended, 26,403,249 dol. 62 c. did not actually pass through the Treasury, having been received and disbursed by postmasters.

Summary of operations. Bonds of the United States amounting to 44,531,350 dol. were redeemed, and applied to the sinking fund. Coupons from bonds of the United States, amounting to 7,557,412 dol. 79 c., were paid by the several assistant treasurers, and forwarded to the Treasury Department, where they were examined. Interest amounting to 42,498,687 dol. 92 c. on registered bonds of the United States, including bonds issued to the various Pacific Railroad Companies, was paid by checks on the Treasury, and assistant treasurers. There were also issued 36,930 drafts in payment of warrants of the Secretary of the Treasury, 72,998 drafts on warrants of the Postmaster General, and 24,539 transfer checks on assistant treasurers, making a total of 370,506 drafts and checks issued by the office during the fiscal year.

There were received for redemption during the year, circulating notes of National Banks amounting to 130,296,606 dol., which amount included 29,557,588 dol. of notes of failed, liquidating, and reducing banks. Coupons from 3·65 per cent. bonds of the District of Columbia, amounting to 105,441 dol. 19 c., were paid and examined, and registered interest, amounting to 416,448 dol. 90 c., was paid by means of checks.

Of bonds held by the Treasurer of the United States in trust for National Banks, 61,042,400 dol. were withdrawn, of which amount 56,925,300 dol. was held to secure circulation, and 4,117,100 dol. was held as security for deposits of public money. The bonds deposited to replace those withdrawn on account of circulation amounted to 20,754,900 dol., and on account of deposits to 6,170,000 dol., making a total decrease of 34,117,500 dol. in the bonds held by the Treasurer for National Banks. The total movement of bonds held for National Banks was 87,967,300 dol. The amount paid by National Banks during the fiscal year on account of semi-annual duty on their circulation was 2,592,021 dol. 33 c., a decrease of 202,562 dol. 68 c. from the amount paid on that account the preceding year.

Worn and mutilated United States' notes, amounting to 63,000,000 dol., were forwarded to the Treasury for redemption during the year, and new notes to a like amount were issued in place thereof.

The issue of silver certificates during the year amounted to 4,600,000 dol., and 28,523,971 dol. were redeemed.

Gold certificates, amounting to 10,188,895 dol., were redeemed during the fiscal year.

The amount to the credit of the disbursing officers of the Government on the books of the Treasury at the close of the year was 17,947,107 dol. 64 c., of which 15,331,354 dol. 53 c. was on deposit in the Treasury, and 2,615,753 dol. 11 c. in the National Bank depositories. The unavailable funds of the Treasury, June 30, 1886, were 29,521,379 dol. 35 c., a decrease of 3,946 dol. 39 c. from last year.

The Treasurer of the United States has taken September 30, 1886, as the date for showing the condition of the Treasury as compared with that on the corresponding date in 1885, in the following tables :— *The state of the Treasury.*

UNITED STATES.

STATEMENT of the Assets and Liabilities of the Treasury of the United States, September 30, 1885.

	Dol. c.	Assets. Dol. c.	Liabilities. Dol. c.	Balances. Dol. c.
Gold.—Coin	180,863,798 65			
Bullion	71,271,013 62	252,134,812 27		
Certificates	140,387,030 00			
Less amount on hand	22,491,510 00		117,895,520 00	
Net gold		...	...	134,239,292 27
Silver.—Standard dollars	165,431,083 00			
Bullion	3,732,336 69	169,163,419 69		
Certificates	125,379,706 00			
Less amount on hand	31,733,440 00		93,646,266 00	
Net silver		...	...	75,517,153 69
United States notes	...	50,926,529 49		
Certificates	24,070,000 00			
Less amount on hand	1,075,000 00		22,995,000 00	
Net United States notes		...	...	27,931,529 49
National Bank notes	...	2,946,127 88		2,946,127 88
Deposits in National Banks—Depositaries	...	15,515,514 23	...	15,515,514 23
Totals		490,686,403 56	234,536,786 00	256,149,617 56
Public debt and interest—				
Interest due and unpaid	1,825,829 19			
Accrued interest	9,393,087 00			
Matured debt	3,871,385 26			
Interest on matured debt	221,332 30			
Debt bearing no interest	2,668 52			
Interest on Pacific Railroad bonds, due and unpaid	26,519 96			
Accrued interest on Pacific Railroad bonds	969,352 68	...	16,310,174 91	
Fractional currency redeemed	2,668 52			
One and two year notes redeemed	...			
Interest checks and coupons paid	145,746 57			
Interest on Pacific Railroad bonds paid	4,500 00	152,915 09		
Totals	...	490,839,318 65	250,846,960 91	
Reserve for redemption of United States notes—Acts of 1875 and 1882	...	...	100,000,000 00	
Fund held for redemption of notes of National Banks "failed," "in liquidation," and "reducing circulation"	38,794,042 60			
Fund held for redemption of National Gold Bank notes	123,259 00			
Five per cent. fund for redemption of National Bank notes	12,482,800 92		51,400,102 52	
National Bank notes in process of redemption	...	3,542,398 35		
Post-office department account	2,917,627 58			
Disbursing officers' balances	24,220,056 14			
Undistributed assets of failed National Banks	411,180 39			
Currency and minor coin redemption account	488,128 35			
Fractional silver coin redemption account	59,605 80			
Interest account, Louisville and Portland Canal Company	1,470 00			
Treasurer's transfer checks and drafts outstanding	4,971,407 14			
Treasurer United States agent for paying interest on D.C. bonds	156,916 92			
Interest on D.C. bonds paid	...	13,930 20	33,226,392 32	
Totals	...	494,395,647 20	435,473,455 75	58,922,191 45
Balance	...	...	...	
Assets not available—				
Minor coin	791,596 84			
Fractional silver coin	23,526,351 44	24,317,948 28	...	24,317,948 28
Aggregate	...	518,713,595 48	435,473,455 75	83,240,139 73

WASHINGTON.

Statement of the Assets and Liabilities of the Treasury of the United States, September 30, 1886.

			Assets.	Liabilities.	Balances.
	Dol.	c.	Dol. c.	Dol. c.	Dol. c.
Gold.—Coin	189,051,398	65			
Bullion	53,509,735	67	242,561,134 32		
Certificates	125,346,127	00			
Less amount on hand	41,036,550	00			
Net gold			...	84,309,577 00	158,251,557 32
Silver.—Standard dollars	181,161,161	00			
Bullion	3,877,541	44	185,038,702 44		
Certificates	117,943,102	00			
Less amount on hand	22,032,850	00			
Net silver			...	95,910,252 00	89,128,450 44
United States notes	...		45,244,640 88		
Certificates	7,895,000	00			
Less amount on hand	280,000	00			
Net United States notes			...	7,615,000 00	37,629,640 88
National Bank notes	...		364,452 50		364,452 50
Deposits in National Banks—Depositaries	...		16,682,286 33		16,682,286 33
Totals	...		489,891,216 47	187,834,829 00	302,056,387 47
Public debt and interest—					
Interest due and unpaid	1,931,702	01			
Accrued interest	8,998,016	50			
Matured debt	7,313,035	26			
Interest on matured debt	201,061	07			
Debt bearing no interest	3,524	75			
Interest on Pacific Railroad bonds, due and unpaid	37,739	96			
Accrued interest on Pacific Railroad bonds	969,352	68			
				19,454,432 23	
Fractional currency redeemed	3,524	75			
One and two year notes redeemed	10	50			
Interest checks and coupons paid	107,370	95			
United States bonds and interest paid	315,849	97	426,756 17		
Totals	...		490,317,972 64	207,289,261 23	
Reserve for redemption of United States notes—Acts of 1875 and 1882	...		...	100,000,000 00	
Fund held for redemption of notes of National Banks "failed," "in liquidation," and "reducing circulation"	65,515,523	35			
Fund held for redemption of National Gold Bank notes	97,024	00			
Five per cent. fund for redemption of National Bank notes	10,856,751	34			
			...	76,469,298 69	
National Bank notes in process of redemption	...		1,917,974 89		
Post-office department account	4,929,621	29			
Disbursing officers' balances	22,676,967	45			
Undistributed assets of failed National Banks	824,411	30			
Currency and minor coin redemption account	433,080	78			
Fractional silver coin redemption account	57,118	00			
Interest account, Louisville and Portland Canal Company	...				
Treasurer's transfer checks and drafts outstanding	6,307,180	95			
Treasurer United States agent for paying interest on D.C. bonds	346,184	73			
			...	35,574,564 50	
Interest on D.C. bonds paid	...		10,318 15		
Totals	...		492,246,265 68	419,333,124 42	
Balance	...		...	...	72,913,141 26
Assets not available—Minor coin	296,021	76			
Fractional silver coin	26,846,612	76			
			27,142,634 52	...	27,142,634 52
Aggregate	...		519,388,900 20	419,333,124 42	100,055,775 78

UNITED STATES.

The balance in the Treasury at the close of the year ending September 30, 1886, was 100,055,775 dol. 78 c. (20,844,953*l.*), an increase over that of 1885 of 16,815,636 dol. 5 c. (3,503,257*l.*).

The available balance was 72,913,141 dol. 26 c., against 58,922,191 dol. 45 c. last year, an increase of 13,990,949 dol. 81 c.

Receipts and expenditures, actual and estimated, for 1887.

For the present fiscal year the revenue, actual and estimated, is as follows:—

Source.	Quarter ended Sept. 30, 1886.	Remaining three-fourths of the Year.	Total.
	Dol. c.	Dol. c.	Dol. c.
Customs	59,177,586 50	150,822,413 50	210,000,000 00
Internal revenue	29,930,043 94	87,069,956 06	116,000,000 00
Sale of public lands	1,827,781 46	4,172,218 54	6,000,000 00
Tax on National Banks	1,252,498 57	1,247,500 43	2,500,000 00
Repayment of interest and sinking fund, Pacific Railroad Companies	516,195 02	1,483,804 98	2,000,000 00
Customs' fees, fines, penalties	232,998 88	767,001 12	1,000,000 00
Fees, Consular, letters patent, and lands	814,359 39	2,685,640 61	3,500,000 00
Proceeds of sales of Government property	48,508 21	201,491 79	250,000 00
Profits on coinage, assays, &c.	582,694 65	4,417,305 35	5,000,000 00
Deposits for surveying public lands	34,961 79	215,038 21	250,000 00
Revenues of the District of Columbia	287,915 70	1,712,084 30	2,000,000 00
Miscellaneous sources	1,240,048 46	6,259,951 54	7,500,000 00
Total receipts	94,945,592 57	261,054,407 43	356,000,000 00

The expenditures, actual and estimated, for the same period are as follows:—

Object.	Quarter ending Sept. 30, 1886.	Remaining three-fourths of the Year.	Total.
	Dol. c.	Dol. c.	Dol. c.
Civil and miscellaneous expenses	20,213,300 11	58,065,623 51	78,278,923 62
Indians	1,621,973 62	4,878,026 38	6,500,000 00
Pensions	20,401,137 52	47,598,862 48	68,000,000 00
Military establishment	9,726,804 09	30,273,195 91	40,000,000 00
Naval establishment	4,603,230 59	12,396,769 41	17,000,000 00
Expenditure on account of District of Columbia	1,287,415 17	2,212,584 83	3,500,000 00
Interest on public debt	13,210,226 86	33,789,773 14	47,000,000 00
Sinking fund	31,588,465 00	16,565,246 14	48,153,711 14
Judgments of the Court of Alabama claims	5,721,076 38	.. ..	5,721,076 38
Total ordinary expenditures	108,373,629 34	205,780,081 80	314,153,711 14

		Dol. c.
Total receipts	.. .. ..	356,000,000 00
Total expenditures	.. .. ..	314,153,711 14
Estimated surplus	.. .. ..	41,846,288 86

WASHINGTON.

The indebtedness of the United States on November 1st, 1885, including therein the bonds issued to the Pacific Railroad Companies, was as follows.

The public debt.

	Dols.	c.
Interest-bearing debt	1,260,778,162	00
Accrued and unpaid interest to date	9,595,948	10
Matured debt not yet presented, and accrued interest	3,593,689	76
Debt bearing no interest	574,012,505	88
Total	1,848,340,335	74
Cash in Treasury	400,682,767	65
Amount of debt, less cash in Treasury	1,447,657,568	09

The indebtedness of the United States on November 1st, 1886, including therein the bonds issued to the Pacific Railroad Companies was as follows:—

	Dols.	c.
Interest-bearing debt	1,153,443,112	00
Accrued and unpaid interest to date	8,993,561	71
Matured debt not yet presented, and accrued interest	12,548,927	49
Debt bearing no interest	549,433,862	52
Total	1,724,419,463	72
Cash in Treasury	370,071,515	86
Amount of debt, less cash in Treasury	1,354,347,947	86

showing the reduction of debt during the above period to be 93,309,620 dol. 23 c.

The balance account of the United States' receipts for the fiscal year 1886, as shown by warrants issued, is given in the following table:—

Receipts Covered in to the Credit of.	Issue of Notes and Bonds.		Net Receipts.		Repayments to Appropriations.		Counter Credits to Appropriations.		Total.	
	Dol.	c.	Dol.	c.	Dol.	c.	Dol.	c.	Dol.	c.
Customs	..		192,905,023	44	1,122,614	78	78,189	10	194,105,827	32
Internal revenue	..		116,805,936	48	47,490	29	294	33	116,853,721	10
Lands	..		5,630,999	34	..		..		5,630,999	34
Miscellaneous sources	..		21,097,767	80	..		..		21,097,767	80
Total net revenue	..		336,439,727	06	..		..		..	
Public Debt—										
Funded loan of 1907	39,850	00	..		..		..		..	
Gold certificates	1,040,000	00	..		..		..		..	
Silver certificates	4,600,000	00	..		..		..		..	
Certificates of deposit (Act of June 8, 1872)	47,635,000	00	..		..		..		..	
United States' notes	63,000,000	00	116,314,850	00	..		..		116,314,850	00
Interest on the public debt			..		2,815	48	..		2,815	48
War department appropriations			..		1,236,888	33	88,035	57	1,324,923	90
Navy " "			..		724,561	45	5,885,169	68	6,609,731	13
Interior " "			..		6,199,668	38	422,712	13	6,622,380	46
" civil			..		83,065	44	3,179	93	86,245	37
Treasury proper "			..		2,664,359	86	513,553	00	3,177,904	86
Diplomatic "			..		24,029	52	34,216	88	58,246	40
Quarterly salary "			..		28	76	..		28	76
Judiciary "			..		191,622	55	41,368	78	232,991	33
Total receipts	..		452,754,577	06	12,297,136	79	7,066,719	40	472,118,433	25
Balance as shown by report, June 30, 1885	..		..		..		..		493,684,383	71
Total receipts	..		..		..		..		965,802,816	96

The balance account of the United States' expenditures for the fiscal year 1886, as shown by warrants issued, is given in the following table:—

Expenditures Authorised by Warrants from Appropriations on Account of.		Net Expenditures.		Repayment of Amounts Unexpended.		Amounts Re-credited to Appropriations.		Total.	
	Dol. c.	Dol.	c.	Dol.	c.	Dol.	c.	Dol.	c.
Customs, light-houses, public buildings	24,165,246 36			1,122,614 78		78,189 10		25,366,050 24
Internal revenue	4,113,319 90			47,490 29		294 33		4,161,104 52
Interior, civil	7,306,224 44			83,065 44		3,179 93		7,392,469 81
Treasury, proper	33,323,749 66			2,664,351 86		513,553 00		36,501,654 52
Diplomatic	1,332,320 88			24,029 52		34,216 88		1,390,567 28
Quarterly salaries	616,379 42			28 76				676,408 18
Judiciary	3,309,689 19			191,622 55		41,368 78		3,542,680 52
Net civil and miscellaneous expenditures		74,166,929 85							
War department		34,324,152 74		1,236,888 33		88,035 57		35,649,076 64
Navy "		13,907,887 74		724,561 45		5,885,169 68		20,517,618 87
Interior "		69,504,022 20		6,199,668 33		422,712 13		76,126,402 66
Interest on the public debt		50,580,145 97		2,815 48				50,582,961 45
Total net expenditure		242,483,138 50							
Redemption of the public debt:									
Gold certificates	10,188,895 00								
Silver "	28,523,971 00								
Certificates of deposit (Act of June 8, 1872)	58,920,000 00								
Refunding certificates	32,800 00								
United States' notes	63,000,000 00								
Fractional currency	10,088 36								
Old demand notes	505 00								
Treasury notes prior to 1846	100 00								
7-30s of 1861	50 00								
" 1864 and 1865	1,900 00								

UNITED STATES.

The balance account of the United States' expenditures for the fiscal year 1886—continued:—

Expenditures Authorised by Warrants from Appropriations on Account of.			Net Expenditures.		Repayment of Amounts Unexpended.		Amounts Re-credited to Appropriations.		Total.	
	Dol.	c.	Dol.	c.	Dol.	c.	Dol.	c.	Dol.	c.
One year notes of 1863	1,290	00								
Two " "	200	00								
Compound interest notes	5,560	00								
Loan of July and August, 1861	2,500	00								
Loan of 1863	1,100	00								
Oregon war debt	100	00								
5-20s of 1862	67,500	00								
" 1864	4,300	00								
" 1865	300	00								
10-40s of 1864	14,250	00								
Consols of 1865	15,900	00								
" 1867	26,950	00								
" 1868	12,250	00								
Funded loan of 1881	49,800	00								
Loan of July 12, 1882	44,044,800	00								
Loan of 1863, continued at 3½ per cent., and August, 1861, continued at 3½ per cent.	96,750	00								
Funded loan of 1881, continued at 3½ per cent.	4,100	00								
	190,750	00	205,216,709	36					205,216,709	36
Total expenditures			447,699,847	86	12,297,136	79	7,066,719	40	467,063,704	05
Balance as shown by warrants issued June 30, 1886									498,739,112	91
Total									965,802,816	96

WASHINGTON.

The larger portion of the revenue is derived from the Customs, the amount obtained from that source for the year 1886 being 192,905,023 dol., an increase of 11,433,084 dol. 10 c. over the preceding year. This sum was collected on values amounting to 413,778,054 dol., the average ad valorem duty being 45·55 per cent.

The expenses of collecting the revenue from Customs amounted to 6,427,612 dol. 67 c., or 570,000 dol. less than the preceding year.

The number of persons employed at the 136 ports was 4,527.

The following are the 11 items which head the list of imports:—

Order.	Articles dutiable.	Values.	Ordinary duties.	Average ad valorem rate of duty.
		Dol. c.	Dol. c.	Per cent.
1	Sugar, molasses, sugar-candy, and confectionery	76,746,461 26	51,778,948 34	67·47
2	Wool and manufactures of—			
	Wool, raw	13,794,212 97	5,126,108 35	37·16
	Manufactures of wool	40,536,509 38	27,278,527 54	67·29
	Total	54,330,722 35	32,404,635 89	59·62
3	Iron and steel, and manufactures of—			
	Iron ore	1,312,322 37	532,956 26	40·61
	Pig-iron	4,041,366 62	1,737,658 19	43·00
	Manufactures of iron and steel	33,278,088 35	12,361,261 30	37·16
	Total	38,631,777 34	14,631,875 75	37·89
4	Flax, hemp, jute, &c., and manufactures of—			
	Unmanufactured—			
	Flax	1,548,800 00	113,138 88	7·30
	Hemp, jute, sisal-grass, and other vegetable substances	8,693,317 66	1,728,587 36	19·88
	Manufactures of	21,370,523 02	7,406,089 86	34·66
	Total	31,612,640 68	9,247,816 10	29·25
5	Cotton, manufactures of	29,236,071 18	11,752,206 89	40·20
6	Silk, manufactures of	28,055,854 94	13,938,096 61	49·68
7	Fruits, including nuts	12,973,307 98	3,498,569 39	26·97
8	Chemicals, drugs, dyes, and medicines	12,796,387 52	4,347,626 05	33·97
9	Leather, and manufactures of	11,466,414 29	3,262,232 87	28·45
10	Tobacco, and manufactures of	10,315,311 00	8,311,114 45	80·57
11	Liquors, spirituous and malt, and wines—			
	Malt liquors	1,206,257 11	585,102 26	48·52
	Spirits, distilled	1,826,059 27	2,834,696 25	155·56
	Wines	6,753,471 97	3,774,348 93	55·91
	Total	9,785,788 35	7,194,147 44	73·58

The following table shows the revenue derived from the Customs for the last 10 years:—

	Dollars.	c.
1877	130,956,493	07
1878	130,170,680	20
1879	137,250,047	70
1880	183,522,064	60
1881	198,159,676	02
1882	220,410,730	25
1883	214,706,496	93
1884	195,067,489	76
1885	181,471,939	34
1886	192,905,023	44

The re-casting of the Customs' collection laws, which have their basis in the law of 1799, is earnestly recommended by the Secretary of the Treasury; a modification would be easily made as soon as the country shall have definitely settled upon the sum and method of a new and better system of taxation.

United States notes outstanding.

The amount of each denomination of United States notes outstanding at the close of the fiscal year, 1886, was as follows:—

Note.	Dol.	c.
One dollar	17,603,922	40
Two dollars	18,204,370	60
Five ,,	85,629,219	00
Ten ,,	66,658,661	00
Twenty ,,	55,078,379	00
Fifty ,,	23,291,265	00
One hundred dollars	31,359,700	00
Five ,, ,,	12,424,000	00
One thousand ,,	37,361,500	00
Five ,, ,,	60,000	00
Ten ,, ,,	10,000	00
	347,681,016	00
Less notes of unknown denominations destroyed in Chicago fire	1,000,000	00
Outstanding	346,681,016	00

Certificates of deposit Act of June 8, 1872.

The deposits of legal tender notes by National Banks during the year for which they received certificates, issued under authority of the Act of June 8, 1872, amounted to 47,650,000 dol.; the amount of certificates redeemed was 58,825,000 dol.; the amount outstanding at the close of the year was 18,110,000 dol.

Gold certificates.

The gold certificates of the old issue, under the Act of March 3, 1863, outstanding at the close of the fiscal year, amounted to 2,427,420 dol.; the redemptions during the year having been 134,860 dol.

Of the new issue under the Act of July 12, 1882, there were nominally outstanding at the close of the fiscal year 128,746,825 dol.; the Treasury offices held 55,129,870 dol. (compared with 13,593,410 dol. at the close of 1885), leaving actually in circulation 73,616,955 dol.; a decrease of 50,550,495 dol. in the year.

Silver certificates.

The amount of silver certificates nominally outstanding at the close of the fiscal year, was 115,977,675 dol., of which amount the Treasury held 27,861,450 dol., leaving 88,116,225 dol. in actual circulation, a decrease of 13,414,721 dol. during the year.

Standard silver dollars.

The following table shows the amount of silver dollars coined, on hand, distributed and outstanding at the close of the year 1886, as compared with the preceding year:—

	Annual Coinage.	Total Coinage.	On Hand at close of Year.	Net Distribution during Year.	Outstanding at close of Year.
	Dollars.	Dollars.	Dollars.	Dollars.	Dollars.
Year ending June 30, 1885	28,528,552	203,884,381	165,535,854	1,196,934	38,342,527
Year ending June 30, 1886	29,838,905	233,723,286	181,253,566	14,121,193	52,469,720

The amount of standard silver dollars coined, in the Treasury and in circulation, and of silver certificates outstanding at the end of the fiscal year 1886, and on November 30, 1886, as compared with the preceding year, was as follows:—

Date.	Standard Silver Dollars Coined.	Standard Silver Dollars in Treasury.	Silver Certificates in the Treasury Cash.	Silver Certificates in Circulation.	Net standard Silver Dollars in Treasury, after deducting Silver Certificates in Circulation.	Standard Silver Dollars in Circulation.
	Dollars.	Dollars.	Dollars.	Dollars.	Dollars.	Dollars.
June 30, 1885	203,884,381	165,413,112	38,370,700	101,530,946	63,882,166	38,471,269
November 30, 1885	215,759,431	165,568,018	32,034,464	92,702,642	72,865,376	50,191,413
June 30, 1886	233,723,286	181,253,566	27,861,450	88,116,225	93,137,341	52,469,720
November 30, 1886	246,673,386	184,911,938	14,137,285	105,519,817	79,392,121	61,761,443

As will appear from this table, there is now in circulation the sum of 61,761,448 dol., the largest sum as yet attained in the circulation of this kind of currency (on June 30, 1878, the amount in circulation was 855,143 dol.). The extreme limit which may be obtained is probably 65,000,000 dol.

Fractional silver coin. The amount of fractional silver coin held by the Treasury on June 30, 1885, was 31,236,899 dol. 49 c., which amount decreased during 1886 to the sum of 28,904,681 dol. 66 c.

Minor coin. At the close of the year 1886, the Treasury held 377,814 dol. in minor coin, i.e., pieces of five, three, two, and one cents, and unassorted, a decrease during the year of 490,651 dol. 64 c.

Mutilated and counterfeit currency. The amount of 4,066 dol. was deducted from the face-value of United States notes redeemed during the year, on account of mutilations; on fractional currency redeemed, the deductions amounted to 50 dol. 62 c. on silver certificates to 339 dol., and on gold certificates to 15 dol.

There were detected in remittances of notes received for redemption, 269 counterfeit United States notes and 233 National Bank notes. There was also detected, counterfeit fractional currency of the nominal value of 186 dol. 70 c. In 48,881,184 standard dollars received in the several Treasury offices during 1886, there were detected 2,829 counterfeits; in dollars, 7,033,456; half dollars, 1,037 counterfeits; and in dollars, 5,340,262 (quarter dollars) 988 counterfeits.

Postal revenue. The amount received from the postal revenues into the Treasury was 26,593,885 dol. 64 c.; the amount received by the Postmaster General's report was 52,997,135 dol. 26 c.; the amount received by the Treasury being about one half of the receipts.

Depository banks. Public moneys amounting to 123,592,221 dol. 68 c., were during the year deposited with National Banks, designated as depositaries. The balances held at the close of the year to the credit of the Treasury, amounted to 14,036,632 dol. 18 c., and to the credit of disbursing officers, to 2,615,753 dol. 11 c.

Bonds of the United States, amounting to 19,659,900 dol., were held by the Treasury to secure the safe keeping and prompt payment of these funds. 160 National Banks acted as depositories during the year, receiving the moneys from collecting officers of the Government; thus saving the risk and expense of transportation to Treasury officers, and disbursing the same on drafts of the treasurer.

UNITED STATES.

The following figures show the transactions with Depository Banks for the years 1885 and 1886:—

Date.	Receipts.	Funds transferred to Depository Banks.	Funds transferred to Treasury by Depository Banks.	Drafts drawn on Depository Banks.	Balances at close of the Year.
	Dol. c.	Dol. c.	Dol. c.	Dol. c.	Dol. c.
1885 ...	119,056,058 94	4,798,782 35	105,952,609 09	17,633,235 03	10,985,141 34
1886 ...	123,592,221 68	8,786,546 55	112,862,815 24	16,464,462 15	14,036,632 18

Pacific Railroad Sinking Funds. At the close of the fiscal year, United States bonds were held in the Treasury for account of the Pacific Railroad Sinking Funds, established by Act of May 7, 1878, as follows:—

	For Union Pacific Railroad Company.	For Central Pacific Railroad Company.	Total.
	Dollars.	Dollars.	Dollars.
Bonds issued to Pacific Railroads, 6 per cents.	361,000	444,000	805,000
Funded Loan of 1907, 4 per cents. ..	4,218,650	199,100	4,417,750
Loan of July 12, 1882, 3 per cents. ..	456,450	194,900	651,350
Total	5,036,100	838,000	5,874,100

Four per cent. bonds to the amount of 1,095,000 dol. were added to the account of the Union Pacific Railroad; and 510,000 dol., called 3 per cent. bonds, were withdrawn for redemption, and the proceeds thereof deposited in the Treasury to the credit of said fund.

Three per cent. bonds to the amount of 320,000 dol. were added to the account of the Central Pacific Railroad; and 1,220,000 dol., called 3 per cent. bonds, were withdrawn for redemption, and the proceeds thereof deposited in the Treasury to the credit of that fund, making bonds and cash to the credit of the respective funds as follows:—

	Bonds.	Cash.	Total.
	Dol.	Dol. c.	Dol. c.
Union Pacific ..	5,036,100	263,631 72	5,299,731 72
Central Pacific ..	838,000	2,152,397 56	2,990,397 56

National Banks. The Comptroller of the Currency, who gives his returns up to November 1, 1886, reports that, on October 7, there were 2,852 National Banks in operation. The following table gives a summary of their state and condition at that date:—

WASHINGTON.

RESOURCES.

	Dol.	c.
Loans and discounts	1,443,668,240	77
Overdrafts	7,288,814	16
U.S. bonds to secure circulation	258,498,950	00
U.S. bonds to secure deposits	20,105,900	00
U.S. bonds on hand	12,326,500	00
Other stocks, bonds, and mortgages	81,825,266	40
Due from approved reserve agents	140,764,579	01
Due from other National Banks	80,526,615	47
Due from State Banks and bankers	20,140,256	27
Real estate, furniture, and fixtures	54,090,071	24
Current expenses and taxes paid	7,438,741	12
Premiums paid	14,303,529	55
Clearing-house loan certificates		
Checks and other cash items	13,277,169	64
Exchanges for clearing-house	95,536,941	15
Bills of other banks	22,734,085	00
Fractional currency	434,220	93
Trade dollars	1,889,794	55
*Specie, viz.—		
Gold coin	71,682,807	13
Gold Treasury certificates	48,426,920	00
Gold clearing-house certificates	24,520,000	00
Silver coin, dollars	6,465,792	00
Silver coin, fractional	2,681,524	87
Silver Treasury certificates	2,610,652	09
Legal-tender notes	68,812,322	00
U.S. certificates of deposit for legal-tender notes	5,855,000	00
Five per cent. redemption fund with treasurer	11,358,014	97
Due from treasurer other than redemption fund	2,592,042	94
Aggregate	2,513,854,751	17
* Total specie	156,387,696	00

LIABILITIES.

	Dol.	c.
Capital stock paid in	548,240,730	00
Surplus fund	157,249,190	87
Other undivided profits	66,503,494	72
National Bank circulation outstanding	228,672,610	00
State Bank notes outstanding	125,002	00
Dividends unpaid	2,227,780	59
Individual deposits	1,172,968,308	64
U.S. deposits	13,842,023	69
Deposits of U.S. disbursing officers	2,721,276	77
Due to other National Banks	218,395,980	54
Due to State Banks and bankers	90,246,483	31
Notes and bills rediscounted	10,917,176	56
Bills payable	1,744,693	48
Aggregate	2,513,854,751	17

During the year 1886, 33 banks were closed, 24 went into voluntary liquidation, one ceased to exist by expiration of charter, and eight failed.

As the laws now stand, a national banking association may be formed by any number (not less than five) of natural persons. The conditions are simple and reasonable, the only one appearing onerous being that which requires the bank to deposit in the Treasury United States' registered bonds, bearing interest. *Organisation, circulation, and dissolution of National Banks.*

Before 1882, every bank with a capital not exceeding 150,000 dol.
(302)

was required to place and keep on deposit with the treasurer such bonds to the amount of at least one-third of its capital; but the Act of July 12, 1882, reduced this minimum requirement to one-fourth the capital. Under the Act of June 20, 1874, 50,000 dol. is the minimum requirement for all other banks, however large the capital.

Every bank, before beginning business, is also required to deposit with the comptroller a copy of its articles of association, a complete list of its shareholders, directors, and principal officers, all duly authenticated, and evidence that at least 50 per cent. of the capital is actually paid in. The comptroller may in his discretion cause a special examination to be made, in order to satisfy himself on any of these points; and he may refuse to authorise any bank to begin business if he has reason to believe that the purposes of its promoters are not in accord with those of the national banking laws. When the comptroller issues his certificate of authority to begin business, the bank is established, and is thenceforth bound to conform to all the requirements of the law governing its business; while, on the other hand, it is entitled to exercise the rights, privileges, and franchises secured to it by the statutes.

By a special provision of law, banks and banking corporations having State charters may be converted into National Banks upon satisfying the comptroller of the currency that they are in sound financial condition; and upon complying with such of the general requirements of the law as are applicable to them. In all such cases, both of conversion and of primary association, applicants for authority to enter the National Bank system, must select a title approved by the comptroller of the currency. The title, "First National Bank," being very much sought after, some cases of contention for it have arisen, and, during the past year, the following general rules have been adopted to govern the concession of this title, which have obviated controversy, and have been accepted by competing applicants as entirely just.

The title of "First National Bank" will not be approved unless:— 1st. The application therefor is really the first application to establish a National Bank in the place named in the title, or, unless all such applications previously made have lapsed or been abandoned. 2nd. Unless no National Bank is located at the time in the place named in the title. 3rd. Unless the title asked for, though once in use, is at the time vacant by reason of the entire extinction of the bank that had it. 4th. Unless every National Bank at the time located in the place named in the title assents to the application. The term "place" means any ward of a city, or any town, city, county, state, or geographical area.

National Bank shareholders.
The capital stock of the 2,868 National Banks now existing is represented by 7,116,894 shares, and of these over 90 per cent. are held by residents of the State in which the bank is located, and less than 10 per cent. by non-residents.

Circulating notes.
Upon the security of its bonds deposited with the treasurer, each bank is entitled to receive, and the comptroller of the currency is by law required to issue to it circulating notes to the amount of 90 per cent. of the market value, and not more than 90 per cent. of the par value of the bonds. Any bank may deposit more than the minimum of bonds, and may take out circulating notes for 90 per cent. of its deposit, provided its entire outstanding circulation against bonds does not exceed 90 per cent. of its capital stock actually paid in. The circulating notes when issued by the comptroller, are in sheets, and are not valid until signed by the bank officers designated by the statute.

Under the present law, the minimum deposit of bonds required to be made by the 2,852 National Banks in operation in the United States

WASHINGTON.

on 7th October, 1886, in order to continue as national banking associations, would be but 84,365,312 dol.

The connection between the banks and the distribution of the funded debt of the United States renders the following statement appropriate:— {Interest bearing funded debt of the United States, and the amount held by National Banks.}

The public debt at its maximum, on 31st August, 1865, amounted to 2,844,649,626 dol., of which, obligations not bearing interest, amounted to 461,616,311 dol., leaving 2,383,033,315 dol. carrying an average rate of interest of about 6·33 per cent. On 1st November, 1886, the interest-bearing debt amounted to 1,153,443,112 dol.

The following table shows the authorising act for each class of bonds held by the treasurer as security for the circulating notes of the National Banks on November 1st, 1886, and a comparison as to the holdings during the years ending Nov. 1st, 1885, and November 1st, 1886. {Security for circulating notes.}

Class of Bonds.	Authorising Act.	Rate of Interest.	Amount, 1885.	Amount, 1886.
		Per cent.	Dol.	Dol.
Funded loan of 1891	July 14, 1870, and January 20, 1871	4½	49,547,250	57,436,850
,, ,, ,, 1907	Ditto	4	116,391,650	115,383,150
,, ,, ,, July 12, 1882	July 12, 1882	3	138,920,650	69,038,050
Pacific railroad bonds	July 1, 1862, and July 2, 1864	6	3,505,000	3,586,000
Total	...	...	308,364,550	245,444,050

It will be seen that the average rate of interest now paid by the United States on the bonds deposited as security for circulating notes is nearly 3·9 per cent. upon their par value, while owing to the high premiums commanded by all but the rapidly, diminishing 3 per cent. bonds, the banks are receiving only 2·41 per cent. per annum upon the present market value of their aggregate bond investments.

Since the establishment of the national banking system, February 25th, 1863, there have been organised 3,580 National Banks. Of these, 456 have gone into voluntary liquidation for the purpose of winding up their affairs; 79 have gone into voluntary liquidation for the purpose of reorganisation; 65 are in liquidation by expiration of charter, of which number 38 have been reorganised, and 112 have been placed in the hands of receivers for the purpose of closing up their affairs; leaving the total number in existence 2,868 on November 1st, 1886. {Dissolution.}

The New York Clearing-house Association is composed of 64 members, of which 45 are National Banks, 18 are State Banks, and the other member is the assistant treasurer of the United States at New York. {Transactions of the New York clearing-house.}

The following is a comparative statement for two years of the transactions of the New York Clearing-house.

NEW YORK CLEARING-HOUSE.

Year Ending.	Aggregate Clearings.	Aggregate Balances.
	Dol.	Dol.
October 1, 1885	25,250,791,440	1,295,355,252
October 1, 1886	33,374,682,216	1,519,565,385
Increase	8,123,890,776	224,210,133

(302)

UNITED STATES.

The clearing-house transactions of the assistant treasurer of the United States at New York, for the year ending October 1st, 1886, were as follows:—

	Dol.	c.
Exchanges received from clearing-house	306,138,237	63
Exchanges delivered to clearing-house	125,494,508	37
Balances paid to clearing-house	182,084,503	84
Balances received from clearing-house	125,494,508	37
Showing that the amount paid by the assistant treasurer to the clearing-house was in excess of the amount received by him	180,643,729	26

The debit balances were paid to the clearing-house as follows:

	Dol.	c.
United States gold certificates	80,128,000	00
Legal tenders and change	101,956,503	84

The comptroller of the currency at the conclusion of his report, says, that the present financial prospects of the country induce the expectation that the funded debt will be paid off as fast as the bonds mature, and, in consequence, a question has arisen as to what changes should be made in the National Bank system, in order that it shall not suffer deterioration or destruction, upon the withdrawal of the support upon which it is based by the present laws, which require every bank, before beginning business, to deposit a certain amount in United States' bonds.

The payment of the 3 per cent. bonds, the maturity in 1891 of the 4½ per cent. bonds, amounting to 250,000,000 dol., and in 1907 of the 4 per cent. bonds, amounting to nearly 738,000,000 dol., have combined to produce a prospective scarcity in the securities available to the banks as a basis for their corporate existence, and this is reflected in the advance of these bonds to a premium so high that every day their enforced purchase becomes more and more onerous.

Banks now holding only 3 per cent. bonds, and newly-organised national banking association, are forced into the market as purchasers of the 4 per cent., or the 4½ per cent. bonds, and this constant demand in connection with the prospective scarcity already referred to, sustains and tends still further to elevate the premium on these bonds.

As the time approaches for the payment of the 4½ per cent. bonds, it is reasonable to expect a still greater demand for the 4 per cent., and it is a question of serious importance whether the banks can afford to hold, or to buy 4 per cent. bonds after 1891. Congress will before long have to take into consideration what legislation may be proper to remove this element of future uncertainty from the national banking system.

Gold and silver, coinage of, in the United States.

The director of the mint reports that the value of gold bullion imported into the United States during the fiscal year 1886 was 4,073,458 dol., and the amount of gold bullion exported during the same period, 27,365,090 dol. The United States, therefore, lost by export of gold bullion during the year 23,291,632 dol. The import of gold coin into the United States during the year was—

	Dollars.
American gold coin	1,687,231
Foreign „	14,982,660
Total	16,669,891

WASHINGTON.

The amount of gold coin exported was: of American, 5,400,976 dol.; and of foreign, 10,039,941 dol. Hence a net export of American gold of 3,713,745 dol., and a gain, by import of foreign coin, of 4,942,719 dol.

The imports of silver bullion during the year amounted to 4,151,438 dol.; the exports during the same year amounted to 18,693,313 dol. The net excess of the exportation of silver bullion over the importation of the same was 14,541,873 dol. The amount of silver bullion, other than bars, imported into the country, was 1,872,628 dol.

The imports of silver coin during the year amounted to:—

		Dollars.
Foreign..	.. ..	13,178,589
American	.. ..	520,280
Total	.. ..	13,698,869

The exports of American coin were 464,738 dol., of which 354,848 consisted of trade dollars. The exports of foreign silver coin were 10,315,918 dol.; the total silver coin exported being 10,780,656 dol.

The total imports of silver, including bullion and coin, foreign and domestic, amounted to 17,850,307 dol., against 29,511,219 dol. exported. The total imports of bullion and coin, gold and silver, during the year, amounted to 38,593,656 dol., and the total exports to 72,463,410 dol.

(The reports of the production of precious metals in the United States, for the year 1886, have not yet been published, so the returns for 1885 are here given.)

The following table gives the comparison in round numbers of the estimates of production of the United States by States and territories for the calendar years 1884 and 1885:—

Estimated production of each State and territory of precious metals.

State or Territory.	Gold. 1884.	Gold. 1885.	Silver. 1884.	Silver. 1885.	Total. 1884.	Total. 1885.
	Dollars.	Dollars.	Dollars.	Dollars.	Dollars.	Dollars.
Alaska	200,000	300,000	...	2,000	200,000	302,000
Arizona	930,000	880,000	4,500,000	3,800,000	5,430,000	4,680,000
California	13,600,000	12,700,000	3,000,000	2,500,000	16,600,000	15,200,000
Colorado	4,250,000	4,200,000	16,000,000	15,800,000	20,250,000	20,000,000
Dakota	3,300,000	3,200,000	150,000	100,000	3,450,000	3,300,000
Georgia	137,000	136,000	...	...	137,000	136,000
Idaho	1,250,000	1,800,000	2,720,000	3,500,000	3,970,000	5,300,000
Montana	2,170,000	3,300,000	7,000,000	10,060,000	9,170,000	13,360,000
Nevada	3,500,000	3,100,000	5,600,000	6,000,000	9,100,000	9,100,000
New Mexico	300,000	800,000	3,000,000	3,000,000	3,300,000	3,800,000
North Carolina	157,000	152,000	3,500	3,000	160,500	155,000
Oregon	660,000	800,000	20,000	10,000	680,000	810,000
South Carolina	57,000	43,000	500	...	57,500	43,000
Utah	120,000	180,000	6,800,000	6,750,000	6,920,000	6,930,000
Washington	85,000	120,000	1,000	70,000	86,000	190,000
Texas, Alabama, Tennessee, Virginia, Vermont, Michigan, and Wyoming	84,000	90,000	5,000	5,000	89,000	95,000
Total	30,800,000	31,801,000	48,800,000	51,600,000	79,600,000	83,401,000

It will be seen that the production of gold increased during the calendar year 1885 over that of the previous year about 1,000,000 dol., and that, notwithstanding the depreciation in the market value of silver, the total production of that metal in the United States increased from 48,800,000 dols. in 1884 to 51,600,000 dol. in 1885—an increase of 2,800,000 dol.

The director of the mint calls attention to this fact, which is remarkable, as it was generally believed that the price of silver had reached such a point that the production would naturally decline. He goes on to say that, considering this question, it is important to remember that the conditions of supply are, as in the case of the precious metals, not so dependent on the conditions of demand as in the case of other commodities. It is also well known that a very large portion of the silver product of the country is, practically, a by-product incidental to the production of gold and the baser metals. In cases where the reduction of silver is alone for the recovery of that metal, a check to production has necessarily followed from the fall in its price. But in other and the more important cases where silver is recovered incidentally to the reduction of gold, copper, or lead, the fall in price has had but little effect upon the production of the mines. While the fall in price naturally tends to reduce the number of producing mines, and to discourage new silver-mining ventures, with the obvious effect of turning the attention of miners from poorer to richer ones, and from deposits carrying largely silver to those carrying more gold, the output of the miscellaneous ores of the previous metals of the mines of the United States has been so great that the fall in the price has not yet had the effect of diminishing the quantity of silver produced, as compared with past aggregates.

Unless the decline in the price of silver is checked, either by improved economic conditions or by legislation, the day cannot be far distant when many of the mines of the United States, at present producing silver, will cease to be profitable, and a falling-off in the production may be expected.

The United States ranks first among the countries in the world as a producer of precious metals, its production of gold and silver for the calendar year 1885 having reached the sum of 83,400,000 dol. (17,375,000*l.*), out of a total production of 219,000,000 dol. (45,625,000*l.*), or about two-fifths of the production of the world.

Use of gold and silver in the arts.

The use of gold and silver as raw material having become so important an element in the estimate of the production of the precious metals, the following tables are given, which have been compiled from answers to letters addressed to firms in the United States, supposed to be engaged in the manufacture or repair of articles of gold and silver.

WASHINGTON.

STATEMENT showing the Value and Character of the Gold and Silver used in the Arts and Manufactures during the Calendar Year 1885, as reported by the Persons and Firms addressed.

GOLD.

Manufactures.	Number addressed.	Replied.	Manufacturing.	United States Coin.	Stamped United States or Refined Bars.	Foreign Coin.	Old Jewellery, Plate and other Old Materials.	Native Grains Nuggets, &c.	Wire or Rolled Plate.	Total.
				Dollars.	Dollars.	Dollars.		Dollars.	Dollars.	Dollars.
Chemicals	341	219	39	32,040	13,903	..	6,063	29	4,341	56,376
Platers	634	348	226	257,741	218,831	801	178,513	24,295	15,537	695,715
Gold-pen manufacturers	34	22	11	7,433	34,886	2,867	990	3,526	6,753	56,455
Gold and silver leaf	72	51	46	58,150	527,453	2,000	31,050	19,700	39,001	677,354
Dental and surgical instruments	154	98	47	3,970	149,186	100	14,942	2,400	4,188	174,786
Spectacles and opticals	383	217	79	52,707	62,420	642	16,269	314	2,291	134,643
Miscellaneous	106	73	27	116,604	44,168	8,000	17,337	1,060	3,835	190,944
Jewellery and watches	6,330	3,352	2,232	2,298,733	5,183,187	164,503	582,554	451,629	485,241	9,165,847
Total	8,054	4,380	2,707	2,827,378	6,234,034	178,913	847,715	502,893	561,187	11,152,120

SILVER.

Manufactures.										
Chemicals	..	..	..	91	305,165	..	73,561	106	2,165	381,088
Platers	..	..	..	32,824	1,990,587	25,434	43,191	12,798	157,922	2,622,756
Gold-pen manufacturers	..	..	..	55	3,191	..	249	558	5	4,058
Gold and silver leaf	..	..	..	..	21,881	..	708	20	23,512	46,121
Dental and surgical instruments	..	..	..	4,682	107,717	1,401	7,057	4,450	2,494	127,801
Spectacles and opticals	..	..	..	2,587	42,424	155	2,750	210	942	49,068
Miscellaneous	..	..	..	838	5,330	..	268	70	1,017	7,523
Jewellery and watches	..	..	..	92,567	1,360,308	35,718	117,629	85,060	28,716	1,719,998
Total	..	..	..	133,644	3,836,603	62,708	245,413	103,272	216,773	4,598,413

UNITED STATES.

Deposits and purchases of gold and silver at the mints and assay offices.

The total value of the gold deposited at the mints and assay offices during the year amounted to 49,606,534 dol. 65 c., of which amount 4,696,785 dol. 42 c. consisted of bars of the several institutions redeposited, leaving the net value of the gold deposited 44,909,749 dol. 23 c., against 52,894,075 dol. 9 c. in the preceding year.

The total value of the silver, computed at its coining rate in standard dollars, deposited, purchased, and parted at the mints and assay offices of the United States during the year amounted to 37,917,026 dol. 36 c. (32,584,944 dol. 61 c. standard ounces). Of this amount the sum of 2,421,843 dol. 12 c. (2,082,130 dol. 83 c. standard ounces) consisted of fine and unparted bars of the several institutions redeposited, leaving the net value of the silver deposited, purchased, and parted during the year 35,494,183 dol. 24 c. (30,502,813 dol. 78 c. standard ounces), against 36,789,774 dol. 92 c. (31,616,212 dol. 91 c. standard ounces) in the preceding year.

Gold coinage.

The coinage of gold amounted during the past fiscal year to 5,050,814 pieces, of the value of 34,077,380 dol., against 1,748,158 pieces, valued at 24,861,123 dol. 50 c., in the preceding year.

Of the gold coinage 4,871,680 dol. was in double eagles, 10,428,470 dol. in eagles, 18,758,145 in half eagles, 303 dol. in three dollar pieces, 10,215 dol. in quarter eagles, and 8,567 in dollars.

Silver coinage.

The silver coinage during the year amounted to 31,627,157 pieces, of the value of 30,022,347 dol. 95 c., against 31,699,096 pieces, of the value of 28,848,959 dol. 65 c., in the preceding year.

Of this amount 29,838,905 dol. consisted of silver dollars, 3,052 dol. 50 c. of half dollars, 3,626 dol. 25 c. of quarter dollars, and 176,764 dol. 20 c. of dimes.

Minor coins.

Minor coins were struck, *i.e.*, 1,706,651 pieces, of the value of 17,377 dol. 65 c. The coinage executed was as follows:—

	Pieces.	Value.
		Dol. c.
Gold	5,050,814	34,077,380 00
Silver	31,627,157	30,022,347 95
Minor coins	1,706,651	17,377 65
Total	38,384,622	64,117,105 60

Coin circulation of the United States.

The stock and ownership of the gold and silver coin in the United States, July 1, 1886, are exhibited in the following table:—

Ownership.	Gold Coin.	Silver Coin.			Total Gold and Silver.
		Full Legal Tender.	Subsidiary.	Total.	
	Dollars.	Dollars.	Dollars.	Dollars.	Dollars.
Treasury	*113,485,228	†93,137,341	28,904,681	122,042,022	235,527,250
National Banks	‡145,977,017	§8,569,553	2,913,304	11,482,857	157,459,874
State Banks, trust companies, and savings banks	‖31,255,789	132,016,392	43,242,952	175,259,344	464,117,130
Other banks, and private hands	257,601,997				
Total	548,320,031	233,723,286	75,060,937	308,784,223	857,104,254

* Exclusive of outstanding gold certificates (76,044,375 dol.).
† Exclusive of outstanding silver certificates (88,116,225 dol.).
‡ Includes Treasury and clearing-house certificates (68,313,430 dol.).
§ Includes silver certificates (1,812,290 dol.).
‖ Reported to Comptroller of the Currency, November 1, 1885. Includes certificates.

The change in the value of silver caused a modification in the value of foreign coins from that proclaimed in the preceding year. *Value of foreign coins.*

The florin of Austria was reduced from 39·3 to 37·1; the boliviano of Bolivia from 79·5 to 75·1; the peso of Ecuador from 79·5 to 75·1; the rupee of India from 37·8 to 35·7; the yen of Japan from 85·8 to 81; the dollar of Mexico from 86·4 to 81·6; the sol of Peru from 79·5 to 75·1; the rouble of Russia from 63·6 to 60·1; the mahbut of Tripoli from 71·7 to 67·7; and the peso of the United States of Colombia from 79·5 to 75·1.

The Secretary of the Treasury, in his report to Congress, points out that the total annual surplus revenue has been nearly 825,000,000 dol. a-year for the last seven years. With this surplus the United States have been paying off funded debt at an average rate of 100,000,000 dol. a-year, the residue being mostly spent on silver dollars. The taxes (duties and excise amounting last year to about 310,000,000 dol.) on commodities entered from abroad or produced at home for consumption in the United States are giving an increase—and an augmenting increase. Congress was anxious to hasten the payment of the funded debt, subject to call. That part of the funded debt has now been reduced to 64,017,800 dol., and in September, 1886, payment to any holder, without regard to future calls, was publicly offered. It will be doubtless practicable to have called for payment the last of the Three per Cents. loan of 1882, by October 1, 1887. A taxation reform is necessary, the surplus taxation amounting to 125,000,000 dol. Employment for this surplus can no longer be found in a rapid payment of the funded debt, the greater portion of which, setting aside the Three per Cents., has been so funded that it cannot be paid except by purchase of a high premium to the bondholder, part of it before September 1, 1891, the remainder before July 1, 1907. *Increase of the revenue of the United States.*

" It is computed that the provisions of the revised statutes as to the sinking fund and the public debt, and compliance therewith, by their continued operation hereafter, will effect the payment of the whole public debt, greenbacks, and bonds by the year 1908, within a twelvemonth after our last great funded loan becomes due and payable. In other words, I am advised that the whole public debt can be thus duly paid without a continuance of our present surplus taxation, but merely by conformity to the sinking-fund law, and the regular annual appropriation therefor from now till 1908—to wit, by the purchase or payment of one per cent. of the entire debt of the United States to be made within each fiscal year, which is to be set apart as a sinking fund, and the interest on which shall, in like manner, be applied to the purchase or payment of the public debt as the Secretary of the Treasury shall from time to time direct.

" But in order to transfer our present and accruing proceeds of surplus taxation from the Treasury vaults to the pockets of the people—in order, also, to effect the most economical appliance with the sinking-fund law above cited, whilst the bonds not yet due are too far beyond our reach; and in order, also, to fulfil the law in which the faith of the United States is solemnly pledged to the payment in coin (redemption is elsewhere separately promised, and, since 1879, has been practised) to the payment in coin or its equivalent, of all the obligations of the United States not bearing interest, known as United States' notes, and mere reduction of our present surplus taxation is not enough.

" Currency reform, and taxation reform, are both necessary and both unavoidable.

" The financial situation, scanned at large and as a whole, plainly indicates our best policy.

"We should reduce taxation immediately to an annual revenue sufficing to pay our annual expenditure, including the sinking fund, and excluding the silver purchase—pay our unfunded debt of 346,681,016 dol. with the present surplus, and the surplus which will accrue before the whole reduction of taxation can be made or take effect, and while no more funded debt can be paid except at a premium during the five years from now until 1891."

The Secretary of the Treasury therefore recommends:—The repeal of the clause in the Act of 1878, making compulsory Treasury purchases of silver. A further reduction of surplus taxation—the chief change to be made being reduction of taxation on raw materials.

The repeal of the Act of 1887-88, making compulsory post-redemption issues and reissues of the U.S. legal tender notes—thus facilitating the gradual purchase and payment of 346,681,016 dols. outstanding promisory notes of the U.S. with the present and accruing Treasury surplus, issuing silver certificates in their room, and gold certificates if need be, without contraction of the present circulating volume of the currency—these notes (called greenbacks) being now the only debt due and payable before 1891, except the Three per Cent. bonds, which are probably all to be called and paid early in the ensuing fiscal year 1887.

Internal Revenue.—The estimates of the receipts of internal revenue for 1886 were 115,000,000; the actual receipts exceeded that sum by 1,902,869 dol. 44 c.

The total receipts from all sources of internal revenue taxation for 1886 were 116,902,869 dol. 44 c., as compared with 112,421,121 dol. 7 c. for the preceding year.

The following statement shows the receipts from the several objects of internal taxation in the United States during the years ended June 30, 1885 and 1886:—

WASHINGTON.

Objects of Taxation.	Receipts during Fiscal Year ended June 30— 1885.	Receipts during Fiscal Year ended June 30— 1886.	Increase.	Decrease.
	Dol. c.	Dol. c.	Dol. c.	Dol. c.
Spirits—				
Spirits distilled from apples, peaches, and grapes	1,321,897 58	1,400,394 48	78,496 90	...
Spirits distilled from grain and other materials	60,920,324 39	62,365,825 13	1,445,500 74	...
Rectifiers (special tax)	167,930 23	178,650 17	10,719 94	...
Retail liquor dealers (special tax)	4,641,783 99	4,714,735 18	72,951 19	...
Wholesale liquor dealers (special tax)	415,503 49	418,406 24	2,902 75	...
Manufacturers of stills (special tax)	1,194 20	1,102 90	...	91 30
Stills and worms, manufactured (special tax)	2,665 45	3,000 00	334 55	...
Stamps for distilled spirits intended for export	39,909 30	10,151 90	...	29,757 40
Total	67,511,208 63	69,092,266 00	1,581,057 37	
Tobacco—				
Cigars and cheroots	10,077,287 50	10,532,804 05	445,516 55	...
Cigarettes	529,535 88	655,569 55	126,033 67	...
Snuff	508,943 52	493,283 80	...	15,659 72
Tobacco, chewing and smoking	13,953,410 31	14,834,095 42	880,685 11	...
Dealers in leaf tobacco (special tax)	53,352 87	53,875 63	522 76	...
Dealers in manufactured tobacco (special tax)	1,159,897 78	1,208,529 17	48,631 39	...
Manufacturers of tobacco (special tax)	5,320 25	5,575 85	255 60	...
Manufacturers of cigars (special tax)	105,139 81	108,695 45	3,555 64	...
Peddlers of tobacco (special tax)	14,200 56	14,933 61	733 05	...
Total	26,407,088 48	27,907,362 53	1,500,274 05	...
Fermented liquors—				
Ale, beer, lager-beer, and porter	17,747,006 11	19,157,612 87	1,410,606 76	...
Brewers (special tax)	183,561 67	186,928 89	3,367 22	...
Dealers in malt liquors (special tax)	300,214 25	332,189 53	31,975 28	...
Total	18,230,782 03	19,676,731 29	1,445,949 26	...
Banks and bankers, not national—				
Bank circulation other than national, and banks, bankers, and other parties liable on amount of any person, State bank, or State banking association, or of any town, city, or municipal corporation, paid out by them	25,000 00	...	...	25,000 00
Miscellaneous—				
Collections not otherwise provided for	24,360 74	32,087 17	7,726 43	...
Penalties	222,681 19	194,422 45	...	28,258 74
Total	247,041 93	226,509 62	...	20,532 31
Aggregate receipts	112,421,121 07	116,902,869 44	4,481,748 37	...

The quantities of distilled spirits, fermented liquors, manufactured tobacco, snuff, cigars, and cigarettes, on which tax was paid during the last two fiscal years, are as follows:—

Articles Taxed.	Fiscal Year ended June 30— 1885.	Fiscal Year ended June 30— 1886.	Increase.	Decrease.
Number of gallons of spirits distilled from apples, peaches, and grapes	1,468,775	1,555,994	87,219	...
Number of gallons of spirits distilled from grain and other materials	67,689,250	69,295,361	1,606,111	...
Number of cigars	3,358,972,633	3,510,898,488	151,925,855	...
Number of cigarettes	1,058,749,238	1,310,961,350	252,212,112	...
Number of pounds of snuff	6,361,794	6,166,047	...	195,747
Number of pounds of tobacco	174,415,619	185,426,193	11,010,574	...
Number of barrels of fermented liquors	19,185,953	20,710,933	1,524,980	...

UNITED STATES.

The sum collected during the past five fiscal years amounted to 641,990,648 dol. 92 c.

The cost of collection for 1886 was 4,299,485 dol. 28 c., being about 3.6 per cent. of the amount collected.

Number and value of internal revenue stamps issued.

During the year ended June 30, 1886, the following was the number, kind, and value of internal revenue stamps issued to collectors:—

Kind of Stamps.	Number.	Value.
	Dol.	Dol. c.
Tax-paid spirit stamps	1,676,550	74,247,705 00
Exportation spirit stamps	106,000	10,600 00
Other than tax-paid stamps	3,856,900	.. ..
Tobacco and snuff stamps	318,603,288	18,682,796 67
Cigar and cigarette stamps	159,042,971	11,398,483 25
Special tax stamps	896,320	9,444,844 00
Fermented liquors' stamps	65,774,560	21,327,820 00
Brewers' permits	104,400	.. ..
Documentary	37	55 70
Total	550,061,029	135,112,304 62

Receipts from tobacco and snuff.

	Dol. c.
Manufactured tobacco tax, 8 c. per pound	14,834,095 42
Snuff tax, 8 c. per pound	493,283 80
Total for the year ended June 30, 1886	15,327,379 22
Total for the year ended June 30, 1885	14,462,353 83
Increase in collections	865,025 39

The increase of collections from chewing and smoking tobacco was 880,685 dol. 11 c. There was a decrease in the collections from snuff of 15,659 dol. 72 c.

Receipts from cigars and cigarettes:—

	Dol. c.
Cigars and cheroots at 3 dol. per 1,000	10,532,586 88
Cigars and cheroots at 6 dol. per 1,000	217 17
Cigarettes taxed at 60 c. per 1,000	655,462 90
Cigarettes taxed at 3 dol. per 1,000	106 65
Total for the year ended June 30, 1886	11,188,373 60
Total for the year ended June 30, 1885	10,606,823 38
Increase in collection from cigars and cigarettes	581,550 22

Production of manufactured tobacco, cigars, cigarettes, &c.

The production of tobacco, snuff, cigars and cigarettes, for the fiscal year ended June 30, 1886, as computed from the receipts of stamps sold for all such goods as were put on the market for consumption, together with those removed in bond for export, was as follows:—

	Pounds.
Tobacco taxed at 8 c. per pound	185,426,193
Snuff taxed at 8 c. per pound	6,166,047
Total of tobacco and snuff for consumption	191,592,240
Increase over last fiscal year	10,814,827
Tobacco and snuff removed in bond for exportation	13,037,474
Total production for 1886	204,629,714
Total increase over 1885	10,798,286

Cigars and cigarettes:—

	Number.
Number of cigars taxed	3,510,898,488
Number of cigarettes taxed	1,310,961,350
Total number	4,821,859,838
Increase of taxed cigars and cigarettes	404,137,967
Cigars removed in bond for exportation	1,427,470
Cigarettes removed in bond for exportation	134,311,180
Total product for 1886	4,957,598,488
Total product for 1885	4,524,090,841
Increase	433,507,647

In the year ended June 30, 1886, there were 6,242 distilleries registered, and 6,034 operated. *Distilled spirits.*

The following is a comparative statement of materials used and spirits produced during the last nine years:— *Grain and materials used for production of spirits.*

Year.	Grain used.	Spirits produced.	Molasses used.	Rum produced.
	Bushels.	Gallons.	Gallons.	Gallons.
1878	14,680,552	54,499,677	1,995,645	1,603,376
1879	18,735,814	69,649,166	2,801,307	2,243,455
1880	24,006,359	87,915,969	3,110,190	2,439,301
1881	31,291,175	115,609,644	2,710,307	2,118,506
1882	27,459,095	104,149,077	2,121,804	1,704,084
1883	18,644,787	72,235,175	2,373,106	1,801,960
1884	18,927,982	73,724,581	2,259,536	1,711,158
1885	17,865,203	72,834,198	2,719,416	2,081,165
1886	19,195,332	78,544,428	2,308,130	1,799,952
Total	190,806,299	729,161,915	22,399,441	17,502,957
Average	21,200,699	81,017,990	2,488,826	1,944,773

The following tables show the stock on hand, production, and movement of spirits for the fiscal years 1882–86:— *Movement of spirits.*

	1882.	1883.	1884.	1885.	1886.
	Gallons.	Gallons.	Gallons.	Gallons.	Gallons.
Quantity of spirits actually in warehouses beginning of fiscal year	64,648,111	89,962,645	80,499,993	63,502,551	54,724,916
Quantity of spirits produced during fiscal year	105,853,161	74,013,308	75,435,739	74,915,363	80,344,380
Total	170,501,272	163,975,953	155,935,732	138,417,914	135,069,296
Quantity of spirits withdrawn, tax paid, during fiscal year	70,730,180	75,441,087	78,342,474	67,649,321	69,096,900
Quantity of spirits withdrawn for exportation during fiscal year	8,092,725	5,326,427	9,586,738	10,671,118	5,646,656
Quantity of spirits withdrawn for scientific purposes, for use of United States, for transfer to manufacturing warehouse destroyed by fire, allowed for loss by leakage in warehouses, &c.	1,715,722	2,708,446	4,503,969	5,372,559	2,229,120
Total	80,538,637	83,475,960	92,433,181	83,692,998	76,972,676
Quantity of spirits remaining in warehouses at end of fiscal year	89,962,645	80,499,993	63,502,551	54,724,916	58,096,620

Number of cattle and hogs fed at grain distilleries.

	Number.	Lbs.
Number of cattle fed at registered grain distilleries in the United States	59,361	..
Average increase in weight of cattle	..	224
Total increase in weight of cattle	..	13,317,198
Number of hogs fed at registered grain distilleries in the United States	28,904	..
Average increase in weight of hogs	..	93
Total increase in weight of hogs	..	2,688,790
Total number of cattle and hogs fed	88,205	..
Average increase in weight of cattle and hogs	..	181
Total increase in weight of cattle and hogs	..	16,005,994

The statement of the public debt of the United States at the close of the calendar year, 1886, is given as a postcript.

WASHINGTON.

STATEMENT of the Public Debt of the United States for the Month of December, 1886.

INTEREST-BEARING DEBT.

Title of Loan.	Authorising Act.	Rate.	When Redeemable.	Interest Payable.	Amount Outstanding.			Interest Due and Unpaid.	Accrued Interest.
					Registered.	Coupon.	Total.		
					Dol. c.	Dol. c.	Dol. c.	Dol. c.	Dol. c.
Loan of July 12, 1882	July 12, 1882	3 per cent.	Option, U.S.	A., N., F., and M.	63,899,000 00	...	63,899,000 00	12,232 01	319,495 00
Funded Loan of 1891	July 14, 1870, and Jan. 20, 1871	4½ per cent.	Sept. 1, 1891	M., J., S., and D.	203,057,800 00	46,942,200 00	250,000,000 00	599,581 60	937,500 00
Funded Loan of 1907	July 14, 1870, and Jan. 20, 1871	4 per cent.	July 1, 1907	J., A., J., and O.	616,434,850 00	121,347,000 00	737,781,850 00	182,327 33	7,377,818 50
Refunding Certificates	February 26, 1879	4 per cent.	...	,,	...	...	190,100 00	57,030 00	1,901 00
Navy-Pension Fund	July 23, 1868	3 per cent.	...	Jan. and July	...	...	14,000,000 00	210,000 00	210,000 00
Bonds issued to Pacific Railroads.	July 1, 1862, and July 2, 1864		2,362,000 dol. matures Jan. 16, 1895; 640,000 dol. matures Nov. 1, 1895; average date of maturity, Mar. 19, 1895; 3,680,000 dol. matures Jan. 1, 1896; 4,320,000 dol. matures Feb. 1, 1896; average date of maturity, Jan. 18, 1896; 9,712,000 dol. matures Jan. 1, 1897; 29,904,952 dol. matures Jan. 1, 1898, and 14,004,560 dol. matures Jan. 1, 1899.			64,623,512 00	...	64,623,512 00	32,129 96	1,938,705 36
Aggregate of interest-bearing debt					948,015,162 00	168,289,200 00	1,130,494,462 00	1,053,300 90	10,785,419 86

UNITED STATES.

STATEMENT of the Public Debt of the United States for the Month of December, 1886—continued.

DEBT ON WHICH INTEREST HAS CEASED SINCE MATURITY.

Title of Loan.	Authorising Act.	Rate.	Matured.	Amount Outstanding.	Interest Due and Unpaid.
				Dol. c.	Dol. c.
Old Debt	Various, prior to 1837	4 to 6 per cent.	At various dates prior to January 1, 1837	57,665 00	64,174 81
Mexican Indemnity Stock	August 10, 1846	5 per cent.	At various dates in 1851 and 1852	1,104 91	85 74
Loan of 1847	January 28, 1847	6 per cent.	December 31, 1867	1,250 00	22 00
Bounty-Land Scrip	February 11, 1847	6 per cent.	July 1, 1849	3,175 00	210 06
Texan Indemnity Stock	September 9, 1850	5 per cent.	December 31, 1864	20,000 00	2,945 00
Loan of 1858	June 14, 1858	5 per cent.	After January 1, 1874	2,000 00	125 00
Loan of 1860	June 22, 1860	5 per cent.	January 1, 1871	10,000 00	600 00
Five-twenties of 1862 (called)	February 25, 1862	6 per cent.	Dec. 1, 1871, and at subsequent dates	267,200 00	431 95
Five-twenties of June, 1864 (called)	June 30, 1864	6 per cent.	Nov. 13, 1875, and at subsequent dates	44,250 00	236 61
Five-twenties of 1865 (called)	March 3, 1865	6 per cent.	Feb. 15, 1876, and at subsequent dates	28,850 00	1,607 79
Ten-forties of 1864 (called)	March 3, 1864	5 per cent.	July 9, 1879, and at subsequent dates	83,800 00	4,923 38
Consols of 1865 (called)	March 3, 1865	6 per cent.	August 21, 1877, and at subsequent dates	183,450 00	116 96
Consols of 1867 (called)	March 3, 1865	6 per cent.	April 1, 1879, and at subsequent dates	405,000 00	17,454 56
Consols of 1868 (called)	March 3, 1865	6 per cent.	July 4, 1879	73,950 00	8,998 19
Loan of February, 1861	February 8, 1861	6 per cent.	December 31, 1880	6,000 00	2,580 00
Funded Loan, 1881 (called)	July 14, 1870; January 20, 1871	5 per cent.	May 21, 1881, and at subsequent dates	134,600 00	213 06
Funded Loan, 1881 (called)	July 14, 1870; January 20, 1871	5 per cent., continued at 3½ per cent.	Dec. 23, 1882, and at subsequent dates	61,250 00	4,100 84
Oregon War Debt	March 2, 1861	6 per cent.	July 1, 1881	3,950 00	730 50
Loan of July and August, 1861	July 17 and August 5, 1861	6 per cent.	June 30, 1881	125,050 00	1,260 50
Loan of July and August, 1861 (called)	July 17 and August 5, 1861	6 per cent., continued at 3½ per cent.	Dec. 24, 1881, and at subsequent dates	100,350 00	949 83
Loan of 1863 (81's)	March 3, 1863	6 per cent.	June 30, 1881	18,250 00	107 90
Loan of 1863 (81's), called	March 3, 1863	6 per cent., continued at 3½ per cent.	August 1, 1882, and at subsequent dates	7,150 00	63 17
Loan of July 12, 1882 (called)	July 12, 1882	3 per cent.	Dec. 1, 1883, and at subsequent dates	6,723,150 00	32,056 66
Treasury Notes prior to 1846	Various, prior to 1846	1/10 to 6 per cent.	At various dates from 1838 to 1844	82,425 35	2,662 06
Treasury Notes of 1846	July 22, 1846	1/10 to 6 per cent.	At various dates in 1847 and 1848	5,900 00	200 60
Treasury Notes of 1847	January 28, 1847	5 to 6 per cent.	At various dates in 1848 and 1849	950 00	57 00
Treasury Notes of 1857	December 23, 1857	3 to 6 per cent.	At various dates in 1858 and 1859	1,700 00	99 00
Treasury Notes of 1861	March 2, 1861	6 per cent.	March 1, 1863	3,000 00	364 50
Seven-thirties of 1861	July 17, 1861	7 3/10 per cent.	August 19 and October 1, 1864	15,800 00	1,011 89
One-year Notes of 1863	March 3, 1863	5 per cent.	At various dates in 1865	36,335 00	1,828 85
Two-year Notes of 1863	March 3, 1863	5 per cent.	At various dates in 1866	29,550 00	1,323 90
Compound-interest Notes	March 3, 1863; June 30, 1864	6 per cent.	June 10, 1867, and May 15, 1868	195,840 00	40,260 56
Seven-thirties of 1864-65	June 30, 1864; March 3, 1865	7 3/10 per cent.	Aug. 15, 1867, and June 15 and July 15, 1868	129,950 00	18,641 99
Certificates of Indebtedness	March 1, 17, 1862; March 3, 1863	6 per cent.	At various dates in 1866	4,000 00	253 48
Temporary Loan	June 30, 1864	4 to 6 per cent.	October 15, 1866	2,960 00	244 19
3 per cent. Certificates	March 2, 1867; July 25, 1868	3 per cent.	February 28, 1873	5,000 00	394 31
Aggregate of debt on which interest has ceased since maturity				8,874,855 26	211,336 84

WASHINGTON.

Debt Bearing no Interest.

		Dol. c.	Total. Dol. c.
Old demand notes	July 17, 1861; February 12, 1862	...	57,325 00
Legal-tender notes	February 25, 1862; July 11, 1862; March 3, 1863	...	346,681,016 00
Certificates of deposit	June 8, 1872	6,710,000 00	
	Less amount held in treasurer's cash	200,000 00	6,510,000 00
Gold certificates	March 3, 1863, and July 12, 1882	124,701,409 00	
	Less amount held in treasurer's cash	27,485,804 00	97,215,605 00
Silver certificates	February 28, 1878	124,585,102 00	
	Less amount held in treasurer's cash	7,338,432 00	117,246,670 00
Fractional currency	July 17, 1862; March 3, 1863; June 30, 1864	15,329,636 52	
	Less amount estimated as lost or destroyed, Act of June 21, 1879	8,375,934 00	6,953,702 52
Aggregate of debt bearing no interest			574,664,318 52

UNITED STATES.

RECAPITULATION.

	Dol.	c.	Principal. Dol.	c.	Interest. Dol.	c.	Totals. Dol.	c.
Interest-bearing debt—Bonds at 4½ per cent.	250,000,000	00						
Bonds at 4 per cent.	737,781,850	00						
Bonds at 3 per cent.	63,899,000	00						
Refunding certificates, at 4 per cent.	190,100	00						
Navy pension fund, at 3 per cent.	14,000,000	00						
Pacific Railroad bonds, at 6 per cent.	64,623,512	00	1,130,494,462	00	11,838,720	76	1,142,333,182	76
			8,874,855	26	211,336	84	9,086,192	10
Debt on which interest has ceased since maturity								
Debt bearing no interest—Old demand and legal-tender notes	346,738,341	00						
Certificates of deposit	6,510,000	00						
Gold certificates	97,215,605	00						
Silver certificates	117,246,670	00						
Fractional currency, less 8,375,934 dol., estimated as lost or destroyed	6,953,702	52	574,664,318	52			574,664,318	52
Total debt			1,714,033,635	78	12,050,057	60	1,726,083,693	38
Less cash items available for reduction of the debt					241,902,564	64		
Less reserve held for redemption of U.S. notes					100,000,000	00	341,902,564	64
Total debt, less available cash items							1,384,181,128	74
Net cash in the Treasury							42,196,632	77
Debt, less cash in the Treasury, January 1, 1887							1,341,984,495	97
Debt, less cash in the Treasury, December 1, 1886							1,351,342,698	29
Decrease of debt during the month							9,358,202	32

CASH IN THE TREASURY.

	Dol.	c.	Dol.	c.
Available for reduction of the public debt—				
Gold held for gold certificates actually outstanding	97,215,605	00		
Silver held for silver certificates actually outstanding	117,246,670	00		
United States notes held for certificates of deposit actually outstanding	6,510,000	00		
Cash held for matured debt and interest unpaid	20,924,912	86		
Fractional currency	5,376	78		
Total available for reduction of the debt			241,902,564	64
Reserve fund—				
Held for redemption of United States notes, Acts January 14, 1875, and July 12, 1882			100,000,000	00
Unavailable for reduction of the debt—				
Fractional silver coin	25,660,935	44		
Minor coin	131,422	34	25,792,357	78
Certificates held as cash—				
Legal-tender	200,000	00		
Gold	27,485,804	00		
Silver	7,338,432	00	35,024,236	00
Net cash balance on hand			42,196,632	77
Total cash in the Treasury as shown by treasurer's general account			444,915,791	19

WASHINGTON.

COMPARISON.

Cash in the Treasury.	January 1, 1887. Dol. c.	January 1, 1887. Dol. c.	December 1, 1886. Dol. c.	December 1, 1886. Dol. c.	Increase. Dol. c.	Decrease. Dol. c.
Available for reduction of the Public Debt:—						
Gold held for gold certificates actually outstanding	...	97,215,605 00	...	90,520,633 00	...	...
Silver held for silver certificates actually outstanding	...	117,246,670 00	...	105,519,817 00	...	...
United States notes held for certificates of deposit actually outstanding	...	6,510,000 00	...	7,025,000 00	...	...
Cash held for matured debt and interest unpaid	...	20,924,912 86	...	21,001,902 51	...	...
Fractional currency	...	5,376 78	...	4,201 01	...	...
Total available for reduction of the debt	...	241,902,564 64	...	224,071,553 52	17,831,011 12	...
Reserve Fund:—						
Held for redemption of United States notes, Acts January 14, 1875, and July 12, 1882	...	100,000,000 00	...	100,000,000 00	...	...
Unavailable for reduction of the debt:—						
Fractional silver coin	25,660,935 44	...	25,808,067 32	...	...	...
Minor coin	131,422 34	25,792,357 78	163,584 53	25,971,651 85	...	179,294 07
Certificates held as cash:—						
Legal tender	200,000 00	...	280,000 00	...	...	...
Gold	27,485,804 00	...	34,469,694 00	...	...	...
Silver	7,338,432 00	35,024,236 00	14,137,285 00	48,886,979 00	...	13,862,743 00
Net cash balance on hand	...	42,196,632 77	...	40,093,556 22	2,103,076 55	...
Total cash in the Treasury as shown by treasurer's general account	...	444,915,791 19	...	439,023,740 59	19,734,087 67	14,042,037 07
Net increase in cash	...	...	...	...	5,892,050 60	...
Cash in the Treasury on account of Deposit Accounts:—						
National Bank-note Redemption Funds	100,201,696 82	...	97,100,946 33	...	...	...
Post-office and Disbursing Accounts, &c.	34,001,530 48	134,203,227 30	39,981,650 97	137,082,597 30	...	2,879,370 00
		579,119,018 49		576,106,337 89		
Deduct certificates held as cash not included in treasurer's statement of assets and liabilities	...	35,024,236 00	...	48,886,979 00	...	13,862,743 00
Total cash by treasurer's statement	...	544,094,782 49	...	527,219,358 89	16,875,423 60	...

The foregoing is a correct statement of the Public Debt, as appears from the books and treasurer's returns in the Treasury Department at the close of business, December 31, 1886.

DANIEL MANNING, Secretary of the Treasury.

LONDON:
Printed for Her Majesty's Stationery Office,
By HARRISON AND SONS,
Printers in Ordinary to Her Majesty.
(1000 11 | 87—H & S 302)

FOREIGN OFFICE.
1888.
ANNUAL SERIES.

No. 262.

DIPLOMATIC AND CONSULAR REPORTS ON TRADE AND FINANCE.

UNITED STATES.

REPORT FOR THE YEAR 1887
ON THE
TRADE AND COMMERCE OF BALTIMORE.

REFERENCE TO PREVIOUS REPORT, Annual Series No. 94.

Presented to both Houses of Parliament by Command of Her Majesty,
MARCH, 1888.

LONDON:
PRINTED FOR HER MAJESTY'S STATIONERY OFFICE,
BY HARRISON AND SONS, ST. MARTIN'S LANE,
PRINTERS IN ORDINARY TO HER MAJESTY.

And to be purchased, either directly or through any Bookseller, from
EYRE AND SPOTTISWOODE, EAST HARDING STREET, FLEET STREET, E.C., and
32, ABINGDON STREET, WESTMINSTER, S.W.; or
ADAM AND CHARLES BLACK, 6, NORTH BRIDGE, EDINBURGH; or
HODGES, FIGGIS, & CO., 104, GRAFTON STREET, DUBLIN.

[C.—5252—39.]

1888.
Price One Penny.

New Series of Reports.

Reports of the Annual Series have been issued from Her Majesty's Diplomatic and Consular Officers at the following places, and may be obtained from the sources indicated on the title-page:—

No.		Price.	No.		Price.
138.	Bolivar	3d.	200.	Tokyo	2d.
139.	Wênchow	1d.	201.	Tamatave	1d.
140.	Chicago	2d.	202.	Mexico	1d.
141.	Fiume	1d.	203.	Chefoo	1d.
142.	Port Saïd	1d.	204.	Nagasaki	5d.
143.	Java	1d.	205.	Cuba	1d.
144.	Puerto Cabello	1d.	206.	Tunis	1d.
145.	Coquimbo	1d.	207.	Réunion	1d.
146.	Vera Cruz	2d.	208.	Hyogo	2d.
147.	Bengazi	1d.	209.	Tangier	1d.
148.	Canary Islands	1d.	210.	Antwerp	1d.
149.	Rome	1d.	211.	Stettin	1d.
150.	Madeira	1d.	212.	Erzeroum	1d.
151.	Tahiti	1d.	213.	Rotterdam	1d.
152.	Corunna	1d.	214.	Nantes	2d.
153.	Vienna	1d.	215.	Newport News	1d.
154.	Cagliari	1d.	216.	Rio Grande do Sul	1d.
155.	St. Petersburg	2d.	217.	Rio de Janeiro	1d.
156.	Taiwan	1d.	218.	Corea	1d.
157.	Foochow	1d.	219.	Kanagawa	1d.
158.	Tonga	1d.	220.	Wurtemberg	1d.
159.	Wuhu	1d.	221.	Tahiti	1d.
160.	Lisbon	1d.	222.	Bangkok	1d.
161.	Ning-po	1d.	223.	St. Petersburg	2d.
162.	Cadiz	2d.	224.	Canton	1d.
163.	Bilbao	1d.	225.	Erzeroum	1d.
164.	Jaffa	1d.	226.	Rio de Janeiro	1d.
165.	Van	1d.	227.	Valparaiso	1d.
166.	Bushire	1d.	228.	St. Thomas	1d.
167.	Riga	1d.	229.	Stockholm	1d.
168.	Santos	1d.	230.	Nyassa	1d.
169.	Charleston	1d.	231.	Buenos Ayres	1d.
170.	Newchwang	1d.	232.	The Hague	1d.
171.	Amsterdam	1d.	233.	Trieste	1d.
172.	Ajaccio	1d.	234.	Vienna	1d.
173.	Chinkiang	2d.	235.	Washington	3d.
174.	Naples	3d.	236.	Odessa	1d.
175.	Smyrna	1d.	237.	Sofia	1d.
176.	Belgrade	1d.	238.	Porto Rico	1d.
177.	Philadelphia	2d.	239.	Palermo	2d.
178.	Stockholm	2d.	240.	Lisbon	2d.
179.	Pernambuco	1d.	241.	Tabreez	1d.
180.	Frankfort-on-Main	1d.	242.	Tunis	1d.
181.	Mogador	2d.	243.	The Hague	1d.
182.	New York	2d.	244.	Fiume	1d.
183.	Swatow	1d.	245.	Venice	1d.
184.	Berlin	1d.	246.	Paris	2d.
185.	Philippopolis	1d.	247.	Ancona	1d.
186.	San Francisco	6d.	248.	St. Petersburg	2d.
187.	Lisbon	1d.	249.	Algiers	2d.
188.	Lisbon	2d.	250.	Bucharest	1d.
189.	Nice	2d.	251.	Christiania	2d.
190.	Tientsin	1d.	252.	Paris	1d.
191.	Hankow	1d.	253.	Bogota	1d.
192.	Erzeroum	1d.	254.	Salonica	1d.
193.	Syra	1d.	255.	Copenhagen	1d.
194.	Athens	3d.	256.	Jeddah	1d.
195.	Vienna	2d.	257.	Russia	2d.
196.	Alexandria	1d.	258.	Paris	1d.
197.	Constantinople	1d.	259.	Patras	1d.
198.	Hakodate	1d.	260.	Brussels	1d.
199.	Shanghai	2d.	261.	Ichang	1d.

No. 262.

Reference to previous Report, Annual Series No. 94.

UNITED STATES.

BALTIMORE.

Consul Segrave to the Marquis of Salisbury.

My Lord,
British Consulate, Baltimore,
January 31, 1888.

I HAVE the honour herewith to transmit to your Lordship my Report on the Trade and Commerce of Baltimore for the year 1887.

I have, &c.
(Signed) W. F. SEGRAVE.

Report on the Trade and Commerce of Baltimore for the Year 1887.

During the year 1887 trade in Baltimore was very satisfactory.

Not only did foreign commerce show a decided advance over 1886, but it was especially remarkable as being the second year in succession in which such increase took place; and that is to be compared with considerable shrinkage of business in New York and Boston, and only a very moderate increase in Philadelphia. *Foreign commerce.*

To illustrate the value of foreign trade here, reference may be made to the figures of the December Report of the United States' Bureau of Statistics, giving the total value of exports from all the Customs' districts of the country for the first eleven months of 1887.

These figures are remarkable, they show that the total increase in value of exports from the United States for the period in question was only 14,000,000 dol., and that of this increase 4,500,000 dol. was at Baltimore, whilst there was a decrease of 5,500,000 dol. at New York, and 1,500,000 dol. at Boston.

Not alone in foreign commerce was great advance made, local industry also shows remarkable progress and development. The Pennsylvania Steel Works, with a capital of many millions of dollars, have purchased a thousand acres of land, with water frontage, within a short distance of this city, and have already commenced work with a plant which it is intended to extend until eight great furnaces, with a daily output capacity of 2,000 tons of pig-iron, a steel-rail mill, to turn out 1,000 tons of rails a-day, a nail-mill, agricultural steel works; and kindred enterprises are in operation. *Local trade.*

It is intended also, ultimately, to establish a steel shipbuilding yard.

These great works, the largest manufacturing enterprise established in the United States in 1887 will, no doubt, exercise enormous influence, not only on the manufacturing and railroad interests of the city, but upon all trade and shipping business as well.

In addition to the above, there are many other important industries carried on in Baltimore, notably, extensive railway carriage and street car works, canning factories, &c., which will no doubt tend in the next few years to increase the growing wealth and population of the city and neighbouring districts *Other industries*

(344)

UNITED STATES.

Labour question.

No limit seems to be placed on the sanguine, nay extravagant, hopes and anticipations entertained by the inhabitants, but a prudent outsider will make due allowance for the possible—if not probable—labour troubles which may arise, and which every day appear to become more and more endemic in this country.

Foreign shipping.

I subjoin (Annex A.) return of all shipping at the port of Baltimore; (Annex B.), return of exports and imports; and (Annex C.) table showing value of all articles exported and imported.

Annex A.—RETURN of all Shipping at the Port of Baltimore in the Year 1887.

ENTERED.

Nationality.	Sailing. Number of Vessels.	Sailing. Tonnage.	Steam. Number of Vessels.	Steam. Tonnage.	Total. Number of Vessels.	Total. Tonnage.
British	37	20,231	478	631,750	515	651,981
American (foreign trade only)	152	49,221	...	...	152	49,221
German	15	17,823	47	127,472	62	145,295
Italian	26	16,445	1	1,628	27	18,073
Spanish	...	...	5	10,066	5	10,066
French	...	...	5	8,580	5	8,580
Swedish and Norwegian	7	4,764	2	2,417	9	7,181
Austrian	4	2,383	...	...	4	2,383
Total for 1887	241	110,867	538	781,913	779	892,780
,, ,, 1886	242	125,189	533	744,044	775	869,233
Increase in 1887	...	...	...	...	4	23,547

CLEARED.

Nationality.	Sailing. Number of Vessels.	Sailing. Tonnage.	Steam. Number of Vessels.	Steam. Tonnage.	Total. Number of Vessels.	Total. Tonnage.
British	35	19,691	483	641,836	518	661,527
American (foreign trade only)	169	40,963	1	418	170	41,381
German	16	18,983	47	127,472	63	146,455
Italian	26	16,445	1	1,628	27	18,073
Spanish	...	...	5	10,066	5	10,066
French	...	...	5	8,580	5	8,580
Swedish and Norwegian	6	3,907	2	2,417	8	6,324
Austrian	5	2,972	...	...	5	2,972
Total for 1887	257	102,961	544	792,417	801	895,378
,, ,, 1886	275	132,527	526	730,041	801	862,568
Increase in 1887	...	...	...	...	...	32,810

BALTIMORE.

Annex B.—RETURN of the Principal Articles of Export from Baltimore during the Year 1887.

Articles.		1887. Quantity.	1887. Value.	1886. Quantity.	1886. Value.
Breadstuffs—					
Wheat	Bushels	10,688,330		10,498,597	
Flour	Barrels	2,790,000		1,916,478	
Maize	Bushels	7,130,230		14,079,835	
Provisions—					
Bacon	Lbs.	4,000,383	All exports 49,563,977 dol.; at 4 dol. 84 c. per £, equal to 10,240,491l. 2s. 4d. sterling.	15,267,859	All exports 46,810,870 dol.; at 4 dol. 84 c. per £, equal to 9,671,667l. 7s. sterling.
Lard	,,	25,501,903		17,625,706	
Canned goods	Cases	143,000		84,365	
Cotton	Bales	121,597		180,417	
Petroleum	Gallons	8,739,334		12,663,560	
Tobacco	Hogsheads	53,286		51,350	
Lumber	Feet	8,508,000		4,551,000	
Staves	Number	3,368,000		2,405,000	
Rosin	Barrels	63,673		32,801	
Coals	Tons	54,255		65,500	
Live stock	Head	16,527		12,458	

Annex BA.—RETURN of the Principal Articles of Import into Baltimore during the Year 1887.

Articles.		1887. Quantity.	1887. Value.	1886. Quantity.	1886. Value.
Metals—					
Iron ore	Tons	401,997		363,462	
,, pig	,,	53,182		51,561	
,, spiegel	,,	14,618		3,000	
,, ,,	Casks	1,445		426	
Tin-plates	Boxes	679,895		621,300	
Steel billets	Number	322,055		43,770	
,, ,,	Tons	7,816	All imports 13,062,695 dol.; at 4 dol. 84 c. per £, equal to 2,698,903l. 18s. 6d. sterling.	2,598	[All imports 11,785,113 dol.; at 4 dol. 84 c. per £, equal to 2,434,940l. 14s. sterling.
,, crop ends	,,	10,175		...	
,, slabs	Number	87,932		321	
,, bars	Bundles	6,094		...	
,, rods	,,	265,331		61,393	
Spelter plates	Plates	31,218		...	
,, ingots	Number	9,711		...	
Rails, old	Tons	6,141		3,624	
,, ,,	Pieces	14,210		10,559	
Chemicals	Packages	31,991		31,149	
Salt	Sacks	100,549		115,842	
,,	Tons	13,780		14,589	
,,	Bushels	70,614		72,517	
,, agricultural	Sacks	31,918		28,846	
,, ,,	Tons	15,974		37,637	
Nitrate of soda	Bags	40,269		27,672	
Guano	Tons	12,896		9,820	
Fruit—					
Cocoa-nuts	Number	1,676,000		1,601,000	
Bananas	Bunches	555,310		304,853	
Pine-apples	Number	273,558		190,503	
Oranges	Packed and loose	925,000		97,000	
Lemons	Boxes	20,898		11,874	
Coffee	Bags	197,568		335,946	
Whisky	Barrels	18,671		...	

(344)

Annex C.—TABLE showing the Total Value of all Articles Exported from and Imported into Baltimore from and to Foreign Countries during the Years 1886 and 1887.

Country.	Exports. 1887.	Exports. 1886.	Imports. 1887.	Imports. 1886.
	£	£	£	£
Great Britain	6,375,000	6,000,000	1,600,000	1,362,700
Germany	1,000,000	825,000	90,000	75,000
Brazil	350,000	500,000	500,000	600,000
Holland	933,800	620,000	60,000	15,000
France	650,000	1,000,000	..	..
Belgium	650,000	330,000	30,000	6,000
Cuba	50,000	30,000	20,000	30,000
Italy	25,000	55,000	70,000	75,000
Spain	6,000	..	200,000	125,000
Algeria	..	10,000	120,000	120,000
Other countries	200,691	301,667	8,903	26,240
Totals	10,240,491	9,671,667	2,698,903	2,434,940

Export trade. The most remarkable increase in any single article of foreign export has been in flour.

Flour. Previous to 1885, the flour exported from Baltimore averaged annually under half-a-million barrels. In 1887, Baltimore exported 3,078,717 barrels. Flour averaged 2 dol. 40 c. per barrel in 1887, against 2 dol. 52 c. in 1886.

Grain trade. The export of grain during the past year shows an increase of about half-a-million bushels of wheat, but a decrease of about 6,000,000 bushels of corn (maize); the very large decrease in this latter article is accounted for by a very short crop.

On the 31st December last the stock in the elevators amounted to:—Wheat, 1,367,451 bushels; corn, 693,660 bushels.

Average prices during the year were approximately:—Wheat, 81¾ c. per bushel; highest in May, 96 c.; lowest in September, 76 c. Corn highest in December, 58 c.; lowest in March, 45¾ c.; average price, 48 cents.

Cotton. There has been a very considerable falling-off in the export of cotton from Baltimore during the past year, this may be attributed partly to the fact that the South Carolina crop, which was formerly exported *via* Baltimore is at present shipped direct from Charleston and Savannah; and partly also to the great extension of railways which now enable the planter to send his cotton direct to the ocean port. The bulk of the 122,000 bales exported from Baltimore was grown in Virginia and North Carolina.

Petroleum. The influence of the Standard Oil Company, which controls and exercises a virtual monopoly of the oil business in this market, has restricted the receipts of this article to the requirements and demands of their own refineries; there has been a decrease of some 6,000,000 gallons, which no doubt is to be attributed to the action of the Company.

Canned goods. The amount of canned provisions exported in 1887 nearly doubles the shipment of the previous year, and that in the face of a partial failure of the peach crop. There is every reason to anticipate further and large increase in this business, as the vegetables, fruit and oysters preserved in Maryland have a universal and well-deserved reputation for excellence.

Cattle trade. There has been a very satisfactory increase in the export of live stock, the facilities afforded by this port are very remarkable, and the large number of steamers leaving Baltimore, at stated regular periods, have no doubt attracted much business; the increase in shipments amounts to 4,069 head.

Freights. The volume of business has been in the aggregate superior to that of the previous year, although restricted in the latter months by scarcity of tonnage; rates not having been satisfactory, owners have sought employment for their ships elsewhere. The number of vessels entered and cleared has been less, but the amount of tonnage is greater.

Imports. Iron. The output of pig-iron in this country in 1887 was 6,500,000 tons, or about 600,000 tons more than in the previous year. The production of Bessemer steel rails shows also a large increase. This, however, does not appear to have had much effect on the import of these articles which have reached this port in considerably increased volume.

Iron-ore came from Spain, Algiers, Elba and Cuba, and gave employment to a large amount of British tonnage.

Coffee. The coffee which comes to Baltimore is imported almost exclusively from Brazil, and shows a very considerable diminution over that of the previous year.

The crop in Brazil was very short, and prices at Rio were almost constantly higher than in the United States; to this fact, and to the advance in prices which commenced about eighteen months back and culminated in the early summer, there is no doubt that much of the decrease is due. Coffee is imported to a great extent in sailing-vessels, most of which are owned in Baltimore.

Chemicals. The receipt of chemicals—which come almost exclusively from England—shows a slight increase; this, however, is not a branch of business in which fortunes are to be made in this country, the importer and wholesale merchant being forced to grant large credits which the depressed condition of agriculture often render very difficult to realise.

Fruit. The fruit trade shows considerable expansion, and no doubt has a profitable future before it, but, as a preliminary, some system must be devised for selecting, packing, and shipping the fruit, so that it may be placed on the market in a sound and wholesome condition. This remark refers especially to bananas, which often heat on the voyage, and arrive in a condition unfit for consumption.

Several local firms are engaged in this business, which is carried on by means of small Scotch steamers, which are chartered by them, and which run regularly all the year between this port and Jamaica.

Whisky. Over 18,000 barrels of whisky are reported to have been received at Baltimore during the past year, a new article to be added to the list of imports. It is explained, however, to the consumer that this whisky is not distilled by the under-paid pauper-labour of Europe, but is of genuine American manufacture.

It is stated that the whisky is sent to Europe, when its period of warehousing has expired, in order to evade the payment of internal revenue charges. As "retour de l'Inde" gave prestige and character to Bordeaux and Madeira, so American whisky, no doubt, on its "return from Europe," finds a readier sale, and at a price which is sufficient to cover cost and freight and leave a margin of profit as well.

Employment of population. In Maryland, as in other countries, the tendency of the population to engage in manufacturing industry in preference to agriculture, is steadily on the increase. As a consequence, wages are probably lower in Baltimore than in most other cities of equal importance in the Union;

there is no reason, moreover, to anticipate any advance in the rates of wages, because of the great increase in the number of hands who look for support to manufacturing industry, as well as in the very large proportionate increase in female labour.

Notwithstanding the comparatively low rate of wages, the condition of the artisan in Baltimore is, in many respects, superior to that of his fellows in other cities. Provisions are cheaper, and he is better housed. Whereas the average number of persons per house is in—

New York	16·37
Brooklyn	9·11
Cincinnati	9·11
Boston	8·26
In Baltimore it is only	6·54

Canning industry. By far the most important of Maryland industries is the canning of fruit, vegetables, and oysters, which gives employment to upwards of 30,000 hands.

The season for packing commences in May and continues until September—in all about 100 days, during this period fruit and vegetables are canned; subsequently, in October, the oyster season commences, and keeps the factories busy until the following April. Should, however, the new process of "muzzling" oysters, as it is termed, prove a success, it will doubtless seriously affect the canning business. It is claimed that the "muzzled" oyster, that is with the shells fastened together by a wire, is preserved in a better condition than when canned, and for a quite long enough period to enable the fish to be sent to Rome or St. Petersburg.

Brickmaking. Numbers of old houses in Maryland are alleged to be built of English bricks, the tradition on the subject being that the vessels, which took tobacco to England 200 years ago, had a return freight of bricks. There is no longer any necessity to import them from England as probably the finest grade of bricks in the world are now made in the immediate vicinity of Baltimore, and the manufacture of which gives employment to over 5,000 at an average wage of 1 dol. 63 c. per day.

Immigration. The arrival of foreign immigrants at this port goes on increasing progressively; during the past year the increase amounted to upwards of 16,000 persons. The table, Annex D, shows the numbers of the different nationalities of the immigrants.

Every possible arrangement is made for their comfort and physical well-being on arrival, and due precaution taken to prevent their being imposed upon by outsiders. As a rule their destination is the Far West, and they are forwarded by railway direct from the ship's side to their future homes.

Annex D.—IMMIGRATION to Baltimore during 1887.

Nationality.	Number.
England	1,056
Ireland	300
Scotland	22
British Possessions	24
	1,402
Austria	1,778
Bohemia	2,550
Denmark	988
Germany	25,600
Hungary	1,109
Norway	990
Poland	55
Russia	3,080
Sweden	1,662
Switzerland	54
United States	969
Other countries	36
	40,273
In 1886	22,660
Increase	17,613

Male, 21,225. Female, 19,048.

LONDON:
Printed for Her Majesty's Stationery Office,
By HARRISON AND SONS,
Printers in Ordinary to Her Majesty.
(1125   3 | 88—H & S   344)

FOREIGN OFFICE.
1888.
ANNUAL SERIES.

No. 266.

DIPLOMATIC AND CONSULAR REPORTS ON TRADE AND FINANCE.

UNITED STATES.

REPORT FOR THE YEAR 1887
ON THE
TRADE AND COMMERCE OF TEXAS.

REFERENCE TO PREVIOUS REPORT, Annual Series No. 104.

Presented to both Houses of Parliament by Command of Her Majesty,
MARCH, 1888.

LONDON:
PRINTED FOR HER MAJESTY'S STATIONERY OFFICE,
BY HARRISON AND SONS, ST. MARTIN'S LANE,
PRINTERS IN ORDINARY TO HER MAJESTY.

And to be purchased, either directly or through any Bookseller, from
EYRE AND SPOTTISWOODE, EAST HARDING STREET, FLEET STREET, E.C., and
32, ABINGDON STREET, WESTMINSTER, S.W.; or
ADAM AND CHARLES BLACK, 6, NORTH BRIDGE, EDINBURGH; or
HODGES, FIGGIS, & Co., 104, GRAFTON STREET, DUBLIN.

1888.

[C.— 5252—43.]   *Price One Penny.*

New Series of Reports.

Reports of the Annual Series have been issued from Her Majesty's Diplomatic and Consular Officers at the following places, and may be obtained from the sources indicated on the title-page:—

No.		Price.	No.		Price.
152.	Corunna	1d.	209.	Tangier	1d.
153.	Vienna	1d.	210.	Antwerp	1d.
154.	Cagliari	1d.	211.	Stettin	1d.
155.	St. Petersburg	2d.	212.	Erzeroum	1d.
156.	Taiwan	1d.	213.	Rotterdam	1d.
157.	Foochow	1d.	214.	Nantes	2d.
158.	Tonga	1d.	215.	Newport News	1d.
159.	Wuhu	1d.	216.	Rio Grande do Sul	1d.
160.	Lisbon	1d.	217.	Rio de Janeiro	1d.
161.	Ning-po	1d.	218.	Corea	1d.
162.	Cadiz	2d.	219.	Kanagawa	1d.
163.	Bilbao	1d.	220.	Wurtemberg	1d.
164.	Jaffa	1d.	221.	Tahiti	1d.
165.	Van	1d.	222.	Bangkok	1d.
166.	Bushire	1d.	223.	St. Petersburg	2d.
167.	Riga	1d.	224.	Canton	1d.
168.	Santos	1d.	225.	Erzeroum	1d.
169.	Charleston	1d.	226.	Rio de Janeiro	1d.
170.	Newchwang	1d.	227.	Valparaiso	1d.
171.	Amsterdam	1d.	228.	St. Thomas	1d.
172.	Ajaccio	1d.	229.	Stockholm	1d.
173.	Chinkiang	2d.	230.	Nyassa	1d.
174.	Naples	3d.	231.	Buenos Ayres	1d.
175.	Smyrna	1d.	232.	The Hague	1d.
176.	Belgrade	1d.	233.	Trieste	1d.
177.	Philadelphia	2d.	234.	Vienna	1d.
178.	Stockholm	2d.	235.	Washington	3d.
179.	Pernambuco	1d.	236.	Odessa	1d.
180.	Frankfort on-Main	1d.	237.	Sofia	1d.
181.	Mogador	2d.	238.	Porto Rico	1d.
182.	New York	2d.	239.	Palermo	2d.
183.	Swatow	1d.	240.	Lisbon	2d.
184.	Berlin	1d.	241.	Tabreez	1d.
185.	Philippopolis	1d.	242.	Tunis	1d.
186.	San Francisco	6d.	243.	The Hague	1d.
187.	Lisbon	1d.	244.	Fiume	1d.
188.	Lisbon	2d.	245.	Venice	1d.
189.	Nice	2d.	246.	Paris	2d.
190.	Tientsin	1d.	247.	Ancona	1d.
191.	Hankow	1d.	248.	St. Petersburg	2d.
192.	Erzeroum	1d.	249.	Algiers	2d.
193.	Syra	1d.	250.	Bucharest	1d.
194.	Athens	3d.	251.	Christiania	2d.
195.	Vienna	2d.	252.	Paris	1d.
196.	Alexandria	1d.	253.	Bogota	1d.
197.	Constantinople	1d.	254.	Salonica	1d.
198.	Hakodate	1d.	255.	Copenhagen	1d.
199.	Shanghai	2d.	256.	Jeddah	1d.
200.	Tokyo	2d.	257.	Russia	2d.
201.	Tamatave	1d.	258.	Paris	1d.
202.	Mexico	1d.	259.	Patras	1d.
203.	Chefoo	1d.	260.	Brussels	1d.
204.	Nagasaki	5d.	261.	Ichang	1d.
205.	Cuba	1d.	262.	Baltimore	1d.
206.	Tunis	1d.	263.	Taganrog	1d.
207.	Réunion	1d.	264.	Oporto	1d.
208.	Hyogo	2d.	265.	Rio de Janeiro	1d.

No. 266.

Reference to previous Report, Annual Series No. 104.

UNITED STATES.

GALVESTON.

Consul Lyall to the Marquis of Salisbury.

My Lord, *Galveston, January* 19, 1888.

I HAVE the honour to enclose a portion of my Report on the Trade and Commerce of Galveston for the Year 1887, and trust to forward the remainder without delay.

I have, &c.
(Signed) WALTER T. LYALL.

Report on the Trade and Commerce of Texas for the Year 1887.

The weather in Texas has, during 1887, been generally favourable to agriculture, the crops including cotton, have therefore been good; there have been no storms or hurricanes along the coast as in 1886.

Trade and progress during the year.

The commercial progress of the city has, during the past year, been highly satisfactory. New enterprises have been established, and old ones duplicated and extended.

A solid breakwater of heavy stone blocks, quarried in the interior of the State and transported to Galveston by railway, is in course of construction; this, it is calculated, will ensure permanent deep water on the bar, the great desideratum, the depth not now averaging more than 14 feet.

Marine ways, for hauling out and docking vessels not exceeding 1,500 tons, have been taken in hand, and are nearly completed; while the wharves have been extended, new *levées* made, and extensive terminal tracks constructed.

The tonnage of vessels entering from and clearing for foreign and home (U.S.) ports, during the year, is as follows:—

	Tons.
Entered, Foreign shipping	129,176
,, United States' vessels	265,037
Cleared, Foreign shipping	104,716
,, United States' vessels	257,031
Total tonnage entered during 1887	394,113
,, cleared ,,	361,747

FOREIGN TRADE, EXPORTS AND IMPORTS.

The great bulk of exports from Galveston (foreign) is cotton, and cotton-seed oil-cake, the total valuation of which for each month during the year 1887, as shown by the Custom-house returns, is as follows:—

(350)

Month.	Amount.
	Dollars.
January	3,213,726
February	1,280,283
March	1,143,964
April	582,588
May	70,899
June	..
July	..
August	1,999
September	940,021
October	4,209,805
November	3,491,897
December	2,560,914
Total	17,476,294

The total value of foreign imports during the year, made up from the Customs' returns, is 1,765,612 dols. Much of this, however, was in bond for Mexican ports.

The importations of home (U.S.) merchandise for 1887 amounted to 80,000,000 dol., while the home (U.S.) exports aggregated a value of 30,000,000 dol.

Liquor law. The principal event during the past year was the defeat of the "Prohibition amendment," by a majority of over 100,000 votes. This was a law to totally prohibit the sale of liquor, of any description, or rather to totally prohibit the retail trade, as has been done in Georgia, Maine, and other States. This attempt, for a time, created considerable excitement, as for a variety of reasons it seemed probable that the Bill would be carried. A great number of good people in Texas, while not particularly opposed to liquor, are opposed to the saloon, or public-house system. Then there is a large class, especially in the rural districts, who, though not opposed to drinking either on moral or sanitary grounds, would like to see its sale prohibited in small country towns and villages, because of the disorder it often occasions.

Immigration. *Immigration.*—An Immigration Movement to invite people to settle in Texas is now going on in the country itself, and will, in all probability, be vigorously "promoted" during the present year in England and Europe generally. The immigration promoters, or "Boomers," are said to be interested in the sale, at a profit, of a considerable area of land, and two opinions exist as to the actual value of these lands. The "Boomers" assert that Texas, which possesses 262,000 square miles of territory, is capable of maintaining a population of 40,000,000. Its present population is between 2,000,000 and 3,000,000.

That without taking the arid Western and North-western districts into account, there is enough good land in Texas to make four considerable "States," having a range of produce from sugar to maize, cotton, wheat, hay, and millet. They allege that Texas is the first cotton, cattle, wool, and hide-producing State in the Union, and could easily be made the first wheat, maize, hay, and dairy-product country. The other side, *per contra*, assert "that whatever may be the wishes of interested parties, the State of Texas lacks population, and always will do so; that although the Eastern and South-eastern portion of the State (*i.e.*, the Cotton Belt) is well adapted to cotton planting, which requires much care and attention; that, nevertheless, by far the greater portion of the State is only fit for cattle-raising, and a great part of it not even fit for that business; that though an old State, having been established half-a-century, Texas does not raise corn enough to supply its own necessities, even the draught animals being fed on imported corn; that as to dairy produce, butter, cheese, and condensed milk have been, and are, imported in immense quantities—all which it is difficult to disprove."

Texas undoubtedly possesses a fruitful soil, and, taken all round, a tolerably healthy climate. In the Western and North-western counties the climate is *very* healthy, but it is just there that unfortunately a scarcity of rainfall and of water prevails.

This will be, in all probability remedied some day or other by irrigation works, undertaken on a large scale, irrigation having succeeded in producing admirable results wherever introduced.

But there are different kinds of immigrant colonists, and the conditions which suit one kind will not suit another.

For young, active, educated men, backed with sufficient capital to purchase a big "ranche" and to stock it, or even a half or quarter share in such a ranche, Texas is a first-class place to come to; but struggling immigrants with small capital, who calculate to farm a plot of 150 or 200 acres of land, had better go to British territory. Without artificial irrigation, I am satisfied that the land now unoccupied, or at any rate 90 per cent. of it, can never be profitably worked, and irrigation is, in Texas, quite in its infancy.

There is any amount, it is true, of unoccupied fertile land to be had cheap; but should a dry season set in, as is usually the case, nothing will grow upon it, and the settler will become bankrupt.

As to chances of getting employment in Texas at present. I am credibly informed that there is not a town where you will not find at least 15 per cent. of the working-classes out of employment, and this applies to every class of working-man, from first-class mechanics downwards. I also know that during the past year thousands of working people have left the State, and if these, who were mostly "old hands," could not get along, how is it likely that new comers could do so?

While on this subject, I will give a *résumé* of some of the drawbacks which attend immigration to the Southern and Western Texas, this being in my opinion a very important affair to British emigrants, possessed of small capital which they, as it were hazard on a throw, and in case they lose it (by emigrating to an unsuitable locality) ruin themselves.

Texas is a good country for certain German immigrants, and for Austrians, Bohemians, Poles, &c. They come out and join already-settled villages and communities, where they find everything going on much as it does in Suabia, Franconia, or Galicia. But for an Englishman or Scotchman, I cannot see what advantages the country possesses over English colonies such as the Cape, Transvaal, or Australia. It is just as hot, or hotter, and in many parts of the country more unhealthy.

One of the first and greatest disadvantages to an emigrant to Texas, or any of the Southern and Western States, is the protective Tariff; however, a few more observations may not be amiss, more especially as it will undoubtedly furnish the great bone of contention in the next Presidential election.

Now under the present Protective Tariff the expenses of a working-man with a wife and six children, or of a small farmer with the same family, will be for the first year, at the most reasonable estimate 900 dol., or about 180*l*. Of this amount very nearly one-third, *i.e.*, 292 dol. 50 c., or almost 60*l.*, is literally a tax which goes into the pockets of the "protected" manufacturers.

The American working-man, who expends annually 900 dol., or 180*l.*, pays about 60*l.* of this sum to aid the manufacturer. He pays a duty of 80 per cent. on woollen clothes, 45 per cent. on cotton clothing, 50 per cent. on "notions," 35 per cent. on shoes, 25 per cent. on leather, 80 per cent. on carpets, 60 per cent. on curtains and hangings, 40 per cent. on bedding, 35 per cent. on table linen, 60 per cent. on china-ware, and 45 per cent. on cutlery. That is to say, he pays something like 49 per cent. taxes, *in toto*, on actual necessaries. The American working-man, it is true, earns higher wages than the European workman, but he has to pay about twice the money for everything he purchases, and gets fewer and inferior articles for his money—for cheap shoddy clothing and household goods are the most expensive of all in the end, requiring constant renewal.

The great argument of the Protectionists is that protection is necessary in the working-man's interest to keep up wages. Let us see whether it does so. Taking the tax on woollen goods—one of the most oppressive in the category, though not the highest—we find that the actual cost of a suit, which in London at a respectable tailor's would be 4*l.* 10*s.* to 5*l.*, is here 50 dol., or 10*l.* The cost of an overcoat, which in London would be 2*l.* 10*s.*, is here 25 dol. to 30 dol., 5*l.* to 6*l.* The protective import tax on woollen goods is now over 67 per cent. From official statistics we find that in 1880, when labour was better paid than now, the whole amount of woollen fabrics manufactured was of a value of 160,606,721 dol., nearly 170,000,000 dol. The cost of production was:—

For material 100,845,611 dol., deducting which from the net value we find there is—

		Dol.
A net profit of	.. ..	160,606,721
Deduct	.. ..	100,845,611
		59,761,110
Deduct amount paid for labour	.. ..	25,836,292
And there remains net profit to capitalist		33,924,818

The hands employed during the year 1880 were a total of 83,504 men, women, and children, who received as above, 25,836,292 dol. for wages. The total capital invested was (as given by the manufacturers themselves) 96,095,564 dol., which capital was making, therefore, over 35 per cent. per annum profit out of the protective import duties.

Much has been written about the "cheapness of provisions" in the United States. This is an entire fiction. The cost of living in the towns, especially in the Southern States, is very high, everything being double or treble the price it is in Europe. Country people, it is true, live cheaply, but this is because they live on their produce, and buy nothing, except flour, tobacco, sugar (or molasses), and coffee. In consequence of the Tariff, they cannot afford to buy decent clothing, and are almost to a man ragged and meanly dressed.

So far from the Tariff being advantageous to the working-classes in raising wages—as Mr. Keith attempts to maintain—it causes terrible misery, and, though these classes do not yet see it clearly (being misled by demagogues), is their greatest enemy. The Tariff being intensely protective against foreign imports fosters manufacturing monopolies, which by combination raises prices of necessaries to three times what they would naturally be, *i.e.*, to three times what they would be if only ordinary European duties of eight or ten per cent. for revenue purposes were levied. The working-man, therefore, in order to be enabled to live, has to demand just about three times as much wages as he would get in Europe; and, as the "combinations," rings, corners, &c., tend to continually heighten the quotations for necessaries, the working-man has to strike for higher and higher wages. But one of the monopolist "combination" systems, and one of the most efficient, is to "shut down" their manufactures or close up their mines and foundries, in order to keep up prices, therefore these strikes do not injure their interests. Nay, it is said that they have been known to organise these strikes as an excuse for "shutting down" and raising prices. The high rate of wages, necessitated by the tariff, injures the working classes in other ways. Well-to-do people will often say, I should like to make this or that improvement, to enclose that piece of ground with a fence or a wall, to build a stable, or build a yacht, &c., but I cannot afford it, it costs too much. In the same way you see people of position, lawyers, accountants, wealthy householders, &c., doing their own carpentering, painting, glazing, roof-mending, and such like odd jobs, which men of their standing would not dream of doing in Europe, simply because it costs too much to employ a craftsman.

All this is so much lost to the working-man through the action of the Tariff.

The Executive in Texas.—Then the administration of law and the executive in Texas, leave much to be desired. There is no doubt that the masses of the Texan population are peaceable and law-abiding; yet the records of crime in this State for 1885–1886 are simply appalling. The Texan criminal statistics show an average of over 500 murders and homicides per year, out of a population of little over 2,000,000. This is five times the criminal percentage of the kingdom of Italy, where the statistics for 1885–1886 show only one murder per 20,000 of population. Train robberies (in which the entire train is taken possession of by armed men, who bring it to a stand-still and then plunder the mails and passengers) have been tolerably frequent this year. We have had five or six, in each of which from 30,000 dol. to 200,000 dol. was secured by the robbers. In only one case have any of them been detected and run down, and in this one case the men were not arrested, being shot by the guard while in the act of plundering the mail.

Government.

There is very little doubt that were it not for the very high rewards offered by the railway companies, these robberies would be still more frequent, for every description of lawlessness prevails in Texas, the reason being, firstly, that there are no police, or next to none; secondly, not only is the law not enforced in cases of murder and other violence, but the laws themselves are inefficient, enabling anyone who has enough money to fee lawyers, to get clear of punishment, (unless lynched).

Another considerable drawback to Texas as a British emigration field is its large negro population, a great per centage of whom are just as savage, ignorant, and brutal, as the Congo tribes from whom they are descended. The negro is now supposed to be on his good behaviour, yet the papers are continually publishing accounts of negro "outrages," such as rape of white women, (usually accompanied by murder) assassinations by negroes, robberies, murders, burglaries, and all sorts of thieving, and this, although any serious crime committed by a negro is, as a rule, promptly avenged by lynching the culprit the moment he is captured, or by riddling him with bullets.

The Southern and Western States contain a population of at least 6,000,000 or 7,000,000 of negroes and negro half-breeds, who are multiplying rapidly. A great per-centage of these are honest, hard-working, good citizens (especially the mulattos), and possessed of considerable property, landed and otherwise, but there is a vast residuum, of low, "mean niggers," who are irrepressible thieves, and habitually insolent to whites.

LONDON:

Printed for Her Majesty's Stationery Office,
By HARRISON AND SONS,
Printers in Ordinary to Her Majesty.
(1125 3 | 88—H & S 350)

FOREIGN OFFICE.
1888.
ANNUAL SERIES.

No. 270.

DIPLOMATIC AND CONSULAR REPORTS ON TRADE AND FINANCE.

UNITED STATES.

REPORT FOR THE YEAR 1887
ON THE
TRADE OF NEW ORLEANS, PENSACOLA, AND MOBILE.

REFERENCE TO PREVIOUS REPORT, Annual Series No. 92.

Presented to both Houses of Parliament by Command of Her Majesty,
MARCH, 1888.

LONDON:
PRINTED FOR HER MAJESTY'S STATIONERY OFFICE,
BY HARRISON AND SONS, ST. MARTIN'S LANE,
PRINTERS IN ORDINARY TO HER MAJESTY.

And to be purchased, either directly or through any Bookseller, from
EYRE AND SPOTTISWOODE, EAST HARDING STREET, FLEET STREET, E.C., and
32, ABINGDON STREET, WESTMINSTER, S.W.; or
ADAM AND CHARLES BLACK, 6, NORTH BRIDGE, EDINBURGH; or
HODGES, FIGGIS, & Co., 104, GRAFTON STREET, DUBLIN.

1888.

[C. 5252—47.] *Price Twopence.*

New Series of Reports.

Reports of the Annual Series have been issued from Her Majesty's Diplomatic and Consular Officers at the following places, and may be obtained from the sources indicated on the title-page:—

No.		Price.	No.		Price.
146.	Vera Cruz	2d.	208.	Hyogo	2d.
147.	Bengazi	1d.	209.	Tangier	1d.
148.	Canary Islands	1d.	210.	Antwerp	1d.
149.	Rome	1d.	211.	Stettin	1d.
150.	Madeira	1d.	212.	Erzeroum	1d.
151.	Tahiti	1d.	213.	Rotterdam	1d.
152.	Corunna	1d.	214.	Nantes	2d.
153.	Vienna	1d.	215.	Newport News	1d.
154.	Cagliari	1d.	216.	Rio Grande do Sul	1d.
155.	St. Petersburg	2d.	217.	Rio de Janeiro	1d.
156.	Taiwan	1d.	218.	Corea	1d.
157.	Foochow	1d.	219.	Kanagawa	1d.
158.	Tonga	1d.	220.	Wurtemberg	1d.
159.	Wuhu	1d.	221.	Tahiti	1d.
160.	Lisbon	1d.	222.	Bangkok	1d.
161.	Ning-po	1d.	223.	St. Petersburg	2d.
162.	Cadiz	2d.	224.	Canton	1d.
163.	Bilbao	1d.	225.	Erzeroum	1d.
164.	Jaffa	1d.	226.	Rio de Janeiro	1d.
165.	Van	1d.	227.	Valparaiso	1d.
166.	Bushire	1d.	228.	St. Thomas	1d.
167.	Riga	1d.	229.	Stockholm	1d.
168.	Santos	1d.	230.	Nyassa	1d.
169.	Charleston	1d.	231.	Buenos Ayres	1d.
170.	Newchwang	1d.	232.	The Hague	1d.
171.	Amsterdam	1d.	233.	Trieste	1d.
172.	Ajaccio	1d.	234.	Vienna	1d.
173.	Chinkiang	2d.	235.	Washington	3d.
174.	Naples	3d.	236.	Odessa	1d.
175.	Smyrna	1d.	237.	Sofia	1d.
176.	Belgrade	1d.	238.	Porto Rico	1d.
177.	Philadelphia	2d.	239.	Palermo	2d.
178.	Stockholm	2d.	240.	Lisbon	2d.
179.	Pernambuco	1d.	241.	Tabreez	1d.
180.	Frankfort on-Main	1d.	242.	Tunis	1d.
181.	Mogador	2d.	243.	The Hague	1d.
182.	New York	2d.	244.	Fiume	1d.
183.	Swatow	1d.	245.	Venice	1d.
184.	Berlin	1d.	246.	Paris	2d.
185.	Philippopolis	1d.	247.	Ancona	1d.
186.	San Francisco	6d.	248.	St. Petersburg	2d.
187.	Lisbon	1d.	249.	Algiers	2d.
188.	Lisbon	2d.	250.	Bucharest	1d.
189.	Nice	2d.	251.	Christiania	1d.
190.	Tientsin	1d.	252.	Paris	1d.
191.	Hankow	1d.	253.	Bogota	1d.
192.	Erzeroum	1d.	254.	Salonica	1d.
193.	Syra	1d.	255.	Copenhagen	1d.
194.	Athens	3d.	256.	Jeddah	1d.
195.	Vienna	2d.	257.	Russia	2d.
196.	Alexandria	1d.	258.	Paris	1d.
197.	Constantinople	1d.	259.	Patras	1d.
198.	Hakodate	1d.	260.	Brussels	1d.
199.	Shanghai	2d.	261.	Ichang	1d.
200.	Tokyo	2d.	262.	Baltimore	1d.
201.	Tamatave	1d.	263.	Taganrog	1d.
202.	Mexico	1d.	264.	Oporto	1d.
203.	Chefoo	1d.	265.	Rio de Janeiro	1d.
204.	Nagasaki	5d.	266.	Galveston	1d.
205.	Cuba	1d.	267.	Tripoli	1d.
206.	Tunis	1d.	268.	Galatz	1d.
207.	Réunion	1d.	269.	Varna	1d.

No. 270.

Reference to previous Report, Annual Series No. 92.

UNITED STATES.

NEW ORLEANS.

Consul de Fonblanque to the Marquis of Salisbury.

My Lord,   New Orleans, February 7th, 1888.
 I HAVE the honour to enclose herewith my annual Trade Reports for this Consular district for the year 1887.
            I have, &c.
      (Signed)   A. de G. de FONBLANQUE.

TRADE REPORT, 1887.

Notwithstanding a long drought, and some labour strikes accompanied (as they usually are in this country) by rioting, the Louisiana agriculturist can look back with satisfaction on the result of his work during the year 1887. *Agriculture.*

The sugar crop has turned out phenomenally large, and promises to be fully 250,000 hogsheads, or 100,000 hogsheads more than last year, and this has been realised on cheaper terms. Not only has the crop been larger, but prices have been also materially higher, which will net to the planters about 7,000,000 dol. more than last season, exclusive of whatever increase there may be from molasses. Although the rice crop was small, fully 33 per cent. less than last year, prices have ruled 1 dol. 50 c. to 2 dol. higher per barrel for rough. Whatever may be the size of the cotton crop, the receipts in this market have been very heavy, with a larger per-centage of factors' cotton than we have had in several years. Besides, prices for cotton have ruled materially higher than last year, and consequently proved very profitable to producers. *Sugar. Cotton.*

According to Bradstreet's estimate the cotton crop in the States forming this Consular district is as follows, and (with the exception of Arkansas) shows an increase over last season. *Cotton crop.*

State.	Yield.	
	1886-7.	1887.
Alabama	770,000	773,000
Arkansas	695,000	638,000
Florida	55,000	55,000
Louisiana	475,000	485,000
Mississippi	925,000	1,034,000

UNITED STATES.

It must be remembered, however, that in Arkansas the farmer does not place his main reliance upon cotton, but cultivates hay, corn, and does a great deal of what is called "truck farming."

The United States' Department of Agriculture gives the acreage and produce thus:—

Comparative acreage and results.

	Acres. 1886.	Acres. 1887.	Bales. 1887.	Per Acre.	Pounds per Acre.
Florida	270,738	262,616	68,280	26	81
Alabama	2,828,713	3,809,599	805,355	287	143
Mississippi	2,548,674	2,548,674	973,593	382	181
Louisiana	1,035,781	1,066,854	461,948	433	210

Diffusion process. Some very interesting and important experiments have been made with a new process for extracting the saccharine matter from sugar-cane by diffusion, at the United States' Government Station at Magnolia Plantation. The result of two "strikes" is said to have been over 200 lbs. of sugar per ton of cane. The official reports have not yet been published: as soon as they are, I shall not fail to send them to the proper authorities for the information of those interested in sugar-making in the colonies.

Cultivation of ramie. Having received several applications for information respecting the cultivation of the Ramie plant from the West India Islands I beg to offer the following data from a practical hand.

Preparing the ground. "Grounds for Ramie-planting must be well-ploughed at the depth of at least 12 inches, thoroughly harrowed and then furrowed.

"The roots are to be planted in rows at a depth of from 5 to 7 inches, according to their length, and at a distance of 18 inches from each other.

Planting. "The planting can be done from February to the end of October, but in the hot season care must be taken to moisten the ground well during the first 14 days after planting. An occasional application of liquid manure, when the soil is not alluvial, will much improve the yield.

In the tropics. "In tropical countries it is best to run the furrows from east to west, in order to prevent the meridian sun drying out the soil. In a temperate, or semi-tropical climate, the direction of the furrows should be from north to south, as experience proves that a **Intemperate climates.** moist soil contributes largely to the growth of height of the plant, without furthering its formation of branches.

Weeding. "The first year of planting the Ramie, some attention must be paid to weeding; after that the vigorous and continuous growth of this perennial plant will subdue all encroaching weeds.

"To plant with a certainty of obtaining a good yield, it will take nearly 5,000 roots per acre.

Sowing the roots. "If you plant 20 acres in February, in the June following you can abstract roots from the 20 acres already planted; to plant out 300 acres more, for each planted root will yield 15 or more bulbs, that is to say, 1,000 planted roots will give, in less than six months, 15,000 roots.

First year. "In October of the first year's planting there will be a fair half-yield, yet it will be sufficient to give a large profit on outlay for labour, &c.

"The second year the planter will be able to cut three full crops, yielding about 20 tons of stalk to the acre of each crop. *Second year.*

"Take as a basis only two crops on 320 acres, your crops yield of 20 tons of stalk per acre, or 6,400 tons, or 12,800,000 pounds of stalk, 8 per cent. of which is marketable fibre,—computing at the lowest market price, will bring 8 c. per pound. *Profits.*

"Ramie can be propagated also from the stalk—for instance, when the stalks are well-grown and not quite ripe, lay them down and cover lightly with earth and they will root from every joint. This is important to know, for the call for roots at this moment makes it difficult to supply the demand. *Propagating from stalks.*

"There is little or no advantage to sow Ramie seed, for it requires two years to realise a favourable result. *From seed.*

"The maturity of the stalk and the time when fit for cutting is indicated by a brownish tint on the lower part of the stalk. *Time for cutting.*

"The Ramie must be decorticated perfectly ripe and dry as a bone; never decorticate Ramie in its green state, although it is unwisely advised by some persons. *Decorticating.*

"In gathering crop cut from two to three inches from the ground, and the leaves left on the ground will serve as a manure.

"Unlike cotton, and other of our southern products, the Ramie seldom or never requires renewing. When the plants once become established, they need little or no attention, further than occasionally fertilising if the land is poor." *Ramie is perennial.*

The same authority—General L. Sewell, of New Orleans—attributing the difficulty in late years of obtaining an appreciable supply of Ramie fibre to the fundamental error of attempting to decorticate the plant when in an unripe condition, says:—"In this opinion I am supported by the practical experience of Senator Feray. It stands to reason, with the stalk in its unripe state—not being matured—that the fibre cannot be as good as the fibre produced from the Ramie stalk when ripe, healthy and dry. Yet, the old error is pursued just like the Chinese themselves, who change nothing. Besides all the machines I have heard of or seen, have not the power to fibrise the Ramie stalk when at its maturity. Messrs. Seigfried, Gruner, and Anderson visited France and satisfied themselves that the Scheifner was a perfect machine in all that is claimed for it. So soon as Messrs. Edwards and Hanbtman have erected the machine the public will be invited to inspect it." *Decorticating unripe material. The Scheifner Decorticator.*

This machine has been erected and works well, but, unfortunately, a sufficient quantity of Ramie to make a thorough test of the system advocated cannot at present be obtained. Farmers will not plant this crop because they think that the machinery for utilising it is not perfected. The machinery cannot be perfected because there is not enough of the raw material to test it with: and so we go round in a vicious circle. *Lack of material for experiment.*

UNITED STATES.

Shipping.

RETURN of all Shipping at the Port of New Orleans in the Year 1887.

ENTERED.

Nationality.	Sailing. Number of Vessels.	Sailing. Tons.	Steam. Number of Vessels.	Steam. Tons.	Total. Number of Vessels.	Total. Tons.
British	75	67,403	392	469,071	467	536,474
American	97	38,680	304	382,503	401	421,183
Austrian	...	...	...	...	8	5,748
French	...	...	10	26,890	10	26,890
German	...	...	...	...	36	44,277
Italian	...	...	...	...	64	30,948
Mexican	1	215	12	1,674	13	1,889
Swedish-Norwegian	11	8,785	...	...	11	8,785
Spanish	...	...	...	...	76	91,041

CLEARED.

Nationality.	Sailing. Number of Vessels.	Sailing. Tons.	Steam. Number of Vessels.	Steam. Tons.	Total. Number of Vessels.	Total. Tons.
British	79	71,129	401	525,986	480	597,115
American	63	31,633	310	411,610	373	443,243
Austrian	...	...	...	...	10	8,072
French	...	...	10	26,890	10	26,890
German	...	...	...	...	34	41,913
Italian	...	...	...	...	63	28,356
Mexican	1	215	12	1,674	13	1,889
Swedish-Norwegian	8	5,083	...	...	8	5,083
Spanish	...	...	...	...	76	93,371

Increase of British shipping.

My returns of British shipping show the entrance of 467 ships of 536,474 tons; as against 372 ships of 444,554 tons in 1886—the best previous year on record. In that year, the entries in direct trade were 84 ships with cargo, and 111 in ballast—in the indirect trade, 75 with cargo, and 102 in ballast. In 1887, the direct entries with cargo were 103, and in ballast 38, and the indirect, with cargo 166, and in ballast 160. Of these latter, 30 cleared also in ballast, making only a nominal entry. It will be seen, therefore, that there must have been a considerable increase in the amount of outward freight gained by our ships.

Port charges.

New Orleans in comparison with other ports.

These remain unchanged since my last report on the subject, and I find that the Chamber of Commerce and other bodies are stating that the port of New Orleans does not compare unfavourably with other deep-water ports of the United States, except in the item of labour. I doubt if this statement will bear a practical test. Take the subject of wharfage for example. A ship may pay the same dues for wharfage here as would be charged her at another port; but how do the services given in return for such payments compare? Here she is moored to an open stage on which she must not place heavy cargo, lest it should break down the rickety structure. She has to pay extra for police, and cover up her cargo at harbour expense. Sometimes she has to subscribe towards mending the road which leads to her wharf, to make it passable for the cotton floats. The shipowner will have, therefore, to take these extras into consideration when he makes his calculations for freight or charter.

Extra charges.

Exports and imports.

The principal exports carried in British ships were:—

Exported.	Packages.	Quantity.
Cotton	Bales	1,016,166
Cotton-seed products—		
Cotton-seed oil	Barrels	10,478
„ „ cake	Sacks	529,683
„ „ meal	„	295,268
Corn	Bushels	6,283,042
Wheat	„	3,465,649

I find that the import of British dry goods (with the exception of Irish linens) is steadily decreasing. A fair quantity of steel rails have been imported, but other sorts of hardware are also on the decline. No serious steps have been taken towards a direct importation of cotton ties. On the other hand, I see that one of the articles recommended by me in former reports, *i.e.*, metal bedsteads (iron and brass) is making its appearance, and I understand that there is a brisk demand for this class of goods from Mexico. In my list of possible imports, I have now to add glass bottles for beer, of which a large quantity is brewed in New Orleans for export, also to Mexico and to Central and South America. A correspondence on this subject has been opened with a Liverpool firm, but there has been an unfortunate delay in sending out samples, which may divert a promising trade into German or Belgian hands. This leads me to repeat previous warnings that illustrated trade magazines and price-lists are of no use. Americans have been educated up to trading by sample in all cases where the thing offered for sale can be seen and handled. Any other plan involves a waste of paper, printing and postage. *[British dry goods and hardware declining. Cotton ties. Metal bedsteads. Glass bottles. Trade by sample.]*

For several years cotton stored on the levées and many of the ships engaged in loading it have been placed literally between two fires. On the river-side tugs and steamboats pass close by throwing up, not merely sparks, but masses of burning wood. I was once shown a charred mass, as large as my fore-arm, which had fallen, red hot, on the deck of a cotton-loading ship. On the land side, the locomotives of two lines of railway—"The New Orleans and Mobile," and "The Texas and Pacific"—are passing constantly, making up and shunting the goods traffic, and these also shed a liberal quantity of burning matter. Latterly a new danger has been added by the electric (Brush) lights, the glasses of which are constantly broken, so that the sparks occasioned by a temporary derangement of the connections, are blown about amongst the cotton bales. The number of ocean-going ships in which fires have occurred since the year 1886 is as follows:— *[Fires in cotton ships. Dangerous position of ships. Sparks.]*

UNITED STATES.

Number of late fires.

Year.	Number of ships.
1866	3
1867	1
1868	2
1869	2
1870	1
1872	4
1873	2
1874	1
1875	1
1876	3
1877	0
1878	2
1879	10
1880	8
1882	2
1883	4
1884	0
1885	1
1886	2
1887	9

Encouraged by salvage.

Case of the "Iron Cross."

In the years 1879–80, sums amounting to 71,300 dol. were awarded as salvage to the owners, officers, and crew of a steam-tug, called the "Protector." Other tugs, notably the "Ella Woods," also reaped a rich harvest out of the fires on board cotton ships. In June, 1880, three men were convicted of setting fire to the British ship "Iron Cross," and it was proved beyond the possibility of doubt that not only in this particular case, but also in a great many others, ships had been set on fire for the purpose of obtaining awards for salvage. The "Protector" Company has ceased to exist, the pretensions of other tugs have been discouraged, the right of the City Fire Association to claim compensation for services in ship fires has been disallowed, and therefore I am of opinion that the causes which led to so many disasters in 1879–80 must not be taken to explain the losses in 1887.

Fires in cotton in general.

Want of care, a cause.

It must be borne in mind that it is not only on sea-going ships that these fires have become so common. In gin houses, on railroad trains, on river steamboats, and in presses, an unprecedented destruction of cotton has taken place during the last six months of this year. I am afraid that want of ordinary care in all cases—be the origin an accident or a crime—a prime factor of the result. During the period I have mentioned, over 2,000,000 dol. worth of cotton has been destroyed by fire, thus—

Loss by fire in cotton.

	Dollars.
Greenville, Texas	200,000
Little Rock, Arkansas	245,000
Memphis, Tennessee (first fire)	175,000
Memphis, Tennessee (second fire)	650,000
Galveston, Texas	55,000
Bryan, Texas	40,000
Steamboat "Chouteau"	175,000
Steamship "Peninah"	55,000
Paris, Texas	5,000
Harriston, Mississippi	22,000
Waynesboro	6,000
Savannah, Georgia (ship)	500,000
Charleston, South Carolina (ship)	10,000
New Orleans, Louisiana (ships)	about 52,000

The *Vindicator*, a paper published in the interests of insurers is responsible for the following statement of the condition of seven presses and warehouses in this Consular district:—

Compress.—All barrels need filling. No water in buckets; several empty, and found scattered about lot. Regular pickery in north-east corner of premises. Loose cotton, paper, and trash all over the floor; lamp-room in very dangerous condition. Stove-pipe in office exposes cotton. Oily rags in lamp-room.

Compress.—No barrels or buckets. Not enough hose. Cotton is opened and picked in the yard. Loose hay on floor. One barrel near door. Four empty barrels on posts. One filled with loose cotton. Large quantity of loose cotton and trash near door.

Warehouse.—No barrels and buckets. Loose cotton piled in three corners. Floor very dirty.

Warehouse.—No barrels or buckets. Loose cotton piled near door.

Warehouse.—No barrels or buckets. Hay, oats, &c., stored here. Floor very dirty. Much loose cotton found here.

—— *Bros.' Storehouse.* Hay, oats, and other merchandise stored therein.

Warehouse.—No barrels or buckets. Every square yard of space covered with cotton just now. Hose was covered with bales of cotton, though in position. Inspector had bales lifted off and freed hose, and cautioned employés about keeping it free. Platform extending 80 feet to side track of railroad. Doors opening on same are plain, with no metal. With little good management and care, risk would be good one, as the water supply is good, and pressure sufficiently great.

Condition of cotton premises.

Want of precaution against fire.

The Captain of the New Orleans Fire Patrol thus reports of a press whose cotton is covered by a 100,000 dol. policy:—

Careless stowage of cotton.

"Owing to the very negligent methods observed in storing the cotton, I found this press to be in a very dangerous condition. Not only was there a very large quantity of cotton found in the open court, covering the greater part of its area, but a great deal was ranged and piled in such a manner that the fire-walls were rendered absolutely useless; and, after carefully looking over the court-room from various points, I found that not only a fire might spread throughout the whole premises, but that it would be almost impossible to prevent its doing so. I found that not only the cotton was piled far out into the court beyond the fire-walls, from one compartment to another, but in several cases the cotton was actually piled beyond the aprons of the sheds.

"I found that no station for a watch-clock had been located in the press-room. I found that the boiler-room was located directly inside of the press-room, and that the press-room was inadequately supplied with barrels and buckets.

"In the adjoining yard to this press, I found the same careless and dangerous storage. There were no hydrants and no hose in this yard. The entire area of the yard was covered with cotton, and should any fire get any headway, it would involve the whole premises, and keep the firemen out, as no one could possibly enter the court in such a case. The court in this yard is so circumscribed that, in my opinion, even if the regulations were faithfully complied with, there would still be much danger of a fire extending clear across the yard; and I am decidedly of the opinion that, in order to place this yard on a footing with the yards of the other presses, it would be necessary to provide the compartments with fire-doors."

A fire-trap.

Now the cotton stored for loading on board ship has not even this amount of protection.

UNITED STATES.

Rapidity of fire in cotton.

Those who have never seen a cotton fire have no idea how rapidly it spreads. At Savannah, the hands were turning out a lot of cotton for delivery, when fire burst forth from a bale and flashed so rapidly over the whole court that nine men and two women were unable to escape, and perished in the flames. I have satisfied myself, after a careful examination of cotton taken at random at various places, that much of this danger might be obviated by using an improved sort of bagging. This is the only thing about a bale of cotton that has not been the object of constant improvements. As soon as the pressure from without, which gives a bale of cotton its prescribed bulk, has ceased, and the ties have been applied, a pressure from within commences. Every fibre becomes a miniature spring, and seeks to free itself outwards. Examine a bale with a magnifying lens, and you will find that through every mesh of the bagging hundreds of minute filaments have thrust themselves. Over these fire will flash as though gunpowder had been spread on the surface, and (if there were nothing more substantial upon which it could feed) would flash and pass. But there are very few bales indeed, wherever found, which have not a tear in them, and loose cotton hanging out of it to take the flash and make it into a fire. Thus a lot of cotton is found to be in flames in half-a-dozen places within a minute or two of the first alarm, and this is supposed to be proof that an incendiary has been at work. Microscopic examination would show that the fire has run over the tops or sides of the bales and stayed only where it could find food.

Bad bagging.

Flashing fire.

Better sort of bagging required.

What, therefore, is required to check this particular source of danger is a closer fabric of bagging. I understand that there need be no increase of material. The same weight of hemp or jute would suffice, only it should be woven closer. If it were possible to induce the negro "rustabout" to be a little more dexterous with his cotton-hook (an instrument for turning bales, shaped something like a book-hook, but with a sharp point) bales would be less ragged, and consequently less inflammable.

Sparks from tugs, &c.

No protection for cotton bales.

Course of sparks in a bale.

Thanks to the exertions of Lloyd's Agent here, steps have been taken to compel the use of spark-interceptors on steam tugs and railway engines, and to have the electric lights on the levées better protected; but so long as cotton is stored on an open levée without material protection of any description (other than tarpaulins) it will be impossible to guard with any amount of efficiency against either carelessness or crime. A spark which has fallen upon a bale of cotton, burns downwards in the shape of an inverted cone, with the apex concealed by ashes, giving no notice of its silent progress either by heat or smoke for many days. At last some shock disturbs the ash, the air enters, and the fire blazes forth. Such an instance occurred in the cotton of the s.s. "Harrogate." A bale in which such an operation as I have attempted to describe had been going on, burst into flames in the slings, just as it fell into the hold. If the spark had had less headway, or the bale had been stowed with less disturbance, this ship might have shared the fate of the "City of Montreal."

Quarantine.

As the system mentioned by Dr. Holt, of the Louisiana Board of Health, has worked admirably, I beg to offer the following from his pamphlet.

THE QUARANTINE SYSTEM OF LOUISIANA.

System of Dr. Holt.

The quarantine system in the Mississippi is a system composed of three stations, the first of which is an advance-guard inspection station, situated at Port Eads, 110 miles below New Orleans, where the waters of South Pass are jettied into the gulf.

When an inward-bound vessel comes into the offing she is immediately boarded by a thoroughly-skilled medical officer, and a careful inspection is made of her sanitary record and present condition. *Inspection of ships.*

If from a non-quarantined port and all is well, she is given pratique, and goes on to the city. If from a quarantined port, but presenting a clean health-record of voyage, and no evidence of sickness of a dangerous or doubtful character, she proceeds to the upper quarantine station, situated on the left bank of the river, 70 miles below the city, where she is subjected to a full course of sanitary treatment, and is detained such length of time, not exceeding five days (except in rare instances wherein further observation may be deemed necessary) as the Board of Health may provide. *Observation and sanitary treatment.*

If, upon inspection of a vessel entering the river, she is found to be foul, she is at once remanded to the lower station, located on Pass à L'Outre, an unused outlet of the Mississippi, 103 miles below the city. The sick, if any, are at once removed to the hospital. The vessel, with the well on board, is dropped down stream a few hundred yards and anchored. In the meantime the quarantine tug-boat with its complete disinfecting outfit has been telegraphed for, and speedily arrives from the upper station, when the work of disinfection begins, and does not cease until the vessel has been subjected to the most rigorous application of the solution of the bichloride of mercury; her atmosphere below deck completely replaced with one heavily charged with sulphurous oxide, and every article of baggage and ship's wardrobe has been saturated with the mercurious solution. *Foul ships.* *Disinfection.*

A ship known to be infested with one of the three great pestilential diseases—small-pox, cholera, or yellow fever—can stand, and must endure extraordinary treatment, even if clothing is wetted and some articles damaged. *Damage to clothing.*

The immediate segregation of the sick and the well, and disinfection of the ship and all baggage (in the case of a cholera-infected vessel), extended to the disinfectant washing out, and refilling of the water-tanks, destruction of the food supply and re-victualling the vessel, constitute the treatment of an infected vessel at this station. The ship, together with all on board, is held for observation, a period of 10 days or more, according to circumstances, when she is released and proceeds to the upper station, where the processes of sanitary treatment are repeated with the addition of the use of moist heat applied to baggage, ship's apparel, &c. (which latter process will be described hereafter) and the vessel is then allowed to proceed to the city. *Cholera-infected ships.*

This course of treatment at the upper station, while probably unnecessary, is enforced purely as an extraordinary precaution.

Inasmuch as infected ships are the exceptions, but inasmuch also as the Board of Health will take no risk in the case of vessels from known infected or suspected ports, regardless of bills of health, the vast majority of vessels are treated at the upper station. *No risks taken.*

Arriving at this station the vessel is brought alongside the wharf. All on board officers, crew, and passengers, are at once sent ashore, where they find ample accommodation in commodious shelter, provided for their entertainment during the time occupied in the sanitary treatment of the ship and all baggage.

As soon as this is completed they are permitted to return aboard ship, where they remain under observation during the prescribed period determined by the remoteness or nearness of the port against which these precautions are taken. The object of this brief detention for observation, after the sanitary treatment of the vessel has been *Detention for observation.*

completed, is to allow for a probable outbreak of an infectious disease already incubating in the system of any one on board.

As an essential part of the service, there is a tugboat of sufficient power to move a sailing-vessel to or from the wharf.

Laboratory tug. In addition to this requirement, this boat is equipped with a complete outfit for generating and applying germ-destroying gas for displacement of the entire atmosphere within the ship, transported perhaps directly from some infected port. In the hold of this tug is constructed a wooden tank of 2000 gallons' capacity to hold the bi-chloride of mercury solution for the treatment of vessels in the lower quarantine, as described. This tank is furnished with a steam-pump (made of iron on account of the greater resistance of that metal to amalgamation) supplied with three-quarter inch rubber-hose.

In the sanitary treatment of a vessel in quarantine, there are three processes of disinfection concurrently applied.

Processes for disinfection. Use of bi-chloride of mercury. The first is the wetting of all available surfaces of the vessel, excepting cargo, but including bilge, ballast, hold, saloons, forecastle, decks, &c., with a solution of the bi-chloride of mercury, made soluble by an equal weight of muriate of ammonia, in the proportion of one part to 1000 of water.

The bold adoption of this poisonous agent in domestic, municipal, and maritime sanitation, at once called forth a flood of most gloomy forebodings of fearful effects upon the human system.

Our declaration at that time is confirmed by an experience of four years' trial on an immense scale, that our standard solution, as used in sanitation, is absolutely harmless to persons unless swallowed, it matters not how extensive or constant the contact. The only objection we have yet discovered is that certain articles, particularly blankets and flannels treated by the solution, sometimes become spotted, and colours liable to "run" when wetted suffer; but unlike all other chemical agents applied as disinfectants, the textile itself is in nowise injured.

Recapitulating its merits, being colourless, stainless (except as stated) odourless, not injurious to fabrics, perfectly safe to handle for months at a time, easily applied and exceedingly cheap, it is impossible to imagine a substance more efficient and as free from objection in practice. The amalgamating powers of the mercuric salt presented many serious obstacles in the contrivance of an apparatus for its application, all of which have been overcome without sacrificing simplicity, efficiency, or economy.

Immediately adjoining the quarantine wharf and near its water edge, is constructed a heavy framework of piles, each 12 ins. in diameter. This structure has an ample base, is pyramidal and 45 feet in height above mean level of the river.

Appliances for use of mercurical solution. On the top of this cover is placed centrally a 60-gallon wooden cask, in which is dissolved the mercuric salt, which is then emptied into the tank through a wooden faucet. 70 lbs. are used for one charge.

In the tank near the lower edge are three heavy galvanised-iron faucets, to each of which is screwed a lead of three-quarter inch, four-ply rubber-hose, the farther ends of which lie on the wharf. These are lengthened by additional sections to reach any part of the largest vessel. To the far extremity of each hose is attached a short wide nozzle, provided with a stop-cock.

During disinfection all three are simultaneously used fore, aft, and amidship.

Spraying with solution. For spraying, we use a perforated heavy block-tin rose, four inches across the face, similar to an ordinary watering-pot spray. These are made with a shank about six ins. long, to fit snugly into the open end of the pipe.

On a single vessel we average 1,500 gallons of solution, but often use 3000. The process requires from 30 minutes to two hours, according to circumstances.

As soon as the men have completed the work of "bi-chloriding" below decks, the fumigating-pipe is then extended from the quarantine tug-boat lying alongside. It is lengthened by sections, being fitted together like stove-pipe, and conducted down a convenient hatchway to the bottom of the hole, or as near the kelson as possible, preparatory to the fumigation of the entire vessel (and cargo if any) with sulphurous oxide. In the case of a sailing-ship one hatchway gives access of the sulphurous gas to the entire hold, but in large steamers the hold is subdivided by bulk heads into two or more distinct compartments which must be treated separately. *Fumigating.*

In undergoing treatment the cargo is not disturbed, except when the removal of bags of coffee is required to permit the passage of the fumigating-pipe, which is 12 inches in diameter, down into the dunnage at the bottom of the cargo. *Cargo undisturbed.*

I have given explicit instructions to coffee importers whereby the expense of removing bags to make this well or shaft through the cargo may be avoided. It is necessary to have an open framework-shaft, allowing a clear inside space of 15 inches, placed in the centre of the main-hatch in a sailing-vessel, or in the centre of each hatch in a steamship having bulkhead compartments. The framework of this shaft is set before loading, and should be cut flush with the top of the cargo. *Special instructions for coffee.*

This simple arrangement avoids all handling and delay.

When the connections are made, and the fumigating-pipe is arranged, the fan on the tugboat is started, and the process of displacing with sulphurous oxide the entire atmosphere within the ship begins. The length of time required to complete the fumigation varies from thirty minutes to three hours, according to size of vessel, number of compartments, &c. *Application of sulphurous oxide gas.*

The quantity of commercial roll sulphur used varies from one hundred to seven hundred pounds per vessel.

The apparatus invented for rapidly evolving, and supplying the germicidal gas consists in a battery of eighteen furnaces, each supplied with a pan to contain the sulphur during combustion. These furnaces open into a common reservoir, to the farther end of which is connected a powerful exhaust-fan.

The gas drawn by the fan is driven into a 12-inch galvanized-iron pipe, through which it is conducted over the side and down the hatchway of the vessel into the bottom of the hold.

The gas, as it is driven into the vessel, is quite hot, but would extinguish rather than create fire.

The outflow should not impinge directly against bags of coffee or bags of textiles if it can be avoided, in order to prevent formation of sulphuric acid and some slight injury therefrom at that point.

In treating coffee, and for convenience in some other instances, the vertical lead of pipe into the hold is made of asbestos cloth, closely and heavily woven for our purpose.

Every opening is closely battened during the process, and remains so for at least eight hours after it is discontinued.

The apparatus throughout is made ample in size and power for rapidity of work and economy in wear-and-tear by lessening velocity and friction. The fan is run by a special engine at a slow rate as compared with its capacity, but driving into the ship 180,000 cubic feet per hour of atmosphere surcharged with sulphurous oxide.

Treatment of clothes, bedding, &c.

While these two processes of sanitary treatment of the vessel are going on, all bedding, ship's linen, cushions, mattresses, flags, mosquito nets, curtains, carpets, rugs—all personal baggage and wearing apparel of whatever description, are removed from the ship to a commodious building in close proximity, in which these articles are treated by moist heat at a temperature of not less than 230° Fahrenheit.

Steaming apparatus.

The apparatus for this work consists in a steel 40 horse-power steam-boiler, for supplying steam to a super-heating chamber a few feet distant, and which I will now describe.

The dimensions of this chamber, taken interiorly or inside measure, are 60 feet long, 11 feet wide, and 7 feet high.

The framework is composed of 3 × 3-inch seasoned pine lumber, joined as in the construction of a frame-house. Upon the outside of this framework (and corresponding to weather-boarding in the case of a house) is nailed, tongued-and-grooved flooring material three-fourths of an inch thick by six inches wide.

The inside, or interior of the ends, rear and top of the chamber, is ceiled with the same material, and a flooring of the same is also laid. Upon these interior surfaces is tacked heavy "Russian hair-cloth or felting," and upon this, at intervals of three feet, are nailed parallel strips of wood $1\frac{1}{2}$ × 2 inches, and, in turn, upon these strips is fastened another sheathing or ceiling of flooring-plank as already described.

This secures an air-space between the air-cloth and inner ceiling. Upon this now smooth interior surface of wood is finally tacked and held in place by very broad-headed nails, or better, by nails supplied with tin discs or washers, a double layer of "Asbestos building felt," well-lapped and securely tacked, thus rendering the interior of the chamber fireproof.

Fireproof chambers.

By the foregoing described construction it will be seen that the walls of the chamber, which are 8 inches in thickness, consist of seven non-conducting media; first, the outer layer of planking; second, 3 inches of air-space; third, an inner ceiling of planking; fourth, 1-inch thickness of "Russian air-cloth;" fifth, $1\frac{1}{2}$-inch air-space; sixth, a third layer of $\frac{3}{4}$-inch planking; seventh, a double layer, or interior lining, of heavy asbestos felting.

The front wall is divided into forty panels, 18 inches wide each, which represents that number of racks contained within the chamber.

Upon the bars of these racks the clothing, &c., is hung for exposure to disinfection by moist heat.

These racks are constructed with a front and rear panel united by horizontal bars, six to each side. Each rack is suspended overhead on travelling rollers upon an iron rod which extends from the rear wall of the chamber to a support ten feet in front of the chamber, the rod therefore being twenty feet in length.

By this arrangement overhead the racks may be drawn out and pushed in with facility, thus avoiding tracks or rods on the floor obstructing the movements of employés.

When drawn out the full length of 10 feet, the rear panels of the racks securely close the chamber, as do the front panels when the racks are pushed in, thus admitting of the heating of the chamber during the time of hanging the articles of clothing, &c., on the rack-bars preparatory to disinfection.

For this admirable device and, indeed, for the entire skeleton of the super-heating chamber, including the dry-heat double steam-coils, we are indebted to the Troy Laundry Machinery Company, Chicago, Illinois. We have found the purchase of this apparatus, constructed to include certain of our specifications, to be the most economical and satisfactory we could have desired.

The interior surface of each front panel is lined with a layer of Russian hair-cloth, over which is applied a double layer of asbestos felting.

At intervals of 7½ feet, a bulkhead of 1-inch tongued-and-grooved flooring is constructed, subdividing the chamber into eight compartments. These bulkheads, or partitions, are made fire-proof by a covering of a double layer of asbestos felting. The object of this arrangement is to provide against the spread of fire in the event of its occurrence. *Fire-proof bulkheads.*

In addition to this provision there is a double lead of 1-inch fire-hose connected with a steam-pump near the boiler, and at all times ready within fifteen seconds' notice to turn on two streams of water upon any rack on which fire might have originated.

These minute specifications concerning provision against fire are particularly appreciated by ourselves. It cost us two fires and the destruction of a large amount of property to learn a lesson which experience alone could teach. Lacking experience and precedent these accidents could not have been foreseen, and therefore could not have been provided against. They were the result of an under-rating and failure to appreciate the prodigious force the contrivance invented placed at our will to invoke.

Under the present arrangement, including early use of free steam, fire is hardly possible, but if it should occur we are prepared to draw out instantly the burning panel, to strip it of clothing, and to put out the fire. With reasonable care and watchfulness on the part of the employés there need be absolutely no danger of loss by fire. *Precautions against fire.*

The super-heating of this chamber is so provided as to furnish at will dry or moist heat, or both, and by a turn of the hand a temperature of 300° F. can be obtained.

Within and at the end of this chamber next to, and connected with the boiler, are two manifolds, one above the other, to which is connected a system of forty-five three-quarter-inch steam-pipes (aggregating 5,509 lineal feet) placed horizontally near the floor of the chamber, running its full length, and supplied with a "bleeder" for conveying off the water of condensation. *Machinery for dry heat.* *Drainage.*

This double coil furnishes the dry heat.

Above and in close proximity to this system of pipes is extended a horizontal screen of galvanised-iron, one half-inch mesh, to catch and so prevent the coming in contact with the super-heating pipes, any article falling from the racks.

The moist heat is supplied by a 1-inch steam-pipe laid centrally in the midst of the above described dry-heat pipes, and running the entire length of the chamber, constituting a steam-main connected with the boiler, and controlled, as the others, by a ball-valve on the outside. *Machinery for moist heat.*

This pipe is perforated by 81 twelve-inch holes, so placed as to furnish steam to each rack.

During the time of hanging the articles of clothing, etc., on the racks the dry heat is turned on, and the temperature raised to about 190° F., made known by a thermometer having a large mercurial column, and suspended near the centre of the chamber, working on a slide or travelling-rod in such a manner when it is desired to make a reading, as to allow of being drawn forward (by a cord extending outside) to a long, narrow pane of glass set in the panel. This thermometer should have a scale of at least 275° F. *Application of dry heat.*

As each rack is filled it is put back into place. By the time the last of the articles have been hung on the racks, the entire mass of the material within the chamber has attained a temperature between

Application of moist heat. 190° and 200° F., when free steam is turned on. The thermometer speedily rises to a point between 230° and 240° F., at which it is maintained for a period of 20 minutes.

The steam-pressure in the boiler at the beginning of this process registers between 100 and 110 lbs. by the steam-guage; at the end of the process of blowing-in steam the pressure will have fallen to about 60 lbs.

The steam is now entirely cut off from the chamber, the racks are drawn out, and their contents removed.

During the process of steaming every article is perceived to be saturated and intensely hot, the steam freely permeating to the interior of mattresses, double blankets, &c., but so great is the heat in the texture of the fabrics as to immediately expel all moisture upon drawing the racks and exposure to the open air. Shirts, collars, &c., instantly assume the crisp dryness they possessed before exposure, losing the musty smell of long packing in a trunk. Silks, laces, the most delicate woollen goods, show no signs of injury whatever from the treatment.

Of course, articles of leather, rubber, and whalebone would be injured by the heat, and are therefore disinfected with the mercuric solution, and not permitted to go into the heated chamber.

Time required. Time required to charge chamber with apparel for disinfection, thirty minutes; time required for moist heat, twenty minutes; for removal of articles, fifteen minutes; a total of sixty-five minutes.

A large steamship, particularly a passenger vessel, may require two or three charges of the chamber. Amount of coal consumed, from two to four barrels per vessel.

Quarantine regulations. The following are the requirements imposed upon all vessels arriving at the quarantine stations in the State of Louisiana during the quarantine period, beginning about May 1st and ending October 31st.

All vessels arriving at the several quarantine stations in the State, together with their crews, passengers, and their cargoes, shall be subjected to the inspection of the quarantine officers at the said stations.

All vessels, together with their cargoes, crews, passengers, and baggage arriving at the Mississippi quarantine station from inter-tropical, American, and West Indian ports, shall be subjected to thorough maritime sanitation, according to the following schedule:—

Classification of ships.
First Class.—Vessels arriving from non-infected ports.
Second Class.—Vessels arriving from suspected ports.
Third Class.—Vessels arriving from ports known to be infected.
Fourth Class.—Vessels which, without regard to regard to port of departure, are infected; that is to say, vessels which have yellow fever, cholera, or other contagious or infectious diseases on board at time of arrival, or have had same on voyage.

Vessels of the first class to be subjected to necessary maritime sanitation at the upper quarantine station, without detention of either vessels or persons, longer than may be necessary to place such vessels in perfect sanitary condition.

Vessels of the second and third classes to undergo the same conditions, together with detention for observation for a period of five full days from hour of arrival in quarantine.

Vessels of the fourth class to be remanded to the lower quarantine station, there to undergo sanitation and detention of vessels and persons such length of time as the Board of Health may order.

The five days' detention, as above provided, shall apply to all ports of the Gulf of Mexico and the Caribbean Sea, exception being made in regard to vessels coming from ports south of the Equator, whose period of detention shall be three days.

All vessels arriving from Mediterranean or other ports known or suspected to be infected with cholera, or which may hereafter become infected, shall be subjected to maritime sanitation and such detentions as the Board of Health may determine. *From cholera ports.*

Vessels arriving from the above-named ports and places, and belonging to the second, third, or fourth class—as set forth in the foregoing schedule—shall not be allowed to pass the Rigolets, or Atchafalaya quarantine stations, or other State quarantine stations which may hereafter be established, without having undergone a period of forty days and thorough cleaning and disinfection.

Special Suggestions to Owners, Agents, Masters of Vessels and Passengers.

The Louisiana State Board of Health recommends the following suggestions to agents, owners, masters of vessels, and passengers for the purpose of facilitating the work of quarantine officers and reducing the period of detention to a minimum:— *Suggestions to owners, &c., of ships.*

1. That vessels should be stripped during the quarantine season of all woollen hangings, carpets, curtains, and such-like materials, and upholstered furniture—as far as practicable. Hair or moss mattresses to be replaced by wire or wicker beds. *Shippers' woollens.*

2. That, as far as possible, vessels trading with tropical ports should be manned with acclimated crews. *Acclimated crews.*

3. Masters of vessels, ship and Consular agents are earnestly requested to instruct passengers from quarantinable ports to dispense, as far as possible, with baggage which may be injured by wetting, in case of pestilential outbreak on board, while undergoing disinfection. Such passengers are especially warned against bringing silks, laces, velvets and other fabrics of delicate texture, as they will be compelled to assume all risks of injury. *Passengers' baggage.*

4. While in ports infected with yellow fever, vessels should be anchored out in the harbour, when this is possible, and the crew prohibited from going ashore, especially at night. *Keep crews on board.*

5. When practicable, cargoes should be loaded in such a manner as to allow access to the pumps, and also to enable the quarantine officials to pump out and wash the bilge. *Loading cargo.*

6. Special attention should be given to cleanliness of vessels and persons, and provision should be made for all possible ventilation of the entire vessel. The best disinfectants and instructions for using the same can be obtained by application to the Board of Health or any of its officers. *Cleanliness.*

7. Masters should, before arrival, see that the bilge is thoroughly pumped out and cleansed, and that the entire vessel be put in such good sanitary condition as to permit of the least possible detention. Fruit-vessels, particularly, should be kept thoroughly cleansed for the purpose of avoiding delay at the quarantine station. *Bilges to be pumped.*

8. Vessels observing the above recommendations will receive special considerations at the quarantine station, detention and cost of cleaning, disinfecting, &c., being materially lessened thereby.

PENSACOLA.

Mr. Vice-Consul Howe reports as follows on the Timber and Lumber Trade of Pensacola:— *British merchants interested in wood trade of Pensacola.*

As a topic of interest, I believe, to many commercial houses in the

(354)

Pitch-pine trade keeps steadily on. Supply equal to demand.

United Kingdom engaged in trade with Pensacola, it affords me much pleasure to be able to give such a report of this post for the past year as will compare favourably with my reports for several years preceding, as regards the staple export—pitch-pine wood. Pensacola keeps steadily on in her pitch-pine trade, and, enormous as the yearly out-put continues to be, the supply is always equal to the demand, without any decrease at present to be looked for in this extensive trade by lack of demand or supply; inasmuch as the markets of the world steadily continue to consume this very desirable wood in its several preparations, and the timber continues to be freely gathered for market. It will be seen by the statement under the head of principal articles of export in this report, that the greatest portion of the exports in pitch-pine wood from Pensacola continues to the United Kingdom; and it is believed that some British firms are interested in the cargoes of pitch-pine timber and lumber that form a large portion of the shipments from Pensacola to some places in South America—Uruguay and the Argentine Republic.

Greatest portion to United Kingdom. British firms believed to be interested in shipments to other markets.

The Timber Trade.

Great Britain the chief centre for pitch-pine. Pensacola the greatest shipping port. Information about Florida's timber supply.

In view of the apparent fact above referred to, and as made manifest in these reports from year to year, that Great Britain is the great centre for the consumption of the pitch-pine wood of this section of the Southern States, (Pensacola being by far the greatest outlet for such commodity from Florida's hitherto—and at present—large supply of pitch-pine wood, as well as being the foremost by far in this trade of any port), it may be interesting in this commercial report for commercial purposes to give, for the information and consideration of those in the United Kingdom engaged in this wood trade (in the handling of shipments, and by the employment of British vessels in the carrying of such cargoes) a statement of "Florida's timber supply," extracted from the "Times-Union," a leading newspaper published in Jacksonville, Florida:—"To Florida the most important publication issued from the Department of the Interior giving the results of the last census is the Forestry Bulletin, No. 2, which gives the estimated amount of merchantable pine timber standing on May 2nd, 1880. From that publication has been compiled the following table giving the timber supply of Florida by counties, which will be found both interesting and valuable.

[Here follow the names of 34 counties giving the timber supply in Florida, on May 2nd, 1880, as equal to 6,615.000,000 ft., board measure.]

"The total as given in this table was the amount of merchantable pine-timber standing at the date of this report, namely, May 3, 1880. In the same report the amount cut during the year ending in May, 1881, is estimated at 208,054,000 ft. Assuming that this represents the average annual amount that has been cut during the six years since the date of the report, we have an aggregate of 1,248,324,000 ft. This amount, of course, is to be deducted from the total that was standing in 1880, which would leave standing in 1886, 5,366,676,000 ft.

"These figures furnish a basis for an estimate of the time when the pine-timber supply of Florida will be exhausted at the present rate of consumption. Multiplying the annual cut, namely, 208,054,000 ft., by 26 we have a product of 5,409,404,000 ft. Deduct this from the amount which, as shown above, was standing in 1886, and we find that at the end of 26 years there would be a deficit of 42,728,000 ft."

The foregoing statement is, I suppose, to be accepted as about correct as regards Florida's timber supply, but I must also point out that shipments of pitch-pine from Pensacola are largely composed of wood brought here by railroad and water-course from the immediately adjacent State of Alabama; and it is said that the supply of wood from this quarter may be relied on for quite as many years as the Florida supply is expected to last—hence it appears that the pitch-pine trade of Pensacola is good for over 50 years yet. *Pitch-pine from Alabama shipped through Pensacola.*

My reference to the present and expected supply of pitch-pine timber is intended, in addition to giving that information, to show that the wood does not appear to be inexhaustible. The pitch-pine forests are of spontaneous growth, indigenous to the sandy soil of the portions of the Southern States where the timber most abounds, principally hereabout. It is estimated "that the timber supply of the pine regions increases at the rate of about five per cent. per annum; but, in Florida, with its loose methods of firing the woods and cutting down timber which is never used for commercial purposes, this annual increase is more than offset by the annual waste." *The supply not inexhaustible. Supposed increase in growth of timber per year.*

As further to show the considered value of pitch-pine wood in comparison with other pine-timber, I take from the publication, "Facts about Florida," the following Government test, recently issued by the Department of the Interior of the United States' Government in the "Reports on the Forests of North America," showing the results of experiments as to the relative value of the different kinds of white and yellow (pitch-) pine. *Government test of pitch-pine.*

	Co-efficient of elasticity, kilogrammes or milomètres.	Ultimate transverse strength in kilogrammes.	Ultimate resistance to longitudinal pressure in kilogrammes.	Ultimate indentations to 1·27 milomètres in kilogrammes.
Pinus strobus (white pine)	·851	·267	6·219	1·194
Pinus resinosa (Norway pine)	1·132	·341	7·274	1·353
Pinus tarda (Loblolly pine)	1·128	·377	6·834	1·719
Pinus metis (Arkansas pine)	1·375	·443	7·628	2·064
Pinus palustris (Florida long-leaf yellow pine)	1·488	·490	10·074	2·508
Quercus alba (white oak)	·971	·386	8·183	3·388
Quercus rubra (red oak)	1·137	·422	8·172	2·825

In the official report, the long table showing the behaviour of these woods under transverse strain, give the first rank in this regard to *pinus palustris*, even above oak. As these tests were made by Government officials, who, without doubt, had no desire to be partial to any kind of wood, the statement that yellow-pine is deservedly growing in popular favour, cannot be gainsaid. *Strength of pitch-pine.*

Exports and Imports.

The tabulated statement in this report shows the business of Pensacola, for the past year in exports, to have been about the usual average in comparison with the export trade for years gone by. *Last year's exports about usual average.*

As regards imports, several cargoes of steel rails were brought here during the past year from England. Also, some cargoes of fertiliser—superphosphate—were received from England to be sent forward to the cotton-planting centres. Several cargoes of salt were also received from Liverpool during the year, to be sent forward to large salt-dealing houses in the States adjacent to Florida. *Cargoes of steel rail from England.*

The chief articles of every-day necessaries of life, as well as nearly all descriptions of general merchandise, as stated from time to time in my previous reports, are brought here by railroad principally, from the large northern, western, and southern markets of the United States. *Every-day commodities from markets in the United States.*

UNITED STATES.

Goods of English manufacture brought from large markets of the United States. Among these supplies it is to be reasonably supposed that fair quantities are of English, Scotch, and Irish manufacture, secured from the large houses north and west, that import largely from the United Kingdom.

RETURN of Principal Articles of Export from Pensacola during the Years 1886–1887.

Articles.	1887. Quantity.	1887. Value. £ s. d.	1886. Quantity.	1886. Value. £ s. d.
Pitch-pine lumber	131,004,501	327,511 5 0	108,125,487	270,313 14 4
Sawn pitch-pine timber	8,651,456	198,262 10 8	8,317,683	190,613 11 4
Hewn ,, ,,	935,889	21,447 9 1	935,078	19,480 15 10
Cotton	3,446	34,747 3 4	1,475	14,596 7 1
Rosin	305	79 8 6	4,434	1,154 13 6
Other articles	...	3,279 10 7	...	2,019 7 2
Total	...	585,327 7 2	...	498,178 9 6

The following, as regards the above table of exports, is descriptive of the values, quantities, weights, and measures; the conversion of money into sterling being at the rate of 4 dol. 80 c. per 1*l*. Lumber at average of 12 dol. (2*l*. 10*s*.) per 1,000 superficial feet; sawn timber at average of 11 c. (5½*d*.) per cubic foot—basis 40 feet average; hewn timber at average of 11 c. (5½*d*.) per cubic foot—basis 100 cubic feet average; cotton at average of 10 c. (5*d*.) per lb. in bales of 484 lbs. average weight each bale; rosin, in barrels, at 1 dol. 25 c. (5*s*. 2½*d*.) per barrel.

RETURN of Principal Articles of Imports to Pensacola during the Years 1886–1887.

Articles.	1887. Value. £ s. d.	1886. Value. £ s. d.
Chief articles	..	..
Other	27,955 9 8	8,629 10 0

NOTE.—The chief articles received at Pensacola are considered to be breadstuffs, grocery goods, hardware, and things generally required as necessaries of life, which goods are received from the large northern, southern, and western markets of the United States. In addition, may be added, as also received from ports in the United States, railroad iron, fertilisers, ice, &c. It is calculated that the entire value of the receipts referred to is not less than 2,000,000 dol. per year. The exact quantities and values cannot be arrived at by me, as no record of such is kept. As regards other articles of import, for which the value is given, they comprise steel rails, superphosphate, salt, &c., which things are mostly from the United Kingdom.

TABLE showing the Total Value of all Articles Exported from Pensacola, and Imported to Pensacola, from and to Foreign Countries during the Years 1886 and 1887.

Country.	Exports. 1887.	Exports. 1886.	Imports. 1887.	Imports. 1886.
	£ s. d.	£ s. d.	£ s. d.	£ s. d.
United Kingdom	224,107 18 0	167,800 16 2	24,355 16 8	7,117 0 0
Argentine Republic	78,129 2 0	34,010 12 11	...	...
Uruguay	45,168 3 0	16,878 1 9	...	...
Italy	40,747 2 9	49,496 11 10	...	...
France	24,279 14 9	23,430 16 4	...	...
Netherlands	20,067 4 10	32,912 13 10	...	...
Spain and Colonies	18,389 18 3	24,405 16 10	...	...
Brazil	14,399 9 5	8,430 17 11	...	...
Belgium	12,279 7 2	11,393 9 6	...	...
United States of Colombia	8,147 10 0	12,647 14 2	...	...
Portugal	8,063 5 8	2,527 10 8	...	...
Germany	2,819 11 8	16,676 16 7	...	...
Other countries	1,428 19 8	2,257 13 11	3,599 13 0	1,512 10 0
Foreign countries—Total	498,027 7 2	402,869 12 5	27,955 9 8	8,629 10 0
Ports in the United States—Total	87,300 0 0	95,308 17 1	*	*
Total	585,327 7 2	498,178 9 6	27,955 9 8	8,629 10 0

* As stated elsewhere in this report, the value of imports from the cities in the United States to Pensacola cannot be arrived at, but the receipts from those markets are calculated at over 2,000,000 dol. per annum, comprising chief articles of import.

Shipping.

This being a subject of much interest in the United Kingdom and Canada, I am induced to refer to the decrease somewhat in British tonnage at Pensacola within the last few years, and to give my opinion as to the causes of such decrease, though temporary, as I believe it to be. It is true that timber freights from Pensacola have been quite low for some time past, and British shipowners have not appeared to seek the business, or to trouble themselves about it, and vessels under the Italian, and Swedish and Norwegian flags have taken the place of the comparatively reduced British tonnage lately at Pensacola. But another way for accounting in part for the falling-off of British tonnage at Pensacola, may be by reason of the fact that many of the old timber-carrying British wooden vessels—in the general carrying trade—that were employed in the Pensacola trade years ago have been sold, and continue to be sold by their British owners to Norwegian and Swedish shipping people principally; and many of the same vessels so disposed of now load here with pitch-pine cargoes, their present owners accepting readily low rates, possibly in many instances being the means of lowering the rates of freight, and able to do so with profit to themselves through low investments in the increase of their tonnage. 1 allude particularly to the sale of British vessels that were owned in the United Kingdom. The British vessels so sold may have been in many cases disposed of as unfit, or as soon to become unfit for further service, according to certain requirements of British law; yet here are the same vessels still plying in this trade under their changed flag (I am informed that in some cases it is managed so that only the flag is changed, but not the British ownership) to the seeming injury of staunch and desirable British vessels. I believe it may be stated that one-fifth or one-fourth of the vessels that have loaded at Pensacola within the last few years under the Norwegian and Swedish flag were formerly under the British flag, and were, if not wholly, mostly owned in the United Kingdom, and the transfers thus appear to be yearly in-

Marginal notes: Decrease somewhat in British shipping at Pensacola lately. Supposed causes of such decrease. British vessels sold to parties in Norway and Sweden. Large portion of Swedish and Norwegian vessels that now load at Pensacola formerly under British flag.

(354)

creasing. During the past year 133 wooden sailing-vessels loaded at Pensacola under the Swedish and Norwegian flag, about one-third of which, I am informed (and have no doubt of, by their names and large tonnage) were formerly under the British flag.

If my propositions are correct (and in making this statement I have, independent of my own observation, sought information on the subject) as regards the withdrawal of British vessels, and if the same vessels are placed under other flags under such circumstances as to bring them in unfair competition with British vessels; or if for any reason the competition contributed to should cease, may not this subject be one for consideration by those in the United Kingdom mostly concerned?

British tonnage expected to be again well represented in Pensacola.

British steamships in Pensacola trade.

Again, as regards British vessels, particularly those of the United Kingdom, I look for the time, as the wooden sailing-vessels continue to reduce in number, and as few of such class are now being built in Great Britain to take their place, when steamers will be so constructed as to be well-fitted for the timber-carrying trade; and as steamships will, in course of time, be more acceptable in the Pensacola trade—in these days of rapid movement—the largest proportion of the carrying business hence will be, I believe, by steamers, and by steamers of the United Kingdom as a natural sequence. A few British steamers have loaded at this port annually for some years past. Also iron sailing-vessels will, I think, be brought into this trade—one or two per year load here now, one recently with cotton. The attention of British steamship owners may be well given, I think, to the foreign carrying trade of Pensacola, which has required, as a yearly average for some years past, about 275,000 tons. This trade surely will not decrease, but is more likely to advance yearly, and continue for a long time yet.

Carrying trade of Pensacola worth looking after by British shipowners.

Yearly average tonnage at Pensacola.

The yearly average tonnage of vessels loaded at Pensacola for the past eleven years—the term of my service at this post—may be put at about 340,000 tons. Of that yearly average tonnage there was a yearly average in number of 103 British vessels—about 84,000 tons. About a yearly average in number of 160 American vessels aggregating about 66,000 tons. The remaining yearly average was about 277 vessels in number of all other flags of about 190,000 tons, of which latter yearly average in number and tonnage vessels under the Norwegian and Swedish flag were largely in advance of other nationalities.

RETURN of all Shipping at the Port of Pensacola in the Year 1887.

ENTERED.

Nationality.	Sailing. Number of Vessels.	Sailing. Tons.	Steam. Number of Vessels.	Steam. Tons.	Total. Number of Vessels.	Total. Tons.
British	76	71,144	5	6,225	81	77,369
American	145	67,253	...	...	145	67,253
Swedish and Norwegian	133	104,731	...	...	133	104,731
Italian	100	66,993	...	...	100	66,993
Russian	30	20,457	...	...	30	20,457
Austrian	19	14,766	...	...	19	14,766
German	6	5,450	...	...	6	5,450
French	4	2,187	...	...	4	2,187
Other countries	7	4,105	...	...	7	4,105
Total	520	357,086	5	6,225	525	363,311
,, for the year preceding	462	289,626	4	4,326	466	293,952

CLEARED.

Nationality.	Sailing. Number of Vessels.	Sailing. Tons.	Steam. Number of Vessels.	Steam. Tons.	Total. Number of Vessels.	Total. Tons.
British	65	59,766	5	6,225	70	65,991
American	144	65,695	...	...	144	65,695
Swedish and Norwegian	136	95,694	...	...	136	95,694
Italian	101	64,721	...	...	101	64,721
Russian	35	23,564	...	...	35	23,564
Austrian	16	11,887	...	...	16	11,877
German	6	5,450	...	...	6	5,450
French	6	3,920	...	...	6	3,920
Other countries	10	5,263	...	...	10	5,263
Total	519	335,950	5	6,225	524	342,175
,, for the year preceding	479	310,561	4	4,326	483	314,887

General Remarks.

In view of the letters that I receive from time to time from parties in the United Kingdom inquiring about this portion of the Southern States—Florida generally—I may be allowed to diverge from statements as regards my immediate post, and to go a little further into Florida matters so far as I am able. — Inquiries received about Florida.

The opportunities at Pensacola and its vicinity are few for persons of the labouring class arriving from abroad, a large portion of the chief employment being the manufacture of timber and lumber by the mills for shipment, unskilled labour being used to a large extent in this industry. In handling and loading cargoes of timber and lumber in vessels for shipment, unskilled labour is also mostly employed, and in these two branches of employment connected with the Pensacola trade, it may be said that the labour is more than abundantly supplied. Another industry that calls for unskilled labour to a large extent throughout Florida, is the felling, gathering together, and bringing to market from the forests the pitch-pine timber for preparation for the trade; but this industry is, and ever has been in the hands of a certain class of people peculiarly adapted to such work, and who, entirely owing to all of its surroundings, actually, I believe, control this branch of Pensacola trade. Most of the labourers — Opportunities for labourers from abroad limited. Industries connected with trade of Pensacola. People of this Southern country better adapted to the work.

UNITED STATES.

Skilled labour abundant.

are, to a large extent, of Florida and the adjacent portion of this Southern country; and a large portion of them are of the coloured or negro race. The gangs that work on the ships in port are divided according to rules of the several labour societies into equal numbers of black and white labourers. In skilled labour, such as carpenters, bricklayers, blacksmiths, &c., Pensacola is abundantly supplied.

Population of Pensacola increases yearly.

The population of Pensacola advances yearly, and the increase is particularly by persons from the milling and timber regions of the nearby Southern States, and from the Western States, and some people from the Northern States. Some of the new-comers are here for the purpose of seeking employment, and seeking chances for investment of capital; others of them come seeking residence in a milder climate.

Ten years ago, population 5,000. Now 13,000. Will be a cotton-shipping port. Population and industries will increase. Information for inquiries.

Ten years ago the population of Pensacola was little over 5,000; it has kept on increasing yearly, however, and it may be said that from 12,000 to 13,000 persons actually reside here now. With Pensacola regularly as a cotton shipping port, in addition to its present staple trade (and it will be a cotton shipping port, it is said, on the completion of the Pensacola and Memphis Railroad), the population of Pensacola would, I think, rapidly increase, and, in turn, many industries —now spoken of—would no doubt be in operation.

To go further into Florida, for the information of inquirers generally, I may state that, in agricultural pursuits, the field, I believe, is quite limited, and the results from such occupation would not, I think, be sufficiently remunerative to those who would require quick returns for any limited means at their disposal. To those well enough off, and simply seeking a change of climate, and able to make outlays without inconvenience, and await returns, there may be investments and operations that would prove satisfactory. Much is stated and circulated about Florida, and sometimes greedily caught at by those unsettled in life, and, for many reasons, desiring to change their places of abode and occupation; but I cannot but caution them against hasty movements. There may be openings in Florida for the investment of money in orange groves and other things, still it would be better, at least so I must advise, that parties having in view the investment of capital in Florida, and settlement in the State, should first visit and satisfy themselves by judicious investigation on the spot before concluding arrangements to emigrate.

Good climate.

As regards climate and every other conceivable thing towards the enjoyment of life, I may say that there are many parts of the State of Florida that would come up to all that could be so desired. I give from "Facts about Florida" some remarks about "West Florida, its location and productions":—

"West Florida has been in no respect an agricultural country, for the reason that heretofore the timber interest has absorbed the entire energies of the country; and, before the construction of the Pensacola and Atlantic Railroad, necessary transportation was wanting.

"The timber wealth is on the surface, but, under the surface, lies hidden wealth, which is yet to be dug out of the soil. The climate is semi-tropical, and devoid of extremes in heat and cold. The completion of the Pensacola and Atlantic Railway through a wilderness has made known its attractions and advantages, and, already, the entire line is dotted with happy homes, churches, schools, and villages. Great fertility by virtue of soil, much of the lands of West Florida do not possess, though some of the richest is within her limits, nor can the combination of extreme fertility and health be found in any new country.

"The 'scuppernong' grape deserves some mention here. Lord Raleigh landed in North Carolina, near Newbern, nearly two centuries ago. He there tasted the scuppernong for the first time, from a vine still in existence, which, three years ago, it is said, yielded 42 barrels of wine."

Mobile, Alabama.

Mr. Vice-Consul Barnewall reports as follows:—

Commercial year commencing September 1, 1886, and ending August 31, 1887. Receipts, 216,142 bales, valued at 9,655,063 dol. 14 c., against 248,526 bales, valued at 10,713,955 dol. 86 c., receipts of the year preceding. Average price per bale 44 dol. 67 c., average price per lb., 8 dol. 97 c., against 43 dol. 11 c. per bale, and 8 dol. 59 c. per lb. the year preceding. *Cotton receipts. Prices.*

This important and growing branch of business of Mobile and South Alabama continues to grow, and the trade of the past year has been larger than for a number of years. Our lumber mills did a good business the past season, and there has been a general improvement in plant, new and improved machinery added, and capacity increased. *Lumber.*

Total foreign exports 12,160,235 feet, valued at 142,439 dol. 94 c., against 14,513,648 feet, valued at 170,418 dol. 30 c. last year, coastwise 17,185,995 feet, against 6,777,805 last year.

The foreign exports, owing to the moderate supply of foreign tonnage, and the situation of the European markets, show a decrease, while the shipments coastwise exhibit a sharp increase, especially to northern ports, for to New York alone there were 9,000,000 feet against 3,000,000 feet last year.

Another year has passed in this important branch of business, but the statement of exports given herewith, would, no doubt, lead many to believe that there has been a decrease in the pitch-pine trade of this section, which is not so. *Timber*

The shipments of timber to Europe have been checked by various causes, many of them unavoidable, especially in sawn-timber, for the mills the past season, owing to steadily increased demand in the West for yellow pine, found it more profitable in shipping in that direction, as well as to other parts of the United States. Shippers had also to contend with a moderate supply of tonnage on this side, and low prices on the other side, and European markets well stocked. The low prices caused shippers to curtail shipments until prices improved on the other side, as I am informed has been the case in hewn timber, especially for timber of large average girth and cubical contents; all that came to market were readily sold at good prices, the supply, however, was curtailed by low rivers, but as logging railroads are now being built, there will, no doubt, be a good supply this season. One of the most important facts in this trade, is that the timber merchants have recently formed an association which have now rules, a classification, and other laws necessary for carrying on the trade successfully the present season. They have adopted a new form of charter covering the various expenses arising from loading vessels at this port, which being much reduced are more acceptable to shipowners, and it is believed that tonnage will be ample and more easily obtained for the increasing business of the port.

Since September 1, there has been a very marked improvement in the timber business, and those engaged in it look with confidence to a profitable and active trade.

UNITED STATES.

Naval stores. The naval store trade continues to be an important branch of business in this Section, and in Sections tributary to Mobile are many stills in operation, situated on the Mobile, and Ohio and Mobile, and Montgomery railways, the Bigbee, Alabama, and Mobile rivers, and on the eastern shore in Baldwin County.

Rosin and turpentine. Receipts: rosin 172,470 barrels, turpentine 40,149 barrels, total value 820,691 dol.; against rosin 175,817 barrels, turpentine 38,733 barrels, total value 1,034,682 dol. the year preceding.

Vegetable shipments. Value. This is a very important industry in this section, as shown by the value of shipments for the year 1886–87, 309,359 dol. against 161,025 dol. 73 c. the preceding year. 33⅓ per cent should be added for shipments from Mobile County not included in above.

My last Consular Report of 1886, gave a full account of the rise and progress of Alabama in commerce and manufactures.

The immense strides of new enterprises and extension of old ones, continue to attract universal attention. This phenomenal progress is not a mere "boom" of any one section, but a steady advance all through the State. As the knowledge of her wonderful success and capabilities increases and spreads, her distinguished future becomes more clear and determined, and it will not be long before her climate, soil, and mineral wealth will make her inferior to none in prosperity and importance.

Real estate. Mobile during the past year feels much encouraged, all branches of business have been satisfactory. In real estate, large transactions have taken place. Purchasers of last year have, in several instances, realised from 25 to 30 per cent. profit; home people are not the only operators in the field, but capitalists from abroad are still hunting and securing options, and her future prosperity is an assured fact.

Shipping. For the year ending December 31, 1887, there have been entered at this port 12 British steamers, total tonnage 14,946; this marks a beginning of a new era in her shipping, all of the said steamers have loaded with cotton at the city wharves, drawing 16 to 17 feet, and passed down the channel without delay.

Annex A.—RETURN of all Shipping at the Port of Mobile in the Year 1887.

ENTERED.

Nationality.	Sailing. Number of Vessels.	Sailing. Tons.	Steam. Number of Vessels.	Steam. Tons.	Total. Number of Vessels.	Total. Tons.
British	39	29,023	12	14,946	51	43,969
American	24	6,019	...	...	24	6,019
Swedish	6	4,416	...	...	6	4,416
Italian	1	626	...	...	1	626
Spanish	2	733	...	...	2	733
German	2	1,332	...	...	2	1,332
Austrian	2	815	...	...	2	815
Honduras	6	240	...	...	6	240
Russian	4	2,661	...	...	4	2,661
Norwegian	12	7,639	...	...	12	7,639
French	1	1,010	...	...	1	1,010
Belgian	...	...	1	1,007	1	1,007
Total	99	54,514	13	15,953	112	70,467
Coastwise	65	28,407	21	14,636	86	43,043
Total	164	82,921	34	30,589	198	113,510
,, year preceding	...	...	...	...	...	67,360

NEW ORLEANS.

CLEARED.

Nationality.	Sailing. Number of Vessels.	Sailing. Tons.	Steam. Number of Vessels.	Steam. Tons.	Total. Number of Vessels.	Total. Tons.
British	41	31,376	8	10,426	49	41,802
American	37	12,303	...	...	37	12,303
Italian	1	626	...	...	1	626
Russian	3	2,038	...	...	3	2,038
French	1	1,010	...	...	1	1,010
Swedish	5	3,592	...	...	5	3,592
Honduras	6	240	...	...	6	240
German	3	2,262	...	...	3	2,262
Norwegian	10	6,396	...	...	10	6,396
Austrian	2	1,267	...	...	2	1,267
Spanish	2	887	...	...	2	887
Belgian	...	...	1	1,007	1	1,007
Total	111	61,997	9	11,433	120	73,430
Coastwise	56	21,365	20	13,971	76	35,336
Total	167	83,362	29	25,404	196	108,766
,, year preceding	...	...	...	...	...	84,235

Annex B.—RETURN of Principal Articles of Import to Mobile during the Years 1886–87 and 1885–86.

Articles.		1886 and 1887. Quantity.	1886 and 1887. Value. £ s. d.	1885 and 1886. Quantity.	1885 and 1886. Value. £ s. d.
Bagging	Pieces	37,476	...	30,366	...
Iron ties	Bdls.	29,550	...	54,417	...
Bacon	Hhds.	15,194	...	15,140	...
Cotton	Bales	216,142	2,011,471 9 9	248,526	2,232,074 2 9
Coffee	Sacks	16,115	...	19,270	...
Corn	,,	349,931	...	371,480	...
Flour	Bbls.	125,129	...	122,517	...
Fertilisers	Sacks	147,360	...	137,769	...
Hay	Bales	53,268	...	43,182	...
Lard	Tierces	3,379	...	2,727	...
Molasses	Bbls.	3,582	...	3,146	...
Oats	Sacks	93,428	...	92,330	...
Potatoes	Bbls.	21,593	...	20,534	...
Pork	,,	2,259	...	2,055	...
Rice	,,	5,120	...	4,833	...
Salt	Sacks	58,436	...	27,019	...
Soap	Boxes	24,432	...	24,414	...
Sugar	Bbls.	17,900	...	15,986	...
Tobacco	Boxes	24,074	...	25,277	...
Whiskey	Bbls.	6,068	...	5,773	...
Coal	Tons	40,142	...	32,338	...
Wool	Lbs.	522,800	29,952 1 8	540,000	27,000 0 0
Various articles from foreign countries to June 30, 1886-87	...	...	13,445 0 0	...	14,465 4 2

Value £ sterling, 4 dol. 80 c.

I cannot enumerate articles imported from foreign countries, nor give the value of above enumerated articles, with exception of cotton and wool.

UNITED STATES.

RETURN of Principal Articles of Export from Mobile during the Years 1886–87 and 1885–86.

Articles.		1886 and 1887.		1885 and 1886.	
		Quantity.	Value.	Quantity.	Value.
			£ s. d.		£ s. d.
Cotton	Bales	233,210	2,170,310 11 3	255,796	2,297,367 15 8
Timber	Cubic ft.	1,836,573	45,022 10 1	2,973,206	70,162 11 0
Lumber	Feet	29,346,230	72,639 19 6	21,435,453	53,771 6 11
Rosin	Bbls.	17,504	5,892 4 6	36,864	14,137 19 8
Staves	...	48,071	949 4 5	79,956	1,968 6 8
Cotton-seed meal	Sacks	25,043	4,758 10 10	...	...
Shingles	...	585,000	340 15 0	345,950	302 5 10
Merchandise	...	...	999 9 10	...	2,139 16 3
Coal	Tons	...	...	200	145 16 8
Vegetables	...	...	64,449 15 10	...	33,547 0 6
Total	...	...	2,365,363 1 3	...	2,473,542 19 2

Value £ sterling, 4 dol. 80 c.

Annex C.—TABLE showing the Total Value of all articles Exported from Mobile and Imported to Mobile from and to Foreign Countries during the Years 1886–87 and 1885–86:—

Exports.

	£ s. d.
1886–87	532,886 5 0
1885–86	550,769 2 4

Imports to June 30th, 1887.

	£ s. d.
1886–87	13,445 0 0
1885–86	14,465 4 2

I have no means of dividing the above as to countries, except as regards cotton, included in above.

	£ s. d.
Great Britain, 1886–87	435,597 12 10
„ 1885–86	425,854 19 0

CONDITION of Dredged Channel, Mobile Harbour, on the 30th day of June, 1887.

Locality.	Dredged, 1881 to 1887.			Examination, 1886 to 1887.	
	From the initial Point.	Width.	Depth.	Minimum Top Width.	Maximum Central Depth.
	Miles.	Feet.	Feet.	Feet.	Feet.
Initial point in Mobile river upper gap obstructions	0·64	145	18 to 20	200	19·3 to 20·7
Upper gap of obstructions to Cluster No. 2 between obstructions	1·07	245	18 „ 19	300	20·1 „ 22·0
Cluster No. 2 to lower gap of obstructions	1·48	155	18 „ 19	190	20·1 „ 20·9
Lower gap of obstructions to Cluster No. 23	11·99	145	18 „ 19	180	16·8 „ 20·5
Cluster No. 23 to Cluster No. 27	13·91	105	18 „ 19	140	15·8 „ 16·8
Cluster No. 27 to Cluster No. 30	15·39	145	18 „ 19	180	16·5 „ 17·2
Cluster No. 30 to Cluster No. 51, or Dumb Beacon, 17 foot-curve	25·91	185	18 „ 19	200	14·6 „ 22·6

FOREIGN OFFICE.

1888.

ANNUAL SERIES.

No. 289.

DIPLOMATIC AND CONSULAR REPORTS ON TRADE AND FINANCE.

UNITED STATES.

REPORT FOR THE YEAR 1887

ON THE

FINANCES OF THE UNITED STATES.

REFERENCE TO PREVIOUS REPORT, Annual Series No. 235.

Presented to both Houses of Parliament by Command of Her Majesty,
APRIL, 1888.

LONDON:
PRINTED FOR HER MAJESTY'S STATIONERY OFFICE,
BY HARRISON AND SONS, ST. MARTIN'S LANE,
PRINTERS IN ORDINARY TO HER MAJESTY.

And to be purchased, either directly or through any Bookseller, from
EYRE AND SPOTTISWOODE, EAST HARDING STREET, FLEET STREET, E.C., and
32, ABINGDON STREET, WESTMINSTER, S.W.; or
ADAM AND CHARLES BLACK, 6, NORTH BRIDGE, EDINBURGH; or
HODGES, FIGGIS, & Co., 104, GRAFTON STREET, DUBLIN.

1888.

[C. 5252—66.] *Price Fourpence.*

New Series of Reports.

Reports of the Annual Series have been issued from Her Majesty's Diplomatic and Consular Officers at the following places, and may be obtained from the sources indicated on the title-page:—

No.		Price.	No.		Price.
163.	Bilbao	1d.	226.	Rio de Janeiro	1d.
164.	Jaffa	1d.	227.	Valparaiso	1d.
165.	Van	1d.	228.	St. Thomas	1d.
166.	Bushire	1d.	229.	Stockholm	1d.
167.	Riga	1d.	230.	Nyassa	1d.
168.	Santos	1d.	231.	Buenos Ayres	1d.
169.	Charleston	1d.	232.	The Hague	1d.
170.	Newchwang	1d.	233.	Trieste	1d.
171.	Amsterdam	1d.	234.	Vienna	1d.
172.	Ajaccio	1d.	235.	Washington	3d.
173.	Chinkiang	2d.	236.	Odessa	1d.
174.	Naples	3d.	237.	Sofia	1d.
175.	Smyrna	1d.	238.	Porto Rico	1d.
176.	Belgrade	1d.	239.	Palermo	2d.
177.	Philadelphia	2d.	240.	Lisbon	2d.
178.	Stockholm	2d.	241.	Tabreez	1d.
179.	Pernambuco	1d.	242.	Tunis	1d.
180.	Frankfort-on-Main	1d.	243.	The Hague	1d.
181.	Mogador	2d.	244.	Fiume	1d.
182.	New York	2d.	245.	Venice	1d.
183.	Swatow	1d.	246.	Paris	2d.
184.	Berlin	1d.	247.	Ancona	1d.
185.	Philippopolis	1d.	248.	St. Petersburg	2d.
186.	San Francisco	6d.	249.	Algiers	2d.
187.	Lisbon	1d.	250.	Bucharest	1d.
188.	Lisbon	2d.	251.	Christiania	2d.
189.	Nice	2d.	252.	Paris	1d.
190.	Tientsin	1d.	253.	Bogota	1d.
191.	Hankow	1d.	254.	Salonica	1d.
192.	Erzeroum	1d.	255.	Copenhagen	1d.
193.	Syra	1d.	256.	Jeddah	1d.
194.	Athens	3d.	257.	Russia	2d.
195.	Vienna	2d.	258.	Paris	1d.
196.	Alexandria	1d.	259.	Patras	1d.
197.	Constantinople	1d.	260.	Brussels	1d.
198.	Hakodate	1d.	261.	Ichang	1d.
199.	Shanghai	2d.	262.	Baltimore	1d.
200.	Tokyo	2d.	263.	Taganrog	1d.
201.	Tamatave	1d.	264.	Oporto	1d.
202.	Mexico	1d.	265.	Rio de Janeiro	1d.
203.	Chefoo	1d.	266.	Galveston	1d.
204.	Nagasaki	5d.	267.	Tripoli	1d.
205.	Cuba	1d.	268.	Galatz	1d.
206.	Tunis	1d.	269.	Varna	1d.
207.	Réunion	1d.	270.	New Orleans	2d.
208.	Hyogo	2d.	271.	Cherbourg	1d.
209.	Tangier	1d.	272.	Suakin	1d.
210.	Antwerp	1d.	273.	Brest	1d.
211.	Stettin	1d.	274.	Barcelona	2d.
212.	Erzeroum	1d.	275.	Barcelona	1d.
213.	Rotterdam	1d.	276.	Antwerp	1d.
214.	Nantes	2d.	277.	Havre	3d.
215.	Newport News	1d.	278.	Odessa	1d.
216.	Rio Grande do Sul	1d.	279.	Tokyo	1d.
217.	Rio de Janeiro	1d.	280.	Saigon	1d.
218.	Corea	1d.	281.	Buenos Ayres	1d.
219.	Kanagawa	1d.	282.	Taganrog	1d.
220.	Wurtemberg	1d.	283.	Tamsui	1d.
221.	Tahiti	1d.	284.	Puerto Plata	1d.
222.	Bangkok	1d.	285.	Wenchow	1d.
223.	St. Petersburg	2d.	286.	Tokyo	1d.
224.	Canton	1d.	287.	Lisbon	2d.
225.	Erzeroum	1d.	288.	La Rochelle	1d.

No. 289.

Reference to previous Report, Annual Series No. 235.

UNITED STATES.

WASHINGTON.

Sir L. S. Sackville-West to the Marquis of Salisbury.

My Lord,   *Washington, March 9, 1888.*

I HAVE the honour to enclose to your Lordship herewith copy of a letter which has been addressed to me by Mr. Edwardes, transmitting his Report on the Finances of the United States for the fiscal year ended June 30, 1887, enclosed herewith.

This Report has been compiled with much care, and gives much valuable information respecting the financial system of this country.

I have, &c.

(Signed)   L. S. SACKVILLE-WEST.

Mr. Edwardes to Sir L. Sackville-West.

Sir,   *Washington, February 25, 1888.*

I have the honour to enclose herewith my Report on the Finances of the United States far the fiscal year ended June 30, 1887.

The chief point of interest in connection with the Finances of this country is the continued yearly increase of Revenue over Expenditure, and I have ventured to dwell at some length on this point (taking for my guidance the Report of the Secretary of the Treasury), and on the expedient put forward to avoid the embarrassments to trade, &c., which must arise, if the present state of things be allowed to continue.

The other information and statistics given in this Report are likewise taken from the Annual Report of the Secretary of the Treasury, and from those issued by the several Departments under his charge.

I have, &c.,

(Signed)   H. G. EDWARDES.

Report on the Finances of the United States of America for the fiscal year ended 30 June, 1887.

The ordinary revenues of the United States during 12 months, ended June 30, 1887, from all sources amounted to 371,403,277 dol. 66 c (77,375,682*l.*), and the expenditures for the same period to

Receipts and expenditure.

(375)

315,835,428 dol. 12 cents (65,799,047*l.*); leaving a surplus of 55,567,849 dol. 54 c. (11,576,635*l.*).

The different items of revenue were—

	Dollars.	c.
From Customs	217,286,893	13
„ internal revenue	118,823,391	22
„ sales of public lands	9,254,286	42
„ profits on coinage, bullion deposits, and assays	8,929,252	83
„ tax on national banks	2,885,851	18
„ fees—consular, letters patent, and land	3,301,647	16
„ Customs fees, fines, penalties, &c.	1,053,037	86
„ sales of Indian lands	1,479,028	81
„ Soldiers' Home, permanent fund	1,226,259	47
„ sinking-fund for Pacific railways	1,364,435	87
„ repayment of interest by Pacific railways	914,793	13
„ sales of old buildings	624,882	20
„ sales of Government property	262,832	32
„ immigrant fund	258,402	50
„ tax on seal-skins	317,452	76
„ deposits by individuals for surveying public lands	94,289	76
„ revenues of the District of Columbia	2,367,869	01
„ miscellaneous sources	1,458,672	04
Total ordinary receipts	371,403,277	66

The ordinary expenditures were—

	Dollars.	c.
For civil expenses	22,072,436	27
„ foreign intercourse	7,104,490	47
„ Indian service	6,194,522	69
„ pensions	75,029,101	79
„ the military establishment, including rivers and harbours and arsenals	38,561,025	85
„ the naval establishment, including vessels, machinery, and improvements at navy-yard	15,141,126	80
„ miscellaneous expenditures, including public buildings, light-houses, and collecting the revenue	52,002,647	46
„ expenditures on account of the District of Columbia	4,085,251	39
„ interest on the public debt	47,741,577	25
„ the sinking-fund	47,903,248	15
Total ordinary expenditure	315,835,428	12

The receipts of the Post Office Department not included in the above statement were 54,752,347 dol. 42 c. (11,406,739*l.*), which is an increase of 1,755,212 dol. 16 c. over the receipts of last year. The expenditures increased from 50,682,585 dol. 72 c. (10,558,872*l.*), in 1886, to 53,583,835 dol. 03 c. (11,163,299*l.*) in 1887, or an increase of 2,901,249 dol. 31 c. (604,427*l.*) of the total receipts; 28,031,949 dol. 72 c. (5,839,989*l.*) was received and disbursed by postmasters without having been deposited in the Treasury.

The above surplus, together with 24,455,720 dol. 46 c. (5,094,942*l.*) drawn from the cash balance in the Treasury, making 80,023,570 dol. (16,671,577*l.*) was applied to the redemption of—

	Dollars.
The loan of 1882	79,864,100
„ funded loan of 1881	54,800
„ loan of July and August, 1861	34,650
„ ten-forty loan of 1864	12,350
Consols of 1865	14,550
„ „ 1867	34,400
„ „ 1868	650
The five-twenty loan of 1862	1,650
„ loan of 1863	350
Oregon war debt	100
The five-twenty loan of 1865	150
Compound-interest and other notes	5,820
	80,023,570

As compared with the fiscal year 1886, the receipts for 1887 have increased 34,963,550 dol. 60 c. (7,284,073*l*.) as follows. The decrease is also shown.

Source.	Increase.	Decrease.	Net increase.
	Dol. c.	Dol. c.	Dol. c.
Customs	24,381,869 69	..	..
Internal revenue	2,017,454 74	..	..
Sales of public lands	3,623,287 08	..	..
Profits on coinage, assays, &c.	3,024,633 57	..	..
Soldiers' Home, permanent fund	980,822 49	..	..
Sales of old public buildings	272,525 07	..	..
Interest repaid by Pacific railways	235,603 70	..	..
Sinking-fund for Pacific railways	266,530 40	..	..
Reimbursement for non-paying Indian stocks	154,426 98	..	..
Reimbursement for cost of Indian reservations	232,941 86	..	..
Material sold to Southern railroads in 1865	95,000 00	..	..
Consular fees	77,336 67	..	..
Immigrant fund	76,855 50	..	..
Customs fines, penalties, &c.	31,561 83	..	..
Sales of ordnance material	28,817 30	..	..
Custom-house fees	17,880 64	..	..
Revenues of the District of Columbia	221,229 57	..	..
Miscellaneous items	83,691 40	..	..
Tax on National Banks	..	307,861 69	..
Registers' and receivers' fees	..	131,347 10	..
Steamboat fees	..	99,786 19	..
Deposits for surveying public lands	..	98,445 87	..
Sales of Indian lands	..	97,429 25	..
Shipping fees	..	54,578 00	..
Sales of condemned vessels	..	40,357 19	..
Fees on letters-patent	..	27,912 60	..
Total	35,821,268 49	857,717 89	34,963,550 60

There was an increase in the expenditure of 25,449,041 dol. 47 c. (5,301,883*l*.) as follows:—

Source.	Increase.	Decrease.	Net increase.
	Dol. c.	Dol. c.	Dol. c.
Civil and miscellaneous	11,097,895 74	..	..
War Department	4,236,873 11	..	..
Navy Department	1,233,239 06	..	..
Interior Department—Indians	95,364 52	..	..
„ „ Pensions	11,624,237 76	..	..
Interest on the public debt	..	2,838,568 72	..
Total	28,287,610 19	2,838,568 72	25,449,041 47

Fiscal year, 1888. For the fiscal year 1888, the revenues, actual and estimated, are as follows:—

Source.	Quarter ended September 30, 1887. Actual.	Remaining three-fourths of the year. Estimated.	Total.
	Dol. c.	Dol. c.	Dol. c.
Customs	62,588,115 92	165,411,884 08	228,000,000 00
Internal revenue	31,422,039 49	88,577,960 51	120,000,000 00
Sales of public lands	2,620,890 23	7,379,109 77	10,000,000 00
Tax on National Banks	912,411 69	1,087,588 31	2,000,000 00
Interest and sinking-fund, Pacific railways	446,090 81	1,553,909 19	2,000,000 00
Customs fees, fines, penalties, &c.	273,201 10	876,798 90	1,150,000 00
Fees—consular, letters-patent, and lands	1,007,660 36	2,492,339 64	3,500,000 00
Sales of Government property	84,926 87	215,073 13	300,000 00
Profits on coinage, assays, &c.	1,113,855 90	7,886,144 10	9,000,000 00
Deposits for surveying public lands	40,450 32	109,549 68	150,000 00
Revenues of the District of Columbia	356,400 11	2,043,599 89	2,400,000 00
Miscellaneous sources	1,462,355 02	3,037,644 98	4,500,000 00
Total receipts	102,328,397 82	280,671,602 18	383,000,000 00

The expenditures for the same period, actual and estimated, are as follows:—

Object.	Quarter ended September 30, 1887. Actual.	Remaining three-fourths of the year. Estimated.	Total.
	Dol. c.	Dol. c.	Dol. c.
Civil and miscellaneous expenses, including public buildings, lighthouses, and collecting the revenue	17,286,572 63	62,713,427 37	80,000,000 00
Indians	1,913,585 65	4,336,414 35	6,250,000 00
Pensions	28,156,382 17	50,843,617 83	80,000,000 00
Military establishment, including fortifications, river and harbour improvements, and arsenals	12,368,225 87	26,631,774 13	39,000,000 00
Naval establishment, including vessels and machinery, and improvements at navy-yards	3,735,240 89	12,264,759 11	16,000,000 00
Expenditures for District of Columbia	1,474,685 28	2,775,314 72	4,250,000 00
Interest on the public debt	12,162,181 68	32,337,818 32	44,500,000 00
Sinking-fund, including premium	43,024,277 84	3,793,507 64	46,817,785 48
Total expenditures	121,121,152 01	195,696,633 47	316,817,785 48

	Dol. c.
Total receipts, actual and estimated	383,000,000 00
„ expenditure, including sinking-fund	316,817,785 48
Estimated surplus	66,182,214 52

In the fiscal year, 1889, the revenue, estimated upon the basis of existing laws, is calculated to being 383,000,000 dol. (79,791,666*l*.), and the expenditures, including the sinking-fund, to amount to 326,530,793 dol. 26 c. (68,027,248*l*.), or an estimated surplus of 56,469,206 dol. 74 c. (11,764,418*l*.).

Fiscal year, 1889.

Excluding the Sinking Fund, the expenditures will be 278,686,634 dol. 36 c. (58,059,715*l*.), showing a surplus of 104,313,365 dol. 54 c. (21,731,951*l*.).

The Balance Account of the United States receipts and expenditures for the year 1887, as shown by warrants issued, is given in the following table:—

UNITED STATES.

Receipts covered in to the credit of—	Issue of notes and bonds.	Net receipts.	Repayments to appropriations.	Counter credits to appropriations.	Total.
	Dol. c.	Dol. c.	Dol. c.	Dol. c.	Dol. c.
Customs	...	217,286,893 13	1,769,895 51	90,860 15	219,147,648 79
Internal revenue	...	118,823,391 22	26,399 36	371 25	118,850,168 83
Lands	...	9,254,286 42	...	...	9,254,286 42
Miscellaneous sources	...	26,038,706 82	...	...	26,038,706 89
Total net revenue	...	371,403,277 66	...		
Public debt—					
Funded loan of 1907	40,900 00	...	...		
Silver certificates	51,852,000 00	...	...		
Certificates of deposit (Act of June 8, 1872)	28,480,000 00	...	...		
United States notes	74,068,000 00	...	...		
	154,440,900 00	...	...		154,440,900 00
Interest on the public debt	...	...	14,372 58	105 00	14,477 58
War Department appropriations	...	...	1,097,727 01	87,807 76	1,185,534 77
Navy Department appropriations	...	...	376,400 34	6,597,469 05	6,973,869 39
Interior Department appropriations, Indians	...	...	208,607 65	29,727 60	238,335 25
Interior Department appropriations, pensions	...	...	2,910,227 66	889,783 89	3,800,011 55
Interior civil appropriations	...	...	96,840 25	9,108 83	105,949 08
Treasury proper appropriations	...	...	2,294,875 42	197,043 02	2,491,918 44
Diplomatic appropriations	...	...	12,193 89	52,096 60	64,290 49
Quarterly salaries' appropriations	...	...	121 29	...	121 29
Judiciary appropriations	...	...	148,637 01	89,974 46	238,611 47
Total receipts	...	525,844,177 66	8,956,297 97	8,044,354 61	542,844,830 24
Balance June 30, 1886, as shown by warrants issued	...	...	...	...	498,739,112 9
Total	...	...	...	...	1,041,583,942 15

WASHINGTON.

Expenditures authorised by warrants from appropriations on account of—	Net expenditure.	Repayments of amounts unexpended	Amounts re-credited to appropriations.	Total.
	Dol. c.	Dol. c.	Dol. c.	Dol. c.	Dol. c.
Customs, lighthouse, public buildings, &c.	23,795,933 12	...	1,769,895 51	90,860 15	25,656,688 78
Internal revenue	4,070,126 59	...	26,399 36	378 25	4,096,904 20
Interior civil	7,821,225 31	...	96,840 25	9,108 83	7,927,174 39
Treasury proper	38,342,337 73	...	2,294,875 42	197,043 02	40,834,256 17
Diplomatic	7,104,490 47	...	12,193 89	52,096 60	7,168,780 96
Quarterly salaries	603,417 47	...	12,1 22	...	603,538 76
Judiciary	3,527,294 90	...	148,637 01	89,974 46	3,765,906 37
Net civil and miscellaneous expenditure		852,64,825 59	...	...	...
War Department	...	38,561,025 85	1,097,717 01	87,807 76	39,746,560 62
Navy Department	...	15,141,126 80	38,400 34	6,597,469 05	22,114,996 19
Interior Department, Indians	...	6,194,522 69	208,607 69	29,727 60	6,432,857 94
Interior Department, pensions	...	75,029,101 79	2,910,927 66	889,783 89	78,829,113 34
Interest on the public debt	...	47,741,577 25	14,372 58	105 00	47,756,054 83
Total net expenditures	...	267,932,179 97	...	...	...
Redemption of the Public Debt—					
Gold certificates	9,687,428 00	...	...	...	...
Silver certificates	22,286,525 00	...	...	...	...
Certificates of deposit (Act of June 8th, 1872)	37,900,000 00	...	...	...	...
Refunding certificates	32,550 00	...	...	...	...
United States' notes	74,068,000 00	...	...	...	...
Fractional currency	7,123 15	...	...	...	...
Old demand notes	315 00	...	...	...	...
7-30s of 1864 and 1865	700 00	...	...	...	...
One year notes of 1863	590 00	...	...	...	...
Two year notes of 1863	350 00	...	...	...	...
Compound interest notes	4,290 00	...	...	...	...
Treasury notes of 1861	500 00	...	...	...	...
Treasury notes of 1857	1,000 00	...	...	...	...
Loan of July and August, 1861	29,200 00	...	...	...	...
Loan of 1863	13,750 00	...	...	...	...
Oregon war debt	100 00	...	...	...	...
Loan of February, 1861	2,000 00	...	...	...	...
5-20s of 1862	2,300 00	...	...	...	...
5-20s of June, 1864	150 00	...	...	...	...
5-20s of 1865	8,000 00	...	...	...	...
10-40s of 1864	13,650 00	...	...	...	...
Consols of 1865	32,750 00	...	...	...	...
Consols of 1867	68,400 00	...	...	...	...
Consols of 1868	1,150 00	...	...	...	...
Funded Loan of 1881	19,750 00	...	...	...	...
Loan of July 12th, 1882	127,612,850 00	...	...	...	...
Loan of July and August, 1861, continued at 3½ per cent.	35,650 00	...	...	...	...
Loan of 1863, continued at 3½ per cent.	8,500 00	...	...	...	...
Funded loan of 188, continued at 3½ per cent.	63,750 00	...	...	...	...
		271,901,321 15	...	...	271,901,321 15
		539,133,501 12	8,956,297 97	8,044354 61	556,834,153 70
Balance June 30, 1887, as shown by warrants issued	...	...	...	...	484,749,789 45
Total	...	...	...	...	1,041,583,943 15

The following is the comparative statement of receipts for 1886 and 1887, as shown by warrants issued :—

Fiscal year.	Customs.	Internal revenue.	Lands.	Miscellaneous sources.	Total net revenue.
	Dol. c.	Dol. c.	Dol. c.	Dol. c.	Dol. c.
1886	192,905,023 44	116,805,936 48	5,630,999 34	21,097,767 80	336,439,727 06
1887	217,286,893 13	118,823,391 22	9,254,286 42	26,038,706 89	371,403,277 66
Increase in 1887	24,381,869 69	2,017,454 74	3,623,287 08	4,940,939 09	34,963,550 60

UNITED STATES.

The following is the comparative statement of expenditures for the fiscal years 1886 and 1887, as shown by warrants issued:—

Fiscal year.	Interest on the public debt.	Civil and miscellaneous.	War Department.	Navy Department.	Interior Department.	Total net Expenditures.
	Dol. c.	Dol. c.	Dol. c.	Dol. c.	Dol. c.	Dol. c.
1886	50,580,145 97	74,166,929 85	34,324,152 74	13,907,887 74	69,504,022 20	942,483,138 50
1887	47,741,577 25	85,264,825 59	38,561,025 85	15,141,126 80	81,223,624 48	267,932,179 97
Decrease, 1887	2,838,568 72	...	...	...	...	...
Increase, 1887	...	11,097,895 74	4,236,873 11	1,233,239 06	11,719,602 28	25,449,041 47

A statement of balances in the Treasury at the close of the fiscal years 1886 is also given:—

Balances as shown by last report, June 30th, 1886		498,739,112 91
Net revenue, 1887	371,403,277 66	
Net expenditure, 1887	267,932,179 97	
Excess of revenue over expenditure		103,471,097 69
		602,210,210 60

Public debt.	Issues during fiscal year.	Redemptions during fiscal year.	Excess of issues over redemptions.	Excess of redemptions over issues.
	Dol. c.	Dol. c.	Dol. c.	Dol. c.
Bonds and securities	...	306,845 00	...	306,845 00
Funded loan of 1907	40,900 00	...	40,900 00	...
Silver certificates	51,852,000 00	22,286,525 00	29,565,475 00	...
Gold certificates	...	9,687,428 00	...	9,687,428 00
Certificates of deposit (Act of June 8, 1872)	28,480,000 00	37,900,000 00	...	9,420,000 00
United States notes	74,068,000 00	74,068,000 00	...	...
Loan of July 12, 1882	...	127,612,850 00	...	127,612,850 00
Refunding certificates	...	32,550 00	...	32,550 00
Fractional currency	...	7,123 15	...	7,123 15
Total	154,440,900 00	271,901,321 15	29,606,375 00	147,066,796 15
Net excess of redemptions over issues	...	...	...	117,460,421 15
Balance, June 30, 1887	...	...	...	484,749,789 45

Receipts for 1887, where deposited.

The gross receipts of the Government amounting during the fiscal year vary, as shown by the above tables, to the sum of 525,844,177 dol. 66 c. (154,440,900 dol. of which were on account of United States' notes, certificates, and conversion of refunding certificates), were deposited as follows:—

	Dol. c.
In the Treasury and Sub-Treasuries	398,534,669 95
„ National Bank depositories	127,309,507 71

Summary of operations.

The following is a brief summary of operations which offers interest and is taken from the report of the Treasurer of the United States.

There were redeemed during the year bonds of the United States amounting to 127,911,950 dol., of which 47,894 dol. were applied to the Sinking Fund.

The payment of interest on the registered bonds of the United States, including bonds issued to the Pacific Railway Companies was made by 219,436 checks, amounting to 39,755,876 dol. 52 c. Coupons were also paid at the Treasury, and the various sub-Treasury offices, amounting to 7,002,094 dol. 83 c.

The payment of the warrants of the Secretary of the Treasury required the issue of 55,157 drafts; 78,453 drafts on warrants of the

Postmaster General, and 26,176 transfer checks on assistant treasurers were issued, making a total of 379,222 drafts and checks issued by the office during the year.

Circulating notes of National Banks amounting to 87,689,687 dol. 15 c. were received for redemption. United States' notes unfit for circulation of the value of 74,068,000 dol. were redeemed and destroyed, and new notes of a like amount were issued.

Silver certificates to the amount of 51,852,000 dol. were issued, 22,286,525 dol. were redeemed, and the amount nominally outstanding at the close of the fiscal year was 145,543,150 dol.

There were redeemed during the year gold certificates amounting to 9,687,428 dol.

The National Banks paid into the Treasury on account of semi-annual duty on their circulation the issue of 2,044,922 dol. 75 c., which was 547,098 dol. 58 c. less than was paid on that account the preceding year.

Interest amounting to 415,120 dol. 70 c. on registered bonds of the District of Columbia was paid by 973 checks, and coupons from such bonds, amounting to 95,250 dol. 16 c. were examined and paid.

The National Banks withdrew 126,188,750 dol. in bonds held by the Treasurer of the United States in trust to secure their circulating notes, and 42,180,650 dol. in bonds were deposited for that purpose.

There were also deposited by National Banks, designated as depositories, 15,251,500 dol. in bonds to secure public funds and 8,425,900 dol. in bonds, so held, were withdrawn.

The total movement of bonds held for National Banks during the year was 192,046,800 dol., and the total decrease of such bonds held by the Treasurer was 77,182,500 dol.

The accounts of the disbursing officers of the Government on the books of the Treasury, show that funds amounting to 22,565,001 dol. 19 c., stood to their credit at the close of the year; 4,162,363 dol. 80 c. of which was on deposit in the various National Bank depositories.

Trade-dollars amounting to 7,254,363 dol. were received in exchange for standard silver, dollars and fractional silver coin.

The unavailable funds of the Treasury, June 30, 1887, were 29,521,579 dol. 35 c., and those of the Post Office Department 37,277 dol. 06 c.

UNITED STATES.

State of the Treasury.

The assets and liabilities of the Treasury of September 30, 1886, and September 30, 1887, and the character of the assets at the latter date are shown by the following statements:—

		Assets	Liabilities.	Balances.
	Dol. c.	Dol. c.	Dol. c.	Dol. c.
Gold.—Coin	189,051,398 65	...	...	...
Bullion	53,509,735 67	...	...	...
		242,561,134 32	...	...
Certificates	125,346,127 00	...	...	...
Less amount on hand	41,036,550 00	...	...	...
		...	84,309,577 00	...
Net gold	...	...	...	158,251,557 32
Silver.—Standard dollars	181,161,161 00	...	...	...
Bullion	3,877,541 44	...	...	...
		185,038,702 44	...	...
Certificates	117,943,102 00	...	...	...
Less amount in hand	22,032,850 00	...	...	...
		...	95,910,252 00	...
Net silver	...	...	...	89,128,450 44
United States' notes	...	45,244,640 88	...	...
Certificates	7,895,000 00	...	...	...
Less amount on hand	280,000 00	...	...	...
		...	7,615,000 00	...
Net United States' notes	...	...	...	37,629,640 88
National Bank notes	...	364,452 50	...	364,452 50
Deposits in National Bank Depositaries	...	16,682,286 33	...	16,682,286 33
Totals	...	489,891,216 47	187,834,829 00	302,056,367 47
Public debt and interest—				
Interest due and unpaid	1,931,702 01	...	...	...
Accrued interest	8,998,016 50	...	...	...
Matured debt	7,313,035 26	...	...	...
Interest on matured debt	201,061 07	...	...	...
Debt bearing no interest	3,524 75	...	...	...
Interest on Pacific Railroad bonds due and unpaid	37,739 96	...	...	...
Accrued interest on Pacific Railroad bonds	969,352 68	...	...	...
		...	19,454,432 23	...
Fractional currency redeemed	3,524 75	...	...	...
One and two-year notes redeemed	10 50	...	...	...
Interest checks and coupons paid	107,370 95	...	...	...
United States' bonds and interest paid	315,849 97	426,756 17	...	...
Totals	...	490,317,972 64	207,289,261 23	...
Reserve for redemption of United States notes, acts of 1875 and 1882	...	...	100,000,000 00	...
Fund held for redemption of notes of National Banks "failed," "in liquidation," and "reducing circulation"	65,515,523 32	...	...	...
Fund held for redemption of National-bank notes	97,024 00	...	...	...
Five per cent. fund for redemption of National-bank notes	10,856,751 34	...	...	...
		...	76,469,298 69	...
National-bank notes in process of redemption	...	1,917,974 89	...	...
Post Office Department account	4,929,621 29	...	...	...
Disbursing officers' balances	22,676,967 45	...	...	...
Undisturbed assets of failed National Banks	824,411 30	...	...	...
Currency and minor coin redemption account	433,080 78	...	...	...
Fractional silver coin redemption account	57,118 00	...	...	...
Treasurer's transfer checks and drafts outstanding	6,307,180 95	...		
Treasurer U.S. agent for paying interest on D.C. bonds	346,184 73	...	...	...
			35,571,564 50	...
Interest on D.C. bonds paid	...	10,318 15	...	...
Totals	...	492,246,265 68	419,333,124 42	...
Balance	...	...	...	72,913,141 26
Assets not available:				
Minor coin	296,021 76	...	...	...
Fractional silver coin	26,846,612 76	...	...	...
		27,142,634 52	...	27,142,634 52
Aggregate	...	519,388,900 20	419,333,124 42	100,055,775 78

WASHINGTON.
SEPTEMBER 30, 1887.

		Assets.	Liabilities.	Balances.
	Dol. c.	Dol. c.	Dol. c.	
Gold.—Coin	182,529,827 80			
Bullion	108,620,986 01			
		291,150,813 81		
Certificates	127,138,971 00			
Less amount on hand	28,945,338 00			
			98,193,633 00	
Net gold				192,957,180 81
Silver.—Standard dollars	213,069,257 00			
Bullion	4,755,319 00			
		217,824,576 49		
Certificates	158,274,667 00			
Less amount on hand	3,435,359 00			
			154,839,308 00	
Net silver				62,985,268 49
United States' notes		24,939,664 13		
Certificates	6,765,000 00			
Less amount on hand	150,000 00			
			6,615,000 00	
Net United States' notes				18,324,664 13
Trade dollars		295,533 00		295,533 00
Trade-dollar bullion		6,799,503 00		6,799,503 00
National-bank notes		227,211 00		227,211 00
Deposits in National-bank depositaries		25,651,000 28		25,651,000 28
Totals		566,888,801 71	259,647,941 00	307,240,360 71
Public debt and interest—				
Interest due and unpaid	2,106,247 47			
Accrued interest	8,323,200 86			
Matured debt	3,739,935 26			
Interest on matured debt	184,432 22			
Interest prepaid, not accrued, per Department Circular No. 90	1,092,988 81			
Debt bearing no interest	452 49			
Interest on Pacific Railroad bonds due and unpaid	16,769 96			
Accrued interest on Pacific Railroad bonds	969,352 68			
			16,433,379 75	
Fractional currency redeemed	452 49			
United States' bonds and interest	1,094,611 70			
Interest checks and coupons paid	4,170,374 05			
Registered and coupon interest prepaid	1,900,195 31	7,165,633 55		
Totals		574,053,935 26	276,081,320 75	
Reserve for redemption of United States' notes, Acts of 1875 and 1882			100,000,000 00	
Fund held for redemption of notes of National Banks "failed," "in liquidation," and "reducing circulation"	102,265,787 60			
Five per cent. fund for redemption of National-bank notes	7,769,057 18			
			110,034,844 78	
National-bank notes in process of redemption		2,764,222 52		
Post-Office Department account	4,986,969 59			
Disbursing officers' balances	32,172,375 47			
Undistributed assets of failed National Banks	1,902,788 02			
Currency and minor coin redemption account	420 00			
Fractional silver coin redemption account	6,920 00			
Redemption and exchange account	435,000 30			
Treasurer's transfer checks and drafts outstanding	4,286,959 07			
Treasurer U.S. agent for paying interest on D.C. bonds	134,743 26			
			43,926,175 71	
Interest on D.C. bonds paid		4,800 00		
Totals		576,822,957 78	530,042,341 24	
Balance				46,780,616 54
Assets not available—				
Minor coin	108,844 46			
Fractional silver coin	24,929,363 54	25,038,208 00		25,038,208 00
Aggregate		601,861,165 78	530,045,341 24	71,818,824 54

Statement of Public Debt.

The following Table gives the Statement of the Public Debt on the 30th June, 1887:—

INTEREST-BEARING DEBT.

Title of Loan.	Authorising Act.	Rate.	When Redeemable.	Interest Payable.	Amounts Outstanding.			Interest Due and Unpaid.	Accrued Interest.
					Registered.	Coupon.	Total.		
					Dollars.	Dollars.	Dollars.	Dol. c.	Dol. c.
Loan of July 12, 1882	July 12, 1882	3 per cent.	Option, U.S.	A., N., F. & M.	$19,716,500	...	19,716,500	7,064 74	98,852 60
Funded Loan of 1891	July 14, '70, and Jan. 20, 1871	4½ per cent.	Sept. 1, 1891	J., M., S. & D.	206,832,650	43,167,350	250,000,000	589,558 69	937,500 00
Refunding Loan of 1907	July 14, '70, and Jan. 20, 1871	4 per cent.	July 1, 1907	J., A., J. & O.	622,020,650	115,779,950	737,800,600	1,100,963 33	7,378,006 00
Refunding certificates	February 26, 1879	4 per cent.	...	J., A., J. & O.	...	...	175,250	56,080 00	1,752 50
Navy-pension fund	July 23, 1868	3 per cent.	...	Jan. & July	...	...	14,000,000	...	210,000 00
Bonds issued to Pacific Railroads	July 1, 1862, and July 2, 1864		2,362,000 dols. matures Jan. 16, 1895; 640,000 dols. matures Nov. 1, 1895: average date of maturity; Mar. 19, 1895; 3,680,000 dols. matures Jan. 1, 1896; 4,320,000 dols. matures Feb. 1, 1896; average date of maturity, Jan. 18, 1896; 9,712,000 dols. matures Jan. 1, 1897; 29,904,952 dols. matures Jan. 1, 1898; and 14,004,560 dols. matures Jan. 1, 1899			64,623,512	...	64,623,512	33,199 96	1,938,705 36
Aggregate of interest-bearing debt	...	...	...	...	913,193,312	158,947,300	1,086,315,862	1,786,786 72	10,564,816 46

WASHINGTON.

Debt on which Interest has Ceased since Maturity.

Title of Loan.	Authorising Act.	Rate.		Amount Outstanding.	Interest due and unpaid.
				Dol. c.	Dol. c.
Old Debt	Various, prior to 1858	1-10 to 6 per cent.	Matured at various dates prior to January 1, 1861	151,920 26	62,489 27
Loan of 1847	January 28, 1847	6 per cent.	,, December 31, 1867	1,250 00	22 00
Texan Indemnity Stock	September 9, 1850	5 ,,	,, ,, 31, 1864	20,000 00	2,945 00
Loan of 1858	June 14, 1858	5 ,,	after January 1, 1874	2,000 00	125 00
Loan of 1860	June 22, 1860	5 ,,	January 1, 1871	10,000 00	600 00
5-20's of 1862, (called)	February 25, 1862	6 ,,	December 1, 1871, and at subsequent dates	266,050 00	219 12
5-20's of June, 1864 (called)	June 30, 1864	6 ,,	November 13, 1875, and at subsequent dates	44,100 00	294 98
5-20's of 1865, (called)	March 3, 1865	6 ,,	February 15, 1876, and at subsequent dates	28,850 00	1,607 79
10-40's of 1864, (called)	March 3, 1865	5 ,,	July 9, 1879, and at subsequent dates	71,450 00	4,526 38
Consols of 1865, (called)	March 3, 1865	6 ,,	August 21, 1877, and at subsequent dates	179,600 00	908 46
Consols of 1867, (called)	March 3, 1865	6 ,,	April 1, 1879, and at subsequent dates	378,750 00	12,927 33
Consols of 1868, (called)	March 3, 1865	6 ,,	July 4, 1879	73,400 00	8,928 92
Loan of February, 1861	February 8, 1861	6 ,,	December 31, 1880	6,000 00	2,580 00
Funded Loan, 1881, (called)	July 14, 1870; January 20, 1871	5 ,,	May 21, 1881, and at subsequent dates	128,950 00	2,549 59
Funded Loan, 1881, (called)	July 14, 1870; January 20, 1871	5 Continued at 3½ per ct.	December 23, 1882, and at subsequent dates	48,200 00	3,945 27
Oregon War Debt	March 2, 1861	6 ,,	July 1, 1881	3,850 00	664 50
Loan of July and August, 1861	July 17 and August 5, 1861	6 ,,	June 30, 1880	124,550 00	1,047 50
Loan of July and August, 1861, (called)	July 17 and August 5, 1861	6 Continued at 3½ per ct.	December 24, 1881, and at subsequent dates	70,200 00	575 00
Loan of 1863, ('81's)	March 3, 1863	6 ,,	June 30, 1881	17,900 00	97 40
Loan of 1863, ('81's)	March 3, 1863	6 Continued at 3½ per ct.	August 1, 1882, and at subsequent dates	7,150 00	62 30
Loan of July 12, 1882, (called)	July 12, 1882	3 ,,	December 1, 1883, and at subsequent dates	4,062,650 00	20,206 09
Treasury Notes of 1861	March 2, 1861	6 ,,	March 1, 1863	2,500 00	364 50
7-30's of 1861	July 17, 1871	7 3-10 per cent.	August 19 and October 1, 1864	15,800 00	1,011 89
1-year notes of 1863	March 3, 1863	5 per cent.	at various dates in 1865	36,205 00	1,822 35
2-year notes of 1863	March 3, 1863	5 ,,	,, ,, 1866	29,400 00	1,303 14
Compound-interest notes	March 3, 1863; June 30, 1864	6 ,,	June 10, 1867, and May 15, 1868	192,880 00	39,686 28
7-30's of 1864-65	June 30, 1864; March 3, 1865	7 3-10 per cent.	August 15, 1867, and June 15 and July 15, 1868	129,600 00	18,351 83
Certificates of indebtedness	March 1, I7, 1862; March 3, 1863	6 per cent.	at various dates in 1866	4,000 00	253 48
Temporary loan	June 30, 1864	4 to 6 per cent.	October 15, 1866	2,960 00	244 19
3 per cent. certificates, (called)	March 2, 1867; July 25, 1868	3 per cent.	February 28, 1873	5,000 00	394 31
Aggregate of debt on which interest has ceased since maturity				6,115,165 26	190,753 87

UNITED STATES.

Debt bearing no Interest.

			Dol. c.	Total. Dol. c.
Old demand notes	..	July 17, 1861; February 12, 1862	..	57,130 00
Legal tender notes	..	February 25, 1862; July 11, 1862; March 3, 1863	..	346,681,016 00
Certificates of deposit	..	June 8, 1872	9,080,000 00	
		Less amount held in Treasurer's cash	310,000 00	8,770,000 00
Gold certificates	..	March 3, 1863, and July 12, 1882	121,486,817 00	
		Less amount held in Treasurer's cash	30,261,380 00	91,225,437 00
Silver certificates	..	February 28, 1878	145,543,150 00	
		Less amount held in Treasurer's cash	3,425,133 00	142,118,017 00
Fractional currency	..	July 17, 1862; March 3, 1863; June 30, 1864	15,322,898 37	
		Less amount estimated as lost or destroyed, Act of June 21, 1879	8,375,934 00	6,946,964 37
		Aggregate of debt bearing no interest		595,798,564 37

WASHINGTON.

RECAPITULATION.

	Principal.	Interest.	Totals.
	Dol. c.	Dol. c.	Dol. c.
Interest-bearing debt	1,086,315,862 00	12,351,603 18	1,098,667,465 18
Debt on which interest has ceased since maturity	6,115,165 26	190,753 87	6,305,919 13
Debt bearing no interest	595,798,564 37	...	595,798,564 37
Total debt	1,688,229,591 63	12,542,357 05	1,700,771,948 68

Cash in the Treasury.

	Dol. c.	
Available for reduction of the Public Debt:		
Gold held for gold certificates actually outstanding	91,225,437 00	
Silver held for silver certificates actually outstanding	142,118,017 00	
United States' notes held for certificates of deposit actually outstanding	8,770,000 00	
Cash held for matured debt and interest unpaid	18,657,522 31	
Cash held for bonds called, not matured, and balance of interest	19,716,500 00	
Fractional currency	2,366 07	
Total available for reduction of the debt		280,489,842 38
Reserve fund:		
Held for redemption of United States' notes, Acts January 14, 1875, and July 12, 1882		100,000,000 00
Unavailable for reduction of the debt:	Dol. c.	
Fractional silver coin	26,977,493 79	
Minor coin	116,698 75	
		27,094,192 55
Certificates held as cash:		
Legal tender	310,000 00	
Gold	30,261,380 00	
Silver	3,425,133 00	
		33,996,513 00
Net cash balance on hand		40,853,369 28
Total cash in the Treasury as shown by the Treasurer's General Account		482,433,917 21

Less cash items available for reduction of the debt	280,489,842 38
Less reserve held for redemption of United States' notes	100,000,000 00
Total debt, less available cash items	1,320,282,106 30
Net cash in the Treasury	40,853,369 28
Debt, less cash in the Treasury, July 1, 1887	1,279,428,737 02
Debt, less cash in the Treasury, June 1, 1887	1,296,281,462 19
Decrease of debt during the month	16,852,725 17
Decrease of debt since June 30, 1886	109,707,646 38

(375)

UNITED STATES.

COMPARISON.

Cash in the Treasury.	July 1, 1887. Dol. c.	July 1, 1887. Dol. c.	June 1, 1887. Dol. c.	June 1, 1887. Dol. c.	Increase. Dol. c.	Decrease. Dol. c.
Available for reduction of the Public Debt:						
Gold held for gold certificates actually outstanding	...	91,225,437 00	...	90,960,977 00		
Silver held for silver certificates actually outstanding	...	142,118,017 00	...	139,143,328 00		
United States' notes held for certificates of deposit actually outstanding	...	8,770,000 00	...	8,990,000 00		
Cash held for matured debt and interest unpaid	...	18,657,522 31	...	18,446,566 59		
Cash held for bonds called, not matured, and balance of interest	...	19,716,500 00	...	19,766,061 34		
Fractional currency	...	2,366 07	...	2,064 40		
Total available for reduction of the debt	...	283,489,842 38	...	277,308,997 33	3,180,845 05	
Reserve fund:						
Held for redemption of United States' notes, Acts January 14, 1875, and July 12, 1882	...	100,000,000 00	...	100,000,000 00		
Unavailable for reduction of the debt:						
Fractional silver coin	26,977,493 79	...	27,064,742 87	...		
Minor coin	113,698 76	27,091,192 55	143,571 41	27,208,314 28		114,121 73
Certificates held as cash:						
Legal tender	310,000 00	...	410,000 00	...		
Gold	30,261,380 00	...	32,101,358 00	...		
Silver	3,425,133 00	33,996,513 00	5,289,164 00	37,800,522 00		3,804,009 00
Net cash balance on hand	...	40,853,369 28	...	23,951,692 44	16,901,676 84	
Total cash in the Treasury as shown by Treasurer's General Account	...	485,433,917 21	...	465,269,526 05	20,082,521 89	
Net increase in cash	...	...	...	...	16,164,391 16	
Cash in the Treasury on account of Deposit Account:						
National Bank Note Redemption Funds	106,106,253 43	...	109,978,707 14	...		
Post office and disbursing accounts, &c.	32,556,323 81	138,662,577 24	42,856,979 88	152,835,687 02		14,173,106 78
		621,096,494 45		619,105,213 07		3,918,130 72
Deduct Certificates held as Cash not included in Treasurer's Statement of Assets and Liabilities	...	33,996,513 00	...	37,800,522 00		3,804,009 00
Total Cash by Treasurer's Statement	...	587,099,981 45	...	281,304,691 07	5,795,290 38	

Debt of the Pacific Railroads for Bonds Issued and Interest Paid by the United States, and Condition of the Sinking-Fund, Act of May 7, 1878.

Name of Railway.	Principal outstanding.	Interest accrued and not yet paid.	Interest paid by the United States.	Interest repaid by Companies. By Transportation Service.	Interest repaid by Companies. By cash payments, 5 p.c. net earnings	Balance of interest paid by the United States.	Sinking Fund. Bonds.	Sinking Fund. Cash.	Total.
	Dol.	Dol. c.	Dol. c.	Dol. c.	Dol. c.	Dol. c.	Dol.	Dol. c.	Dol. c.
Central Pacific	25,885,120	776,553 60	28,888,430 47	5,496,849 96	658,283 26	22,733,297 25	2,590,000	98,545 13	2,688,545 13
Kansas Pacific	6,303,000	189,090 00	7,452,963 09	3,517,642 95	......	3,935,320 14	......	......	......
Union Pacific	27,236,512	817,095 36	30,677,517 93	11,370,902 40	438,409 53	18,868,205 95	5,881,650	77,057 10	5,958,707 10
Central Branch, U.P.	1,600,000	48,000 00	1,885,808 26	298,523 60	6,926 91	1,580,357 75	......	......	......
Western Pacific	1,970,560	59,116 80	2,082,066 54	9,367 00	......	2,072,699 54	......	......	......
Sioux City and Pacific	1,628,320	48,849 60	1,806,244 69	126,504 96	......	1,679,739 73	......	......	......
Total	64,623,512	1,938,705 36	72,793,030 98	20,819,790 87	1,103,619 75	50,869,620 36	8,471,650	175,602 23	8,647,252 23

(375)

UNITED STATES.

Sinking Fund. By an Act of February, 1862 one per cent. of the entire debt of the United States must be annually set aside as a Sinking Fund, and applied to the purchase or payment of the public debt in such a manner as the Secretary of the Treasury may from time to time direct, together with a sum equal to the interest on all bonds so redeemed; and an Act of 1876 provides that fractional currency redeemed by the Treasury shall also form a part of the Sinking Fund.

The requirements of the Fund for the fiscal year 1887, including a balance of 1,597,407 dol. 23 c. from the previous year, were met by the redemption of bonds, interest notes, and fractional currency to the extent of 47,903,248 dol. 15 c.

The requirements of the present year are estimated at 46,817,785 dol. 48 c.

SURPLUS REVENUE, &c.

From the returns given in this Report it will be easily recognised that the United States may be said to offer the very rare—if not the only—instance of a country suffering in a measure from the difficulties caused by a surplus of revenue. By surplus revenue is meant the money which annually remains in the Treasury of the country after the officers of the Treasury have collected the taxes laid on the people by the laws of Congress, and have paid all the expenses and obligations of the Government, except the principal of the interest-bearing debt. The Surplus Revenue, says the Secretary of the Treasury in his Report, is the question on account of which the earnest attention of the Legislative and Executive Branches of the Government is urgently demanded in the direction of taxation reform. He points out that for 22 years there has been such a surplus; and although the ordinary expenditures, exclusive of interest on the public debt, have increased, the surplus still increases yearly. During the present fiscal year ending June 30, 1888, the surplus taxation will amount to 113,000,000 dol. The question is what shall be done with this surplus revenue, which comes into the Treasury in the form of gold coin, silver coin, gold certificates, silver certificates, and United States' notes.

These various forms of money and representatives of money are provided by the Government at a large annual cost as a circulating medium between the people of the country and the other peoples of the world. But, if larger amount of these circulating media are taken into the Treasury as payment of taxes, &c., than that which is paid out, the inadequate amount of money left in the hands of the people for the purposes of business, will bring about such a diminution of consumption of necessaries and luxuries that the taxes on such will not exceed the expenditures of Government. This is an evil and a cure to be avoided. The surplus revenue, he goes on to say, could be reduced, and the derangement to business set forth above could be avoided by various expedients—by the purchase of the interest-bearing debt of the Government, by expenditures by Government for other purposes than the purchase of bonds; or by reduction of the revenue from taxation to the amount actually required to meet necessary expenses.

The Secretary of the Treasury does not recommend the purchase of bonds with the view to the spending by the Government of its present surplus revenues. The Government has purchased during the present fiscal year some bonds for the Sinking Fund, and had to pay such a price for them that the annual saving in interest upon the purchases is only about $2\frac{1}{2}$ per cent. Should the Government attempt to spend its surplus revenues in this manner, the price would go much higher. On two other occasions the Government has paid a premium in gold for its bonds—in 1880 and in 1881. With these exceptions, the Government has always been able to purchase or call its bonds at par or less, and almost the whole of the vast surplus revenue for the 22 years ended June 30, 1887, amounting to 1,491,845,953 dol. (310,801,240*l*.) has been consequently applied to the reduction of the debt upon fairly good terms. This cannot, however, be done as to any considerable portion of the remaining debt.

As stated elsewhere, a total of 127,612,850 dol. three per cents. were retired in 1887. All the three per cent. bonds have been now cancelled. The Sinking Fund requirements for the fiscal year, 1888, have been met. The available funds in the Treasury on December 1, 1887, amounted to 55,258,701 dol., and at the end of the present fiscal year this sum will have, under existing laws, increased to 140,000,000 dols. There exists no way of putting this surplus money out again among the people, except it be under an Act of 1881, authorising the Secretary of the Treasury to purchase bonds in the market at such price and to such amount as he may think fit. The Secretary of the Treasury points out in his report that this is a power which ought not to be given, and a responsibility which ought not to be put on any officer of the Government.

Expenditure, such as would be incurred in the construction of public buildings, &c., in excess of the needs of Government, and any other unnecessary expenditure should, equally with the purchase of bonds, be rejected as an expedient for the disposal of surplus revenue.

Reduction of taxation is, in the opinion of the Secretary of the Treasury, the only fit remedy for the existing evil. He does not recommend the abolition or reduction of internal revenue taxation. To do away with the whole of this revenue would so diminish the receipts of the Government as to make necessary the imposition of duties on articles of importation now free, such as tea and coffee; or to suspend the Sinking Fund requirement, and also materially diminish other expenses of Government. Moreover, internal-revenue taxation is a tax upon whiskey, beer, and tobacco—and if such be looked upon as necessaries to any man, they are at least far less necessary than many other articles taxed by Government.

Where reduction of taxation should take place, is, the Secretary of the Treasury maintains, in Customs taxation. Reduction of duty upon every dutiable article should be made to the lowest possible point, the present situation of labour and business being always kept in mind when this possible point has to be ascertained.

On this all-important point the Secretary of the Treasury says:—
"One argument urged in favour of the continuance of the present highly protective tariff would, if admitted to be true, establish the claim that the majority of the labour and people of this country have made a compact with the minority that the majority will pay the minority more for certain articles to be made by the latter, than the price at which the people of other countries are willing to sell the same; that the evidence of this is found in our tariff laws, which have kept duties at a highly protective rate since early in the war, and in the continued existence of those laws for so long a time; and that under these conditions many labouring men have become so employed in certain industries that it might be difficult for them at once to get work.

"While not admitting that labour elsewhere can injure labour as a whole in this country by giving it clothing and tools at less cost than it can make them here for itself, no more than the sun, the winds, the waters, and, indeed, all the forces of nature injure the labour of the world because they do for mankind far more of man's work than he does himself; yet it must be admitted that the cheaper labour of other countries might now injure a portion of the labour of this country if the articles made by the former were admitted here upon terms which would enable our people to buy them for the prices at which they are sold in the other countries. If this obligation, which it is claimed that labour, as a whole, has assumed towards labour engaged in particular industries in this country, does exist, it should be sacredly kept, however unwise and ill-considered we may believe its assumption to have been; and whether the existence of this obligation is admitted or not, the fact of this present employment of a portion of the labourers of the country should always be borne in mind when making changes in the tariff, to the end that their interests may not suffer thereby.

"Under the encouragement offered by the tariff laws, large sums of money have been invested in manufacturing enterprises, and the capital thus invested must also be remembered, for it is important to the country that it should receive reasonable reward, and its power to pay fair wages to the labour which it employs depends upon its own prosperity. But it must also be borne in mind that it was no part of the alleged compact, nor should it be claimed on any other ground that the labour engaged in the tariff-protected industries should be rewarded beyond the general labour of the country, due allowance being made for skill and experience, or that the capital invested in them should return vast fortunes to its owners.

"The country was promised the benefit of whatever competition might naturally arise among the manufacturers when they should be once established, and to this it has a right. The tariff laws are the country's laws. They do not belong to any section or to any class. Their amendment should be approached in a spirit of justice, and with full consideration of all the obligations which exist between sections of the country towards each other, and of those engaged in one pursuit towards those engaged in other pursuits; but it should also be approached with courage, and with a determination to dispose of this business in the same way that other business is disposed of, and with full regard to the rights and equities as well as the interests of all concerned. After paying due regard to all these equities, after providing for due observance of every obligation, it will be found that great reductions can be made in tariff taxation. So many compensations will be thereby given to this and that industry that most of them will find themselves in fully as good a state as now—many of them in a much better state. Patient labour, coupled with a firm determination to lay aside every consideration save the lasting good of the whole country, will enable the Congress to accomplish its task with honour."

President's Message. The Message of the President of the Republic to Congress on December 6, 1887, is for the most part devoted to the condition of national finances and the dangers which may arise to trade, &c. by the hoarding of money in the Treasury, brought about by surplus revenue. To meet the situation, the President recommends an immediate revision and amendment of the tariff laws; the reduction of taxation demanded being so measured as not to necessitate or justify either the loss of employment by the working-man, nor the lessening of his wages. The message recommends a radical reduction of the duties imposed upon raw material used in the manufacture of the necessaries of life, or even its free importation. By such a change as this a very large reduction of the revenue would be arrived at.

It is believed that the Committee of Ways and Means have this very important question under their serious consideration, but up to the present date no Bill for the reduction of Customs' taxation has been laid before Congress.

With regard to the employment of the surplus money already in the Treasury, the Secretary of the Treasury recommends that this surplus, which amounted on December 1, 1887 to 55,288,701 dol., and will probably amount to 140,000,000 dol. on June 30, 1888, be disposed of by diminishing taxation to such an extent that the annual revenues will be less for some years to come than the appropriations. The accumulated surplus would be used for ordinary expenses, and the people would gain all possible good from it.

Judging by experience, it can be held that, by the time the money was thus expended, the revenues would have so increased as to be sufficient to meet the proper annual expenditures. In the mean time a portion of this money could lie in banks and be available for business.

With reference to the difficulties encountered in the collection of Customs duties, the Secretary of the Treasury recommends as remedies for these troubles, which are daily increasing in number and importance, the reduction of high *ad valorem* rates of duty, the simplification of the Tariff by the elimination of ambiguities, and by decreasing the number of dutiable articles, and the rearrangement and simplification of the Customs laws. He strongly advises that in revising and reducing rates of duty, such rates be made specific instead of *ad valorem*, as far as the nature of the merchandise will permit. By such a change, he is of opinion that devices to gain improper advantages at the Custom-house would be to a large extent frustrated.

United States' Customs.

The chief source of revenue is from the Customs. The revenue therefrom amounted in the past fiscal year to 217,286,893 dol. 13 c (45,268,902*l*.); an increase of 24,381,869 dol. 69 c. over that of the preceding year.

The value of imported merchandise entered for consumption,* including entries for immediate consumption and withdrawal from warehouse for consumption, was in 1886, 625,308,814 dol., and in 1887, 683,418,181 dol. The average rate of ordinary duty collected on dutiable merchandise was, in 1886, 45·55 per cent., and in 1887, 47·10 per cent. The imports of 1887 show thus an increase over those of 1886 of 58,110,167 dol., or 9.3 per cent. This increase in the total value of imports entered for consumption, is found principally in the following articles:—

---

* Imports for consumption embrace imported articles entered for immediate consumption, and imported articles withdrawn from warehouse for consumption. The term "entry for consumption" is the technical name of the entry of imports made at the Custom-house, and does not imply that the goods are actually consumed, but simply that they have been delivered into the custody of the importer, and that the duties have been paid on the dutiable portion. Portions of these goods may be subsequently exported.

UNITED STATES.

Articles and Classes of Articles.

Articles.	1886.	1887.	Increase.
	Dollars.	Dollars.	Dollars.
Free of duty—			
Coffee	42,675,600	56,360,701	13,685,101
Tin, in bars	5,873,773	6,927,710	1,053,937
Ores (emery, gold, and silver)	1,343,294	3,840,925	2,497,631
Dutiable—			
Iron and steel, and manufactures of:			
Ores	1,312,322	2,112,128	790,806
Pig-iron	4,041,367	6,510,126	2,468,759
Scrap-iron and steel	557,402	3,723,471	3,166,069
Railroad-bars, iron and steel	274,878	1,000,329	725,451
Bars, billets, &c., of steel	1,859,827	5,529,704	3,669,877
All other	30,585,981	31,743,228	1,157,247
Total	38,631,777	50,618,986	11,987,209
Wool, and manufactures of—			
Wools	13,794,213	16,351,370	2,557,157
Manufactures	40,536,509	44,235,244	3,698,735
Total	54,330,722	60,586,614	6,255,892
Silk, manufactures of	28,055,855	31,264,277	3,208,422
Jewellery and precious stones	8,367,838	10,981,192	2,613,354
Flax, hemp, jute, and manufactures of	31,612,641	33,807,283	2,194,642
Fruits and nuts	12,973,308	15,088,074	2,114,766

Coffee. The increase in the value of coffee was caused rather by the enhanced price of this commodity than by increased consumption; the average import price having advanced from 7·5 c. per pound in 1886, to 10·7 c. per pound in 1887.

The principal articles on which there was an increase in 1887 in the amount of ordinary duty collected over that collected in 1886, were as follows:—

Classes of articles.	Duty collected.		Increase.
	1886.	1887.	
	Dollars.	Dollars.	Dollars.
Sugar-sugar candy, and molasses	51,778,948	58,016,686	6,237,738
Iron and steel, and manufactures of	14,631,876	20,713,234	6,081,358
Wool, and manufactures of:			
Wools	5,126,108	5,899,817	773,709
Manufactures	27,278,528	29,729,717	2,451,189
Silk, manufactures of	13,938,097	15,540,301	1,602,204
Tobacco, and manufactures of	8,311,114	9,127,758	816,644
Glass and glassware	3,694,924	4,510,312	815,388
Fruits, including nuts	3,498,569	4,210,099	711,530

WASHINGTON.

The following are the leading articles of imported merchandise entered for consumption in the United States during the year ended June 30, 1887:— *Leading articles of imports.*

Free of Duty.

Order.	Articles.	Values.
		Dollars. c.
1	Coffee	56,360,701 42
2	Chemicals, drugs, dyes, and medicines..	27,025,787 62
3	Hides and skins, other than fur-skins ..	24,225,776 21
4	Silk, unmanufactured, cocoons, eggs, &c.	19,640,397 00
5	Tea..	16,373,422 66
6	India-rubber and gutta-percha ..	13,762,627 00
7	Tin, bars, blocks, or pigs, grain or granulated..	6,927,710 00
8	Fruits, including nuts ..	4,767,628 58
9	Paper-stock, crude	4,538,719 21
10	Ores (emery, gold, and silver) ..	3,840,925 00
11	Wood, unmanufactured ..	3,550,191 83
12	Spices, unground..	3,315,964 92
13	Animals ..	3,136,081 52
14	Household effects, &c., of immigrants ..	2,659,700 47
15	Furs and fur-skins, undressed ..	2,471,279 60
16	Hair	2,404,423 00
17	Eggs	1,960,405 39
18	Fertilisers..	1,773,367 98
19	Oils, fixed or expressed and volatile or essential	1,736,239 58
20	Cocoa, or cacao, crude, leaves and shells of	1,670,008 00
21	Cork-wood, or cork-bark, manufactured	1,239,247 00
22	Fish	1,098,561 82

UNITED STATES.

DUTIABLE.

Order.	Articles.	Values.	Ordinary duties collected.	Average *ad valorem* rates of duty.
1	Sugar, confectionery, and molasses:	Dollars.	Dol. c.	Per cent.
	Molasses	5,336,729 63	1,496,863 32	28·05
	Sugar and confectionery	68,905,549 57	56,519,823 02	82 03
	Total	74,242,279 20	58,016,686 34	78 15
2	Wool, and manufactures of:			
	Wool, raw	16,351,369 97	5,899,816 63	36·08
	Manufactures of	44,235,243 64	29,729,717 50	67·21
	Total	60,586,613 61	35,629,534 13	58·81
3	Iron and steel, and manufactures of:			
	Iron-ore	2,112,128 00	855,995 83	40·53
	Pig-iron	6,510,126 08	2,811,026 05	43·18
	Manufactures of	41,996,731 52	17,046,212 01	40·59
	Total	50,618,985 60	20,713,233 89	40·92
4	Flax, hemp, jute, etc., and manufactures of:			
	Unmanufactured—	Dol. c.	Dol. c.	Per cent.
	Flax	1,908,845 00	154,508 63	8·09
	Hemp, jute, sisal grass, and other vegetable substances	9,971,276 00	1,775,831 39	17·81
	Manufactures of	21,927,161 55	7,567,641 72	34·52
	Total	33,807,282 55	9,497,981 74	28·10
5	Silk, manufactures of	31,264,276 58	15,540,300 70	49·71
6	Cotton, manufactures of	29,150,058 83	11,710,719 88	40·17
7	Fruits, including nuts	15,088,073 82	4,210,098 64	27·90
8	Chemicals, drugs, dyes, and medicines	13,285,225 75	4,654,165 24	35·03
9	Jewellery and precious stones	10,981,191 66	1,162,300 19	10·58
10	Tobacco, and manufactures of	10,955,125 03	9,127,758 26	83·32
11	Leather, and manufactures of	10,933,569 77	3,286,862 17	30·06
12	Liquors: Malt, spirituous, and wines:			
	Malt liquors	1,267,309 25	614,186 73	48·47
	Spirits, distilled	1,909,899 96	2,939,923 04	154·01
	Wines	7,013,737 19	3,848,133 05	54·90
	Total	10,190,946 40	7,402,242 82	72·68
13	Wood, and manufactures:			
	Unmanufactured	15,087 39	2,977 26	19·73
	Manufactures of	8,208,416 67	1,500,206 83	18·28
	Total	8,223,504 06	1,503,184 09	18·28

The following figures show the value of imported merchandise entered for consumption at the seven principal ports of the United States, with the amounts of duty collected at each port during the years 1886 and 1887. The enormous preponderance of the port of New York is interesting.

Duties collected at the principal ports.

Customs Districts and Ports.	1885. Values.	1885. Amount of duty collected.	1885. Per cent. of total duty collected.	1887. Values.	1887. Amount of duty collected.	1887. Per cent. of total duty collected.
	Dols.	Dols.		Dols.	Dols.	
New York, N. Y.	412,541,583	130,253,615	68.77	450,070,946	114,356,282	67.39
Boston and Charlestown, Mass.	57,745,323	20,724,833	10.94	61,940,909	22,684,804	10.59
Philadelphia, Pa.	36,548,209	14,438,121	7.62	40,293,229	17,668,472	8.24
San Francisco Cal.	37,674,563	5,791,484	3.06	40,330,099	6,601,180	3.08
Chicago, Ill.	10,488,945	4,037,293	2.12	12,112,275	4,540,931	2.12
Baltimore, Md.	11,675,999	2,512,722	1.32	12,292,853	2,975,674	1.39
New Orleans, La.	7,448,182	1,3'0,321	0.69	9,207,421	2,289,843	1.07

It may be appropriate to give here the following estimation of the value of foreign coins, which was proclaimed on 1st January, 1888, by the Secretary of the Treasury to be the value of those coins in the money of account of the United States, and to be taken in estimating the values of all foreign merchandise made out in any of the said metallic currencies, imported into the United States on or after the above date.

Estimate of values of foreign coins.

UNITED STATES.

Estimate of Values of Foreign Coins.

Note.—The "Standard" of a given country is indicated as follows, namely: *Double*, where its standard silver coins are unlimited legal tender, the same as its gold coins; *Single Gold* or *Single Silver*, as its standard coins of one or the other metal are unlimited legal tender. The par of exchange of the monetary unit of a country with a single gold, or a double, standard is fixed at the value of the gold unit as compared with the United States Gold unit. In the case of a country with a single silver standard, the par of exchange is computed at the mean price of silver in the London market for a period commencing October 1 and ending December 24, 1887, as per daily cable despatches to the Bureau of the Mint.

Country.	Standard.	Monetary unit.	Par of exchange or equivalent value in terms of U.S. gold dollar.	Coins.
Argentine Republic	Double	Peso	Dols. e. 0.96,5	Gold: argentine (4 dols. 82,4c.) and ½ argentine. Silver: peso and divisions.
Austria	Single Silver	Florin	.34,5	Gold: 4 florins (1 dol. 91,9c.), 8 florins (3 dols. 85,8c.) ducat (2 dols. 28,7c.) and 4 ducats (9 dols. 15,8c.). Silver: 1 and 2 florins.
Belgium	Double	Franc	.19,3	Gold: 10 and 20 francs. Silver: 5 francs.
Bolivia	Single silver	Boliviano	.69,9	Silver: Boliviano and divisions.
Brazil	Single gold	Milreis of 1,000 reis	.54,6	Gold: 5, 10, and 20 milreis. Silver: ½, 1, and 2 milreis.
British Possessions, N.A.	Single gold	Dollar	1.00	
Chili	Double	Peso	.91,2	Gold: escudo (1 dol. 82,4c.), doubloon (4 dols. 56,1c.), and condor (9 dols. 12,3c.). Silver: peso and divisions.
Cuba	Double	Peso	.92,6	Gold: doubloon (5 dols. 01,7c.) Silver: peso.
Denmark	Single gold	Crown	.26,8	Gold: 10 and 20 crowns.
Ecuador	Single silver	Sucre	.69,9	Gold: condor (9 dols. 64,7c.) and double-condor. Silver: sucre and divisions.
Egypt	Single gold	Pound, (100 piastres)	4.94,3	Gold: pound (100 piastres), 50 piastres, 20 piastres, 10 piastres, and 5 piastres. Silver: 1, 2, 5, 10, and 20 piastres.
France	Double	Franc	.19,3	Gold: 5, 10, 20, 50, and 100 francs. Silver: 5 francs.
German Empire	Single gold	Mark	.23,8	Gold: 5, 10, and 20 marks.
Great Britain	Single gold	Pound sterling	4.86,6½	Gold: sovereign (pound sterling) and ½ sovereign.
Greece	Double	Drachma	.19,3	Gold: 5, 10, 20, 50, and 100 drachmas. Silver: 5 drachmas.
Guatemala	Single silver	Peso	.69,9	Silver: peso and divisions.
Hayti	Double	Gourde	.96,5	Silver: gourde.
Honduras	Single silver	Peso	.69,9	Silver: divisions of peso.
India	Single silver	Rupee of 16 annas	.33,2	Gold: mohur (7 dols. 10,5c.). Silver: rupee and divisions.
Italy	Double	Lira	.19,3	Gold: 5, 10, 20, 50, and 100 liras. Silver: 5 liras.
Japan	*Double	Yen { Gold / Silver	.99,7 / .75,3	Gold: 1, 2, 5, 10 and 20 yen. Silver: yen.
Liberia	Single gold	Dollar	1.00	
Mexico	Single silver	Dollar	.75,9	Gold: dollar (98,3c.), 2½, 5, 10, and 20 dollars. Silver: dollar (or peso) and divisions.
Netherlands	Double	Florin	.40,2	Gold: 10 florins. Silver: ½, 1, and 2½ florins.
Nicaragua	Single silver	Peso	.69,9	Silver: peso and divisions.
Norway	Single gold	Crown	.26,8	Gold: 10 and 20 crowns.
Peru	Single silver	Sol	.69,9	Silver: sol and divisions.
Portugal	Single gold	Milreis of 1,000 reis	1.08	Gold: 1, 2, 5, and 10 milreis.
Russia	Single silver	Rouble of 100 copecks	.55,9	Gold: imperial (7 dol. 71,8c.) and ½ imperial† (3 dols. 86.0c.). Silver: ¼, ½, and 1 rouble.
Spain	Double	Peseta of 100 centimes	.19,3	Gold: 25 pesetas. Silver: 5 pesetas.
Sweden	Single gold	Crown	.26,8	Gold: 10 and 20 crowns.
Switzerland	Double	Franc	.19,3	Gold: 5, 10, 20, 50, and 100 francs. Silver: 5 francs.
Tripoli	Single silver	Mahbub of 20 piastres	.63	
Turkey	Single gold	Piastre	.04,4	Gold: 25, 50, 100, 250, and 500 piastres.
United States of Colombia	Single silver	Peso	.69,9	Gold: condor (9 dols. 64.7c.) and double-condor. Silver: peso.
Venezuela	Single silver	Bolivar	.14	Gold: 5, 10, 20, 50, and 100 bolivars. Silver: 5 bolivars.

* Gold the nominal standard. Silver practically the standard.
† Coined since January 1, 1886. Old half-imperial = 3 dol. 98·6 c.

WASHINGTON.

NATIONAL BANKS.

The Comptroller of the Currency reports that on October 5, 1887, 3,049 National Banks were in operation. The following table gives a summary of their state and condition as reported up to the year ending October 31, 1887.

	October 5.	
Resources.	3,049 banks.	
	Dol.	c.
Loans and discounts	1,580,045,647	14
Overdrafts	7,503,486	62
U.S. bonds to secure circulation	189,083,100	00
U.S. bonds to secure deposits	27,757,000	00
U.S. bonds on hand	6,914,350	00
Other stocks, bonds, and mortgages	88,831,009	96
Due from approved reserve agents	140,873,587	98
Due from other National Banks	93,302,413	94
Due from State banks and bankers	22,103,677	18
Real estate, furniture, and fixtures	57,968,159	71
Current expenses and taxes paid	8,253,890	72
Premiums paid	17,288,771	35
Checks and other cash items	14,691,373	38
Exchange for clearing-house	88,775,457	99
Bills of other banks	21,937,984	00
Fractional currency	540,594	50
Trade dollars	509	25
*Specie, viz:		
Gold coin	73,782,489	62
Gold Treasury certificates	53,961,690	00
Gold clearing-house certificates	23,981,000	00
Silver coin, dollars	6,683,368	00
Silver coin, fractional	2,715,526	76
Silver Treasury certificates	3,961,380	00
Legal-tender notes	73,751,255	00
U. S. certificates of deposit for legal-tender notes	6,190,000	00
Five per cent. redemption fund with Treasurer	8,310,442	35
Due from Treasurer other than redemption fund	985,410	14
Aggregate	2,620,193,475	59
Total specie	165,085,454	38
Liabilities.		
Capital stock paid in	578,462,765	00
Surplus fund	173,913,440	97
Other undivided profits	71,451,167	02
National-bank circulation outstanding	167,283,343	00
State-bank notes outstanding	98,699	00
Dividends unpaid	2,495,127	83
Individual deposits	1,249,477,126	95
U.S. deposits	20,392,284	03
Deposits of U.S. disbursing officers	4,831,666	14
Due to other National Banks	227,491,984	15
Due to State banks and bankers	102,094,625	68
Notes and bills rediscounted	17,312,806	39
Bills payable	4,888,439	43
Aggregate	2,620,193,475	59

During the year 25 banks went into voluntary liquidation, and eight failed.

A bill for a National Bank Code will probably be laid shortly before Congress. The proposed Code conforms in a great part to the existing law, but it contains some important modifications.

UNITED STATES.

(Reference to the last report on this subject will show the laws, &c., relative to the organisation, &c., of National Banks).

During the year ended October 31, 1887, there were organised in the United States 225 National Banks with an aggregate capital of 30,546,000 dol.

Under the present law, the minimum deposit of bonds required to be made by the 3,049 National Banks in operation on October 5, 1887, amounts to 89,912,347 dol.

The connection between the banks and the distribution of the funded debt of the United States renders the following statement appropriate:

The public debt at its maximum amounted to 2,844,649,626 dol., of which obligations not bearing interest amounted to 461,616,311 dol. leaving interest-bearing debt 2,383,033,315 dol. On October 31, 1887, the interest-bearing debt amounted to 1,041,770,742 dol.

United States' bonds held for National Banks.

The United States' Bonds held in limit by the Treasurer of the United States at the close of the fiscal year to secure circulating notes issued to National Banks, amounted to 191,966,700 dol.; a decrease of 84,008,100 dol. from the amount held on the same account last year. The amount of bonds held for security of deposits of public funds on June 30, 1887, was 25,485,500 dol., an increase of 6,825,600 dol., over the amount held at the same time in 1886.

The amount of bonds deposited during the year was 57,432,150 dol., and of bonds withdrawn 134,614,650 dol.; a total movement of 192,046,800 dol., and a total decrease of 77,182,500 dol. in bonds, held in trust for National Banks.

The following is a statement of the amount of gold, silver, &c., held by National Banks and other banking associations, according to returns last received.

Classification.	National Banks.	1,360 other banking associations.	Total.
	Dollars.	Dollars.	Dollars.
Gold coins	73,782,489	27,015,952	100,798,441
Gold certificates	53,961,690	937,710	54,899,400
Gold clearing house certificates	23,981,000	..	23,981,000
Silver dollars	6,683,368	} 1,824,657	} 11,223,551
Silver, fractional	7,715,526		
Silver certificates	3,961,380	598,313	4,559,590
National Bank notes	21,937,884	} 35,462,589	} 131,151,728
Legal tenders	73,751,255		
Specie (not classified)	..	13,744,873	13,744,873
Total	260,774,592	79,584,094	340,358,686

Redemption of loan of July 2, 1882.

Since the last annual report the whole of this loan, known as the 3 per cent. bonds, has been called in for redemption. The amount of the original issue of this loan was 305,581,259 dol. Changes in the debt have induced corresponding changes in the bonds held by the National Banks.

Security for circulating notes.

This table shows the amount of bonds held by the Treasurer as security for the circulating notes of the National Banks on October 31, of each year from 1882 to 1887 inclusive, the amount held by the banks for all other purposes, and the total of these two:—

Year.	Number of banks.	United States bonds held as security for circulation.					United States' bonds held for other purposes at nearest date.	Total.
		4½ per cent. bonds.	4 per cent. bonds.	3 per cent. bonds.	Pacific 6 per cent. bonds.	Total.		
		Dollars.	Dollars.	Dollars.	Dollars.	Dollars.	Dollars.	Dollars.
1882	2,301	33,754,650	104,927,500	{ 40,621,950 / 179,675,550 }	3,526,000	362,505,630	37,563,750	400,069,400
1883	2,522	41,319,700	106,164,850	{ 602,000 / 201,327,750 }	3,463,000	352,877,300	30,674,050	383,551,350
1884	2,671	49,537,450	116,705,450	155,604,400	3,469,000	325,316,300	30,419,600	355,735,900
1885	2,727	49,547,250	116,391,650	138,920,650	3,505,000	308,364,550	31,780,100	340,144,650
1886	2,868	57,436,850	115,383,150	69,038,050	3,586,000	245,444,050	32,431,400	277,875,450
1887	3,061	69,696,100	115,731,400	144,500	3,256,000	188,828,000	34,671,350	223,499,350

The New York Clearing House Association is composed of 65 members, of which 45 are National Banks, 19 are State Banks, and the other member is the Assistant-Treasurer of the United States at New York. The aggregate amount of clearings of the New York Clearing House for the year ended October 1, 1886, was 33,374,682,216 dol. and on the same date in 1887, 34,872,848,785 dol.; an increase of 1,498,166,569 dol. The aggregate balance was in 1886, 1,519,565,385 dol.; in 1887, 1,569,626,324 dol.; an increase of 50,060,939 dol.

New York Clearing House.

The clearing house transactions of the Assistant-Treasurer of the United States at New York for the year ending October 1, 1887, were as follows:—

	Dollars.	c.
Exchanges received from clearing house	359,788,103	42
Exchanges delivered to clearing house	111,471,810	74
Balances paid to clearing house	248,497,702	25
Balances received from clearing house	181,409	57
Showing that the amount paid by the Assistant Treasurer to the clearing house was in excess of the amount received by him	248,316,292	68

The debit balances were paid to the clearing house as follows:—

	Dollars.	c.
United States' gold certificates	248,343,000	00
Legal tenders and change	154,702	25
Total	248,497,702	25

From the following table will be seen the amount of United States' notes outstanding at the end of the each of the last four fiscal years, and on September 30, 1887:—

United States' notes.

Denomination.	1884.	1885.	1886.	1887.	Sept. 30, 1887.
	Dollars. c.	Dollars. c.	Dollars. c.	Dollars. c.	Dollars. c.
One dollar	26,660,184 80	24,952,061 80	17,603,922 40	8,797,376 50	7,667,871 10
Two dollars	24,897,886 20	25,295,069 20	18,204,369 60	9,008,572 00	7,746,823 40
Five dollars	75,552,915 00	75,997,805 00	85,629,219 00	95,064,850 50	94,224,182 50
Ten dollars	69,527,016 00	64,539,386 00	66,658,661 00	80,371,471 00	83,269,839 00
Twenty dollars	58,054,629 00	55,126,509 00	55,078,379 09	63,929,361 00	68,792,345 00
Fifty dollars	23,208,895 00	23,459,895 00	23,291,265 00	21,908,985 00	21,295,455 00
One hundred dollars	33,640,990 00	32,896,790 00	31,359,700 00	29,643,400 00	29,743,000 00
Five hundred dollars	16,914,000 00	16,557,000 00	12,424,000 00	7,704,500 00	7,484,000 00
One thousand dollars	19,034,500 00	28,716,500 00	37,361,500 00	31,197,500 00	27,402,500 00
Five thousand dollars	130,000 00	100,000 00	60,000 00	45,000 00	45,000 00
Ten thousand dollars	60,000 00	40,000 00	10,000 00	10,000 00	10,000 00
Total	347,681,016 00	347,681,016 00	347,681,016 00	347,681,016 00	347,681,016 00
Less unknown denominations destroyed in sub-treasury in Chicago fire	1,000,000 00	1,000,000 00	1,000,000 00	1,000,000 00	1,000,000 00
Outstanding	346,681,016 00	346,681,016 00	346,681,016 00	346,681,016 00	346,681,016 00

UNITED STATES.

Certificates of Deposit Act of June 8, 1872.
During the past fiscal year certificates amounting to 34,900,000 dol. were issued (under the Act of June 8, 1872) upon deposits of United States' notes received from National Banks. There were received 43,990,000 dol., leaving outstanding at the close of the year 9,020,000 dol., the smallest amount outstanding at the close of any year since the commencement of the issue. In 1885 the amount was 29,285,000 dol., and in 1886 18,110,000 dol.

Gold Certificates.
The amount outstanding of the issue of Gold Certificates under the Act of March 3, 1863, at the end of the fiscal year, was 2,375,700 dol. The certificates, authorised by the Act of July 12, 1882, outstanding at the close of the year amounted to 119,111,117 dol., making a total amount of gold certificates outstanding at the close of the fiscal year of 121,486,817 dol., of which 30,261,380 dol. were held in the cash of the Treasury offices of both issues, and 91,225,437 dol. actually in circulation.

Silver Certificates.
At the close of the fiscal year the amount of Silver Certificates outstanding had increased to 145,543,150 dol., as compared with 115,977,675 dol. on June 30, 1886. The amount held in the Treasury, June 30, 1887, was 3,425,133 dol.; the amount in actual circulation was 142,118,017 dol.; this latter amount showing an increase over that of 1886 of 54,001,792 dol., which was partly due to the demand for notes of small denominations, caused by the discontinuance of the issue of 1·00 dol. and 2·00 dol. legal tender notes.

Trade dollars.
Trade dollars were coined under the Act of February 12, 1873, which made them legal tender at their nominal value for any amount not exceeding 5 dol. in any one payment. They were originally intended to meet a supposed demand for export; but, although a large portion of the amount issued, viz., 35,965,924 dol., is held to have gone to China and India, where they were melted down, it was discovered that many were placed in domestic circulation. At the recommendation of the Secretary of the Treasury, the withdrawal of this coin from circulation, its value having fallen to 86 cents, was determined, and, under the Act of March 3, 1887, trade dollars to the number of 7,689,036 have been redeemed at the Treasury and Sub-Treasuries, standard dollars and fractional silver coin being given in exchange. The loss by this redemption amounted to 40,215 standard ounces of silver. Very few of these coins are now to be found in the country.

Currency circulation.
The following tables show the increase and changes in the circulation of money and its representatives, and of money and bullion in the Treasury since July 1, 1886:—

COMPARATIVE Statement showing the changes in circulation from July 1, 1886, to November 1, 1887.

	In circulation July 1, 1886.	In circulation Nov. 1, 1887.	Decrease.	Increase.
	Dollars.	Dollars.	Dollars.	Dollars.
Gold coin	358,790,428	392,585,770	...	33,795,342
Standard silver dollars	52,469,720	62,934,625	...	10,464,905
Subsidiary silver	46,156,256	51,290,051	...	5,133,795
Gold certificates	76,044,375	99,684,773	...	23,640,398
Silver certificates	88,116,225	160,713,957	...	72,597,732
United States notes'	323,812,700	331,419,950	...	7,607,250
National Bank notes	304,475,950	267,883,223	36,592,727	...
Total	1,249,865,654	1,366,512,349	36,592,727	153,239,422
Net increase	...	...	...	116,646,695

WASHINGTON.

COMPARATIVE Statement showing the Changes in the Money and Bullion held by the Treasury from July 1, 1886, to November 1, 1887.

	In Treasury July 1, 1886.	In Treasury Nov. 1, 1887.	Decrease.	Increase.
	Dollars.	Dollars.	Dollars.	Dollars.
Gold coin	189,529,603	182,342,103	7,187,500	...
Standard silver dollars	181,253,566	214,175,532	...	32,921,966
Subsidiary silver	28,904,681	24,468,135	4,436,546	...
United States' notes	22,868,316	15,261,066	7,607,250	...
National Bank notes	4,034,416	4,157,980	...	123,564
Gold bullion	43,308,520	120,202,502	...	76,893,982
Silver bullion	3,092,198	4,721,996	...	1,629,798
Trade-dollars as bullion	...	6,961,036	...	6,961,036
Total	472,991,300	572,290,350	19,231,296	118,530,346
Net increase	...	...	...	99,299,050

Nearly the whole of this increased circulation was in coin and paper of denominations of 20 dol. and less. The demand for coin and paper of small denominations was enormous, and the Government was unable to supply it more rapidly on account of the lack of a sufficient appropriation for the Bureau of Engraving and Printing.

The amount of standard silver dollars coined in the fiscal year was 33,216,831 dol., an increase of 3,377,926 dol. over 1886. The amount held in the Treasury, June 30, 1887, was 211,483,970 dol., and the amount in circulation 55,456,147 dol. *Standard silver dollars.*

The following figures show the amount of silver dollars coined, on hand, distributed, and outstanding at the close of the fiscal year 1887, as compared with the preceding year:—

Fiscal Year.	Annual coinage.	Total coinage.	On hand at close of year.	Net distribution during year.	Outstanding at close of year.	Percentage of annual coinage distributed.	Percentage of total coinage outstanding.
	Dollars.	Dollars.	Dollars.	Dollars.	Dollars.	Dollars.	Dollars.
1886	29,838,905	233,723,286	181,253,566	14,121,193	52,469,720	47·3	22·4
1887	33,216,831	266,940,117	211,483,970	2,986,427	55,456,147	8·9	20·7

The Secretary of the Treasury in his report points out that from the decrease in the number of standard silver dollars owned by the Government, and from the increased use of the same money by the people in the form of silver certificates, as shewn by the figures relative to currency circulation and standard silver dollars, it is evident that it is waste to coin and store any more silver dollars at present. The amount now in the Treasury will more than suffice to redeem, on presentation, the silver certificates. He recommends that the law should be so amended as to authorise the Secretary of the Treasury to issue certificates against the coining value of the bullion bought, and to coin only such number of dollars as he may deem expedient hereafter.

The Treasury held on June 30, 1887, 26,977,493 dol. 79 c. in fractional silver coin (pieces of 50, 25, 20, 10, 5, and 3 c., and unassorted) a decrease of 1,927,187 dol. 87 c. from the amount held at the same date in 1886. *Fractional silver coin.*

From June 30, 1886, to October 31, 1887, the minor coins (pieces of 5, 3, 2, and 1 cent, and unassorted) held by the Treasury, decreased from 377,814 dollars to 51,400 dol. 61 c. *Minor coin.*

UNITED STATES.

Mutilated and counterfeit currency.

There were deducted from the face-value of United States' notes redeemed during the fiscal year on account of mutilations, 7,266 dollars; from fractional currency, 63 dol. 23 c.; from silver certificates, 943 dol. 00 c.; from gold certificates, 32 dol. 00 c.; making a total of 8,304 dol. 23 c.

There were detected in counterfeit National Bank notes, 2,924 dollars; in counterfeit United States' notes, 4,496 dollars; and 214 dollars in fractional currency. The number of counterfeit National Bank notes detected was 242; of United States' notes, 312.

In 44,537,167 standard silver dollars received in the several Treasury offices during the year, there were detected 4,292 counterfeits; in the amount of 7,162,723 half-dollars, 921 counterfeits; and in the amount of 5,766,520 quarter-dollars, 1,236 counterfeits.

Postal revenues.

The moneys received and disbursed on account of the Post Office Department are not included in the statement of receipts and expenditures of the United States' Government. The total amount of such receipts and expenditures exceeds 50,000,000 dollars, the greater portion of which is received and disbursed by postmasters without going into the Treasury at all. The amount, however, is carried into and out of the Treasurer's accounts with the Post Office Department by postal warrants, issued at the close of each quarter for the total amounts involved.

The expediency and desirability of altering this system, and of requiring all moneys received by the Post Office Department to be deposited in the Treasury, and all payments to be made by warrants of the Secretary of the Treasury issued upon the requisition of the Postmaster-General, have been frequently urged by the authorities of the Treasury Department.

Speakers' certificates.

The amount disbursed by the Treasury during the year in payment of Speakers' certificates for salary and mileage of Members, and Delegates of the House of Representatives, amounted to 1,766,543 dol. 40 c. (368,029*l*. 17*s*. 6*d*.).

Pacific Railroad sinking funds.

United States' bonds and first-mortgage railroad bonds were held in the Treasury Department for account of the Pacific Railroad sinking funds at the close of the fiscal year, as follows:—

Class of bonds.	For Union Pacific Railroad Company.	For Central Pacific Railroad Company.
	Dollars.	Dollars.
United States' bonds issued to Pacific Railroads, 6 per cents	1,043,000	2,548,000
United States' funded loan of 1907, 4 per cents	4,478,650	..
Union and Central Pacific Railroad Company, first-mortgage 30-year, 6 per cents	360,000	42,000
Total	5,881,650	2,590,000

During the year all the three per cent. bonds held for the sinking funds, amounting to 651,350 dol. were withdrawn and paid by the Government, and the proceeds placed to the credit of the respective funds.

Four per cent. bonds held for the Central Pacific Railroad Co., amounting to 199,100 dol., were withdrawn and sold, and the proceeds invested in Union and Central Pacific Railroad first-mortgage bonds, some of which were purchased after the close of the fiscal year, and consequently do not appear in the above table. United States' six per cent. bonds, amounting to 2,104,000 dol. were added to the fund.

United States' six per cent. bonds, amounting to 682,000 dol., and Union and Central Pacific Railroad first-mortgage bonds, amounting to 360,000 dol., were added to the sinking fund of the Union Pacific Railroad Co.

The bonds and cash to the credit of the respective funds June 30, 1887, were as follows:—

Road.	Bonds.	Cash.	Total.
	Dollars.	Dollars. c.	Dollars. c.
Union Pacific	5,881,650	77,057 10	5,958,707 10
Central Pacific	2,590,000	98,545 13	2,688,545 13

Gold and Silver, coinage of, in the United States.

The Director of the Mint, in his yearly report, states that the value of the gold bullion imported during the fiscal year 1887, was 19,770,714 dol.; of this there was afterwards exported, 18,932 dols. There was also exported gold bullion, principally stamped United States' bars, of the value of 2,154,534 dol.; leaving a net gain to the country by imports of gold bullion, of the value of 17,597,248 dol. Gold coin was imported to the value of 23,139,887 dol., of which 5,862,509 dol. were United States' coins and 17,277,378 dol. were foreign.

There were exported 3,550,770 dol. of United States' gold coin, and 3,976,951 dol. of foreign gold coin. The total gain in gold bullion and gold coin amounted to 33,209,414 dol., as will be seen from the following table:—

Imports and exports of gold and silver.

MOVEMENT of Gold Coin and Gold Bullion in Fiscal Year 1887.

IMPORTS.

	Dollars.
Bullion	19,770,714
Foreign coin	17,277,378
Total	37,048,092
United States' coin	5,862,509
Total	42,910,601

EXPORTS.

Foreign bullion	18,932
Domestic bullion	2,154,534
Foreign coin	3,976,951
Total	6,150,417
United States' coin	3,550,770
Total	9,701,187
Excess of imports	33,209,414

The imports of silver bullion amounted to 4,932,697 dol., and the exports of silver bullion of native production amounted to 16,941,713 dol., showing a net export of 12,009,016 dol.

The value of silver coin imported into the United States was

UNITED STATES.

12,327,494 dol., of which 1,239,605 dol. was domestic, and 11,087,889 dol., foreign. There were exported 63,323 dol. of United States' silver coin, and 9,291,468 dol. in foreign coin.

The excess of exports of silver bullion and coin over the imports was 9,036,313 dol., as shown in the following table:—

MOVEMENT of Silver Bullion and Coin, Fiscal Year 1887.

IMPORTS.

	Dollars.
Silver bullion	4,932,697
Foreign coin	11,087,889
Total	16,020,586
United States' coin	1,239,605
Total	17,260,191

EXPORTS.

	Dollars.
Domestic bullion	16,941,713
Foreign coin	9,291,468
Total	26,233,181
United States' coin	63,323
Total	26,296,504
Excess of exports	9,036,313

Stock of coin in the United States. The total metallic stock in the United States on July 1, 1887, including bullion belonging to the Government and awaiting coinage in the mints and assay offices, amounted to—gold, 654,520,335 dol.,—silver, 352,993,566 dol.; making a total of 1,007,513,901 dol. (209,898,729*l*.)

Production of gold and silver in the United States. The production of the precious metals in the United States for the calendar year 1886, was gold, 35,000,000 dol.; silver, 51,000,000 dol. Silver being reckoned at its coining rate in silver dollars.

The following table gives the comparison in round numbers of the estimated total of production of the various States and Territories, for the calendar years 1885 and 1886.

	1885.			1886.		
	Gold.	Silver.	Total.	Gold.	Silver.	Total.
	Dollars.	Dollars.	Dollars.	Dollars.	Dollars.	Dollars.
Alaska	300,000	2,000	302,000	446,000	2,000	448,000
Arizona	880,000	3,800,000	4,680,000	1,110,000	3,400,000	4,500,000
California	12,700,000	2,500,000	15,200,000	14,725,000	1,400,000	16,125,000
Colorado	4,200,000	15,800,000	20,000,000	4,450,000	16,000,000	20,450,000
Dakota	3,200,000	100,000	3,300,000	2,700,000	425,000	3,125,000
Georgia	136,000	...	136,000	152,500	1,000	153,500
Idaho	1,800,000	3,500,000	5,300,000	1,800,000	3,600,000	5,400,000
Montana	3,300,000	10,060,000	13,360,000	4,425,000	12,400,000	16,825,000
Nevada	3,100,000	6,000,000	9,100,000	3,090,000	5,000,000	8,090,000
New Mexico	800,000	3,000,000	3,800,000	400,000	2,300,000	2,700,000
North Carolina	152,000	3,000	155,000	175,000	3,000	178,000
Oregon	800,000	10,000	810,000	990,000	5,000	995,000
South Carolina	43,000	...	43,000	37,500	500	38,000
Utah	180,000	6,750,000	6,930,000	216,000	6,500,000	6,716,000
Washington	120,000	70,000	190,000	147,000	80,000	227,000
Texas, Alabama, Tennessee, Virginia, Vermont, Michigan, and Wyoming	90,000	5,000	95,000	5,000	205,000	210,000
Total	31,801,000	51,600,000	83,401,000	34,869,000	51,321,500	86,190,500

The world's production of gold and silver, arranged by countries for the years 1885 and 1886, compiled from recognised statistics, is given here for sake of comparison.

UNITED STATES.

	1885.					1886.			
Countries.	Gold.		Silver.			Gold.		Silver.	
	Kilos.	Dollars.	Kilos.	Dollars.		Kilos.	Dollars.	Kilos.	Dollars.
United States	47,848	31,800,000	1,241,578	51,600,000		52,663	35,000,000	1,227,141	51,000,000
Australasia	41,287	27,439,000	25,220	1,048,000		39,761	26,425,000	29,403	1,222,000
Mexico	1,304	867,000	772,670	32,112,000		924	614,000	794,033	33,000,000
European countries:—									
Russia	38,125	25,338,000	15,550	646,000		30,872	20,518,000	12,707	528,000
Germany	1,378	916,000	142,340	5,916,000		1,065	708,000	156,400	6,500,000
Austria-Hungary	1,664	1,106,000	50,310	2,091,000		1,664	1,106,000	50,310	2,091,000
Sweden	47	31,000	2,326	96,000		67	45,000	3,031	129,000
Norway	..	..	7,200	299,000		..	..	7,200	299,000
Italy	142	94,000	29,259	1,216,000		142	94,000	29,259	1,216,000
Spain	..	..	54,335	2,258,000		..	..	54,335	2,258,000
Turkey	10	7,000	1,323	55,000		10	7,000	1,323	55,000
France	..	..	51,000	2,120,000		..	..	51,000	2,120,000
Great Britain	..	..	7,607	316,000		..	..	10,124	421,000
Dominion of Canada:—	1,080	720,000	..	..		1,000	665,000	..	..
South American countries:—									
Argentine Republic	118	78,000	11,500	478,000		118	78,000	11,500	478,000
Colombia	3,762	2,500,000	9,625	400,000		3,762	2,500,000	9,625	400,000
Bolivia	109	72,000	384,985	16,000,000		109	72,000	384,985	16,000,000
Chili	260	173,000	180,342	7,495,000		260	173,000	180,342	7,495,000
Brazil	1,204	800,000	2,640	110,000		1,502	998,000	141	6,000
Venezuela	7,033	4,674,000	..	..		5,020	3,336,000	..	..
Peru	226	150,000	47,840	1,988,000		170	113,000	96,246	4,000,000
Japan	265	176,000	23,085	960,000		333	221,000	24,855	1,033,000
Africa	2,083	1,384,000	1,274	53,000		2,163	1,438,000	3,165	132,000
China (Amoor district)	6,997	4,650,000	..	..		5,492	3,650,000	..	..
Total	154,942	102,975,000	3,062,009	127,257,000		147,097	97,761,000	3,137,175	130,383,000

WASHINGTON.

It will be seen that the production in the United States of gold increased from 31,801,000 dollars in 1885, to 34,869,000 dol. in 1886, while that of silver showed a small decrease of 51,600,000 dol. in 1885, against 51,321,500 dol. in 1886.

Deposits of gold and silver.

The value of the total deposits of gold at the mints and assay offices of the United States during the fiscal year 1887, including re-deposits, that is, United States' mint or assay-office bars returned was 83,416,779 dol., against 49,606,534 dol., in the preceding year—an excess in 1887 of 33,810,244 dol. The value of the total of deposits and re-deposits of silver was 48,219,031 dol., against 37,917,026 dol. in the preceding year—an excess of 10,302,005 dol. The value of silver is computed at the coining rate in standard silver dollars equivalent to 1·16$\frac{4}{11}$ per standard ounce.

The total value of both gold and silver deposited and purchased at the mints of the United States during the year 1887 was, including re-deposits, 131,635,811 dol.

Coinage.

The gold coinage of the year was 3,724,720 pieces, of the value of 22,393,279 dol. The silver coinage consisted of 44,231,288 pieces, of the coinage value of 34,366,483 dol. 75 c. The minor coinage consisted of 50,166,509 pieces, of the nominal value of 943,650 dol. 65 c. The following table shows the coinage by denomination of pieces during the fiscal years 1886 and 1887:—

Denomination.	1886. Pieces.	1886. Value.	1887. Pieces.	1887. Value.
Gold—		Dollars. c.		Dollars. c.
Double-eagles	1,106	22,120 00	1,114	22,280 00
Eagles	1,062,160	10,621,600 00	756,067	7,560,670 00
Half-eagles	3,656,432	18,282,160 00	2,960,075	14,800,375 00
Three-dollars	1,142	3,426 00	1,167	3,501 00
Quarter-eagles	4,088	10,220 00	104	260 00
Dollars	6,016	6,016 00	6,193	6,193 00
Total gold	4,730,944	28,945,542 00	3,724,720	22,393,279 00
Silver—				
Dollars	31,423,886	31,423,886 00	33,266,831	33,266,831 00
Half-dollars	5,886	2,943 00	5,831	2,915 50
Quarter-dollars	5,886	1,471 50	5,831	1,457 75
Dimes	6,584,094	658,409 40	10,952,795	1,095,279 50
Total silver	38,019,752	32,086,709 90	44,231,288	34,366,483 75
Minor—				
Five-cents	3,330,290	166,514 50	11,047,523	552,376 15
Three-cents	4,290	128 70	4,232	126 96
One-cent	17,654,290	176,542 90	39,114,754	391,147 54
Total minor	20,988,870	343,186 10	50,166,509	943,650 65
Total coinage	63,739,566	61,375,438 00	98,122,517	57,703,413 40

UNITED STATES.

Coin circulation of the United States.

The stock and ownership of the gold and silver coin in the United States on July 1, 1887, are exhibited in the following table:—

Ownership.	Gold coin.	Silver coin. Full legal tender.	Silver coin. Subsidiary.	Silver coin. Total.	Total gold and silver coin.
	Dollars.	Dollars.	Dollars.	Dollars.	Dollars.
Treasury	*101,143,478	†69,365,953	26,977,493	96,343,446	197,486,924
National Banks	‡152,412,379	§9,878,692	2,813,138	12,691,830	165,104,209
Banks other than National (values specifically reported)	‖41,698,535	2,422,970	...	2,422,970	44,121,505
Banks other than National (values not specifically reported), and in private hands	273,753,673	185,322,502	45,757,168	231,079,670	504,833,243
Total	569,008,065	266,990,117	75,547,799	342,537,916	911,545,981

		Dollars.
*	Gold coin in the Treasury, exclusive of outstanding gold certificates	(91,225,437)
†	Silver dollars in the Treasury, exclusive of outstanding silver certificates	(142,118,017)
‡	Includes gold, Treasury, and clearing house certificates	(79,318,940)
§	Includes Treasury silver certificates	(3,535,479)
‖	As partially reported to Comptroller of the Currency at close of fiscal year 1887, viz.:—	

	Dollars.	Dollars.
Gold coin	27,015,952	
Gold certificates	937,710	
Specie, miscellaneous	13,744,873	
		41,698,535 (total taken as gold).
Silver coin	1,824,657	
Silver certificates	598,313	(total taken as gold and silver).
		2,422,970 (total taken as full legal tender silver).
		44,121,505 (total taken as gold and silver).

Use of gold and silver in the Arts.

The following is a revised table showing the value and character of gold and silver used in the Arts and Manufactures during the calendar year 1885, in which will be found some additions and corrections over the table given in my last Report. The Director of the Mint points out that reports on this subject can only be undertaken at intervals of several years, as they involve excessive labour and correspondence:—

Manufactures.	Number addressed.	Replied.	Manufacturing.	United States' coin.	Stamped United States or refined bars.	Foreign coin.	Old jewellery, plate, and other old material.	Native grains, nuggets, &c.	Wire or rolled plate.	Total.
Gold—				Dols.	Dols.	Dols.	Dols.	Dols.	Dols.	Dols.
Chemicals	341	219	39	32,040	13,903	...	6,063	29	4,341	56,376
Plating	634	348	226	257,741	218,831	801	178,510	24,295	15,537	695,715
Gold pens	34	22	11	7,433	34,886	2,867	990	3,526	6,753	56,455
Gold and silver leaf	72	51	46	58,150	527,453	2,000	31,050	19,700	39,001	677,354
Dental and surgical instruments	154	98	47	3,970	149,186	100	14,942	2,400	4,188	174,786
Spectacles and opticals	384	218	80	207,907	62,420	642	17,169	314	2,291	290,743
Miscellaneous	106	73	27	116,604	44,168	8,000	17,337	1,000	3,835	190,944
Jewellery and watches	6,329	3,351	2,231	2,143,533	5,183,187	164,503	581,654	451,629	485,241	9,009,747
Total	8,054	4,380	2,707	2,827,378	6,234,034	178,913	847,715	502,893	561,187	11,152,120
Silver—										
Chemicals	...	...	...	91	305,165	...	73,561	106	2,165	381,088
Plating	...	...	...	32,824	1,990,587	25,434	43,191	12,798	157,922	2,262,756
Gold pens	...	...	...	55	3,191	...	249	558	5	4,058
Gold and silver leaf	...	...	...	...	21,881	...	708	20	23,512	46,121
Dental and surgical instruments	...	...	...	4,682	107,717	1,401	7,057	4,450	2,494	127,801
Spectacles and opticals	...	...	...	8,587	48,424	155	4,250	210	942	56,568
Miscellaneous	...	...	...	838	5,330	...	268	70	1,017	7,523
Jewellery and watches	...	...	...	86,567	1,354,308	35,718	116,129	85,060	28,716	1,712,498
Photography and mirrors (silver nitrate), estimated	...	...	...	...	600,000	...	...	...	...	600,000
Total	...	...	...	133,644	4,436,603	62,708	245,413	102,272	216,773	5,198,413

Internal Revenue.

The estimates of the receipts of internal revenue for the year ended June 30, 1887, was 118,000,000 dol. The actual receipts for that were 118,837,301 dol. exceeding the estimate by 837,301 dol.

UNITED STATES.

Cleared.

Nationality.	Sailing. Number of Vessels.	Sailing. Tons.	Steam. Number of Vessels.	Steam. Tons.	Total. Number of Vessels.	Total. Tons.
British	55	41,515	23	2,430	78	43,945
United States of America	173	111,162	655	291,087	828	402,249
Norwegian	19	15,766	...	...	19	15,766
Chilian	10	7,625	...	...	10	7,625
German	8	5,458	...	...	8	5,458
Swedish	7	5,617	...	...	7	5,617
Bolivian	2	1,136	...	...	2	1,136
Belgian	1	865	...	...	1	865
Italian	1	823	...	...	1	823
Nicaraguan	1	609	...	...	1	609
French	1	413	...	...	1	413
Hawaiian Islands	1	382	...	...	1	382
Total	279	191,371	678	293,517	957	484,888
,, for year 1885	176	113,728	873	350,675	1,049	464,403

Annex B.—RETURN of Principal Articles of Export from Port Townsend during the Years 1886 and 1885.

Articles.		1886. Quantity.	1886. Value. £	1885. Quantity.	1885. Value. £
Cattle	No. of head	314	1,923	521	4,171
Hogs	,, ,,	3,559	2,081	2,703	3,376
Horses, mules	,, ,,	124	2,174	516	11,606
Sheep	,, ,,	21,730	8,451	21,774	10,912
Oats	Bushels	44,133	3,391	62,126	3,703
Wheat	,,	14,983	2,406	273,421	41,831
Flour	Barrels	38,605	27,542	43,747	35,500
Other bread stuffs	...	...	1,270	...	} 18,959
Butter, cheese, eggs	...	...	11,855	...	
Bacon, hams, lard	Lbs.	617,407	11,069	640,913	12,601
Potatoes	Bushels	11,875	894	14,434	943
Oil, illuminating and lubricating	Gallons	215,261	8,785	181,653	7,500
Iron and steel manufactures, &c.	...	...	11,911	...	9,068
Fish	...	...	3,625	...	...
Furs, hides	...	...	4,266	...	...
Lumber, boards	M. feet	92,795	183,693	89,171	194,910
Laths, pickets, shingles	...	...	8,397	...	7,621
Other articles	...	...	83,614	...	108,785
Total	...	...	377,347	...	471,486

RETURN of Principal Articles of Import from Port Townsend during the Years 1886 and 1885.

Articles.		1886. Quantity.	1886. Value. £	1885. Quantity.	1885. Value. £
Furs, hides	...	...	52,219	...	...
Iron ore	Tons	5,101	2,091	...	...
Oil, fish	Gallons	29,613	2,009	...	...
Rice	Lbs.	475,650	2,006	838,307	3,527
Live stock	No. of head	255	1,723	...	...
Opium, crude	Lbs.	992½	1,035	...	...
Coal	Tons	651	458	...	...
Liquors	...	...	371	3,405	589
Tea	Lbs.	2,140	119	2,705,663	83,628
Beef (fresh)	,,	5,277	76	3,549	93
Sugar	,,	1,550	8	15,106	175
Other articles	...	...	21,415	...	37,667
Total	...	...	83,530	...	125,679

WASHINGTON.

The quantities of distilled spirits, fermented liquors, manufactured tobacco, snuff, cigars, cigarettes, and oleomargarine, on which tax was paid during the last two fiscal years, are as follows:—

Articles taxed.	Fiscal year ended June 30. 1886.	Fiscal year ended June 30. 1887.	Increase.	Decrease.
Number of gallons of spirits distilled from apples, peaches, and grapes	1,555,994	1,211,532	...	344,462
Number of gallons of spirits distilled from materials other than apples, peaches, and grapes	69,295,361	66,168,859	...	3,126,502
Number of cigars	3,510,898,488	3,788,305,443	277,406,955	...
Number of cigarettes	1,310,961,350	1,584,505,200	273,543,850	...
Number of pounds of snuff	6,166,047	6,561,778	395,731	...
Number of pounds of tobacco	185,426,193	199,937,743	14,511,550	...
Number of barrels of fermented liquors	20,710,933	23,121,526	2,410,593	...
Number of pounds of oleomargarine	...	21,796,202	21,796,202	...

The cost of collection during the year amounted to 4,065,148 dol., being about 3·4 per cent. of the amount collected. *Cost of collection.*

The estimated cost of collection for the current year amounts to 4,125,280 dol.

It is estimated that the sum of 120,000,000 dol. will be collected from the sources of Internal Revenue during the current year, an increase of 2,000,000 dol. over the estimates for the past year. *Collections for current fiscal year.*

UNITED STATES.

The following table of the receipts for the first quarter of the fiscal years 1887 and 1888 shows a large increase in the present year:—

Objects of taxation.	Amount of tax paid during first three months of fiscal year. 1887. Dol. c.	1888. Dol. c.	Increase. Dol. c.	Decrease. Dol. c.
Spirits—				
Spirits distilled from apples, peaches, and grapes	179,560 49	173,810 23	...	5,750 26
Spirits distilled from materials other than apples, peaches, and grapes	14,648,801 49	15,468,387 38	819,585 89	...
Wine made in imitation of champagne, &c.	...	...	...	...
Rectifiers (special tax)	6,733 41	5,262 50	...	1,470 91
Retail liquor dealers (special tax)	279,176 40	260,071 64	...	19,104 76
Wholesale liquor dealers (special tax)	16,954 23	12,482 79	...	4,471 44
Manufacturers of stills, and stills and worms manufactured (special tax)	1,115 84	1,460 42	344 58	...
Stamps for distilled spirits intended for export	859 90	499 20	...	360 70
Total	15,133,201 76	15,921,974 16	788,772 40	...
Tobacco—				
Cigars and cheroots	2,963,574 50	3,103,130 98	139,556 48	...
Cigarettes	206,413 85	255,393 51	48,979 66	...
Manufacturers of cigars (special tax)	4,907 35	4,738 49	...	168 86
Snuff of all descriptions	122,609 12	143,790 66	21,181 54	...
Tobacco manufactured, of all description	3,979,201 59	4,759,097 72	779,896 13	...
Dealers in leaf-tobacco (special tax)	2,375 33	2,855 00	479 67	...
Dealers in leaf-tobacco, not over 25,000 pounds (special tax)	613 32	842 63	229 31	...
Retail dealers in leaf-tobacco (special tax)	125 00	...	...	125 00
Dealers in manufactured tobacco (special tax)	97,222 16	101,547 33	4,325 17	...
Manufacturers of tobacco (special tax)	211 00	336 25	125 25	...
Peddlers of tobacco (special tax)	1,703 65	1,281 35	...	422 30
Total	7,378,956 87	8,373,013 92	994,057 05	...
Fermented liquors—				
Fermented liquors, tax of 1 dol. per barrel on	6,300,580 99	6,823,279 37	522,698 38	...
Brewers (special tax)	4,452 12	4,239 57	...	212 55
Retail dealers in malt liquors (special tax)	24,015 97	22,463 61	...	1,552 36
Wholesale dealers in malt liquors (special tax)	15,981 33	17,415 17	1,433 84	...
Total	6,345,030 41	6,867,397 72	522,367 31	...
Oleomargarine—				
Oleomargarine, domestic and imported	...	125,623 30	125,623 30	...
Manufacturers of oleomargarine (special tax)	...	3,000 00	3,000 00	...
Retail dealers in oleomargarine (special tax)	...	14,016 00	14,016 00	...
Wholesale dealers in oleomargarine (special tax)	...	15,040 00	15,040 00	...
Total	...	157,679 30	157,679 00	...
Banks, Bankers, &c.—				
Bank circulation	...	...	...	...
Notes of persons, State banks, towns, cities, &c., paid out	...	332 35	332 35	...
Total	...	332 35	332 35	...
Miscellaneous—				
Penalties	42,385 92	39,366 52	...	3,019 40
Collections not otherwise herein provided for	5,328 88	6,301 59	972 71	...
Total	47,714 80	45,668 11	...	2,046 69
Aggregate receipts	28,904,903 84	31,366,065 56	2,461,161 72	...

Tobacco.

The aggregate amount of taxes collected from tobacco during the last fiscal year was 30,108,067 dol., an increase over 1886 of 2,200,704 dol.

In 1887, 15,995,019 dol. was collected on manufactured tobacco with a tax of 8 c. per pound; and 524,942 dol. on snuff with a similar tax. This total of 16,519,961 dol. shows an increase over the collections of 1886 of 1,192,582 dol.

The receipts on cigars and cheroots at 3 dol. per 1,000 were 11,364,916 dol.; on cigarettes at 50 c. per 1,000, 792,247 dol.; and on cigarettes at 3 dol. per 1,000, 32 dol.; making a total of 12,157,195 dol.; an increase over the previous year of 968,822 dol.

The production of snuff, cigars and cigarettes for the fiscal year ended June 30, 1887, computed from the receipts of stamps sold for all such goods as were put on the market for consumption, together with those removed in bond for export, including importation, was:— *Production of tobacco, &c.*

TOBACCO AND SNUFF.

	Pounds.
Tobacco taxed at 8 c. per lb.	199,937,743
Snuff taxed at 8 c. per lb.	6,561,778
Total of tobacco and snuff for consumption	206,499,521
Increase over last fiscal year	14,907,281
Tobacco and snuff exported	13,728,933
Total production for fiscal year 1887	220,228,454
" " " 1886	204,629,714
Total increase over fiscal year 1886	15,598,740

CIGARS AND CIGARETTES.

	Number.
Cigars taxed	3,788,305,443
Cigarettes taxed	1,584,505,200
Total	5,372,810,643
Increase of taxed cigars and cigarettes	550,950,805
Cigars exported	1,895,050
Cigarettes exported	139,935,300
Total product for fiscal year 1887	5,514,640,993
" " " 1886	4,957,598,488
Increase	557,042,505

There were in the United States at the close of the calendar year 1886, 971 tobacco factories, the amount of tobacco and snuff produced being 209,964,174 lbs.

During the fiscal year 1887 there were 5,156 distilleries (of grain, molasses and fruit) registered, and 4,905 operated. The following is a comparative statement of materials used, and spirits produced during the last ten years:— *Distilled spirits.*

UNITED STATES.

Year.	Grain used.	Spirits produced.	Molasses used.	Rum produced.
	Bushels.	Gallons.	Gallons.	Gallons.
1878	14,680,552	54,499,677	1,995,645	1,603,376
1879	18,735,814	69,649,166	2,801,307	2,243,455
1880	24,006,359	87,915,969	3,110,163	2,439,301
1881	31,291,175	115,609,644	2,710,307	2,111,506
1882	27,459,095	104,149,077	2,121,804	1,704,084
1883	18,644,787	72,235,175	5,373,106	1,801,960
1884	18,927,982	73,724,581	2,259,536	1,711,158
1885	17,865,203	72,834,118	2,719,416	2,081,165
1886	19,195,332	78,544,428	2,308,130	1,799,952
1887	17,959,565	75,974,376	2,421,783	1,857,223
Total	208,765,864	865,136,291	24,828,224	19,360,180
Average	20,876,586	10,513,629	2,482,822	1,936,018

The number of gallons produced from grain during the year shows a decrease of 2,570,052 gallons from the production of the previous year, and is over 4,500,000 gallons less than the average production of the last 10 years. The quantity of molasses used for the production of rum during the fiscal year is 54,039 gallons less than the average for the last 10 years. The quantity of rum distilled from molasses during the fiscal year is 78,795 gallons less than the average production for the last 10 years.

Although the production of rum in 1887 shows an increase over 1886, the production of spirits shows a marked decrease; and these figures, I venture to think, may be held to strengthen the opinion which I have expressed in a report drawn up on the liquor traffic legislation in the United States, published elsewhere, to the effect that the decrease of the production of spirits in the United States, notwithstanding the rapidly increasing population, is a proof of the advance of the cause of temperance.

Decreased production of spirits.

The quantity of spirits (77,831,599 gallons) produced and deposited in distillery warehouses during the fiscal year ended June 30, 1887, is less than the production (80,344,380 gallons) of the year 1886 by 2,512,781 gallons. The difference is distributed among the different kinds known to the trade as follows:—

Increase in the production of—	Gallons.
Rum	57,271
Gin	90,418
High wines	14,675
Pure, neutral, or Cologne spirits	527,638
Miscellaneous	540,744
Total increase	1,230,746

Decrease in the production of—	Gallons.
Bourbon whisky	2,303,785
Rye whisky	528,900
Alcohol	910,842
Total decrease	3,743,527
Net decrease	2,512,781

Spirits removed in bond for export.

The quantity of distilled spirits removed in bond for export during the fiscal year 1886 was 5,646,656 gallons, or 7·02 per cent. of production, while in 1887 it fell to 2,223,913 gallons, or 2·85 per cent. of production; this decrease being mainly due to the decreased withdrawals for export of Bourbon and Rye whiskies and of alcohol.

OLEOMARGARINE.

As this is a subject which for the present is occupying a certain attention, the following details taken from the report of the Commissioner of Internal Revenue may be of interest.

The Act of August 2, 1886, defining butter, and imposing a tax upon and regulating the manufacture, sale, importation and exportation of oleomargarine, was in force for eight months of the fiscal year ended June 30, 1887. The receipts under this Act during these eight months amounted to 723,948 dol., of which 435,924 dol. is the tax on 21,796,202 pounds of oleomargarine at 2 c. per pound, the remainder being derived from special taxes paid by manufacturers and by wholesale and retail dealers.

The Commissioner of Internal Revenue reports in great detail on the increasing revenue derived from the taxation of oleomargarine.

He goes on to say, "The addition of nearly 1,000,000 dol. to the receipts of the United States through the operation of an internal revenue law taxing an imitation, is unprecedented. Heretofore, manufacturers of the article taxed, either quit business or managed to evade the law. The result was the same in either case. No revenue was derived. In this instance, although the results of the first year's work are encouraging, they are not entirely satisfactory. The experience of the year has shewn that although the law was modelled upon existing internal revenue laws in cases most nearly analogous, some changes of the law are needed in order to insure its complete success. It cannot, as an internal revenue measure be regarded as entirely successful until the tax is paid on all of the article consumed; and, if the question were one of internal revenue simply, I would merely urge that Congress by a joint resolution construe the law as this office (of Internal Revenue) construed it in the regulations of August 25, 1886, to impose the tax of 2 c. per pound upon the manufactured substances, such as oleomargarine oil, which are intended as substitutes for butter fat, also upon the mixtures of such substances with butter, and upon imitations made by mixing butter with beef fat, lard, &c."

When the Bill above referred to was reported back to the Senate it was stated that the purpose of the Bill was not to raise revenue, but that it was necessary in order to protect the people from having a counterfeit article sold to them for the genuine, to protect the public health, and to protect the dairy interests, the chief farming interest of the country.

It was said in the debate on the question "This legislation is necessary because the States have not been able thus far to either suppress or properly control the great evil of which I have spoken, and because a sufficient remedy can be found nowhere, in my judgment, save under the Federal Government."

The Commissioner of Internal Revenue is of opinion that the United States' Oleomargarine Law when passed was intended to be regulatory rather than prohibitory. The Bill when introduced was perhaps intended as a prohibitory measure, but the reduction of the tax to 2 c. per pound rendered it possible for manufacturers to continue the business except where, as in New York and Pennsylvania, the State law is prohibitory.

Although the office of Internal Revenue has not been called upon to make any decision relative to the healthfulness of any sample of oleomargarine, the office has received information as to the kind and character of the ingredients used in its manufacture. This information is uniformly favourable, and it is believed that the manufacturers whose products bear the proper internal revenue stamps and brands, are earnest in their endeavours to render their manufactures not deleterious to public health. The Commissioner in the interest of the public welfare recommends amendments to the above law, with the view to arriving at proper supervision, &c.

The quantity of oleomargarine exported free of tax during the eight months ended June 30, 1887 was 667,831 pounds. This quantity includes, of course only oleomargarine, taxable if put upon the domestic market, and does not include oleo oil, of which the export is very considerable.

The statement of the Public Debt of the United States at the close of the calendar year 1887 is given as a postscript.

WASHINGTON.

INTEREST-BEARING DEBT.

Title of Loan.	Authorising Act.	Rate.	When Redeemable.	Interest Payable.	Amount Outstanding. Registered.	Amount Outstanding. Coupon.	Amount Outstanding. Total.	Interest Due and Unpaid.	Accrued Interest.
Funded Loan of 1891	July 14, 1870, & Jan. 20, 1871	4½ per cent.	Sept. 1, 1891	M., J., S., and D.	Dol. 191,956,050	Dols. 38,588,550	Dols. 230,544,600	Dol. c. 417,389 78	Dol. c. 864,542 25
Funded Loan of 1907	July 14, 1870, & Jan. 20, 1871	4 per cent.	July 1, 1907	J., A., J., and O.	620,131,650	112,310,450	732,442,100	973,717 33	7,824,421 00
Refunding Certificates	February 26, 1879	4 per cent.	...	J., A., J., and O.	...	...	151,530	51,520 20	1,515 30
Navy Pension Fund	July 23, 1868	3 per cent.	...	Jan. and July	...	...	14,000,000	210,000 00	210,000 00
Bonds issued to Pacific Railroads	July 1, 1862, & July 2, 1864	...	...	2,362,000 dols. matures Jan. 16, 1895; 640,000 dols. matures Nov. 1, 1895; average date of maturity, Mar. 19, 1895; 3,680,000 dols. matures Jan. 1, 1896; 4,320,000 dols. matures Feb. 1, 1896; average date of maturity, Jan. 18, 1896; 9,712,000 dols. matures Jan. 1, 1897; 29,904,952 dols. matures Jan. 1, 1898; and 14,004,560 dols. matures Jan. 1, 1899.	64,623,512	...	64,623,512	9,989 96	1,938,705 36
Aggregate of interest-bearing debt	...	...	...	...	876,711,212	150,899,000	1,041,761,742	1,662,617 27	10,339,183 91

UNITED STATES.

Debt on which Interest has Ceased.

Title of Loan.	Authorizing Act.	Rate.		Amount Outstanding.	Interest due and unpaid.
				Dol. c.	Dol. c.
Old Debt	Various, prior to 1858	1-10 to 6 per cent.	Matured at various dates prior to January 1, 1861	151,920 26	62,489 27
Loan of 1847	January 28, 1847	6 per cent.	December 31, 1867	1,250 00	22 00
Texan Indemnity Stock	September 9, 1850	5 ,,	,, 31, 1864	20,000 00	2,945 00
Loan of 1858	June 14, 1858	5 ,,	after January 1, 1874	2,000 00	125 00
Loan of 1860	June 22, 1860	5 ,,	January 1, 1871	10,000 00	600 00
5-20's of 1862, (called)	February 25, 1862	6 ,,	December 1, 1871, and at subsequent dates	264,450 00	343 67
5-20's of June, 1864, (called)	June 30, 1864	6 ,,	November 13, 1875, and at subsequent dates	44,100 00	288 98
5-20's of 1865, (called)	March 3, 1865	6 ,,	February 15, 1876, and at subsequent dates	27,350 00	1,415 05
10-40's of 1864, (called)	March 3, 1864	5 ,,	July 9, 1879, and at subsequent dates	66,800 00	4,437 90
Consols of 1865, (called)	March 3, 1865	6 ,,	August 21, 1877, and at subsequent dates	153,700 00	469 53
Consols of 1867, (called)	March 3, 1865	6 ,,	April 1, 1879, and at subsequent dates	304,150 00	10,632 22
Consols of 1868, (called)	March 3, 1865	6 ,,	July 4, 1879	73,050 00	8,889 75
Loan of February, 1861	February 8, 1861	6 ,,	December 31, 1880	6,000 00	2,580 00
Funded Loan 1881, (called)	July 14, 1870; Jan. 20, 1871	5 ,,	May 21, 1881, and at subsequent dates	128,950 00	2,397 09
Funded Loan 1881, (called)	July 14, 1870; Jan. 20, 1871	5 ,, continued at 3½ per ct.	December 23, 1882, and at subsequent dates	45,800 00	3,853 95
Oregon War Debt	March 2, 1861	6 ,,	July 1, 1881	3,700 00	655 50
Loan of July and Aug., 1861	July 17, and Aug. 5, 1861	6 ,,	June 30, 1881	116,000 00	662 00
Loan of July and Aug., 1861, (called)	July 17, and Aug. 5, 1861	6 ,, continued at 3½ per ct.	December 24, 1881, and at subsequent dates	69,300 00	563 53
Loan of 1863, ('81s)	March 3, 1863	6 ,,	June 30, 1881	17,900 00	31 40
Loan of 1863, ('81's) (called)	March 3, 1863	6 ,, continued at 3½ per ct.	August 1, 1882, and at subsequent dates	7,150 00	62 30
Loan of July 12, 1882, (called)	July 12, 1882	3 ,,	December 1, 1883, and at subsequent dates	1,235,100 00	11,952 37
Treasury Notes of 1861	March 2, 1861	6 ,,	March 1, 1863	2,500 00	364 50
7-30's of 1861	July 17, 1861	7 3-10 per cent.	August 19 and October 1, 1864	15,800 00	1,011 89
1-year notes of 1863	March 3, 1863	5 per cent.	at various dates in 1865	35,555 00	1,789 85
2-year notes of 1863	March 3, 1863	5 ,,	at various dates in 1866	28,800 00	1,224 39
Compound interest notes	March 3, 1863	6 ,,	June 10, 1867, and May 15, 1868	191,270 00	39,373 94
7-30's of 1864-65	March 3, 1865; June 30, 1864	7 3-10 per cent.	August 15, 1867, and June 15 and July 15, 1868	129,400 00	18,318 98
Certificates of Indebtedness	March 1, 17, 1862; March 3, 1863	6 per cent.	at various dates in 1866	4,000 00	253 48
Temporary loan	June 30, 1864	4 to 6 per cent.	October 15, 1866	2,960 00	244 19
3 per cent. Certificates (called)	March 2, 1867; July 25, 1868	3 per cent.	February 28, 1873	5,000 00	394 31
Aggregate of debt on which interest has ceased since maturity				3,163,955 26	178,392 04

WASHINGTON.

DEBT bearing no Interest.

			Total.
		Dol. c.	Dol. c.
Old demand notes	July 17, 1861; February 12, 1862		57,105 00
Legal-tender notes	February 25, 1862; July 11, 1862; March 3, 1863		346,681,016 00
Certificates of deposit	June 8, 1872	7,115,000 00	
	Less amount held in Treasurer's cash	130,000 00	6,985,000 00
Gold certificates	March 3, 1863, and July 12, 1882	127,744,451 00	
	Less amount held in Treasurer's cash	31,010,394 00	96,734,057 00
Silver certificates	February 28, 1878	183,194,993 00	
	Less amount held in Treasurer's cash	6,339,570 00	176,855,423 00
Fractional currency	July 17, 1862; March 3, 1863; June 30, 1864	15,318,148 12	
	Less amount estimated as lost or destroyed, Act of June 21, 1879	8,375,934 00	6,942,214 12
Aggregate of Debt bearing no Interest			634,254,815 12

UNITED STATES.

RECAPITULATION.

	Principal.	Interest.	Totals.
	Dol. c.	Dol. c.	Dol. c.
Interest-bearing debt	1,041,761,742 00	12,001,801 18	1,053,763,543 18
Debt on which interest has ceased since maturity	3,163,955 26	178,392 04	3,342,347 30
Debt bearing no interest	634,254,815 12	...	634,254,815 12
Total debt	1,679,180,512 38	12,180,193 22	1,691,360,705 60

Cash in the Treasury.

	Dol. c.		
Available for reduction of the Public Debt:			
Gold held for gold certificates actually outstanding	96,734,057 00		
Silver held for silver certificates actually outstanding	176,855,423 00		
United States' notes held for certificates of deposit actually outstanding	6,985,000 00		
Cash held for matured debt and interest unpaid	15,344,148 48		
Fractional currency	796 02		
Total available for reduction of the debt	295,919,424 50		
Reserve fund:			
Held for redemption of United States' notes, Acts January 14, 1875, and July 12, 1882	100,000,000 00		
Unavailable for reduction of the debt:	Dol. c.		
Fractional silver coin	24,327,528 62		
Minor coin...	55,761 08	24,383,289 70	
Certificates held as cash:			
Legal tender	130,000 00		
Gold	31,010,394 00		
Silver	6,339,570 00	37,479,964 00	
Net cash balance on hand...		69,842,879 11	
Total cash in the Treasury as shown by Treasurer's General Account		527,625,557 31	

Less cash items available for reduction of the debt...	295,919,424 50	
Less reserve held for redemption of United States' notes	100,000,000 00	395,919,424 50
Total debt, less available cash items		1,295,441,281 10
Net cash in the Treasury		69,842,879 11
Debt, less cash in the Treasury, January 1, 1888...		1,225,598,401 99
Debt, less cash in the Treasury, December 1, 1887		1,240,183,052 67
Decrease of debt during the month		14,584,650 68
Decrease of debt since June 30, 1887		53,830,335 03

COMPARISON.

WASHINGTON.

Cash in the Treasury.	January 1, 1888. Dol. c.	January 1, 1888. Dol. c.	December 1, 1887. Dol. c.	December 1, 1887. Dol. c.	Increase. Dol. c.	Decrease. Dol. c.
Available for reduction of the Public Debt:						
Gold held for gold certificates actually outstanding	...	96,734,057 00	...	90,780,753 00	...	...
Silver held for silver certificates actually outstanding	...	176,855,423 00	...	168,149,274 00	...	...
United States' notes held for certificates of deposit actually outstanding	...	6,985,000 00	...	6,835,000 00	...	...
Cash held for matured debt and interest unpaid	...	15,344,148 48	...	14,345,446 80	...	...
Interest prepaid, not accrued, per Department Circular No. 90	...	...	...	262,652 50	...	...
Fractional currency	...	796 02	...	1,780 26	...	...
Total available for reduction of the debt	...	295,919,424 50	...	280,374,906 56	15,544,517 94	...
Reserve Fund:						
Held for Redemption of United States' notes, Acts January 14, 1875, and July 12, 1882	...	100,000,000 00	...	100,000,000 00	...	...
Unavailable for reduction of the debt:						
Fractional silver coin	24,327,528 62	...	24,158,003 77	...	...	...
Minor coin	55,761 08	24,383,289 70	50,270 34	24,208,274 11	175,015 59	...
Certificates held as cash:						
Legal-tender	130,000 00	...	320,000 00	...		
Gold	31,010,394 00	...	39,974,838 00	...		
Silver	6,339,570 00	37,479,964 00	4,413,446 00	44,708,284 00	...	7,228,320 00
Net cash balance on hand	...	69,842,879 11	...	55,258,701 19	14,584,177 92	...
Total cash in the Treasury as shown by Treasurer's General Account	...	527,625,557 31	...	504,550,165 86	30,303,711 45	7,228,320 00
Net increase in cash	...	...	...	...	23,075,391 45	...
Cash in the Treasury on account of Deposit Account:						
National Bank Note Redemption Funds	110,413,466 98	...	109,379,076 69	...		
Post Office and Disbursing Accounts, &c.	42,081,139 99	152,494,606 97	54,236,576 54	163,615,653 23	...	11,121,046 26
	...	680,120,164 28	...	668,165,819 09	...	...
Deduct certificates held as Cash not included in Treasurer's Statement of Assets and Liabilities	...	37,479,964 00	...	44,708,284 00	...	7,228,320 00
Total Cash by Treasurer's Statement	...	642,640,200 28	...	623,457,535 09	19,182,665 19	...

DEBT of the Pacific Railroad for Bonds Issued and Interest Paid by the United States, and Condition of the Sinking-Fund, Act of May 7, 1878.

Name of Railway.	Principal Outstanding.	Interest accrued and not yet paid.	Interest paid by the United States.	Interest repaid by Companies. By Transportation Service.	Interest repaid by Companies. By cash payments, 5 p.ct. net earnings	Balance of interest paid by the United States.	Sinking Fund. Bonds.	Sinking Fund. Cash.	Sinking Fund. Total.
	Dol.	Dol. c.	Dol. c.	Dol. c.	Dol. c.	Dol. c.	Dol.	Do. c.	Dol. c.
Central Pacific	25,885,120	776,553 60	29,664,984 07	5,574,932 83	658,283 26	23,431,767 98	2,743,000	76,905 49	2,819,905 49
Kansas Pacific	6,303,000	189,090 00	7,642,053 09	3,563,485 83	......	4,078,567 26			
Union Pacific	27,236,512	817,095 36	31,494,613 29	11,523,832 70	438,409 58	19,532,371 01	6,273,650	77,531 05	6,351,181 05
Central Branch, U.P.	1,600,000	48,000 00	1,933,808 26	319,832 62	6,926 91	1,607,048 73			
Western Pacific	1,270,560	59,116 80	2,141,183 34	9,367 00	......	2,131,816 34			
Sioux City and Pacific	1,628,320	48,849 60	1,855,094 29	134,573 32	......	1,720,520 97			
Totals...	64,623,512	1,938,705 36	74,731,736 34	21,126,024 30	1,103,619 75	52,502,092 29	9,016,650	154,436 54	9,171,086 54

The foregoing is a correct Statement of the Public Debt, as appears from the Books and Treasurer's Returns in the Treasury Department at the close of business, December 31, 1887.

LONDON :
Printed for Her Majesty's Stationery Office,
By HARRISON AND SONS,
Printers in Ordinary to Her Majesty.
(1125 4 | 88—H & S 375)

FOREIGN OFFICE.
1888.
ANNUAL SERIES.

No. 296.

DIPLOMATIC AND CONSULAR REPORTS ON TRADE AND FINANCE.

UNITED STATES.

REPORT FOR THE YEAR 1887
ON THE
TRADE OF CHARLESTON.

REFERENCE TO PREVIOUS REPORT, Annual Series No. 169.

Presented to both Houses of Parliament by Command of Her Majesty,
APRIL, 1888.

LONDON:
PRINTED FOR HER MAJESTY'S STATIONERY OFFICE,
BY HARRISON AND SONS, ST. MARTIN'S LANE,
PRINTERS IN ORDINARY TO HER MAJESTY.

And to be purchased, either directly or through any Bookseller, from
EYRE AND SPOTTISWOODE, EAST HARDING STREET, FLEET STREET, E.C., and
32, ABINGDON STREET, WESTMINSTER, S.W.; or
ADAM AND CHARLES BLACK, 6, NORTH BRIDGE, EDINBURGH; or
HODGES, FIGGIS, & Co., 104, GRAFTON STREET, DUBLIN.

1888.

[C. 5252—73.] *Price One Penny.*

New Series of Reports.

Reports of the Annual Series have been issued from Her Majesty's Diplomatic and Consular Officers at the following places, and may be obtained from the sources indicated on the title-page:—

No.		Price.	No.		Price.
172.	Ajaccio	1d.	234.	Vienna	1d.
173.	Chinkiang	2d.	235.	Washington	3d.
174.	Naples	3d.	236.	Odessa	1d.
175.	Smyrna	1d.	237.	Sofia	1d.
176.	Belgrade	1d.	238.	Porto Rico	1d.
177.	Philadelphia	2d.	239.	Palermo	2d.
178.	Stockholm	2d.	240.	Lisbon	2d.
179.	Pernambuco	1d.	241.	Tabreez	1d.
180.	Frankfort-on-Main	1d.	242.	Tunis	1d.
181.	Mogador	2d.	243.	The Hague	1d.
182.	New York	2d.	244.	Fiume	1d.
183.	Swatow	1d.	245.	Venice	1d.
184.	Berlin	1d.	246.	Paris	2d.
185.	Philippopolis	1d.	247.	Ancona	1d.
186.	San Francisco	6d.	248.	St. Petersburg	2d.
187.	Lisbon	1d.	249.	Algiers	2d.
188.	Lisbon	2d.	250.	Bucharest	1d.
189.	Nice	2d.	251.	Christiania	2d.
190.	Tientsin	1d.	252.	Paris	1d.
191.	Hankow	1d.	253.	Bogota	1d.
192.	Erzeroum	1d.	254.	Salonica	1d.
193.	Syra	1d.	255.	Copenhagen	1d.
194.	Athens	3d.	256.	Jeddah	1d.
195.	Vienna	2d.	257.	Russia	2d.
196.	Alexandria	1d.	258.	Paris	1d.
197.	Constantinople	1d.	259.	Patras	1d.
198.	Hakodate	1d.	260.	Brussels	1d.
199.	Shanghai	2d.	261.	Ichang	1d.
200.	Tokyo	2d.	262.	Baltimore	1d.
201.	Tamatave	1d.	263.	Taganrog	1d.
202.	Mexico	1d.	264.	Oporto	1d.
203.	Chefoo	1d.	265.	Rio de Janeiro	1d.
204.	Nagasaki	5d.	266.	Galveston	1d.
205.	Cuba	1d.	267.	Tripoli	1d.
206.	Tunis	1d.	268.	Galatz	1d.
207.	Réunion	1d.	269.	Varna	1d.
208.	Hyogo	2d.	270.	New Orleans	2d.
209.	Tangier	1d.	271.	Cherbourg	1d.
210.	Antwerp	1d.	272.	Suakin	1d.
211.	Stettin	1d.	273.	Brest	1d.
212.	Erzeroum	1d.	274.	Barcelona	2d.
213.	Rotterdam	1d.	275.	Barcelona	1d.
214.	Nantes	2d.	276.	Antwerp	1d.
215.	Newport News	1d.	277.	Havre	3d.
216.	Rio Grande do Sul	1d.	278.	Odessa	1d.
217.	Rio de Janeiro	1d.	279.	Tokyo	1d.
218.	Corea	1d.	280.	Saigon	1d.
219.	Kanagawa	1d.	281.	Buenos Ayres	1d.
220.	Wurtemberg	1d.	282.	Taganrog	1d.
221.	Tahiti	1d.	283.	Tamsui	1d.
222.	Bangkok	1d.	284.	Puerto Plata	1d.
223.	St. Petersburg	2d.	285.	Wenchow	1d.
224.	Canton	1d.	286.	Tokyo	1d.
225.	Erzeroum	1d.	287.	Lisbon	2d.
226.	Rio de Janeiro	1d.	288.	La Rochelle	1d.
227.	Valparaiso	1d.	289.	Washington	4d.
228.	St. Thomas	1d.	290.	Beyrout	1d.
229.	Stockholm	1d.	291.	Algiers	2d.
230.	Nyassa	1d.	292.	Varna	1d.
231.	Buenos Ayres	1d.	293.	Algiers	1d.
232.	The Hague	1d.	294.	Port Said	1d.
233.	Trieste	1d.	295.	Manila	1d.

No. 296.

Reference to previous Report, Annual Series No. 169.

UNITED STATES.

CHARLESTON.

Consul Cridland to the Marquis of Salisbury.

My Lord,   *Charleston, February* 25, 1888.

I HAVE the honour to enclose herewith a Report on the Trade and Commerce of Charleston for the past year, and of the principal productions of the State of South Carolina for the same period.

I have, &c.
(Signed)   FREDERICK J. CRIDLAND.

Report on the Trade and Commerce of Charleston, and of the principal productions of the State of South Carolina for 1887.

The city of Charleston, South Carolina, is situated on a tongue of land between the Ashley and Cooper rivers, which unite immediately below the city, and form a spacious harbour, communicating with the ocean—about seven miles distant—in latitude 32, 41 N., longitude 79, 52 W. The land upon which the city is built is elevated eight or nine feet above the level of the water, at high-tide, which rises about six feet, flowing by the city with a strong current, and thus assisting both in the drainage and salubrity of the port. *[Charleston and its port. Latitude and longitude.]*

The harbour is well-sheltered, and safe for shipping. The depth on the bar between Fort Sumpter and the ocean is 12 feet at low water, and 16 feet at high-tide. Vessels, however, drawing 17 feet do cross at times. In the harbour the depth is from 25 to 30 feet, and at the wharves 15 to 25 feet. The bed of the harbour is mud and good holding-ground. *[Depth of water on bar. Anchorage.]*

The railroads entering the city have a large area of wharf-frontage; are connected with elevators and warehouses, offering every facility for through-shipments, and quick despatch of freight arriving or departing. *[Railroads and freight.]*

There is also a dry dock and marine railway employing skilled mechanics. *[Dry dock.]*

The imports consist principally of West India fruits; salt, cotton ties, ale, porter, hardware, and crockery from England; kainite from German ports; brimstone from Italy; cement and general merchandise. *[Articles of import.]*

The exports are principally Upland and Sea-island cotton, cotton-seed, rice, lumber, rosin, pitch, tar, turpentine, and phosphate-rock; also fertilisers and cotton goods manufactured in the State. *[Exports.]*

The receipts of cotton at the port of Charleston for the past year were 400,346 bales, against 505,168 bales in 1886, and 512,039 bales in *[Receipts of cotton.]*

(883)

UNITED STATES.

Cotton acreage.

1885; showing a decrease of 104,822 bales compared with 1886, and 111,693 bales compared with 1885.

The report of the Agricultural Department of South Carolina for 1887, states that the area planted in cotton last year was, in the State, 1,714,937 acres, or a decrease of 35,000 acres as compared with 1886; notwithstanding which, owing to more favourable weather than in the previous year, the yield is said to be 605,000 bales, or about 9,000 bales above the crop of 1886, and, under favourable advices from Europe—cotton having advanced two cents per pound between the 1st of October and the 1st of December—all interested have derived much benefit therefrom.

Cotton yield.

Cotton receipts and exports.

Receipts of cotton:—

In 1886 .. .. 505,168 bales.
„ 1887 .. .. 400,346 „

Exports of Cotton from Charleston.

	In 1886.	In 1887.
	Bales.	Bales.
To Liverpool	90,935	90,444
„ France	22,471	43,966
„ Continental ports	207,011	143,206
Total to Foreign ports	330,417	277,616
To Boston	20,290	16,626
„ New York	130,380	84,826
„ Philadelphia	9,380	7,690
Total to Coast ports	160,050	109,142
Grand total	490,467	386,758

Rice-crop.

The rice crop of South Carolina for 1887 is estimated by the State Department of Agriculture at 67,782,920 pounds, and is probably correct; compared with the year previous, it is 1,843,000 pounds short. The rice-planters, in common with other agriculturists, have not prospered for several years. The decreasing yield of the crop is attributed to many causes; one is the low price at which the article is sold, $4\frac{3}{4}$c. to $5\frac{1}{2}$c. per pound ($2d.$ and $2\frac{1}{2}d.$ sterling); another is that foreign rice is admitted into the United States at a duty of $2\frac{1}{2}$c. per pound cleaned, and the uncleaned at a duty of $1\frac{1}{2}$c. per pound. The rice-planters inform me that the worst difficulty they have to contend with is the high price of negro labour, and its uncertainty at the most necessary period of the rice season. The planter finds that the cost of production is greater than what he obtains for his crop when marketed.

The rice-crop of South Carolina for the past two years:—

For 1886 .. .. 101,329 barrels.
„ 1887 .. .. 107,986 „

Receipts of Rice at Charleston for the past two years.

Receipts of rice.

		Average weight.
	Barrels.	Lbs.
1886	86,126	325
1887	96,280	„

In 1867, six tons of phosphate rock were mined in Charleston County. In 1887 the amount mined was 285,000 tons, giving employment to hundreds of workmen, increasing the tonnage of this port, and the freight for the railroads—also the banking business of the city and State for discount and interest. The trade of this port has been greatly sustained by this industry, valuable works have been established on the banks of the Ashley and Cooper rivers, and several railroad connections made with these works. The royalty on river-mining has contributed to the State's Treasury, reduced taxation, centralised many millions in value round this city, and supplies the basis of many fertilising companies in the United States, and in foreign countries also, opening a field for new devices and machinery, for the more efficient mining of the rock, and for labour-saving appliances for the economic handling of the material.

Phosphate rock: Weight 2,240 pounds.

During the past year, land- and river-mining have been both satisfactory, and of nearly equal amounts.

The price of phosphate rock ruling for some time past has been far too low for profit to the owners of the mines, and an adequate adjustment of the matter can only be secured by the mining companies coming to a clear understanding among themselves, and mutually co-operating for their own interests.

Price of rock, average 4$75c. (19s. 9d).

PRODUCTION of Phosphate Rock in South Carolina.

Year.	Land.	River.	Total.
	Tons.	Tons.	Tons.
1886	294,000	191,174	485,174
1887	230,000	202,757	432,757

Phosphate-rock mined.

SHIPMENTS Coastwise from Charleston of Crude and Ground.

	In 1886.	In 1887.
	Tons.	Tons.
Phosphate-rock	170,459	147,735
To interior towns	23.129	31,748
Local consumption	68,000	60,000
Shipped to Foreign ports	9,583	7,800
Total	271,171	247,283

Shipments of phosphate-rock.

In the report from this Consulate for 1886, No. 88, more information was given in reference to the phosphates and fertilisers of South Carolina.

The trade in lumber and timber for the past year at this port has been more than heretofore localised. The great demand for repairs and rebuilding since the destruction of property by the earthquake, has given work to the City Mills, and has been the occasion for the consumption of a large per-centage of the production of the railroad and river mills. But few foreign orders were offered, while those from the Coast ports were larger than during the previous year. The stock of lumber and timber now on hand is good and large.

Lumber.

UNITED STATES.

Exports of Lumber and Timber for the past two years.

Export of lumber and timber in feet.

	1886.	1887.
To Coast ports of the United States	24,625,371	30,281,085
„ Foreign ports, same period	2,235,223	2,391,650
Total feet	26,860,594	32,672,735

Naval stores.

The receipts of naval stores at Charleston was larger last year than during the previous one, and though prices for turpentine and rosin ruled low, the difference in value was nearly set off by the increased production. It is necessary to lessen the manufacture of naval stores so as to allow the heavy stock on hand to be reduced, and thereby improve the prices.

Receipts and exports of naval stores.

The following comparative statement shows the receipts and exports of naval stores at Charleston for the past two years:—

Average weight of a barrel of rosin, 415 lbs. Do. contents of cask of turpentine, 51 gallons.

	Receipts, 1886.		Receipts, 1887.	
	Turpentine.	Rosin.	Turpentine.	Rosin.
	Casks.	Barrels.	Casks.	Barrels.
Stock on hand	1,181	26,475	4,304	21,784
Receipts	40,575	160,066	49,645	183,182

Exports.

	1886.		1887.	
	Turpentine.	Rosin.	Turpentine.	Rosin.
	Casks.	Barrels.	Casks.	Barrels.
To Great Britain	9,261	37,173	18,982	32,247
„ Holland	11,044	52,399	9,668	33,796
„ Belgium	1,485	3,092	3,500	7,357
„ Germany	5,951	21,084	10,652	31,860
„ Austria	650	22,476	350	18,047
Other countries	2,000	10,911	..	20,412
	30,391	147,135	43,152	149,719
To Coast ports and interior towns	6,861	17,618	9,397	21,435

Price of turpentine and rosin. Currency and sterling.

The price of turpentine last year was from 28 to 36 cents per gallon, or 1s. 2d. to 1s. 6d. sterling.

The price of rosin per barrel is regulated according to its quality. 80 c. to 2 dol. 37 c. was paid for the lower grade, and the highest during the season at 3s. 4d. to 9s. 10d.

CHARLESTON.

PRODUCTIONS of the Soil in South Carolina in 1887.

Article.	Measure.	Quantity.	Acres.	Average.	Value.
				per acre.	£
Indian corn	Bushels	13,453,000	1,487,341	9·0	1,569,516
Wheat	,,	1,170,000	220,030	5·3	268,125
Rye	,,	32,000	8,036	4·0	6,696
Oats	,,	3,510,000	413,963	8·5	394,375
Barley	,,	16,000	1,236	12·9	3,682
Potatoes	,,	235,000	3,911	60·0	35,665
Hay	Tons	4,336	4,336	1·0	12,420
Cotton	Bales	605,000	1,714,937	·32	6,250,000
Rice	Pounds	67,782,920	80,000	..	302,000
Fodder	,,	..	..	..	166,666
Peas	,,	..	..	..	167,207
Sugar-cane	,,	..	..	..	120,273
Orchard and garden produce	,,	..	..	..	240,000
Total value	..	..	..	..	9,536,625

Productions of South Carolina.

Value.

NUMBER and value of Live Stock in South Carolina in 1887.

	Number.	Average price.	Value in sterling.
		Dol. c.	£ s. d.
Horses	64,673	88 17	18 7 4
Mules	73,253	94 04	19 11 10
Cows	144,748	18 25	3 16 0
Oxen	216,858	10 67	2 3 6
Sheep	108,418	1 53	0 6 4
Hogs	550,166	3 76	0 15 8

Live stock in South Carolina and value.

The currency in this report is reduced into sterling at 4·80 per £. *Quarantine regulations.*
Quarantine.—The quarantine laws are enforced from sunrise, May 1st, until sunset, October 31st, unless otherwise ordered. Vessels arriving within these periods will be left at the quarantine ground, about four miles from the port of Charleston, by the pilot. The quarantine officer will then board the vessel and give instructions. Vessels coming to quarantine will have flag at half-mast on the foremast on crossing the Bar.

The harbour-master attends to the strict enforcement of the port regulations, looking to the safety and convenience of vessels arriving, remaining, and leaving the same; to this end he is required from time to time, and as often as may be necessary, to inspect the wharves, docks, and places of anchorage in the port and observe the location of vessels using the same. *Harbour-master and his duties.*

For the purpose of meeting expenses attendant upon the execution of the regulations of the port and proper accommodation of vessels, the following fees are imposed upon all vessels coming into the port of Charleston: *Port fees on home and foreign ships.*

	Dollars.
On Coasting steamers, yearly	20
,, ,, schooners, per trip	2
,, ,, brigs, ,,	2
,, Foreign steamers, ,,	12
,, ,, barques, ,,	6
,, ,, brigs, ,,	3

UNITED STATES.

Commission on vessels.

On collecting freight	2½ per cent.
„ disbursements	2½ „
„ procuring freight	5 „

Commission and charges on vessels arriving in distress and their cargoes reshipped, 2½ per cent. When the ship-broker or commission merchant transacts the entire business of a vessel, no charge is made for collecting freights or for disbursements, unless the vessel leaves in debt, when 2½ per cent. is charged and interest.

Cost of water. The cost of water for vessels, ¾ cent per gallon.
„ coal. The cost of steam-coal per ton, 4 dol. 25 c. to 5 dol.
„ stores. The cost of ships-stores, a small advance on New York prices.

Rates of Pilotage at Charleston.

	Currency.	Sterling.
	Dol. c.	£ s. d.
For vessels drawing 6 feet water or under	15 00	3 2 6
„ „ „ 7 „ „ „	16 50	3 8 9
„ „ „ 8 „ „ „	18 50	3 17 1
„ „ „ 9 „ „ „	21 00	4 7 6
„ „ „ 10 „ „ „	28 50	5 18 9
„ „ „ 11 „ „ „	33 00	6 17 6
„ „ „ 12 „ „ „	40 00	8 6 8
„ „ „ 12½ „ „ „	44 00	9 3 4
„ „ „ 13 „ „ „	45 00	9 7 6
„ „ „ 13½ „ „ „	50 00	10 8 4
„ „ „ 14 „ „ „	54 00	11 5 0
„ „ „ 14½ „ „ „	60 00	12 10 0
„ „ „ 15 „ „ „	66 00	13 15 0
„ „ „ 15½ „ „ „	69 00	14 7 6
„ „ „ 16 „ „ „	84 00	17 10 0
„ „ „ 16½ „ „ „	100 00	20 16 8
„ „ „ 17 „ „ „	120 00	25 0 0
„ „ „ 17½ „ „ „	150 00	31 5 0
„ „ „ 18 „ „ „	180 00	37 10 0

Same rates of pilotage on vessels in and out.
For docking vessels, 4 dol. (16s. 8d.).

Dock charges.

	Currency.	Sterling.
	Dollars.	£ s. d.
Dock charges on vessels up to 100 tons per day	1	0 4 2
From 100 tons to 300 tons	2	0 8 4
„ 300 „ 500 „	3	0 12 6
„ 500 „ 700 „	4	0 16 8
„ 700 „ 900 „	5	1 0 10
„ 900 „ 1,000 „	6	1 5 0
„ 1,000 „ 1,100 „	7	1 9 2
„ 1,100 „ 1,200 „	8	1 13 4
„ 1,200 „ 1,300 „	9	1 17 6
Over 1,300 tons	10	2 1 8

CHARLESTON.

Annex A.—Return of all Shipping at the Port of Charleston in the Year 1887.

Entered.

Nationality.	Sailing. Number of Vessels.	Sailing. Tons.	Steam. Number of Vessels.	Steam. Tons.	Total. Number of Vessels.	Total. Tons.
British	18	9,279	48	52,954	66	62,233
American	415	390,985	273	188,739	688	579,724
Norwegian-Swedish	43	20,240	3	1,910	46	22,150
Italian	30	14,809	...	...	30	14,809
Spanish	14	5,291	3	2,533	17	7,824
German and Austrian	...	...	...	...	...	...
Russian and French	...	...	...	...	...	...
Danish	19	9,250	4	5,484	23	14,734
Total	539	449,854	331	251,620	870	701,474
,, for the year preceding	469	191,911	205	263,049	674	454,960

Cleared.

Nationality.	Sailing. Number of Vessels.	Sailing. Tons.	Steam. Number of Vessels.	Steam. Tons.	Total. Number of Vessels.	Total. Tons.
British	19	9,167	50	54,937	69	64,104
American	412	386,013	263	174,293	675	560,306
Norwegian-Swedish	42	19,860	...	...	42	19,860
Italian	26	12,744	...	...	26	12,744
Spanish	14	5,291	2	1,728	16	7,019
German and Austrian	...	...	...	...	...	...
Russian and French	17	8,447	4	5,484	21	13,931
Total	530	441,522	319	236,442	849	677,964
,, for the year preceding	475	193,485	205	264,799	680	458,284

Annex B.—Return of Principal Articles of Export from the Port of Charleston, South Carolina, to Home and to Foreign Markets, during the Years 1887 and 1886.

Articles.		1887. Quantity.	1887. Value in Sterling. £	1886. Quantity.	1886. Value in Sterling. £
Cotton, Upland	Bales	392,861	3,683,071	495,547	4,645,728
,, Sea Island	Bags	7,485	148,140	9,621	240,525
Rice	Barrels	96,280	300,875	70,017	233,390
Turpentine	Casks	49,645	165,483	62,854	183,324
Rosin	Barrels	183,182	64,876	273,309	99,643
Phosphate rock	Tons	209,427	207,245	225,660	266,312
,, ground	,,	37,856	59,150	15,511	29,083
Lumber and crossties	Feet	44,672,735	93,220	27,615,715	108,333
Fertilisers	Tons	130,633	544,304	141,287	573,978
Fruits and vegetables	Packages	85,385	186,458	89,611	182,291
Cotton goods, manufactured in Charleston	Bales	52,708	658,850	46,725	486,718
Total		...	6,111,672	...	7,049,328

UNITED STATES.

Return of Principal Articles of Import to Charleston during the Years 1887 and 1886.

Articles.	Value. 1887.	Value. 1886.
	£	£
The principal articles imported are salt, iron, ties, beer, brimstone, and kainite, also tropical fruit ..	111,771	148,180

Annex C.—Table showing the Total Value of all Articles Exported from Charleston, and Imported to Charleston, from and to Foreign Countries during the Years 1887 and 1886.

Countries.	Exports. 1887.	Exports. 1886.	Imports. 1887.	Imports. 1886.
	£	£	£	£
Great Britain, France, Germany, Italy, Holland, Belgium, Spain, Russia	3,047,755	3,695,852	111,771	148,180

The Statistics of Commerce published by the United States' Government at Washington and by the Port Authorities of this city, give only returns from July 1 to 30th of next June, or from August 30 in each year to September 1 in next year; consequently it is impossible to obtain the proper information for Annex C. as desired.

LONDON:
Printed for Her Majesty's Stationery Office,
By HARRISON AND SONS,
Printers in Ordinary to Her Majesty
(1125 4 | 88—H & S 383)

415

FOREIGN OFFICE.
1888.
ANNUAL SERIES.

No. 310.

DIPLOMATIC AND CONSULAR REPORTS ON TRADE AND FINANCE.

UNITED STATES.

REPORT FOR THE YEAR 1887
ON THE
AGRICULTURE OF BALTIMORE AND DISTRICT.

REFERENCE TO PREVIOUS REPORT, Annual Series No. 262.

Presented to both Houses of Parliament by Command of Her Majesty,
APRIL, 1888.

LONDON:
PRINTED FOR HER MAJESTY'S STATIONERY OFFICE,
BY HARRISON AND SONS, ST. MARTIN'S LANE,
PRINTERS IN ORDINARY TO HER MAJESTY.

And to be purchased, either directly or through any Bookseller, from
EYRE AND SPOTTISWOODE, EAST HARDING STREET, FLEET STREET, E.C., and
32, ABINGDON STREET, WESTMINSTER, S.W.; or
ADAM AND CHARLES BLACK, 6, NORTH BRIDGE, EDINBURGH; or
HODGES, FIGGIS, & Co., 104, GRAFTON STREET, DUBLIN.

1888.

[C. 5252—87.]   *Price One Penny.*

New Series of Reports.

Reports of the Annual Series have been issued from Her Majesty's Diplomatic and Consular Officers at the following places, and may be obtained from the sources indicated on the title-page:—

No.		Price.	No.		Price.
186. San Francisco		6d.	248. St. Petersburg		2d.
187. Lisbon		1d.	249. Algiers		2d.
188. Lisbon		2d.	250. Bucharest		1d.
189. Nice		2d.	251. Christiania		2d.
190. Tientsin		1d.	252. Paris		1d.
191. Hankow		1d.	253. Bogota		1d.
192. Erzeroum		1d.	254. Salonica		1d.
193. Syra		1d.	255. Copenhagen		1d.
194. Athens		3d.	256. Jeddah		1d.
195. Vienna		2d.	257. Russia		2d.
196. Alexandria		1d.	258. Paris		1d.
197. Constantinople		1d.	259. Patras		1d.
198. Hakodate		1d.	260. Brussels		1d.
199. Shanghai		2d.	261. Ichang		1d.
200. Tokyo		2d.	262. Baltimore		1d.
201. Tamatave		1d.	263. Taganrog		1d.
202. Mexico		1d.	264. Oporto		1d.
203. Chefoo		1d.	265. Rio de Janeiro		1d.
204. Nagasaki		5d.	266. Galveston		1d.
205. Cuba		1d.	267. Tripoli		1d.
206. Tunis		1d.	268. Galatz		1d.
207. Réunion		1d.	269. Varna		1d.
208. Hyogo		2d.	270. New Orleans		2d.
209. Tangier		1d.	271. Cherbourg		1d.
210. Antwerp		1d.	272. Suakin		1d.
211. Stettin		1d.	273. Brest		1d.
212. Erzeroum		1d.	274. Barcelona		2d.
213. Rotterdam		1d.	275. Barcelona		1d.
214. Nantes		2d.	276. Antwerp		1d.
215. Newport News		1d.	277. Havre		3d.
216. Rio Grande do Sul		1d.	278. Odessa		1d.
217. Rio de Janeiro		1d.	279. Tokyo		1d.
218. Corea		1d.	280. Saigon		1d.
219. Kanagawa		1d.	281. Buenos Ayres		1d.
220. Wurtemberg		1d.	282. Taganrog		1d.
221. Tahiti		1d.	283. Tamsui		1d.
222. Bangkok		1d.	284. Puerto Plata		1d.
223. St. Petersburg		2d.	285. Wênchow		1d.
224. Canton		1d.	286. Tokyo		1d.
225. Erzeroum		1d.	287. Lisbon		2d.
226. Rio de Janeiro		1d.	288. La Rochelle		1d.
227. Valparaiso		1d.	289. Washington		4d.
228. St. Thomas		1d.	290. Beyrout		1d.
229. Stockholm		1d.	291. Algiers		2d.
230. Nyassa		1d.	292. Varna		1d.
231. Buenos Ayres		1d.	293. Algiers		1d.
232. The Hague		1d.	294. Port Saïd		1d.
233. Trieste		1d.	295. Manila		1d.
234. Vienna		1d.	296. Charleston		1d.
235. Washington		3d.	297. Kiungchow		1d.
236. Odessa		1d.	298. Pakhoi		1d.
237. Sofia		1d.	299. Wuhu		1d.
238. Porto Rico		1d.	300. Boulogne		2d.
239. Palermo		2d.	301. Marseilles		1d.
240. Lisbon		2d.	302. Bordeaux		2d.
241. Tabreez		1d.	303. Ancona		1d.
242. Tunis		1d.	304. Swatow		1d.
243. The Hague		1d.	305. Ssŭ-ch'uan		1d.
244. Fiume		1d.	306. Antwerp		1d.
245. Venice		1d.	307. Cadiz		1d.
246. Paris		2d.	308. Genoa		1d.
247. Ancona		1d.	309. Marseilles		1d.

No. 310.

Reference to previous Report, Annual Series No. 262.

UNITED STATES.

BALTIMORE.

Consul Segrave to the Marquis of Salisbury.

My Lord,   *Baltimore, March* 23, 1888.

IN compliance with instructions, I have the honour herewith to transmit to your Lordship a Report on Agriculture in Maryland and Virginia.

I have, &c.
(Signed)   W. F. SEGRAVE.

Report on Agriculture in the States of Maryland and Virginia.

The area of Maryland is about 8,000,000 of acres, and that of Virginia about 27,000,000 acres. In Maryland 2,000,000 acres is forest area; in Virginia forest area is 13,000,000 acres, or 50 per cent. of total area. Maryland contains 40,517 agricultural holdings, and Virginia 118,517. It may be taken as a general rule that the whole of this land is freehold.

The assessed value of property in the rural districts of Maryland is, in round numbers, 45,000,000*l.* sterling, and the land-tax—or what can be compared approximately to the land-tax—is at the rate of $1\tfrac{3}{4}d.$ in the £. It is not easy to arrive at any definite estimate of the average saleable value of land for the two States, but it may be taken roughly as about 20 dol. an acre. It varies, however, greatly from a maximum of 100 dol. an acre to a minimum of infinitesimal low value, some lands in the mountain districts of Virginia being to be had as low as one dollar—or even less—an acre, market facilities being considered more in testing the saleable value of land than its actual productiveness.

There is comparatively little land which is not capable of improvement, although a large quantity is lying idle which good farming would render valuable and productive. These States offer many inducements to immigrants, and are far superior to those of the Western States.

The mildness of the climate, the fertility of the soil, and the great variety of products, offer profitable openings to farm-labour backed by moderate capital. Although heat and cold are at times intense, the extremes are rarely of long duration, and there is probably no portion of the United States that can count on longer periods of pleasant enjoyable weather. The country is singularly healthy, with the exception of the low-lying districts bordering on Chesapeake Bay, where a certain amount of malaria prevails at some seasons of the year.

In so extensive a tract of country land varies greatly in its nature, and, as a consequence, in its produce and value. A large portion

(398)

Soil; Maryland and Virginia.

of these States is hilly, even mountainous, and is more adapted for stock-raising than for agriculture; whilst on the lowlands bordering on the Chesapeake Bay—an alluvial region with light warm soil easily tilled—fruit-growing, market-gardening, and cotton, are most in favour and the best paying crops; a cheap and commodious system of water-carriage giving them great market facilities with the neighbouring cities of New York, Philadelphia, and Baltimore. The red soil of Piedmont at the foot of the mountains, is very fertile, and is the great apple-growing and wine-producing district; whilst the Shenandoah Valley, a broad belt of rolling country between two mountain ranges, has a stiff clayey loam well adapted for grain and grass.

Not so long ago, the opinion prevailed amongst farmers in this country that it was cheaper to wear out their land and then clear up fresh land than to improve the old. At the present time, however, land in the Eastern States is more or less exhausted, and it is only under exceptional circumstances that the farmer can make wheat, maize, or tobacco pay.

Land in these States has, of late years, greatly fallen in price, and more especially that given up to growing the above-mentioned crops.

In the hills where stock-breeding and fruit-growing are the staple industries, and which are generally much more profitable, land fetches comparatively better prices.

A farmer in Eastern Virginia, holding 1,000 acres, is generally a poor man, and probably could not get more than 10 dol. to 15 dol. an acre if he wanted to sell it. In the Northern States such land would be worth 50 dol. an acre, yet the climate of Virginia is far superior to that of the North, the land is naturally as productive, the price of produce is, as a rule, higher, and labour is cheaper; yet, nevertheless, with so many circumstances in its favour, land in Virginia is of much less value. The reason assigned here is that land is always most valuable where grass and forage-plants are grown.

Crops; Virginia and Maryland.

As may be seen by the accompanying tables, farmers in the States turn their attention chiefly to wheat, Indian-corn, minor cereals, hay, cattle-breeding, and dairy-farming, fruit, vegetables, and market-gardening, cotton, and tobacco.

Land improvements.

The first thing that preoccupies the farmer is, how to get the largest and most profitable crop out of his land with the most economical expenditure in fertilisers, for it is now quite understood that if the farmer does not improve his land it will deteriorate.

It is not, however, everyone who can afford expensive commercial fertilisers, nor is it every expensive fertiliser which is adapted to the special soil for which it is used. To understand exactly the nature of the fertiliser to apply to the land, and that which is suited to the special crop to be grown, requires a knowledge of agricultural chemistry which is by no means so general as it ought to be amongst men who undertake the business of agriculture with a view to profit.

And, in point of fact, it is by no means unusual in some parts of the country to find farmers who spend their money in highly manuring good land, and leave light, bad land entirely unimproved; their idea being that, in view of the great cost of commercial fertilisers, it is more profitable to take a short crop out of bad land than to spend money in improving it; or in other words, that the cost of the fertilisers is out of proportion to the prospective gain in produce.

Every farmer has his own theory—and, unfortunately, his own practice as well—for the most effective and economical means of improving his land.

It is generally conceded that lime, followed by green fallow, is of all the cheapest and most effective means for bringing land into good order.

In some parts of the States farmers are much in favour of clover as an improver of land, and some even declare that, with clover and lime, you can improve any land, and that no fertiliser is equal to them. *Clover.*

There has been much difference of opinion as to the respective advantages of deep and shallow ploughing; where the subsoil is good deep ploughing is always profitable, and even where the subsoil is indifferent, a small expenditure in fertilisers will amply repay the cost. The opinion is generally finding favour that sheep are the most useful, profitable, and economical improvers of land; but, in view of the difficulty of folding, as well as the ravages of stray dogs and occasional wolves, it is more than doubtful whether any large extension of sheep-breeding will take in the country. *Ploughing* *Sheep as improvers.*

The labour question has become a difficult problem. Few farmers would object to pay the present increased wages were it possible in return to get as good a day's work from their men as the fathers of the latter gave for less money. Notoriously this is not the case. *Labour.*

The labourers' children go to school and there acquire a distaste for agricultural work and disdain the manual labour of rural life, they flock into the towns, leaving the least competent of their companions to work on the farms. So that, having to pay a school-rate in addition to his other heavy burdens, the farmer finds the cost of labour increased and its efficiency diminished. Indeed, it is a current saying in this part of the country that a spelling-book given to a negro spoils for ever a good field-hand.

About 50 per cent. of the labour of Virginia is engaged in agriculture, and the greater proportion is coloured. In Maryland the larger proportion of labour is manufacturing. Engaged men receive 12 dol. a-month, with board; at harvest-time hired hands obtain 1 dol. 50 c. a-day without board. The waifs and strays of the large towns take advantage of this season for an outing, and pour into the country districts in the same manner as hop-pickers migrate from London into Kent. As the bulk of them have no practical knowledge of the labour they undertake to perform, it can be imagined how inefficient and extravagant their work is. Agricultural machinery, however, of the latest and most improved models, is in almost general use throughout these States. *Machinery.*

In Maryland and Virginia there are about 1,231,000 acres under wheat, but the area diminishes yearly. Nor is this to be wondered at, as the average return for the two States is only about $6\frac{1}{2}$ bushels an acre. With such a return it can be easily understood that farmers must grow wheat at a loss, and indeed it is difficult to see why they grow wheat at all, unless for domestic consumption. No doubt high farming and the lavish use of fertilisers will produce on certain lands a greater yield, but in view of the steady fall in the price of wheat, and which has by no means reached its lowest point as yet—if the opinion of practical men has any weight—farmers look upon putting expensive commercial fertilisers into their land as throwing good money after bad, when wheat in these parts only fetches 92 c. a bushel, or about 30s. 6d. a quarter. To ensure anything like a paying crop off his land the farmer must put in a 200 lb. bag of stuff an acre, at the cost of 35 dol. to 40 dol. a ton—that is 3 dol. 50 c. to 4 dol. an acre. *Wheat.*

No doubt these fertilisers stimulate the land, and, in some cases, produce surprising results, but, like opium smoking and dram drinking, they require to be constantly repeated, otherwise the land becomes so exhausted as to be practically worthless. In fine, the general opinion

UNITED STATES.

is that, taking the whole wheat area of Maryland and Virginia into consideration, commercial fertilisers do not pay.

No farmer in this part of the country should put land in wheat unless he has the prospect of a paying crop in the majority of years; on such land he may expect, with the proper use of a well-selected fertiliser, to get such an addition to his crop as may pay him, and, at the same time, a good stand of clover and grass.

Land well set in these may be considered, with proper management, on the high road to improvement.

But much of the land in these States will not, even with fertilisers, produce clover. In such a case they sow in peas with some fertiliser containing potash, to secure a good crop; they then turn these under and sow with wheat, and in the spring with clover, and generally a catch will be secured.

They let the land stand in clover for two or three years' fallow, then lime and sow in wheat again with clover in the spring.

Pure bone meal has proved on most soils—in these two States—the very best fertiliser for wheat and clover, but stable or farmyard manure is no doubt the best for all lands. As, however, the supply of it is always short, it should be supplemented by a good commercial fertiliser, sown regularly without regard to the manure.

A gentleman in this city, who in England would be called a gentleman farmer, as he is independent of his farm for his support, has furnished me with a Dr. and Cr. Account of the cost of cultivation of an acre of wheat. He writes to me, "I farm 350 acres of land of the same character as prevails within a radius of 20 miles of Baltimore, and have yearly about 70 acres of wheat and 50 acres of Indian corn. I calculate the cost of growing an acre of wheat, and the product thereof as follows:—

Dr.	Dol. c.	Cr.	Dol. c.
Seed	2 18	Crop of 25 bushels at 90 c...	22 50
Fertilisers	3 50		
Labour	6 37½		
Cost—exclusive of taxes, insurance and interest	12 05½		
Profit	10 44½		
	22 50		22 50

But a reference to the accompanying Tables will show that this gentleman is peculiarly favourably situated, as the average return of wheat for the two States only amounts to about 6½ bushels an acre.

And now to follow that bushel of wheat from the farmer's barn until it is placed on the Liverpool market, and see what profit is to be made out of it:—

	Dol. c.
Original cost, say	0 90
Hauling, handling and transport to seaboard	0 04
Freight to Europe	0 06
Handling at Liverpool	0 02
per bushel	1 02

or 34s. 0½d. per quarter, exclusive of insurance, commission, primage, &c. It is quite evident, therefore, that the farmer in this part of the United States, at any rate, cannot compete with the Englishman in his own market.

Indian corn A reference to the accompanying Tables will show that in Maryland

and Virginia there are about 2,850,000 acres cropped with Indian corn, the average product being 18 bushels an acre, and the average price $46\frac{1}{2}$ c. a bushel. It is seeded in May.

It is a well-established fact that corn can be grown for many years continuously on the same land without any permanent damage to it, provided that the ground does not wash, and that it is not worked when too wet. Some help should, however, be given, as for instance, peas or buckwheat sowed in the row at the last working of the corn and turned under along with the corn-stalks as manure for the next crop.

An excellent fertiliser to produce a large crop is Peruvian or fish guano and muriate of potash.

Every farmer should grow corn, not only because it is a certain crop but because it is the "staff of life" to the farmer, who should always endeavour to grow at least enough for his own use; indeed, in many districts in these States, corn has been made the money crop, and farmers have had a very satisfactory return. The farmer needs it for his family, his hands and his stock, and, if he has to buy, the stock are sure to suffer, for, as the proverb has it, "Stock will not get fat on bought corn." That corn is a certain crop is proved by the fact that a fairly good return can be obtained in even exceptionally dry seasons if the land is good and well-tilled. In fact its value is incalculable, for not only are the leaves a very superior forage—more of which can be grown to the acre than any other forage plant—but it has assumed additional importance from the system of ensilage which has recently been adapted to it.

About 750,000 acres of land in Maryland and Virginia are generally sown in oats, the average crop being $13\frac{1}{2}$ bushels to the acre, and price about 41 c. a bushel. Oats are a precarious crop in most parts of the country, but winter oats are said to do fairly well in some districts. *Oats.*

On the low lands near the Bay, farmers declare that there is more money in winter oats than in wheat—which at best, is but negative praise.

Oats are here seeded about two bushels to the acre, and even more occasionally, but never less; they should be put in, if possible, before September 15, but better by the end of August, and then grazed down if there is any danger of their running into straw.

If, however, they are sown in autumn, in the hilly, cold upland districts, they are liable to be killed off in the winter. Spring-seeded oats are very uncertain, and rarely fill well except on very good land; whereas the worst land on the farms is generally given up to them.

The acreage under these several grains is unimportant and does not, as a consequence, call for any special mention. *Rye, barley buckwheat.*

The following is the average product and price:—

	Bushels.	Cents.
Rye..	7	66
Barley	19	66
Buckwheat..	11	60

The old proverb says—"No grass no cattle, no cattle no manure, no manure no grass." *Hay, forage plants.*

The unanimity with which the better class of agriculturists are turning their thoughts to pastoral farming in this part of the country is very striking; the more they think over the situation, the more convinced they become that breeding horses and cattle, and growing fruit and vegetables, will ultimately prove the chief occupation of farmers in Maryland and Virginia.

No subject is more important to them than that of forage and pasture, and no crop pays better than hay. Moreover, whilst most crops wear out land, it steadily improves under grass, yet the ordinary farmer is very ignorant and very prejudiced on this subject.

For years tobacco, corn, and wheat have been the money crops, and grass has been looked upon as the deadly enemy of the two first. Some parts of these States are more adapted to grass than others, the hilly regions are especially favourable to its growth and in no part of the continent are they more productive. But in all parts of these States, artificial grasses do well except in very sandy soil, and fodder corn, rye, sorghum and lucerne thrive everywhere.

Blue grass. — In the mountain sections "Blue Grass," whose great nutritive and fattening properties are so well-known, grows spontaneously, and where "blue grass" grows fat cattle may be looked for, and the facility of fattening cattle in these regions is what makes the profit out of the cattle trade with England.

Red clover. — Red clover is considered the most valuable crop, whether as forage or as an improver of land. It makes excellent hay, bears grazing well and thrives on moderately good land. It will not do on wet lands, unless they are fairly well-drained, and the ploughing should be as deep as practicable.

Clover is usually seeded in the spring on wheat, oats, or rye; it is not always easy to get a stand, but most farmers think the best plan is to sow on wheat early in the spring, using the harrow to get the seed in—but the safest plan is to harrow, then sow, re-harrow and roll. Many farmers object to sowing clover without grain, as they say they can ill spare the land, but a good clover crop is more valuable than a wheat crop.

A gallon of clover-seed an acre is the old rule, but the modern practice is to put in a gallon and a half, or two gallons for choice.

The difficulty of curing clover-hay is one of the drawbacks to its cultivation; it should be cured as much as possible in the shade, and not subjected to the effects of the hot sun. Good land, if the clover be well set, should yield at least two tons of hay an acre.

Clover should not be allowed to stand for more than two years, as what does not die out is superseded by weeds and coarse grasses.

Orchard grass. — Orchard grass (*Dactylis glomerata*) is very valuable grass, ranking next to clover for hay and pasturage, and superior to it in this, that it is, for grazing, 10 or 12 days earlier than any other grass.

It is not in its prime until the third year, but it will stand for years; it resists drought better than any other grass, keeping green when other sorts are dried up.

Sorghum (Sorghum nigrum). — Sorghum is much used as a forage plant, especially for fattening pigs; it is not considered a safe feed for cattle after the grain and stalk harden, as the stalk is very flinty; as a sugar-producing plant it is a failure in these States, the stalk being deficient in saccharine matter.

Other forage plants. — Many other forage plants are grown over these States, whether for hay or pasture; notably may be mentioned timothy, herds-grass, meadow oat-grass, lucerne, sainfoil, &c., and which suit the varieties of soil very well.

In a country like this where so much of the land is still under bush and timber, it is important to be able to turn the same, when practicable, into pasture. *Making wood pastures.*

By thinning out the trees, which may be used for firewood or fencing, very valuable pasture may be formed of land which is now all but worthless.

The refuse of the trees is burned and the ashes scattered carefully over the ground, then lime, 50 bushels to the acre, harrow, sow grass-seed, and roll.

A wood pasture thus formed is useful for grazing stock and for shelter in bad weather.

Of late years, machinery has greatly lessened the labour of saving hay and enabled the farmer to do so in about half the time, thus giving him more command over the weather. The saving is considered quite equal to one half in a moderate, and more than that in a large crop, the implements in use here are the mower, rake-jedder (for turning), hay-lift and loader. *Haymaking.*

Stock-breeding is every year becoming more important and necessary in these States, as the farmers are becoming alive to the fact that they can no longer compete with the West in cereals. The time, however, may come when, giving up the latter crops and devoting their land to cattle and sheep, they may so improve them as to be ultimately in a better position to compete with the now rich lands of the West. Farmers with diminished capital and the increased price of labour can no longer till their land in a profitable manner, and the only way in which they can do justice to their holdings and themselves, is by laying down a large breadth in grass and breeding stock to consume it. *Stock breeding.*

One of the great difficulties the grazing farmer has to deal with is the increased cost of fencing. To build permanent fences would cost much money, and to keep them up much labour is required, the very item it is most essential to economise. Good strong fences are indispensable to successful grazing, and they are becoming more costly as timber gets dearer; but labour is going up in price and inefficiency more rapidly than fencing. *Fencing.*

A really good portable fence, easy to move, and not too expensive, would save the farmers millions, and it is singular that a people so remarkable for inventive ingenuity has as yet done so little in this direction.

Appended are Tables showing the number and average price of horses and farming stock held in these States. Their number and quality have been gradually and steadily improving, but more especially their quality. *Stock.*

The live-cattle trade with England has given considerable impulse to the business, and large tracts in the hilly parts of these States, which were formerly considered almost worthless, and which have been consequently acquired at small cost, have been taken up for stock breeding.

In Western Maryland special attention is given to horse and cattle breeding, and Clydesdale and Percheron horses, and Alderney, Holstein and Hereford cattle; and the finest breeds of sheep and pigs are now to be found where, ten years back, the common and least profitable breeds were alone raised.

In Central Maryland, where dairy farming is extensively carried on, the Jersey cow is the favourite, whilst breeders of beef-cattle prefer the Shorthorn; the Berkshire is the favourite pig.

In addition to breeding fat cattle for the foreign market, Virginia has long been noted for its high-bred horses, and which are claimed to have quality, stamina, and style superior to any other stock of the kind bred on this continent; to a stranger, however, just arrived in the country from abroad, they do not appear to be especially remarkable for these qualities.

Sheep. — The opinion amongst practical agriculturists is gradually gaining ground that in Virginia there is a great and profitable opening for sheep husbandry, and, of late years, there has been a large increase in the number held in this State. It is maintained that no stock so improve land, whether by cleaning it in destroying coarse grasses, weeds and bushes, or by the nutritive quality of its manure and its adaptability for forming a turf sod. Southdowns, Cotswolds and Merinos are the breeds most fashionable in Virginia.

It is asserted that there is more money in sheep than in grain, cotton, or tobacco; but the great drawback is the difficulty of fencing, and the damage and destruction caused by stray dogs. In the part of the country specially adapted for sheep-raising, every man has a dog and—a vote; it is, consequently, hopeless to look for any legislation for the protection of the flocks.

Dairy farming. — Dairy farming has, of late years, been the subject of more attention and closer investigation than any other branch of agriculture, and concurrently with the improvements in cattle and dairy management, there has been a vast increase in the consumption of dairy products, especially of butter and milk.

It is, therefore, surprising that in these States dairy management should be in a deplorably bad condition, and that a large per-centage of the butter sent to market is almost unfit for human consumption.

Hence, the better classes of butter are, as a rule, imported from the Northern States; this gives an opening for the introduction in large quantities of oleomargarine, and which is, in many cases, preferred to the often dirty, tallowy, rancid butter of the country. And yet this is the more remarkable as the demand for really good butter is so great that, when once a dairy has established its reputation, it can ask almost what it likes for its produce. It is said that there are dairymen in New York and New Jersey who can always get a dollar (4s. 2d.) a pound for their butter.

It is almost impossible to get really fresh butter in this part of the country, unless specially ordered; the so-called American fresh butter is always more or less salt; and yet there is no reason why good butter should not be made here. It is made in limited quantities in private dairies, and, more recently, in "Creameries" (the local name for central co-operative dairies), and which system is growing in favour as well with the farmers who supply the milk as with the consumer. One great difficulty which dairy farmers have hitherto had to contend with, has been the necessity of employing coloured labour, and the difficulty of teaching these people that cleanliness is essential for the production of good butter.

As the system of "Creameries," or central dairies, extends, however, this difficulty will, no doubt, be surmounted by employing exclusively white labour.

Dairies are here managed more on the Continental than the English system: chilling the milk immediately after milking is generally practised, and is said largely to increase the yield of cream and butter. The lower the temperature is brought between 40° and 35°, the greater the yield. American dairy farmers have great facilities for attaining the proper temperature from the constant and cheap supply of ice.

Jerseys and Holsteins are reported to have made the most astonishing yields of milk in America, and far larger than any with which they are credited to Europe—they are gradually superseding Ayrshires and Shorthorns, which were once so formidable here.

Certain districts in these States are admirably adapted for the growth of fruit and vegetables, and full advantage has been taken of their fitness for such culture. {Market gardening and fruit raising.}

The Eastern shore of Maryland, *i.e.*, that part of the State lying to the east of Chesapeake Bay, with its light sandy loam, is largely cropped with early vegetables.

The peach crop is, however, the great stand-by of the farmers in this part of the State, and on which they mainly depend for profit. Peach cultivation was first commenced here some 25 years back, since which time it has attained enormous extension. Few farmers are without a peach orchard. Many extend over 100 acres, and there are some that cover even 250 acres. Last year the peach crop was a total failure; but in previous and exceptionally good years, single orchards are stated to have cleared over 10,000 dol. {Peaches.}

In the central part of the State, a large acreage is under tomatoes and Indian corn, grown for the packing-houses; it may be stated that the latter is canned in Maryland alone. {Tomatoes.}

Sweet and ordinary potatoes and melons pay well in most places, as does market gardening generally, whenever it is undertaken in the vicinity of towns, or where water-carriage is available. {Potatoes and melons.}

In Maryland, fruit-growing is profitable, but the reverse in Virginia, with the exception of apples and grapes, which, with good management, may be made to pay; and yet there is no apparent reason why this latter State should not become a great wine-producing district. It has climate and soil admirably adapted for the purpose; and, indeed, it is stated that over 2,000 acres are now under grapes, which produce 225,000 gallons of wine to the value of over 200,000 dol.

This wine, generally termed Virginia claret, is sound and palatable, and much superior to the modern, third-growth vintage which passes by the name of claret at Bordeaux. It can be purchased at a reasonable price—about 1 dol. a gallon—and, as a guarantee of its excellence, it took a silver medal at the Paris Exhibition of 1878.

Apples and pears give large returns in the hilly districts when they escape the "blight," which, unfortunately, is very prevalent, and for which no remedy has been as yet discovered.

Maryland may be considered as the chief centre of the canning industry on the Atlantic seaboard, and it is probably the most important business in the State, and not the less so in consequence of the vast amount of employment which it supplies. {Fruit and vegetable canning.}

Corn and tomatoes are the staple articles packed in the rural district, the canning of fruit and the other vegetables being mainly carried on in this city.

In 1882, when the canning business was in its most prosperous condition, Harford county, in this State, alone packed more than 38,000,000 cans of hermetically-sealed goods. Since then, however, many of the small growers of fruit and vegetables have collapsed; their lands became impoverished through the constant growth of a special crop, and they were unable to afford the large outlay required in fertilisers, as just at that time occurred a heavy fall in the price of canned goods, which forced them to turn their attention to more remunerative culture. There is no doubt, however, that growing fruit and vegetables for the canning-houses is the most profitable business that the farmer can engage in.

The season for packing commences in May, and continues until

UNITED STATES.

September, and includes generally about 100 days. Fruit and vegetables are packed in the following order:—

1. Early peas.	10. Blackberries.
2. Pineapples.	11. Greengages.
3. Strawberries.	12. Damsons.
4. Gooseberries.	13. Tomatoes.
5. French beans.	14. Peaches.
6. Cherries.	15. Pears.
7. Marrowfat Peas.	16. Apples.
8. Raspberries.	17. Beans.
9. Whortle berries.	18. Indian corn.

A large per-centage of the labour employed in the packing-houses is of Bohemian nationality. The general working-hours are from 6 A.M. to 6 P.M. Work is paid for by the piece, and the average earnings may be computed at about 4 dol. 50 c., or 18s. a-week.

The packing-houses of this city can put up 40,000 bushels of peas and 100,000 bushels of tomatoes a day, each bushel being equivalent to 13 tins. The raw material, except pineapples and greengages, is grown exclusively in this State. During the past year Maryland and Virginia turned out 968,646 cases of preserved tomatoes, of two dozen tins to the case, or a total of 23,247,504 tins; which, at the wholesale price of 1 dol. a dozen 3 lb.-tins, represents a sum of 1,937,292 dol.

Appended is Table C., showing the average wholesale price of canned fruit and vegetables per dozen tins.

Evaporation, preserving fruit by. Another mode of treating fruit, which is becoming very popular, and which has, no doubt, a great future in store for it, is by evaporation; this system is more practised in Virginia than in Maryland.

Fruit thus preserved. While a great saving to the grower, it is a luxury to the consumer, for it is said that fruit thus treated, when cooked or used in pies or tarts, is quite as good as when plucked fresh from the trees.

The Zimmerman Fruit Drying Company, of Cincinnati, manufacture an evaporator at a cost of from 45 dol. to 50 dol., which, besides drying fruit, may be used to bake and roast. It is stated that this implement will bake 15 loaves of bread and 40 pies at a time, that it will roast meat, poultry, and game to perfection, that it will dry clothes, and, when not in use, may serve as a meat-safe.

There only remains of the staple crops of these States tobacco and cotton, and, although their cultivation can have little interest for English farmers, a few remarks about them may not be out of place.

Tobacco. The area sown in tobacco in these States has been much reduced since last year; the fact staring the farmer in the face that it had not proved a paying crop; in fact, last year the crop was so short that a reaction in prices will probably take place, and, as a consequence, larger planting next year.

As a crop it is, no doubt, an impediment to the improvement of land; cut down and wear out, and then repeat the operation, has been the rule followed for a long series of succeeding years, whereas the secret of making tobacco pay is to have a small acreage, and that highly fertilised.

There is no crop more exacting; whoever would succeed as a tobacco planter must give his whole time and attention to it; it must be expensively fertilised and constantly worked, and, if he intends to do justice to his tobacco, it must be at the expense of his other crops.

Cotton. No cotton is grown in Maryland, but, as may be seen in the appended Table A, a considerable area is under that crop in Virginia.

Like tobacco, cotton is a most exacting crop, especially about the picking season. The cotton-worm, too, is a great trouble, and requires constant attention.

Cotton is planted early in April, it blooms from the 1st to 20th June, when about 15 inches high. Picking commences in August, and ends in November. Fresh upland, unmanured, returns under good tillage 300 lb. to 1,000 lb. to the acre, and five crops may be taken off the land without a sensible diminution in yield. As compared with other crops in Virginia, it is more than doubtful whether cotton pays.

Cotton-seed is extensively used as a fertiliser, chiefly in composts, and cotton-seed meal is considered one of the best and most nutritive feeds; when used with judgment, it is worth 6*l*. a ton: 1 lb. of cotton-seed meal is considered equal to 2 lb. of corn meal, but it is excessively rich, and must be used sparingly.

Cotton-seed oil has become quite important as an article of food. It is shipped in vast quantities to Spain and Italy, whence it returns to this country, labelled "Pure Olive Oil"; for adulterating purposes it enters largely into all fatty substances for domestic consumption, such as lard, butter, cheese, &c.; and there is quite an extensive demand for it in the Northern States for the manufacture of "Pure French Sardines" out of a small local herring.

The worst feature in cotton cultivation is the improvidence which it engenders amongst the farmers, in consequence of the prevailing practice of taking advances on the growing crop, and which has for so many years devoured the proceeds of the industry and labour of the cotton planter. It is reported, however, that as the country settles down this practice is declining.

If comfort is to be derived from the misfortunes of one's neighbours, the British farmer may take consolation in the fact that in many respects he is better off than his American fellow.

If, on the one hand, he is hampered with rent, land-tax and rates, he has, as compensation, comparatively cheap labour, and his land yields him a return at least fourfold that of the American farmer. Indeed, the life of the latter in these States is wanting in many factors that help to make existence enjoyable.

He is comparatively without other society than that of his own family, and the excessive cost of labour forces him to be in a great measure his own servant, and to employ his children in farm work when they ought to be at school. Indeed it is doubtful whether, from an economical point of view, the freehold of the land is in this country an unmixed blessing, at least for the present. If there is plenty in the homestead there is also waste and extravagance, and no one who has not gone over a farm in these States can realise what really dirty land is. Not the unobtrusive weeds, which are the despair of the English farmer, but tall, hardy, tough plants, almost arriving at the dignity of bushes, overshadow the fields of grain and ruin the pastures.

The answer of the American farmer to enquiries on the subject is usually the same, that labour is dear and the land is his own.

He also has his, no doubt, well-founded grievance on the small profit to be got out of farming, on the terrible competition and consequent low price of produce. For some reason known only to himself, he dreads above all things the abrogation of the land-tax in England, which he professes to consider inevitable, and which he declares would prove the death-knell of the American farmer. It is, he says, inconceivable that a country wedded to Free Trade, as England is, should, by persisting in maintaining this tax, place indirectly a burden on their own home produce, whilst at the same time they are admitting, nay welcoming, that of the foreigner free.

TABLE showing the product of Cereals, Potatoes, Tobacco, Hay and Cotton of the following States, the total Acreage, the yield per Acre, Average Price in each State, and Value of Crop.

MARYLAND.

Products.		Number of Acres each Crop.	Quantity Produced.	Average Yield per Acre.	Value per Unit of Quantity.	Total Valuation.
					Dol. c.	Dol.
Indian corn	Bushels	726,336	15,999,000	22·0	0 46	7,359,540
Wheat	,,	580,482	5,534,000	9·5	0 91	5,035,940
Rye	,,	30,759	240,000	7·8	0 65	155,948
Oats	,,	111,100	2,475,000	22·3	0 35	806,250
Barley	,,	277	6,000	21·7	0 68	4,083
Buckwheat	,,	11,106	144,000	13·0	0 60	80,627
Potatoes	,,	20,378	1,528,000	75·0	0 49	748,892
Tobacco	Lbs.	43,065	28,552,000	663·0	0 7$\frac{3}{10}$	2,084,303
Hay	Tons	286,355	272,000	·95	13 75	3,740,509

VIRGINIA.

Products.		Number of Acres each Crop.	Quantity Produced.	Average Yield per Acre.	Value per Unit of Quantity.	Total Valuation.
					Dol. c.	Dol.
Indian corn	Bushels	2,132,230	31,838,000	14·9	0 47	14,963,860
Wheat	,,	651,140	2,848,000	4·4	0 93	2,634,690
Rye	,,	48,216	328,000	6·7	0 67	216,441
Oats	,,	621,230	8,666,000	13·9	0 41	3,552,240
Barley	,,	1,175	20,000	17·0	0 65	12,984
Buckwheat	,,	20,734	187,000	9·0	0 61	113,830
Potatoes	,,	35,037	2,102,000	60·0	0 51	1,072,132
Tobacco	Lbs.	164,445	107,711,000	655·0	0 7$\frac{4}{10}$	7,970,649
Hay	Tons	295,930	251,541	·85	13 28	3,340,464
Cotton	Bales	44,913	14,821	·33	Per lb. 8½ c.	579,500

KENTUCKY.

Products.		Number of Acres each Crop.	Quantity Produced.	Average Yield per Acre.	Value per Unit of Quantity.	Total Valuation.
					Dol. c.	Dol.
Indian corn	Bushels	3,551,667	90,560,000	25·5	0 35	31,699,150
Wheat	,,	1,055,760	3,759,000	3·6	0 95	3,571,650
Rye	,,	93,347	493,000	5·3	0 71	351,265
Oats	,,	491,545	10,223,000	20·8	0 33	3,374,250
Barley	,,	19,564	342,000	17·5	0 67	229,388
Buckwheat	,,	1,152	11,000	9·5	0 67	7,419
Potatoes	,,	50,556	3,387,000	67·0	0 62	1,422,646
Tobacco	Lbs.	265,093	209,423,000	790	0 ·6·5	13,612,526
Hay	Tons	313,200	313,200	1	10 25	3,210,300

TABLE showing the Estimated Number and Value of Animals on Farms.

MARYLAND.

Animals.	Number.	Average Price.	Value.
		Dol. c.	Dol.
Horses	129,026	83 15	10,728,077
Mules	13,358	96 16	1,284,544
Cows	133,684	29 50	3,948,678
Oxen	139,578	24 56	3,469,213
Sheep	165,210	3 30	544,383
Swine	275,879	6 49	1,789,077
			21,763,972

VIRGINIA.

Animals.	Number.	Average Price.	Value.
		Dol. c.	Dol.
Horses	238,548	70 11	16,725,673
Mules	35,372	86 46	3,058,096
Cows	255,241	23 00	5,870,543
Oxen	428,041	18 59	7,958,353
Sheep	449,233	2 30	1,034,134
Swine	787,730	4 11	3,237,570
			37,884,369

KENTUCKY.

Animals.	Number.	Average Price.	Value.
		Dol. c.	Dol.
Horses	386,864	67 83	26,242,445
Mules	122,943	72 26	8,883,535
Cows	310,485	27 23	8,464,309
Oxen	534,362	23 82	12,727,433
Sheep	858,062	2 33	1,997,569
Swine	1,808,603	3 82	6,905,247
			65,220,538

UNITED STATES.

Average Wholesale Prices of Canned Goods per dozen tins.

	Tins.	Price.
	lb.	s. d.
Peaches	2	7 0
"	3	9 8
Pine-apples	2	6 0
Tomatoes	2	3 2½
"	3	4 0
Green Indian-corn	2	4 0
Strawberries	2	4 0
Blackberries	2	4 0
Raspberries	2	6 0
Green peas	2	5 0
French beans	2	3 4
Red cherries	..	6 0
White "	..	8 0
Common pears	..	4 5
Bartlett "	..	5 0
Damsons	..	5 0
Lima beans (broad beans)	..	5 0
Whortle berries	..	4 5
Gooseberries	..	7 0

LONDON:
Printed for Her Majesty's Stationery Office,
By HARRISON AND SONS,
Printers in Ordinary to Her Majesty.
(1125 4 | 88—H & S 398)

FOREIGN OFFICE.
1888.
ANNUAL SERIES.

No. 311.

DIPLOMATIC AND CONSULAR REPORTS ON TRADE AND FINANCE.

UNITED STATES.

REPORT FOR THE YEAR 1887
ON THE
TRADE OF SAVANNAH.

REFERENCE TO PREVIOUS REPORT, Annual Series No. 136.

Presented to both Houses of Parliament by Command of Her Majesty,
APRIL, 1888.

LONDON:
PRINTED FOR HER MAJESTY'S STATIONERY OFFICE,
BY HARRISON AND SONS, ST. MARTIN'S LANE,
PRINTERS IN ORDINARY TO HER MAJESTY.

And to be purchased, either directly or through any Bookseller, from
EYRE AND SPOTTISWOODE, EAST HARDING STREET, FLEET STREET, E.C., and
32, ABINGDON STREET, WESTMINSTER, S.W.; or
ADAM AND CHARLES BLACK, 6, NORTH BRIDGE, EDINBURGH; or
HODGES, FIGGIS, & Co., 104, GRAFTON STREET, DUBLIN.

1888.

[C. 5252—88.] *Price One Penny.*

New Series of Reports.

Reports of the Annual Series have been issued from Her Majesty's Diplomatic and Consular Officers at the following places, and may be obtained from the sources indicated on the title-page:—

No.		Price.	No.		Price.
187.	Lisbon	1d.	249.	Algiers	2d.
188.	Lisbon	2d.	250.	Bucharest	1d.
189.	Nice	2d.	251.	Christiania	2d.
190.	Tientsin	1d.	252.	Paris	1d.
191.	Hankow	1d.	253.	Bogota	1d.
192.	Erzeroum	1d.	254.	Salonica	1d.
193.	Syra	1d.	255.	Copenhagen	1d.
194.	Athens	3d.	256.	Jeddah	1d.
195.	Vienna	2d.	257.	Russia	2d.
196.	Alexandria	1d.	258.	Paris	1d.
197.	Constantinople	1d.	259.	Patras	1d.
198.	Hakodate	1d.	260.	Brussels	1d.
199.	Shanghai	2d.	261.	Ichang	1d.
200.	Tokyo	1d.	262.	Baltimore	1d.
201.	Tamatave	1d.	263.	Taganrog	1d.
202.	Mexico	1d.	264.	Oporto	1d.
203.	Chefoo	5d.	265.	Rio de Janeiro	1d.
204.	Nagasaki	1d.	266.	Galveston	1d.
205.	Cuba	1d.	267.	Tripoli	1d.
206.	Tunis	1d.	268.	Galatz	1d.
207.	Réunion	2d.	269.	Varna	1d.
208.	Hyogo	1d.	270.	New Orleans	2d.
209.	Tangier	1d.	271.	Cherbourg	1d.
210.	Antwerp	1d.	272.	Suakin	1d.
211.	Stettin	1d.	273.	Brest	1d.
212.	Erzeroum	1d.	274.	Barcelona	2d.
213.	Rotterdam	2d.	275.	Barcelona	1d.
214.	Nantes	1d.	276.	Antwerp	1d.
215.	Newport News	1d.	277.	Havre	3d.
216.	Rio Grande do Sul	1d.	278.	Odessa	1d.
217.	Rio de Janeiro	1d.	279.	Tokyo	1d.
218.	Corea	1d.	280.	Saigon	1d.
219.	Kanagawa	1d.	281.	Buenos Ayres	1d.
220.	Wurtemberg	1d.	282.	Taganrog	1d.
221.	Tahiti	1d.	283.	Tamsui	1d.
222.	Bangkok	1d.	284.	Puerto Plata	1d.
223.	St. Petersburg	2d.	285.	Wênchow	1d.
224.	Canton	1d.	286.	Tokyo	1d.
225.	Erzeroum	1d.	287.	Lisbon	2d.
226.	Rio de Janeiro	1d.	288.	La Rochelle	1d.
227.	Valparaiso	1d.	289.	Washington	4d.
228.	St. Thomas	1d.	290.	Beyrout	1d.
229.	Stockholm	1d.	291.	Algiers	2d.
230.	Nyassa	1d.	292.	Varna	1d.
231.	Buenos Ayres	1d.	293.	Algiers	1d.
232.	The Hague	1d.	294.	Port Saïd	1d.
233.	Trieste	1d.	295.	Manila	1d.
234.	Vienna	1d.	296.	Charleston	1d.
235.	Washington	3d.	297.	Kiungchow	1d.
236.	Odessa	1d.	298.	Pakhoi	1d.
237.	Sofia	1d.	299.	Wuhu	1d.
238.	Porto Rico	1d.	300.	Boulogne	2d.
239.	Palermo	2d.	301.	Marseilles	1d.
240.	Lisbon	2d.	302.	Bordeaux	2d.
241.	Tabreez	1d.	303.	Ancona	1d.
242.	Tunis	1d.	304.	Swatow	1d.
243.	The Hague	1d.	305.	Ssŭ-ch'uan	1d.
244.	Fiume	1d.	306.	Antwerp	1d.
245.	Venice	1d.	307.	Cadiz	1d.
246.	Paris	2d.	308.	Genoa	1d.
247.	Ancona	1d.	309.	Marseilles	1d.
248.	St. Petersburg	2d.	310.	Baltimore	1d.

No. 311.

Reference to previous Report, Annual Series No. 136.

UNITED STATES.

SAVANNAH.

Report by Vice-Consul Robertson on the Trade and Commerce of Savannah for the Year 1887.

The year of 1887 proved for Savannah one of unprecedented prosperity. The growth and general improvements of the city has been most satisfactory, and is of itself a pure indication that business has been prosperous. New and palatial private residences, stores, roadways and railroads, were started and pushed forward with all the energy of a prosperous and enterprising people.

Introductory.

The commerce of the port, particularly in exports, compares most favourably with all preceding years, and the future outlook for still greater prosperity and advancement was never brighter.

The work on the river improvements alluded to in my last report, continued to be carried on throughout the year now under review, and I am pleased to state with very gratifying results. The least mean high-water depth in the Channel between the city and sea, being at the present time a fraction over 20 feet, this depth it is hoped will be materially increased in the near future, it having been proved practicable to obtain a depth of 28 feet at mean high-water in the shallowest part of the Channel.

Works.

The general health of the city during the past year has been most gratifying to the community at large—fewer cases of malarial fever having been reported than in any previous year; and it is hoped that by continuing the drainage of the swamps and low-lying ground around Savannah—on which work the convicts are kept busily employed—that this direful malady may soon be wiped out entirely, thus making Savannah one of the healthiest ports in the Southern States.

Health.

One cloud alone arose to darken the bright prosperity of the year, viz: the cotton fires on shipboard. These fires at one time threatened to materially injure the future prospects of the port, coming as they did in such rapid succession. The most alarming thing in connection with the fires, was not only the frequency of their occurrence, but also the peculiarity of their development, nearly all the fires breaking out after the ships were loaded and ready for sea.

Fires on ship board.

All classes of the community were aroused to a sense of the danger which threatened them.

The City Council were appealed to, to enforce the ordinance prohibiting smoking along the wharves where cotton is handled. This was immediately done, and a new ordinance passed compelling the carriers of cotton and other inflammable material—by lighters—to protect all such cargoes with tarpaulins, and also prohibiting smoking on all vessels lying within the jurisdictional limits of the city.

(399)

These steps appear to have had the desired effect, no fires having occurred since the ordinances were enforced.

Imports and exports generally.

The imports and exports at this port have on the whole been satisfactory.

Imports.

The annexed Table A will show a marked falling-off in the imports for the present year over that of 1886. This is accounted for by the fact that during the latter part of last year, very heavy importations took place, which filled the markets; consequently importers have been holding back as long as possible.

Fertilisers.

Fertilisers—one of the principal articles of importation from Great Britain—shows a decrease of nearly 30,000*l.* sterling. This great falling-off I attribute to the fact that during the year of 1886, large tracts of virgin land were brought under cultivation necessitating the use of more fertilisers at that time than for some years afterwards.

Cotton ties.

The stock of cotton-ties at the opening of the cotton season entirely ran out, both here and at the North, and 35,200 bundles were imported direct. This article is usually obtained through a northern firm—rarely coming direct.

Salt.

A slight increase is observable in this article of importation.

All other articles.

Under this heading many articles were imported direct for the first time comprising, among other things, cement, potatoes, household effects, &c. &c. None of them amounted to any great value. I have therefore not enumerated them in detail.

Exports.

All articles of export have materially increased, as will be shown by the annexed tables.

Cotton.

The exceptionally fine weather at the early part of the summer was most beneficial to the cotton crop, and will account for the increase in this article of export.

Cotton-seed.

Cotton-seed previous to the year 1886 was not shown as an article of export. In that year 1,341,018 lbs. were exported, and, during 1887, 2,663,854 lbs., or nearly double the quantity was sent from this port, and the demand for same is ever on the increase.

Lumber and timber.

The trade in this article has increased in quantity, but diminished somewhat in value. This is, I think, alone attributable to the fluctuations of the market.

Spirits of turpentine.

This article of exportation also shows an increase, both in quantity and value, and is a source of great revenue to the port.

All other articles.

There is nothing very startling to report under this heading; a steady increase is, however, visible.

AGRICULTURE.

Georgia as an Agricultural State may be justly called a variety State; varied as to people, production, and climate.

People.

The population by the last census (1880) was 1,542,180, 725,103 of whom were coloured. Of the total population, 432,324 were engaged in agricultural pursuits. Of this number 145,062 were farmers and planters, 3,202 nurserymen, florists, &c., and 284,060 labourers.

Productions.

The productions of the State under this heading are too numerous to enumerate in detail, and may properly be divided under two great heads: money crops, and provision, or domestic crops. Of the former, cotton takes the lead, surpassing all the others combined. There are also rice, sugar, tobacco, vegetables, and fruits raised for export.

Still more varied are the provision crops, or crops raised strictly for the home market. They include all the cereals, the leguminous crops, peas, beans, the root crops, and all sorts of vegetables and fruits—in fact they embrace almost everything for food for man and beast which is not tropical.

The soil differs materially in different portions of the State. In **Soil.**
the North-west the soil is composed of disintegrated lime-stone, &c.
In the North-east, of granite and like stones; in Middle Georgia are
red clay and gray soils; and in Southern Georgia the better lands
contain lime and marl.

The choice of climate is very wide, ranging from the invigorating **Climate.**
climate of the mountains in North Georgia to the debilitating summer
climate of the South.

The rainfall of Georgia is considerably above the average of the **Rainfall.**
United States. The quantity is everywhere abundant, the only needful
condition being its proper distribution.

The average for the State for 5 years being 13·44.

CROPS.

This is by far the most valuable crop. Of this great staple the **Cotton**
production in 1887 amounted to 875,000 bales of 450 lbs. each, and
realised an average price of 9 c. per lb.

The total corn crop of the State for 1887 was about 30,000,000 **Corn.**
bushels, and realised an average price of 66 c. per bushel.

The acreage sown to wheat has slightly decreased of late years: **Wheat.**
the total yield of last year amounted to 2,250,000 bushels, the market
price of which was about 1 dol. 25 c. per bushel.

FERTILISERS.

Georgia is by far the largest consumer of fertilisers of any State
in the Union, using in value, in 1879—the last record to hand—
4,347,000 dol.

HIGH CULTURE.

It is a pretty-generally acknowledged fact that the true secret
of success in all agricultural ventures, is a judicious outlay of both
care and money in the yearly operations of the farm.

Nothing of any moment can be accomplished by inadequate means
in any department of human industry, and more particularly in
agriculture.

It would doubtless be interesting to quote here the results of a
prize of 800 dol. offered, in 1884, by Messrs. G. W. Scott & Co., of
Atlanta, Georgia, manufacturers of the Gossypium-Phospo-Fertiliser,
for the best yield made on ground enriched by their fertiliser. The
highest yield was for cotton, 1,545 lbs. to the acre. The lowest
430 lbs., or one bale, to the acre.

The average yield of the 75 contestants was 774 lbs. to the acre,
and to secure this yield an average of 888 lbs. of fertilisers was used,
at a total cost of 15 dol. 54 c.

The highest yield for corn was $116\frac{1}{2}$ bushels, and the lowest 103
bushels per acre.

Taking into consideration the advantages offered to fruit-growers **Fruit.**
in Georgia, in point of climate, soil, and general adaptedness, it cannot
but be noticed that this industry has not had that attention to which
it is entitled. There are few States in the Union which can equal the
Georgia fruits, which attain the highest perfection on the soil.

Among the most notable kinds which are grown, may be mentioned
the apple, pear, peach, grape, cherry and fig. This latter fruit—the
fig—is very extensively grown, but in most cases with little or no

profit. No one in this State has yet been able to satisfactorily prepare the fruit for market, dried and pressed; consequently, the greater portion of what might and could be made a valuable crop is lost.

CATTLE.

There is probably no country in the world in which cattle are more exempt from disease, or in which they are subject to so few diseases, as in the Southern States. Notwithstanding this, however, cattle-rearing is, one might say, entirely neglected in Georgia, it being merely incidental to other branches of the farm. Little attention is bestowed upon them, further than to secure a supply of milk and butter for family use.

SHEEP FARMING.

The people of Georgia have given so little attention to sheep husbandry, that they are naturally unfamiliar with the management of flocks; consequently, they are slow to abandon industries with which they are familiar to embark in one which they know but little, even though the prospect for profit may be better, and the expenses less than cultivating crops.

The climate of Georgia corresponds with that of the best wool-growing regions of the world; and, with but little more expense than the first cost of the sheep, this industry, under proper management, could be made one of the most paying branches of agriculture.

Annex A.—RETURN of all Shipping at the Port of Savannah in the Year 1887.

ENTERED.

Nationality.	Sailing. Number of Vessels.	Sailing. Tons.	Steam. Number of Vessels.	Steam. Tons.	Total. Number of Vessels.	Total. Tons.
British	38	26,092	71	85,332	109	111,424
American	30	12,603	340	466,012	370	478,615
Norwegian	109	53,365	...	...	109	53,365
German	23	12,093	1	1,202	24	13,295
Other countries	44	24,283	3	3,600	47	27,883
	244	128,436	415	556,146	659	684,582

CLEARED.

Nationality.	Sailing. Number of Vessels.	Sailing. Tons.	Steam. Number of Vessels.	Steam. Tons.	Total. Number of Vessels.	Total. Tons.
British	31	26,092	81	98,814	112	124,906
American	9	3,165	343	466,322	352	469,487
Norwegian	103	50,718	...	...	103	50,718
German	24	13,034	1	1,202	25	14,236
Other countries	50	37,504	2	2,835	52	40,339
	217	130,513	427	569,173	644	699,686

SAVANNAH.

Annex B.—RETURN of Principal Articles of Export from Savannah, during the Years 1887-1886.

Articles.		1887.		1886.	
		Quantity.	Total.	Quantity.	Value.
			£		£
Cotton	Lbs.	223,225,757	4,188,454	211,872,323	3,700,101
Cotton-seed	,,	2,663,854	4,672	1,341,018	2,384
Lumber and timber	Feet	25,310,000	37,044	17,727,340	48,386
Spirits of turpentine	Gallons	3,785,389	340,381	3,498,244	229,302
All other articles		...	139,831	...	139,461
		...	4,610,382	...	4,119,634

RETURN of Principal Articles of Import to Savannah, during the Years 1887-1886.

Articles.		1887.		1886.	
		Quantity.	Value.	Quantity.	Value.
			£		£
Fertilisers	Tons	9,925	17,568	25,940	45,714
Coffee	Lbs.	...	...	1,211,714	43,900
Cotton-ties	Bds.	35,200	4,386	...	...
Salt	Lbs.	15,846,305	3,296	14,550,153	3,053
Cigars	,,	129	638	255,000	1,223
Molasses	Gallons	26,743	836	29,321	829
All other articles		...	9,497	...	5,134
		...	36,221	...	99,853

TABLE showing the Total Value of all Articles Exported from Savannah, and Imported to Savannah, from and to Foreign Countries during the Years 1886-87.

Country.	Exports.		Imports.	
	1887.	1886.	1887.	1886.
	£	£	£	£
British	1,514,116	2,067,439	18,860	40,943
Germany	907,361	836,667	9,436	10,571
Spain	466,869	229,804	2,199	23,314
Russia	955,128	282,814	..	..
Netherlands	164,708	199,848	..	..
Belgium	193,699	172,080	1,008	..
Brazil	2,580	..	..	23,911
Other countries	405,921	331,082	4,718	1,114
Total	4,610,382	4,119,634	36,221	99,853

LONDON:
Printed for Her Majesty's Stationery Office,
By HARRISON AND SONS,
Printers in Ordinary to Her Majesty.
(1125 4|88—H & S 399)

FOREIGN OFFICE.
1888.
ANNUAL SERIES.

No. 312.
DIPLOMATIC AND CONSULAR REPORTS ON TRADE AND FINANCE.

UNITED STATES.

REPORT FOR THE YEAR 1887
ON THE
TRADE OF BOSTON.

REFERENCE TO PREVIOUS REPORT, Annual Series No. 110.

Presented to both Houses of Parliament by Command of Her Majesty,
APRIL, 1888.

LONDON:
PRINTED FOR HER MAJESTY'S STATIONERY OFFICE,
BY HARRISON AND SONS, ST. MARTIN'S LANE,
PRINTERS IN ORDINARY TO HER MAJESTY.

And to be purchased, either directly or through any Bookseller, from
EYRE AND SPOTTISWOODE, EAST HARDING STREET, FLEET STREET, E.C., and
32, ABINGDON STREET, WESTMINSTER, S.W.; or
ADAM AND CHARLES BLACK, 6, NORTH BRIDGE, EDINBURGH; or
HODGES, FIGGIS, & Co., 104, GRAFTON STREET, DUBLIN.

1888.

[C. 5252–89.] *Price One Penny.*

New Series of Reports.

Reports of the Annual Series have been issued from Her Majesty's Diplomatic and Consular Officers at the following places, and may be obtained from the sources indicated on the title-page:—

No.		Price.	No.		Price.
190.	Tientsin	1d.	251.	Christiania	2d.
191.	Hankow	1d.	252.	Paris	1d.
192.	Erzeroum	1d.	253.	Bogota	1d.
193.	Syra	1d.	254.	Salonica	1d.
194.	Athens	3d.	255.	Copenhagen	1d.
195.	Vienna	2d.	256.	Jeddah	1d.
196.	Alexandria	1d.	257.	Russia	2d.
197.	Constantinople	1d.	258.	Paris	1d.
198.	Hakodate	1d.	259.	Patras	1d.
199.	Shanghai	2d.	260.	Brussels	1d.
200.	Tokyo	2d.	261.	Ichang	1d.
201.	Tamatave	1d.	262.	Baltimore	1d.
202.	Mexico	1d.	263.	Taganrog	1d.
203.	Chefoo	1d.	264.	Oporto	1d.
204.	Nagasaki	5d.	265.	Rio de Janeiro	1d.
205.	Cuba	1d.	266.	Galveston	1d.
206.	Tunis	1d.	267.	Tripoli	1d.
207.	Réunion	1d.	268.	Galatz	1d.
208.	Hyogo	2d.	269.	Varna	1d.
209.	Tangier	1d.	270.	New Orleans	2d.
210.	Antwerp	1d.	271.	Cherbourg	1d.
211.	Stettin	1d.	272.	Suakin	1d.
212.	Erzeroum	1d.	273.	Brest	1d.
213.	Rotterdam	1d.	274.	Barcelona	2d.
214.	Nantes	2d.	275.	Barcelona	1d.
215.	Newport News	1d.	276.	Antwerp	1d.
216.	Rio Grande do Sul	1d.	277.	Havre	3d.
217.	Rio de Janeiro	1d.	278.	Odessa	1d.
218.	Corea	1d.	279.	Tokyo	1d.
219.	Kanagawa	1d.	280.	Saigon	1d.
220.	Wurtemberg	1d.	281.	Buenos Ayres	1d.
221.	Tahiti	1d.	282.	Taganrog	1d.
222.	Bangkok	1d.	283.	Tamsui	1d.
223.	St. Petersburg	2d.	284.	Puerto Plata	1d.
224.	Canton	1d.	285.	Wênchow	1d.
225.	Erzeroum	1d.	286.	Tokyo	1d.
226.	Rio de Janeiro	1d.	287.	Lisbon	2d.
227.	Valparaiso	1d.	288.	La Rochelle	1d.
228.	St. Thomas	1d.	289.	Washington	4d.
229.	Stockholm	1d.	290.	Beyrout	1d.
230.	Nyassa	1d.	291.	Algiers	2d.
231.	Buenos Ayres	1d.	292.	Varna	1d.
232.	The Hague	1d.	293.	Algiers	1d.
233.	Trieste	1d.	294.	Port Saïd	1d.
234.	Vienna	1d.	295.	Manila	1d.
235.	Washington	3d.	296.	Charleston	1d.
236.	Odessa	1d.	297.	Kiungchow	1d.
237.	Sofia	1d.	298.	Pakhoi	1d.
238.	Porto Rico	1d.	299.	Wuhu	1d.
239.	Palermo	2d.	300.	Boulogne	2d.
240.	Lisbon	2d.	301.	Marseilles	1d.
241.	Tabreez	1d.	302.	Bordeaux	2d.
242.	Tunis	1d.	303.	Ancona	1d.
243.	The Hague	1d.	304.	Swatow	1d.
244.	Fiume	1d.	305.	Ssŭ-ch'uan	1d.
245.	Venice	1d.	306.	Antwerp	1d.
246.	Paris	2d.	307.	Cadiz	1d.
247.	Ancona	1d.	308.	Genoa	1d.
248.	St. Petersburg	2d.	309.	Marseilles	1d.
249.	Algiers	2d.	310.	Baltimore	1d.
250.	Bucharest	1d.	311.	Savannah	1d.

No. 312.

Reference to previous Report, Annual Series No. 110.

UNITED STATES.

BOSTON.

Report by Consul Henderson on the Trade and Commerce of Boston and the Boston Consular District for the Year 1887.

There was no new feature calling for special notice in the character or methods of business in Boston, and the Boston Consular district, during the past year. *Domestic trade and industry.*

Prices continued low, and trade was somewhat curtailed by uncertainty as to the result of proposed Tariff reforms; but, on the other hand, speculative enterprises were not indulged in, labour strikes were comparatively few and unimportant, trading firms increased in number, the amount of liabilities of bankrupts was greatly reduced, the stock and money markets were free from disturbance; and, speaking generally, there was a marked improvement not only in the actual volume and profits, but also in the condition and prospects of Trade and Industry throughout the district.

REVIEW OF BOSTON MARKETS FOR THE YEAR.

An increased demand for cotton goods, which commenced in the year 1886, after a protracted term of depression (principally occasioned by over-production) was well maintained in 1887, and mills were kept actively employed in filling orders for home consumption and exportation, and prices advanced even beyond the equivalent of a moderate rise which took place in raw cotton. *Cotton and cotton goods.*

The price of wool fell steadily throughout the year, and those who held stocks, or speculated for a rise, sustained heavy losses. The cause of the continuous decline was ascribed to uncertainty as to the result of proposed changes in the Tariff, and, to the inability of manufacturers at the present rate of duty on wool, to make certain kinds of woollen goods in competition with importers. *Wool and woollens.*

The goods on which the manufacturers found themselves undersold were cloth for men's clothing, and worsted goods, the production of which was entirely unprofitable and was curtailed or discontinued.

Sterling amounts are given at the rate of 4s. to the dollar. Comparisons of increase and decrease, when not otherwise stated, have reference to quantities or values in the year 1886.

(400)

Clothing trade.

The demand for home manufactures of flannels and light materials for women's wear was, however, steady at fair prices.

Wholesale and retail clothiers did an active and profitable business in spring, summer, and autumn clothing; but the winter trade was slack, owing to mild weather up to the latter part of December.

Hides and leather.

The market for hides was weak, and the lowest prices for many years were ultimately reached, and did not subsequently rally. All kinds of leather declined in the same ratio, and, notwithstanding a fair demand, tanners, who had large stocks on hand, were obliged to curtail production to save themselves from serious loss.

Boot and shoe trade.

Some strikes occurred in the trade in the early spring, but they were of short duration and were satisfactorily adjusted. The steady fall in leather was in favour of manufacturers, who merely bought enough at a time to supply their immediate wants. The volume of business was the largest on record, the output amounting to over 3,000,000 cases (averaging 24 pairs of boots and shoes) and, with fairly-maintained prices and few bad debts, the business of the year was an exceptionally prosperous one.

India-rubber and rubber-goods.

The india-rubber market fluctuated considerably during the year, the range for Pará being from 68 c. to 75 c. (2s. 8d. to 3s.).

The demand for rubber-goods was very large, and a fairly profitable business was done, notwithstanding greatly reduced prices and active competition amongst manufacturers.

Iron, steel and other metals.

The market was active throughout the year, with a rise in iron and steel, and a "boom" in copper and tin. With the exception of nails, prices of manufactures of metal showed a slight improvement.

Fish trade.

The mackerel catch in 1886 was small, but, owing to a heavy stock of old fish, prices continued low. In 1887 the catch was no better, but, as the old stock had been disposed of, prices advanced about 40 per cent. In cod and other kinds of fish, there was also a marked improvement in prices, but this gain was off-set by the small amount of business done.

Flour and grain.

The price of flour continued low during the greater part of the year, but business was very active, and, with an additional demand for exportation in the latter months, prices for the lower grades improved and were maintained.

The local grain market, which is almost entirely limited to Indian corn and oats, was steady at a small advance on the previous year; but Boston business has been very much reduced since the recent enactment of a law on Inter-State transportation which has rendered it expedient for North-eastern markets to obtain their supplies of grain direct from the West, instead of purchasing them here.

Mercantile failures.

The number of trading firms in the Boston Consular district was 78,046, or an increase of 1,260; and the number of bankrupts was 905, with liabilities amounting to 2,241,000*l.*, or a decrease of 985,000*l.*

Foreign commerce.

Foreign imports at Boston during the year amounted to 12,514,000*l.*, an increase of 167,000*l.*; and foreign exports were valued at 11,340,000*l.*, a decrease of 166,000*l.*

Maritime trade.

According to the Custom-house Returns, the number of vessels which arrived at Boston in the foreign trade was 2,428, of 1,304,489 tons, or an increase of 45,965 tons; namely, British 1,801, of 975,558 tons, an increase of 82,661 tons; American 492, of 229,429 tons, a decrease of 25,268 tons; all other nationalities 135, of 99,502 tons, a decrease of 11,428 tons.

American and foreign vessels arriving from foreign ports *viâ* other United States' ports, are not included in these returns.

The Consulate Records of entries of British vessels show 1844 vessels of 987,631 tons, of which 432, of 758,324 tons, being an increase of 79,278 tons, were steamers; and 1,412, of 229,307 tons, an increase of 6,823 tons, were sailing-vessels.

Ocean freights, especially on outward cargoes, were indirectly affected by the difficulty experienced in adjusting rates under the recent law for the regulation of Inter-State transportation, and they fluctuated considerably, and were on an average lower than in 1886. *Maritime freights.*

Very few and very gradual variations occurred in exchange, the extremes—which were not long maintained—being 4 dol. 84 c. and 4 dol. 87 c. per £ for bankers' bills at sight. *Rate of Exchange.*

The assessed valuation of real and personal property in the State of Massachusetts, for state, county, and town taxes for the year 1887, was 386,500,000*l.*, an increase of 17,000,000*l.*; and the amount of taxes levied was 5,766,000*l.*; and the valuation of property in the city of Boston was 149,525,000*l.*, showing an increase of 7,405,000*l.* *Property and taxation in Massachusetts.*

The Massachusetts decennial Census of the State was taken in the year 1885, and is to be published in three volumes, namely, Vol. I. (in two parts), relating to Population and Social Statistics; Vol. II. to Manufactures, Fisheries, and Commerce; and Vol. III. to Agriculture and Mines. *Census of the State of Massachusetts.*

Part 1 of Vol. I., which is all that has so far been printed and distributed, quotes the United States' decennial Census for the year 1880, showing that in that year Massachusetts had 1,783,085 inhabitants, and was seventh as to number, and second as to density, of population, which was then 221·8 to the square mile; and contains voluminous tables, giving minute particulars in regard to date of incorporation and former censuses of each township, and to increase, age, sex, parentage, place of birth, and nationality, of the population.

From the tables thus far published, it appears that the population of the State in 1885 was 1,942,141, showing an increase of 290,229, or 17·57 per cent. since the date of the decennial State Census of 1875; that the number of males was 932,884, or 48·03 per cent., and the number of females, 1,009,257, or 51·97 per cent.; the number of native-born, 1,415,274, and the number of foreign-born, 526,867; that of the latter, 99,131 males, 20 years of age or over, were aliens, and 206,227 were originally, or had become, citizens; that 1,922,944 were white, 19,197 were black, mulatto, Chinese, Japanese, or Indian. The number of inhabitants under 15 years of age was 536,731; 15, and under 60 years, 1,258,674; 60, and under 80 years, 131,076; 80, and under 100 years, 15,430; and from 100 to 111 years, 86. The number of families was 424,415, averaging 4·58 persons to each family. Of native and foreign-born, 44·05 per cent. were of native, 47·36 per cent. of foreign, and 6·17 per cent. of mixed parentage; 55·10 per cent. of the population were single, 38·08 per cent. were married, 6·66 per cent. were widowed, and 0·15 per cent. were divorced.

The average age of the whole population was 28·75 years, and that of all over 20 years of age, was 40·75 years; whilst the average death age for all was 34·23 years.

In conjunction with the inquiries set on foot for the purposes of the Census, the Chief of the State Bureau of Statistics of Labour obtained specific answers on the subject of unemployed labour for the 12 months to the 1st of May, 1885, when the inquiry commenced; and has embodied the information thus collected in the interesting and instructive 18th Annual Report of the Bureau, which has just been published. In this report, which gives the population, as per the Census returns, at 1,942,191, the number of persons of both sexes, and of all ages, from 10 to 80 years, engaged in remunerative occupations, *Report on unemployed labour.*

is placed at 816,470, the number fully employed in their special occupations at 574,881; the number unemployed in their special occupations for terms varying from one to twelve months, at 241,589, and the number so unemployed who found other employment, at 10,758; the average time of unemployment of each person, taking the whole number engaged in remunerative occupations, is stated as 1·22 per month; the average time of unemployment in his special occupation of each one of those unemployed in such occupation, as 4·11 months, and the average time of unemployment of each of those unemployed in any occupation, as 3·91 months.

Of the 241,589 unemployed for a long or short term in their special occupations, the per-centage of unemployed in each class of occupation as compared with the other classes, is thus given:—Government and professional occupations, 3·27 per cent.; domestic service, 2·03; personal service, 1·72; trade, 3·94; transportation, 2·91; agriculture, 6·28; fisheries, 1·46; manufactures, 69·14; mining, 0·29; labourers, 8·43; apprentices, 0·53.

The relative per-centage of employed and unemployed in each class of occupation is not given.

The causes and relative time of unemployment in manufacturing establishments (which show by far the largest per-centage of unemployment) are thus stated:—

Repairs in factories, 0·20 month; slack trade, 2·72 months; strikes and lock-outs, 0·02 month; total, 2.94 months.

Boston, March 15, 1888.

Annex A.—RETURN of all Shipping in the Foreign Trade at Ports in the Boston Consular District in the Fiscal Year ended June 30th, 1887.

ENTERED.

Nationality.	Sailing.		Steam.		Total.	
	Number of Vessels.	Tons.	Number of Vessels.	Tons.	Number of Vessels.	Tons.
Foreign	3,592	484,778	754	929,890	4,346	1,414,668
American	844	223,672	254	251,200	1,098	474,872
Total 1887	4,436	708,450	1,008	1,181,090	5,444	1,889,510
„ 1886	4,370	701,780	938	1,040,066	4,894	1,655,596

CLEARED.

Nationality.	Sailing.		Steam.		Total.	
	Number of Vessels.	Tons.	Number of Vessels.	Tons.	Number of Vessels.	Tons.
Foreign	3,564	464,795	632	751,400	4,196	1,216,195
American	1,397	318,419	248	244,377	1,645	562,796
Total 1887	4,961	783,214	880	995,777	5,841	1,778,991
„ 1886	4,740	771,950	850	904,548	5,590	1,676,498

Annex B.—RETURN of Principal Articles of Export from, and Imports to, Ports in the Boston Consular District, during the Fiscal Years ended June 30th, 1887 and 1886.

EXPORTS.

Articles.	Value. 1887.	Value. 1886.
	£	£
Meat and dairy products	2,785,961	2,887,437
Horned cattle	758,874	818,143
Corn, flour, and other breadstuffs	2,980,247	2,632,982
Raw cotton	1,749,047	1,972,883
Cotton manufactures	268,446	243,645
Tobacco in leaf and manufactured	525,451	545,769
Iron, steel, and manufactures of	285,002	285,090
Sugar and molasses	154,187	130,600
All other domestic merchandise	2,873,677	2,177,693
Foreign merchandise re-exported	309,646	233,767
Coin and bullion	440	6,604
Total	12,690,978	11,934,333

IMPORTS.

Articles.	Value. 1887.	Value. 1886.
	£	£
Sugar and molasses	2,658,134	2,609,885
Wool	1,340,386	1,512,043
Woollen goods	784,381	767,148
Hides, goat and fur skins, and furs	1,279,866	1,222,393
Iron-ore, iron, steel, and manufactures of	1,192,423	960,518
Chemicals, drugs, and dyes	966,339	817,591
Flax, hemp, and jute	879,083	515,583
Cotton manufactures	305,683	345,899
Fish	331,870	286,314
All other merchandise	4,437,569	4,636,918
Coin and bullion	15,164	59,924
Total	14,190,903	13,733,716

UNITED STATES.

Annex C.—TABLE showing the Total Value of all articles Exported from San Francisco, and Imported to San Francisco, from and to Foreign Countries during the years 1886-87.

Country.	Exports. 1887.	Exports. 1886.	Imports. 1887.	Imports. 1886.
	£	£	£	£
Great Britain	3,311,481	4,095,300	888,325	589,470
China	614,053	749,150	1,278,437	1,225,090
Hawaiian Islands	524,585	655,470	1,881,056	2,140,550
Mexico	297,235	228,050	91,401	58,940
Central America	216,043	146,600	563,595	382,550
Australia	204,904	281,040	290,707	264,880
Canada	160,167	267,450	262,102	192,450
Japan	152,391	117,760	1,933,993	2,042,480
France	30,652	533,880	308,194	287,750
Germany	13,905	22,700	191,157	156,150
Spanish Possessions	4,040	3,560	153,291	121,350
India	347	750	224,443	243,250
Belgium	40	122,930	98,026	52,600
Domestic ports and other countries	1,788,305	753,660	156,612	158,990
Total	7,318,148	7,978,300	8,321,337	7,916,500

LONDON:
Printed for Her Majesty's Stationery Office,
By HARRISON AND SONS,
Printers in Ordinary to Her Majesty.

(1125 4 | 88—H & S 401)

447

FOREIGN OFFICE.
1888.
ANNUAL SERIES.

No. 313.
DIPLOMATIC AND CONSULAR REPORTS ON TRADE AND FINANCE.

UNITED STATES.

REPORT FOR THE YEAR 1887
ON THE
TRADE OF SAN FRANCISCO.

REFERENCE TO PREVIOUS REPORT, Annual Series No. 186.

Presented to both Houses of Parliament by Command of Her Majesty,
APRIL, 1888.

LONDON:
PRINTED FOR HER MAJESTY'S STATIONERY OFFICE,
BY HARRISON AND SONS, ST. MARTIN'S LANE,
PRINTERS IN ORDINARY TO HER MAJESTY.

And to be purchased, either directly or through any Bookseller, from
EYRE AND SPOTTISWOODE, EAST HARDING STREET, FLEET STREET, E.C., and
32, ABINGDON STREET, WESTMINSTER, S.W.; or
ADAM AND CHARLES BLACK, 6, NORTH BRIDGE, EDINBURGH; or
HODGES, FIGGIS, & Co., 104, GRAFTON STREET, DUBLIN.

1888.

[C. 5252–90.] *Price One Penny.*

New Series of Reports.

Reports of the Annual Series have been issued from Her Majesty's Diplomatic and Consular Officers at the following places, and may be obtained from the sources indicated on the title-page:—

No.		Price.	No.		Price.
191.	Hankow	1d.	252.	Paris	1d.
192.	Erzeroum	1d.	253.	Bogota	1d.
193.	Syra	1d.	254.	Salonica	1d.
194.	Athens	3d.	255.	Copenhagen	1d.
195.	Vienna	2d.	256.	Jeddah	1d.
196.	Alexandria	1d.	257.	Russia	2d.
197.	Constantinople	1d.	258.	Paris	1d.
198.	Hakodate	1d.	259.	Patras	1d.
199.	Shanghai	2d.	260.	Brussels	1d.
200.	Tokyo	2d.	261.	Ichang	1d.
201.	Tamatave	1d.	262.	Baltimore	1d.
202.	Mexico	1d.	263.	Taganrog	1d.
203.	Chefoo	1d.	264.	Oporto	1d.
204.	Nagasaki	5d.	265.	Rio de Janeiro	1d.
205.	Cuba	1d.	266.	Galveston	1d.
206.	Tunis	1d.	267.	Tripoli	1d.
207.	Réunion	1d.	268.	Galatz	1d.
208.	Hyogo	2d.	269.	Varna	1d.
209.	Tangier	1d.	270.	New Orleans	2d.
210.	Antwerp	1d.	271.	Cherbourg	1d.
211.	Stettin	1d.	272.	Suakin	1d.
212.	Erzeroum	1d.	273.	Brest	1d.
213.	Rotterdam	1d.	274.	Barcelona	2d.
214.	Nantes	2d.	275.	Barcelona	1d.
215.	Newport News	1d.	276.	Antwerp	1d.
216.	Rio Grande do Sul	1d.	277.	Havre	3d.
217.	Rio de Janeiro	1d.	278.	Odessa	1d.
218.	Corea	1d.	279.	Tokyo	1d.
219.	Kanagawa	1d.	280.	Saigon	1d.
220.	Wurtemberg	1d.	281.	Buenos Ayres	1d.
221.	Tahiti	1d.	282.	Taganrog	1d.
222.	Bangkok	1d.	283.	Tamsui	1d.
223.	St. Petersburg	2d.	284.	Puerto Plata	1d.
224.	Canton	1d.	285.	Wênchow	1d.
225.	Erzeroum	1d.	286.	Tokyo	1d.
226.	Rio de Janeiro	1d.	287.	Lisbon	2d.
227.	Valparaiso	1d.	288.	La Rochelle	1d.
228.	St. Thomas	1d.	289.	Washington	4d.
229.	Stockholm	1d.	290.	Beyrout	1d.
230.	Nyassa	1d.	291.	Algiers	2d.
231.	Buenos Ayres	1d.	292.	Varna	1d.
232.	The Hague	1d.	293.	Algiers	1d.
233.	Trieste	1d.	294.	Port Saïd	1d.
234.	Vienna	1d.	295.	Manila	1d.
235.	Washington	3d.	296.	Charleston	1d.
236.	Odessa	1d.	297.	Kiungchow	1d.
237.	Sofia	1d.	298.	Pakhoi	1d.
238.	Porto Rico	1d.	299.	Wuhu	1d.
239.	Palermo	2d.	300.	Boulogne	2d.
240.	Lisbon	2d.	301.	Marseilles	1d.
241.	Tabreez	1d.	302.	Bordeaux	2d.
242.	Tunis	1d.	303.	Ancona	1d.
243.	The Hague	1d.	304.	Swatow	1d.
244.	Fiume	1d.	305.	Ssŭ-ch'uan	1d.
245.	Venice	1d.	306.	Antwerp	1d.
246.	Paris	2d.	307.	Cadiz	1d.
247.	Ancona	1d.	308.	Genoa	1d.
248.	St. Petersburg	2d	309.	Marseilles	1d.
249.	Algiers	2d.	310.	Baltimore	1d.
250.	Bucharest	1d.	311.	Savannah	1d.
251.	Christiania	2d.	312.	Boston	1d.

No. 313.

Reference to previous Report, Annual Series No. 186.

UNITED STATES.

SAN FRANCISCO.

Consul Donohoe to the Marquis of Salisbury.

My Lord, San Francisco, March 7, 1888.

I HAVE the honour to enclose my Annual Report on the Trade and Commerce of San Francisco for the year 1887.

I have, &c.
(Signed) DENIS DONOHOE.

Report on the Trade and Commerce of California for 1887.

The year 1887 has been, speaking in general terms, a good one for California in most branches of trade, though there has been a great falling-off in the export of wheat during the year, as will be seen by the tables appended to this report. The quantity received at this port for 1887 was 10,493,433 centals,* whilst in 1886, 16,552,939 centals were received; nearly all of this been exported to the United Kingdom. [General trade fair. Wheat.]

The average price of best shipping wheat for the year has been as follows:— [Price of wheat.]

	Per Cental.	
	Dol. c.	Dol. c.
January	1 52½ to	1 60
February	1 47½	1 52½
March	1 47½	1 67½
April	1 67½	1 80
May	1 70	1 85
June	1 80	2 10
July	1 80	1 95
August	1 90	1 25
September	1 25	1 35
October	1 25	1 35
November	1 30	1 37½
December	1 32½	1 40

A syndicate was formed here early in the year to purchase the control of the entire stock of No. 1 Wheat in the State, and it was pretty successful in doing so, and was able in June to run the price up to 2 dol. 10 c. per cental. It is unnecessary to say that during this period the shipments to foreign ports were few and far between. In August the crash came, and wheat fell in price until the close of the year. [Speculation in wheat.]

The export of flour from this port to the United Kingdom shows a large decrease: 168,645 barrels in 1887, as compared with 471,636 in [Flour.]

* A cental equals 100 lbs.

1886, is remarkable. This is probably caused by the difference in freight, and the manipulation of the wheat market, as much as by anything else.

Salmon. — The total packing of 1887 for the entire Pacific Coast amounts to 997,890 cases, the total for 1886 being 933,354 cases. The Columbia River is the most prolific source of supply, and the Territory of Alaska comes next, having produced 190,200 cases in 1887. It is estimated there will be at least seven new canneries put in operation in Alaska during the coming season. About one-half of the pack of 1887 was shipped to the Eastern States. The stock on hand in January, 1888, on this Coast is 67,064 cases.

Coal. — The fluctuations in the price of coal during the year have been very great, and there has been a clear advance of 3 dol. per ton for the month of December, as compared with the price ruling for January. The price for "spot" cargoes was as follows:—

	January.	December.
	Dol. c.	Dol. c.
Australian	6 25	9 00
English steam	6 00	9 00
Scotch splint	6 50	9 50
West Hartley	7 00	9 50

The total receipts from all sources is 1,113,878 tons.

Sugar. — The bulk of the raw sugar received here comes from the Sandwich Islands, and there is a falling-off in the amount entered for the first time since the passage of the Reciprocity Treaty with the Islands.

The production of sugar from beetroot was very small, owing to an accident of a boiler explosion at the refinery at Alvarado in this State. These works will be enlarged, and it is expected that they will have a capacity for 200 tons of beets per day. Another large factory is in course of construction at Watsonville in this State, and will probably be in operation this autumn.

Wine. — The production of wine in the State of California for the year 1887 has not reached the expectations of those engaged in the culture of the vine—the estimated production is placed at 13,900,000 gallons, whilst 18,000,000 gallons is given for 1886. The long, dry, hot summer of 1887, with frosts in the early spring, has had a good deal to do with this decrease; but, though there has been so much less wine produced, *Increase in raisins.* the increase in the raisin crop is remarkable. This industry may be said to have had its inception in 1873, when 6,000 boxes were produced. It has steadily increased ever since, and the production of 1887 is given as 800,000 boxes. The raisin-grape seems to flourish all over the State, and, at the lowest estimate, an acre will yield 100 boxes, worth 20*l*.

Dried fruits. — The product of the State in dried fruits, honey, beeswax, &c., for the year is given as follows:—

SAN FRANCISCO.

Articles.		Quantity.
Raisins	20 lb. boxes	800,000
Honey, extracted	Lbs.	1,090,000
,, comb	,,	250,000
Beeswax	,,	25,000
French prunes	,,	1,750,000
German prunes	,,	75,000
Apples, sun-dried	,,	200,000
Peaches ,,	,,	1,750,000
Plums ,,	,,	400,000
Pears ,,	,,	40,000
Grapes ,,	,,	600,000
Apricots ,,	,,	200,000
Nectarines, sun-dried	,,	100,000
Figs, sun-dried	,,	90,000
Apples, evaporated	,,	550,000
Apricots, ,,	,,	} 3,000,000
,, bleached	,,	
Peaches, evaporated, peeled	,,	500,000
Peaches, evaporated, unpeeled	,,	750,000
Plums, evaporated	,,	50,000
Nectarines, evaporated	,,	50,000
Walnuts	,,	1,500,000
Almonds	,,	500,000
Pea-nuts	,,	250,000

Green fruits. There has been a very considerable increase in the shipment of green fruits by rail to the Eastern and Middle States, and a good market has been opened up for the farmer in this direction, with quick returns for the value of his products. About 566,000*l.* value of green fruit has been sent by rail.

Canned fruit and vegetables. The pack of the season is estimated at about 40 per cent. over that of 1886, and, as canneries are being put up in various directions through the interior of the State, there will be a steady increase in the output. The total estimated pack of the season is given at 1,121,500 cases; and though the export by sea is but small, the quantity sent by rail for distribution throughout the country is enormous.

Metal product. From the circular of Messrs. Wells, Fargo, and Co., the net product of metals in the States and Territories west of the Missouri River, excluding British Columbia and Mexico, for the last two years, are given as follows:—

Year.	Gold.	Silver.	Copper.	Lead.	Total.
	£	£	£	£	£
1887	6,500,013	10,166,777	2,072,549	1,926,215	20,665,554
1886	5,912,285	10,427,370	1,855,351	1,837,038	20,032,044

The exports of silver during the past year to Japan, China, the Straits, &c., from San Francisco, have been as follows:—2,888,981*l.*

Cement, increase in imports. The importation of cement is largely on the increase. Vessels have brought their entire cargo of it in some instances. The quantity used in San Francisco is very great for the roadways of the cable railways, as well as for the sidewalks of the streets, and there is a large demand for it from other towns throughout the State.

Tin-plates, increase in imports. With the large demand for the use of the canneries, the importation of tin-plates is likely to assume a considerable increase.

UNITED STATES.

Labour. The canning business of the Pacific Coast is steadily increasing from year to year.

The demand for skilled labour during the year has been good throughout the State, and, during the spring and summer, ordinary labourers have been in demand. Men who work on farms flock to the city during the winter, and the numbers of unemployed wandering about the streets have been very large.

Wages. There is no change to be reported under this head. The very ample table given in Mr. Acting-Consul Mason's report of last year conveys an accurate idea on this subject.

Railways. There has been great activity in railway building throughout the State during 1887, and about 300 miles of new lines have been opened to traffic.

Much grading has been done and many new lines are projected and under survey, and extensions of old lines are being made. The most important new railway connection during the year has been the completion of the California and Oregon line connecting Puget Sound and Portland with the Californian system extending to the city of Mexico. This line runs through a very fertile section of this State, throwing open to settlement much valuable land.

The traffic on all the lines has been so great as to cause freight-blockades during the winter on the Atchison, Topeka and Santa Fé, as well as on the Central Pacific; but, by the acquisition of more rolling-stock and increased motive power, these difficulties will soon be overcome.

Although the different Trans-continental lines have been able to agree upon rates all through the year, still there has been much competition between them for the overland traffic.

At a meeting of the managers in November last at Chicago, the Trans-continental Association was re-organised, and the Canadian Pacific then joined in the pool, receiving, however, some differential concession as to rates. Since then all the Trans-continental lines have apparently acted in a harmonious manner.

NOTE.—All values in this Report are reduced to sterling at the rate of five dollars to the pound.

Annex A.—RETURN of all Shipping at the Port of San Francisco in the Year 1887.

ENTERED.

Nationality.	Sailing. Number of Vessels.	Sailing. Tons.	Steam. Number of Vessels.	Steam. Tons.	Total. Number of Vessels.	Total. Tons.
British	209	301,162	38	64,034	247	365,196
American, from foreign countries	242	196,889	165	226,936	407	423,825
American, from Atlantic ports of the Union	37	61,562	3	1,681	40	63,243
Hawaiian	9	3,310	17	29,134	26	32,444
German	22	24,420	1	368	23	24,788
Bolivian	11	9,526	...	...	11	9,526
French	2	917	1	101	3	1,018
Others	15	9,879	8	8,727	23	18,606
Total	547	607,665	233	330,981	780	938,646
,, for the year preceding	594	630,445	244	341,498	838	971,943

SAN FRANCISCO.

CLEARED.

Nationality.	Sailing. Number of Vessels.	Sailing. Tons.	Steam. Number of Vessels.	Steam. Tons.	Total. Number of Vessels.	Total. Tons.
British	196	277,187	41	68,199	237	345,386
American, from foreign countries	215	190,753	167	230,857	382	421,610
American, from Atlantic ports of the Union	13	22,068	...	...	13	22,068
Hawaiian	9	3,310	18	29,245	27	32,555
German	20	22,295	1	368	21	22,663
Bolivian	14	11,038	...	...	14	11,038
French	...	...	...	...	...	...
Others	13	8,923	11	7,998	24	16,921
Total	480	535,574	238	336,667	718	872,241
,, for the year preceding	581	658,116	248	342,264	829	1,000,380

The entries and clearances of American ships do not include the Coasting Trade or Whaling and Fishing voyages.

Annex B.—RETURN of Principal Articles of Export from San Francisco during the Years 1886-87.

Articles.		1887. Quantity.	1887. Value.	1886. Quantity.	1886. Value.
			£		£
Wheat and flour	Tons	511,809	3,621,241	580,425	5,121,800
Tinned salmon	Cases	196,724	193,424	181,300	183,000
Tinned fruit and vegetables	,,	148,749	109,449	98,700	86,300
Borax	Lbs.	7,350,073	82,466	7,934,000	80,000
Quicksilver	Flasks	9,545	79,812	7,000	46,000
Timber	Feet	17,135,868	65,202	15,352,600	59,000
Lead	Lbs.	7,359,174	63,329	10,611,700	103,000
Leather	Rolls	5,137	58,449	4,100	46,000
Wine	Gallons	274,063	44,175	757,600	74,700
Other articles	...	...	2,995,601	...	2,178,500
Total		...	7,318,148	...	7,978,300

RETURN of Principal Articles of Import to San Francisco during the Years 1886-87.

Articles.		1887. Quantity.	1887. Value.	1886. Quantity.	1886. Value.
			£		£
Raw silk	Lbs.	3,286,450	2,461,855	4,455,700	2,546,700
Sugar	Tons	99,612	1,831,807	101,451	2,095,700
Coffee	Lbs.	18,080,837	458,069	20,432,190	358,000
Coals	Tons	512,646	324,478	548,000	340,600
Tea	Lbs.	8,028,068	222,956	8,949,800	260,400
Rice	Tons	19,456	220,628	24,340	205,600
Tin-plates	Boxes	211,205	138,800	152,450	104,950
Cement	Barrels	329,926	82,481	159,000	33,130
Scrap-iron	Tons	30,429	68,875	14,903	30,770
Pig-iron	,,	14,410	34,650	14,200	21,000
Other articles	...	...	2,476,738	...	1,919,650
Total		...	8,321,337	...	7,916,500

UNITED STATES.

Annex C.—Table shewing the Value of all Articles Exported from, and Imported to Ports in the Boston Consular District during the Fiscal Years ended June 30, 1887 and 1886.

Country.	Exports. 1887.	Exports. 1886.	Imports. 1887.	Imports. 1886.
United Kingdom and Colonies	11,581,756	10,758,772	8,006,895	7,648,477
Spain and Colonies	97,745	91,685	2,280,768	1,338,417
Germany	21,992	14,786	834,674	535,349
France and Colonies	129,873	159,518	752,804	676,587
Argentine Republic	149,934	104,542	466,144	606,346
Italy	14,732	18,980	279,091	230,385
Belgium	233,111	99,422	191,707	194,063
Sweden and Norway	1,248	4,095	182,501	171,861
Mexico	249	10	159,173	65,984
Chili	108,429	116,483	105,561	38,253
Brazil	1,995	3,584	113,368	218,880
Turkey	11,185	11,439	93,384	79,503
Netherlands and Colonies	4,798	51,814	87,926	149,520
All other countries	334,331	499,213	656,407	1,781,091
Total	12,690,978	11,934,333	14,190,903	13,733,716

LONDON:
Printed for Her Majesty's Stationery Office,
By HARRISON AND SONS,
Printers in Ordinary to Her Majesty.

(1125   4 | 88—H & S   400)

FOREIGN OFFICE.
1888.
ANNUAL SERIES.

No. 330.

DIPLOMATIC AND CONSULAR REPORTS ON TRADE AND FINANCE.

UNITED STATES.

REPORT FOR THE YEAR 1887
ON THE
TRADE OF THE CONSULAR DISTRICT OF CHICAGO.

REFERENCE TO PREVIOUS REPORT, Annual Series No. 140.

Presented to both Houses of Parliament by Command of Her Majesty,
MAY, 1888.

LONDON:
PRINTED FOR HER MAJESTY'S STATIONERY OFFICE,
BY HARRISON AND SONS, ST. MARTIN'S LANE,
PRINTERS IN ORDINARY TO HER MAJESTY.

And to be purchased, either directly or through any Bookseller, from
EYRE AND SPOTTISWOODE, EAST HARDING STREET, FLEET STREET, E.C., and
32, ABINGDON STREET, WESTMINSTER, S.W.; or
ADAM AND CHARLES BLACK, 6, NORTH BRIDGE, EDINBURGH; or
HODGES, FIGGIS, & Co., 104, GRAFTON STREET, DUBLIN.

1888.

[C. 5252—107.] *Price Twopence.*

New Series of Reports.

REPORTS of the Annual Series have been issued from Her Majesty's Diplomatic and Consular Officers at the following places, and may be obtained from the sources indicated on the title-page:—

No.		Price.	No.		Price.
204.	Nagasaki	5d.	267.	Tripoli	1d.
205.	Cuba	1d.	268.	Galatz	1d.
206.	Tunis	1d.	269.	Varna	1d.
207.	Réunion	1d.	270.	New Orleans	2d.
208.	Hyogo	2d.	271.	Cherbourg	1d.
209.	Tangier	1d.	272.	Suakin	1d.
210.	Antwerp	1d.	273.	Brest	1d.
211.	Stettin	1d.	274.	Barcelona	2d.
212.	Erzeroum	1d.	275.	Barcelona	1d.
213.	Rotterdam	1d.	276.	Antwerp	1d.
214.	Nantes	2d.	277.	Havre	3d.
215.	Newport News	1d.	278.	Odessa	1d.
216.	Rio Grande do Sul	1d.	279.	Tokyo	1d.
217.	Rio de Janeiro	1d.	280.	Saigon	1d.
218.	Corea	1d.	281.	Buenos Ayres	1d.
219.	Kanagawa	1d.	282.	Taganrog	1d.
220.	Wurtemberg	1d.	283.	Tamsui	1d.
221.	Tahiti	1d.	284.	Puerto Plata	1d.
222.	Bangkok	1d.	285.	Wênchow	1d.
223.	St. Petersburg	2d.	286.	Tokyo	1d.
224.	Canton	1d.	287.	Lisbon	2d.
225.	Erzeroum	1d.	288.	La Rochelle	1d.
226.	Rio de Janeiro	1d.	289.	Washington	4d.
227.	Valparaiso	1d.	290.	Beyrout	1d.
228.	St. Thomas	1d.	291.	Algiers	2d
229.	Stockholm	1d.	292.	Varna	1d.
230.	Nyassa	1d.	293.	Algiers	1d.
231.	Buenos Ayres	1d.	294.	Port Said	1d.
232.	The Hague	1d.	295.	Manila	1d.
233.	Trieste	1d.	296.	Charleston	1d.
234.	Vienna	1d.	297.	Kiungchow	1d.
235.	Washington	3d.	298.	Pakhoi	1d.
236.	Odessa	1d.	299.	Wuhu	1d.
237.	Sofia	1d.	300.	Boulogne	2d.
238.	Porto Rico	1d.	301.	Marseilles	1d.
239.	Palermo	2d.	302.	Bordeaux	2d.
240.	Lisbon	2d.	303.	Ancona	1d.
241.	Tabreez	1d.	304.	Swatow	1d.
242.	Tunis	1d.	305.	Ssŭ-ch'uan	1d.
243.	The Hague	1d.	306.	Antwerp	1d.
244.	Fiume	1d.	307.	Cadiz	1d.
245.	Venice	1d.	308.	Genoa	1d.
246.	Paris	2d.	309.	Marseilles	1d.
247.	Ancona	1d.	310.	Baltimore	1d.
248.	St. Petersburg	2d.	311.	Savannah	1d.
249.	Algiers	2d.	312.	Boston	1d.
250.	Bucharest	1d.	313.	San Francisco	1d.
251.	Christiania	2d	314.	Guayaquil	1d.
252.	Paris	1d.	315.	Santos	1d.
253.	Bogota	1d.	316.	Carthagena and Santa Martha	1d.
254.	Salonica	1d.	317.	San José	1d.
255.	Copenhagen	1d.	318.	Boulogne	1d.
256.	Jeddah	1d.	319.	Tahiti	1d.
257.	Russia	2d.	320.	Fiume	1d.
258.	Paris	1d.	321.	Warsaw	1d.
259.	Patras	1d.	322.	Vera Cruz	2d.
260.	Brussels	1d.	323.	Rio Grande do Sul	1d.
261.	Ichang	1d.	324.	Gothenburg	2d.
262.	Baltimore	1d.	325.	Philippopolis	1d.
263.	Taganrog	1d.	326.	Mogador	2d.
264.	Oporto	1d.	327.	Havana	2d.
265.	Rio de Janeiro	1d.	328.	La Rochelle	1d.
266.	Galveston	1d.	329.	Corunna	2d

No. 330.

Reference to previous Report, Annual Series No. 140.

UNITED STATES.

CHICAGO.

Consul Hayes Sadler to the Marquis of Salisbury.

My Lord,   *Chicago, April* 5, 1888.

I HAVE the honour to transmit, herewith, a report on the Trade and Commerce of Chicago during the year 1887.

Reports from the Vice-Consuls at St. Louis, St. Paul, and Denver are likewise transmitted herewith.

I have, &c.,
(Signed)   J. HAYES SADLER.

Report of Consul Hayes Sadler on the Trade and Commerce of Chicago during the Year 1887.

THE CITY OF CHICAGO.

Trade in general.

The city of Chicago, while retaining its position as the centre of the grain and provision trade, is every year extending its manufactures, and is still growing as a point of supply and distribution for the domestic and other necessities required by the ever-increasing development of the west. The year 1887 has been marked by a large increase in all branches of trade, except in corn and hog packing: the most prominent advance was in wheat and cattle, while in manufacturing industries the greatest increase is shown in the manufacture of iron, a general advance in prices being also noticeable. The passing of the Interstate Commerce Bill caused unusual large purchases early in the year, from the belief that freight for goods arriving from distant points would be raised by the terms of the Act, which regulates that goods shall not be taken at a less rate for a long distance than a short one.

Activity, however, continued after the Act took effect in April, and the money value of the total trade of the city is said to exceed that of the previous year by 10½ per cent., and to have reached the sum of 227,000,000*l.* sterling, or a higher figure than at any preceding period. Where the returns in this report are not derived from absolutely official sources, and with regard to many of the industries there is no such return made, they are taken from published estimates compiled by a recognised authority.

Growth of the city.

The enormous increase in the business at the Post-office will give some idea of the progressive activity of the city. Ten years ago, when the population was about 450,000, there were 61,000,000 pieces handled in the city delivery division; there are now 248,000,000. In the dead-letter division 2,000,000 pieces were handled in 1887 against 286,593 in 1878, and the postal receipts exceeded those of the latter year by 269,943*l*. The population is now reckoned at nearly 800,000, and including the adjoining suburbs at 950,000.

To meet the growing demand, important works are being carried on for the purpose of increasing the water supply, which is at present barely sufficient. New pumping works are to be erected, and a second tunnel four miles long is being thrown out under the lake, while the existing tunnel will be extended two miles further to the same distance, at which a purer supply will be obtained. The number of buildings erected was 4,833, with a frontage of 115,506 feet, costing about 4,000,000*l*.; a greater number but of rather a less costly character than in the preceding year.

Finance. Chicago is now a central reserve city, and national banks are obliged to keep constantly on hand 25 per cent. of their net deposits. The amount of deposits in these banks at the end of December last was estimated at 16,500,000*l*. sterling, whereas 10 years ago they were barely 5,000,000*l*. The aggregate bank clearings amounted to about 612,000,000*l*. sterling, or an advance of 14½ per cent. over the total of the preceding year.

Money was somewhat scarce from the great demand for railway and other enterprise and for the west, and 7 to 8 per cent. were the ruling rates in the latter months.

Receipts and Shipments.

Cereals. The receipts of breadstuffs are estimated at 161,000,000 bushels, or an excess of 7 per cent. on those of the previous year; the largest increase having been 50 per cent. in flour and 25 per cent. in wheat, and the greatest decrease 20 per cent. in corn. The large increase in *Flour.* flour receipts, which reached a total of 6,250,000 barrels, is in some measure due to direct shipments from mills to consumers in the east and in Europe. Mills are fast extending in the north-west, and it is thought that the relative receipts of flour to those of wheat will every year increase, till most of the milling is done in this country.

Wheat. The receipts of wheat were 21,411,249 bushels, and the shipments 26,850,576 bushels, the average price having been 3*s*. 2½*d*., or about 75 per cent. higher than in 1886. The first six months the receipts were unusually heavy, and prices rose till, on June 7, they reached 3*s*. 11*d*., owing to the operations of a clique, but fell in a few days to 2*s*. 10*d*. on the collapse of the corner. It was the biggest corner in wheat ever run, and it was not till the speculative purchases amounted to 25,000,000 bushels, and resources were exhausted, that the crash came, before the completion of the plan, which was apparently to wait for a further inflation of the market. These speculative dealings have a wide influence on the market for leading commodities here, and there was a general feeling of satisfaction when the deal met with merited punishment, but the losses of many of the victims were heavy, and a general dulness in speculative operations has succeeded.

Corn and other grain. The price of corn rose steadily throughout the year from short supply consequent on the drought, the value being 2*s*. per bushel at the end of December, and the average price for the year 1*s*. 7½*d*. There were in round numbers 51,500,000 bushels received, and 50,500,000 bushels shipped. The receipts of oats, 40,500,000 bushels, were very large, and the prices of 1886 were not maintained; the shipments amounted to nearly 40,000,000. The demand for rye seems to be yearly on the decrease, but the market for barley was active at an advance of about 7 per cent. in value.

CHICAGO.

The capacity of the Chicago elevators is now 27,670,000 bushels, one large elevator having been recently built. Owing to the high price charged here, the storage of grain has been largely on the increase in country and roadside elevators, which have become much more numerous. A considerable reduction has, however, been lately made with a view to maintain Chicago as the great grain market of the world, and it is supposed some benefit will ensue to the producer and consumer. Quotations largely depend on the cost of holding the property in store, and the premium on carrying wheat into a period of a few months has been at times extremely heavy.

The receipts of cattle were unprecedentedly large, amounting to 2,382,000 head, and exceeding those of 1886 by 418,108. A great number of animals were pushed on the market on account of paucity of feed from want of rain, and through fear of a recurrence of those terrible losses from cold and exposure which marked the preceding winter. The price consequently was low, at fully 8 per cent. below that of 1886, while Texan cattle, which arrived in large numbers, owing to increased railway facilities, were poor at about 20 per cent. reduction in value. The shipments amounted to 791,483 head. *Cattle.*

A remarkable increase occurred in the receipt of horses, 46,404 having entered at Chicago against 27,599 in 1886, and large draught horses were in special demand. The shipments were 46,155. *Horses.*

The receipts of sheep show an increase of 35 per cent. over those of 1886, and amounted to 1,360,862, and the shipments to 445,094. They arrived chiefly from the north-west and Texas, but the latter were mostly of an inferior quality. *Sheep.*

The receipts of hogs amounted to 5,470,850, or 1,250,000 less than in the preceding year, and competition for the short supply caused a rise of nearly 20 per cent. in price. The shipments were 1,812,000. *Hogs.*

The Provision Trade.

The business of hog packing shows a further decline in volume of product, owing to a diminished supply of hogs, and there are now only 13 houses in operation against 18 in 1886. The labour troubles of the preceding year have been the main cause of decadence, and there seems no sign of the industry resuming its former proportions, in view of the extension given to trading houses in the west, many of which are branches of Chicago houses. These new centres of the trade, Kansas City, Omaha, and other cities, are more nearly situated for the supplies from Iowa and Missouri, the two great swine-producing States, and from the west, and the transport cost of product is far less than that of the live animal. The terminal charges at the stockyards here are heavy, as well as the railway freight for animals, and a very slight difference in the cost of conducting a business is of great importance where the profit per head is small. *Hog packing.*

The manufacture of butterine decreased nearly 50 per cent in value, and there were fewer licenses taken out than during the period for which the Oleomargarine Bill was in operation in 1886. The production of lard was extremely large, and there is no Act affecting its adulteration. All prime steam lard is regularly inspected by an inspector appointed by the Board of Trade in accordance with a regulation which came into force last year, and requires that " standard prime steam lard shall be solely the product of the trimmings and other fat parts of hogs, rendered in tanks by the direct application of steam, and without subsequent change in grain or character by the use of agitators or other machinery, except as such change may unavoidably *Butterine and lard.*

(419)

come from transportation. It shall have proper colour, flavour, and soundness for keeping, and no material which has been salted shall be included. The name and location of the renderer and the grade of the lard shall be plainly branded on each package at the time of the packing." A very large quantity of lard, however, is manufactured and sold as "refined steam lard," or under other denominations, which carries no certificate of inspection, and is partly composed of other materials than those required by the above regulation.

Beef canning. The beef canning and packing trade is a growing industry, and would appear to be fast taking the place of shipments on the hoof. The value of product last year was equal to two-thirds of that of the hog-packing trade. The three leading establishments are said to have slaughtered 1,026,147 head against 844,517 in 1886, and the total product is valued at nearly 6,000,000*l*. sterling.

Iron and other Manufactures.

Iron and steel. The great development of the railway system in the west caused an immense increase in the manufacture of steel rails, boilers, engines, and other machinery, and gave an impetus to all iron industries. Many of the foundries and factories were enlarged and new premises erected, and a new mill was established at Springfield. The total output of the iron manufactories of Chicago and its vicinity in 1887 is valued at 12,615,877*l*., against 9,647,433*l*. in 1886. The five works of the North Chicago Rolling Mill Company, the Union Steel Company, and the Joliet Steel Company produced 695,000 net tons of pig-iron, 710,000 tons of steel rails, and 823,000 tons of steel ingots, besides angle-bars, iron and steel bars, and nails. The Joliet Company's product shows an increase of 23 per cent., and 200,000 tons of steel rails were turned out. Steel rails varied in price from 8*l*. 17*s*. 4*d*. in June to 7*l*. 8*s*. 5*d*. per ton in December; at present there is a lack of fresh orders, and there has been a gradual closing from that cause, or for the purpose of repairs. The output of the 40 foundries is estimated at about 2,000,000*l*. sterling, and that of the 60 machinery establishments at 1,650,000*l*. The five car-wheel works turned out to the value of about 870,000*l*., and a new mill has been erected lately for the manufacture of a car-wheel rolled entirely out of a solid steel bloom, which is said to be 30 per cent. lighter and much stronger than the composite wheel now in use. There are 20 boiler shops, many galvanised iron and wire works, and numerous manufactories of stoves, iron safes, tools, nails, and every variety of iron and steel, all of which have been in full operation and kept hard at work to meet increased demand. Steel is fast taking the place of iron in almost every branch, and steel nails are superseding iron nails at a very small increase of cost. Prices of manufactured iron in many of the leading goods have advanced, in some instances being regulated by combinations of manufacturers, and wages of skilled labour have made an appreciable advance. As duty is paid at the sea-board ports, there is no possibility of ascertaining the quantity of steel rails or iron goods imported into this district, but some companies are believed to have made large purchases.

Brass, copper, &c. The four smelting and refining works, as well as the various manufactories of brass, copper, and tin, have largely increased their output, the latter wares having greatly increased in price. The total value of product under this head increased from 3,341,237*l*. in 1886 to 4,822,680*l*. in 1887.

Iron and wood. The value of agricultural implements manufactured is estimated at 2,300,000*l*.; and the total product of the 80 industries of iron and wood, including wagons, carriages, cars, bridges, elevators, and sewing machines at nearly 6,500,000*l.* sterling, or an advance of 10 per cent.

Business has largely increased at the planing-mills, sash, door, and other manufactories of wood. There are 390 establishments, of which 200 are furniture manufactories, employing 10,200 workmen, and 53 picture-frame and looking-glass establishments. The only business showing a decrease is that of billiard-tables, which depreciated 20 per cent., owing to diminution in the number of saloons relative to population on account of the prohibition and high license laws. *Wood.*

The manufactures of textile fabrics and clothing, the boot trade, the tanneries, chemical works, and the stone and marble works show a general advance in business, as well as the miscellaneous manufactures of toys, glass, sails, and other articles. The 258 printing and book-binding firms have increased their volume of trade to nearly 3,500,000*l.* sterling, or an advance of nearly 1,000,000*l.* *Other manufactures.*

The total number of manufacturing firms at Chicago is now stated to be 2,396, with a capital of about 23,500,000*l.* sterling, and employing 134,600 workers. The value of product is estimated at 83,000,000*l.*, or a gain of 15½ per cent. on that of the preceding year. They have all been actively employed, and the heavy duties and cost of transport protect them from much foreign competition, and enable them to make large profits, except as regards the finer cutlery, woollen and dress fabrics, and dry goods, which are largely imported, and which local manufacture is unable to equal.

Wholesale Trade.

The amount of business done in the wholesale trade last year is estimated at 92,500,000*l.* sterling. The volume was larger, while values increased in most lines of business, and there was fair profit, notwithstanding the tightness in money. The method adopted by so many houses of supplying to their customers a great variety of goods has become so prevalent that it is in some cases difficult to define their special line of business. There are many houses where almost every description of goods can be purchased, and the tendency of the system is to throw more business into the hands of the larger firms, and to restrict that of the smaller houses with some special trade, which may not have the capital to compete with their more powerful neighbours. The dry goods business increased about 15 per cent., and amounted to about 15,000,000*l.* sterling, while the clothing, millinery, and similar trades did an immense business. Wholesale groceries are estimated to have done business to the value of nearly 13,000,000*l.*; sugar, out of which little profit was formerly made, was forced up in price by the formation of a trust late in the autumn. The lumber trade is represented by 225 firms, with a capital of 4,000,000*l.*, and the product in 1887 is valued at 8,000,000*l.* sterling. The sales of jewellery, books, stationery, musical instruments, and almost every description of goods are constantly increasing. Chicago is now the second city in the States as a publishing centre.

Shipping.

The shipping at the port of Chicago is given in Annex A. *Shipping.*

Imports and Exports.

Annex B. shows the principal articles of import and export entered at the Customs of Chicago, and Annex C. gives the value of all articles *Imports and exports.*

exported to and imported from foreign countries during the years 1886-7.

These returns, however, afford a very imperfect idea of the quantity of goods imported and exported; the greater part of the exports are either shipped direct viâ Huron and Detroit to the seaboard, or sent direct by rail, and enter into the Customs returns of seaboard ports, only such exports being represented as are shipped direct to Canada. In the same manner the imports represent only such goods as pay duty at Chicago having been forwarded on in bond, and the majority of goods pay duty at New York or other Atlantic ports, from whence they are forwarded into the interior. There are therefore no means of forming a definite idea of the aggregate imports of foreign merchandise, or the amount of each separate article imported; and the demand for any special British or other goods cannot be adequately judged from the Customs returns here, where the country from which each separate article is imported is not recorded. A comparison between the relative imports from different countries in one year with another is also in a measure imperfect, as much depends on any preference which may be given to direct shipments.

Freights. Lake freights, though subject to considerable fluctuations, ruled materially higher last season than during the previous year, partly on account of the operations of the Interstate Commerce Act. The highest point reached was in June, when freights to Buffalo were $2\frac{1}{2}d.$ for corn and $3d.$ for wheat, but the general rate was $2d.$ and $2\frac{1}{4}d.$ Rates to Georgian ports were about $1\frac{1}{2}d.$ below the above rates, and to ports on Lake Ontario about $1d.$ higher. Railway freights were not subject to much fluctuation after the Interstate Law took effect, and rates were generally $1s. \frac{1}{2}d.$ per 100 lbs. to New York on grain and flour, and about $1s. 3d.$ on provisions.

Trusts, Labour, and Strikes.

Trusts. One of the most striking incidents in the past year has been the widespread development of monopolies and trusts, and the consequent check to competition. Pooling on the part of railroad companies has been checked by the Interstate Commerce Act, but the market price of many commodities is now regulated by these combinations, and in some instances the volume of production restricted. The system has extended to some of the necessaries of life, and has a direct influence on the cost of coal, gas, coffee, sugar, and other articles. Some of the large manufacturing interests are in the hands of trust associations, and the value of iron, steel, oil, castor-oil, as well as the production of some of the mineral ores greatly depends on a few large capitalists, who can monopolise the trade by means of the great power that combination gives them, and can fix the price that shall be paid within that point where foreign competition would step in and the high tariff duty allow of importation. These trusts, not only local but those originated by capitalists elsewhere, have increased their power over a wide area during the year.

Labour. The wages of the workman or the hired labourer are undoubtedly high compared with those in Great Britain, though in so large a district and with such a variety of trades and occupations it would be difficult to fix a definite scale. Yet it may be doubted if they go farther than they do at home, or that the workman is better off than where the purchasing power of money is greater. Rent, clothing, firing, and many of the necessaries of life are far higher. It is not so much the original cost of the article or its production which makes living expensive, but rather the large profit on capital and the high charges made in the various channels of distribution: many articles are directly or indirectly enhanced in value by trusts, or their cost affected by speculation or commission before they reach the consumer. On account too of the severity of the winter labour is not constant in every trade all the year round: building ceases during that season, and in farms many labourers are thrown out of work. Co-operation and profit-sharing have taken little hold in this district. Wages are higher, and there is therefore less object in small savings, and the working population are in general not so stationary in one place as in those countries where the systems are more developed.

Business was not generally so interrupted by strikes as in 1886, Strikes. with the exception of the building trade. Masons and bricklayers struck for an advance of wages at the very commencement of the season, and operations were impeded during the greater part of the summer. Hod carriers refused to work unless their pay was increased from 10$d.$ and 11$d.$ to 1$s.$ $\frac{1}{2}d.$ and 1$s.$ 3$d.$ an hour, and carpenters struck for 1$s.$ 5$d.$ an hour and eight hours a day, with extra pay for night or Sunday work, and nearly 30,000 hands were idle for months till an arrangement was eventually come to. While this report is in course of being framed a serious strike occurred among the engineers and firemen of the Chicago, Burlington, and Quincy Railway, and the whole of that system extending with many branches to Denver and Kansas city was temporarily paralysed and traffic suspended. The members of the brotherhood on strike were gradually replaced by new hands, and the attempt to boycott the line and prevent other railways from handling its freight has been ruled as contrary to the provisions of the Interstate Commerce Act, but at the moment when the line was again open for traffic the switchmen struck in a body, and traffic is again impeded.

Railroad Building.

Extension of the railway system in the west progresses with great rapidity, the mileage built in 1887 having exceeded that of any previous period. The greatest increase has been in Kansas and Nebraska, where 2,070 and 1,101 miles of new line are respectively reported. Next follow Dakota with 717 and Montana with 626 miles, exclusive of those which have been partially graded. In all other States and Territories of this district there has been some increase either by extending the existing system or building fresh branches.

The St. Paul, Minneapolis, and Manitoba Railway has extended a new track from Devil's Lake through North Dakota and Montana to Helena, running about midway between the Canadian Pacific and the Northern Pacific. This line cuts through a rich country, past Minot, till it joins the Upper Missouri, follows that valley to the point where the Milk River flows in, and then proceeds up the latter river to Assiniboine: it then turns south-west till it again joins the Missouri at Fort Benton, and, passing Great Falls, pursues its course to Helena under the name of the Montana Central. The whole distance from Grand Forks, on the direct line from St. Paul to Winnipeg, is 850 miles, and a great part of the line was completed at the rate of five to 10 miles a day. It runs through well-watered plains in a rich grazing and farming country, hitherto unoccupied from want of communication, with vast coalfields at no great distance, the extent of which is as yet unknown. The continuation of the Montana Central to Butte City, the centre of the mining industry of the Territory, is in course of completion. The

Fremont, Elkhorn, and Missouri line, known also as the Chicago and North-western, has been extended through the whole length of Nebraska into the centre of Wyoming, and settlements and towns are springing up in this hitherto unknown district; it passes through rich valleys and lately discovered coalfields, and will soon reach the oil region. The Cheyenne and Northern is now in operation for 90 miles north of Cheyenne, and other lines and extensions are projected or already pushing their way into Wyoming. A branch line is now opened to the Black Hills in Dakota, and the Chicago and North-western and the Chicago, Milwaukee, and St. Paul lines are cutting through the Sioux reservations.

The Union Pacific, Missouri Pacific, and the Atcheson, Topeka, and Santa Fé railroads have opened out a large extent of fresh country, while the Kansas City, Memphis and Birmingham, and other lines have lately developed trade with Texas and the South.

Progress in the West.

Whenever the steel rail is laid the tide of immigration continues to flow, communities are formed, and cities and towns grow and thrive at a marvellous rate. Land which but a few years ago had but a nominal value suddenly rises to a high price, and building lots soon become extremely valuable property. Wealth is thus constantly on the increase, and is greatly self-created, while capital is for ever flowing in from the east. A large area of fresh land has been entered on during the year in the Territories of Dakota, Wyoming, and Montana. In Dakota alone there were 13,855 new filings under the general land laws, comprising 2,067,281 acres and 10,750 final proofs, covering an area of 1,586,672 acres. The population of the Territory is now about 600,000. In Wyoming, from the 1st September, 1886, to the 30th June, 1887, there were 303,185 acres filed on under the various headings, and the population is estimated at 90,000: in this Territory a "Mammoth Canal" is to be at once constructed, which will give irrigation to 270,000 acres of rich land in the Green River basin. There are still many millions acres of Government land unoccupied in these Territories. No doubt a good deal of land taken up and many farms in this district are mortgaged. According to an estimate made after thorough investigation by one of the leading banks of this city, the amount of farm mortgages varies in the different States from a half to a quarter of the total assessed value of real estate according to the census of 1880, which is about one-third of the real value. The loans, from 5s. to 30s. per acre, are chiefly made by insurance corporations, and are considered safe investments; the money is borrowed to enable the parties to complete their purchases or to pay off a previous mortgage, and the rate of interest varies from 6 to 8 per cent.

Kansas city. Among the cities which have taken the most rapid stride, and become prominent centres of trade and distribution, may be mentioned Kansas city, which is peculiarly favoured by its situation, both as to the agriculture and commerce of the country. It is surrounded by about 300 miles of some of the richest agricultural land in the world, and its concentration of railway system makes it a central trading point between the south and north-west. The estimated population is now 200,000, including the 40,000 residents of Kansas city, in the State of Kansas, which adjoins and practically forms part of the same city. Enormous sums of money have been profitably invested by eastern capitalists, and building lots fetch a large price; in one instance, in a central situation, as high as 15l. per square foot has been paid.

CHICAGO.

Many fine structures have been erected during the last year, amongst them the New York Life Insurance building and the Midland Hotel, each costing 200,000*l*. Sales of real estate during nine months in the year amounted to about 17,000,000*l*. sterling, and the bank clearings during the same period to 60,000,000*l*., or an increase of 48 per cent. over the preceding year. The packing-houses are now calculated to turn out a product of about 10,000,000*l*. sterling in value.

Omaha is also becoming a great centre of trade and manufacture. The population is reckoned at 112,000. and the buildings erected during the year at a value of 2,000,000*l*. sterling. The packing business has largely increased, and the smelting and refining works last year turned out a value of nearly 500,000*l*. sterling. Omaha.

The port of Duluth, the most westerly point of the great lake system, is rapidly rising in importance. In 1887, 974 vessels, with an aggregate tonnage of 888,475 tons, entered in the coasting trade, and 263 vessels, of an aggregate tonnage of 122,419 tons, in the foreign trade. The total lake grain shipments amounted to more than 20,000,000 bushels, about 2,000,000 more than in 1886, and the value, at 3*s*. 2*d*. per bushel, to about 3,500,000*l*. sterling, more than three-fifths being wheat. The great development of Dakota and North-western Minnesota in wheat growing, and the extended operations at the iron and other mines north of Duluth, in conjunction with the large increase in railway communication, point to a yearly increase of shipping at this port. The port of Ashland, in Wisconsin, is also rapidly growing from the opening out of the Gogsbic and other mines, and iron works have been erected. Duluth.

MINES AND THEIR PRODUCT.

The vast mineral resources of the west, the full extent of which is even yet imperfectly known, constitute an ever-increasing source of industry and production: each year fresh mineral-bearing land is discovered, and there appears to be an inexhaustible supply of all those metals which so largely contribute to the wealth and industry of a country.

The chief iron mines worked are those in the Lake Superior region and in Missouri, but good ores are found in great abundance in many other parts, and are known to exist in districts as yet unexplored. The so-called Lake Superior region comprehends the Marquette region in Michigan, the Menominee range, partly in Michigan and partly in Wisconsin, the Gogsbic range, chiefly in Wisconsin, and the Vermillion district in Minnesota. The two former turned out respectively 1,621,887 tons and 880,000 tons in 1886. The progress of the latter two districts has been marvellous, considering that four years ago they were wholly unbroken wildernesses. The Gogsbic range was discovered in 1885, and in the last two years 53 mining companies were incorporated, with a nominal capital of nearly 12,000,000*l*. sterling. Some of these speculative operations have already failed, having been started without capital or on loans, and the stock of others has depreciated to a quarter of its par value; but as regards the richness of the range there is no question. The ore is a high grade of red hematite, mostly of the best Bessemer class, and all low in phosphorus, the shipments being confined to those which have ·06 phosphorus in an ore containing 60 per cent. of iron. The range has been practically explored for 30 miles, but properties held as iron lands extend both east and west beyond that limit along the ridge. The production in 1886 was 756,281 tons, the leading mines, the "Colby" and the Iron mines.

"Norris," turning out respectively 257,432 tons and 124,844 tons, and the output of 1887 is said to have been considerably larger. Another range parallel to the Gogsbic, 12 miles south, is now being explored for magnetic iron ores. The Vermillion range lies 80 miles north of Duluth; the ore is a hard specular of unusual richness. An analysis of a number of specimens gives 68 per cent. of iron, ·05 of phosphorus, and 1·25 of silica. The output in 1886 was 304,396 tons, which quantity will soon be largely exceeded. Other ridges, notably the Messaba range in the neighbourhood, are commencing active operations, and it seems that Minnesota will vie with Wisconsin and Michigan in production.

In Missouri iron occurs over nearly the whole of the south and centre of the State, and extremely valuable deposits of limonite and specular ores abound between the Mississippi and Upper Osage rivers, and in the centre of the State, forming one great iron belt. The output of the Iron Mountain and neighbouring mines in 1886 was 379,776 tons. The central district sustains a number of blast furnaces, and has extensive mines, the percentage of ore ranging between 44 and 67, and of phosphorus from ·13 to ·025. In the State of Iowa there are some valuable mines, and in Colorado, Montana, and parts of Dakota ore is found in great abundance, though as yet the mines are but little developed.

Pig and rolled iron are manufactured in all the States, chiefly in Illinois, though considerable quantities are turned out in Missouri and Wisconsin. Steel rails are produced largely in Illinois, with smaller quantities in Missouri and Colorado. Illinois is a great manufacturing State for other products of iron, but the various industries are fast increasing in other parts of this district.

Coal. The approximate area of the five States of Illinois, Missouri, Iowa, Nebraska, and Kansas is estimated at 110,887 square miles. No precise information is available regarding the vast coal basins of Colorado, Montana, Wyoming, and Dakota, but they are surmised to comprehend even a larger area. The coalfields of Illinois extend over 36,000 square miles, and a low estimate places the amount of commercial coal in the State at 30,000 million tons, which supply, at the present rate of production, would last for 3,000 years, but the amount has been estimated at a much higher figure. In 1887 there were 801 mines of all kinds operated, the greater number being small openings, and the output was 10,278,890 tons, or nearly 400,000 tons in excess of the average of the last five years. The average value at the mines was 4s. 5d. per ton, and the average price paid for mining was 3s. per ton. In Missouri the coal basin is estimated to extend over 26,887 square miles, and the annual production is about 1,750,000 tons. In Iowa the annual production is about 4,000,000 tons, from a coalfield extending over 18,000 square miles. In Kansas the area of the coal basin is reckoned at 17,000 square miles, now annually producing about 1,500,000 tons, and in Nebraska the area is estimated at 3,000 square miles. About 1,000,000 tons are annually mined from the coalfields of Wyoming, 50,000 tons in Montana, 30,000 in Dakota, and 1,250,000 in Colorado. The area of these coalfields is little known, but they are supposed to be of enormous extent and value, and in Montana it is said there are workable beds of good bituminous and lignite coal, underlying large areas, in nearly every county. As yet no anthracite has been found in this district, except in Colorado and Nebraska, where a small quantity is worked. Coke is made only to a small extent, but good coking coal has lately been discovered in parts of Colorado. A patent has lately been taken out by two Wisconsin farmers, named Raymond, for a machine called the "Cyclone pulveriser," which it is stated can reduce almost anything to the finest powder, and is to be used in Mr. McCauley's process of spraying pulverised coal with a combustion chamber attached to a furnace, whereby it is computed 50 per cent. of the coal now consumed in furnaces and rolling mills will be saved. The carrying out of Mr. McCauley's invention had hitherto been delayed from want of means to pulverise coal sufficiently fine. More capital has been invested and more mines developed last year in Montana than in any year in the history of the Territory, notwithstanding the depreciation in the value of silver, which is by far the most important and valuable portion of the mines. No separate statement of the yield of 1887 is at hand, but an official statement places the value of gold, silver, copper, and lead produced at not less than 5,100,000*l.* The product of gold in 1886 was 912,370*l.*, and of silver 2,536,082*l.*, and is now nearly equal to that of Colorado. The Territory of Dakota produced gold to the value of 536,000*l.* in 1886, and silver to that of 87,833*l.*, while a small quantity came from Wyoming, where mines are being opened and smelters erected. *Gold and silver.*

After a long period of depression, during which production was greater than demand, the price of copper took a sudden rise, greatly owing to the operations of the Paris syndicate. The chief deposits are in Minnesota and Montana. The Hecla and Calumet mines in the Lake Superior district of the former State produced, in 1886, half the 70,000 tons, the total product of the country, and they are largely adding to their capacity; the cost of production has decreased 10 per cent. in the last 10 years. In Montana great improvements have been made in the works, and the tendency is to refine at home. The Anaconda mine was working, in 1887, with 22 furnaces, at the rate of 1,500 tons of ore a day, and the product is stated to have been 79,000 tons, or double the product of the year before. *Copper.*

The supply of zinc ore comes from South-west Missouri and Kansas, these States supplying respectively about 60,000 and 30,000 a year, and a small quantity from Wisconsin. The price of ore has advanced to about 3*l.* or 3*l.* 5*s.* per ton, and 5*l.* for superior quality. The production of spelter in the United States is almost wholly confined to the States of Illinois, Missouri, and Kansas, which turned out, in 1886, respectively 21,077 tons, 8,932 tons, and 5,870 tons. There are altogether 12 institutions, but the only two manufactories of sheet zinc are at La Salle, in Illinois. Production yearly increases, and many of the companies, notably the Collinsville Zinc Works, have largely increased their number of retorts. Messrs. Matthiessen's and Hegeler's works at La Salle cover 50 acres, and constantly employ 800 men, the daily produce being 20 tons of sulphuric acid, and from 35 tons to 40 tons of spelter, which is chiefly rolled into sheet zinc. The Illinois Zinc Company employs about 500 men, and produced 8,000 tons of spelter in 1886, mostly transformed into sheet zinc, and valued at 200,000*l.* The present price of spelter is 19*s.* 9½*d* an oz., and sheet zinc 1*l.* 2*s.* 3*d.* an oz., fractionally less than foreign production could be sold at after paying the heavy duty, and a large profit is made. *Zinc.*

Almost all the non-argentiferous lead is produced in Illinois, Missouri, Kansas, and Wisconsin, the output being about 21,000 tons. The seat of the desilverised lead industry is in the Rocky Mountains; Colorado produces about 60,000 short tons. In Montana the principal works have been enlarged, and a small quantity of smelting is done in Dakota. *Lead.*

The discovery of tin in the Black Hills must be regarded as of the highest importance, and there is now little doubt that the mines are of *Tin.*

enormous extent and value. The district known as the Black Hills is an isolated group of mountains lying principally in Dakota and partly in Wyoming, between the two main forks of the Cheyenne River. The group is of nearly an oval form, about 90 by 60 miles, rising from an arid plain; it is thickly wooded and covered with verdure, and has rich, deep soil in the well-watered valleys. Geologically it consists of a central nucleus or mass of granite, successively surrounded by the up-turned edges of singularly regular though eccentric bands of Archæan schists and slates, Cambrian (Potsdam), carboniferous, red beds, jura, cretaceous, and tertiary. Almost every mineral is found in these formations. The Potsdam is rich in deposits of gold, silver, and copper, the base of the rocks being everywhere auriferous. The same metals appear in veins in the Archæan, and it is here that the rich veins of tin have been discovered. Of the two known tin districts the southern section, four miles wide, lies round the north and west sides of, and probably runs all round, the central mass of granite called "Harney's Peak;" and the other, or northern section, is about 20 miles west of Deadwood. Professor Carpenter, Dean of the Dakota School of Mines, states in his recent report as follows:—"The tin-stone is found in granitic veins or dykes in the earlier or schistose Archæan, which vary in width from a few inches to hundreds of feet. In some sections the veins consist of an albitic greisen, that is, a rock composed of albitic feldspar and mica, through which are disseminated crystals of cassiterite. In other sections, as upon the west side of Harney's Peak, the veins are composed of typical greisen, that is, quartz and mica. The crystals of cassiterite vary much in size, some having been found of several pounds weight; but generally they seem to partake of the nature of the greisen, that is, if the individual crystals of feldspar or quartz and mica are large, the accompanying crystals of cassiterite are large and *vice versâ*. That through which the tin is finely disseminated is usually richer than the coarsely-crystallised rocks. The percentage of tin-stone in the greisen varies, but there are many veins carrying rock yielding from 2 to 4 per cent." Later on Professor Carpenter states that he last year personally examined all the districts, making numerous assays of the ore, and that "when sampled in quite large quantities it seldom runs below 2 per cent., and often yields 4, 6, 8, and even 12 per cent. These assays refer to averages taken across veins, dumps, sample lots, &c., for, of course, picked specimens can be easily had which are nearly pure cassiterite."

Tin was first discovered here in 1883, but the miners were only in search of the precious metals, and little attention was at first paid to it. Some of the mines are now commencing regular operations, sinking shafts and erecting machinery, and before long there will probably be a regular supply of metal. The quantity of ore appears to be unlimited, and as it lies near and crops out from the surface, and on lofty, wooded hills, the cost of working and transport will not be great. Little has, however, yet been done, except the production of specimen bars, and the examination of localities which appear to be most likely to yield paying quantities of ore, though there are considerable quantities extracted ready for concentration. The first company to operate was the Etta Mine in the Southern Hills, which produced seven tons of tin from 400 tons of ore in 1886, but through imperfect machinery and management, and the mine not being sufficiently opened, the works were closed. Other claims have since been purchased, and a plan for further operations has been adopted by this company, and other companies are preparing to work. In the northern, or Nigger Hill district, the Cleveland Company have sunk a shaft to the depth of 100 feet, and here, where a cross cut has been driven, the vein is found to be 200 feet wide, and to carry tin throughout; they expect shortly to operate on a large scale. Chicago as well as other cities west are large consumers of tin, which has hitherto been wholly imported, and great interest is taken in the development of the discovery of this metal.

Recent Legislation.*

Aliens.

The rights of aliens with regard to holding or acquiring land or real estate have been abolished or restricted in the greater part of this district by Acts passed during the past year. In the Territories, by Act of Congress, the ownership of real estate is restricted to United States citizens. In the States of Illinois, Minnesota, Wisconsin, Nebraska, and Colorado, Acts were passed by the different legislative assemblies in 1887 either entirely or in various degrees depriving aliens, unless they naturalise, of the right to acquire, or hold, or inherit land or real estate, subject to existing treaties, the general effect being to wholly prohibit non-resident aliens from holding the property referred to, as well as alien corporations, and any corporation more than 20 per cent. of the stock of which is held by aliens.

Annex A.—RETURN of all Shipping at the Port of Chicago in the Year 1887.

ENTERED.

Nationality.	Sailing.		Steam.		Total.	
	Number of Vessels.	Tons.	Number of Vessels.	Tons.	Number of Vessels.	Tons.
British	95	30,295	66	27,155	161	57,450
American	6,153	1,491,488	4,514	2,319,527	10,667	3,811,015
Total	6,248	1,521,783	4,580	2,346,682	10,826	3,868,465
,, for the preceding year	6,615	1,656,331	4,542	2,269,987	11,157	3,926,318

CLEARED.

Nationality.	Sailing.		Steam.		Total.	
	Number of Vessels.	Tons.	Number of Vessels.	Tons.	Number of Vessels.	Tons.
British	95	30,536	68	27,935	163	58,471
American	6,187	1,590,488	4,570	2,340,656	10,757	3,931,144
Total	6,282	1,621,024	4,638	2,368,591	10,920	3,989,615
,, for the preceding year	6,635	1,664,234	4,580	2,286,528	11,215	3,950,762

* For further information on this subject, *vide* Parliamentary Papers, Commercial Nos. 4 and 6 of 1888, and Commercial No. 18 of 1887.—ED.

14 — UNITED STATES.

Annex B.—RETURN of Principal Articles of Export by Lake from Chicago during the Years 1887 and 1886.

Articles.		1887. Quantity.	1887. Value in Sterling.	1886. Quantity.	1886. Value in Sterling.
			£		£
Wheat	Bushels	1,166,526	174,497	1,092,909	177,310
Corn	,,	1,529,512	134,389	2,396,221	193,889
Oats	,,	25,895	1,319	2,016	127
Flour	Barrels	1,014	736	1,170	776
Cornmeal	,,	625	460	1,000	523
Pork	,,	4,979	13,838	12,127	25,555
Lard	Lbs.	40,788	548	59,370	875
Cured meats	,,	7,530	163	62,534	984
Timothy seed	,,	18,634	206	...	...
Other articles	...	34,329	1,599	...	1,648
Total		...	327,755	...	401,687

RETURN of Principal Articles of Import to Chicago during the Years 1887 and 1886.

Articles.		1887. Quantity.	1887. Value in Sterling.	1886. Quantity.	1886. Value in Sterling.
			£		£
Free goods	...	...	636,604	...	527,979
China and glassware	...	...	82,166	...	71,162
Caustic soda	...	...	49,430	10,782,486	46,003
Cigars and tobacco, and manufacture of	...	...	125,546	...	69,677
Dry goods	...	...	959,724	...	946,143
Iron, pig; manufacture of, and wire, &c.	...	...	37,564	...	...
Leather manufactures	...	...	46,531	...	44,896
Metal manufactures	...	...	27,470	...	...
Musical instruments	...	...	46,798	...	40,804
Steel bars, bloom, and needles	...	...	13,870	...	...
Tin plate	...	...	289,656	32,290,414	211,429
Wines and liquors	...	...	69,423	...	41,961
Other articles	...	...	325,643	...	302,848
Total		...	2,710,425	...	2,302,902

Annex C.—TABLE showing the total value of all Articles exported from Chicago and imported to Chicago from and to Foreign Countries during the Years 1886 and 1887.

Country.	Exports. 1887.	Exports. 1886.	Imports. 1887.	Imports. 1886.
	£	£	£	£
Great Britain	..	..	1,102,502	947,196
British Colonies and Possessions	327,255	401,687	101,653	71,037
Germany	..	..	334,633	304,667
France	..	..	297,817	315,105
Austria	..	..	21,180	23,189
Sweden	..	..	24,332	23,675
Switzerland	..	..	94,338	88,914
Japan	..	..	233,829	337,528
China	..	..	60,344	54,963
Cuba	..	..	96,987	90,758
Other countries	..	..	57,315	45,870
Total	327,255	401,687	2,427,930	2,302,902

NOTE. – Values converted at the rate of 4 dol. 85 c. per £ sterling.

ST. LOUIS.

Mr. Vice-Consul Bascome reports as follows:—

The Commerce of St. Louis has been very considerably increased during the year 1887, and the present condition of trade in all its branches is excellent, while the outlook for the future is encouraging.

St. Louis is making rapid progress not only as a commercial centre, but her manufactures are also increasing and reaching out to all portions of the United States, and some, particularly her beer and agricultural implements, are known and sought after in the foreign markets of the world.

Her jobbing trade has branched out until it covers, not only the territory which geographically belongs to her, but enters into competition in districts hitherto claimed by other trade centres.

The tonnage receipts by railways and river increased from 7,882,010 in 1886 to 9,272,717 tons in 1887, a gain of 17·65 per cent., while the shipments increased from 4,178,985 tons in 1886 to 5,086,342 tons in 1887, a gain of 21·71 per cent.; or, taking receipts and shipments together, 12,060,995 tons of freight were handled in and out during 1886, against 14,359,059 tons in 1887, a gain of 19½ per cent.

Progress has been made in internal improvements, evidenced by miles of reconstructed streets, and a number of magnificent public and commercial buildings on the principal thoroughfares.

New railroads are seeking entrance into the city, and existing roads are extending their lines into new territory.

The project for another bridge across the Mississippi River is being pushed forward, and terminal facilities have been secured for access thereto.

The river trade, although hampered during the past season by low water, is developing, and forms an important outlet to the sea, viâ New Orleans, for the foreign grain trade.

16   UNITED STATES.

In articles handled in the Exchanges the volume has been very marked. Flour, grain, cotton, lead, provisions, live stock, lumber, and tobacco, all show an increase, as will be shown by the following table:—

Articles handled in Exchanges.

Articles.		1886.	1887.
Flour, amount manufactured	Bbls.	1,807,956	1,985,717
,, ,, handled	,,	3,198,383	3,633,194
Wheat, total receipts	Bush.	12,309,364	14,510,313
Corn ,, ,,	,,	16,387,071	16,576,386
Oats ,, ,,	,,	7,426,915	9,765,545
Rye ,, ,,	,,	447,842	236,726
Barley ,, ,,	,,	2,529,731	2,932,192
All grain received (including flour reduced to wheat)	,,	42,918,799	48,748,562
Cotton, receipts	Bales	400,236	520,063
Hemp ,,	,,	645	448
Bagging, manufactured	Yards	16,000,000	15,000,000
Hay, receipts	Tons	85,975	85,394
Tobacco ,,	Hhds.	32,113	37,592
Lead, receipts in 80 lbs.	Pigs	1,138,854	1,432,054
Hog product, total shipment	Lbs.	174,907,899	220,613,987
Cattle, receipts	Head	377,550	464,828
Sheep ,,	,,	328,985	417,425
Hogs ,,	,,	1,264,471	1,052,240
Horses and mules, receipts	,,	42,032	57,048
Lumber and logs	Feet	557,196,554	675,144,047
Shingles	Pcs.	55,136,000	77,288,735
Lath	,,	37,254,600	43,334,705
Wool, total receipts	Lbs.	18,563,614	17,347,186
Hides ,, ,,	,,	19,978,698	26,175,972
Sugar, received	,,	115,806,240	105,670,926
Molasses, shipped	Galls.	1,301,100	1,952,265
Coffee, received	Bags	240,685	184,312
Rice, receipts	Pkgs.	72,079	79,604
Coal ,,	Bush.	61,258,525	66,524,925
Nails kegs	Kegs	908,817	706,472
Potatoes, receipts	Bush.	812,950	1,301,636
Salt ,,	Bbls.	400,358	394,676
,, ,,	Sacks	51,992	32,060
,, ,,	Bush. in bulk	247,160	320,490
Butter	Lbs.	8,605,230	9,234,043

Bank clearings.

The aggregate clearings of the St. Louis banks in 1887 was 178,905,546*l*., and in 1886, 162,159,012*l*., showing an increase of 10·3 per cent., or 16,746,534*l*.

Capital.

The banking capital of the city is 3,000,000*l*., and money has been loaned by the banks at 8 per cent. for a portion of the year when most needed to move the crops, but at other times as low as 6 per cent. per annum, and a large amount of city bonds were floated here at a rate of 3·65 per cent.

City bonded debt.

At the close of the fiscal year, April, 1887, the bonded debt was 4,421,000*l*., and showed a reduction of 167,500*l*. during the year The maturing bonds amounted to 867,800*l*. Of this amount 843,400*l*. were 6 per cents., 19,400*l*. 7 per cents., and 5,000*l*. 8 per cents.

To provide for those maturing, 600,000*l*. renewal bonds were placed at 3·65 per cent.

At the close of the fiscal year, April, 1888, the city's bonded debt will amount to about 4,366,000*l.*, and the interest on nearly 20 per cent. of it has been reduced from 6, 7, and 8 per cent. to 3·65 per cent.

It would be impracticable for me to attempt to report on the trade and commerce of this district, which comprises all the counties of the State of Missouri, except that of Jackson, in which the city of Kansas is situated, and I shall therefore content myself by chronicling the fact that the general business of the district has been prospering the past year.

District.

FOREIGN IMPORTS.

There was a slight increase in value of imports during 1887, which amounted to 712,348*l.*, against 663,037*l.* 8*s.* in 1886—increase 49,310*l.* 12*s.*, as will appear in the following table:—

Imports.

CONDENSED Report of Commodities Imported into St. Louis during 1886-1887, showing Foreign Values and Duties.

	1886.		1887.	
Articles.	Value.	Duties.	Value.	Duties.
	£ s. d.	£ s. d.	£ s. d.	£ s. d.
Ale and beer	1,981 8 0	540 16 0	1,639 8 0	449 10 9
Anvils	2,710 8 0	848 11 3	4,678 4 0	1,503 0 10
Barley	10,170 8 0	1,235 2 10	48,216 15 0	6,806 17 0
Chemicals	21,149 0 0	7,441 18 8	20,266 0 0	6,515 3 2
China and earthenware	26,309 8 0	14,474 18 0	28,989 8 0	16,215 18 2
Cutlery	17,997 4 0	8,707 17 10	18,919 0 0	9,062 16 0
Free goods	57,126 12 0	...	74,348 0 0	...
Glass and glass-ware	24,851 16 0	10,259 12 7	25,006 4 0	15,727 2 1
Guns and firearms	13,753 0 0	4,377 14 2	19,349 12 0	6,198 11 3
Hops	28,760 12 0	12,877 5 4	20,963 0 0	6,540 1 8
Manufactures of cotton	36,823 12 0	11,946 7 2	43,619 8 0	17,720 9 1
,, ,, iron and steel	110,982 0 0	39,820 18 4	198,526 0 0	76,885 17 1
,, ,, wool	33,033 0 0	22,400 2 11	37,743 16 0	25,593 10 2
Rice, granulated	6,449 12 0	1,289 18 5	19,389 16 0	3,877 19 2
Sugar	142,353 4 0	102,053 5 0	8,717 12 0	6,116 16 8
Tobacco, cigars and cigarettes	23,670 16 0	21,831 2 9	24,137 4 0	29,963 9 3
Wines and spirits	20,347 8 0	11,980 13 4	14,276 4 0	9,345 8 8
Liquors re-imported	...	...	16,396 0 0	14,595 3 10
Other articles	84,568 0 0	28,493 19 5	187,166 9 0	49,165 18 2
Totals	663,037 8 0	303,581 3 0	712,348 0 0	280,274 13 0

Articles, value and duties.

The duties on foreign imports received at the St. Louis Customhouse were 323,581*l.* 3*s.* in 1886, and 280,274*l.* 13*s.* in 1887, showing a falling-off in 1887 of 43,306*l.* 10*s.*

(419)

UNITED STATES.

Imports.

MERCHANDISE Imported into St. Louis through various Ports of Entry showing Foreign Values and Duties Collected.

Ports, value and duties.

Ports.	1886. Value.	1886. Duties.	1887. Value.	1887. Duties.
	£ s. d.	£ s. d.	£ s. d.	£ s. d.
Baltimore	29,142 8 0	6,164 10 7	21,975 16 0	8,564 11 9
Boston	3,445 4 0	764 10 5	3,182 12 0	724 3 2
Chicago	102 12 0	67 13 6	5,985 12 0	1,075 18 9
Detroit	2,226 4 0	168 12 7	2,928 0 0	523 19 2
Galveston	...	...	10,899 8 0	1,643 9 6
Newport News	...	...	30,181 16 0	5,104 4 6
New Orleans	228,592 12 0	105,221 7 5	141,938 0 0	34,624 12 9
New York	248,222 4 0	117,045 9 7	312,422 12 0	159,728 0 4
Philadelphia	101,259 0 0	53,761 10 0	106,112 8 0	51,967 4 9
Port Huron	30,042 0 0	12,761 3 8	45,883 16 0	7,184 2 6
Portland	19,304 8 0	7,576 0 8	30,691 4 0	9,128 8 9
San Francisco	700 16 0	50 4 7	146 16 0	5 15 1
Totals	663,037 8 0	303,581 3 0	712,348 0 0	280,274 13 0

FOREIGN TRADE.

Exports. Seaboard and jetty routes.

The foreign export trade showed a large increase over 1886, both by the Atlantic sea-board and by the jetty route, *viâ* New Orleans, the total amount exported being 453,964 tons, as against 263,205 tons in 1886. The export trade *viâ* the Mississippi river and the jetties in corn and wheat was very large during the first six months of the year, and would have continued so the entire season, had it not been for the low state of water in the river after July, due to the prolonged drought and failure of the Government to continue the work of improvement. Notwithstanding these drawbacks, the amount of corn and wheat exported amounts to 7,365,340 bushels of corn and 3,973,737 bushels of wheat.

The jetty route now stands only second to New York in exportation of corn, and fifth in exportation of wheat—the eastern cities and San Francisco leading in this cereal—corn.

Shipments on through bills of lading.

The foreign shipments from St. Louis on through bills *viâ* the Atlantic seaports were largely increased on the following articles:— Tobacco, 1,919 hogsheads; corn, 698,588 bushels; bacon, 10,199,548 lbs.; lard, 4,775,047 lbs.; wheat, 169,400 bushels; cotton, 19,578 bales; flour, 146,387 barrels; hides, 143,240 lbs.; tallow, 2,113,009 lbs.

Exports.

To Great Britain.

The shipments by this route to Great Britain were as follows. In 1887, cotton 136,380 bales, being an increase of 10,115 bales over the previous year; to Canada, 22,600 bales, being an increase of 8,671 bales; all other countries 7,065 bales.

Flour to Great Britain in 1887, 226,329 barrels, an increase of 118,354 barrels; to Canada, 65,225 barrels, an increase of 30,012 barrels; to other countries, 28,653 barrels; tobacco to Great Britain, 3,871 hhds., an increase of 1,961 hhds.; corn to England, 798,294 bushels, against 103,550 in 1886; meats to Great Britain, 13,290,000 lbs., against 3,146,872 in 1886; lard to Great Britain, 3,295,700 lbs., there being none exported by this route in 1886; tallow, 191,000 lbs., against 174,000 lbs. in 1886; and to all other places 2,834,600 lbs., against 738,000 lbs. in 1886.

CHICAGO.

The direct shipments of bulk grain to foreign countries in tons was:— Bulk grain.

	1887.	1886.	Increase.
	Tons.	Tons.	Tons.
By rail, eastward	128,522	30,853	97,669
„ river, viâ New Orleans	325,412	232,352	93,060
Total	453,934	263,205	190,729

The quantity of corn shipped abroad viâ New Orleans was as follows:—

	1886.	1887.	Increase or Decrease.
	Bushels.	Bushels.	Bushels.
To Great Britain	3,668,955	4,091,961	403.006
„ all other countries	4,466,988	3,109,270	−1,357,718
Total	8,135,943	7,201,231	− 934,712

To Great Britain.

The quantity of wheat shipped abroad viâ New Orleans was:—

	1886.	1887.	Increase.
	Bushels.	Bushels.	Bushels.
To Great Britain	474,909	1,962,817	1,487,908
„ all other countries	513,717	2,427,309	1,913,692
Total	988,626	4,390,126	3,401,600

The average rates of freight on bulk grain viâ New Orleans to Liverpool were in 1887 about 7½d. per bushel, and in 1886 about 8¼d., the rate viâ New York being 11¼d. in 1887 and 11d. in 1886.

Freight rates.

UNITED STATES Internal Revenue Taxes.

United States Internal Revenue taxes.

	1886.	1887.
	£ s. d.	£ s. d.
Lists (chiefly banks)	1,140 8 0	884 19 0
Spirits stamps	412,744 4 5	369,533 3 3
Tobacco „	496,840 17 8	644,554 16 0
Cigars „	26,151 16 4	24,089 15 9
Snuff „	717 19 3	755 10 6
Bee „	223,363 9 4	258,789 2 0
Special tax stamps	23,786 9 6	24,636 16 2
*Oleomargarine	..	8 8 9
Total	1,184,745 4 6	1,323,202 11 2

* There are no Oleomargarine manufactures in St. Louis; the tax was on illicit goods seized and released under compromise.

UNITED STATES.

Receipts of Post Office.

Post Office receipts.

	1886.	1887.
	£ s. d.	£ s. d.
Postage stamps, letters	124,136 0 0	133,084 0 0
,, ,, periodicals	10,009 7 2	11,277 18 5
,, ,, postage due	693 19 2	797 18 10
Envelopes	18,221 4 7	18,847 1 0
Special request envelopes	13,317 9 7	14,236 12 0
Waste paper	132 5 9	125 6 11
Box rent	409 8 9	442 15 4
Total	166,919 15 0	178,811 12 6
Increase in 1887	11,891 17 6	..

Mails Dispatched and Distributed. Class of Mail Matter.

Postal matter handled.

	1886.	1887.	Increase.
Letters originating at St Louis	468,732	544,643	75,910
Postal cards ,, ,,	43,531	45,313	1,782
Newspapers and periodicals, regular	5,005,111	5,594,166	589,055
,, transient, books, circulars	1,609,638	1,839,487	229,849
Merchandise originating in St. Louis	201,015	225,610	24,595
Total in pounds	7,328,028	8,249,219	921,191

Mail Matter received from Postal Routes and other Post Offices for Distribution and Dispatch.

	1886.	1887.	Increase.
Letters, postal cards, and circulars	59,796	46,881	12,915
Papers and merchandise	655,583	992,482	336,899
Total in pounds	702,464	1,052,278	349,814
Grand total in pounds	8,030,492	9,301,497	1,271,005

Fire Record.

Fire losses.

The fire losses in 1886 and 1887 were excessive compared with those of 1885, as will appear by the following table:—

Year.	Number of Fires.	Average Loss each Fire.	Amount of Losses.	Amount of Insurance.	Losses to Insurance Companies.	Per Cent. is to Insurance.
		£	£ s. d.	£ s. d.	£ s. d.	
1885	727	133	96,960 0 0	783,908 8 9	95,038 18 4	12·03
1886	827	484	360,449 14 3	858,835 0 0	265,036 13 3	30·86
1887	953	480	457,937 16 11	1,354,943 11 9	398,135 19 9	34·03

Population.

The population of St. Louis in the year 1799 was only 925. In 1880 the United States census reported it 350,522, and the estimated population in 1887 is 450,000.

CHICAGO.

The real and personal property assessed for taxation was in 1886 43,654,252*l.*, rate of taxation 2·55. Assessed value in 1887 was 43,428,464*l.*, and the rate of taxation 2·50 per cent. *Assessed value. Taxable property.*

The total cost of new buildings erected in 1887, as reported by the Commissioner of Public Buildings, was 1,032,583*l.*, which includes improvements to old buildings. *Buildings.*

The city has an area of 30,276·25 acres, equal to 61·37 square miles, with a river front of 19·15 miles. *Area.*

The public parks are eighteen in number, and contain 2,095 acres exclusive of the fair grounds, race-course, and zoological gardens of 143 acres. *Public parks.*

The streets were for many years prior to 1870 constructed of limestone macadam, which proved very unsatisfactory. Since that time the principal streets have been reconstructed with asphaltum, granite, and wood blocks, laid on a concrete base at the expense of abutting property. The re-construction to date is as follows:— *Streets.*

	Miles.	Cost.
		£
With granite blocks	38·25	594,475
„ wood	2·72	39,849
„ sheet asphaltum	3·86	52,316
Reconstruction to December 31, 1887	44·83	686,640

Re-construction.

Re-constructed during 1887—

	Miles.	Cost.
		£
With granite blocks	2·32	41,210
„ wood	0·37	6,182
Total	2·69	47,392

St. Louis is admirably located for drainage purposes, rising from the river in a succession of hills not so abrupt as to interfere with walking or driving, but sufficiently abrupt as to give excellent drainage through nearly 300 miles of sewers. *City drainage.*

The city consumes about 30,000,000 gallons of water daily, which is pumped from the Mississippi river into settling tanks, and from there into settling reservoirs. *Water supply.*

An improvement is now in progress, to cost 500,000*l.*, which is expected to materially improve the supply.

The climate is rather a trying one, being subject to extreme changes. For the year 1887—barometer, mean, 30·01; highest, 30·75, Feb. 4; lowest, 29·31, Jan. 13; absolute range, 1·44. *Climate. Meteorological.*

Temperature—mean, 57·5; normal, 55·3; highest, 100, July 17; lowest, 9·6 below zero, Jan. 3; absolute range, 109·6.

Total rainfall—35·30 inches; normal, 38·98 inches; greatest amount in any 24 hours fell on Nov. 26, 2·32 inches; mean humidity, 60·3 per cent.; average cloudiness, 43 per cent.; number of clear days, 149; fair, 133; cloudy, 83.

Street railways.
There are 154⅖ miles of street railways, of which seven miles are moved by cable, which have carried 52,054,242 passengers during the year.

Libraries.
There are ten or more libraries, three of which are deserving of mention: the Mercantile, ranking among the finest in the United States; the St. Louis Public School; and the Law Library.

Educational.
Some of the finest educational institutes in the United States are to be found in St. Louis: the Washington University, with its Polytechnic Department, Academy, and Training School; the St. Louis University; and the Academy of the Christian Brothers.

Public schools.
The Public School system is said to be perfect. Scholars enrolled number 49,885, with a daily average attendance of 40,388, an increase of 1,000 over the preceding year.

Hotels.
The city possesses a fine hotel system. Its large hotels, ten in number, with its smaller hostelries, bring the total capacity above 50,000 guests. During the fall of the year, when there are 100,000 visitors in the city at one time, no difficulty is found in accommodating them.

Newspapers.
There are four daily newspapers printed in the English language, and four in the German, the principal ones being the "Globe Democrat" (a Republican paper), and the "Republican" (a Democratic party paper), both English.

St. Paul, Minnesota.

Mr. Vice-Consul McNeale reports as follows:—

Wholesale trade and manufactures.
The commerce and manufactures of St. Paul during 1887 show a remarkable increase, compared with preceding year. The manufactures established during the year, and the increased output, is given elsewhere, and careful estimates and comparisons with the general trade of 1886 show that the increase in the value of the business of 1887 would amount to 54 per cent. in dry goods and groceries; 25 per cent. to 35 per cent. in leather and findings, and boots and shoes; and hardware shows an increase of about 40 per cent. In all other lines the increase would average 25 per cent. This rapid increase and development of trade is mainly the result of the building of several new lines of railroad in Minnesota, Dakota, and Montana, and consequent influx of population in these territories, of which St. Paul is the natural business centre and principal point of exchange.

The wholesale trade has been and is the principal feature of St. Paul's prosperity; the table, showing the comparative business of seven years, will give some idea of St. Paul as a wholesale centre. The St. Paul Jobbers' Union is an organisation of the leading wholesale firms of the city, the object of which is to unite the mercantile community for the purpose of advancing and increasing the trade and business of the city of St. Paul, and to support such means as may be deemed best to promote this end, and to use its influence, as a body, to protect their rights and influence as citizens and merchants.

The St. Paul Jobbers' Union has gained a power and influence which has increased the facilities of doing business, and marvellously increased the importance of St. Paul as a commercial and manufacturing centre.

In 1886 was formed the St. Paul and Minneapolis Freight Bureau, composed of the Transportation Committees of the St. Paul Jobbers' Union and the Jobbers' Association of Minneapolis. The Bureau employs a salaried Commissioner, to give his entire time and attention to the protection of the transportation interests of the two cities, and his work has been productive of great benefit to the merchants and the people of the North-west, and even greater benefits may be expected in the future.

St. Paul, as a distributing point, reaches far out for its supplies, bringing to this market the products of the countries of Europe upon one hand, and of Asia on the other. Fifty-five firms paid import duties to the St. Paul Custom-house in 1887, amounting to 875,027 dol. on goods valued at 1,154,713 dol. In addition to these figures, there was imported 166,819 dol. of free goods. St. Paul is a great central depôt for imported goods that come across the Atlantic and Pacific Oceans. Nearly the entire supply of China and Japan teas for the North-west are imported direct by the jobbers of St. Paul and Minneapolis.

The vast area supplied by the merchants of these two cities extends northwards into the British possessions, southwards into the States of Iowa and Nebraska, eastward into Wisconsin and Michigan, across the great territories of Dakota and Montana, and on the Pacific coast. New fields of trade are being continually opened up within this great area, as new railroads and settlements each year fill up this great fertile country. The travelling men of St. Paul are to be found in every part of this extensive field of trade, pushing to the frontiers with a persistency and energy which rapidly brings each new settlement and district into trade relations with this commercial centre. The productive resources of this great tributary are so numerous and varied that the prosperity of the jobbing and manufacturing trade has been uninterrupted by any serious drawbacks. A few of the many resources are: the agricultural products of varied farming; stock-raising upon the immense grazing fields in the West, where pasturage and water are insured for every month in the year; stock-raising by the farmers of the States and Territories; the great mining interests of the North and West, including gold, silver, copper, lead, and iron—all of which are as yet but in their infancy. The following table shows the amount of wholesale and manufacturing business done in St. Paul during the last seven years:—

	Wholesale.	Manufactures.
	Dollars.	Dollars.
1881	46,555,999	15,466,201
1882	66,628,494	22,390,589
1883	72,448,771	25,855,471
1884	74,829,700	26,662,000
1885	81,596,000	29,437,000
1886	84,138,000	31,043,000
1887	105,234,000*	38,803,650

* Estimated.

Custom-house Business.

	1881.	1882.	1883.	1884.	1885.	1886.	1887.
	Dollars.	Dollars.	Dollars.	Dollars.	Dollars.	Dollars.	Dollars.
Value of dutiable goods	62,783	115,851	144,822	128,097	186,574	313,495	1,154,718
Total duties collected	26,983	41,264	60,212	60,462	78,368	139,031	875,027
Value of free goods	...	...	...	...	...	...	166,819

Custom-house business.

Public Improvements in St. Paul in 1887.

Public improvements.

	Costing Dollars.
6 Miles of streets graded	999,000
11 „ „ paved	500,000
17 „ of sewers constructed	640,000
41 „ of side-walks, wood	64,000
8 „ „ „ stone and cement	20,000
Bridge work done	67,000
Total	2,290,000

Total miles of paved streets in St. Paul	22
„ „ graded streets in St. Paul	330
„ „ wooden side-walks in St. Paul	333
„ „ stone and cement side-walks in St. Paul	25
„ „ sewers in St. Paul	69

Population of St. Paul.

Population.

The books of the St. Paul Directory are for the fiscal year ending May 31, 1887. The number of names in the Directory is 62,231, indicating that, on the estimate of 2½ persons to the name, St. Paul then had a population of 155,577. The increase in names for 1887 over 1886 was 12,873. The publishers of the Directory are now at work upon the statistics for the fiscal year ending May 31, 1888, and they report that present indications warrant the belief that even the record of the last year will be beaten; it is safe, therefore, to estimate, at least upon the same proportion of increase, that St. Paul has added to its population (May 31, 1888) 187,759 inhabitants, using the multiple 2½ persons to each name.

The most notable feature in the rapid growth of St. Paul is the tremendous strides that it has taken during the last seven years. By the census of 1880 it had a population of 41,498, so that its population has quintupled within that brief period; but it has simply kept pace with the immense growth of the country tributary.

Within that period the Manitoba has covered the Red River Valley, and North-western Minnesota and Dakota, with its great network of railroad lines, the Northern Pacific has extended across the continent, and an energetic farming population has poured into the region which was opened to settlement. The same phenomenal development has followed the rapid extension of railroad lines all over Western and South-western Minnesota and Dakota, and the growth of St. Paul has simply responded to the demands of these vastly increased areas of production and population upon its trade.

More than 1,000,000 of people have been added to the territory tributary to St. Paul since the census of 1880, and its rapid rise has been simply coincident with the extraordinary growth of the Upper North-west during that period.

The following table gives the population of St. Paul from 1838 to May 31, 1888:—

Year	Population	Year	Population
1838	3	1873	27,023
1847	50	1875	33,178
1849	400	1880	41,498
1850	850	1881	50,900
1855	4,400	1882	75,835
1856	5,630	1883	88,878
1860	10,600	1884	99,322
1865	13,100	1885	111,397
1870	20,300	1886	123,395
1871	24,200	1887	155,577
1872	25,500	1888 (estimated)	187,759

Banks and Bankers.

St. Paul is the financial centre of the great North-west. The high-standing, sound, and conservative character of the banks of St. Paul has gained for them a prestige second to those of no other city in the United States. The bankers of St. Paul have reason to be proud of the rapid growth of their business, and the record they have made. It is this record that has done much towards building up the magnificent business this city now enjoys. Many of the banks of Minnesota, Dakota, and Montana, Northern Iowa, and Wisconsin, now keep their reserves in St. Paul, instead of in eastern cities as they have formerly done.

The St. Paul's banks at the close of the year 1887 were as follows:—

First National Bank.	Germania Bank.
Second National Bank.	West Side Bank of St. Paul.
Merchants' National Bank.	Scandinavian-American Bank.
St. Paul National Bank.	Seven Corners Bank.
National German-American Bank.	Savings Bank of St. Paul.
Commercial National Bank.	St. Paul Trust Co.
Bank of Minnesota.	A. M. Peabody's Banking House.
Capital Bank.	C. W. Benson & Co., Foreign Bankers.*
People's Bank.	

* Not included.

Having the combined showing of:—

	Dollars	c.
Capital and surplus	9,325,524	42
Deposits	17,915,814	22
Loans	19,659,577	55

The St. Paul Clearing House records for eight years are:—

	Dollars	c.		Dollars	c.
1880	29,267,804	93	1884	101,636,568	07
1881	56,242,292	93	1885	118,340,977	91
1882	80,276,100	38	1886	153,615,117	50
1883	105,635,291	99	1887	205,012,122	78

Furnished from the Records and Banking Firms by H. P. Upham, Esq., President, St. Paul Clearing House.

DENVER.

Mr. Vice-Consul Pearce reports as follows:—

The value of the imports of British goods on which duty has been paid through the Denver Custom-house in 1887 is 5,043*l.* sterling; this shows a gain of some 2,000*l.* over 1886. A portion of this gain may, perhaps, be accounted for from the fact that it is more generally known that Denver is a port of entry, and a larger percentage of goods are sent direct to Denver than, as formerly, through the different ports of the Atlantic coast.

UNITED STATES.

RETURN of Principal Articles of Import to Denver from Great Britain during the Year 1887.

	£	s.	d.
Earthenware, common brown	545	4	0
,, decorated china	194	14	0
Manufactured silk, clothing, &c.	239	4	0
,, wool cloths	542	16	0
,, ,, carpets	1,159	16	0
,, silver cutlery	159	12	0
,, brass balance	34	0	0
,, steel pocket-knives and cutlery	52	12	0
,, cotton curtains	215	14	0
,, linen clothing	102	8	0
Personal and household effects	393	8	0
Books	834	0	0
Varnish	65	8	0
Glass, cut	25	8	0
Fur and felt hats	55	0	0
Wines and spirits	354	16	0
Biscuits	17	16	0
Manufactured leather	5	0	0
Lime juice cordial	13	0	0
Miscellaneous articles	33	16	0
Total	5,043	12	0

Exports. There are practically no exports to Europe from Colorado.

Industries. The value of metals (gold, silver, copper, lead) produced in Colorada for 1887 has been estimated at about 4,928,000*l.* sterling.

	£
Gold	1,000,000
Silver	2,800,000
Lead	1,080,000
Copper	48,000
Total	4,928,000

These figures show a falling-off from the production of 1886, which is partly owing to a depreciation in the value of the silver produced.

Coal. The coal-fields of Colorado which have been partially or fully explored cover about 1,500 square miles. The output for 1887 shows an increase over 1886 of 300,000 tons. The total product for 1887 is estimated at 1,791,735 tons (2,000 lbs. each).

The average value of the coal on the cars at the mines is 9*s.* 2*d.* per ton; thus the coal production for 1887 is valued at the mines at about 358,347*l.* sterling.

The average number of persons employed in and around the mines during the year is estimated at 5,000.

The average thickness of the coal seams now being worked throughout the State is 5 feet 7 inches; the thickest is 14 feet, and the thinnest is 3 feet.

The average price paid to miners for digging and loading coal and timbering the workings is about 3*s.* 11*d.* per ton of 2,000 lbs. of screened coal.

Coal-miners earn from 10*s.* to 16*s.* per day. The mining of coal is rapidly becoming an important industry in Colorado, and almost every variety is found within the limits of the State.

Iron and steel. The iron industry of Colorado may be said to be in its infancy.

The Colorado Coal and Iron Company established the first and only iron smelting establishment west of Chicago, some nine years ago.

The production of the works for 1887 was: pig-iron, 25,293 tons (2,000 lbs.); steel rails, 18,500 tons (2,000 lbs.); together with sundry castings, rails, bar-iron, &c.

The only English steel rails laid in the State are those on the Denver, Texas, and Gulf Railway, between Denver and Pueblo; they have not been in use long enough to test their comparative wearing qualities.

They cost, laid down in Denver, 11*l*. 8*s*. per ton, whilst the price of steel rails made in Colorado or purchased from Eastern markets is 9*l*. 4*s*. to 9*l*. 12*s*. per ton.

Owing to the recent Tariff agitation, all contracts which had been made with the Colorado Coal and Iron Company for steel rails have been cancelled, and the rail-mill is now idle.

During the year 1887 considerable progress has been made in the development of the oil industry in Colorado. At present, the only locality in which oil is found is at or near the town of Florence, in Fremont County. *Petroleum.*

The number of wells is 30; the deepest well, 3,047 feet; number of oil refineries, two.

During the year 1887, 800 miles of railroad have been completed, making a total in the State of 4,000 miles. Railroad construction seems to keep pace with the general development of the country. This extension to the railroads has been made at a cost of about 4,000*l*. sterling per mile. *Railroad building.*

The valuation of live stock for 1887 is estimated at 3,441,629*l*. *Live stock.*

The condition of the trade and commerce of Colorado during 1887 has been remarkably prosperous. The growth of Denver has been unprecedentedly large. A comparison of sales of real estate for 1886 and 1887 shows an increase of about 250 per cent. It is estimated that over 2,000 buildings were erected in Denver during 1887, at a cost amounting to nearly 1,000,000*l*. sterling, and this prosperity is prevalent throughout the whole State. It is indicated by the Returns of the value of taxable property in the State for 1886 and 1887, which show an increase of nearly 3,500,000*l*. sterling. *Trade and commerce in general.*

An Act was passed by the Legislature during 1887 preventing non-resident aliens from acquiring real estate in Colorado, and requiring the forfeiture of such property hereafter acquired to the State. The following is a copy of the Act:— *Rights of aliens to real estate.*

"Be it enacted by the General Assembly of the State of Colorado, 36 S:—

"Section 1. Non-resident aliens shall, on and after the passage of this Act, be for ever prohibited from acquiring, by any form of purchase, to them, or to their use, any agricultural, arid, or range lands within the State of Colorado, or any interest, use, or benefit in such agricultural, arid, or range lands.

"Section 2. When any such lands, use, interest, or benefit therein shall, in violation of the intent of this Act, be acquired, or purport to be acquired, upon notice thereof, in any form, to the Attorney-General, it shall be his duty to cause proceedings to be instituted in the district court of the proper county or counties, to cause the same to be forfeited to the people of the State of Colorado.

"Section 3. To such proceedings the non-resident alien whose claim is to be inquired into and affected shall be made a party, and all persons having liens, trusts, or encumbrances shall also be made parties, and upon forfeiture of any such lands or interest therein the lawful claims of any such party not being a non-resident alien shall be protected; and the decree shall provide for the sale of the interest sought to be forfeited in such form and under such terms as is usual in decrees in Chancery, so as to provide for the payment of any lawful money liens, and for the enforcement of any valid trust, and the securing of any rightful estate lawfully held; subject, however, in all cases, to the forfeiture of the interest of all non-resident aliens, and with the proviso that the State shall not be liable for the payment of any liability in excess of the fund.

"Section 4. Whenever any interest, such as is mentioned in Section 1 of this Act, shall come to any non-resident alien by devise or descent, or by purchase at foreclosure or judicial sale in aid of a lien or loan, such non-resident alien shall hold the same with right of alienation for the period of three years, after which period the lands, if not in the meantime sold, shall become forfeited, as in the case of like lands purporting to be acquired by purchase.

"Section 5. This Act shall not apply to foreign corporations, syndicates, or individuals acquiring, owning, holding, or working mines, or for engaging in any industry other than the holding of agricultural, arid, or range lands outside of incorporated towns and cities.

"Section 6. This Act shall not apply when the value of the land or interest therein is of an assessed value of less than five thousand dollars ($5,000), but the entire land held in the State in any number of tracts by any person to be affected by this Act shall be considered in ascertaining such valuation, and the holding of the land in the name of one in trust, secret or declared, for the benefit of another, shall be considered as an evasion of this Act.—Approved, April 2, 1887"

LONDON:
Printed for Her Majesty's Stationery Office,
By HARRISON AND SONS,
Printers in Ordinary to Her Majesty.
(1125 5 | 88—H & S 432)

FOREIGN OFFICE.
1888.
ANNUAL SERIES.

No. 340.

DIPLOMATIC AND CONSULAR REPORTS ON TRADE AND FINANCE.

UNITED STATES.

REPORT FOR THE YEAR 1887
ON THE
AGRICULTURE OF NORTH CAROLINA.

REFERENCE TO PREVIOUS REPORT, Annual Series No. 296.

Presented to both Houses of Parliament by Command of Her Majesty,
MAY, 1888.

LONDON:
PRINTED FOR HER MAJESTY'S STATIONERY OFFICE,
BY HARRISON AND SONS, ST. MARTIN'S LANE,
PRINTERS IN ORDINARY TO HER MAJESTY.

And to be purchased, either directly or through any Bookseller, from
EYRE AND SPOTTISWOODE, EAST HARDING STREET, FLEET STREET, E.C., and
32, ABINGDON STREET, WESTMINSTER, S.W.; or
ADAM AND CHARLES BLACK, 6, NORTH BRIDGE, EDINBURGH; or
HODGES, FIGGIS, & Co., 104, GRAFTON STREET, DUBLIN.

1888.

[C. 5252—117.] *Price One Penny.*

New Series of Reports.

Reports of the Annual Series have been issued from Her Majesty's Diplomatic and Consular Officers at the following places, and may be obtained from the sources indicated on the title-page:—

No.		Price.
216.	Rio Grande do Sul	1d.
217.	Rio de Janeiro	1d.
218.	Corea	1d.
219.	Kanagawa	1d.
220.	Wurtemberg	1d.
221.	Tahiti	1d.
222.	Bangkok	1d.
223.	St. Petersburg	2d.
224.	Canton	1d.
225.	Erzeroum	1d.
226.	Rio de Janeiro	1d.
227.	Valparaiso	1d.
228.	St. Thomas	1d.
229.	Stockholm	1d.
230.	Nyassa	1d.
231.	Buenos Ayres	1d.
232.	The Hague	1d.
233.	Trieste	1d.
234.	Vienna	1d.
235.	Washington	3d.
236.	Odessa	1d.
237.	Sofia	1d.
238.	Porto Rico	1d.
239.	Palermo	2d.
240.	Lisbon	2d.
241.	Tabreez	1d.
242.	Tunis	1d.
243.	The Hague	1d.
244.	Fiume	1d.
245.	Venice	1d.
246.	Paris	2d.
247.	Ancona	1d.
248.	St. Petersburg	2d.
249.	Algiers	2d.
250.	Bucharest	1d.
251.	Christiania	2d.
252.	Paris	1d.
253.	Bogota	1d.
254.	Salonica	1d.
255.	Copenhagen	1d.
256.	Jeddah	1d.
257.	Russia	2d.
258.	Paris	1d.
259.	Patras	1d.
260.	Brussels	1d.
261.	Ichang	1d.
262.	Baltimore	1d.
263.	Taganrog	1d.
264.	Oporto	1d.
265.	Rio de Janeiro	1d.
266.	Galveston	1d.
267.	Tripoli	1d.
268.	Galatz	1d.
269.	Varna	1d.
270.	New Orleans	2d.
271.	Cherbourg	1d.
272.	Suakin	1d.
273.	Brest	1d.
274.	Barcelona	2d.
275.	Barcelona	1d.
276.	Antwerp	1d.
277.	Havre	3d.

No.		Price.
278.	Odessa	1d.
279.	Tokyo	1d.
280.	Saigon	1d.
281.	Buenos Ayres	1d.
282.	Taganrog	1d.
283.	Tamsui	1d.
284.	Puerto Plata	1d.
285.	Wênchow	1d.
286.	Tokyo	1d.
287.	Lisbon	2d.
288.	La Rochelle	1d.
289.	Washington	4d.
290.	Beyrout	1d.
291.	Algiers	2d.
292.	Varna	1d.
293.	Algiers	1d.
294.	Port Saïd	1d.
295.	Manila	1d.
296.	Charleston	1d.
297.	Kiungchow	1d.
298.	Pakhoi	1d.
299.	Wuhu	1d.
300.	Boulogne	2d.
301.	Marseilles	1d.
302.	Bordeaux	2d.
303.	Ancona	1d.
304.	Swatow	1d.
305.	Ssŭ-ch'uan	1d.
306.	Antwerp	1d.
307.	Cadiz	1d.
308.	Genoa	1d.
309.	Marseilles	1d.
310.	Baltimore	1d.
311.	Savannah	1d.
312.	Boston	1d.
313.	San Francisco	1d.
314.	Guayaquil	1d.
315.	Santos	1d.
316.	Carthagena and Santa Martha	1d.
317.	San José	1d.
318.	Boulogne	1d.
319.	Tahiti	1d.
320.	Fiume	1d.
321.	Warsaw	1d.
322.	Vera Cruz	2d.
323.	Rio Grande do Sul	1d.
324.	Gothenburg	2d.
325.	Philippopolis	1d.
326.	Mogador	2d.
327.	Havana	2d.
328.	La Rochelle	1d.
329.	Corunna	2d.
330.	Chicago	2d.
331.	Foochow	1d.
332.	Taiwan	1d.
333.	Loanda	1d.
334.	Loanda	1d.
335.	Noumea	1d.
336.	Trieste	1d.
337.	Nice	1d.
338.	Bordeaux	1d.
339.	Mogador	1d.

No. 340.

Reference to previous Report, Annual Series No. 296.

UNITED STATES.

WILMINGTON.

Consul Cridland to the Marquis of Salisbury.

My Lord,   *Charleston, March* 29, 1888.

IN accordance with the instructions, I have the honour to enclose herewith a Report on Agriculture in North Carolina, received from Mr. Vice-Consul Sprunt, of Wilmington.

I have, &c.

(Signed)   FREDERICK J. CRIDLAND.

Vice-Consul Sprunt to Consul Cridland.

Sir,   *Wilmington, N.C., March* 24, 1888.

The number of acres of land in farms in the State of North Carolina, according to the last census, was 6,481,191 acres of improved land, and 15,882,367 acres of unimproved land; since the last census, however, a larger proportion, supposed to be fully 10 per cent., has been improved. The whole number of farms in the State of North Carolina, according to the census of 1880, is 157,609. The classification, according to acreage, is as follows:— *Extent of farms.*

Number of farms under 3 acres							277
,,	,,	over 3	,, and under	10 acres			13,314
,,	,,	,, 10	,, ,,	,, 20	,,		34,143
,,	,,	,, 50	,, ,,	,, 100	,,		34,007
,,	,,	,, 100	,, ,,	,, 500	,,		61,806
,,	,,	,, 500	,, ,,	,, 1,000	,,		5,063
,,	,,	of 1,000	,, and over				1,721

The classification, according to tenure, is as follows:—

Number of farms kept by owners		104,887
,, ,, rented for fixed money rental		8,644
,, ,, ,, ,, shares of produce		44,078

It is shown by the census that three-fourths of the population of the State of North Carolina are engaged in agriculture, one-seventh in professional and personal services, one-fifteenth in manufacturing, mining, and mechanical operations, and one-thirtieth in trade and transportation. *Followings of the population.*

There are several Agricultural Societies in the State, and their transactions and annual meetings are productive of much good, in bringing together the farmers, and in competitive exhibitions of the products of their skill and labour. *Agricultural societies.*

(432)

UNITED STATES.

Products.

The principal agricultural products of the State in acres and production are about as follows:—

Cotton	893,153 acres,	producing	389,598 bales.
Indian corn	2,305,419 „	„	28,019,839 bushels.
Oats	500,415 „	„	3,838,068 „
Rice	10,846 „	„	5,609,191 lbs.
Rye	61,953 „	„	285,160 bushels.
Tobacco	57,208 „	„	26,986,213 lbs.
Wheat	646,829 „	„	3,391,393 bushels.

The acreage of the principal products, cotton and tobacco, has increased largely since this Report was made, and will probably continue to increase with the facilities for transportation which are becoming more abundant.

Functions of Raleigh Board of Agriculture.

To the Board of Agriculture at Raleigh, established by the State Legislature, belongs the enforcement and supervision of the laws and regulations relating to fertilizers, the sellers of which are compelled, under a heavy penalty, to submit samples to the State Commissioner for analysis whenever so required by him. In the exercise of this jurisdiction the Board have always proceeded upon certain cardinal principles. First, never to resort to seizure except when the violation of the law was clear. Second, when seizure became necessary, that it should be so controlled as to cause the least possible interruption to trade. Third, when the violation of the law proceeded from misapprehension or mistake, simply to vindicate the law by exacting payment of the license, and take no steps towards a criminal prosecution. A constant inspection has been exercised, to prevent the introduction of fertilizers in fraud of the law, and nothing has been found so efficacious for this end as frequent visits by the Inspector to the principal markets of the State. In the efforts of the Board to enforce the law, the moral support of the great manufacturers and of the principal dealers has not been wanting. Of late the trade in fertilizers has been remarkably free from any attempt of evasion of the law, or irregularities of any kind. The vigorous enforcement of the law against offenders, and the exercise of a constant vigilance through the Inspectors, has resulted in placing the manufacture and trade in fertilizers generally in the hands of men as much distinguished by the spirit of honour in their transactions as in any other branch of business whatsoever. In the original draft of the Department Act for regulating the sale of fertilizers, dealers in fertilizers were required to make oath at certain times to the Registrar of Deeds of the quantities of fertilizers sold. By Section 20 penalties are imposed for bringing into the State any fertilizers in violation of this section. Other special duties of the Board of Agriculture are defined as follows:—First, such investigations as may seem best adapted to promote the adoption and improvement of sheep husbandry, and more particularly for the suppression of the ravages of dogs, which have hitherto played havoc with this important and interesting industry. The number of dogs owned throughout the State, especially by the negroes in the eastern part, is simply appalling to one desiring the development of sheep husbandry. Efforts have been made from time to time to enact a law imposing a State tax upon each dog, but, for reasons unknown to me, they have failed. I have noticed among the poorest of the farming population, in countries adjoining this Vice-Consulate, a much larger number of dogs than of children; and it is a remarkable fact that a negro family on the verge of starvation, with probably not more than one or two meals in advance of their immediate necessities, will support as many as half-a-dozen of the vilest curs imaginable, who are left to prey upon anything convenient

Dogs.

for their food. Until more stringent measures are adopted for protection against the ravages of these creatures, there is little encouragement for the development of this industry, sheep being the most timid and helpless of our domestic animals.

Second, investigations with reference to the diseases of stock and the ravages of insects. I am pleased to report, upon official authority, that neither of these evils has prevailed in this State to any extent. The crops have been remarkably exempt from insect ravages. *Insects.*

Third, as to the culture of silk, grapes, other fruits, and new agricultural industries. The culture of grapes is extending with every year. The grape has an advantage over other summer fruits in that it can be marketed by the ordinary freight train. Peaches are more perishable, hence have to be sent to market by express. The higher rate of freight by express, and the liability to decay, have prevented the cultivation of peaches to the same extent as other fruits, which are being cultivated in increasing quantities each year. *Fruit culture.*

The Board is also charged to inquire into the conditions under which fences may be dispensed with altogether. Under the present arrangement, this subject presents difficulties which are apparently unsurmountable by any law that shall be uniform in its operations through the State. Over a large part of the State the forest abounds, indeed, may be said to be practically unbroken. It is but a small area, comparatively, that demands legislation for the preservation of timber. How to make a law that will apply equally to a state of things where the interests are so directly opposed is the problem to be solved. Legislation that would meet the ends of one section would be regarded as unnecessary, perhaps oppressive, by the other. It is not easy to see how this difficulty can be better met than in the mode which has been advised by the Legislature, that is, by a general statute allowing fences to be dispensed with whenever the qualified voters of a county, township, or district shall adopt its provisions. *Fences.*

By reference to the mean parallels of latitude of the United States, it will be seen that North Carolina is situated nearly midway of the Union; and, inasmuch as those States lie entirely within the temperate zone, it follows that North Carolina is situated upon the central belt of that zone. This position gives to the State a climate not excelled by any in the world. It is exempt from the extreme cold which prevails in the Northern States, and, to a considerable extent, from the early frosts which visit the States immediately north of it, on the one hand, and from the torrid heat and malarial influences which prevail in the States to the south of it, on the other. Other causes, apart from its position, concur to produce this result. On the west, the lofty Appalachian chain interposes its mighty barrier between the bleak winds of the north-west and the general surface of the State. On the east, the coast is swept by the Gulf Stream, the ameliorating effect of which is felt far inland. From these causes combined, the temperature of the seasons ranges within moderate limits. The spring comes in with less of those fickle variations which mark its advent elsewhere on this continent. The summers are not oppressive, even in the low country, or, if so, for a few days only. But, in the autumn, nature here exhibits herself in the most benignant mood in her most favoured zone. From the incoming of October to the latter part of December there is an almost uninterrupted succession of bright sunny days, during which the air is dry, crisp, and pure—a season equally favourable to the ingathering of the crops and to active exertion of every kind. The reign of winter, as respects cold and wet, is short, and field labour is carried on throughout that season, with the *Geographical; and climate.*

exception of two or three days at a time. Frost makes its appearance about the 15th of October, and sometimes there is not enough to nip the tender vegetation until the end of November. From the blue ridge to the sea-board ice rarely forms of a thickness to be gathered, except in localities overhung and deeply shaded by high southern bluffs. When snow falls, it covers the ground for only a few inches, and is quickly dissipated by the sun. Fogs are of rare occurrence, and then mainly in the form of a belt of light vapour, marking the course of the larger streams in the latter part of summer and during the autumn months. The average rainfall throughout the State is 53 inches, which is pretty uniformly distributed through the year.

Professor Kerr, in his Geological Report, classes the climate of the different sections of North Carolina, with reference to their isothermal ranges, as follows: "Middle and Eastern North Carolina correspond to Middle and Southern France, and Western North Carolina to Northern France and Belgium. And all the climates of Italy, from Palermo to Milan and Venice, are represented."

The following tables, computed by Prof. Kerr, partly from observations taken in all sections of the State for a term of years, and partly from Blodgett, will show the range and character of the climate better than any description:—

Mean annual temperature for the State		59° Fahr.
„ summer „ „		75° „
„ winter „ „		43° „
„ rainfall „ „		45 inches.

Middle Section.

	deg.	deg.	deg.	inches.
Raleigh, N.C.	60	76	44	48
Florence, Italy	59	75	44	27

Eastern Section.

	deg.	deg.	deg.
Beaufort, N.C. (on the coast)	62	78	46
Genoa, Italy	61	75	47
Smithville, N.C. (sea-coast)	66	80	51
Mobile, Ala.	66	79	52
Nicolosi, Sicily	64	79	51

Western Section.

	deg.	deg.	deg.
Asheville, N.C. (in the mountains)	54	71	38
Venice, Italy	55	73	38
Bordeaux, France	57	71	43

"Thus," he says, "it will be seen that the range of climate in the State is the same as that from the Gulf of Mexico to New York. The influence of this circumstance is seen in the wide range of natural and agricultural products, from the Palmetto and Magnolia grandiflora to the white pine, hemlock, and balsam fir, and from the sugar-cane and rice to Canadian oats and buckwheat."

LONDON:
Printed for Her Majesty's Stationery Office,
By HARRISON AND SONS,
Printers in Ordinary to Her Majesty.
(1125 5 | 88—H & S 419)

FOREIGN OFFICE.
1888.
ANNUAL SERIES.

No. 356.

DIPLOMATIC AND CONSULAR REPORTS ON TRADE AND FINANCE.

UNITED STATES.

REPORT FOR THE YEAR 1887
ON THE
AGRICULTURE OF CALIFORNIA.

Presented to both Houses of Parliament by Command of Her Majesty,
JUNE, 1888.

LONDON:
PRINTED FOR HER MAJESTY'S STATIONERY OFFICE,
BY HARRISON AND SONS, ST. MARTIN'S LANE,
PRINTERS IN ORDINARY TO HER MAJESTY.

And to be purchased, either directly or through any Bookseller, from
EYRE AND SPOTTISWOODE, EAST HARDING STREET, FLEET STREET, E.C., and
32, ABINGDON STREET, WESTMINSTER, S.W.; or
ADAM AND CHARLES BLACK, 6, NORTH BRIDGE, EDINBURGH; or
HODGES, FIGGIS, & Co., 104, GRAFTON STREET, DUBLIN.

1888.

[C. 5252—133.] *Price One Penny.*

New Series of Reports.

Reports of the Annual Series have been issued from Her Majesty's Diplomatic and Consular Officers at the following places, and may be obtained from the sources indicated on the title-page:—

No.		Price.	No.		Price.
234.	Vienna	1d.	295.	Manila	1d.
235.	Washington	3d.	296.	Charleston	1d.
236.	Odessa	1d.	297.	Kiungchow	1d.
237.	Sofia	1d.	298.	Pakhoi	1d.
238.	Porto Rico	1d.	299.	Wuhu	1d.
239.	Palermo	2d.	300.	Boulogne	2d.
240.	Lisbon	2d.	301.	Marseilles	1d.
241.	Tabreez	1d.	302.	Bordeaux	2d.
242.	Tunis	1d.	303.	Ancona	1d.
243.	The Hague	1d.	304.	Swatow	1d.
244.	Fiume	1d.	305.	Ssŭ-ch'uan	1d.
245.	Venice	1d.	306.	Antwerp	1d.
246.	Paris	2d.	307.	Cadiz	1d.
247.	Ancona	1d.	308.	Genoa	1d.
248.	St. Petersburg	2d	309.	Marseilles	1d.
249.	Algiers	2d.	310.	Baltimore	1d.
250.	Bucharest	1d.	311.	Savannah	1d.
251.	Christiania	2d.	312.	Boston	1d.
252.	Paris	1d.	313.	San Francisco	1d.
253.	Bogota	1d.	314.	Guayaquil	1d.
254.	Salonica	1d.	315.	Santos	1d.
255.	Copenhagen	1d.	316.	Carthagena and Santa Martha	1d.
256.	Jeddah	1d.	317.	San José	1d.
257.	Russia	2d.	318.	Boulogne	1d.
258.	Paris	1d.	319.	Tahiti	1d.
259.	Patras	1d.	320.	Fiume	1d.
260.	Brussels	1d.	321.	Warsaw	1d.
261.	Ichang	1d.	322.	Vera Cruz	2d.
262.	Baltimore	1d.	323.	Rio Grande do Sul	1d.
263.	Taganrog	1d.	324.	Gothenburg	2d.
264.	Oporto	1d.	325.	Philippopolis	1d.
265.	Rio de Janeiro	1d.	326.	Mogador	2d.
266.	Galveston	1d.	327.	Havana	2d.
267.	Tripoli	1d.	328.	La Rochelle	1d.
268.	Galatz	1d.	329.	Corunna	2d.
269.	Varna	1d.	330.	Chicago	2d.
270.	New Orleans	2d.	331.	Foochow	1d.
271.	Cherbourg	1d.	332.	Taiwan	1d.
272.	Suakin	1d.	333.	Loanda	1d.
273.	Brest	1d.	334.	Loanda	1d.
274.	Barcelona	2d.	335.	Noumea	1d.
275.	Barcelona	1d.	336.	Trieste	1d.
276.	Antwerp	1d.	337.	Nice	1d.
277.	Havre	3d.	338.	Bordeaux	1d.
278.	Odessa	1d.	339.	Mogador	1d.
279.	Tokyo	1d.	340.	Wilmington	1d.
280.	Saigon	1d.	341.	Amoy	2d.
281.	Buenos Ayres	1d.	342.	Trebizond	1d.
282.	Taganrog	1d.	343.	Lisbon	1d.
283.	Tamsui	1d.	344.	Java	1d.
284.	Puerto Plata	1d.	345.	Brest	1d.
285.	Wênchow	1d.	346.	Odessa	2d.
286.	Tokyo	1d.	347.	Cavalla	1d.
287.	Lisbon	2d.	348.	Bussorah	1d.
288.	La Rochelle	1d	349.	Mollendo	1d.
289.	Washington	4d.	350.	Cadiz	5d.
290.	Beyrout	1d.	351.	Cagliari	4d.
291.	Algiers	2d.	352.	Cagliari	1d.
292.	Varna	1d.	353.	Ajaccio	1d.
293.	Algiers	1d.	354.	Copenhagen	1d.
294.	Port Said	1d.	355.	Vienna	1d.

No. 356.

UNITED STATES.

SAN FRANCISCO.

Consul Donohoe to the Marquis of Salisbury.

My Lord,   *San Francisco, April* 3, 1888.

I HAVE the honour to enclose my report on Agricultural Matters in the State of California.

I also enclose reports from the Vice-Consuls at Astoria and Los Angeles.

I have, &c.,
(Signed)   DENIS DONOHOE.

Report on Agriculture in the State of California.

Agriculture

California is one of the richest agricultural tracts of land in the United States, with much fine soil and favourable climate, often producing two crops a year on the same field. The area of the State is 158,360 square miles, with a coast line of over 700 miles. The mean winter temperature of San Francisco is 43 degrees, and the mean summer temperature is 74 degrees; the average rainfall at Sacramento, the capital of the State, is 20 inches. A State extending over such a vast area, and with a great diversity of altitude, must naturally possess a very varied climate, and its agricultural productions must be likewise of the most varied descriptions.

Wheat.

The acreage planted in wheat in 1887 was not as great as in former years, as the farmers have found that other products, such as fruit, realise a larger profit. The amount of wheat harvested in the State was, however, about 1,000,000 tons. I have no statistics at hand as to average product per acre.

Barley.

The barley crop of 1887 was about 400,000 tons, with a yield of about 19 bushels to the acre, but prices have been very low.

Fruit production.

California produces every kind of fruit that grows in a semi-tropical and temperate climate. There is no county in the State which does not produce the fruits of one or other of these two zones. Of the temperate zone fruits, apples, pears, plums, cherries, and peaches of the finest quality are produced, as well as currants, gooseberries, blackberries, raspberries, and strawberries. Of the semi-tropical fruits the orange, lemon, citron, shaddock, and other citrus fruits, with the olive and pomegranate, the fig, banana, apricot. nectarine, walnuts and almonds, besides the grape-vine producing wine and raisins, and the olive with its oil.

(448)

UNITED STATES.

Green fruit trade.

The green fruit trade of the State has increased most extensively, and during the summer and autumn car loads of green fruit from the Pacific coast are shipped to the Middle and Eastern States, making a good return to the farmer. In 1886 22,758,000 lbs. of green fruit was shipped over the Southern Pacific lines of railway, and it is estimated that in 1887 about 35,000,000 lbs. have been forwarded to the Eastern States. Now that it has been found that the middle countries of California produce oranges and peaches, as well as further south, a great impetus has been given to the planting of trees.

Canned fruit and vegetables.

The establishment of canneries in the farming and fruit districts of California has been of great use to the farmer. The output of the various canneries for 1886 amounts to 659,950 cases of fruit, 203,500 cases of vegetables, and 22,500 cases of jellies and jams. Allowing an average of 45 lbs. of fruit to a case, makes the amount of fruit put up in this way about 30,000,000 lbs.

An estimate of the canned-goods pack of 1887 is made as follows by one of the leading canning firms:—

	Cases.
Apples	5,500
Asparagus	5,500
Apricots	175,500
Blackberries	25,000
Cherries	60,000
Currants	5,000
Gooseberries	15,000
Grapes	35,000
Nectarines	3,000
Pears	150,000
Peas	25,000
Peaches	220,000
Plums	40,000
Quinces	6,500
Raspberries	6,500
Strawberries	15,000
Total	792,500

Dried and evaporated fruits and vegetables.

Dried and evaporated fruits and vegetables are another source of income to the farmer. The product of 1887 was:—

Raisins (20 lb. boxes)	800,000	
Honey (extracted)	1,090,000	lbs.
Honey (comb)	250,000	,,
Bees'-wax	25,000	,,
French prunes	1,750,000	,,
German ,,	75,000	,,
Apples (sun dried)	200,000	,,
Peaches ,,	1,750,000	,,
Plums ,,	400,000	,,
Pears ,,	40,000	,,
Grapes ,,	600,000	,,
Apricots ,,	200,000	,,
Nectarines ,,	100,000	,,
Figs ,,	90,000	,,
Apples (evaporated)	550,000	,,
Apricots ,, / ,, (bleached)	3,000,000	,,
Peaches (evaporated, peeled)	500,000	,,
,, ,, (unpeeled)	750,000	,,
Plums ,,	50,000	,,
Nectarines ,,	50,000	,,
Walnuts	1,500,000	,,
Almonds	500,000	,,
Peanuts	250,000	,,

CALIFORNIA.

Raisins. The growing of grapes for raisins has proved a most profitable crop, with a ready market for all that can be made. The farmer sells them to the packer, and, according to quality, receives from 4 c. to 6 c. a lb. In the larger factories throughout the State the packing is done by steam power, and they sell in New York at from 2 dol. to 2 dol. 25 c. the box of 20 lbs. In Fresno County alone some 225,000 boxes were put up last year. Californians believe that the raisin crop of their State will eventually drive the foreign product from the markets of the United States, and from statistics of the trade I am inclined to believe that such will be the case

Wine. The crop of last year is estimated at somethiing over 13,000,000 gallons. Wine of 1886, up to August, 1887, sold at from 14 c. to 16 c. a gallon, and at the end of the year fetched from 25 c. to 28 c. New wine of 1887 sells at 17 c. to 20 c. The following are the average prices paid per tun during the vintage of 1887 for the prominent varieties of wine grapes:—Cabernet, 25 dol. to 30 dol.; Petit Pinot, 25 dol. to 30 dol.; black Burgundy, 18 dol. to 20 dol.; Meunier, 18 dol. to 20 dol.; Riesling, 18 dol. to 20 dol.; Matro, 16 dol. to 18 dol.; Zinfaudel, 14 dol. to 16 dol.; Carbono, 13 dol. to 15 dol.; Malvoisie, 8 dol. to 9 dol.; and Mission, 7 dol. to 8 dol. It is, of course, understood that these prices varied in different localities, conforming to the universal rule of supply and demand.

Acres in grapes. The State Board of Viticulture estimate that about 150,000 acres in this State are planted with vines, and that not less than 90 per cent. of these are foreign varieties. That the improvement in the quality of wine produced is very marked there can be no doubt, and the former California wine, with its disagreeable, harsh, foxy taste is fast becoming a thing of the past. This is due to the importation of the best varieties of foreign vines, and a more careful system of cultivation, manufacture, and preservation of the wine. There still remains much prejudice against the California wines in the Eastern States, and they are mostly sold under French labels; though it is but fair to say that there are houses now in New York and elsewhere which sell solely the Californian wines and brandies, and mark them as such.

Must condensing. The process of condensing grape-must has been introduced, and is said to be successful. By this process it is claimed that the must is condensed to one-third of its original density, thus preventing fermentation. In this state it is said that it can be transported to foreign countries and entered as fruit juice without paying custom-house duties as wine, and that 50 gallons of condensed must will keep for years without fermentation, and will improve by age as much as wine, so that a good quality of wine can be produced at any time by the addition of water to the must. 50 gallons of condensed must will make 150 gallons of wine.

When it passes through the hands of the skilful manipulators abroad, I doubt very much if the consumer will receive an article that can be designated "unsophisticated juice of the grape," but probably it will be just as pure as many of the wines we drink at present.

Wool. The number of sheep in the State is from four to four and a half millions. The clip in 1854 was 175,000 lbs., and in 1876 it had reached to 56,550,970 lbs.: after this it fell off, and in 1887 was 31,564,231 lbs., but with a great improvement in quality.

Root crops. All the varieties of roots, such as beetroot, mangolds, turnips, cabbage, &c., are produced in this State.

Prices of farm produce.

The following are the San Francisco prices of market produce ruling on 16th March, 1888:—

		Dol. c.		Dol. c.
Wheat, No. 1	per cental	1 30	to	1 32½
Barley, brewing	,,	0 92½		1 2½
Oats, best	,,	1 65		1 70
Corn, large yellow	,,	1 30		0 0
Rye	,,	2 0		0 0
Hay, alfalfa	per ton	12 0		14 0
,, clover	,,	13 0		15 0
Butter, various	per lb.	0 22		0 27
Cheese ,,	,,	0 12½		0 18
Eggs	per doz.	0 18		0 21
Poultry, hens and cocks	,,	6 0		9 0
,, broilers	,,	5 0		8 0
Ducks	,,	9 0		11 0
Geese	per pair	2 0		2 50
Turkeys, live	per lb.	0 19		0 21
,, dressed	,,	0 22		0 24
Honey, extracted	,,	0 6½		0 7½
,, comb	,,	0 8		0 17
Oranges, California	per box	1 0		2 0
,, Los Angeles Navel	,,	2 50		3 0
,, Riverside Navel	,,	5 0		6 0
Lemons	,,	1 0		2 50
Limes	,,	0 50		1 0
Apples, California	,,	0 50		2 0

Dried fruits—

Pears, sliced	per lb.	0 5		0 6
,, machine dried	,,	0 0		0 10
Peaches, peeled	,,	0 20		0 22½
,, unpeeled	,,	0 8		0 12
Apricots, bleached	,,	0 15		0 17
,, sun dried	,,	0 9		0 11
Plums, pitted	,,	0 10		0 12½
,, unpitted	,,	0 5		0 6
Prunes	,,	0 4		0 11
Blackberries	,,	0 9		0 11
Apples, sliced and quartered	,,	0 4		0 6
Figs, pressed	,,	0 0		0 5
,, unpressed	,,	0 3		0 3½
Nectarines	,,	0 0		0 9
Raisins, California, London layers	per box	2 0		2 50

Vegetables—

Cabbage	per cental	1 0		0 0
Carrots	per sack	0 35		0 40
Beets	per cental	0 75		1 0
Parsnips	,,	1 0		1 50
Turnips	,,	1 0		1 35
Cauliflower	per doz.	0 50		1 0
Artichokes	,,	0 20		0 25
Peppers, dried	per lb.	0 8		0 10
Asparagus	,,	0 6		0 17
Rhubarb	,,	0 8		0 10
Potatoes, various	per sack	0 75		1 20
,, sweet	,,	2 0		3 0
Onions	per cental	1 50		2 0
Beans, various	,,	2 40		4 0

Wool—

Northern, fall clip	per lb.	0 13	0 15
Middle counties, fall clip	,,	0 10	0 12
San Joaquin, fall clip	,,	0 8	0 12
Southern, fall clip	,,	0 7	0 9

CALIFORNIA.

ASTORIA, OREGON.

Mr. Vice-Consul Cherry reports as follows:—

This district, comprising as it does the slope of the coast range of Northern Oregon and Western Washington Territory, has but a small proportion of land immediately available for agriculture.

The cost of clearing land from the heavy forest growths is too great to allow the settlers to do it for agricultural purposes, but on the banks of the numerous streams and rivers flowing into the bays and inlets on the coast are rich bottom lands covered with a growth of small trees which are easily cleared off; and on the shores of the bays are large tracts of submerged "tide lands," which are exceedingly productive when protected by dykes. This is now being done to a comparatively large extent, and have proved to be capable of producing large crops of grasses and roots.

All of the cleared land in this district, with the exception of sufficient to grow vegetables for the use of the settlers, and to supply the demand of the towns and villages in the district, are put down for grasses, both for pasture and hay.

The climate is too cool during the summer months to be certain to ripen wheat, and the productiveness of the alluvial lands for hay is such that as much as from four tons to six tons are produced per acre, besides grazing stock on them during the winter and early spring.

The demand for hay is now nearly always greater than the supply for local uses of stock farms and lumber-logging camps where teams of oxen are used, and the local production is supplemented by oat hay from California.

The whole agricultural output of this Vice-Consular district may be said not to be sufficient for the local demand, excepting potatoes, which are shipped to San Francisco.

WILMINGTON AND LOS ANGELES.

Mr. Vice-Consul Mortimer reports as follows:—

Owing chiefly to the difference in climate, the cultivation of the soil is carried on in a manner wholly different from the methods in use in England. The specialty of this district is the cultivation of the grape, and semi-tropic fruits, oranges, limes, lemons, &c. The grain ranches are very large, many of them containing 15,000 to 25,000 acres, and several over 50,000 acres, and this industry is consequently in the hands of a few people who carry it on scientifically. The following figures are taken from the books of a 25,000 acre grain ranch, and may be relied upon as strictly accurate.

Cost of ploughing, preparing the land for seed, and sowing 1s. 3d. per acre; cost of harvesting, 1s. 2d. per acre: total cost, exclusive of seed, 2s. 5d. per acre.

On many of the large ranches steam-ploughs are used, and on others gang-ploughs, which turn four to six furrows, and are drawn by from eight to fourteen mules. The soil is turned to a depth of from three to four inches only, as it is found that deep ploughing causes the grain to rust. A patent machine for sowing seed is employed, by means of which one man and a team can sow 100 acres of grain in a day. The owner of one very large ranch tells me that the average net returns for a period of six years were only 7s. per acre. This land cost him, 10 years ago, 1l. per acre; it is now valued, and is saleable in small tracts, at 8l. per acre. As these figures apply to other large ranches, it will be seen that grain farming is not profitable here at the present price of land. As the population increases I look for a decrease in the acreage in grain. Owing to lack of moisture (in "dry" years), the crop of grain is a total or partial failure about every third year.

The rainfall is very irregular. The precipitation in inches for the past six years has been as follows :—10·40 ; 12·11 ; 38·22 ; 9·25 ; 22·58 ; and 13·76. From present indications the crop will be very abundant this year.

LONDON :

Printed for Her Majesty's Stationery Office,

By HARRISON AND SONS,

Printers in Ordinary to Her Majesty.

(1125 5 | 88—H & S 448)

FOREIGN OFFICE.
1888.
ANNUAL SERIES.

No. 362.

DIPLOMATIC AND CONSULAR REPORTS ON TRADE AND FINANCE.

UNITED STATES.

REPORT FOR THE YEAR 1887
ON THE
AGRICULTURAL CONDITION OF THE STATE OF COLORADO.

Presented to both Houses of Parliament by Command of Her Majesty,
JUNE, 1888.

LONDON:
PRINTED FOR HER MAJESTY'S STATIONERY OFFICE,
BY HARRISON AND SONS, ST. MARTIN'S LANE,
PRINTERS IN ORDINARY TO HER MAJESTY.

And to be purchased, either directly or through any Bookseller, from
EYRE AND SPOTTISWOODE, EAST HARDING STREET, FLEET STREET, E.C., and
32, ABINGDON STREET, WESTMINSTER, S.W.; or
ADAM AND CHARLES BLACK, 6, NORTH BRIDGE, EDINBURGH; or
HODGES, FIGGIS, & Co., 104, GRAFTON STREET, DUBLIN.

1888.

[C. 5252—139.] *Price One Penny.*

New Series of Reports.

Reports of the Annual Series have been issued from Her Majesty's Diplomatic and Consular Officers at the following places, and may be obtained from the sources indicated on the title-page:—

No.		Price.	No.		Price.
236.	Odessa	1d.	299.	Wuhu	1d.
237.	Sofia	1d.	300.	Boulogne	2d.
238.	Porto Rico	1d.	301.	Marseilles	1d.
239.	Palermo	2d.	302.	Bordeaux	2d.
240.	Lisbon	2d.	303.	Ancona	1d.
241.	Tabreez	1d.	304.	Swatow	1d.
242.	Tunis	1d.	305.	Ssŭ-ch'uan	1d.
243.	The Hague	1d.	306.	Antwerp	1d.
244.	Fiume	1d.	307.	Cadiz	1d.
245.	Venice	1d.	308.	Genoa	1d.
246.	Paris	2d.	309.	Marseilles	1d.
247.	Ancona	1d.	310.	Baltimore	1d.
248.	St. Petersburg	2d.	311.	Savannah	1d.
249.	Algiers	2d.	312.	Boston	1d.
250.	Bucharest	1d.	313.	San Francisco	1d.
251.	Christiania	2d.	314.	Guayaquil	1d.
252.	Paris	1d.	315.	Santos	1d.
253.	Bogota	1d.	316.	Carthagena and Santa Martha	1d.
254.	Salonica	1d.	317.	San José	1d.
255.	Copenhagen	1d.	318.	Boulogne	1d.
256.	Jeddah	1d.	319.	Tahiti	1d.
257.	Russia	2d.	320.	Fiume	1d.
258.	Paris	1d.	321.	Warsaw	1d.
259.	Patras	1d.	322.	Vera Cruz	2d.
260.	Brussels	1d.	323.	Rio Grande do Sul	1d.
261.	Ichang	1d.	324.	Gothenburg	2d.
262.	Baltimore	1d.	325.	Philippopolis	1d.
263.	Taganrog	1d.	326.	Mogador	2d.
264.	Oporto	1d.	327.	Havana	2d.
265.	Rio de Janeiro	1d.	328.	La Rochelle	1d.
266.	Galveston	1d.	329.	Corunna	2d.
267.	Tripoli	1d.	330.	Chicago	2d.
268.	Galatz	1d.	331.	Foochow	1d.
269.	Varna	1d.	332.	Taiwan	1d.
270.	New Orleans	2d.	333.	Loanda	1d.
271.	Cherbourg	1d.	334.	Loanda	1d.
272.	Suakin	1d.	335.	Noumea	1d.
273.	Brest	1d.	336.	Trieste	1d.
274.	Barcelona	2d.	337.	Nice	1d.
275.	Barcelona	1d.	338.	Bordeaux	1d.
276.	Antwerp	1d.	339.	Mogador	1d.
277.	Havre	2d.	340.	Wilmington	1d.
278.	Odessa	1d.	341.	Amoy	2d.
279.	Tokyo	1d.	342.	Trebizond	1d.
280.	Saigon	1d.	343.	Lisbon	1d.
281.	Buenos Ayres	1d.	344.	Java	1d.
282.	Taganrog	1d.	345.	Brest	1d.
283.	Tamsui	1d.	346.	Odessa	2d.
284.	Puerto Plata	1d.	347.	Cavalla	1d.
285.	Wênchow	1d.	348.	Bussorah	1d.
286.	Tokyo	1d.	349.	Mollendo	1d.
287.	Lisbon	2d.	350.	Cadiz	5d.
288.	La Rochelle	1d.	351.	Cagliari	4d.
289.	Washington	4d.	352.	Cagliari	1d.
290.	Beyrout	1d.	353.	Ajaccio	1d.
291.	Algiers	2d.	354.	Copenhagen	1d.
292.	Varna	1d.	355.	Vienna	1d.
293.	Algiers	1d.	356.	San Francisco	1d.
294.	Port Said	1d.	357.	Vera Cruz	1d.
295.	Manila	1d.	358.	Philippopolis	1d.
296.	Charleston	1d.	359.	Greytown	1d.
297.	Kiungchow	1d.	360.	Tangier	1d.
298.	Pakhoi	1d.	361.	Lisbon	1d.

No. 362.

UNITED STATES.

CHICAGO.

Consul Hayes Sadler to the Marquis of Salisbury.

My Lord,   *Chicago, April* 18, 1888.

I HAVE the honour to transmit herewith a Report on Agriculture in my Consular district during the year 1887, together with a Report on the Agriculture of the State of Colorado, which has been forwarded to me by Mr. Vice-Consul Pearce from Denver.

I have, &c.
(Signed)   J. HAYES SADLER.

Report on Agriculture in the District of Chicago for the Year 1887.

THE CROPS.

Throughout this district, which includes the States and territories west of Lake Michigan, and the State of Illinois to the Rocky Mountains, there was almost as great deficiency of rain as in the preceding season of 1886, and a consequent shortness in crops. The temperature was above the average, especially in the early part of the year, and with the absence of moisture told heavily on spring crops, corn, and potatoes, causing an increase in value of those products as well as of hay. In north-western Minnesota, in Nebraska, and notably in Dakota, there was some seasonable rain, and certain crops suffered less, but in Illinois, Iowa, and Kansas the harvest was seriously affected by long continued drought.

The total produce of corn in this district was 701,039,000 bushels on 32,352,819 acres, showing a decrease of nearly 160,000,000 bushels produced and of 2,781,021 acres harvested as compared with the year 1886, the total crop in which was about 18 per cent. less than in 1885. The decrease in acreage harvested in the State of Illinois amounted to 1,211,000 acres, in Iowa to 731,000 acres, and in Kansas to 519,000 acres, a considerable area having failed to mature. In Illinois the yield declined by 68,750,000 bushels, and in Kansas by 50,000,000. On account of a short supply for two seasons an increase in the price of corn has been general except in Dakota, where from the large crop grown there has been a slight decline in value. In Nebraska the farm value of corn rose from 10*d.* per bushel in 1886 to 1*s.* 3*d.* in 1887; in Kansas from 1*s.* 1*d.* to 1*s.* 6*d.*; in Illinois from 1*s.* 3½*d.* to 1*s.* 8*d.*, and in other States in a less degree. *[Indian corn.]*

The total crop of wheat in this district was 221,676,000 bushels grown on 17,355,540 acres, against 206,275,000 bushels on 16,425,849 acres in 1886, while the total farm value is estimated at 27,434,189*l.*, *[Wheat.]*

(456)

against 25,572,342*l.* in 1886. The farm price of wheat varied little from that of the previous year beyond local fluctuations. The rate of yield is constantly varying in different localities, consequent on drought or the prevalence of insects. The wheat crop of Minnesota showed last year a decrease in quantity of 6,500,000 bushels, and scarcely exceeded 36,250,000 bushels produced on 3,129,208 acres. On the contrary, the acreage in wheat in Dakota increased from 2,675,350 acres in 1886 to 3,664,737 in 1887, and, conditions having been favourable, and the crop generally free from clinch bug, the yield amounted to 52,406,000 bushels, the largest quantity ever grown in any State or territory. In Kansas the area under wheat in 1887 was only 792,304 acres, and the yield 9⅝ bushels per acre, whereas in 1880 there were 2,444,434 acres sown, and in 1884 the yield was 21½ bushels per acre. This decline is in some measure due to the ravages of the Hessian fly and clinch bug, which caused some farmers to change the crop for other grain.

Oats and other grain. There has been an increased area sown in oats in this district, amounting to nearly 2,000,000 acres. The yield in 1887 was 404,727,000 bushels grown on 14,010,259 acres, against 361,767,000 bushels on 12,084,515 acres in 1886, and the farm value is estimated at 21,805,532*l.*, against 19,064,301*l.* in the preceding year. Notwithstanding the large yield, the largest ever grown, the price shows a fractional advance, which may be attributed to an increased demand for oats both for human and animal food. Rye and buckwheat also show a slight advance in average price.

Potatoes. Potatoes suffered severely from the drought in the early part of the season, and, though the acreage grown was larger than in the previous year, the yield was not sufficient to meet the demand for consumption. In Illinois and Iowa, which are large potato-growing States, not 50 per cent. of an average crop was secured, the yield in Illinois having been scarcely 33 bushels per acre. There was a consequent increase in price, and foreign potatoes were imported to make up the deficiency at a cost to the importer of about 6*s.* 7*d.* per bushel, including duty and carriage.

STOCK-RAISING.

Cattle ranges. The series of prosperity which marked the period from 1881 to 1885, and caused a great advance in ranch property and a corresponding upward movement in cattle, has been very seriously checked during the last two years, and some large failures have taken place. The drought of 1886, and consequent shortness of pasture, especially in those parts of the north-west where ranches were somewhat overstocked, and the intense cold of the winter of 1886-87, caused enormous losses; and these, combined with the low price of cattle, have had a depressing effect on the industry. The losses from cold and exposure in that winter in Montana are said to have been 40 per cent., and I have been assured by some large ranchers that their losses were fully 80 per cent., it having been impossible to reach the herds during the extreme severe weather, and cattle died before assistance could reach them. The losses in other districts were also heavy, though steers generally survived, and prices have been kept down by a rush to send animals to market, shipments having continued to be heavy throughout the year from a general feeling to diminish stock. Railroads also have opened the Texan ranches to compete with the north-west in these markets; but the class of animals is poorer, and they fetch a lower price. This last winter losses have been comparatively small, and a larger quantity of grain and hay had been cut and stored for feed.

In Dakota, where almost all the land is tillable and covered with Reducing the grasses which cure to hay on the ground, costing only the expense of size of herds. cutting, cattle are held by farmers who are in the habit of feeding in the winter; but in the large range districts of Montana and Wyoming, as well as in those parts of Nebraska where conditions are similar, cattle were almost entirely left to take care of themselves; and here the industry is now undergoing a great change. After late experiences it has been found that the risks of allowing cattle to range at will are too great, and that it pays better to keep smaller herds and take better care of them. Already the cultivation of grain and grasses is increasing as the country is filling up with settlers; large herds are being cut down, and more regard paid to winter feeding, while the grade of cattle is also improving. In future there will probably be more attention paid to the production of tame grasses, there will be smaller ranges, and cattle will be kept in smaller herds, within convenient distance of feed, with closer regard to quality and condition; and with this change, and the prospect of markets nearer home, there is still a wide field open to cattle ranching. The number of cattle, other than milch cows, in 1887, in the four range districts of Montana, Wyoming, Nebraska, and Dakota, is now estimated at 4,012,000.

There are many who consider the horse business more profitable Horse and safer than cattle breeding; it is yearly becoming more important in ranching. the north-west; the losses are undoubtedly less, and there is always food for horses during the severest part of the season, when snow is on the ground, where cattle are unable to provide for themselves. Excellent, sure-footed, and strong animals are bred from the hardy Montana mare, or cayouse, and a well-bred stallion. There are now 946,780 horses in the range districts above mentioned.

Dehorning cattle has been practised to a limited extent during the Dehorning last few years, and the system seems taking hold, some farmers having cattle. dehorned their whole herd. It has been calculated that 200,000 cattle and horses die each year from horn thrusts in the United States. It is claimed by the advocates of the system that, besides lessening this loss and that of human life, much shed room is saved—that there is a saving in feed of hay, less turmoil from restive animals, and that cows, being more quiet and docile, give more milk. In the case of calves, the horn is extracted by a gouge or punch, when two or three months old, and with full-grown animals the horn is sawn off at the point where the matrix joins the bone horn, and should be done early in the spring. If sawn higher than the point mentioned, the horn would again grow, and, if below, the process of granulation would not take place.

In the other States of this district the character of stock raised on Breed of farms has immensely improved. It is but comparatively a few years stock. ago when first a few head of the different English and Scotch breeds were imported; there are now thoroughbred cattle everywhere, and centres of pure blood, which are raising the standard of cattle throughout the country. Purchasers can now procure in their own neighbourhood a perfectly genuine animal of any of the choice breeds. In the State of Illinois a Law was passed last year to protect farmers against damage resulting from breeding to sires advertised with fraudulent pedigrees, and to secure to the owner of sire payment for service. Every owner of a sire charging a service fee must now procure a certificate by filing statement on oath as to name, age, description, and pedigree, and in virtue of such certificate has a lien on the get for payment of service for a period of four months after birth of such get.

Much inconvenience in the interchange of animals was experienced Cattle disease. in the different States from the quarantine, which was generally

(456)

imposed in consequence of the outbreak of pleuro-pneumonia at Chicago in 1886; fortunately the disease has been stamped out by the energetic measures taken, as it was extirpated in Missouri in 1885, and the fears that it might have been disseminated west have not been realised. There were 24,161 head of cattle examined in Cook County, Illinois, to which the outbreak was confined; 7,693 animals were slaughtered, and out of that number 1,435 were found on post-mortem examination to be affected with pleuropneumonia, and about 600 sheds or stables were destroyed or disinfected.

The restrictions placed on inter-State traffic have now been almost wholly removed, and no signs of disease exist now in this district. Several new Acts have been lately passed for preventing the spread of contagious diseases, and for the suppression and extirpation of pleuro-pneumonia. The Act of Illinois, of 1887, was originated in consequence of the difficulty in meeting the emergency caused by imperfect legislation, and is to the following effect:—A Board of Commissioners has been appointed, whom it is the duty of any person to notify in the event of having any knowledge or reason to suspect the existence of disease, when they are immediately to cause proper examination to be made. They are to order all diseased and exposed animals to be strictly quarantined, as well as any premises or farms where disease exists, or has recently existed, or which have been exposed, and have the power to order the slaughter of all such diseased or exposed animals, and to cause to be destroyed all such premises or property as may be necessary to prevent the spread of the disease, where the same cannot be properly disinfected. The Board may agree with the owner upon the value of such animals or property, or, in case such agreement cannot be made, shall appoint three disinterested persons to appraise the same when the value fixed is refunded. The penalty fixed for any violation of the Act is a fine of from 20*l.* to 200*l.*, or imprisonment of not more than six months, or both.

Hog breeding and disease. In the more settled localities, and mostly throughout this district, there has been sufficient admixture of some recognised high-class breed to bring the swine up to a high standard, and there is little to be desired in the form or quality of hogs which are brought to the packing houses. Simultaneously with this improvement in grade, however, various diseases appear to have developed; formerly, the ugly-shaped native hog roamed in a half wild state, and found its own living; now they are bred in a more artificial manner, kept and fed in pens, and possibly this more civilised and indolent existence may be one cause of the increased disorders they are subject to. A great many theories have been formulated, and much investigation has been made into the character and cause of hog cholera and other diseases, without yet any definite decision being arrived at, though it is not improbable that the researches made will eventually lead to the discovery of some specific. In the meantime, losses are enormous, and entire herds of hogs are sometimes carried off in a week by disease, arising from no known cause, with no known means of checking the disaster. And, with reference to these losses, rumours exist regarding the occasional sale of such dead animals, and even of their entering into the manufacture of lard and butterine, or in the composition of soap, which is almost as bad. These rumours have called forth stout denial, and it seems scarcely possible to credit them without substantial proof by fact, and in face of the inspection which exists at the stockyards. Nevertheless it may be regretted that there is no general law for the disposal of such hogs as may die of disease, either by deep burial or cremation, and their disposal should have even such protection as is allowed under the laws of Iowa where rendering such dead hogs into lard, and selling it, is permitted, providing it is marked " Lard from Hogs which have died of Disease."

DAIRY PRODUCTS.

The magnitude of the dairy interest in the prairie States, which is continually on the increase, cannot be shown without the statement of a few facts. On January 1, 1887, there were 1,243,000 milch cows in the State of Iowa, 937,476 in Illinois, 729,959 in Missouri, 609,601 in Kansas, 548,222 in Wisconsin, 417,275 in Minnesota, and 333,836 in Nebraska, making a total in these seven States of 4,819,371 milch cows, besides 8,836,016 other cattle. Statistics are wanting to show the exact quantity of butter and cheese made, but Iowa alone produced 86,000,000 lbs. of butter, and the produce of its dairy farms sold outside the State is estimated at 4,200,000l. for the year 1887; Minnesota produced 40,000,000 lbs. of butter, and the other States may be calculated to have produced comparatively, according to the number of cows, while with the rich fertile soil their capabilities are many times the present produce. Chicago handles to a great extent the shipments of the north-west; in 1887 the receipts are estimated at 127,750,000 lbs. of butter, and the shipments at 116,500,000 lbs. The cheese receipts were 46,425,000 lbs., and the shipments 42,000,000 lbs. Direct exports from Chicago are small, and amounted last year to 500,000 lbs. of butter and 2,400,000 lbs. of cheese. By far the greater quantity is made at creameries and factories, which are largely increasing in number; better butter can be made by the creameries at $1\frac{1}{2}d.$ less a pound than by the home churn, and the former are destined wholly to supplant the latter. Dairy interests have greatly suffered from the manufacture of oleomargarine, butterine, and other products of animal fat, which, though excluded by recent legislation from entering into the manufacture of butter, injure the genuine article by force of competition, and still enter largely in the composition of cheese, little of which is comparatively consumed in the country, as so little good is made. It is stated that in the last few years the dairy industry has not made the advance it would, had fraud not been practised on its product, but that during the last year, as a result of the Oleomargarine Act, butter has very generally improved about 2d. per lb., and that there is now a great demand for churn apparatus. Most of the States have local laws, either prohibiting or controlling the sale of oleomargarine and the adulteration of the products of milk, but they are for the most part inoperative, and dairy associations would gladly welcome further Federal legislation.

NOTES ON CULTIVATION IN THE WEST.

The increase of area under cultivation throughout this district is remarkable, and is especially noticeable in the more western States and territories. Each year, as fresh railroads are built and immigration from the east extends, a fresh area of land is occupied, and hitherto unknown regions of rich and fertile soil are brought under the plough or occupied as grazing farms, while in the arid region, which but a few years ago it was thought could not be cultivated without irrigation, it is found that almost any crop can be grown with little or no recourse to artificial assistance. And when all the vast territory yet unsettled is improved, and more careful gardening practised, it is impossible to overestimate the agricultural resources of the future.

The progress in the State of Kansas in the last seven years is worthy of remark; the area under cultivation in 1860, including prairie under fence, was 372,855 acres, or ·70 of the area of the State; in 1880 it had increased to 8,868,885 acres, or 18·86 per cent., and in 1886 to 15,473,495 acres or 29·43 per cent., and is still extending at the same rate. The western or arid part seven years ago was solely occupied by scattered ranches; there are now thousands of farms which have transformed the aspect of the country, and but little land remains unoccupied. It consists of high rolling prairies, with a gentle slope eastward, and has a general altitude of from 1,500 feet to 3,500 feet, and the undulating plains are for the most part from 100 feet to 200 feet above the streams. The rainfall, however, is very limited, and, though the rivers, which have an eastward course, are subject to overflow during the early summer rains, many of the smaller streams are lost in their sandy beds in a dry season, leaving here and there a pool; but much can be done by irrigation, and pure water is everywhere obtainable from wells at a varying depth of a few feet to 300 feet, and in many instances the bottom lands present an expanse of level plain. The soil is a rich alluvium and adapted, with favourable climatic conditions, to all forms of vegetation produced in that latitude, but the last two seasons' crops have suffered severely from drought. The average temperature is 52° 92′, ranging from a maximum of 106° to a minimum of 18° below zero, and the rainfall throughout the State is usually 35 inches.

Territory of Dakota. It has been seen that Dakota now leads in the production of wheat. This territory alone contains 96,500,000 acres of land, including Indian reservations, and as yet only 36,000,000 acres have been disposed of, leaving an immense field open for grain-growing; the land, which is almost entirely tillable, and is covered with native grass, which cures to hay on the ground and costs little more than 5s. a ton to cut and stack, is passing into the hands of actual settlers at the rate of 4,000,000 acres each year. Dakota wheat is extremely rich in albuminoids, and contains a remarkably small amount of water, the average percentage of albuminoids in its composition being 14·95, and of water 8·84. The average investment by the farmer in his farm property is only 2l. 10s. per acre, and mortgaged farms, taking the high average of 1l. per acre, pay only a mortgage interest of 2s. per acre, while taxes are low. The cost of wheat production has been estimated at 1s. 6d. per bushel as follows:—Ploughing one acre, 4s.; seeding, 5s.; cultivation and sowing, 2s.; harvesting and stacking, 5s.; threshing and marketing, 8s. Total, 1l. 4s.; or, taking the yield at 20 bushels per acre, and counting 10 per cent. interest on capital, at fractionally less than 1s. 6d. per bushel.

Grasses. The vast prairies of the so-called arid region (which includes the western half of Dakota, Nebraska, and Kansas, and the eastern portion of Colorado) as well as the plains of Montana and Wyoming are covered with wild grasses which have supplied the rancher and the farmer with an apparently inexhaustible supply of food for his cattle. These natural grasses are of very great variety, but many of them have not the quality of resisting drought and tramping. They have already failed in some measure in dry seasons, and where ranches have been overstocked; and it is a question whether they will not further fail as civilisation increases, or lose many of their feeding qualities when cultivated. Attention is now being largely paid to the cultivation of those varieties which appear the most suitable, as well as to the planting of timothy, alfalfa, and other tame grasses and clovers for feeding purposes, and, as these trials and experiments of forage plants lead to further knowledge of their adaptation to different localities, the feeding capacity of these regions will be greatly increased.

"Arbor Day. In the above-mentioned districts there is an almost total absence of

trees, which accounts for the deficiency of moisture, while in the timber regions and in the mountains the reckless cutting, especially of young trees, has led to a serious decrease in lumber and firewood. Various Acts have been passed checking and restraining the unlimited waste which formerly prevailed, and the disposal of land under the Timber Culture Law will, no doubt, have a beneficial effect. It was in the State of Nebraska 15 years ago that a voluntary movement first originated to set apart one day in the year, called "Arbor Day," for the purpose of encouraging the planting of trees and forestry in general. The example has been followed in almost every State and territory in this district, and a public holiday is proclaimed by the Legislature, the day being fixed generally by the Governor, when trees are planted by local authorities and other notable persons; planting of shade trees in streets is carried on by town councils, and the people generally are encouraged to memorialise the day by similar acts. The white elm is considered the best tree, being hardy and of rapid growth. The different varieties of oak, walnut, and maple, the elm, ash, catalpa, linden, tulip-tree, pine, and other trees, are variously recommended to the public as experiments have proved them to thrive in the different localities or are suitable to the purposes desired, and the holiday is very generally observed with its intended object. In Kansas there are now more than 250,000 acres of artificial forest, and a large number in Nebraska; and the observation of "Arbor Day" promises to be of great eventual benefit to the country.

Sorghum was introduced about 30 years ago, and has been largely cultivated as a syrup-producing plant, though it was only last year that the experiments in Kansas have proved that the manufacture of sugar from sorghum can be carried on as a profitable industry. It has now for a very few years been attracting attention as a forage plant. In the dry West it is said to give a surer and cheaper supply of forage than corn, and is largely cultivated, while the demand for seed, which was formerly thrown away as worthless, is rapidly increasing, especially for the western ranches. It is deep-rooted, stands drought well, and produces more by planting in rows and cultivating it than when sown broadcast. The best variety for forage is found to be the early amber, which ripens 90 days after planting. *Sorghum.*

Some attention is now being paid to silk culture in some parts of this district, especially in Kansas and Wisconsin, and it appears that cocoons can be raised to advantage. The mulberry-tree grows well where the climate is not severe, and in those northern latitudes where the varieties grown for silk culture in Italy and France do not do well the Russian mulberry is found to thrive. The osage orange also, which has, however, the objection of spiky thorns, is generally abundant, and affords good food, though some kinds of worms prefer the mulberry. The experiments made in this culture are likely to be further developed. *Silk culture.*

Denver.

Mr. Vice-Consul Pearce reports as follows:—

Owing to the arid condition of the agricultural lands in Colorado, the successful growth of crops depends almost entirely on the facilities for artificial irrigation. Since meteorological observations have been recorded, the annual rainfall has never exceeded 20 inches, and during some seasons it has fallen as low as 9 inches. For 29 years the average has been less than 15 inches, or one-third of the amount necessary for raising crops in districts depending entirely on the rainfall.

UNITED STATES.

Altitude. The altitude of farming lands in the State ranges from 3,500 feet to 8,000 feet above sea-level. Attempts have recently been made to cultivate that portion of the eastern part of the State closely bordering on Nebraska without the aid of irrigation, and, judging from the increased immigration, and rapid settlement of this part of the State, the success of the enterprise seems to be assured.

Irrigation. The area of irrigated land has increased considerably in the State during 1887, the number of new irrigating ditches (canals) recorded from July 14, 1887, to January 1, 1888, being over 200. The greater number of these new ditches get their supply of water from the Rio Grande, the Grand, and the White Rivers. The area of land which is now under irrigation is estimated at from 1,500,000 to 1,800,000 acres, and out of this about 1,250,000 acres are under cultivation.

The system of irrigating was first introduced in 1859, and its growth has been so rapid that at the present time the total length of irrigating canals is about 3,000 miles, not including lateral ditches.

The total value of the whole of the irrigating system of the State is now estimated to be nearly 3,000,000l.

Soil. The soil of Colorado is found to contain every element of fertility necessary for the growth of all plants adapted to this latitude, and suitable in a remarkable degree to the growth of grain, grasses, and vegetables, as well as standard and small fruits, also forest trees of all kinds.

Cost of irrigation. The expense of irrigation is from 4s. to 12s. per acre annually, and this charge is not considered excessive when the many advantages are considered and the certainty of large average crops. The application of water to the crops when it is most needed results in the seed being of a much better quality, grass and forage much more nutritive, fruits and vegetables much superior in size, yield, and flavour.

Cereals. In the case of wheat, oats, barley, and rye the soil, aided by irrigation, is better adapted to the growth and habits of these cereals than is usually found in rainy districts. The grain is much heavier, of better quality, and more prolific; so improved do they become as to be very superior to the seed of other localities. The dry climate has a tendency to make all white grain whiter, and all coloured seed much more defined in colour and texture. All the cereals except rice grow and mature most successfully, the average production being in all cases larger than reported from districts where they are grown under different conditions.

Wheat. The cost of producing wheat is about 2l. 10s. per acre. This includes sowing, irrigating, harvesting, and preparing for market.

Many farms are so conveniently situated as regards water that crops can be produced for one-half the above amount per acre.

The largest yields recorded in the State are 48, 54, 66, and even 70 bushels per acre; and by experimental work, under the most favourable circumstances, 90 bushels per acre have been produced. Taking an average, however, throughout the State, the yield in 1886 was 23 bushels and in 1887 27·5 bushels per acre.

Oats. Oats yield more per acre, and weigh from 40 to 50 lbs. per bushel. The dry climate and strong mineral soil, and the timely application of water to the crops, have a tendency to increase the weight of all grain and at the same time improve its quality.

Barley and rye. The same may be said of barley and rye; the grain is nearly double the size of the original seed, and the common winter rye becomes in many instances a perennial, producing crop after crop from the same roots.

Unlike the smaller grains, the growth of corn for some years was not a success—mainly on account of climatic influences, the result of cold nights and high altitude. But for the past three or four years certain varieties have been so improved that in nearly all portions of the State they are as successfully grown as elsewhere, producing 35, 40, and even 60 bushels per acre, and the fodder is of a superior quality. The cost of producing corn varies; the average throughout the State is about 2*l.* 6*s.* per acre, and if it be harvested with a view of saving the fodder the latter will cover the cost of cultivation. *Corn (maize).*

The grasses, both tame and wild, are, of all the products, the most important. All the tame species grow successfully, making large returns of nutritive hay, as is shown, not only by analysis, but by feeding. The analyses show the valuable albuminoids to be nearly double those of the same grasses raised in rainy sections, hence in stock-feeding it takes less to fatten stock. Over 200 different species of wild grasses are known in the State, many of which are valuable for hay and pasture. The gramma (*Bontelona oligostachya*), the buffalo (*Buchloë dactyloides*), and the blue stem (*Agropyrum glaucum*) constitute from 75 to 90 per cent. of the entire grass product upon which the range stock subsist. *Grasses.*

The comparative analyses of these grasses show their nutritive value to be superior to all others, and certainly the condition of the stock that feeds upon them verifies the analyses. When domesticated by cultivation and irrigation, these grasses lose much of their nutriment and value as pasture and hay.

The clovers are among the best and most reliable forage plants. They are well adapted to the soil and climate, as is clearly proven by the amount and value of the hay they produce. The common red clover makes three crops of hay annually; the second and third cuttings make as good hay as the first. It also makes two crops of seed a year by the careful management of the application of water. In July the first crop for seed is cut, making five and six bushels per acre, and in October the second crop produces 1½ to 2 bushels more. Thus far clover has not suffered from any disease as in other States. *Clovers.*

Alfalfa is the king of all clovers and forage plants in this arid region. It is a favourite food for all kinds of stock. Its growth with water is rapid and abundant. When once the plant is established, it tenaciously defies all efforts to eradicate it; ploughing it up and turning it over make it grow and produce better. Three or four crops are cut a year, averaging 1½ tons per cutting per acre. In some portions of the State it is cut every month from June to October. The value of alfalfa in stack on the ranches ranges from 26*s.* to 36*s.* per ton; the average is probably 30*s.* to 32*s.* per ton. *Alfalfa.*

When wheat, oats, or barley are sown upon its sod a large average crop is made, and the alfalfa itself grows with the grain, making excellent hay, and yielding sometimes 100 lbs. of seed per acre besides.

The soil is most admirably adapted to the cultivation of tobacco, for four years it has been grown experimentally with great success. The quality is pronounced to be equal to that of any grown in this country, and the yield is fully equal to that of any other State. *Tobacco.*

Flax ranks high in quality and quantity, the common kind producing from 21 to 26 bushels of seed per acre, and the large seeded European flax 35 to 40 bushels per acre. *Flax.*

Other products, such as buckwheat, millet, lupins, lentils, broom corn, hops, and all the vegetables, under the system of irrigation in use in Colorado, succeed in producing full crops every year. *Other plants.*

UNITED STATES.

It is very difficult to obtain any reliable data concerning the yield of agricultural products in Colorado.

Some idea of the progress of agricultural interests may be gathered from a comparison of the yield of certain crops for the years 1883 and 1886, as given by the President of the State Agricultural College.

The returns for 1887 are not yet published.

		1883.	1886.
Wheat	Bushels	1,750,000	2,200,000
Oats	,,	1,000,000	1,500,000
Barley	,,	125,000	175,000
Rye	,,	25,000	30,000
Corn	,,	400,000	1,000,000
Potatoes	,,	1,200,000	2,000,000
Small fruits	Quarts	1,225,000	2,800,000
Orchard fruits	Bushels	8,000	40,000
Alfalfa grass	Tons	15,000	150,000
Clover and tame grass	,,	5,000	30,000
Native	,,	100,000	200,000

With all this, Colorado does not produce sufficient agricultural products for its own consumption, and it has to depend largely on neighbouring States for supplies.

LONDON:
Printed for Her Majesty's Stationery Office
By HARRISON AND SONS,
Printers in Ordinary to Her Majesty.
(1125 6 | 88—H & S 456)

FOREIGN OFFICE.
1888.
ANNUAL SERIES.

No. 370.

DIPLOMATIC AND CONSULAR REPORTS ON TRADE AND FINANCE.

UNITED STATES.

REPORT FOR THE YEAR 1887
ON THE
TRADE OF NEW YORK.

REFERENCE TO PREVIOUS REPORT, Annual Series No. 182.

Presented to both Houses of Parliament by Command of Her Majesty,
JUNE, 1888.

LONDON:
PRINTED FOR HER MAJESTY'S STATIONERY OFFICE,
BY HARRISON AND SONS, ST. MARTIN'S LANE,
PRINTERS IN ORDINARY TO HER MAJESTY.

And to be purchased, either directly or through any Bookseller, from
EYRE AND SPOTTISWOODE, EAST HARDING STREET, FLEET STREET, E.C., and
32, ABINGDON STREET, WESTMINSTER, S.W.; or
ADAM AND CHARLES BLACK, 6, NORTH BRIDGE, EDINBURGH; or
HODGES, FIGGIS, & Co., 104, GRAFTON STREET, DUBLIN.

1888.

[C. 5252—147.] *Price Twopence.*

New Series of Reports.

Reports of the Annual Series have been issued from Her Majesty's Diplomatic and Consular Officers at the following places, and may be obtained from the sources indicated on the title-page:—

No.		Price.	No.		Price.
248.	St. Petersburg	2d.	309.	Marseilles	1d.
249.	Algiers	2d.	310.	Baltimore	1d.
250.	Bucharest	1d.	311.	Savannah	1d.
251.	Christiania	2d.	312.	Boston	1d.
252.	Paris	1d.	313.	San Francisco	1d.
253.	Bogota	1d.	314.	Guayaquil	1d.
254.	Salonica	1d.	315.	Santos	1d.
255.	Copenhagen	1d.	316.	Carthagena and Santa Martha	1d.
256.	Jeddah	1d.	317.	San José	1d.
257.	Russia	2d.	318.	Boulogne	1d.
258.	Paris	1d.	319.	Tahiti	1d.
259.	Patras	1d.	320.	Fiume	1d.
260.	Brussels	1d.	321.	Warsaw	1d.
261.	Ichang	1d.	322.	Vera Cruz	2d.
262.	Baltimore	1d.	323.	Rio Grande do Sul	1d.
263.	Taganrog	1d.	324.	Gothenburg	2d.
264.	Oporto	1d.	325.	Philippopolis	1d.
265.	Rio de Janeiro	1d.	326.	Mogador	2d.
266.	Galveston	1d.	327.	Havana	2d.
267.	Tripoli	1d.	328.	La Rochelle	1d.
268.	Galatz	1d.	329.	Corunna	2d.
269.	Varna	1d.	330.	Chicago	2d.
270.	New Orleans	2d.	331.	Foochow	1d.
271.	Cherbourg	1d.	332.	Taiwan	1d.
272.	Suakin	1d.	333.	Loanda	1d.
273.	Brest	1d.	334.	Loanda	1d.
274.	Barcelona	2d.	335.	Noumea	1d.
275.	Barcelona	1d.	336.	Trieste	1d.
276.	Antwerp	1d.	337.	Nice	1d.
277.	Havre	3d.	338.	Bordeaux	1d.
278.	Odessa	1d.	339.	Mogador	1d.
279.	Tokyo	1d.	340.	Wilmington	1d.
280.	Saigon	1d.	341.	Amoy	2d.
281.	Buenos Ayres	1d.	342.	Trebizond	1d.
282.	Taganrog	1d.	343.	Lisbon	1d.
283.	Tamsui	1d.	344.	Java	1d.
284.	Puerto Plata	1d.	345.	Brest	1d.
285.	Wenchow	1d.	346.	Odessa	2d.
286.	Tokyo	1d.	347.	Cavalla	1d.
287.	Lisbon	2d.	348.	Bussorah	1d.
288.	La Rochelle	1d.	349.	Mollendo	1d.
289.	Washington	4d.	350.	Cadiz	5d.
290.	Beyrout	1d.	351.	Cagliari	4d.
291.	Algiers	2d.	352.	Cagliari	1d.
292.	Varna	1d.	353.	Ajaccio	1d.
293.	Algiers	1d.	354.	Copenhagen	1d.
294.	Port Said	1d.	355.	Vienna	1d.
295.	Manila	1d.	356.	San Francisco	1d.
296.	Charleston	1d.	357.	Vera Cruz	1d.
297.	Kiungchow	1d.	358.	Philippopolis	1d.
298.	Pakhoi	1d.	359.	Greytown	1d.
299.	Wuhu	1d.	360.	Tangier	1d.
300.	Boulogne	2d.	361.	Lisbon	1d.
301.	Marseilles	1d.	362.	Chicago	1d.
302.	Bordeaux	2d.	363.	Jerusalem and Jaffa	1d.
303.	Ancona	1d.	364.	Truxillo	1d.
304.	Swatow	1d.	365.	Ningpo	1d.
305.	Ssŭ-ch'uan	1d.	366.	Chefoo	1d.
306.	Antwerp	1d.	367.	Bushire	1d.
307.	Cadiz	1d.	368.	Stockholm	2d.
308.	Genoa	1d.	369.	Santiago	1d.

No. 370.

Reference to previous Report, Annual Series No. 182.

UNITED STATES.

NEW YORK.

Consul-General Booker to the Marquis of Salisbury.

My Lord,   *New York, April* 19, 1888.

I HAVE the honour to transmit herewith my Annual Report upon the Trade of New York, with some information with regard to other parts of my Consular district.

I have, &c.,
(Signed)   WM. LANE BOOKER.

Report on the Trade of New York.

The great improvement in the business of this city in 1886 was continued throughout the past year, and nearly all branches of trade participated in the improvement. The jobbing trade was satisfactory, inasmuch as it was large, with fair profits and smaller losses than usual.

The year was marked by gigantic speculations in wheat and coffee, but the efforts to monopolise these great staples resulted disastrously to those concerned. Exports of wheat and flour were greatly checked in the spring months by the speculation referred to, but, with its collapse in June and July, prices rapidly fell, and the increased shipments during the third quarter of the year fully made up for the previous falling-off. *General report on trade.*

The satisfactory state of business interests is to be traced in a great measure to the construction of over 12,700 miles of railroads, causing an expenditure of over 250,000,000 dollars, a large proportion of which was necessarily disbursed in payments for labour. The consuming demand was also less interrupted by strikes. The unprecedented activity in railroad building is not likely to result in the depression in railroad interests which marked the years succeeding those of 1881 and 1882, in which over 21,000 miles of roads were constructed, as a large proportion of them were built by new companies in parallelling trunk lines, while those of 1887 have been the work of established companies in extending their lines through newly settled parts of the country, chiefly to the west and south-west of the Missouri River; it is probable that some of these may be in advance of any prosperous trade, but, if the lands be capable of supporting a population, it is sure to follow when railroad facilities are offered.

The total bank clearances in New York city in 1887 were a small fraction of 1 per cent. less than in 1886, but this does not represent the volume of trade, as there was a falling-off in 1887 of 1,377,000,000 dollars (284,000,000*l.*) in the stock sales, which, it is calculated, represent bank clearances of 3,442,000,000 dollars (707,000,000*l.*), a decrease of over 23 per cent. on those of 1886, and, deducting the amount representing stock transactions from the total clearances, there is shown an increase of about 17 per cent. to represent trade transactions. The receipts for duties at this port show an increase over 1886 of about 7 per cent.

The earnings of the railroads in 1887 were beyond those of any previous year, but, notwithstanding this, there has been no activity in the stock market. In the early part of the year prices recovered the decline of the close of 1886, but from June to October there was a steady retrograde movement, which was checked in November, and to the end of December the market was upheld, but without animation. Almost all the leading stocks were considerably lower at the close than at the commencement of 1887. The decline was in some degree due to the uncertainty of an Inter-State Commerce Law, which went into effect in April—also to the active demand for money for interior enterprises, and the constant fear of financial pressure.

The demand for money was much more active, and the rates higher, throughout 1887 than in 1886, not so much for stock speculations as for carrying new railroad bonds in the hands of bankers and syndicates, and to meet a large interior demand for railroad building and land and merchandise speculations.

The rates for call loans ranged in the first quarter from 2 to 6 per cent., in the second and third quarters from 3 to 8 per cent., and in the last quarter from 4 to 7 per cent., the demand being more regular.

In August and September there was trouble in borrowing on Railroad Collaterals, except that of first-class, and there was a fear of a tight money market, which was relieved by the Treasury purchasing over 5,000,000*l.* of bonds, and in October by offering to place its surplus with depository banks on government bond security. Up to the end of the year about 10,500,000*l.* had been thus deposited.

First-class commercial paper ranged in the first quarter from $4\frac{1}{2}$ to 6 per cent., in the second from $4\frac{1}{2}$ to $5\frac{1}{2}$ per cent., in the third and fourth from $5\frac{1}{2}$ to $6\frac{1}{2}$ per cent.

Bank returns. The condition of the 63 associated banks of the city at different periods of the year is shown in the following table:—

Associated Banks of New York City.

1887. Week ending	Average amount of				
	Loans and Discount.	Specie.	Legal Tenders.	Net Deposits other than U.S.A.	Circulation.
	£	£	£	£	£
January 8	71,786,750	17,614,894	4,493,300	76,248,600	1,626,750
April 2	75,325,900	16,067,200	4,014,400	76,717,400	1,639,850
July 2	74,891,950	15,097,350	4,559,450	75,618,750	1,711,650
October 1	71,027,850	15,179,800	4,187,700	71,240,150	1,690,250
December 31	73,447,240	14,654,700	5,615,500	74,028,100	1,633,900

The annual Report of the Superintendent of the State Bank Department has just been submitted to the Legislature, and from it I extract the following items:—

NEW YORK.

The resources of the State banks on January 1 were 203,545,350*l*., divided as follows:— Bank resources.

	£
Savings banks	121,634,500
Banks of discount and deposit	39,824,800
Trust companies	41,217,970
Safe deposit companies	868,200

The total shows an increase during five years of 45,307,280*l*.
The following shows the amount of deposits:—

NUMBER of Open Accounts and Average Deposits on January 1, 1888, and January 1, 1887.

	1888.			1887.		
	£	s.	d.	£	s.	d.
Deposits	104,033,656	0	0	64,441,560	0	0
Open accounts	1,325,062	0	0	844,550	0	0
Average deposits	78	7	6	76	6	0

At present the rate of interest is between 3 and 4 per cent. The difference between the amount of resources of the savings banks and of deposits indicates a sound financial condition, but this is represented in a great measure by the excess of the market over the par values of securities held by them. The Report states that half the counties of the State are still without savings banks.

The following gives the rates of bankers' sterling exchange during the year:— Sterling exchange.

	Sixty Days.	Sight.
	Dol. c.	Dol. c.
January, highest	4 84½	4 88
,, lowest	4 80¾	4 84¾
February, highest	4 85½	4 88¾
,, lowest	4 85	4 88¼
March, highest	4 85½	4 88
,, lowest	4 83¼	4 86½
April, highest	4 86¾	4 88½
,, lowest	4 84¾	4 87
May, highest	4 86¾	4 88½
,, lowest	4 85¼	4 87
June, highest	4 85½	4 87
,, lowest	4 83	4 84
July, highest	4 83½	4 85
,, lowest	4 82½	4 83¾
August, highest	4 82	4 84¼
,, lowest	4 80½	4 83¾
September, highest	4 80½	4 86
,, lowest	4 79¾	4 83¾
October, highest	4 81¾	4 86
,, lowest	4 79½	4 83¼
November, highest	4 81¾	4 85¾
,, lowest	4 81¼	4 85¼
December, highest	4 83	4 86½
,, lowest	4 81	4 85

UNITED STATES.

Annex B. Imports generally.

The import returns in Annex B. show an increase in receipts of about 6,000,000*l.* over those of 1886, of which the largest excess is in coffee, which is nearly 3,500,000*l.* The largest decrease is in sugar, which approaches 2,000,000*l.*

The value of imports from Great Britain, excluding specie, varies little from that of 1886.

Annex C. Exports generally.

The export returns in Annex B. are nearly 5,000,000*l.* less than in the previous year, but, excluding specie, they are about 1,000,000*l.* in excess. The decrease in refined sugar, which was considerable in 1886, from a reduction in the drawback allowed by Government on the raw importation, is still more noticeable in the past year's return. The exports of manufactured articles show no important variations.

Dry Goods Trade.

Dry goods: Cottons.

The demand for cotton fabrics was active at an average advance of fully 10 per cent. The mills were worked nearly to their full capacity, and the market has not been so clear of stock for many years. The uncertainty as to the working of the Inter-State Act stimulated the trade in the early part of the year, but the enquiry continued active and regular throughout.

The importations varied little from those of 1886, and the quantity thrown on the market by entries for consumption and withdrawals from bonded warehouse was a little less.

Woollen trade.

The woollen trade has been as inactive and irregular as the cotton was the contrary. The imports were nearly 5 per cent., and the quantity thrown on the market 8 per cent. in excess of those of 1886; the stocks were not, however, large, many of the mills having greatly reduced their output, but in face of this prices were unsatisfactory.

There is nothing special to note in regard to the trade in British goods.

Grain shipments.

The following table shows the total grain shipments by steam and sail from this port to Great Britain and the Continent in 1887, the number of vessels, and their nationality.

Under Steam.

Nationality.	No. of Vessels loaded.	Bushels.
American	5	249,576
British	705	32,962,609
Belgian	78	5,263,129
Danish	25	797,971
Dutch	45	1,768,165
French	58	3,064,025
German	140	3,614,574
Italian	25	1,560,878
Portuguese	2	127,809
Spanish	16	990,841
Swedish and Norwegian	8	361,999
Total	1,107	50,761,576

NEW YORK.

UNDER SAIL.

Nationality.	No. of Vessels loaded.	Bushels.
American	1	34,400
Austrian	16	489,584
Brazilian	1	45,000
British..	3	129,006
Danish..	2	15,305
German	4	113,014
Italian..	24	676,935
Portuguese	18	398,242
Spanish	1	8,000
Swedish and Norwegian	4	83,435
Total	74	1,992,921

The number of sailing vessels engaged in the trade is diminishing year by year: in 1880, when there was not an exceptionally large quantity of grain exported, 1,879 sailing vessels were engaged in carrying it to Europe.

Canals. The New York canals were open for 208 days, six days less than in 1886, but the Report of the Superintendent shows that 5,553,805 tons (2,000 lbs.) passed through, against 5,293,982 tons in 1886. Of the 5,553,805 tons, 3,986,767 tons went east, of the value of 60,075,597 dollars (12,375,572l.), and consisted chiefly of the following merchandise:—

Wheat	30,471,478 bushels.
Maize	15,645,306 ,,
Oats	2,076,710 ,,
Barley	887,792 ,,
Timber	56,282,916 feet.
Flax-seed	71,899,452 lbs.
Pig-iron	2,292 tons.

Freights were lower than in 1886, averaging about 4·5 cents per bushel, equal to about 7s. per ton of 2,240 lbs. Freights on wheat by lake from Chicago to Buffalo averaged a little over 4 c. per bushel, equal to about 6s. 4d. a ton.

The rates of transportation by the railroads of the State were well maintained throughout the year. The through rates, when the canals were open, from Chicago to New York, were 25 c. for grain and 30 c. for provisions per 100 lbs., equal to 22s. 6d. at 27s. per ton of 2,240 lbs.; after the canals closed, the rates were advanced to 27½ and 32½ c. per 100 lbs. 2,914,266 tons (2,000 lbs.) were sent eastward from Buffalo, Pittsburg, &c., to New York, and 1,333,290 tons arrived at those points from New York in the year. The railroads which this merchandise passed over were the—

New York Central and Hudson River Railroad.
New York, Lake Erie, and Western Railroad.
Pennsylvania Railroad.
Baltimore and Ohio Railroad.
West Shore Railroad.
Delaware, Lackawanna, and Western Railroad

UNITED STATES.

Railroad bridge at Poughkeepsie. The bridge in course of construction at Poughkeepsie, about midway between this city and Albany, referred to in my last Annual Report, will, it is expected, be completed by the end of the year, but complaints are made that the cantilever spans are not high enough above the water to admit of the passage of the largest vessels navigating the Hudson River. The completion of this bridge will change the course of the railroad traffic between the South and the New England States, as at present there is no bridge crossing the river.

CITY TRAFFIC.

City traffic. The question is now under consideration and discussion as to the best mode of increasing transit facilities through the city. The surface and elevated road cars are insufficient for present travel, and with the increasing population it becomes a necessity to make further provision both as to the accommodation and rapid transit of passengers. Business is pushing its way into the present residential quarters, and must, before long, force residents further north.

The Island of Manhattan, on which the city is situated, but the limits of which now extend far beyond the Harlem River, the northern boundary of the island, is so shaped that in the near future the residential part will be from five to ten miles distant from the commercial quarter, rendering a rapid mode of communication very essential. The Mayor of the city, a man of unusual energy and foresight, has had the matter under consideration, and looks upon the underground system as the only one feasible.

LABOUR.

Labour. The full Report for 1887 of the Labour Commission for this State has not yet been published, but a summary has been given to me in advance. From it I gather the following statistical information:—

		1886.	1887.
As to strikes.	Number of establishments affected by strikes	2,061	1,604
	Number of trades and callings affected by strikes	137	144
	Results of strikes—		
	Successful	751	694
	Compromised, or partly successful	426	190
	Doubtful	212	3
	Unsuccessful	524	695
	Pending	147	22
	Number of persons engaged in strikes	127,392	51,731
	Do. engaged in threatened strikes		1,005
	Do. refused work after strike	6,391	8,176
	Loss of wages as result of strike	$2,552,554	$2,013,229
	Amount expended by labour organisations for the relief of members and the conduct of strike	$329,080	$217,070
	Number of establishments closed during strikes	572	708
	Number of women and girls engaged in strikes	29,361	5,015
	Number of threatened strikes	57	71
	Number of persons engaged in sympathetic strikes	10,905	5,220
	Number of firms discriminating against labour organisations	152	171
	Number of boycotts	163	242
	Breaches of the peace and arrests	371	48
	Mode of settlement of strikes—		
	Arbitration	11	6
	Conciliation	249	21
	Do. with employés	81	121
	Do. with labour organisations	832	667
	No formal settlement	20	52
	Abandoned	430	696

NEW YORK.

The causes of the strikes, as returned by answers to the questions sent out by the Bureau, were as follows:—

Abolition of piecework	2
Change of pay-day	3
Discharge of union men	11
„ of employés	5
„ of foremen	2
Employment of non-union men	113
Equalisation of wages	3
Increase of hours	9
„ of wages	469
„ of wages, and abolition of payment in saloons	42
„ of wages, and reduction of hours	55
„ of wages, and union rules	41
„ of wages, &c.	15
Miscellaneous	33
Non-payment of wages	12
Number of apprentices	100
Objectionable employés	2
Obnoxious fines	6
Obnoxious foreman	7
Obnoxious rules	15
Opposed to contract system	2
Opposed to Saturday night-work	2
Opposed to use of wheelbarrows	2
Reduction of hours	158
Reduction of wages	20
Refusal to handle boycotted coal	59
„ „ coal and freight	34
„ „ boycotted freight	25
„ „ „ patterns	18
„ „ non-union material	3
„ to recognise Knights of Labour	12
„ „ Knights of Labour rules	9
„ „ union rules	89
„ „ „ relative to hours of labour	29
Rival labour organisations	8
Saturday half-holiday	28
To assist other trades	148
Use of machinery	4

Board of Arbitration. The State Board of Arbitration, which is vested with powers of original jurisdiction under an amended Act of March, 1887, has made its report to the Legislature, but, like the Labour report, I have it only in an incomplete form.

The Commissioners state that the number of labour difficulties in 1887 legitimately coming under the head of grievances and disputes, and susceptible of settlement by mediation or arbitration, was much smaller than in 1886. In many cases where trouble arose it was settled by the parties themselves without formal intervention by the Board, thus avoiding investigation and publicity. The marked and distinguishing feature of division in the field of industry in the State the past year has not been in disagreement as to wages alone, or to other ordinary considerations and conditions, as between an individual employer and his employés, but has been on a well-marked and clearly defined line of principle, presenting the question whether employers should respectively control and direct their several manufactories and enterprises without interference and dictation from any outside quarter, or whether employés, combined in organisation of trades of a common nature or of all natures, should exercise a power of control and direction over the labour in such manufactories and enterprises.

Two cases that came before the Commissioners are quoted as

showing the difference between contention for redress of a legitimate labour grievance and contention for power to control. One was a strike of printers employed in the job and book trade, who were members of Typographical Union No. 6, in New York, and the other the lockout of the chandelier manufacturers of New York and Brooklyn.

The Printers' Union presented to the employers a scale of wages and other matters peculiar to the trade, and also the proposition that all offices in that branch of the trade must be made "card offices"; that is, the employers were required to agree that they would employ no one who could not present a card showing that he was a member of Typographical Union No. 6. The employing printers, who were also united in organisation, conceded all that the scale called for, except the "card office" proposition. That they refused to subscribe to, but offered to leave to the Board the question whether it was right and proper that they should do so or not. The president of the union and the strike committee declined the offer upon the ground that there was no ordinary labour grievance or dispute to settle. There was, they said, "nothing to arbitrate." Their proposition of a "card office" involved a principle of control of and limitation upon labour which they could not yield to the judgment of anyone, under any circumstances. The issue, thus made up, must be fought out to the end of the superior endurance of one or the other of the parties. It was so fought out, and the "card office" proposition was defeated in all establishments where strikes occurred, with few exceptions.

The chandelier manufacturers had united in a lock-out of their employés in consequence of disagreements, among which a Saturday half-holiday figured most conspicuously. A half-holiday on Saturday had been conceded to the employés, and the manufacturers had resolved to discontinue it upon the ground that it left them at a disadvantage with competitors in neighbouring cities in other States where work was continued six days in a week. In this case it was the employés who were willing to submit the matter involved to arbitration by the Board, and the employers who would not, because, like the printers, they considered that there was a principle involved, and they were not willing to leave it to the judgment and decision of anyone. Sooner than do so, or yield, they said they would close their factories in New York and Brooklyn and go out of business, or go elsewhere. It was a contest of endurance, and the result was that the employers won.

The report states that the Board has been called upon to adjust difficulties in a number of factories and workshops throughout the State.

In one case the strike took place on the 30th of April, and it was not until the 23rd of June that the Board was informed of the fact. For the most part these disturbances of the relations of employer and employé were during the early portion of the year, at a time when the Board was not vested with power of intervention unless called upon by the parties in principal interest. Since June 1st, however, the counsel and advice of the Board have been sought in many instances by both employer and employé, and with few exceptions settlements have been made without resort to strike or lock-out. It is the experience of the past year that when either side submits a proposition to the other, and it is arbitrarily repelled, a strike or lock-out invariably follows; the industry is brought to a stand-still; offers of meditation are rejected; and, after a test of endurance, the side that has shown the greatest strength insists upon the unconditional surrender of the side that has proven weakest. Whereas, if before breaking entirely apart, both sides had tried the virtue of mediation by the Board, injury to trade and loss to labour might have been averted, and a more friendly feeling established between employer and employé. The party vanquished in a prolonged strike or lock-out, as a rule, devote their time and energy to securing and fortifying a position for a renewal of the struggle at the first favourable opportunity, thereby maintaining unfriendly feeling and keeping up continual warfare. It is to the interest of employers to see to it that the grievances of employés, whether real or fancied, receive due attention and consideration, and, if adjudged to be without cause, that the complainants be advised accordingly in a friendly spirit and manner. It is to the interest of employés, on the other hand, to calmly and fully consider the answer of employers before going to the extreme of last resort in a strike. Hasty and inconsiderate action is unwise. Time and reflection, with continued negotiation between employer and employé, will bring better results. If this course be pursued, the number of strikes during the coming year will be comparatively few.

The settlement of labour disputes through voluntary arbitration by the appointment of standing committees, representative of employers on the one side and of employés on the other, in each branch of industry, the powers and duties of such committees being defined, and stated meetings being appointed for the consideration and redress of grievances that may arise on one side or the other, is a system that is attaining perceptible growth throughout the State, and one worthy of every encouragement. It is a step in the right direction.

The Factory Inspection Law of New York was amended in May last in regard to the employment of women and children in manufacturing establishments. The amended Act reads :— *Factory Law.*

Section 1.—No minor under the age of eighteen years nor any woman under twenty-one years shall be employed at labour in any manufacturing establishment in this State for a longer period than sixty hours in any one week, unless for the purpose of making necessary repairs.

Section 2.—No child under thirteen years of age shall be employed in any manufacturing establishment within this State. It shall be the duty of every person so employing children to keep a register in which shall be recorded the name, birthplace, age, and place of residence of every person so employed by him under the age of sixteen years. And it shall be unlawful for any manufacturing establishment to hire or employ any child under the age of sixteen years without there is first provided and placed on file an affidavit made by the parent or guardian stating the age, date, and place of birth of said child; if said child have no parent or guardian, then such affidavit shall be made by the child, which affidavit shall be kept on file by the employer, and which said register and affidavit shall be produced for inspection on demand made by the inspector, assistant inspector, or any of the deputies appointed under this Act. (*As amended by Chapter* 462, *Laws of* 1887.)

Section 3.—Every person, firm, or corporation employing women under twenty-one years, or minors under eighteen years of age, in any manufacturing establishment, shall post and keep posted in a conspicuous place in every room where such help is employed a printed notice stating the number of hours per day for each day of the week required of such persons, and in every room where children under sixteen years of age are employed a list of their names, with their age.

UNITED STATES.

Section 4.—Any person who knowingly violates or omits to comply with any of the foregoing provisions of this Act, or who knowingly employs or suffers or permits any child to be employed in violation of its provisions, shall, on conviction, be punished by a fine of not less than 50 dol. nor more than 100 dol., and, in default of payment of such fine, by imprisonment for not less than 30 nor more than 90 days.

Section 5.—No person or corporation employing less than five persons or children, excepting in any of the cities of this State, shall be deemed a manufacturing establishment within the meaning of this Act.

Strikes.

"Bradstreet," a reliable authority, reports the strikes as much less numerous in 1887 than in 1886, and gives the following as occurring in my district—New York, New Jersey, Connecticut, Rhode Island, and Delaware—in which more than 1,000 employés were involved:—

Carpet makers	New York City	2,400	successful.
Rubber Works	Preston, Rhode Island	1,500	,,
Coal handlers	Jersey City	3,000	unsuccessful.
Tobacco workers	,, ,,	3,500	,,
Longshoremen	New York, Brooklyn, and Jersey City	15,500	,,
Boatmen	New York, Brooklyn, and Jersey City	1,000	,,
Grain handlers	New York, Brooklyn, and Jersey City	5,000	,,
Coal handlers	New York, Brooklyn, and Jersey City	2,000	,,
Grain ceilers	New York, Brooklyn, and Jersey City	6,000	,,
Freight handlers	Jersey City	1,200	,,
Carpet factory	New York City	2,400	,,
Silk dyers	Paterson, New Jersey	1,600	,,
Cotton-mill hands	Cohoes, New York	4,000	,,
Brass workers	New York and Brooklyn	3,000	,,
Reading Railroad Company	New Jersey	6,000	,,

The total number of strikers is given as 62,656 in New York State and 27,508 in New Jersey. There has been no material change in wages in any of the States of my district during the year.

Labour statistics of the State of Connecticut.

The Commissioner of the Labour Bureau of Connecticut states in his Report, in connection with the law requiring weekly payments of wages, and the 10-hour law for women and children, that there has been a spirit shown on the part of some employers which, while it did not directly threaten the employés with discharge, was understood by them to indicate that discharge would follow an attempt on their part to avail themselves of their legal privileges, and the Commissioner believes that the weekly payment law is generally observed by Corporations and a large proportion of private employers, but that the 10-hour law for women and children has been very frequently disregarded, and states that complaints have frequently come to the Bureau from employers as well as employés, the former because their conscientious scruples would not permit them to violate a law of the State, while their observance of the law placed them at a disadvantage with competitors who disregarded the law.

New Jersey Act limiting hours of labour.

The Legislature of New Jersey, at their last Session, passed an Act limiting the labour on all cable traction and horse-car street surface railroads, and all cable traction and steam elevated railroads owned and operated by Corporations incorporated under the laws of the State, to 12 hours per day.

The law prohibiting the immigration of aliens under contract to perform labour in the United States is strictly enforced against those arriving at this port.

IMMIGRATION.

There were 362,853 immigrants landed at this port in 1887, and they were of the following nationalities:—

England	45,746	Roumania	834
Scotland	14,864	Greece	612
Ireland	56,860	Luxemburgh	572
Wales	5,449	Spain	485
Canada	734	West Indies (not British)	466
British East Indies	11	Syria	175
Australasia	47	Turkey	169
Malta	298	Burmah	170
South Africa	11	Armenia	161
Italy	44,274	Iceland	158
Sweden	37,862	Mexico	151
Norway	13,011	South America (not specified)	144
Germany	81,864	Central America (not specified)	131
Russia	33,203	Portugal	75
Hungary	17,719	China	64
Austria	11,762	Arabia	22
Denmark	8,375	Japan	13
Bohemia	6,449	Brazil	9
France	5,999	India (not British)	9
Netherlands	5,500	Africa " "	11
Switzerland	4,537	Hawaiian Islands	4
Finland	4,031	Peru	1
Belgium	2,362		

The Commissioners of Emigration have heretofore exercised the right to determine what immigrants are not entitled to land under the Act to regulate immigration, viz., "convicts, lunatics, idiots, and persons unable to take care of themselves without becoming a public charge," but, under a decision in August last of the United States' Secretary of the Treasury, they are to report the cases to the Collector of the Port, who has the final decision and the power to return immigrants to the country from whence they came.

PRISONS.

The State prisons have for several years been self-supporting, but under a change in the system of employing the prisoners there was in 1887 a deficiency.

Prisoners have been employed under contracts with outside parties, but as the contracts have expired they have been set to work on State account, and with regard to this the Superintendent of State Prisons, in his Annual Report to the Legislature, states:—

"The deficiency in the last year is the greatest since 1878. It reflects the great disturbances of the year which have been mentioned elsewhere. Yet comparison of its salient features contains the promise of a much better result in the coming year, unless new disorganisations and demoralisations shall be forced upon the prisons. The statement shows the progressive movement in the transformation which new legislation required to be made. An extensive expiration of contracts occurred in Auburn the previous year, and the deficit in that prison was more than 80,000 dollars. In the last year new industries had become settled at Auburn, and the prisoners were more fully employed during the year; in consequence, the deficiency in Auburn falls to less than 54,000 dollars. Auburn passed its turning-point in 1886.

"But in that year Sing Sing Prison was engaged in work all the year, and carried a surplus of 75,000 dollars. In the last year, however, the contracts in Sing Sing expired, and it went rapidly through the same experience that Auburn did in the year before. In consequence, the surplus of the prison fell from 75,000 dol. to less than 19,000 dol., a loss of 56,000 dol., or nearly the entire deficit of the prisons during the year. There is now the prospect that Sing Sing will follow the example in the coming year of Auburn, and make a large gain in its earnings and in its surplus over the past year, and it may be remarked here that the earnings for the last year would have been 6,000 dol. larger in Sing Sing but for the unavoidable loss of time and productive work which was caused by the fire in the laundry building."

The earnings and expenditure of the three State prisons during the year 1887 were as follows:—

	£
Sing Sing, earnings	47,420
,, expenditure	42,500
Auburn, earnings	16,960
,, expenditure	35,390
Clinton, earnings	17,765
,, expenditure	24,310

The Superintendent, in connection with the employment of prisoners, adds that the controlling question has not been what would pay the best, but what would be most useful to the convicts and would produce the least competition with free labour.

The proportion of State convicts to the general population is less than it was ten years ago. In 1877 there was one prisoner in the State prisons to every 1,359 persons, whereas in 1887 there was one to every 1,669 persons in the State.

The prisoners numbered 3,296 on the 30th September last (end of the fiscal year), and were divided amongst the prisons as follows:—

Sing Sing prison	1,425
Auburn ,,	1,111
Clinton ,,	760

NEW YORK STATE FINANCES.

New York State Finances.

At the close of the fiscal year (September 30) the total funded debt of the State was 1,558,935*l*., classified as follows:—

	£
Indian annuities	25,275
Canal debt	1,368,728
Niagara reservation fund	164,800
	1,558,803
Aggregate sinking fund	836,605
Total debt unprovided for	722,198

NEW YORK.

The above favourable exhibit shows that the State is practically out of debt. The debt was last year reduced 352,040*l*. The tax rate for the current fiscal year is $2\frac{7}{10}$ mill, which on the present assessed valuation will yield 1,869,460*l*.

NEW YORK CITY FINANCES.

The total funded debt of the city of New York on January 1, 1888, amounted to 26,423,366*l*., against which there is a sinking fund on hand of 8,141,508*l*.

Valuation and tax rates for the past five years are given in the following table:—

Year.	Real estate.	Personal.	City tax.
	£	£	Per cent.
1887	258,425,300	52,148,655	2·16
1886	248,011,860	44,707,606	2·29
1885	240,699,285	41,750,816	2·40
1884	230,670,888	45,018,570	2·25
1883	222,300,918	40,694,578	2·29

VITAL STATISTICS, NEW YORK CITY. 1887.

The vital statistics of the past year show that there were over 1,500 more deaths than in 1886. The contagious diseases, such as small-pox, scarlet fever, diphtheria, and croup, have furnished the principal part of the increase. There was an increase of 300 deaths by diarrhœal diseases, occurring for the most part during the summer.

Vital Statistics, New York City.

	1887.	1886.
Births	33,971	31,319
Marriages	14,710	12,216
Deaths	38,949	37,351

The causes of deaths in 1887 were as follows:—

Small-pox	100
Measles	760
Scarlatina	597
Diphtheria	2,143
Croup	888
Whooping cough	180
Typhus fever	..
Typhoid „	318
Cerebro-spinal fever	246
Malarial fevers	230
Diarrhœal diseases, under 5 years of age	3,267
„ „ all ages	3,769
Cancer	813
Bronchitis	1,810
Pneumonia	3,662
Heart disease	2,006
Bright's disease	2,355
Suicide	238
Deaths of persons 70 years and over	2,458
Deaths of children under 1 year	10,003
„ under 2 years	13,197
„ under 5 years	16,617

UNITED STATES.

Annex A.—Return of all Shipping at the Port of New York in the Year 1887.

Entered.

Nationality.	Sailing. Number of Vessels.	Sailing. Tons.	Steam. Number of Vessels.	Steam. Tons.	Total. Number of Vessels.	Total. Tons.
Great Britain	1,411	741,972	1,353	2,333,848	2,764	3,075,820
United States	1,344	583,037	265	406,947	1,609	989,984
Germany	197	188,204	255	604,490	452	792,694
France	6	2,449	101	330,990	107	333,439
Norway and Sweden	284	189,508	117	56,082	401	245,590
Belgium	2	1,803	87	248,156	89	249,959
Italy	181	107,997	26	50,649	207	158,646
Mexico	3	430	...	...	3	430
Netherlands	17	7,583	53	112,786	70	120,369
Austria	47	20,320	...	...	47	20,320
Spain	22	6,390	74	95,573	96	101,963
Denmark	8	1,695	28	58,818	36	55,513
Other European countries	32	16,410	2	2,224	34	18,634
South America	2	705	...	...	2	705
Central America	9	1,827	...	...	9	1,827
Other countries	2	503	...	...	2	503
Totals	3,567	1,870,833	2,361	4,295,563	5,928	6,166,396
„ for preceding year	3,756	1,802,307	2,251	4,047,157	6,007	5,849,464

Cleared.

Nationality.	Sailing. Number of Vessels.	Sailing. Tons.	Steam. Number of Vessels.	Steam. Tons.	Total. Number of Vessels.	Total. Tons.
Great Britain	1,441	757,748	1,345	2,320,049	2,786	3,077,797
United States	883	383,052	250	383,912	1,133	766,964
Germany	191	182,472	240	568,938	431	751,410
France	8	3,266	100	327,712	108	330,978
Norway and Sweden	275	183,503	112	53,697	387	237,200
Belgium	3	2,705	86	245,304	89	248,009
Italy	180	107,401	26	50,649	206	158,050
Mexico	5	717	...	...	5	717
Netherlands	13	5,799	53	112,786	66	118,585
Austria	49	21,185	...	...	49	21,185
Spain	26	7,552	68	87,824	94	95,376
Denmark	6	1,271	27	51,896	33	53,167
Other European countries	30	15,385	2	2,224	32	17,609
South America	4	1,409	...	...	4	1,409
Central America	3	609	...	...	3	609
Other countries	5	1,258	...	...	5	1,258
Totals	3,122	1,675,332	2,309	4,204,991	5,431	5,880,323
„ for preceding year	3,259	1,733,501	2,231	4,020,054	5,490	5,753,555

NEW YORK.

Annex B.—Return of Principal Articles of Import to New York during the Years 1887-86.

Articles.		1887. Quantity.	1887. Value.	1886. Quantity.	1886. Value.
			£		£
Cocoa	Bags	73,196	329,095	74,596	299,891
Coffee	,,	2,844,466	10,643,992	...	7,155,173
China, glass, and earthenware	...	...	1,780,310	...	1,591,779
Cotton	Bales	5,329	99,063	8,420	89,915
Dry goods—					
Manufactures of cotton	...	...	4,626,968	...	4,668,728
,, ,, Flax	...	...	3,222,050	...	3,183,793
,, ,, Silk	...	...	7,739,556	...	7,142,501
,, ,, Wool	...	...	6,762,412	...	6,428,724
,, ,, Miscellaneous	...	...	2,599,040	...	2,362,168
Fancy goods	...	...	187,530	...	179,770
Furs	Packages	...	1,152,675	23,305	1,105,667
Fruits	...	...	3,636,920	...	2,940,232
Hair	...	...	366,845	...	372,474
Hemp	Bales	373,768	1,453,386	...	994,870
Hides, dressed	No.	...	836,339	7,424	969,116
,, undressed	,,	...	3,144,795	19,449,213	4,011,446
Hops	Bales	17,964	224,545	...	488,848
India-rubber	...	...	2,646,710	...	2,642,811
Jewellery, watches, and precious stones	...	...	2,477,572	...	2,082,797
Jute and jute butts	...	...	393,094	...	456,831
Linseed	Packages	56,996	116,995	83,219	56,356
Molasses	...	...	361,602	...	278,341
Paper stock	...	...	555,210	...	446,960
Metals—					
Cutlery	...	...	380,435	...	330,383
Iron, pig	Tons	128,752	341,895	95,816	222,490
,, spiegel	,,	117,399	514,543	102,124	471,949
,, other	...	...	910,646	...	446,430
Metal goods	...	...	369,500	...	322,990
Steel	...	...	1,241,236	...	849,380
Tin plates	Boxes	2,052,539	1,603,695	2,099,876	1,613,376
,, slabs	Tons	11,964	1,304,298	12,240	1,256,927
Soda, ash	...	...	211,706	...	290,946
,, caustic	...	...	161,160	...	167,094
Spices	...	...	591,730	...	510,373
Stationery and books	...	...	1,004,830	...	922,655
Sugar	Tons	786,823	8,536,698	849,870	10,335,201
Specie and bullion	...	...	8,359,291	...	7,991,090
Tea	Packages	1,225,815	2,132,264	1,367,920	2,412,010
Tobacco and cigars	...	...	1,937,858	...	1,635,110
Wines, spirits, &c.	...	...	1,807,330	...	1,741,390
Wood	...	...	1,396,320	...	1,307,026
Wool	Lbs.	44,880,077	1,106,538	63,607,927	1,595,520
Other articles	...	...	14,994,304	...	13,736,884
Total		...	104,262,981	...	98,108,315

UNITED STATES.

Return of Principal Articles of Export from New York during the Years 1887 and 1886.

Articles.		1887. Quantity.	1887. Value.	1886. Quantity.	1886. Value.
			£		£
Agricultural implements	...	...	459,800	...	397,142
Bacon and hams	Lbs.	234,971,670	4,164,560	259,300,838	4,196,542
Beef, fresh	,,	46,269,995	861,823	52,541,703	1,032,421
,, canned	,,	20,956,643	354,410	23,234,590	380,080
Butter	,,	9,625,891	343,536	11,904,885	359,228
Cattle, live	Number	33,362	661,980	53,117	975,466
Cotton, domestic	Packages	...	2,408,447	207.285	2,317,906
,, raw	Bales	828,665	8,071,365	939,369	8,820,886
Cheese	Lbs.	75,289,602	1,563,077	74,524,037	1,343,595
Flour	Barrels	4,431,010	3,860,194	3,466,840	3,046,846
Hops	Lbs.	4,359,607	176,913	...	...
Indian corn	Bushels (56 lbs.)	12,347,567	1,081,770	20,504,141	2,104,676
Lard	Lbs.	198,224,165	4,002,278	250,334,625	3,482,870
Oilcake and meal	,,	227,130,883	595,269	...	789,385
Oleomargarine	,,	43,711,480	898,446	35,279,363	741,630
Pork and beef, salt	,,	64,990,060	861,943	59,354,315	724,699
Petroleum, refined	Gallons	329,489,258	5,225,280	341,665,783	5,708,513
,, crude	,,	42,216,556	569,432	42,127,133	598,975
,, lubricating	,,	19,546,375	706,030	13,160,266	254,249
Sewing machines	...	...	404,687	...	411,310
Sugar	Lbs.	95,846,967	1,152,780	162,659,280	2,138,431
Specie and bullion	...	...	4,016,814	...	9,837,013
Tallow	Lbs.	43,482.750	386,777	25,024,416	248,570
Wheat	Bushels (60 lbs.)	41,071,750	7,739,716	31,267,839	5,770,904
Other articles	...	...	18,015,037	...	17,621,945
Total	...	...	68,582,364	...	73,303,282

Annex C.—TABLE showing the Total Value of all Articles Exported from and Imported to New York from and to Foreign Countries during the Years 1887 and 1886.

Country.	Exports. 1887.	Exports. 1886.	Imports. 1887.	Imports. 1886.
	£	£	£	£
Great Britain	28,969,595	29,739,216	21,075,220	20,944,192
British Possessions	4,999,235	4,414,691	6,159,300	6,209,516
Germany	5,685,360	6,004,875	13,151,025	13,147,638
France and Possessions	4,087,015	3,781,752	12,570,720	11,266,408
Belgium	3,372,165	3,196,287	1,255,590	1,248,767
Spain and Possessions	3,392,785	3,003,798	8,222,770	8,817,506
Netherlands and Possessions	2,835,845	2,761,568	2,886,475	2,136,778
United States of Columbia	993,255	965,720	741,700	809,553
Central American States	432,235	300,855	871,920	610,514
Italy	1,300,165	1,168,905	3,092,895	2,896,677
Brazil	839,825	924,495	10,134,395	7,309,586
China	1,031,440	1,227,350	2,295,710	2,489,152
Denmark	746,625	698,467	135,895	110,102
Venezuela	633,215	542,215	2,030,065	1,534,612
Portugal	770,945	750,725	259,350	298,908
Argentine Republic	980,335	857,015	423,070	306,558
Mexico	686,925	533,764	1,664,150	1,138,756
Hayti	759,705	491,866	293,950	374,946
Sweden and Norway	519,400	467,085	440,975	328,725
Japan	372,810	268,167	1,070,285	867,136
Chili	318,765	247,363	329,585	232,153
St. Domingo	195,515	198,025	262,650	296,648
Uruguay	218,690	223,982	393,060	708,987
Austria	37,520	25,692	1,701,420	1,319,473
Russia	104,960	64,158	535,165	687,093
Peru	131,215	..	47,735	..
Switzerland	7,680	10,262	2,597,985	2,738,965
Other countries	137,325	606,827	1,260,630	1,487,976
Total	64,565,550	63,475,125	95,903,690	90,117,225

UNITED STATES.

The Tables do not include specie, of which there was exported in 1887 and 1886 to—

	1887.	1886.
	£	£
Great Britain	2,232,849	4,422,611
France	196,281	2,501,570
Germany	254,467	1,148,792
West Indies	610,518	1,414,588
Mexico	4,502	..
South America	529,238	159,754
All other countries	188,959	180,842

And imported from—

	1887.	1886.
	£	£
Great Britain	1,199,455	1,508,344
France	1,769,475	2,497,177
Germany	3,688,484	2,705,738
West Indies	1,319,658	938,343
Mexico	19,153	78,621
South America	102,311	186,568
All other countries	260,755	76,299

NEW YORK.

Annex D.—RETURN of the Number of Seamen who have been Engaged, Discharged, Left Behind, reported Dead or Deserted, or who have been Relieved at the British Consulate General, New York, and showing the Total Number of British and Foreign Sailors who were Engaged, Discharged, &c., from British Ships, with the Amount of Wages paid at the Consulate to Seamen on Discharge from their Ships, and from Hospital or Gaol; and also showing the Number of New Agreements entered into during the Year 1887:—

Seamen.										Wages.			Agreements.
Engaged.	Discharged.	Left Behind.			Dead.			Deserted.	Relieved.	Nationality.		Total Number of Seamen.	Paid on Discharge from Vessels.	Paid on Discharge from Hospital or Gaol.	Total Wages Paid.	Number Opened.
		In Gaol.	In Hospital.	Total.	At Sea.	On Shore.	Total.			British.	Foreign.					
12,603	8,072	16	185	201	51	26	77	5,594	289	16,714	10,122	26,836	Dol. c. 367,046 27	Dol. c. 5,530 50	Dol. c. 372,576 77	288
										Last year..		24,203				
										Increase ..		2,633				

(464)

UNITED STATES.

Providence, Rhode Island.

Mr. Vice-Consul Stockwell reports as follows:—

During the year 1887 general business has been fairly prosperous and of usual volume. In the manufacture of cotton goods there is some improvement over 1886. Demand has been good, and employment steady. The depression in the manufacture of woollen goods, due ostensibly to the presence of foreign goods and confusion in the tariff, continues. The record in the jewellery trade is better than in 1886, and ahead of that of 1885. The building of machinery has been unusually active in some lines, notably the manufacture of locomotives and stationary engines. One company employing about 1,200 men has been running full time throughout the year. The output of some engine-builders is fully fifty per cent. greater than in 1886. The extension of railways has stimulated the manufacture of machinists' tools, for railway companies more and more establish machine-shops of their own. In the manufacture of mill and other machinery the record of 1887 is better than the average for five or six years back.

The labour market.

There has been no conflict between capital and labour during the year to interfere seriously with the peace and profit of either. The members of the Masons' Union last year attempted to establish nine hours as a work-day. They have been unsuccessful. Non-union men have been employed, and some members of the union have withdrawn in order to obtain labour. In all machinists' and builders' trades wages are quoted (by the Secretary of the Mechanics' Exchange) as unchanged from last year. There has been a good demand for ordinary and skilled labour. During the year in the city of Providence alone 441 new buildings have been erected at an estimated cost of 1,329,990 dol., and 189 buildings have been improved at a cost of 172,585 dol., making total cost of new buildings and improvements 1,502,575 dol.

Labour.

Average wages for average workmen:—

		Dollars.	Cents.
Carpenters	per day	2	25
Masons, bricklayers	,,	3	50
,, stone	,,	2	75
,, plasterers	,,	3	50
Painters	,,	2	50
Plumbers	,,	3	0
Gas pipers	,,	3	0
Moulders	per week	14	76
,, helpers	,,	7	50

Another quotation:—

		Dollars.	Cents.
Machinists	per day	2	50
,, helpers	,,	1	35

Machinists' prices are ·012 per cent. lower than in 1886.

		Dollars.	Cents.
Tailor	per week	18	0
Labourer, city	per day, 150 to 225 dol.		
Farm hands, boarded	per month, 16 to 18 dol.		
House servants, city, boarded	per week, 3 to 4 dol.		
Operatives (cotton)—adult males—			
*Weavers	per week		
Spinners	,,		
Operatives (woollens)—adult males—			
Weavers	,,	8	75
Spinners	,,	7	50
Children, worsted	per day	0	80
Carders, worsted	,,		
Dyers	,,	7	0

* On and after February 13, 1888, wages in Fall River will be:—
Cotton, print cloth, spinners, per week, 10 dol. 30 c.
,, ,, ,, weavers ,, 9 dol.

NEW YORK.

Statistics of the Port.

Arrivals from foreign countries:— *Foreign arrivals.*

British	85
Italian	3
American	34
Total	122

Foreign vessels brought:— *Foreign receipts.*

Lumber	3,736,000 feet
Laths	7,974,000 ,,
Pickets	9,080 ,,
Clapbards	5,400 ,,
Piling	1,500 ,,
Pulpwood	3,921 cords
Salt	7,350,749 lbs.
Logwood	4,822 tons
Brimstone	630 ,,
Potatoes	36,950 bushels
Starch	738 casks
Cliff-stone	1,050 tons

The price of cotton in the market for the year is as follows:— *Price of cotton and sale of print cloths.* Middlings, lowest, February, 6¾ c.; highest, June, 10⅝ c.; price, December, 10½ c. and 10¾ c. Sold in the market, exclusive of cotton shipped direct from the South to manufacturers, 187,807 bales.

The price of print cloths in the market for the year, 64 × 64, fluctuated between 3¼ c. and 3½ c.

The bank clearings for the year aggregate 240,156,000 dol. Price *Clearings.* of money, good paper, 5½ to 7 per cent. Interest paid by savings banks, exclusive of dividends, 4 per cent. Money on call, subject to check at sight, 2 to 3 per cent.

A daily paper here published the statement that liquor may be *Prohibition.* bought at 591 places, while under license the number of places was only 466.

From the Rhode Island State Census for 1885 are taken the following *Population.* facts and figures:—

	1865.	1875.	1885.
Providence	54,595	100,675	118,070
Newport	12,688	14,028	19,566
Pawtucket	5,000	18,464	22,906
State	184,965	258,239	304,284

Rhode Island is the most densely-populated State in the United *Area and density of population.* States.

Area, 1,053 square miles.
Persons to a square mile, 1875 .. .. 245·2
,, ,, ,, ,, 1885 .. .. 288·9

Ward 7, City of Providence, 1885, had 25,089·5 persons to the square mile.

The State:—Houses, wood, 47,135; brick, 1,058; stone, 334; total, *Houses.* 48,527.

White, 296,942; black, 6,137; Mulatto, 975; Indian, 119. *Colour and race of inhabitants.*

The Narragansett tribe of Indians maintained its tribal relations till 1880, when they were dissolved by legislative Act. *Over 21 years of age (men). Nativity.*

The State:—Native, 53,814; foreign born, 31,913; total, 87,727.

The State, 1885:—Native, 218,723; foreign, 85,561.

UNITED STATES.

Occupations. The State:—

Government	2,399
Professional	4,547
Domestic	78,942
Personal service	2,920
Trade	14,443
Transportation	6,636
Agriculture	12,839
Fisheries	848
Manufacture and mechanics	71,695
Mining	188
Labour and apprentices	5,746
Indefinite	235
Retired	6,318
Not gainful	43
Not productive	2,247
Unemployed over 16	4,406
At home, 15 to 20	2,124
Students	3,497
Unemployed under 16	83,911
Aggregate	304,248

School attendance. The State:—Public, 34,319; private, 5,581: total, 39,900; absentees, 5,982: total population, 7 to 14, 45,882.

Illiteracy. The State:—Read, but not write, native, 3,583; foreign, 20,221; total, 26,313. Neither read nor write, native, 3,583; foreign, 14,829; total, 18,402.

The State:—

Valuation.

	Dol.
1875	270,415,023
1885	328,530,559
Providence	124,202,000
Newport	29,492,200
Pawtucket	17,610,813

TAX on 100 dol.

Tax.

	Dol. c.
Providence	1 45
Newport	1 1
Pawtucket	1 25

Savings banks. Account on deposit, 51,311,330 dol. 62 c.
Number of depositors, 1885, 116,381.
Average deposit, 445 dol. 23 c.; per capita, 170 dol. 29 c.; per cent. of deposit to population, 38·2.

School statistics. The State buildings, 458. Estimated value, including land, 2,229,135 dol.; support of schools, 1885, 780,003 dol. 9 c.; current expenses, 547,995 dol. 44 c.; average salary, teacher, man, 745 dol. 95 c.; woman, 406 dol. 50 c.; pupils per teacher, 35; cost per pupil, 15 dol. 54 c.

Natives of other countries. England, 16,784; Scotland and Wales, 3,872; Ireland, 38,895; British American, 18,584; Germany, 26,114; France, 424.

Farmers in Rhode Island. Under 1 acre, 521; 1 acre and over, 763; 1 to 21, 400; 3 to 9, 830; 10 to 19, 774; 20 to 49, 1,550; 50 to 99, 1,761; 100 to 199, 1,339; 200 to 299, 285; 300 to 399, 70; 400 to 499, 21; 500 to 999, 31; 1,000, 4.

Total acreage, 479,690; value per acre, 45 dol. 30 c.; value, farm property, 38,655,786 dol.; value of products, 7,204,642 dol.

Fisheries. The State:—Capital, 698,838 dol. (Oyster, 191,102 dol.)

NEW YORK.

Persons employed, 1,373—all Fisheries.

	Number.	Value.
		Dol.
Steamers	14	118,000
Schooners	66	31,950
Sail-boats	312	56,000
Row-boats	908	34,991

Manufactures.

All industries, number of establishments	23,393
Capital	59,616,229 dol.
Average employés, men	37,481
„ „ women	21,468
„ „ children	4,400
Paid in wages, year	23,353,099 dol.
Materials	48,271,448 „
Products	95,452,085 „

	Dol. c.
Average daily wages, under 15, males	0 64
„ „ „ „ 15, females	0 53
„ „ „ over 15, males	1 68
„ „ „ „ 15, females	1 5

Jewellers.

Establishments	169
Capital	153,189 dol.
Wages paid	1,801,429 „
Materials	2,283,840 „
Products	6,991,093 „
Employés	3,511

Annex A.—Return of all Vessels Entered from, and Cleared for, a Foreign Port.

Entered.

Nationality.	Sailing.		Steam.		Total.	
	Number of Vessels.	Tons.	Number of Vessels.	Tons.	Number of Vessels.	Tons.
British	85	10,800	...	...	85	10,800
American	34	6,977	...	...	34	6,977
Italian	3	1,577	...	...	3	1,577
Total	122	19,354	...	...	122	19,354
„ for 1886	85	1,400	...	626	86	14,627

Cleared.

Nationality.	Sailing.		Steam.		Total.	
	Number of Vessels.	Tons.	Number of Vessels.	Tons.	Number of Vessels.	Tons.
British	78	9,658	...	...	78	9,658
American	7	1,528	...	...	7	1,528
Total	85	11,186	...	...	85	19,354
„ for 1886	62	...	1	626	63	14,627

UNITED STATES.

Annex B.—RETURN of Principal Articles of Export from Providence, R.I., during the Years 1887 and 1886.

Articles.	1887. Quantity.	1887. Value.	1886. Quantity.	1886. Value.
	Tons.	£	Tons.	£
Coke	450	233	659	339
Coal	70	78	36	35
Schooner	..	124	..	..
Total	..	435	..	374

RETURN of Principal Articles of Import into Providence, R.I., during the Years 1887 and 1886.

Articles.	1887. Quantity.	1887. Value.	1886. Quantity.	1886. Value.
	Tons.	£	Tons.	£
Dry goods	..	45,410	..	49,985
Chemicals	..	26,775	..	21,504
Metals, and manufactures of	..	16,969	..	10,340
All others	..	42,456	..	25,330
Total	..	131,610	..	107,159

Annex C.—TABLE showing the Total Values of all Articles Exported from Providence, and Imported into Providence, from and to Foreign Countries during the Years 1887 and 1886.

Country.	Exports 1887.	Exports 1886.	Imports 1887.	Imports 1886.
	£	£	£	£
New Brunswick	202	..	..	..
Cuba	233	339	2,347	..
Nova Scotia	..	35	14,528	..
England	..	..	60,165	40,385
British West Indies	..	..	6,504	..
Scotland	..	..	1,299	..
Ireland	..	..	91	..
Germany	..	..	13,982	13,809
France	..	..	11,185	9,252
Hayti	..	..	9,766	..
Austria	..	..	3,693	3,691
Switzerland	..	..	3,243	..
Italy	..	..	2,313	..
Greece	..	..	1,435	..
All others	..	..	1,059	40,023
Total	435	374	131,610	107,159

(1125 6 | 88—H & S 464)

FOREIGN OFFICE.
1888.
ANNUAL SERIES.

No. 375.

DIPLOMATIC AND CONSULAR REPORTS ON TRADE AND FINANCE.

UNITED STATES.

FURTHER REPORT FOR THE YEAR 1887
ON THE
TRADE OF THE CONSULAR DISTRICT OF SAN FRANCISCO.

REFERENCE TO PREVIOUS REPORT, Annual Series No. 313.

Presented to both Houses of Parliament by Command of Her Majesty,
JUNE, 1888.

LONDON:
PRINTED FOR HER MAJESTY'S STATIONERY OFFICE,
BY HARRISON AND SONS, ST. MARTIN'S LANE,
PRINTERS IN ORDINARY TO HER MAJESTY.

And to be purchased, either directly or through any Bookseller, from
EYRE AND SPOTTISWOODE, EAST HARDING STREET, FLEET STREET, E.C., and
32, ABINGDON STREET, WESTMINSTER, S.W.; or
ADAM AND CHARLES BLACK, 6, NORTH BRIDGE, EDINBURGH; or
HODGES, FIGGIS, & Co., 104, GRAFTON STREET, DUBLIN.

1888.

[C. 5252—152.]   *Price Twopence.*

New Series of Reports.

Reports of the Annual Series have been issued from Her Majesty's Diplomatic and Consular Officers at the following places, and may be obtained from the sources indicated on the title-page:—

No.		Price.	No.		Price.
257.	Russia	2d.	316.	Carthagena and Santa Martha	1d.
258.	Paris	1d.	317.	San José	1d.
259.	Patras	1d.	318.	Boulogne	1d.
260.	Brussels	1d.	319.	Tahiti	1d.
261.	Ichang	1d.	320.	Fiume	1d.
262.	Baltimore	1d.	321.	Warsaw	1d.
263.	Taganrog	1d.	322.	Vera Cruz	2d.
264.	Oporto	1d.	323.	Rio Grande do Sul	1d.
265.	Rio de Janeiro	1d.	324.	Gothenburg	2d.
266.	Galveston	1d.	325.	Philippopolis	1d.
267.	Tripoli	1d.	326.	Mogador	2d.
268.	Galatz	1d.	327.	Havana	2d.
269.	Varna	1d.	328.	La Rochelle	1d.
270.	New Orleans	2d.	329.	Corunna	2d.
271.	Cherbourg	1d.	330.	Chicago	2d.
272.	Suakin	1d.	331.	Foochow	1d.
273.	Brest	1d.	332.	Taiwan	1d.
274.	Barcelona	2d.	333.	Loanda	1d.
275.	Barcelona	1d.	334.	Loanda	1d.
276.	Antwerp	1d.	335.	Noumea	1d.
277.	Havre	3d.	336.	Trieste	1d.
278.	Odessa	1d.	337.	Nice	1d.
279.	Tokyo	1d.	338.	Bordeaux	1d.
280.	Saigon	1d.	339.	Mogador	1d.
281.	Buenos Ayres	1d.	340.	Wilmington	1d.
282.	Taganrog	1d.	341.	Amoy	2d.
283.	Tamsui	1d.	342.	Trebizond	1d.
284.	Puerto Plata	1d.	343.	Lisbon	1d.
285.	Wênchow	1d.	344.	Java	1d.
286.	Tokyo	1d.	345.	Brest	1d.
287.	Lisbon	2d.	346.	Odessa	2d.
288.	La Rochelle	1d.	347.	Cavalla	1d.
289.	Washington	4d.	348.	Bussorah	1d.
290.	Beyrout	1d.	349.	Mollendo	1d.
291.	Algiers	2d.	350.	Cadiz	5d.
292.	Varna	1d.	351.	Cagliari	4d.
293.	Algiers	1d.	352.	Cagliari	1d.
294.	Port Saïd	1d.	353.	Ajaccio	1d.
295.	Manila	1d.	354.	Copenhagen	1d.
296.	Charleston	1d.	355.	Vienna	1d.
297.	Kiungchow	1d.	356.	San Francisco	1d.
298.	Pakhoi	1d.	357.	Vera Cruz	1d.
299.	Wuhu	1d.	358.	Philippopolis	1d.
300.	Boulogne	2d.	359.	Greytown	1d.
301.	Marseilles	1d.	360.	Tangier	1d.
302.	Bordeaux	2d.	361.	Lisbon	1d.
303.	Ancona	1d.	362.	Chicago	1d.
304.	Swatow	1d.	363.	Jerusalem and Jaffa	1d.
305.	Ssŭ-ch'uan	1d.	364.	Truxillo	1d.
306.	Antwerp	1d.	365.	Ningpo	1d.
307.	Cadiz	1d.	366.	Chefoo	1d.
308.	Genoa	1d.	367.	Bushire	1d.
309.	Marseilles	1d.	368.	Stockholm	2d.
310.	Baltimore	1d.	369.	Santiago	1d.
311.	Savannah	1d.	370.	New York	2d.
312.	Boston	1d.	371.	Pernambuco	1d.
313.	San Francisco	1d.	372.	Söul	1d.
314.	Guayaquil	1d.	373.	Chinkiang	2d.
315.	Santos	1d.	374.	Pernambuco	1d.

No. 375.

Reference to previous Report, Annual Series No. 313.

UNITED STATES.

SAN FRANCISCO.

Consul Donohoe to the Marquis of Salisbury.

My Lord,   *San Francisco, May* 11, 1888.

I HAVE the honour to transmit herewith commercial reports on the Trade of Portland and Astoria, Oregon, and Los Angeles and San Diego, California, for the year 1887.

I have, &c.

(Signed)   DENIS DONOHOE.

PORTLAND.

Mr. Vice-Consul Laidlaw reports as follows :—

Merchants generally report a large increase of trade during the year, and say that their sales have increased by fully 25 per cent. It will be seen, however, by a reference to Annex B. that the values of exports have fallen off very materially. This comparison is hardly a fair one, as the greater proportion of the wheat harvest of 1885 was shipped during the first months of 1886, and a like proportion of that of 1886 during the last months of the same year, while in the first months of the year now closed exports were in consequence comparatively light, and the harvest of 1887 will be largely shipped in 1888. The harvest in the eastern sections of Oregon and Washington Territory was much larger than that of 1886, while that of the great Willamette Valley seems to be about the same, and until this section is farmed by a more careful and pushing set of farmers we can hardly look for anything like the increase that should be the case. I refer to the wheat harvest particularly, the yield of other grains having been light. Prices of most farm produce were very low during the entire year, but on the whole trade generally has been very good, and with a decided tendency to improve. The British tonnage employed in the foreign trade reached 90 per cent. of the whole, which is a very satisfactory increase.

The tea transit trade referred to in my last report has been nipped in the bud, and the Canadian Pacific Railway is doing nearly all this trade. The greater proportion of the import trade was (as has

Trade generally.

Exports fallen off.

Harvest.

British tonnage.

Imports.

always been the case) done by way of San Francisco, or by sail and rail from the Eastern States, and there is no means of estimating the value with anything like accuracy.

Tin-plates. Imports of tin-plates were much larger than last year, and prices averaged about 19s. per box for B.V. grades of coke.

Salt. Direct imports of salt were more than double those of last year.
Rice. The same was the case with respect to imports of rice from China and the Hawaiian Islands. In addition to the receipts noted in Annex B.,
Coal. 25,445 tons of coal were received from domestic ports. The receipts of foreign coal were:—1,205 tons from Great Britain, 2,071 tons from British Columbia, and 16,203 tons from Australia.

Coke. There is an opening for Cardiff coke for smelting purposes, and the consumption is likely to increase; 567 tons were imported. Market prices of Australian coal averaged about 24s. per ton for Sydney, 28s. per ton for Newcastle, and of Scotch and English 30s. to 32s. per ton,
Cement. while cannel sold at about 36s. per ton. Imports of cement were greater than last year, and there is a good, steady, and increasing
Pig iron. demand. Pig iron imports were light, and there were no stocks in first hands at close of the year. The Oregon Iron and Steel Company produced none during the year. The consumption of grain bags and
Grain bags. wool packs is large, but, as these are usually received viâ San Francisco from Calcutta, it is impracticable to obtain any correct statistics. Market prices were low, averaging a little over 2½d. for standard 22–36 grain bags. Deducting the transit tea trade included in last
Increase in imports. year's returns there has been an increase of fully 32 per cent. in the value of direct imports from foreign countries during the year.
Exports generally. The total value of exports to foreign countries and by rail to Eastern States and coastwise was about 18 per cent. less than during the previous year. Shipments of produce by rail to the Eastern States
Coastwise and rail shipments. and exports coastwise are valued at 1,799,100l. against a valuation in 1886 of 1,778,845l., the decrease being in the foreign trade. The above figures do not include shipments by the Oregon Pacific Railway viâ Yaquina Bay to San Francisco, of which it is difficult to procure
Breadstuffs. statistics. The wheat crops of Eastern Oregon and Washington Territory were greater than in 1886, but 28 per cent. was shipped to San Francisco and Puget Sound, while only 9 per cent. was so shipped in 1886. In like manner 30 per cent. of the flour was so shipped as against 23 per cent. It will be noted from the tables that some quantity of wheat was sent to Peru, and that flour shipments to China and Japan have largely increased. The Portland Flour Mills Company grind largely for export to England, and the old Burr Mills throughout the State are being rapidly superseded by mills using the roller process, and with the latest improved machinery.

During the cereal year ended July 31 the following were the receipts at this port from the tributary districts:—

| Year. | Willamette Valley. || Eastern Oregon and Washington Territory. ||
	Wheat.	Flour.	Wheat.	Flour.
	Quarters.	Sacks.	Quarters.	Sacks.
1886–1887	272,010	142,539	610,099	80,595
1885–1886	281,672	150,221	968,950	96,675
August to December, 1887	43,727	51,529	553,472	48,837
„ „ 1886	199,040	78,015	465,590	33,705

The total shipments of breadstuffs, both foreign and coastwise, were 695,664 quarters of wheat valued at 866,214*l.*, and 320,928 sacks of flour valued at 347,850*l.*

The average market price of wool during the year was about 23 c. Wool. or 11½*d.* per pound for valley, and 17½ c. or 8¾*d.* per pound for wool grown east of the Cascades Mountains. The quality was generally good, but heavier in shrinkage than last year.

Receipts and shipments at this port were as follows:—

	Receipts.		Shipments.	
	Valley.	Eastern.	Viâ San Francisco.	By Rail.
	Lbs.	Lbs.	Lbs.	Lbs.
During 1887	852,445	11,682,040	7,824,907	4,581,359
" 1886	1,785,560	11,755,566	5,347,407	7,879,693

Shrinkage of valley wools was about 52 per cent., and of these from other sections about 68 per cent. The consumption of Oregon woollen mills was about the same as last year.

Contracts were made in March and April at 8*d.* to 9*d.* (16 c. to Hops. 18 c.), but later there was little demand at lower prices, and at the close of the year prices fell to 3*d.* to 4*d.* (6 c. to 7 c.) Receipts were lighter than for years past, being only 1,625,496 pounds, which included 347,715 pounds of Puget Sound growth, and shipments by rail were 1,964,872 pounds, while last year shipments were 6,520,036 pounds, but these included Puget Sound hops, which this year were shipped direct.

A large coastwise trade has been done, and the trade with eastern Timber. cities viâ the Union Pacific Railway has developed very much, shipments last year averaging 4,000,000 feet per month. Mills have all been running to full capacity, and prices have been remunerative. The foreign trade has been infinitesimal.

Salmon was sent east in some quantity in refrigerator cars, and also Fish. some sturgeon; but the great bulk of the salmon catch is, and always will be, tinned. Very little salt salmon is now packed on the Columbia River. The product of the Columbia River packing establishments last year was about 340,000 cases of spring catch, and 40,000 cases of fall catch. Each case contains four dozen 1 lb. tins, or this equivalent in other sizes, and the shipments by railway from this district were 308,357 cases, which included some quantity from other points than the Columbia River. All foreign shipments of this product are made at Astoria, which is the headquarters of this business. Prices advanced steadily, though the largest portion of the product was contracted early at an average of 1 dol. 30 c., or 5*s.* 3*d.* per dozen 1 lb. tins. From the constantly decreasing pack it would appear that the river is being fished out.

There has been no scarcity of money during the year, and on Money good securities advances have been readily obtainable below the legal market. rate of interest (8 per cent.). Sixty days' bills on London fluctuated between 4 dol. 78½ c. and 4 dol. 86½ c. per pound sterling for bank, and from 4 dol. 78 c. to 4 dol. 85⅞ c. for mercantile.

The aggregate capital of mercantile houses doing business here is Mercantile given as 10,800,000*l.*; of these 21 firms represent over 200,000*l.* each. capital.

UNITED STATES.

Banks. There are six national banks, besides savings banks and private banks, representing a capital of 496,470*l.*, and two British banks, with a capital aggregating 9,650,006*l.*

Shipping.
British. The shipping returns show that 75 British vessels, registering 88,931 tons, entered this port during the year, while last year 121 ships, of a register tonnage of 130,941, were entered. The ships generally have been much larger, as small vessels lose money at the low rates of freight now ruling. The engagements of tonnage during the last three years, exclusive of coasting voyages, have been as under:—

Tonnage engagements.

	Registered Tons.		
	1887.	1886.	1885.
Grain and flour cargoes	89,856	146,824	105,026
Salmon and assorted cargoes	3,227	5,873	6,288
Timber cargoes	6,020	3,136	2,885
Miscellaneous voyages	850	2,961	803
Total	99,953	158,794	115,002

Rates of freight. Freights were still lower than last year, though much higher than those ruling at other Pacific Coast ports. Average rates for the year were 38*s.* 3*d.* iron vessels, and 34*s.* 9*d.* wooden vessels, to a port in the United Kingdom: all of the wooden vessels, and many iron, giving the option of continental ports at same rates as United Kingdom. Highest rates paid during the year 42*s.* 6*d.* and 37*s.* 6*d.*, and the lowest 34*s.* and 30*s.* for iron and wood respectively.

Steam tonnage. There has been no increase in the steam tonnage employed in the coasting trade, but a small British steamer made several voyages from Vancouver, B.C., in connection with the Canadian Pacific Railway. The freight carried to and from San Francisco by the allied lines was:—

	From San Francisco.	To San Francisco.
	Tons.	Tons.
During 1887	72,396	100,387
„ 1886	87,090	78,400

Sailors.
Crimps. Seamen's wages out of this port have averaged 6*l.* per month for able seamen, and a bonus has generally been exacted from masters requiring crews of about 9*l.* 10*s.* per man. It is openly asserted that many masters profit by this buying and selling of crews, and are very lukewarm in their hostility to the crimps engaged in the trade. These rascals at Astoria have become so bold and aggressive that few masters have dared to engage crews at this port in face of the almost absolute certainty of losing the men at Astoria by desertion or open intimidation. The local courts seem powerless to protect seamen in their right of contract. The number of and changes in crews of British ships entering this port during this year have been:—

Changes in crews.

Total Number of Crews.	Deserted.	Discharged.	Engaged.	Reported Dead.	Percentage of Desertion.	Hospital Permits.
1,378	316	91	232	3	14·3	13

IMPROVEMENT OF RIVERS AND HARBOURS.

Last Congress appropriated no additional funds for this work, and there was, therefore, little done during the year 1887. *River bars and channels.*

On the improvement of the Columbia and Willamette Rivers between Portland and the sea over 400,000 dols. had been spent up to the close of the fiscal year ending June 30, 1887. The object of this improvement is to afford a ship channel of 20 feet depth at low water, by contraction and shore protection works, at four bars and shoal places between Portland and Astoria. During the fiscal year St. Helens Dyke was extended 1,010 feet.

A considerable amount of work was done in clearing out the upper reaches of the Columbia and Willamette rivers navigable for light draught river steamers.

On this great work of improvement 132,950 dol. had been spent at the close of the fiscal year. A jetty is to be built of brush and stone, beginning at Fort Stevens, and running to a point three miles south of Cape Hancock. At the close of the year 2,700 feet of jetty had been constructed. It is expected by this means to secure a wide, direct, and stable channel carrying 30 feet at low water. *Mouth of the Columbia.*

A high tide brush and stone jetty is being built on the south side of the entrance to Yaquina Bay, with shore protection to close a rock-obstructed channel, for the purpose of providing a central free channel not less than 12 feet deep at mean low water. The rise of tide is 7 feet 1 inch. At the close of the year nearly 3,000 feet of this jetty had been finished. *Yaquina Bay.*

At Coquille a half-tide jetty or deflecting dyke 3,400 feet long is being built from the left bank, the object being to afford a channel to the sea 10 feet deep through the former North Cape; 2,030 feet of this jetty had been constructed at the end of the year. *Coquille.*

A similar jetty to that at Coquille is being built at Coos Bay; 1,825 feet has been finished. When completed this jetty will be 2,400 feet long, running from Fossil Point towards Coos Head, and giving a channel of 14 feet depth at mean low water. *Coos Bay.*

All Columbia River pilots are now carried in two cutters, and rates have advanced again to the old legal tariff of 8 dol. per foot draught up to 12 feet, and 10 dol. per foot for any excess. This is an excessively high charge for the service, and is likely to be reduced. *Pilotage.*

Competition having been withdrawn, rates are a matter of agreement, and are generally excessively high. *Towage.*

On account of the low prices ruling for most descriptions of farm produce, farming generally has not been profitable throughout the year. The weather was favourable for harvesting operations, and the crops were got in in good condition. *Agriculture.*

The wheat harvest east of the Cascades Mountains was greater than last year, but in Oregon, west of this, there has been a decline of production. *Wheat.*

The oat crop of 1886 was small, and that of the past year smaller still. Receipts here were 183,052 centals. In 1886 the receipts were 284,467 centals. Good prices were realised throughout the year. *Oats.*

Hops.	Hop growers only who contracted their crops before delivery or early in the season secured good prices. I am informed that it costs the grower 8 c., or 4d., before the hops are ready for market, and at the close of the year they were not saleable at even this price. Taking one year with another, I think hop vineyards pay very well, but the market is subject to very violent fluctuations.
Fruit culture.	Last year's fruit crop was small owing to late frosts, and in consequence orchardists secured good prices for their products. At the close of the year apples sold very high. Much attention is now given to orchards, which were neglected for a long series of years, and as there is a good market in several of the Western States, this branch of agriculture is growing more profitable; 94,336 boxes of green fruit were received here, against 120,782 in 1886.
Sheep and cattle.	During the month of February exceptionally severe weather was experienced on the ranges, but, as more provision is now made by stockmen for such contingencies, the losses of sheep and cattle were not over 12 per cent., and this has been more than made up during the year. This branch of business is undoubtedly very profitable.
Population and industries. Immigration.	There has been a large immigration into Oregon and Washington Territory by rail, and the Board of Immigration estimates that the population has been increased by at least 100,000. The arrivals at this port by sea were only 8,388, and the departures 7,324.
Manufactures.	The number of hands employed in various manufacturing enterprises, and also the estimated value of manufactured produce, show a considerable increase. The following are the figures:—

	Persons employed.	Value. Dol.
During 1887	3,380	1,560,800
„ 1886	2,770	1,089,500

Reduction works.	The capacity of the works built here last year for the treatment and smelting of ores has been increased, and also the capital stock. Operations, however, have been retarded on account of the excessive freights charged by the railroad companies on ores from the mining districts.
Cordage works.	A company, with a capital of 20,000l., has been incorporated during the year to engage in the manufacture of cordage. The factory is three stories in height, built of brick, and is fitted with the most improved modern machinery. It occupies an area of 50 by 100 feet, and at present has a capacity of 4,000 pounds per day. The other buildings connected with this factory are: a boiler and engine house, a tar house, and a warehouse, two stories high, 28 by 100 feet, all built of stone and brick.
Oregon Iron and Steel Company.	Although the Oregon Iron and Steel Company has done no smelting during the year, it is increasing its capacity to an output of 50 tons per day, and putting up a plant for casting water pipe. It is also intended to engage in the manufacture of bar-iron and steel. The iron mines are close at hand, and everything necessary for their operations.
Paper.	The Columbia River Paper Company has its mills at La Cames, W.T., and has a capacity of eight tons per day. The wood-pulp mills have a capacity of three tons per day.
Mining.	In no other year has there been so much development work carried on in the mining districts of Oregon, Washington Territory, and the northern districts of Idaho, but the results of this will not appear until next year. The mining counties of Oregon are: Jackson, Coos, Curry, Josephine, and, to a limited extent, Douglas, in Southern Oregon; Union, Baker, and Grant counties in Eastern Oregon; and, on the

western slope of the Cascades in Linn county, some little mining is carried on. Idaho is pre-eminently the richest centre of the mining interests of the north-west, and the mines of the north and south forks of the Coeur d'Alene, in the northern section of the territory, are proving enormously rich (in silver principally), though comparatively little developed. The gold, silver, and lead yield of Northern Idaho is estimated by a competent authority at 693,400*l*. for the year. The following is the product of Oregon mines by counties:— *Coeur d'Alene. Bullion and lead yield. North Idaho.*

		£		£
Jackson	.. ..	11,000		
Josephine	.. ..	15,000		
Douglas	.. ..	5,000		
Coos and Curry	.. ..	5,000		
			Southern Oregon ..	36,000
Baker	.. ..	26,000		
Grant	.. ..	30,000		
Union	.. ..	19,000		
			Eastern Oregon ..	75,000
Other counties	.. ..	.. ..	.. ..	3,000
Total for State	.. ..	.. ..	.. ..	114,000

Oregon.

The product of Eastern Washington Territory mines is only about 20,000*l*., principally from the Okanagon and Colville districts. *Eastern Washington Territory.*

Little attention has been given to the valuable deposits known to exist in this State of the baser metals and coal. *Base metals.*

Some excavation has been done at the lock gates of the Cascades Canal, and stone is being got ready for the locks. The United States' Government has spent already 228,500*l*. on this project, and the engineers estimate 370,000*l*. more will be required to complete it. *Public works. Canal.*

The drawbridge mentioned in my last report connecting Portland and East Portland has been completed, and is now in successful operation. A fine steel railroad bridge connecting the suburb of Albina with Portland is now rapidly nearing completion. It will have a 340-feet draw span and a 320-feet fixed span, and will have a carriage way and foot walk above the railroad tracks. *Bridges.*

Considerable progress has been made with the construction of railroad shops and other terminal works at Albina, and ere long the facilities for handling freight will be of the best kind. As soon as the bridge is completed, it is intended to proceed with the construction of a Union passenger station on this side of the river. *Terminal works.*

There has been no construction in my district, with the exception of a portion of the Portland and Willamette Valley Railroad, which connects the narrow gauge system of the Oregonian Railway Company, Limited (the stock of which is principally owned in Dundee), with Portland. The control of this line has passed into the hands of the Southern Pacific Company of California. The Oregon and California has also been completed to a junction with the California and Oregon line, making a through line in connection with the Central and Southern Pacific Railroad system. *Railroads.*

UNITED STATES.

Mileage.

The mileage of railways in Oregon is now:—

Oregon Railway and Navigation Company—main line	404
,, ,, ,, ,, branches	324
Northern Pacific in Oregon	45
Oregon and California	475
Oregon Pacific	83
Total broad gauge	1331
Oregonian Railway Company, Limited	148
Portland and Willamette Valley Railroad	29
Total narrow gauge	171

Projected railroads.

Over 1,300 miles of branch roads are projected by the Oregon Railway and Navigation Company; but it may be many years before some of these are constructed. The Oregon Pacific Company has done a good deal of work on their line running eastward, and, if funds are forthcoming, this line should be far on its way to Boise City, Idaho, which is its objective point, during the next year.

Railway traffic.

The traffic over the lines of the Oregon Railway and Navigation Company (which includes nearly all the through traffic of the Northern and Union Pacific Railroads), also that of the Oregon and California, is given below:—

	Forwarded.		Received.	
	1887.	1886.	1887.	1886.
	Tons.	Tons.	Tons.	Tons.
Oregon Railway and Navigation	158,455	213,115	255,245	325,519
,, and California, east side	29,095	33,352	51,154	89,307
,, ,, west side	11,311	12,234	31,427	56,359

City finances.

The bonded debt of this city at the close of the year was 100,000 dol., or 20,000*l.*, bearing interest at 6 per cent., besides which the city has outstanding water bonds to the extent of 100,000*l.*, bearing interest at 5 per cent. The waterworks have proved a very paying investment. The total revenue was 271,858 dol., or 54,312*l.*, and the expenditures were equal to 45,478*l.* This is exclusive of the cost of street improvements, which are done at the expense of holders of property adjacent to the street to be improved. The same is the case with respect to sewers.

Taxation.

The State, county, and city tax rates were as under:—

	Per cent.
State tax	0·52
,, school tax	0·50
County tax	0·65
City tax	1.00
School district tax	0·35
Total	3·02

Remarks.

The city tax levy for 1888 is the same as last year, on a valuation of 40 per cent. of actual value.

City property. Real estate transactions.

City property has been continually advancing throughout the year, and the transfers and sales have been larger than ever before. Real estate transactions recorded in this county of Multnomah during the last four years were as under:—

	Dollars.
1884	1,695,856
1885	1,566,740
1886	2,135,000
1887	5,824,770

There has been a vast improvement in the architecture of buildings, both brick and frame, that have been erected here during the last four years. Last year about 180 dwellings were constructed in this city at a cost of about 55,600*l*. A brick and stone county armoury was built, costing 7,000*l*. On business buildings and wharves 142,000*l*., and on churches and schools 6,200*l*., was expended. *Buildings.*

In the various suburbs, including East Portland and Albina, it is estimated that the amount expended on buildings and improvements during the year was about 208,200*l*., which includes 105,000*l*. for the North Pacific terminal buildings at Albina. *Suburban.*

There has been a good demand for labourers last year, and men willing to work have had no difficulty in finding employment. Skilled labour has also been in good demand. Direct communication with the Eastern States has introduced numbers of idle, useless tramps into the country. *Labour.*

Note.—The values given in this report are reduced to sterling, at the average rate of 5 dol. to the pound sterling.

Annex A.—RETURN of all Shipping at the Port of Portland, Oregon, in the Year 1887.

ENTERED.

Nationality.	Sailing. Number of Vessels.	Sailing. Tons.	Steam. Number of Vessels.	Steam. Tons.	Total. Number of Vessels.	Total. Tons.
British	72	88,322	3	609	75	88,931
United States—						
Foreign	2	2,469	...	...	2	2,469
Atlantic	4	4,918	...	...	4	4,918
Coastwise	19	8,736	118	253,704	137	262,440
German	2	2,350	...	...	2	2,350
Norwegian	2	2,137	...	...	2	2,137
Total	101	108,932	121	254,313	222	363,245
,, for the year preceding	...	...	...	...	261	387,597

CLEARED.

Nationality.	Sailing. Number of Vessels.	Sailing. Tons.	Steam. Number of Vessels.	Steam. Tons.	Total. Number of Vessels.	Total. Tons.
British	71	86,133	3	609	74	86,742
United States—						
Foreign	5	6,480	...	...	5	6,480
Coastwise	16	7,960	107	252,184	123	260,144
German	1	624	...	...	1	624
Norwegian	2	2,137	...	...	2	2,137
Total	95	103,334	110	252,793	205	356,127
,, for the year preceding	...	...	...	...	272	394,836

UNITED STATES.

Annex B.—Return of Principal Articles of Export from Portland, Oregon, during the Years 1887–86.

Articles.		1887.		1886.	
		Quantity.	Value.	Quantity.	Value.
			£		£
Wheat	Quarters	495,596	610,796	895,489	1,106,374
Wheat flour	Sacks	226,700	235,423	324,579	339,559
Timber	Mil. feet	150	500	3,310	7,017
Fish oil	...	...	2,600	...	...
Tea in transit	Lbs.	...	...	465,121	13,508
Other articles	...	...	15,578	...	2,514
Total exports, foreign	...	...	864,897	864,897	...	1,468,972

Return of Principal Articles of Import to Portland, Oregon, during the Years 1887–86.

Articles.		1887.		1886.	
		Quantity.	Value.	Quantity.	Value.
			£		£
Coals	Tons	19,479	12,628	24,921	13,900
Tin and terne plates	Lbs.	2,237,806	12,921	1,339,976	8,377
Rice	,,	3,114,439	11,389	1,534,401	5,760
Earthenware and glass	...	...	9,020	...	5,820
Salt	Lbs.	14,105,047	8,769	6,441,212	4,689
Cement	Bbls.	26,427	5,586	19,317	3,995
Cigars and tobacco	...	...	5,463	...	...
Wines and liquors	...	...	3,136	...	1,090
Beer, porter, and ale	Gallons	12,382	2,143	7,156	1,364
Soda and chemicals	...	...	1,992	...	2,742
Oils	Gallons	24,816	1,441	19,170	1,151
Pig-iron	Tons	463	1,401	347	829
Fire-bricks	No.	135,000	255	...	...
Tea	Lbs.	52,054	1,865	270,990	8,179
All other articles	...	...	16,963	...	12,251
Hemp	Tons	...	...	80	1,399
Tea in transit	Lbs.	...	...	2,879,102	91,527
Total	...	...	94,972	...	163,064

Note.—The above returns do not include exports or imports coastwise or by rail with the exception of articles transported in bond.

Annex C.—Table showing the Total Value of all Articles Exported from Portland and Imported to Portland, Oregon, from and to Foreign Countries during the Years 1887–86.

Country.	Exports.		Imports.	
	1887.	1886.	1887.	1886.
	£	£	£	£
Great Britain	640,973	1,411,227	51,106	33,779
Belgium	124,099	27,725	..	..
British Columbia	17,253	6,982	3,010	5,977
China	30,170	1,812	21,999	12,27_
Japan	..	..	..	99,005
Australia	..	..	10,250	7,349
Uruguay	..	4,540	..	..
Peru	13,322	..	..	..
France	39,080	..	626	..
Germany	..	..	1,907	..
Cuba	..	..	5,044	..
All other countries	..	16,686	1,030	4,683
Total	864,897	1,468,972	94,972	163,064

ASTORIA, OREGON.

Mr. Vice-Consul Cherry reports as follows:—

General business still shows a steady improvement, but in a way that affects British imports but slightly. *General business for 1887.*

Imports show a good increase in values of fully 38 per cent. on the year before, and an increase over 1885, all of which is from the United Kingdom. *Imports.*

The retail price of tin-plates, in lots, was 19s. 7d. per box of 108 lbs. *Tin-plates.*

But little difference in the price of salt is noted for Liverpool F.F., 3l. per ton. *Salt.*

A decrease in the importation of coals is to be noted owing to the large orders from the Australian mines for Southern California, and consequently the use of domestic coals from Puget Sound. Australian Wallend coals are selling from 1l. 6s. to 1l. 13s. per ton. *Coals.*

Twine, as last year, comes by rail from Boston and New York, and is becoming altogether of United States manufacture. *Twine.*

Block tin still comes from Australia viâ San Francisco, the average price being 1s. per lb. *Block tin.*

Exports show a decrease in the quantities and amounts: this is owing first to the still smaller quantity of salmon exported, which decrease has been steady for the past three years; and secondly, to the influence that the great wheat combination has on the exports of breadstuffs during the first part of the export season, retarding the usual season at least two months, lumber being the only export that shows an increase. *Exports.*

The total number of cases of canned salmon exported directly, all to the United Kingdom, was 120,400, each containing 48 lbs. of preserved salmon, which was of a greater average value than the preceding season. *Canned salmon.*

A great decrease in quantities of wheat and flour can be seen, the reason being already given under the head of exports. *Wheat and flour.*

The export of lumber shows a relatively large and steady increase from the years previously noticed, the bulk of the foreign export going to South America, the domestic markets both of the California Coast and the interior States taking the very large proportion of lumber manufactured in this district. *Lumber.*

The two staple manufacturing industries of salmon-canning and lumber show a gain in this Vice-Consular district. *Manufactures and industries.*

Lumbering shows the more steady advance on the Columbia River, as well as the bays and rivers to the north and south of the port. Logging railways in several places are used, and extensions of the same may be noted. The output of the mills is mostly, as yet, going for the domestic demand in neighbouring States. *Lumbering.*

Owing to the fact of the persistent fishing, together with the use of pound-traps and fish-wheels, without any corresponding effort to restock the river, the salmon catch by gill-nets has fallen off very much; the price paid to the fishermen ranged from 3s. to 4s. per fish. *Salmon fishing.*

The prices of canned salmon ranged a great deal higher than in 1886, but owing to the increased price of raw fish and the greatly decreased quantity put up, the canning industry has not been very profitable, either directly on the Columbia River or on the adjacent rivers and bays on the coast. The total pack of the district amounted to 507,000 cases, divided as follows:— *Canned salmon.*

Columbia River, spring catch	350,000
,, ,, fall catch	27,000
Coast north of Columbia River	55,000
,, south ,, ,,	75,000

UNITED STATES.

Shipping.

I have still to call attention to the fact of a great deal of fish that is unfit for food being put up; all of it is the so-called "fall catch." This, however, is sent into the interior for United States domestic consumption. The average price per case (f.o.b.) was—Columbia River salmon, 26s. 8d. per case; coast fish, 24s. 6d. per case.

As already shown, the effect of the "wheat combination" of the spring of 1887 being to retard the export season by fully two months, has had the effect of preventing the engagements of the vessels at the usual time, and has therefore affected the returns, which will doubtless show in the present year.

A still larger class of vessels are arriving, and the proportion of tonnage under the British flag is still more noticeable.

Government improvements.

The jetty at the mouth of the Columbia River is slowly progressing, and, as far as the work has proceeded, shows good results both in its stability and the effect on the depth of water.

Labour.

The prices paid for all kinds of skilled labour continue very good; no workmen above the manual labourer need be without remunerative employment.

Immigration.

The wealth in forest and rivers still continues to attract the class of persons adapted to the pursuits of lumbering and fishing, although other settlers are coming in mostly for stock-raising on a limited scale.

Health.

The health of the district still remains perfectly good.

Annex A.—RETURN of all Shipping at the Port of Astoria, Oregon, U.S., during the Year 1887.

ENTERED.

Nationality.	Sailing. Number of Vessels.	Sailing. Tons.	Steam. Number of Vessels.	Steam. Tons.	Total. Number of Vessels.	Total. Tons.
British	83	94,980	...	...	83	94,980
American	10	9,943	...	...	10	9,943
German	2	2,349	...	...	2	2,349
Norwegian	2	2,137	...	...	2	2,137
Total	97	109,409	...	...	97	109,409
,, for preceding year	...	...	...	...	152	162,647

CLEARED.

Nationality.	Sailing. Number of Vessels.	Sailing. Tons.	Steam. Number of Vessels.	Steam. Tons.	Total. Number of Vessels.	Total. Tons.
British	84	99,409	...	...	84	99,409
American	22	21,913	...	...	22	21,913
German	1	623	...	...	1	623
Norwegian	2	2,137	...	...	2	2,137
Total	109	124,082	...	...	109	124,082
,, for preceding year	...	...	...	...	180	172,362

SAN FRANCISCO.

Annex B.—RETURN of Principal Articles of Export from Astoria, Oregon, U.S., during the Year 1887.

Articles.		1887.		1886.	
		Quantity.	Value in Sterling.	Quantity.	Value in Sterling.
			£		£
Preserved salmon	Qrs.	142,482	146,800	156,187	155,265
Wheat	Bushels	543,940	80,000	814,264	121,762
Flour	Barrels	18,781	14,600	26,991	20,248
Lumber	M. feet	3,297	7,800	2,346	4,973
Sundries	...	...	891	...	2,804
Total	...	...	250,091	...	305,052

RETURN of Principal Articles of Import for 1887.

Articles.		1887.		1886.	
		Quantity.	Value in Sterling.	Quantity.	Value in Sterling.
			£		£
Tin plates	Boxes	69,704	44,744	45,704	30,795
Salt	Tons	75	89	85	110
Coals	,,	3,381	2,222	4,228	2,635
Sundries	...	...	...	...	400
Total	...	...	47,055	...	33,940

Annex C.—TABLE showing the Total Value of all Articles Exported from Astoria, Oregon, and Imported to Astoria, Oregon, from and to Foreign Countries during the Years 1887 and 1886.

Country.	Exports.		Imports.	
	1887.	1886.	1887.	1886.
	£	£	£	£
Great Britain	240,000	273,000	44,750	30,954
British colonies	73	168	2,274	2,779
Other countries	9,095	31,851	..	..
Total	249,168	305,019	47,024	33,733

LOS ANGELES.

Mr. Vice-Consul Mortimer report as follows:—

Introductory remarks. For the past four years I have annually called attention to the extraordinary increase of this city and district in wealth and population. Each year has seen so marked an increase as to appear almost phenomenal. The year 1887 is marked by an advance in business, population, and general prosperity even greater than any of its predecessors. The following brief statements will illustrate this:—In the year 1880 the population of Los Angeles was about 11,000; in the year 1887 it increased from 50,000 to 75,000. The principal architects of this city have furnished statements showing the construction of buildings during the year to the value of 1,500,000*l.*, an increase of 700,000*l.* on the operations of 1886. The number of passenger and freight trains which arrive and depart from the city daily is 136, as against about 80 per day in 1886.

The books of the County Recorder show that, in the year 1885, 6,471 transfers of real estate were made, the aggregate consideration of which amounted to nearly 2,000,000*l*. In 1886 the number of transfers was 13,559, and the aggregate consideration exceeded 5,600,000*l*. In 1887 the number of transfers increased to 33,287, and the aggregate consideration exceeded 19,000,000*l*. From these figures it will be seen that there has been a great deal of activity in the real estate market, or, as it is called here, a "boom." There is so much English capital invested here, and so many English people are interested in the prosperity of this district, that I venture to give elsewhere in this report, under the heading "The Boom in Real Estate," some particulars about present and prospective values which might otherwise be regarded as of local interest only.

The Trans-Continental Railways report that the local freight received at Los Angeles during the year 1887 exceeded that received at San Francisco by 50,000 tons, and that the total amount received exceeded that of the year 1886 by 77 per cent.

Trade and Commerce.

Chief exports. The chief exports from this district are grain, wine, oranges, raisins, and other fruits and honey.

Grain. The acreage in grain is steadily increasing. The yield of wheat, barley, and corn in Los Angeles County in 1887 exceeded 7,000,000 bushels.

Wine. The State Viticultural Commissioner reports an increase in the acreage in vines for 1887 of 2,500 acres. Although the acreage in grapes is increasing annually at a very rapid rate, the best authorities agree that there is no danger of over-production for many years to come.

Experiments in wine making. The wine-makers of Southern California have made experiments as to the best vines suited to this district. It has not yet, however, been demonstrated that a good dry wine can be produced here. They have succeeded in making a really good sweet sherry and an excellent quality of brandy.

The necessity for the irrigation of the vineyards in the dry season is the cause assigned for the want of success in the production of choice clarets and Rhine wines.

The product of wine and brandy for the year was about 5,000,000 gallons.

Orange crop decreased. Owing partly to the ravages of the "White Scale," but principally to the division of orange groves into town lots, the crop in Los Angeles County this year is considerably less than that of 1886; 1,400 carloads (14,000 tons) are reported for 1887, as against 2,000 carloads for 1886.

Quality of raisins. The product in this district for 1886 was about 600,000 boxes. The estimated product for 1887 is 800,000 boxes. The quality is excellent. The counties of Fresno and San Bernardino are becoming famous for the ripening and curing of the well-known raisin grape, the Muscat of Alexandria.

Increased facilities for shipping fruit. The marked increase in the shipments of fresh and dried fruits from this district to the Eastern States is due partly to increased production, and partly to the increased railway facilities consequent upon the competition between the Trans-Continental Railways. In 1869, when the experiment of shipping fresh fruit from

California to the Eastern States was first tried, the railroad freight was 240*l.* a car on express trains and 160*l.* by goods trains. The present rates are 120*l.* and 50*l.* respectively. There is a further gain in time of three and a half days on express trains, and ten days on goods trains, owing to increased speed.

The principal imports are coal, pig iron, Portland cement, coke, soda, potash, paints, patent medicines, and crockery. _{Chief imports}

The average price of coal for several years past has been, wholesale, 2*l.* 10*s.* per ton; retail, 3*l.* 10*s.* This winter there has been a "coal famine," and the price has been from 4*l.* to 6*l.* per ton. As I stated last year Australian coal can be laid down at this port for 1*l.* 10*s.*, inclusive of 3*s.* per ton duty. As the cost of importing has not materially increased, it will be seen that the profits to the importer are very large. It is openly stated in the Press that the Southern Pacific Railroad gives a special rate on coals from the port to Los Angeles (25 miles) to one firm, and has been subsidised to do so. I applied to the company last year for their rate on coals from Wilmington to this city, but did not succeed in getting a reply. _{Coal.}

An immense quantity of Portland cement has been used during the past year in the construction of side-walks in this city and in the new cities in the vicinity, also in the manufacture of irrigation and drainage pipes. The Los Angeles Cable Railroad Company have in store and en route 20,000 barrels to be used in laying some 14 miles of cable railways. There have been no direct importations here during the year. I am glad to see, however, that a British ship is now discharging a cargo of 1,600 tons. Importations of Portland cement, iron, &c., viâ San Francisco, increase the cost to the consumer here by about 32*s.* per ton for railway freight. _{Increased demand for Portland cement.}

Crockery is imported viâ New York and New Orleans. One firm tells me that they have of late dealt solely in crockery made in the Eastern States, that they are not satisfied with it, and that they will recommence importing from the United Kingdom. _{English and American crockery.}

Stationery is very expensive here, so much so that I think it possible for English manufacturers to compete, notwithstanding the duty. _{Paper.}

Notwithstanding the fact that the wholesale price of the best fruit here is about one halfpenny per pound, I find that the jams of Messrs. Crosse and Blackwell are extensively sold here. _{English preserves.}

The supply of lumber for this city is controlled by a "lumber ring." I am informed, on good authority, that lumber from Oregon can be laid down at the port for 3*l.* per 1,000 feet. The average price here for several years past has been 6*l.* per 1,000 feet. Of late lumber has been shipped to Southern California from the State of Michigan; the fact that Michigan lumbermen can pay railroad freights for 2,500 miles shows the large profits accruing to the dealers in Oregon lumber here. _{Price of lumber.}

I have received circulars from a large number of British manufacturers, and have redirected them to the principal dealers in this city. I am not aware, however, that business has resulted in consequence. In view of the large increase in population, and of the fact that it appears probable that a like increase will continue until Southern California is thickly populated, I feel justified in advising British manufacturers who are competing for the trade of the Western States to send agents to represent them here. _{Manufacturers' agents.}

In my report for 1886 I stated that the Government had expended 140,000*l.* in improving Wilmington Harbour; that in

Wilmington harbour; its drawbacks and advantages.

so far as foreign-going shipping is concerned this expenditure has been almost barren of results; that foreign-going ships have still to anchor in the outer harbour, and discharge and receive cargo in lighters; that there they are entirely unprotected from the south-east wind, and that several have been driven ashore and wrecked in gales from the south-east. The apathy of the people here in not securing a safe harbour has driven a great deal of shipping to San Diego. A survey of Wilmington Harbour has recently been made by the Government engineer. In his report he directs attention to the fact that Wilmington possesses several advantages over San Francisco for the overland transportation of Asiatic commerce, the chief being that the railway haul is about 500 miles less, and as two considerable mountain ranges have to be crossed in this 500 miles, the distance is equal to 800 miles. He advocated the construction of a breakwater from Point Firmin (see map accompanying my report for the year 1886) in an easterly direction, the estimated cost of which is 800,000l. The matter is now before Congress. The Southern Pacific Railway is constructing a line to Point Firmin, and it is stated in the Press here that the company intends building a pier half a mile in length, at which the largest ships will be able to discharge cargo.

A breakwater to enclose the outer harbour.

Low freights from Australia.

Most of the British ships come here with coals from Australia. I am at a loss to understand why they come here. The freight from Australia barely pays expenses, and as there is practically no grain here for shipment they have to take away sand ballast, for which they pay 7s. per ton delivered on board. The past four years the average rate from Australia has been 14s. per ton. I am informed that in the past four months the rates have been advanced to about 22s. per ton. Even at this increased rate the profit must be nominal, when, as has frequently happened, ships clear in ballast for South America and the Indian Ocean.

Seamen's wages.

Owners should also consider, in chartering for this port, that the chances are the sailors will be enticed away from the ship, and new men will have to be shipped at about 8l. per month, the average current rate of wages on this coast.

Deserters.

Desertions were numerous during the year, even among crews receiving the high wages paid in Australia and on this coast. The crew of the "Zuleika," who shipped at San Francisco six or seven months previously at the rate of from 6l. to 8l. per month, deserted after they had discharged the cargo, leaving large sums due them.

Ballona harbour.

In my last report I stated that private parties were attempting to make a harbour for foreign-going shipping at Ballona, a small lake or pond about 15 miles from this city. They have expended a large sum of money, and have succeeded in dredging a channel sufficiently deep to admit small coasting schooners at high water.

Proposed new harbour.

A number of local capitalists have formed a company to construct a harbour at Redondo Beach, about half-way between Ballona and Wilmington. A number of costly improvements have been made. They claim that this harbour when completed will admit foreign-going shipping and control the Asiatic commerce. There are several other embryo harbours in this district which, when carried to completion, are to control the Asiatic commerce.

The collection district of Wilmington includes as ports of delivery Santa Barbara, San Buenaventura, and Hueneme. The area of the counties of which these are the ports aggregates nearly 40,000 square miles.

Agriculture.

I am indebted to Mr. D. Freeman, a Canadian gentleman who owned and farmed a ranch of 25,000 acres, for the following particulars as to the cost of harvesting, &c. :—Cost of ploughing, preparing the land for seed, and sowing, 1s. 3d. per acre; cost of harvesting, 1s. 2d. per acre: total cost, exclusive of seed, 2s. 5d. per acre. On many of the large ranches steam ploughs are used, and on others gang ploughs, which turn four to six furrows, and are drawn by from eight to 14 mules. Not unfrequently the ploughs are run in a straight line for a distance of six or eight miles. A patent machine for sowing seed is employed, by means of which one man and a team can sow 100 acres of grain in a day. The acreage in grain is increasing largely every year in this district. In consequence, however, of the growth in population the surplus for export remains about the same and is sent to Arizona. A number of large grain ranches have been subdivided and sold in small tracts during the past year.

The vintage of 1887 was not good, owing to a disease which attacked the vines. Beginning at the tips this disease slowly spreads down to the roots. The second season after its appearance there is but half a crop, and in the third season the vines die. It is attributed to cellular degeneration, and is stated to be similar to that which attacked the vineyards in Sicily and Madeira some years ago.

The *Phylloxera*, which is doing damage some 400 miles north, has not yet appeared here, and until recently the vines of this district were singularly free from disease. It has been supposed that vines grafted on the *V. Californica* would resist the attacks of the *Phylloxera*. Professor Pierre Viala, of Montpellier, in a recent report to the Minister of Agriculture, says, however, that the *V. Californica* would not offer much resistance.

The "white scale" is still doing a great deal of damage in the orange groves. I stated in my last report that Mr. Wolfskill was about to patent an apparatus for applying gas to orange and other trees, which, it was claimed, would kill all scale bugs without injuring the trees. I have heard nothing further, however, of this invention. The crop on the Wolfskill orchard (29 acres) was sold a few years ago for 5,000l.; this year it is not worth gathering, and the trees are being cut down.

Mr. Chapman, of San Gabriel, Commissioner of Agriculture, states, in his annual report, "The black scale has ceased to be a pest, owing to the parasite fly, which has kept it in subjection. The red scale is very bad, but Professor Coquillete has found a parasite feeding on it, and yet looks to nature for relief. The white scale has been steadily increasing, notwithstanding the efforts to keep it in subjection. One internal parasite has been found feeding on it, which will be watched with interest. The apple crop this year was very heavy. The nut crop and English walnut crop both yielded and sold well, though the price has since receded from 9 to 7 c. on the buyer's hands. There is a great future for California lemons. This fruit keeps well, sells well, and is ripening every month in the year. The crop matures in December and January, but the fruit is kept till June, when the market is better."

Population and Industries.

The population of this city has increased about 25,000 in the past year, and there has been a corresponding increase in the counties comprising this district.

Want of fuel. A list of the factories in this city will be found in my reports for 1884 and 1886. The want of a cheap and abundant supply of fuel has heretofore prevented the development of manufacturing industries on a large scale. The owners of the flowing oil wells in Los Angeles and Ventura counties state that they intend piping the oil to this city. Should this scheme be carried out, and should the fuel so provided be sold at a reasonable cost, extensive manufactories will probably be established, as the variety and number of raw materials produced here only await an abundant supply of fuel in order to be converted into articles of commerce.

Increase in yield of oil. The yield of oil from the wells of Los Angeles and Ventura counties exceeds 2,000 barrels per day, being a little more than double the yield of last year. New oil fields are constantly being discovered and developed in this district. It is estimated that the yield will shortly reach 5,000 barrels a day. The product is not of very good quality, and is used principally for fuel.

Iron ore. Iron ore in very large quantities has been discovered here. The lack of cheap fuel makes the discovery of very small value, however.

Ostriches. A number of ostriches were imported from Africa several years ago, and there are now four or five ostrich farms here. This industry is almost entirely in the hands of Englishmen, and, I am informed, is not proving very remunerative.

Piping. Owing to the large number of new "cities" laid out, the manufacture of iron and cement piping has largely increased. Iron is imported principally from the United Kingdom by way of San Francisco. Some Portland cement has been shipped direct to this port, but the bulk has come viâ San Francisco.

Public companies. In my report for 1886 I gave a list of the public companies incorporated here during that year, the aggregate capital stock of which amounted to something less than 6,000,000*l*. The aggregate capital stock of the companies incorporated here during the year 1887 exceeds 18,000,000*l*.

Electric and cable tramways. The electric railway referred to in my last report has been extended in different directions, and is being still further extended. About eight miles are now operated. I also stated that upwards of 26 miles of street railroads—horse, cable, and electric—were in operation in this city; this has since increased to over 40 miles.

The horse-cars are being superseded by a system of cable roads, the estimated cost of which is 300,000*l*.

Mining. An English company is investing a very large sum of money in the development of some gold and silver mines in the San Gabriel Cañon, about 25 miles east of this city. An English mining engineer of good standing, who was sent here by the company to examine and report, assured me that the mines are exceedingly valuable.

The output of bullion from the mines of this district has increased in the past year.

New railways. A map of this district accompanied my report for the year 1886 to show the harbours and the railways constructed and in course of construction. A new map would now be necessary to give a correct idea of railway development in the past year. The most important of the lines projected of which there is any reasonable probability of completion in the immediate future is a line from Los Angeles to Salt Lake City, a distance of 641 miles. The company has incorporated and, it is stated, has secured the necessary capital, about 4,000,000*l*. This line will lessen the distance between Los Angeles and Chicago by 600 miles. In view of the large shipments of fruit from this district to cities in the Eastern States, the importance of a gain of 24 hours will be readily seen.

It is stated that the proposed line will pass through some very large coalfields in Southern Utah as yet undeveloped. The other lines projected, and which it is proposed to build shortly, are so numerous that I will not refer to them. The following lines were completed in 1887, or are in course of construction:—

(1.) A branch of the Southern Pacific from Newhall, Los Angeles County, to Santa Barbara, 77 miles.

(2.) The California Central Railroad (working with the Atlantic and Pacific, and the Atchison, Topeka, and Santa Fé as a transcontinental line in opposition to the South Pacific Railway, and referred to in this report as the Atlantic and Pacific) is constructing a line from Riverside to Los Angeles viâ Santa Ana, 77 miles.

(3.) The same company has also built a line from Los Angeles to Ballona Harbour, 15 miles.

(4.) The Los Angeles County Railroad is constructing a line from Los Angeles to Santa Monica, 16 miles: this line is completed to the ostrich farm, a distance of eight miles.

(5.) The Rosecrans Railway has completed a line from Los Angeles to Rosecrans, a distance of eight miles.

(6.) The San Gabriel Valley Rapid Transit Railway is building from Los Angeles to Mourovia, a distance of 18 miles.

(7.) The Los Angeles and Glendale Railway has completed a line to Glendale, seven miles.

General Remarks.

There are 20 banks in the city and county of Los Angeles. The assets of these banks aggregate a little over 4,000,000*l*. The rate of interest on the best first mortgage security is from 8 to 12 per cent. per annum. *Bank assets. 4,000,000l.*

On small sums—200*l*. to 400*l*.—the rate is even higher. I have anticipated a decline in the rate of interest for the past six years: no variation has taken place, however, and indications now point to a continuance of present rates for several years. *Rate of interest on mortgage. Horse raising.*

In my last report I directed attention to the fact that there is an excellent opening here for those wishing to raise thoroughbred racehorses. Owing chiefly to the mildness and equability of the climate, horses can be raised here at a very moderate cost. It is, I think, worthy of consideration whether horses for the British Army could not be raised in Southern California and shipped to England viâ New Orleans. *Horse breeding.*

The price of real estate has advanced steadily for the past four years, and in this city has reached such a figure that the prospect of a further rise can only be predicated on the assumption that within four years the population will have reached 250,000, which I think by no means improbable. The extraordinary demand for landed property is best illustrated by the fact that in this city alone there are nearly 2,000 persons paying license as land agents. 8,000*l*. was recently paid for a lot 20 by 100 feet, or at the rate of 400*l*. a front foot; 600*l*. per front foot was offered and refused for another lot in the centre of the city. At this rate an acre divided into lots 100 feet deep would be worth over 260,000*l*., or a good deal more than twice as much, as by cablegram I see was recently paid for land in Cecil and Salisbury-streets, London. *Value of land.*

Upwards of 100 towns and settlements have been laid out within the past year in this district, and I am informed that there are 40 new

The "Boom" in real estate.

cities on the line of the Atlantic and Pacific Railroad between Los Angeles and San Bernardino, a distance of 60 miles. At the first sales of lots in many of these new cities in May and June last, many persons remained standing in line in front of the places of sale for more than 24 hours for the privilege of buying a lot. As a specimen of the mode of advertising lots in these embryo cities the following, taken from the Los Angeles daily papers, will strike English readers as peculiar: "In God's all-seeing eye there is no place like ———." "A lot in ——— is better than being in Abraham's bosom," &c. It has been stated half seriously that one can walk on "city" lots from Ontario to Los Angeles, a distance of 40 miles. Several of these new-born cities are being built up very rapidly, and are increasing marvellously in population; many of them, however, are destined to revert to farming lands. The frantic speculation in lots in almost all the new cities has entirely ceased, and the "boom" has to some extent abated throughout the whole district. In this city the permanent improvements now being completed, and for which contracts have been made, preclude the possibility of any material decline in prices. The estimated value of the buildings now being constructed exceeds 500,000*l*. United States Government and Municipal buildings to the value of 200,000*l*. will be erected this year. A company has commenced work on the construction of cable railways through the streets of the city, which, when completed, will cost not less than 300,000*l*. The fact that Los Angeles is connected with the Eastern States by two competing trans-continental lines of railway, and that a third, the Los Angeles and Salt Lake City Railway, is projected, and will probably be carried to completion in the near future, is the best indication of the estimation in which this district is held throughout the country.

Permanent improvement in Los Angeles.

Warning to non-resident speculators.

I am informed that persons in Canada and England have invested in real estate here tempted by glowing advertisements. The risk of speculating in real estate to persons living at a distance, and whose information as to values, &c., is obtained merely through some advertising medium, is enormous. The mere fact that a real estate firm is highly commended in a daily paper proves nothing. A short time ago a firm described as "gentlemen," "honest," "trustworthy," "enterprising," and "energetic" was a few days later fully exposed as an organised set of swindlers; and this is by no means an isolated instance.

Transfer of land.

The system in use here for transferring and mortgaging land is a poor one. Private enterprise has, however, supplemented the deficiencies of the official records. A company has taken copies of such records, and is now keeping them in accordance with the system in use in the province of Ontario, Canada. This company now issue title insurance policies guaranteeing the owners of the lands insured against loss on account of defects in title.

Climate.

A report on this district in which no reference was made to climate would be incomplete, as the prosperity of Southern California is unquestionably due to the fact that, taking it all the year round, the climate is one of the best in the world. The rainfall is irregular. The precipitation in inches for the past six years has been as follows:— 10·40; 12·11; 38·22; 9·25; 22·58; and 13·76. For full information respecting the climate I refer to my report for the year 1884. I may also refer to a recent publication, entitled "California of the South," edited by two physicians here, Drs. J. P. Widney and H. Lindley. As this volume contains maps and information useful to strangers, intending emigrants would do well to purchase it. Address, Messrs. Merrill and Cook, stationers, Los Angeles; price 8*s*.

New book about Southern California.

In my last report I stated, "Many Englishmen who have come here have been unsuccessful owing to the unpractical education they had received." In the past year so many cases have come under my notice of young Englishmen of good education and position who have been unsuccessful here, and who now occupy the humble positions of farm labourers and waiters in restaurants, that I venture to call attention to what I conceive to be the explanation of the matter. The principal element of success in this country is the ability to adapt oneself to the ways, habits, manners, and business methods of the people; and it must be remembered that a good education without knowledge of business methods, and without special training in a trade or profession, is in many respects worse than useless. *Immigration.*

Elements of success.

In my report for 1885 I stated that "domestic servants who are willing to do the work that two or three servants would be employed to do in England can readily get employment at from 5*l.* to 6*l.* per month, and board." This is still the case, it being understood that the term domestic servant means a general servant who understands cooking, &c. *Domestic servants.*

Efforts are being made to establish an Episcopal bishopric in Los Angeles. At present there is but one Episcopal bishopric for the whole State. A diocese will be established here if sufficient funds can be collected to ensure the Bishop an income of 600*l.* per annum. In 1880 there were only four Episcopal clergymen in Southern California. I am informed by the Rev. the Dean of Southern California that there are now 24 clergymen ministering to 38 parishes and missions. I give these statistics in consequence of numerous letters received from English clergymen who contemplate settling here. *New bishopric.*

Visitors complain of the high prices and inferior accommodation at the hotels and boarding-houses. The best boarding-houses charge from 10*l.* to 15*l.* per month for board and lodging, and not unfrequently boarders have to resort to a restaurant to get something to eat. An hotel which, when completed, will cost upwards of 200,000*l.* is now in course of erection. *Inferior hotel accommodation. High prices.*

The system of "high license" for public-houses (here called saloons) has been adopted with the following results:—In June, 1886, the saloon license was 2*l.* per month; the population was about 40,000, and there were 200 saloons. In June, 1887, the population of the city had increased about 20,000; the saloon license was 10*l.* per month, and there were only 139 saloons. The council of the city of Pasadena passed an ordinance prohibiting saloons and the sale of liquor within the limits of the municipality. This ordinance the Supreme Court of this State recently decreed to be valid and constitutional. *Liquor traffic.*

I am indebted to Mr. Hinds, collector of customs at Wilmington, for the statistics in Annexes A., B., and C.

Note.—In this report dollars have been converted into £ at the rate of 5 dol. per £.

UNITED STATES.

Annex A.—RETURN of all Shipping at the Port of Wilmington (San Pedro), California, in the Year 1887.

ENTERED.

Nationality.	Sailing. Number of Vessels.	Sailing. Tons.	Steam. Number of Vessels.	Steam. Tons.	Total. Number of Vessels.	Total. Tons.
British	43	62,450	3	3,990	46	66,440
American	18	23,590	...	...	18	23,590
Other countries	3	3,864	...	...	3	3,864
Total	64	89,904	3	3,990	67	93,894
" for the year preceding...	50	70,222	...	...	50	70,222

NOTE.—This return does not include 784 sailing and steam coasting vessels, aggregate tonnage 343,074.

CLEARED.

Nationality.	Sailing. Number of Vessels.	Sailing. Tons.	Steam. Number of Vessels.	Steam. Tons.	Total. Number of Vessels.	Total. Tons.
British	40	58,276	3	3,990	43	62,266
American	20	25,665	...	...	20	25,665
Other countries	3	3,864	...	...	3	3,864
Total	63	87,805	3	3,990	66	91,795
" for the year preceding...	56	77,975	...	...	56	77,975

Annex B.—RETURN of the Principal Articles of Export from Wilmington, California, during the Years 1886–87.

Articles.	1886. Value.	1886. Quantity.	1887. Value.	1887. Quantity.
	£	Tons.	£	Tons.
Wheat	30,342	5,776	6,800	1,190
Honey	184	9	...	...
Total	30,526	5,785	6,800	1,190

RETURN of the Principal Articles of Import to Wilmington, California, during the Years 1886-87.

Articles.	1886. Value.	1886. Quantity.	1887. Value.	1887. Quantity.
	£	Tons.	£	Tons.
Coal	155,124	77,562	262,000	131,000
Pig iron	226	106	1,800	405
Other articles	485	224	2,400	567
Total	155,835	77,892	266,200	131,972

NOTE.—The trans-continental railways cannot furnish the statistics called for in this return for the city of Los Angeles.

Annex C.—TABLE showing the Total Value of all Articles Exported from Wilmington, and Imported to Wilmington, from and to Foreign Countries during the Years 1886–87.

Countries.	Exports.		Imports.	
	1886.	1887.	1886.	1887.
Great Britain	£ 30,526	£ 6,800	£ 155,835	£ 266,200
Total	30,526	6,800	155,835	266,200

SAN DIEGO.

Mr. Vice-Consul Winchester reports as follows:—

The rapid growth and development reported, as exhibited by San Diego in the year 1886, has continued and been still more marked in its character in 1887.

The British vessels entered at this port in 1886 numbered four. In 1887 their number was 29. In my last Report I mentioned that nine British ships were then named as on the way here, and that there was known to be 13,000 tons of cargo contracted to be delivered here, for which vessels had not then been named. At the date of this writing there are 34 British ships under charter, besides 22 others of European nationality (principally Norwegian), and 10 American, of an aggregate tonnage of 71,422 tons, reported under charter for this Bay from distant ports. Of these, the greater number consist of vessels bringing coal from Newcastle and Sydney, N.S.W., for railroad use. Five vessels are from London with cement, earthenware, bricks, and groceries, and one each from Glasgow, Liverpool, and Antwerp.

Shipping.

Port facilities have been overtaxed during the later months of the year, and vessels were detained through insufficient discharging and ballasting appliances. These have been increased, and vessels now have good despatch, which is also likely to be given in the future.

Port charges are as follows:—Inward pilotage, 5 dol. per foot draught, and 4 c. per ton register additional. Outward pilotage, same rates as inward. Vessels leaving without pilots pay half rates.

The following is a schedule of the contract rates for tugs belonging to Spreckels Bros.' Commercial Co. Shipmasters not under contract will have to make the best bargains when met outside. The price fixed should, if possible, include all shifting required inside the harbour as well as towage in and out. Actual rates will vary according to the degree of competition and the needs of vessels.

Tugs.

Towage Contract Rates.

Per net registered tonnage.	Tons, 400 and under 600.	Tons, 600 and under 800.	Tons, 800 and under 1000.	Tons, 1000 and under 1,250.	Tons, 1,250 and under 1,500.	Tons, 1,500 and under 1,750.	Tons, 1,750 and under 2,000.	Tons, 2,000 and under 2,250.	Tons, 2,250 and under 2,500.
	Dol.	Dol.	Dol	Dol.	Dol.	Dol.	Dol.	Dol.	Dol.
From Whistling Buoy to San Diego, or San Diego to Whistling Buoy, once docking and undocking at San Diego included in these rates...	40	52	60	75	80	90	100	110	125
Docking and undocking at San Diego	15	17½	20	22½	25	27½	30	32½	35
Additional to above, if from or to National City	10	12½	15	17	20	22½	25	27½	30
San Diego, to or from National City...	20	25	30	35	40	45	50	55	60
Single moves from wharf to wharf, San Diego, or Coronado	8	15	17	20	22	24	26	28	30

Stevedoring. Present rates are: coal 50 c., cement 40 c. per ton, general cargo subject to arrangement. It is expected that before long these rates will be reduced, and the work be performed as cheaply as at San Francisco.

Half-weighing charges on coal cannot be charged to ships by the custom of the port, though they are sometimes provided for by charterparty.

Dockage rates are as follows:—2 dol. for first 200 registered tons, and ⅜ cent for each additional ton, per diem. This charge is one-half of schedule rates in San Francisco.

Ballasting. Sand is delivered alongside for 60 c. per ton, down hatch for 1 dol., or trimmed in hold for 1 dol. 20 c. per ton (of 2,000 lbs.).

Water is ½ c. to 1 c. per gallon, according to quantity taken, and whether put on board alongside wharf or in the stream.

Seamen. Desertions are frequent, many vessels losing their entire crews; but it has been found practicable to obtain men at as low rates as are current anywhere on the coast. At present 25 dol. per month is paid for northern ports, and 4l. to 5l. for long voyages. Shipping masters' fees are 2½ dol. to 5 dol.

Crimping. A bad case of crimping occurred in November, when over 60 men belonging to the Coast Seamen's Union forcibly removed three non-union sailors from the British barque "Darra" while lying at anchor in the Bay. The authorities at once yielded to representations made to them, and appointed Bayfront police. Additional men were sent on board with an armed guard, and the vessel sailed with a complete non-union crew. There has since been no violence perpetrated on British sailors. The Seamen's Union has been ignored, and crews have been shipped through an independent shipping master.

Marine ways. Ways, and the necessary machinery for docking vessels up to 1,500 tons, have just been completed. Overhaul and repairs can now be given with satisfactory appliances and at a reasonable cost.

Railroads. The short cut to Los Angeles, mentioned in my last report, is not yet open, though construction is so far forward that it is expected to be in operation at the end of June. The opening of this road will have an important effect upon the trade of the port, as it will allow of coals and general merchandise being delivered at Los Angeles through San Diego as cheaply as through San Pedro, and without the injury through extra handling, and the occasional losses in transhipment, experienced at the latter place.

There are several branch roads surveyed, and it is probable that building will shortly commence to connect the Southern Pacific system with this port, at the same time opening out interior districts of great productiveness. At present the California Southern Railroad (affiliated with the Atchison Topeka and Santa Fé System) is the only one having terminal facilities here. The advent of the Southern Pacific road would enormously increase the import business of the place.

Considerable immigration has taken place into the adjoining Mexican province of Lower California under the auspices of the International Colonisation Company of Mexico. A serious check has been given to this Company's operations lately so far as relates to settlement of agricultural and fruit lands, but an excitement has been initiated in regard to mining projects in the district, and active explorations are being made. It appears that considerable mineral wealth exists in the district covered by the concession to the Company, but it is yet uncertain whether the deposits are sufficiently permanent in character to allow of their being profitably worked. Deficient water supply, complications in Mexican titles, and the unavoidable drawbacks incident to operating among a non-English speaking community, and under a tariff which, as regards many necessaries of life, is severely felt, all operate to restrain development that, under other circumstances, might be undertaken with an assurance of success.

<small>Lower California.</small>

The phenomenal character of the growth of San Diego during 1887 is well shown in the following statistics, which have been compiled by the statistical secretary of the Chamber of Commerce from the best data procurable.

		End of 1886.	End of 1887.
City population		12,000	35,000
County ,,		30,000	65,000
City assessed values	Dollars	4,582,213	13,433,971
County ,,	,,	14,522,238	24,396,735
Cost of new buildings erected during the year	,,	250,000	3,350,000
Street railroads in operation	Miles	6¾	9¼
Motor roads in operation (electric and steam)	,,	..	26¼
Wharves in operation (berthing space)	Feet	6,300	9,300
Wharves under construction	,,	..	13,310
Capital in public enterprises, viz.:—			
Water and irrigation companies	Dollars	350,000	2,200,000
Street railroads and motor lines	,,	60,000	1,035,000
Gas and electric lighting works	,,	100,000	500,000
Streets graded	Miles	9½	22
Main sewers laid	,,	..	11½
,, in course of construction	,,	..	32½

The reputation of the district as a winter resort has been sustained, and among the hotels lately built is one accommodating 750 guests on Coronado Beach—a peninsula between San Diego Bay and the ocean, reached by a short ferry—that is unsurpassed for elegance and completeness of equipment in the Western States.

As a sanitarium it is being recognised that the coast climate of San Diego, though enjoyable by the healthy, and helpful to many invalids, is not suitable for persons suffering from pulmonary diseases, but these can obtain relief, and often permanent cure, from residence in the interior at an elevation of 1,500 to 2,500 feet above sea level, and at such a distance from the coast that the air is less charged with humidity from the ocean.

British immigrants have come in in good numbers. Those bringing capital, skilled mechanics and steady labourers, have done well, though at present the supply of labour of all kinds is in excess of the demand. It is almost impossible for clerks and shopmen to obtain employment No one should come without some capital to fall back upon.

Values of lands within the city limits (which are extensive enough for a population of 1,000,000) have enhanced enormously. Up to December the advance was continuous and by rapid strides. Little discrimination was shown by many of the buyers, and many purchases were effected under contracts by which 20 to 40 per cent. of the purchase money was paid in cash, the balance becoming due by instalments extending over 6 to 24 months. Over-speculation resulted, and upon instalments becoming due many holders found themselves involved in respect of property in undesirable locations for which no investment buyers could be found. Such property was then forced on the market, and a time of financial stringency followed. There has since been a re-adjustment of values, the highest class of business and residence property maintaining firmness, and less desirable finding a fair relative level.

The settlement of country lands has progressed at a fair rate, and will be further stimulated by the railroad extensions projected. Values have not been inflated, as in some other sections of Southern California. Lands well adapted for fruit-growing can be had at very moderate prices, and this pursuit is found by those having an aptitude for it both pleasant and profitable. Those seeking lands should investigate the capabilities of irrigation as well as the character of the soil, and with reasonable care success may be expected. The price of good fruit lands capable of irrigation is 100 dol. to 350 dol. per acre.

Wheat, barley, and maize are grown in the district, but, owing to the rainfall being precarious and frequently insufficient, crops are uncertain and the industry on the whole is unprofitable.

Capitalists can realise 7 to 10 per cent., clear of taxes, on good mortgage security, lending not over 30 to 40 per cent. of the value of the property mortgaged.

Annex A.—RETURN of all Shipping at the Port of San Diego in the Year 1887. (This return does not include steamers and sailing vessels engaged in United States coasting trade, and in the coasting trade to Lower California, Mexico, or vessels sailing in ballast to United States ports on the Pacific coast.)

ENTERED.

Nationality.	Sailing. Number of Vessels.	Sailing. Tons.	Steam. Number of Vessels.	Steam. Tons.	Total. Number of Vessels.	Total. Tons.
British...	28	32,511	1	857	29	33,368
American (United States)	9	11,993	2	1,494	11	13,487
Other countries	4	3,340	1	849	5	4,189
Total	41	47,844	4	3,200	45	51,044
,, for the year preceding	11	12,118	1	101	12	12,219

SAN FRANCISCO.

Cleared.

Nationality.	Sailing. Number of Vessels.	Sailing. Tons.	Steam. Number of Vessels.	Steam. Tons.	Total. Number of Vessels.	Total. Tons.
British...	20	23,585	1	857	21	24,442
American (United States)	4	5,054	1	747	5	5,801
Total	24	28,639	2	1,604	26	30,243
,, for the year preceding	3	2,183	1	80	4	2,263

Annex B.—RETURN of Principal Articles of Export from San Diego during the Years 1886-87.

Articles.	Value. 1887.	Value. 1886.
	£	£
No direct foreign exports other than to Lower California (Mexico). These consist of live stock, lumber, provisions, farm machinery, &c., not classified	67,299	15,671
Total	67,299	15,671

Annex C.—TABLE showing the Total Value of all Articles Exported from and Imported to San Diego during the Years 1886-87.

Country.	Exports. 1887.	Exports. 1886.	Imports. 1887.	Imports. 1886.
	£	£	£	£
Great Britain	..	..	46,907	502
British Possessions	..	..	32,915	10,358
Belgium	..	..	2,373	..
Germany	..	..	119	..
Guatemala	..	..	15	..
Lower California (Mexico)	67,299	15,671	18,585	16,312
Total	67,299	15,671	100,914	27,172

UNITED STATES.

RETURN of Principal Articles of Import to San Diego during the Years 1886–87.

Articles.		1887.		1886.	
		Value.	Quantity.	Value.	Quantity.
		£		£	
Coal—					
Great Britain	Tons	1,752	3,048	...	...
British Possessions	...	...	...	...	...
,, Columbia	,,	21,709	28,287	...	...
Australia	,,	11,056	20,240	...	...
Total	,,	34,517	51,575	10,860	16,141
Cement	Bbls.	5,119	28,045	...	...
Liquors	Packages	260	556	...	...
Window glass	,,	1,427	7,394	...	...
Steel rails	Tons	39,469	6,504	...	...
Fish-plates and bolts	,,	716	66	...	...
Fire and common bricks	Number	49	29,000	...	...
Household effects	...	757	...	...	...
Bird skins	...	15	...	...	...
Lower California (Mexico): Sundries, not classified	...	18,585	...	16,312	...
Total	...	100,914	...	27,172	...

LONDON:
Printed for Her Majesty's Stationery Office,
By HARRISON AND SONS,
Printers in Ordinary to Her Majesty.
(1125 6 | 88—H & S 469)

FOREIGN OFFICE.
1888.
ANNUAL SERIES.

No. 392.
DIPLOMATIC AND CONSULAR REPORTS ON TRADE AND FINANCE.

UNITED STATES.

FURTHER REPORT FOR THE YEAR 1887
ON THE
TRADE OF THE CONSULAR DISTRICT OF SAN FRANCISCO.

REFERENCE TO PREVIOUS REPORTS, Annual Series Nos. 375 and 313.

Presented to both Houses of Parliament by Command of Her Majesty,
JULY, 1888.

LONDON:
PRINTED FOR HER MAJESTY'S STATIONERY OFFICE,
BY HARRISON AND SONS, ST. MARTIN'S LANE,
PRINTERS IN ORDINARY TO HER MAJESTY.

And to be purchased, either directly or through any Bookseller, from
EYRE AND SPOTTISWOODE, EAST HARDING STREET, FLEET STREET, E.C., and
32, ABINGDON STREET, WESTMINSTER, S.W.; or
ADAM AND CHARLES BLACK, 6, NORTH BRIDGE, EDINBURGH; or
HODGES, FIGGIS, & Co., 104, GRAFTON STREET, DUBLIN.

1888.

[C. 5252—169.] *Price One Penny.*

New Series of Reports.

Reports of the Annual Series have been issued from Her Majesty's Diplomatic and Consular Officers at the following places, and may be obtained from the sources indicated on the title-page:—

No.		Price.	No.		Price.
278.	Odessa	1d.	335.	Noumea	1d.
279.	Tokyo	1d.	336.	Trieste	1d.
280.	Saigon	1d.	337.	Nice	1d.
281.	Buenos Ayres	1d.	338.	Bordeaux	1d.
282.	Taganrog	1d.	339.	Mogador	1d.
283.	Tamsui	1d.	340.	Wilmington	1d.
284.	Puerto Plata	1d.	341.	Amoy	2d.
285.	Wênchow	1d.	342.	Trebizond	1d.
286.	Tokyo	1d.	343.	Lisbon	1d.
287.	Lisbon	2d.	344.	Java	1d.
288.	La Rochelle	1d.	345.	Brest	1d.
289.	Washington	4d.	346.	Odessa	2d.
290.	Beyrout	1d.	347.	Cavalla	1d.
291.	Algiers	2d.	348.	Bussorah	1d.
292.	Varna	1d.	349.	Mollendo	1d.
293.	Algiers	1d.	350.	Cadiz	5d.
294.	Port Saïd	1d.	351.	Cagliari	4d.
295.	Manila	1d.	352.	Cagliari	1d.
296.	Charleston	1d.	353.	Ajaccio	1d.
297.	Kiungchow	1d.	354.	Copenhagen	1d.
298.	Pakhoi	1d.	355.	Vienna	1d.
299.	Wuhu	1d.	356.	San Francisco	1d.
300.	Boulogne	2d.	357.	Vera Cruz	1d.
301.	Marseilles	1d.	358.	Philippopolis	1d.
302.	Bordeaux	2d.	359.	Greytown	1d.
303.	Ancona	1d.	360.	Tangier	1d.
304.	Swatow	1d.	361.	Lisbon	1d.
305.	Ssŭ-ch'uan	1d.	362.	Chicago	1d.
306.	Antwerp	1d.	363.	Jerusalem and Jaffa	1d.
307.	Cadiz	1d.	364.	Truxillo	1d.
308.	Genoa	1d.	365.	Ningpo	1d.
309.	Marseilles	1d.	366.	Chefoo	1d.
310.	Baltimore	1d.	367.	Bushire	1d.
311.	Savannah	1d.	368.	Stockholm	2d.
312.	Boston	1d.	369.	Santiago	1d.
313.	San Francisco	1d.	370.	New York	2d.
314.	Guayaquil	1d.	371.	Pernambuco	1d.
315.	Santos	1d.	372.	Söul	1d.
316.	Carthagena and Santa Martha	1d.	373.	Chinkiang	2d.
317.	San José	1d.	374.	Pernambuco	1d.
318.	Boulogne	1d.	375.	San Francisco	2d.
319.	Tahiti	1d.	376.	Riga	1d.
320.	Fiume	1d.	377.	Newchwang	2d.
321.	Warsaw	1d.	378.	San Salvador	1d.
322.	Vera Cruz	2d.	379.	Frankfort	2d.
323.	Rio Grande de Sul	1d.	380.	Hankow	2d.
324.	Gothenburg	2d.	381.	Bucharest	1d.
325.	Philippopolis	1d.	382.	Lisbon	1d.
326.	Mogador	2d.	383.	Tunis	1d.
327.	Havana	2d.	384.	Tangier	1d.
328.	La Rochelle	1d.	385.	Santiago	2d.
329.	Corunna	2d.	386.	Diarbekir	1d.
330.	Chicago	2d.	387.	Shanghai	2d.
331.	Foochow	1d.	388.	Rome	2d.
332.	Taiwan	1d.	389.	Buenos Ayres	1d.
333.	Loanda	1d.	390.	Amsterdam	1d.
334.	Loanda	1d.	391.	Warsaw	1d.

No. 392.

Reference to previous Report, Annual Series Nos. 375 and 313.

UNITED STATES.

SAN FRANCISCO.

Consul Donohoe to the Marquis of Salisbury.

My Lord,   *San Francisco, June* 7, 1888.

I HAVE the honour to transmit herewith Commercial Reports on the trade of Port Townsend, Washington Territory, and Eureka, California, for the Year 1887.

I have, &c.,
(Signed)   DENIS DONOHOE.

Vice-Consul Alexander to Consul Donohoe.

Sir,   *Port Townsend, Washington Territory, May* 4, 1888.

I HAVE the honour to submit to you, most respectfully, my fourth Annual Report of the British Vice-Consulate at Port Townsend for the year ending the 31st December, 1887, containing a brief summary of the commerce and trade of Washington Territory, particularly that of the Puget Sound district.

It is not as full and complete as I should wish it to be, from the fact that it is almost an impossibility to procure trustworthy information upon every subject; however, I am able to say that the statistical matter contained in the several Annexes is correct, since, in the compilation of the various items, I was permitted, through the courtesy of the Collector of Customs at this port, to whom I am very much indebted, to have access to original documents kept on file.

I have in previous Reports given full descriptions of this comparatively new and undeveloped, but growing, country, so I shall review only those items which are subject to change year by year, and which I think will be matters of interest and afford useful information to our Government at home.

The commerce of Washington Territory is very extensive; vessels are constantly coming from and departing for all parts of the world from Puget Sound. The central office of this collection district is at Port Townsend, with sub-ports at Roche Harbour and O'Sooyoos. Since the completion of the Canadian Pacific Railway a large amount of business that formerly was transacted through this collection district has been deflected. Large shipments were made by sea of oats and other produce from the surrounding country to San Francisco, of which no accurate account can be obtained, and merchandise to the value of 200,000*l.* was carried from the Sound ports north on the Alaskan steamers, and other sailing vessels. No account has been

Commerce and industry.

Imports and exports.

Annexes B and C.

UNITED STATES.

taken of these shipments in the tabulated statements contained in the Annexes B and C, to which I would refer for the value of the imports and exports of articles of commerce of this territory.

Shipping. Annex A.

The number of steam vessels registered at the Custom-house is 104, with an aggregate tonnage of 11,582$\frac{32}{100}$. These vessels only ply upon the waters of Puget Sound to supply the local need. The steamers that ply between Sound ports and San Francisco, Portland, and Alaska are all registered either in San Francisco or Portland.

There are 168 vessels of all kinds documented at this Custom-house, with an aggregate tonnage of 40,306.

The total tonnage of British and foreign vessels, both sailing and steam, which entered and cleared at the ports in this district, either with cargoes or in ballast, to and from foreign countries, during the year, is shown in the appended table, marked Annex A; by referring to it, the numbers for 1887, compared with those for 1886, show, during the year, a decline in entrances of 117 in the number of vessels, and of 25,895 tons in the tonnage; and, in clearances, a decline of 131 in the number of vessels and of 40,189 tons in the tonnage.

I cannot let this statement go forward without offering some explanation, as it may mislead in the interests of British trade and shipping. The number of British vessels which entered at this port, either with cargoes or in ballast, for 1887, compared with those for 1886, show a decline of nine in the number of sailing vessels, but an increase of 1,651 tons in the tonnage; and, in the number of steam vessels, there is an increase of 25, with 1,542 tons in the tonnage. In the clearances a decline of 18 appears in the number of sailing vessels, but an increase of 1,044 tons in the tonnage; and in the number of steam-vessels there is an increase of 24, with 1,402 tons in the tonnage. From this statement it is clear that the class of British vessel which now seeks trade in this district is very much improved, and it is only reasonable to expect that, as the shipping facilities at the Sound ports improve, and trade with the surrounding country developes, the number and tonnage of British vessels will no doubt increase proportionately.

Forests and the production of lumber.

The yellow and red fir constitutes the bulk of the vast forests in every section of Washington Territory west of the Cascade Mountains, and will, with proper care, afford a timber supply for many years to come; it is these varieties of timber which furnish the largest and most important article of export, being generally classed as "Oregon pine" in the price lists of foreign dealers. Many other classes of trees exist, such as white and red cedar, spruce, larch, ash, oak, cherry, laurel, cottonwood, and maple, all of which are utilised in some way or other.

It has been estimated that the capacity of the sawmills of Washington Territory for the year, in superficial feet, amounted to 645,440,000.

370 cargoes of lumber were sent in American vessels to coastwise ports, amounting to 257,689,438 feet, and valued at 686,295*l*.; the freight money received for transportation averaged 1*l*. 6*s*. per 1,000 feet, the freight money received in transporting lumber, foreign, averaged 2*l*. 12*s*. per 1,000 feet.

Within this year a trade in timber with the east as far as Chicago has been inaugurated, and the quantity carried by the railways is becoming larger each month.

Fisheries.

One of the leading industries of Washington Territory is the salmon fisheries of the Columbia River, Shoalwater Bay, Gray's Harbour, and Puget Sound. The business of taking salmon with traps on the Columbia, and packing them in brine, in kits and barrels, or smoking them, has been pursued from the earliest period of settlement; and those who engaged in the business derived considerable profit, and all materials used were cheap, while there was a ready demand for the product at fair prices. About 1865 or 1866 the first experiment of preserving salmon fresh in hermetically sealed tins was tried on the Columbia River.

The fish were of the very best variety, called Chinook. They were very fat, were taken shortly after leaving salt water, were so abundant that only the finest specimens need be used, and great pains were taken in putting them up: consequently the Columbia River canned salmon obtained a world-wide reputation as an article of luxury, and, being in great demand, commanded a very high price.

The large profits made induced others to enter the business, which was rapidly developed, and at the present time it is claimed that 6,000 persons and more than 400,000*l*. are required to conduct the different operations on the Columbia River alone.

Fisheries in this territory are now established in all the open bays and sounds, where the salmon are taken with gill and purse nets.

It is very difficult to get the quantity of salmon exported, as no official records seem to be kept; very large shipments are made, principally by steamers, to San Francisco, and by railway to eastern markets, for home consumption. The foreign supply is sent direct from the Columbia at Astoria.

Up to the present time very little has been done towards developing the fisheries of Puget Sound and the coast line of the territory, with the exception of salmon and halibut, but several experienced fishermen, with their crafts and gear, from the Atlantic coast, are now making these waters their objective point, and it is expected that this industry will grow rapidly and become very important.

The United States Fish Commissioner has recently introduced carp and shad into these waters, and it is contemplated to send lobsters also.

Oysters brought overland from the Atlantic coast are being transplanted in suitable localities, and these experiments, made by private companies, it is hoped will turn out very successful.

The proportion of productive area differs considerably in the two divisions of the territory; a much greater increase of acreage must be expected in the eastern than in the western counties. The former are nearly all left clear by nature, and ready for the plough. In the latter there is very little that must not be cleared by the hand of man—a task, in many districts, of arduous difficulty, and involving great expense.

Agriculture.

To give, in any detail, the productions of Eastern Washington would not be easy, nor could it, in all cases, be safe to class among its productions, as yet, what many persons regard as such, but which are at present only experimental growth. Besides many staple crops (it is the great wheat-producing region), it will produce hops, tobacco, sweet potatoes, melons, peaches, apricots, and grapes in many districts.

The crops of the western section are less various than those of the eastern. Corn or maize, barley and rye, do not do well. Wheat also is of an inferior quality, but oats are first-rate and yield enormously. The crops of hay and hops are wonderful; the latter crop for 1887 may be estimated at 25,000 bales, bringing about 200,000*l*. to the producers.

For vegetables of several kinds this section can hardly be surpassed; the yields in the potato, beet, carrot, and turnip crops are enormous, and quality excellent. Whatever requires much heat does not flourish.

Plums, pears, apples, cherries, strawberries, cranberries, and other

(489)

small fruits are grown in large quantities in this section, the crops being most abundant, of excellent flavour and quality. Fruit-growing is very extensively followed, with great profit; the mild climate of this section, being free from the severe frost of winter, and the hot and dry weather of the summer, makes it naturally adapted to fruit-growing.

The Eastern Division of the territory, once devoted almost exclusively to stock-raising, is now being divided up into farms and put into cultivation; consequently the area of wild land is diminishing very rapidly, and stockmen are obliged to pay attention more to quality than quantity, not only in cattle, but in horses and sheep: in fact, the stock used for breeding purposes in all kinds of animals is selected with great care and judgment; the high prices given for good animals, and the introduction of agricultural shows, which are becoming very popular, have no doubt brought about this beneficial change. The shipment of stock from this section of the country to the Eastern States by road and rail is very considerable, but no estimates are obtainable. Very little loss has occurred this winter on the ranges, and no infectious or contagious diseases have been reported.

Mineral produce.
The mineral resources of the territory are undoubtedly very great upon both sides of the Cascade Mountains. Gold, silver, copper, cinnabar, lead, marble, limestone, sandstone, and coal are found in various quantities. In some instances the development of the mines is advanced, in others they are yet unopened deposits awaiting facilities of transportation.

Of the class of deposits that have been thoroughly tried, and are now affording an important industry to the territory, is coal; the fields are reported to be numerous and very extensive, the character of the coal being chiefly lignite and semi-bituminous. The coal-fields of Western Washington are all within a radius of 40 miles of tide-water, and afford every means for rapid shipment. The cost of mining coal in this section, with transportation to tide-water, varies from 2s. to 3s. 6d. per ton. The mines have produced 2,461,108 tons, and are steadily increasing their outputs monthly to supply the great demand. The principal markets are those of California and Oregon.* Fine timber of varied growth covers the coal-lands, and is of untold value in constructing tramways, houses, sheds, and other buildings and devices necessary in mining work and development.

The mining of precious metals has not, up to the present, been carried on on a very extensive scale, but recent explorations and tests have shown that the Eastern Division has at least three fields of rich deposits of gold and silver, situated chiefly in the north-east portion.

Several deposits of iron ore, discovered some time ago along the east side of the Cascade Mountains, are now being opened up; the supply seems almost inexhaustible, and is very rich; want of means of transportation has hitherto prevented their being operated. A gentleman, representing an English syndicate, has just made arrangements to work the deposits at Cleelum, where smelters will be erected as soon as the Northern Pacific Railway completes this branch of its line and affords means of shipment to market.

Railways.
The past two years have been the most important in the history of railway enterprise in Washington Territory. Within that period the Northern Pacific Railway has completed its line across the Cascade Mountains, the Canadian Pacific has been finished, as well as the

---

* There were 251 cargoes of coal shipped during the year from Puget Sound to coastwise ports, amounting to 520,520 tons, valued at 534,799l.; the freight money received for transportation was 267,399l.

Oregon and California. The loss of either one of them would now be seriously felt. In the completion of the Northern Pacific across the Cascade Mountains the territory has been freed from a disadvantage which was very great. It was an almost intolerable burden to the farmers of the eastern section that they had only one line by which they could ship their crops to the seaboard, belonging to the Oregon Railway and Navigation Company; this company, possessing a monopoly of the finest wheat-producing region in the territory, charged rates, during many years, that were altogether exorbitant. The completion of the "Cascade Division" meant to these people new markets, which before, though near enough to hand, they had not been able to reach.

Besides these main lines, the territory is much interested in the Seattle, Lake Shore, and Eastern Railway. This line is building from Seattle in an easterly direction, has 40 miles under construction, and a part of its rolling stock.

Its immediate objective point is the Danny Iron Mines, but it is eventually to cross the mountains to the wheat region, and to connect with some of the eastern trunk lines that appear to be aiming at this section.

The preceding, with one or two branches, are the chief lines that have been actually constructed. There are about eight other railways projected, some in actual operation, others only existing upon paper.

The total mileage of the railways of the territory is about 1,060 miles, of which the Northern Pacific owns nearly 570.

Shipyards, with the facilities for the construction of large vessels, exist at nearly all the large milling establishments, and at the ports on Puget Sound, Gray's Harbour, Shoalwater Bay, and at Skomokawa, on the Columbia River. All raw materials are found here for the construction of vessels, and the number of skilled workmen is every year growing greater. The industry has become so permanent that most of the yards are putting in expensive special machinery, and all modern appliances for saving labour and securing accuracy of design. Most of the vessels built here are intended for coasters, many having auxiliary steam power. The number of vessels of various kinds built during the year, as shown by the report of the Custom-house at Port Townsend, is 29, and their net tonnage $4,854\frac{36}{100}$, of which 12 were steam-vessels with $612\frac{38}{100}$ net tonnage, and 17 were sail-vessels with $4,241\frac{98}{100}$ net tonnage. *Shipbuilding.*

One of the minor industries of the territory, and which is in a fair way to become very important, is the manufacture of flour; there are 65 flouring mills, the capacity of which is estimated to be about 479,700 barrels per year. *Other industries.*

Paper mills, machine shops with foundries, sash, door, and furniture factories, brick-yards, biscuit manufactories, and book-binding establishments, &c., are all in operation in the various parts of the country, and do a good and profitable business.

The population of the territory, according to the Governor's report, is placed at 150,000, and is rapidly growing.

The climate is very healthy, and remarkably free from diseases; although a few cases of small-pox occurred, few proved fatal, and the disease, which was brought into the country, was soon eradicated.

As the country developes, and the demand increases, it opens up an extensive market for Great Britain, and English manufactures principally, among which may be mentioned pig-iron, fire-brick, fire-clay, cement, salt, hop cloth, and grain bags. Shipments of merchandise are now being made from Great Britain direct to Puget Sound. The extension of the railway system of the territory will create a still *Future prospects and trade with Great Britain.*

further demand for English goods, principally rails. The completion of the Cascade Tunnel, giving the Sound country direct communication with Eastern Washington, will enable merchants to furnish return cargoes of grain, &c.; and, although there was only one cargo of wheat shipped last season, large quantities were brought to tide-water and warehoused. It is computed that during the coming year shipments to the extent of 150,000 tons will be made from the port of Jacoma alone, where the Northern Pacific Railway and private enterprise are erecting large and commodious warehouses necessary for this business.

Annex A.—RETURN of all Shipping at the Port of Port Townsend in the Year 1887.

ENTERED.

Nationality.	Sailing. Number of Vessels.	Sailing. Tons.	Steam. Number of Vessels.	Steam. Tons.	Total. Number of Vessels.	Total. Tons.
British	46	45,266	48	3,972	94	49,238
United States of America	50	37,370	656	347,664	706	385,034
Norwegian and Swedish	28	21,063	...	...	28	21,063
German	9	6,500	...	...	9	6,500
Chilian	7	6,398	...	...	7	6,398
Hawaiian	2	1,220	...	...	2	1,220
Nicaraguan	1	609	...	...	1	609
Total	143	118,426	704	351,636	847	470,062
,, for the year 1886	295	212,834	669	283,123	964	495,957

CLEARED.

Nationality.	Sailing. Number of Vessels.	Sailing. Tons.	Steam. Number of Vessels.	Steam. Tons.	Total. Number of Vessels.	Total. Tons.
British	37	42,559	47	3,832	84	46,391
United States of America	62	42,766	641	319,165	703	361,931
Norwegian and Swedish	32	23,067	...	...	32	23,067
German	8	5,661	...	...	8	5,661
Chilian	6	5,820	...	...	6	5,820
Hawaiian	2	1,220	...	...	2	1,220
Nicaraguan	1	609	...	...	1	609
Total	148	121,702	688	322,997	826	444,699
,, for the year 1886	279	191,371	678	293,517	957	484,888

SAN FRANCISCO.

Annex B.—RETURN of Principal Articles of Export from Port Townsend during the Year 1887.

Articles.		1887.		1886.	
		Quantity.	Value.	Quantity.	Value.
			£		£
Cattle	Head	1,193	7,610	...	...
Hogs	,,	4,043	2,870	...	...
Horses	,,	100	2,613	...	...
Sheep	,,	22,802	10,806	...	...
Other animals		...	762	...	...
Wheat	Bush.	76,835	10,472	...	...
Oats	,,	1,935	140	...	...
Flour	Barrels	33,784	25,951	...	...
Other breadstuffs		...	4,948	...	...
Potatoes	Bush.	1,119	159	...	...
Butter, eggs, etc.		...	3,792	...	...
Bacon, hams	Lbs.	639,531	12,336	...	...
Fish		...	680	...	...
Oil	Gals.	232,767	918	...	...
Liquors	...	...	1,262	...	...
Iron manufactures		...	10,263	...	...
Furs, hides		...	3,361	...	...
Lumber	1000 ft.	69,655	135,003	...	...
Laths, pickets	,,	10,067	6,693	...	...
Other articles		...	68,693	...	...
Total		...	309,332	...	377,347

RETURN of Principal Articles of Import to Port Townsend during the Year 1887.

Articles.		1887.		1886.	
		Quantity.	Value.	Quantity.	Value.
			£		£
Furs	...	...	25,507	...	...
Railway bars, steel	Tons	4,359	21,471	...	...
Pig iron	,,	1,020	2,248	...	...
Iron manufactures		...	110	...	...
Coal	Tons	365	392	...	...
Cement	Barrels	2,056	469	...	...
Cloth and woollen manufactures		...	88	...	...
Oil	Gals.	9,310	629	...	...
Rice	Lbs.	364,905	1,504	...	...
Tobacco	,,	720	45	...	...
Spirits	Gals.	4,513	808	...	...
Other articles		...	11,798	...	...
Total		...	65,069	...	83,530

The rate of exchange is calculated at 4$8665 to the £1 sterling.

Annex C.—TABLE showing the Total Value of all Articles Exported from Port Townsend, and Imported to Port Townsend, from and to Foreign Countries, during the Year 1887.

Country.	Exports. 1887.	Exports. 1886.	Imports. 1887.	Imports. 1886.
	£	£	£	£
Great Britain	10,143	..	24,644	..
British Columbia	136,999	..	40,134	..
British Possessions—				
Australia	86,244	..	6	..
Hong Kong	4,127	..	5	..
Hawaiian Islands	28,448	..	62	..
Chile	27,625	..	..	..
Peru	6,544	..	..	..
Mexico	3,840	..	..	..
Uruguay	1,152	..	..	..
Argentine Republic	3,333	..	..	..
French Possessions—				
Australasia	877	..	10	..
Japan	..	..	191	..
China	..	..	17	..
Total	309,332	377,347	65,069	83,530

Consular Agent Hodgson to Consul Donohoe.

Eureka, California, June 5, 1888.

Shipping.

I HAVE the honour to submit this my first Annual Report on the trade and commerce of Eureka, Humboldt County, State of California, for the year 1887, and regret the unavoidable delay in its preparation.

The arrivals of ships to load at this port for foreign ports during the year 1887, as per Annex A. to this Report, numbered 14, their total tonnage amounting to 4,765 tons; the departures numbered 17, the aggregate tonnage being 5,993. The vessels belonged to the following nationalities, viz., British, 4; American, 9; Hawaiian, 1; Swedish, 1; French, 2; and German, 2.

Annex B. hereto shows approximately the quantity and value of our foreign and domestic exports. This return, as regards the principal articles of import for the year 1887, refers to foreign imports only, which are very light to this port, consisting of coals only. Nearly all vessels to load foreign arrive here in ballast.

Annex C. will also be found to this Report, showing the total value of foreign and domestic exports and of foreign imports for 1887.

The general business of Eureka during the year 1887 has shown a rapid and very marked growth, far beyond that of former years. The town and vicinity are steadily increasing in size, and the new buildings and other improvements are of a very substantial and permanent description. Our population is now about 7,500, and rapidly increasing.

The shipbuilding interest on Humboldt Bay is a very important one, and continues to flourish. There are two regular ship-yards; also a marine railway capable of taking out the largest class of vessels. The latter has proved of great convenience to shipowners. The very best kind of ship timber is to be found in abundance within a short distance of Humboldt Bay. There are three vessels on the stocks at present, and a number more will be built soon. Over 100 handsome superior vessels have been built here. This industry can advantageously be enlarged, and offers one of the best openings for shipbuilders.

Our safe and land-locked harbour—the length of which is 15 miles, with an average width of 3 miles—is likely in the near future to be made available for deep-water ships of the largest draught, an appropriation of 342,500 dol. (68,000*l.*), having already been made by the United States Government towards the cost of building a sea-wall and other improvements, so as to deepen the channel at the entrance, the Government having a clear conception of the importance of this port as a shipping centre and a safe harbour of refuge for distressed vessels. *Harbour.*

Railroad communication between Eureka, San Francisco, and the Eastern States will no doubt be completed in a few years from now. When this is accomplished and the harbour improvements completed it is not difficult to predict that Eureka will become a shipping port of great importance, enjoying, as no doubt she then will, a very large foreign shipping trade. *Railways.*

From the annexed return of exports it will be seen that this is a lumber-manufacturing city, but there are also numbers of enterprises, also manufacturing and otherwise, which should, but do not, exist here, and which would yield good profits to capital and to men of enterprise, energy, and perseverance. The acreage of our peerless redwood alone is set at 450,000 acres, and this is exclusive of pine, fir, spruce and cedar, laurel, madrone, and black oak, which grow in abundant quantities, and are unexcelled for furniture and wooden-ware manufacture. *Exports. Lumber.*

The total area of Humboldt County is 2,297,600 acres. One-half may be set down as timber land, 1,000,000 acres as agricultural and grazing land,* and the remainder contains much valuable mineral land. About 1,250,000 acres are upon the assessment roll of the county, with an assessed valuation of 8,300,000 dol. (1,660,000*l.*), leaving about 1,000,000 acres of Government land yet to be secured, suitable for almost any character of productive industry. Hundreds of opportunities exist for entering upon good land here—land that will make comfortable and profitable homes for those who have the head, the heart, the muscle, and the courage—like the hundreds of stalwart Nova Scotians here—to go into isolated districts.† *Area of Humboldt County.*

The soil on the bottom lands is black (next to the coast), while that on the hills is of a sandy loam.

The lands produce as follows:—Oats, 35 to 90 bushels to the acre; barley, 30 to 85 bushels to the acre; wheat, 30 to 60 bushels; and potatoes, 7 to 8 tons per acre.

Stock-raising and wool-growing has been a very successful and remunerative business ever since the country was first opened to settlement, Humboldt wool at all times bringing the highest figures in the market.

The climate of the coast is very equable, the temperature ranging from about 30° for winter to about 70° for summer. Average rainfall, 35 inches; very little snowfall. Ice sometimes forms. Of course there are extreme cases of weather at times. The rainy season, or winter, sets in during November, and continues till the end of May. Fogs are more or less frequent during the latter part of summer and

---

* Prices:—Grazing land, 5*s.* to 3*l.* an acre; improved farms, 3*l.* to 40*l.* per acre; timber land, per ¼-section of 160 acres, 8*l.* up to 4,000*l.*

† For fuller details as to tenure of land in California by aliens see p. 24 of Parliamentary Paper, No. 17 Commercial, 1887 [C. 5170], price 5*d.*—Ed.

fall, but some of the most delightful weather is experienced during winter.

The school districts in the county number 74, the schoolhouses 94; teachers employed, 102; and school children, 5,262.

Churches of various denominations are found in every town and hamlet, with good church buildings and an efficient ministry.

Mining is carried on with success in many parts of the county, but the timber resources and stock-raising, and some farming, are the sources of the chief industries. The mines, however, will doubtless sustain their character as an important item in the material value of the county.

To the courtesy of the United States Customs Department at this port, the officers of the Eureka Chamber of Commerce, and J. N. Lentell, Esq., city surveyor, the writer is indebted for much of the information contained in the foregoing Report and its Appendices.

I have, &c.,
(Signed) J. H. HODGSON.

Annex A.—RETURN of all Shipping at the Port of Eureka, Humboldt County, California, in the Year 1887, omitting the Coasting Vessels trading to the Ports of San Francisco, San Pedro, and San Diego, and which do not enter and clear through the United States Customs Department.

ENTERED.

Nationality.	Sailing. Number of Vessels.	Sailing. Tons.	Steam. Number of Vessels.	Steam. Tons.	Total. Number of Vessels.	Total. Tons.
British	4	2,125	...	...	4	2,125
American	7	1,661	...	...	7	1,661
Hawaiian	1	108	...	...	1	108
Swedish	1	367	...	...	1	367
French	1	504	...	...	1	504
German	...	...	...	...	...	...
Total	14	4,765	...	...	14	4,765

Note.—Arrivals: Steamers, 148; barkentines, 16; barks, 8; brigs, 5; schooners, 494; total, 671.

CLEARED.

Nationality.	Sailing. Number of Vessels.	Sailing. Tons.	Steam. Number of Vessels.	Steam. Tons.	Total. Number of Vessels.	Total. Tons.
British	2	1,087	...	...	2	1,087
American	9	2,479	...	...	9	2,479
Hawaiian	1	108	...	...	1	108
Swedish	1	367	...	...	1	367
French	2	975	...	...	2	975
German	2	977	...	...	2	977
Total	17	5,993	...	...	17	5,993

Note.—Departures: Steamers, 141; barks, 10; barkentines, 17; brigs, 4; schooners, 502; total, 674.

The entries and clearances of American ships do not include the coasting trade, in which eight steamers and a fleet of over 200 sailing vessels were engaged during the year 1887.

Annex B.—RETURN of Principal Articles of Export from Eureka, Humboldt County, California, during the Year 1887.

Articles.		1887. Quantity.	1887. Value.
			£
Lumber	Feet	104,519,726	418,072
Shingles	Thousand	191,700,985	37,510
Shakes	"	17,040,525	3,208
Posts	Number	82,153	800
Pickets	"	234,723	1,408
Hoop poles	"	39,550	156
Stave bolts (cords)	"	927	1,019
R. R. ties	"	35,520	2,769
Fruit boxes	"	8,000	400
Mouldings (lineal feet)	Bundles		17,601
Redwood doors	Number		2,770
House material	Sup. Feet		676
Redwood windows	Number		1,250
Produce—Apples	Boxes	6,733	1,211
Butter	Lbs.	92,000	5,520
Barley	Sacks	1,951	595
Cheese	Lbs.	2,000	60
Beans	"	4,479	27
Baskets	Bundles	11	..
Eggs	Boxes	237	191
Fish	Lbs.	428,000	440
Fruit	"	496,000	260
Furs, hides, and pelts	Bundles	540	Value not ascertained.
Glue stock	Barrels	49	"
Leather	Rolls	177	"
Oats	Sacks	26,840	7,427
Potatoes	"	40,100	9,624
Peas	"	6,020	1,685
Salmon	Barrels	408	612
"	Half-brls.	179	145
"	Cases, can'd	7,360	1,987
"	" fresh	172	46
Sheep	Head	1,197	297
Other live stock	"	988	400
Wool	Lbs.	1,594,925	57,417
Tan bark	Cords	1,800	5,760
Miscellaneous	Tons	347	Not ascertained.
Exports, foreign and domestic—Total	..	..	581,343

Note.—This return does not include the output for mouldings, doors, windows, &c., of two or more lumber-manufacturing mills located in Springville and Port Kenyon, in Humboldt County, California.

UNITED STATES.

RETURN of Principal Articles of Import to Eureka during the Year 1887 (Foreign Ports only).

Article.	1887.	
	Quantity.	Value.
Coal	Tons. 768	£ 393
Total	..	393

Annex C.—TABLE showing the Total Value of all Articles Exported from and Imported to Eureka, Humboldt County, California, during the Year 1887.

Country.	Exports.	Imports.
	£	£
Great Britain	..	..
Australia, British Possessions in ..	..	393
Hawaiian Islands	581,343	..
Mexico		
Domestic or American Ports		
Total	581 343	393

LONDON:
Printed for Her Majesty's Stationery Office,
By HARRISON AND SONS,
Printers in Ordinary to Her Majesty.
(1125   8 | 88—H & S   497)

FOREIGN OFFICE.
1888.
ANNUAL SERIES.

No. 398.

DIPLOMATIC AND CONSULAR REPORTS ON TRADE AND FINANCE.

UNITED STATES.

REPORT ON THE
AGRICULTURAL CONDITION OF MASSACHUSETTS.

Presented to both Houses of Parliament by Command of Her Majesty,
AUGUST, 1888.

LONDON:
PRINTED FOR HER MAJESTY'S STATIONERY OFFICE,
BY HARRISON AND SONS, ST. MARTIN'S LANE,
PRINTERS IN ORDINARY TO HER MAJESTY.

And to be purchased, either directly or through any Bookseller, from
EYRE AND SPOTTISWOODE, EAST HARDING STREET, FLEET STREET, E.C., and
32, ABINGDON STREET, WESTMINSTER, S.W.; or
ADAM AND CHARLES BLACK, 6, NORTH BRIDGE, EDINBURGH; or
HODGES, FIGGIS, & Co., 104, GRAFTON STREET, DUBLIN.

1888.

[C 5252—175.] *Price One Penny.*

New Series of Reports.

Reports of the Annual Series have been issued from Her Majesty's Diplomatic and Consular Officers at the following places, and may be obtained from the sources indicated on the title-page:—

No.		Price.	No.		Price.
276.	Antwerp	1d.	337.	Nice	1d.
277.	Havre	3d.	338.	Bordeaux	1d.
278.	Odessa	1d.	339.	Mogador	1d.
279.	Tokyo	1d.	340.	Wilmington	1d
280.	Saïgon	1d.	341.	Amoy	2d.
281.	Buenos Ayres	1d.	342.	Trebizond	1d.
282.	Taganrog	1d.	343.	Lisbon	1d.
283.	Tamsui	1d.	344.	Java	1d.
284.	Puerto Plata	1d.	345.	Brest	1d.
285.	Wênchow	1d.	346.	Odessa	2d.
286.	Tokyo	1d.	347.	Cavalla	1d.
287.	Lisbon	2d.	348.	Bussorah	1d.
288.	La Rochelle	1d.	349.	Mollendo	1d.
289.	Washington	4d.	350.	Cadiz	5d.
290.	Beyrout	1d.	351.	Cagliari	4d.
291.	Algiers	2d.	352.	Cagliari	1d.
292.	Varna	1d.	353.	Ajaccio	1d.
293.	Algiers	1d.	354.	Copenhagen	1d.
294.	Port Saïd	1d.	355.	Vienna	1d.
295.	Manila	1d.	356.	San Francisco	1d.
296.	Charleston	1d.	357.	Vera Cruz	1d.
297.	Kiungchow	1d.	358.	Philippopolis	1d.
298.	Pakhoi	1d.	359.	Greytown	1d.
299.	Wuhu	1d.	360.	Tangier	1d.
300.	Boulogne	2d.	361.	Lisbon	1d.
301.	Marseilles	1d.	362.	Chicago	1d.
302.	Bordeaux	2d.	363.	Jerusalem and Jaffa	1d.
303.	Ancona	1d.	364.	Truxillo	1d.
304.	Swatow	1d.	365.	Ningpo	1d.
305.	Ssŭ-ch'uan	1d.	366.	Chefoo	1d.
306.	Antwerp	1d.	367.	Bushire	1d.
307.	Cadiz	1d.	368.	Stockholm	2d.
308.	Genoa	1d.	369.	Santiago	1d.
309.	Marseilles	1d.	370.	New York	2d.
310.	Baltimore	1d.	371.	Pernambuco	1d.
311.	Savannah	1d.	372.	Söul	1d.
312.	Boston	1d.	373.	Chinkiang	2d.
313.	San Francisco	1d.	374.	Pernambuco	1d.
314.	Guayaquil	1d.	375.	San Francisco	2d.
315.	Santos	1d.	376.	Riga	1d.
316.	Carthagena and Santa Martha	1d.	377.	Newchwang	2d.
317.	San José	1d.	378.	San Salvador	1d.
318.	Boulogne	1d.	379.	Frankfort	2d.
319.	Tahiti	1d.	380.	Hankow	2d.
320.	Fiume	1d.	381.	Bucharest	1d.
321.	Warsaw	1d.	382.	Lisbon	1d.
322.	Vera Cruz	2d.	383.	Tunis	1d.
323.	Rio Grande do Sul	1d.	384.	Tangier	1d.
324.	Gothenburg	2d.	385.	Santiago	2d.
325.	Philippopolis	1d.	386.	Diarbeker	1d.
326.	Mogador	2d.	387.	Shanghai	2d.
327.	Havana	2d.	388.	Rome	2d.
328.	La Rochelle	1d.	389.	Buenos Ayres	1d.
329.	Corunna	2d.	390.	Amsterdam	1d.
330.	Chicago	2d.	391.	Warsaw	1d.
331.	Foochow	1d.	392.	San Francisco	1d.
332.	Taiwan	1d.	393.	Alexandria	1d.
333.	Loanda	1d.	394.	Salonica	2d.
334.	Loanda	1d.	395.	Palermo	1d.
335.	Noumea	1d.	396.	Mexico	4d.
336.	Trieste	1d.	397.	Naples	3d.

No. 398.

UNITED STATES.

BOSTON.

Report by Consul Henderson on Agriculture in the State of Massachusetts.

The third volume of the census of Massachusetts for the year 1885, relating exclusively to agriculture, and containing nearly 1,000 pages of detailed statements and figures for the several counties and townships, has been recently printed and distributed, and the following are the general totals and deductions for the whole State. {Summary of third volume of census.}

The total value of agricultural property in the State in the year 1885 was—land, 22,140,000*l.*; buildings, 14,884,000*l.*; machinery, implements, and other appliances, 1,480,000*l.*; domestic animals, 3,411,000*l.*; fruit trees, 1,332,000*l.*: total, 43,247,000*l.*; total in 1875, 37,500,000*l.*

The total value of agricultural products in 1885 was 9,551,000*l.*, against 7,415,000*l.* in 1875, and 6,406,000*l.* in 1865.

The above, in common with all the census figures in the volume, have reference to agricultural property and products on farms, market gardens, orchards, nurseries, and other agricultural establishments cultivated and used for business purposes, but do not comprise those maintained by private persons for their own use.

The number of persons engaged in agriculture, amount of agricultural wages paid, number of farms, and acreage and sub-division of land in 1885, as compared with 1875, were:— {Number of persons engaged in agriculture.}

		1885.	1875.
Owners of farms	Number..	36,526	35,457
Farm labourers and other servants ..	,, ..	41,135	35,488
Total	,, ..	77,661	70,945
Amount of wages paid ..	Value £	1,278,050	1,000,164
Farms worked by owners	Number..	40,112	..
,, ,, on shares	,, ..	683	..
,, rented	,, ..	3,243	..
,, conditions not ascertained	,, ..	972	..
Total	,, ..	45,010	44,549

UNITED STATES.

Total acreage of farms.

The total acreage of these farms in 1885 was 3,898,429 acres, or an average of 86·61 acres, against an average of 76 acres in 1875; and the total value of farms and buildings in 1885 was 37,023,400*l*., or an average value of 823*l*., against 732*l*. in 1875.

	1885.	1875.
	Acres.	Acres.
Cultivated land	939,260	912,521
Unimproved land	1,479,454	1,469,988
Unimprovable land	90,212	89,457
Woodland	1,389,501	936,402

Acreage included in cultivated land:—

		1885.	1875.
Laid down in Indian corn	Acres	48,885	29,194
,, ,, rye	,,	18,351	21,351
,, ,, oats	,,	18,235	14,614
,, ,, buckwheat	,,	4,202	3,609
,, ,, barley	,,	2,220	1,828
,, ,, wheat	,,	254	677
,, ,, tobacco	,,	2,674	3,758
,, ,, hay	,,	618,710	668,183
Market gardens	,,	8,862	3,989
Ensilage pits	Number	1,029	...

The comparative quantities or values of the more important crops produced in Massachusetts in each decennial census year from 1845 to 1885 inclusive were:—

Articles and Units.		1845.	1855.	1865.	1875.	1885.
Indian corn	Bushels	1,985,215	2,595,096	2,015,771	1,040,290	2,147,390
Oats	,,	1,238,159	792,982	678,779	457,710	619,667
Rye	,,	446,925	523,777	271,016	250,113	232,107
Wheat	,,	47,986	41,003	39,709	13,749	7,160
Poultry and eggs	Value £	10,356	21,073	118,181	233,350	409,433
Pork	Lbs.	...	...	29,440,447	12,786,062	16,546,752
Beef	,,	...	...	70,825,396	12,258,542	10,668,941
Mutton	,,	...	...	8,989,506	589,323	954,179
Milk	Gallons	2,850,412	3,300,916	10,079,180	35,698,159	72,528,628
Butter	Lbs.	7,688,556	8,116,009	3,745,293	7,922,431	9,685,539
Cheese	,,	7,262,637	5,762,776	3,560,481	1,280,234	359,124
Green vegetables	Value £	...	...	...	424,424	664,594
Apples	Bushels	...	...	...	3,252,957	4,545,833
Other fruits	Value £	...	...	83,087	137,723	242,368
Cider	Gallons	...	...	271,680	5,613,846	4,865,193
Tobacco	Lbs.	265,560	...	9,306,067	5,993,666	4,210,903
Wool	,,	1,016,230	416,156	610,255	206,935	257,544
Charcoal	Bushels	775,925	2,657,212	2,301,235	1,015,073	290,778
Ice	Tons	...	387,100	650,359	395,184	174,274

NOTE.—Sterling amounts in this report are given at the rate of 4*s*. to the dollar.

BOSTON.

The value, in 1885, of the several agricultural products, of which the total value is stated on the first page of this report, was:— *Value of agricultural products.*

	£
Indian corn	264,300
Oats	54,664
Rye	32,840
Barley	10,210
Buckwheat	7,470
Wheat	1,590
Hay	1,935,380
Other dry fodder	265,000
Roots	68,262
Straw	57,715
Poultry and eggs	414,089
Pork	212,636
Beef	143,800
Veal	78,234
Mutton	14,728
Game	1,186
Milk	2,062,552
Butter	506,214
Cream	40,541
Cheese	6,797
Green vegetables	664,600
Potatoes	380,845
Apples	234,900
Cranberries	108,182
Strawberries	81,379
Pears	29,403
Grapes	23,404
All other fruits	58,903
Cider	70,092
Other beverages	8,943
Vinegar	24,050
Maple sugar	15,435
Maple syrup	9,065
Tobacco	95,000
Wool	12,286
Hides, skins, &c.	31,365
Manure	600,038
Firewood	366,500
Lumber and wood products	219,134
Charcoal	6,067
Ice	43,554
Trees, flowers, and plants	180,247
Other farm products	109,600
Total	9,551,200

The number of animals on farms in 1885 was:—

Horses	61,104
Colts	4,202
Cows	162,847
Oxen	10,433
Bulls, steers, heifers, calves	88,870
Swine	135,429
Sheep	55,140
Lambs	18,384

The following are some additional particulars given in the volume on agriculture:—

Between the years 1875 and 1885 cultivated land increased nearly 5 per cent. in value and nearly 3 per cent. in acreage; horses declined over 5 per cent. in value, but increased nearly 15 per cent. in number; milch cows declined nearly 12 per cent. in value, but increased nearly 30 per cent. in number; pigs declined 30 per cent. in value, but increased 70 per cent. in number; apples fell off one-third in value, but production increased nearly 40 per cent.; cheese declined 18·30 per cent. in value, but the apparent decline of nearly three-fourths in quantity was in great measure due to its manufacture having been generally transferred to factories by farmers, who thenceforward merely supplied the milk; Indian corn fell off nearly one-third in value, but the quantity more than doubled; poultry and eggs more than doubled in quantity, but declined 15 per cent in value.

Of the value of all agricultural products in 1885, dairy products represented 27·39 per cent.; hay, straw, and fodder, 24·36 per cent.; vegetables, 10·95 per cent.; and all other products, 37·30 per cent.

The conclusion arrived at by the Census Commissioner is that, whilst Massachusetts is not a great farming State, and does not compete with the West in the great staple products of the soil, it has succeeded in gradually replacing these products by minor, but which have nevertheless proved to be more remunerative, crops, the increasing value of which offers great encouragement to the further development of the farming interests of the commonwealth.

Boston, June 11, 1888.

LONDON:
Printed for Her Majesty's Stationery Office,
By HARRISON AND SONS,
Printers in Ordinary to Her Majesty.
(1125 7 | 88—H & S 489)

FOREIGN OFFICE.
1888.
ANNUAL SERIES.

No. 427.
DIPLOMATIC AND CONSULAR REPORTS ON TRADE AND FINANCE.

UNITED STATES.

REPORT ON THE
AGRICULTURE OF SOUTH CAROLINA.

REFERENCE TO PREVIOUS REPORT, Annual Series No. 340.

Issued during the Recess and Presented to both Houses of Parliament by Command of Her Majesty.

LONDON:
PRINTED FOR HER MAJESTY'S STATIONERY OFFICE,
BY HARRISON AND SONS, ST. MARTIN'S LANE,
PRINTERS IN ORDINARY TO HER MAJESTY.

And to be purchased, either directly or through any Bookseller, from
EYRE AND SPOTTISWOODE, EAST HARDING STREET, FLEET STREET, E.C. and
32, ABINGDON STREET, WESTMINSTER, S.W.; or
ADAM AND CHARLES BLACK, 6, NORTH BRIDGE, EDINBURGH; or
HODGES, FIGGIS, & Co., 104, GRAFTON STREET, DUBLIN.

1888.

[C. 5252—204.]   *Price One Penny.*

New Series of Reports.

Reports of the Annual Series have been issued from Her Majesty's Diplomatic and Consular Officers at the following places, and may be obtained from the sources indicated on the title-page:—

No.		Price.	No.		Price.
301.	Marseilles	1d.	364.	Truxillo	1d.
302.	Bordeaux	2d.	365.	Ningpo	1d.
303.	Ancona	1d.	366.	Chefoo	1d.
304.	Swatow	1d.	367.	Bushire	1d.
305.	Ssŭ-ch'uan	1d.	368.	Stockholm	2d.
306.	Antwerp	1d.	369.	Santiago	1d.
307.	Cadiz	1d.	370.	New York	2d.
308.	Genoa	1d.	371.	Pernambuco	1d.
309.	Marseilles	1d.	372.	Söul	1d.
310.	Baltimore	1d.	373.	Chinkiang	2d.
311.	Savannah	1d.	374.	Pernambuco	1d.
312.	Boston	1d.	375.	San Francisco	2d.
313.	San Francisco	1d.	376.	Riga	1d.
314.	Guayaquil	1d.	377.	Newchwang	2d.
315.	Santos	1d.	378.	San Salvador	1d.
316.	Carthagena and Santa Martha	1d.	379.	Frankfort	2d.
317.	San José	1d.	380.	Hankow	2d.
318.	Boulogne	1d.	381.	Bucharest	1d.
319.	Tahiti	1d.	382.	Lisbon	1d.
320.	Fiume	1d.	383.	Tunis	1d.
321.	Warsaw	1d.	384.	Tangier	1d.
322.	Vera Cruz	2d.	385.	Santiago	2d.
323.	Rio Grande do Sul	1d.	386.	Diarbekir	1d.
324.	Gothenburg	2d.	387.	Shanghai	2d.
325.	Philippopolis	1d.	388.	Rome	2d.
326.	Mogador	2d.	389.	Buenos Ayres	1d.
327.	Havana	2d.	390.	Amsterdam	1d.
328.	La Rochelle	1d.	391.	Warsaw	1d.
329.	Corunna	2d.	392.	San Francisco	1d.
330.	Chicago	2d.	393.	Alexandria	1d.
331.	Foochow	1d.	394.	Salonica	2d.
332.	Taiwan	1d.	395.	Palermo	1d.
333.	Loanda	1d.	396.	Mexico	4d.
334.	Loanda	1d.	397.	Naples	3d.
335.	Noumea	1d.	398.	Boston	1d.
336.	Trieste	1d.	399.	Hakodate	1d.
337.	Nice	1d.	400.	Nantes	1d.
338.	Bordeaux	1d.	401.	Madeira	1d.
339.	Mogador	1d.	402.	Hakodate	1d.
340.	Wilmington	1d.	403.	Nagasaki	1d.
341.	Amoy	2d.	404.	Hiogo	2d.
342.	Trebizond	1d.	405.	Tonga	1d.
343.	Lisbon	1d.	406.	Adana	1d.
344.	Java	1d.	407.	Valparaiso	1d.
345.	Brest	1d.	408.	Bilbao	1d.
346.	Odessa	2d.	409.	Santiago	1d.
347.	Cavalla	1d.	410.	Paramaribo	1d.
348.	Bussorah	1d.	411.	Nantes	1d.
349.	Mollendo	1d.	412.	Bangkok	1d.
350.	Cadiz	5d.	413.	Yokohama	2d.
351.	Cagliari	4d.	414.	Mozambique	1d.
352.	Cagliari	1d.	415.	Canton	2d.
353.	Ajaccio	1d.	416.	Kiungchow	1d.
354.	Copenhagen	1d.	417.	Damascus	1d.
355.	Vienna	1d.	418.	Syra	1d.
356.	San Francisco	1d.	419.	Aleppo	1d.
357.	Vera Cruz	1d.	420.	Sandakan	1d.
358.	Philippopolis	1d.	421.	Barcelona	1d.
359.	Greytown	1d.	422.	Königsberg	1d.
360.	Tangier	1d.	423.	Tabreez	1d.
361.	Lisbon	1d.	424.	Guayaquil	1d.
362.	Chicago	1d.	425.	St. Petersburg	1d.
363.	Jerusalem and Jaffa	1d.	426.	Tokio	1d.

No. 427.

Reference to previous Report, Annual Series No. 340.

UNITED STATES.

CHARLESTON.

Consul Cridland to the Marquis of Salisbury.

My Lord, Charleston, August 21, 1888.

I HAVE the honour to enclose herewith a Report of the Natural Productions and Agriculture of the State of South Carolina. The statements contained in the enclosed report are, I believe, correct, and it can also be said that there is now a greater state of prosperity amongst the agriculturists of South Carolina than ever existed before.

I have, &c.
(Signed) FREDERICK J. CRIDLAND.

Report on the Natural Productions and Agriculture of the State of South Carolina.

Area. The State of South Carolina lies between north latitude 32° 4' 30" and longitude west from Washington 1° 30' and 60° 54'. The United States census of 1880 states that there are 30,170 square miles within its borders; and the Agricultural Bureau gives the State in 1885 19,308,800 acres. Of this 9,000,000 acres are forest lands, 4,500,000 acres cultivated in farms, leaving 5,808,800 acres waste and uncultivated.

Population. Geographical division. The present population consists of 400,000 whites and 600,000 blacks. The State seems to have two principal divisions—the up-country or mountain region, and the low country, intersected by a very large number of rivers—the sea islands forming almost a continuous coast line to the State.

Climate. The climate of South Carolina is mild and genial: snow is seldom seen, except in the mountains, and rarely along the sea coast. The pine lands of the State are considered very healthy, and of great benefit to consumptives. The dry atmosphere of the mountain region has also proved wonderfully beneficial for bronchial and pulmonary complaints. The sea islands furnish many with a summer retreat from the unhealthy rice plantations, and the mountains in the upper part of the State abound in beautiful scenery and are a favourite resort for the whites from the coast ports, and even from the neighbouring States, from the end of April till November. Hotels and private residences are numerous in the mountains, and since 1886 the railroads afford every facility for the mountain tourists. For nearly a century, or between 1742 and 1848, it appears that indigo was cultivated in South Indigo. Carolina, and at one time on a large and remunerative scale, but

(531)

UNITED STATES.

Productions. at present the plant is rarely seen, cotton, rice, Indian corn, wheat, and oats being now the great crops of the State, the soil evidently being well adapted for their cultivation.

Soil. The soil in the low country is remarkably fertile, the river swamps and reclaimed marshes being admirably adapted to the cultivation of rice, while the sandy loam of the sea islands and surrounding main produces the finest long staple cotton, called sea island cotton, of silky fibre. Away from the salt atmosphere the staple becomes shorter and less luxuriant in growth. The rice produced in this State is considered by the people as the finest grown anywhere. The seed was introduced from Madagascar in 1693 in a vessel. Abundant crops are raised of wheat, rye, maize, or white Indian corn, oats, barley, buckwheat, peas, beans, sugar cane, tobacco, brown corn, potatoes, sweet potatoes, hemp, flax, and hops.

Crops.
Cereals.
Fruit. Orchards all over the State furnish apples, pears, quinces, plums peaches, cherries, and near the coast the fig comes to perfection.

Berries. The raspberry, blackberry, and whortleberry grow well, and the strawberry in particular, the latter being extensively shipped to the northern cities in the spring. The grape grows well, and much wine is made therefrom, and its cultivation is extending very much.

Vegetable gardens. The gardens and farms produce turnips, cabbages, beets, parsnips, carrots, mustard, rhubarb, water and musk melons, cucumbers, kale, lettuce, okra, pumpkins, onions, beans, radishes, celery, and tomatoes, but one of the most profitable is the asparagus, fabulous amounts having been made by its culture and sale in the northern markets early in the season. Valuable and almost inexhaustible forests extend over a large portion of the State; the long leaf, or yellow pine, confined chiefly to the low country, covering probably 10,000,000 acres, and furnishing immense quantities of timber, pitch, tar, and turpentine and resin. Here and elsewhere are found the white, water, red, and live oak, black walnut, elm, maple, ash, cyprus, chestnut, beech, poplar, and other trees.

Forests.
Pine.
Oak.

Game. Game is plentiful, the forests abounding in deer, wild turkeys, foxes, rabbits, otter, &c. Partridges, wild pigeons, woodcock, snipe, and immense flocks of wild ducks are found in large numbers, the latter especially all along the shores of the numerous fresh water creeks and rivers. Fish, shrimps, turtle, crabs, and oysters are abundant, the sport being free to everybody.

Fish.

Stock. Stock farming has been found very profitable, and any quantity of grazing land can now be had for sheep or cattle, the farmers considering their pasturage for stock one of their most important concerns. The short winters are of course favourable to the raising of sheep and cattle. Horses and mules are reared at very little cost. Sheep thrive away from the salt, and are profitable in the mountain region. Jersey, Ayrshire, Devon, Holstein, Guernsey, shorthorns, and other cattle, besides the Merino, Southdown, Oxforddown, and broad-tail sheep are raised in many parts of the State, also Essex and Berkshire hops.

Horses.
Mules.
Sheep.
Cattle.

The statistical information published in the annual reports of the Department of Agriculture is compiled from monthly returns of county and township agents during the current year.

Estimated crops. The estimates of yields are based on returns to the Department of an average date of October 1, and as this date is rather early to obtain accurate statements of some crops, particularly cotton, the estimates are considered as showing the "indicated yield" on October 1. In late years, however, the cotton crop has been pushed forward to maturity so rapidly by the free use of commercial fertilisers that a reasonably accurate statement of yield can be made on the date mentioned. The seasons of 1887 were much more favourable than for the previous year, and consequently the yield of the principal crops increased over the production of 1886.

AREA of the Principal Crops in South Carolina for 1886 and 1887, with comparative Increase or Decrease.

Area of crops.

Crop.	Area. 1886.	Area. 1887.	Area. Increase.	Area. Decrease.
	Acres.	Acres.	Acres.	Acres.
Cotton	1,630,856	1,564,370	..	66,486
Corn	1,484,851	1,553,462	68,611	..
Rice	80,504	79,528	..	976
Wheat	192,746	185,557	..	7,189
Oats	311,406	298,591	..	12,815
Sugar cane	12,754	13,375	621	..
Tobacco	827	729	..	98
Peas	142,500	156,750	14,250	..
Potatoes	4,413	4,417	4	..
Potatoes, sweet	41,123	41,647	524	..
Total	3,901,980	3,898,426	84,010	87,564

YIELD of the Principal Crops in South Carolina for 1886 and 1887, with comparative Increase or Decrease.

Yield of crops.

Crop.		Yield. 1886.	Yield. 1887.	Yield. Increase.	Yield. Decrease.
Cotton	Bales	530,102	605,216	75,114	...
Corn	Bushels	13,925,168	17,490,690	3,565,522	...
Rice	Pounds	69,625,922	67,782,920	...	1,843,002
Wheat	Bushels	1,161,097	1,121,442	...	39,655
Oats	,,	3,700,757	4,001,075	300,318	...
Sugar cane	Gallons	1,015,962	949,391	...	66,571
Tobacco	Pounds	465,309	333,623	...	131,686
Peas	Bushels	781,886	795,310	13,424	...
Potatoes	Irish	471,532	371,329	...	100,203
,,	Sweet	3,990,339	3,197,791	...	792,548

The yield of hay in 1887 was 33,417 tons, the yield of corn fodder 164,666 tons, and the yield of pea-vine hay 108,157 tons, making the total yield of long forage in 1887 306,240 tons, 13,238 tons in excess of the harvest of 1886.

The year 1887 was a very unfavourable one for fruit, the late frosts in the spring having very much diminished the crop, and the following table does not show a fair account of the annual production with a favourable season:—

Yield of fruit.

UNITED STATES.

Fruit.	Area in Acres.	Value.
		£ s. d.
Apples	9,228	7,708 0 0
Peaches	15,451	7,581 0 0
Grapes	2,473	11,521 0 0
Pears	1,668	1,739 0 0
Melons	8,100	16,460 0 0
Total	36,920	45,009 0 0

Truck farming. Truck farming is carried on in the State on a large scale, especially where railroad or steamship facilities afford the means for shipments of fruit and vegetables to the markets north of Virginia. It is especially carried on in the vicinity of Charleston, and every year increasing.

In 1886, 89,611 packages of vegetables, and in 1887, 85,385 packages of vegetables were sent by rail and steamer to the north from this city. In 1887, 7,000 crates of asparagus were shipped to New York, realising from 2s. 6d. to 3s. per bunch.

Value of fruit shipped. In 1886 800,000 melons were shipped from the State, and in 1887 924,000.

	£
Value of strawberries shipped in 1887	16,438
" potatoes " "	71,920
" melons " "	19,521
" fruits and vegetables "	76,030
	183,909

Increase of truck farms. The area in truck farming in the State will be largely increased in this and the coming year, large tracts of land heretofore left uncultivated and considered almost unfit for culture having been found to be most suitable for the raising of fruit and vegetables in the early spring, even with the uncertain labour available in this region. Another matter in favour of the truck farmer is that the most approved means of transportation are increasing yearly.

Means of marketing produce. Prices obtained for crops. The following table shows the price per pound, bushel, or gallon, the value of each crop, and the aggregate value of the principal agricultural productions of the State for the year 1887:—

	Per	Price.	Value.
		Dol. c.	£
Cotton	Lb.	0 08·62	4,890,901
Indian corn	Bushel	0 66	2,404,969
Rice	Lb.	0 02	282,428
Peas	Bushel	0 78	129,237
Irish potatoes	"	0 85	65,756
Sweet "	"	0 48	319,779
Hay	100 lbs.	0 65	90,504
Pea-vine hay	" "	0 60	270,392
Fodder	" "	0 78	535,164
Sugar-cane syrup.	Gallon	0 51	31,844
Sorghum "	"	0 47	64,231
Tobacco	Lb.	0 10	6,950
Wheat	Bushel	1 04	243,230
Oats	Bushel	0 54	450,120
Total			9,785,505

CHARLESTON.

Machinery. The fact of farmers having had better crops last year has caused a better demand for every kind of agricultural machinery, and the agents report much larger sales than for years past.

Farm labour. Farm labour during 1887 was abundant, and it is reported that the labourers are more efficient than formerly.

Condition of cattle. Horses and other work animals throughout the State are reported in good condition and free from diseases.

Wages. It seems impossible to find out what wages agricultural labourers receive in this State from the fact that very few planters or landowners employ labour on wages. Probably three-fourths of the farmers or planters work their lands on the share system, a settlement being made between them and the labourer when the crops are sold.

The planters who have accumulated money since the late war prefer the wages system, and probably a good farm hand is paid on an average from 20s. to 30s. a week, with a very small one-storey house or hut to live in.

Number of cattle and value in South Carolina. The following statement of the number of cattle, &c., in South Carolina is taken from the Agricultural Report for 1887 published in Washington:—

	Number.	Average Price.	Value.
		£ s. d.	£ s. d.
Horses	64,673	18 7 4	1,187,901 5 0
Mules	73,253	19 11 10	1,435,079 15 10
Cows	144,748	3 16 0	550,343 19 2
Oxen	216,858	2 3 5	482,124 15 10
Sheep	108,418	6 4	33,648 15 0
Hogs	550,166	15 8	430,963 10 10
Total	1,158,116		4,120,062 1 8

Phosphate rock. One of the most useful and valuable natural formations in South Carolina is the phosphate rock, mined on the land and dredged from the river beds. Since the discovery of its value in 1870, when about 2,000 tons were mined, the production has been steadily increasing till, in 1887, 432,757 tons were brought to the surface on land and water. It is carried to many foreign countries as a valuable fertiliser, and affords employment to a vast number of people, and since 1870 5,000,000l. has been received here from the sale of the phosphate rock in the home and foreign markets. **Production or mined.**

Gold. The gold mines in South Carolina yield annually about 20,000l. **Kaolin.** Kaolin of very fine quality, used in the manufacture of china, is also obtained in large quantities in this State, and is about to be made of considerable value by manufacturers. Copper, iron, lead, manganese, **Metals.** bismuth, soapstone, coal, limestone, and the finest blue and grey granite **Coal, &c.** are also found. Mineral springs exist in the mountain region of the **Mineral** State, the water being impregnated with iron, magnesia, potash, **springs.** sulphur, iodine, and an excess of carbonic acid, and are much resorted to by invalids.

Temperature. The mean annual temperature of the State is said to be 62°. The mercury during the last three winters has marked from 20° to 60° Fahrenheit, and from 70° to 95° in the summer in the low country **Death rate.** region. The death rate per 1,000 of the population amongst the whites is 20·83 in Charleston, and among the blacks 50 per 1,000 per year, and the monthly reports of the Board of Health are very accurate.

UNITED STATES.

The death-rate in the months of July, August, and September is almost double compared with the winter months. The class of diseases most fatal are zymotic and those produced in the respiratory organs, pneumonia giving the largest per centage.

Price of provisions, &c.

WHOLESALE Price of Provisions and other Necessaries.

	Per	Price.	
		s. d.	s. d.
Apples	Barrel	12 6 to	14 7½
Bacon	Lb.	0 4	0 5
Beef	,,	0 3½	0 4
Butter	,,	0 10	1 0
Cheese	,,	0 6	0 7
Coal, bituminous	Ton	16 8	21 0
,, anthracite	,,	17 0	25 0
Coffee, Rio	Lb.	0 7	0 9
Eggs	Dozen	0 7½	0 10
Flour	Barrel	18 9	27 0
Hams	Lb.	0 5½	0 6
Hay	Ton	70 10	75 0
Indian corn	Bushel	2 11	3 1
Lard	Lb.	0 3	0 4
Mackerel	Barrel	31 3	35 5
Molasses	Gallon	1 0	1 8
Mutton	Lb.	0 3½	0 4
Oats	Bushel	1 10	2 1
Onions	Barrel	16 8	18 9
Pork	Lb.	0 4	0 5
Potatoes	Barrel	11 5½	13 6½
Rice	Lb.	0 2	0 3
Salt	Sack	3 1½	3 6½
Sugar, brown	Lb.	0 3½	0 4
,, white	,,	0 4	0 4½

Crops of 1888.

From all accounts published the condition of the present crops of cotton, rice, corn, &c., in South Carolina is fully up to the average of past years, the season having been a most favourable one for the planter and farmer.

LONDON:
Printed for Her Majesty's Stationery Office,
By HARRISON AND SONS,
Printers in Ordinary to Her Majesty.
1125 10 | 88—H & S 531)

FOREIGN OFFICE.
1888.
ANNUAL SERIES.

No. 431.

DIPLOMATIC AND CONSULAR REPORTS ON TRADE AND FINANCE.

UNITED STATES.

REPORT FOR THE YEAR 1888
ON THE
AGRICULTURE OF THE STATES OF NEW YORK, NEW JERSEY, CONNECTICUT, RHODE ISLAND, AND DELAWARE.

REFERENCE TO PREVIOUS REPORT, Annual Series No. 370.

Issued during the Recess and Presented to both Houses of Parliament by Command of Her Majesty.

LONDON:
PRINTED FOR HER MAJESTY'S STATIONERY OFFICE,
BY HARRISON AND SONS, ST. MARTIN'S LANE,
PRINTERS IN ORDINARY TO HER MAJESTY.

And to be purchased, either directly or through any Bookseller, from
EYRE AND SPOTTISWOODE, EAST HARDING STREET, FLEET STREET, E.C., and 32, ABINGDON STREET, WESTMINSTER, S.W.; or
ADAM AND CHARLES BLACK, 6, NORTH BRIDGE, EDINBURGH; or
HODGES, FIGGIS, & Co., 104, GRAFTON STREET, DUBLIN.

1888.

[C. 5252—208.] *Price Twopence.*

New Series of Reports.

Reports of the Annual Series have been issued from Her Majesty's Diplomatic and Consular Officers at the following places, and may be obtained from the sources indicated on the title-page:—

No.		Price.	No.		Price.
307.	Cadiz	1d.	369.	Santiago	1d.
308.	Genoa	1d.	370.	New York	2d.
309.	Marseilles	1d.	371.	Pernambuco	1d.
310.	Baltimore	1d.	372.	Söul	1d.
311.	Savannah	1d.	373.	Chinkiang	2d.
312.	Boston	1d.	374.	Pernambuco	1d.
313.	San Francisco	1d.	375.	San Francisco	2d.
314.	Guayaquil	1d.	376.	Riga	1d.
315.	Santos	1d.	377.	Newchwang	2d.
316.	Carthagena and Santa Martha	1d.	378.	San Salvador	1d.
317.	San José	1d.	379.	Frankfort	2d.
318.	Boulogne	1d.	380.	Hankow	2d.
319.	Tahiti	1d.	381.	Bucharest	1d.
320.	Fiume	1d.	382.	Lisbon	1d.
321.	Warsaw	1d.	383.	Tunis	1d.
322.	Vera Cruz	2d.	384.	Tangiers	1d.
323.	Rio Grande do Sul	1d.	385.	Santiago	2d.
324.	Gothenburg	2d.	386.	Diarbekir	1d.
325.	Philippopolis	1d.	387.	Shanghai	2d.
326.	Mogador	2d.	388.	Rome	2d.
327.	Havana	2d.	389.	Buenos Ayres	1d.
328.	La Rochelle	1d.	390.	Amsterdam	1d.
329.	Corunna	2d.	391.	Warsaw	1d.
330.	Chicago	2d.	392.	San Francisco	1d.
331.	Foochow	1d.	393.	Alexandria	1d.
332.	Taiwan	1d.	394.	Salonica	2d.
333.	Loanda	1d.	395.	Palermo	1d.
334.	Loanda	1d.	396.	Mexico	4d.
335.	Noumea	1d.	397.	Naples	3d.
336.	Trieste	1d.	398.	Boston	1d.
337.	Nice	1d.	399.	Hakodate	1d.
338.	Bordeaux	1d.	400.	Nantes	1d.
339.	Mogador	1d.	401.	Madeira	1d.
340.	Wilmington	1d.	402.	Hakodate	1d.
341.	Amoy	2d.	403.	Nagasaki	1d.
342.	Trebizond	1d.	404.	Hiogo	2d.
343.	Lisbon	1d.	405.	Tonga	1d.
344.	Java	1d.	406.	Adana	1d.
345.	Brest	1d.	407.	Valparaiso	1d.
346.	Odessa	2d.	408.	Bilbao	1d.
347.	Cavalla	1d.	409.	Santiago	1d.
348.	Bussorah	1d.	410.	Paramaribo	1d.
349.	Mollendo	1d.	411.	Nantes	1d.
350.	Cadiz	5d.	412.	Bangkok	1d.
351.	Cagliari	4d.	413.	Yokohama	2d.
352.	Cagliari	1d.	414.	Mozambique	1d.
353.	Ajaccio	1d.	415.	Canton	2d.
354.	Copenhagen	1d.	416.	Kiungchow	1d.
355.	Vienna	1d.	417.	Damascus	1d.
356.	San Francisco	1d.	418.	Syra	1d.
357.	Vera Cruz	1d.	419.	Aleppo	1d.
358.	Philippopolis	1d.	420.	Sandakan	1d.
359.	Greytown	1d.	421.	Barcelona	1d.
360.	Tangier	1d.	422.	Königsberg	1d.
361.	Lisbon	1d.	423.	Tabreez	1d.
362.	Chicago	1d.	424.	Guayaquil	1d.
363.	Jerusalem and Jaffa	1d.	425.	St. Petersburg	1d.
364.	Truxillo	1d.	426.	Tokio	1d.
365.	Ningpo	1d.	427.	Charleston	1d.
366.	Chefoo	1d.	428.	Amsterdam	1d.
367.	Bushire	1d.	429.	Hamburg	4d.
368.	Stockholm	2d.	430.	Trieste	1d.

No. 431.

Reference to previous Report, Annual Series No. 370.

UNITED STATES.

NEW YORK.

Consul-General Booker to the Marquis of Salisbury.

My Lord Marquis,　　　　　　　　　　　New York, September 7, 1888.

I HAVE the honour to transmit herewith a Report upon the Agriculture of the States of New York, New Jersey, Connecticut, Rhode Island, and Delaware.

I have, &c.
(Signed)　　WM. LANE BOOKER.

Report upon the Agriculture of the States of New York, New Jersey, Connecticut, Rhode Island, and Delaware for the Year 1888.

NEW YORK.

The product of the cereals, &c., of the State of New York in 1886 and 1887 is given in the following table:—

		1886. No. of Acres in each Crop.	1886. Quantity Produced.	1886. Average Yield per Acre.	1887. No. of Acres in each Crop.	1887. Quantity Produced.	1887. Average Yield per Acre.
Wheat	Bushels	680,493	11,093,000	16·3	666,883	10,137,000	15·2
Indian corn	,,	716,572	22,426,000	31·3	709,406	23,410,000	33·0
Barley	,,	350,544	7,712,000	22·0	\multicolumn{3}{No statistics available.}
Oats	,,	1,399,097	40,223,000	28·7	1,413,088	33,268,000	23·6
Rye	,,	236,875	2,890,000	12·2			
Buckwheat	,,	317,663	4,543,000	14·3	No statistics available.		
Potatoes	,,	349,934	27,995,000	80·0			
Hay	Tons	5,111,023	5,418,677	1·06			

The north-western counties, south of Lake Ontario, have always been the greatest grain-producing counties, and from a section of this part of the country came the "Genessee" wheat, which was so well known in the English market before the Western States assumed such prominence as grain-producers. At the present time, out of an average crop of about 11,500,000 bushels, nearly 9,000,000 bushels are raised in the counties referred to. Indian corn, oats, and barley are also largely grown. A well-known agriculturist, President of one of the County Agricultural Societies, writes to me, in reference to the farming in this section of the State:—"The counties of Monroe, Yates, Ontario, Wayne, Livingston, Genessee, Orleans, and Niagara are peculiarly adapted to the growth of cereals and grass. The soil is sufficiently alluvial to plough under a clover sod for the planting of Indian corn,

North-Western principal grain-growing counties of State.

Mode of farming in North-Western counties.

(538)

one of our most necessary and profitable crops, yielding from 50 to 100 bushels of ears per acre; the following year we take the same corn stubble and sow it to barley (in some instances oats), from which we expect from 25 to 40 bushels per acre; in July and August of the same year we plough and 'fit' the same land for winter wheat, the yield of which is determined by the season, &c.; but for many years the yield has been from 15 to 40 bushels per acre. In many localities, through the counties named, potato and bean raising has increased to a large extent. With wheat we seed the ground again to clover and timothy, for the purpose of pasture or mowing for hay. Our usual custom is to let the land lie about two years in grass, and then go through the same round again. Some of our best farmers think a one-year-old clover sod the best to break up for Indian corn or potatoes."

Another correspondent, the President of the County Agricultural Society of Livingston (one of the counties referred to), writes:—" As I understand your letter, the term 'your farms' means the farms of the county, not my personal ones; so I can only answer as to their character in a general way, by saying that Livingston county is composed of parts of the valley of the Genessee and its tributaries, so that the farms can be roughly divided into upland and lowland, or 'flats.' The upland is generally a pretty stiff clay, but well adapted to wheat or pasturage; the lowlands are better for Indian corn and beans. Wheat pays well enough if we get a good crop, but of course it does not pay to raise wheat at 87 c. (about $3s.\ 6\frac{3}{4}d.$) per bushel, otherwise I should call 20 bushels or better a good crop. I have 36 to-day in some places. It is not the custom to seed down land unless with some other crop, and that is, almost universally, wheat. The ordinary rotation here is: Indian corn or beans, first year; oats or barley, second year; wheat, third year; grass, fourth year; pasture, fifth year. This generally makes a six-years' rotation, otherwise the pasture is left out, and the clover ploughed under. I do not think commercial fertilisers are as generally used here as some years since. The farming of the county is general; hops, roots, apples, peaches, and grapes are raised, but the staples are Indian corn, wheat, beans, oats, and some barley."

The President of the Genessee Agricultural Society writes:—"We cannot compete with the Western States in growing Indian corn, but in winter wheat, oats, barley, potatoes, beans, and hay we can hold our own against any of the States. Apples are produced in great quantities in the southern part of the county, and I believe it is generally admitted that our long-keeping varieties are unsurpassed in their quality; new orchards are being extensively planted, and the production is rapidly increasing. A system of rotation much practised here is to turn over the sod land in the spring, first manuring with stable manure; then plant with Indian corn or beans, or any crop which may be hoed; fallow the next season with oats or barley, using about 200 lbs. of superphosphate per acre; after harvest, plough the stubble and sow to winter wheat, with another application of phosphate; then lay down to grass for about two years. With this system the wheat yield is 15 to 40 bushels per acre, oats 40 to 60 bushels, and barley 30 to 50 bushels per acre. The hay is generally 2 to 3 tons the first year, and $1\frac{1}{2}$ to 2 tons the second. Commercial fertilisers are extensively used, and increase the crops greatly."

Farming in Schuyler, a western county.

The President of the Agricultural Society of Schuyler, in the western part of the State, and south of those previously referred to, writes: "The county of Schuyler has a soil of varied formation on the shores of the beautiful Seneca Lake, which heads near the south line of the county, and runs north through the county; the character of the soil is mostly gravelly loam, with an admixture of clay sufficient to prevent teachiness. The general surface of the county is rolling, with some valleys and table lands. The land in the valleys is mostly of a gravelly loam with a mixture of muck, on the hills and table lands mostly a clay loam. In respect to the products of the county, I believe that almost everything in the line of grass, grain, and fruit that grows in any of the northern states of the Union is raised within the county; on either shore of the lake spoken of, for a distance of three miles back from the shore, peaches, plums, pears, apricots, prunes, cherries, grapes, raspberries, blackberries, currants, gooseberries are largely raised as a market crop: apples, pears, cherries, and plums are grown more or less over the whole county. The principal grain grown for market is barley and wheat, also buckwheat; oats are raised and corn to a great extent, but are mostly used in the county for feeding cattle and sheep, which are fed in large numbers for the New York market. There is, comparatively speaking, but little grazing land in the county, consequently a general rotation of crops becomes necessary, beginning with the ploughing of sod fields, planting to corn. The next year sowing to barley, followed by wheat in the fall; with the wheat, timothy and clover are sown, which develop the next year and are either mown for hay or pastured for one or two years and sometimes longer, when the land is manured and again ploughed. Others practise the rotation by ploughing and sowing to buckwheat, the next year to oats, and seeding to clover and timothy, and either mowing or pasturing as before. Dairying is carried on as a business to a small extent, yet the county produces quite a quantity of butter for export above what is needed for home consumption. Large numbers of horses for road and coach purposes are raised, also early lambs for market and winter feeding. But few beef cattle are grown, as the demand for veal calves is so great that they are sold when but a few weeks old. I have thus given a general outline of the products of the county."

The President of the Agricultural Society of Steuben, a very large county adjoining Schuyler, writes: "In this county there is a large acreage of land under grain cultivation, such as rye, barley, oats, corn, and wheat, but the latter is not a profitable crop and is only sown to seed after. The rotation of crops is Indian corn or potatoes, then barley and oats, then wheat or rye to seed after; in some parts of the county, potatoes are very extensively grown, and are a profitable crop. In the lake region there are over 20,000 acres set to grapes. Fertilisers are used to most crops. *Farming in Steuben, a western county.*

In the eastern part of the State, wheat is only sown to seed after, except in a few well-favoured localities. The growth of barley is confined to the north-western and northern parts, that of oats mainly to the same sections, but in every county there is some raised. Indian corn is not confined to any particular county, although the greatest production is in the north-west and north. Buckwheat is grown almost entirely in the eastern parts of the State, from this point to the river St. Lawrence. Hops are grown in the central counties, chiefly from 150 to 200 miles north of this city. 150,000 bales (180 lbs.) was the result of last year's crop, which may be considered about the average of late years, except that of 1886, which was almost a total failure. *General farming of the State. Hops.*

Fruit-growing is an important factor in the husbandry of the State, the value of the orchard products being estimated at about 8,500,000 dols. (1,750,000*l.*), one-sixth of the product of the whole of the United States. *Fruit.*

The most profitable and extensive farming in the State is in connec- *Dairy farming.*

(538)

tion with the dairy, the value of the product of which is estimated at over 70,000,000 dols. (about 13,600,000*l.*) The Hudson river counties have always been dairy counties; their proximity to the large cities, their abundance of spring water, and their great area of natural meadow-land (so much desired in the earlier days of farming) made them, notwithstanding the irregular and broken face of the country, the chosen spot for dairying. The northern counties have been obliged to adopt this system of farming from necessity, on account of the generally poor soil and the inability to raise grain to advantage. Formerly the Hudson river counties were noted for the excellence and quantity of their butter, but of late years the demand for milk and cream for New York and other cities, and to supply condensing factories, has been so great that the making of butter has been in a great measure given up. Twenty-five years ago the dairy product of Orange county just north of this was chiefly marketed in butter, but to-day the farmers buy the greater part of the butter consumed in the county. In this State there were last year 1,540,000 milch cows (20 per cent. high grade), of which two-thirds were in the eastern part between this point and the river St. Lawrence, and one-third in the north-western and western, south of Lake Ontario. Nine-tenths of the cheese which was estimated at 135,000,000 of pounds in 1887 was the product of factories. I give below an extract from the report of the manager of one of the leading cheese factories, situated in the central part of the State in regard to the method of cheese making as adopted there:—

Method of cheese-making

"Lyon Brook Factory is situated in the Chenango valley. The locality is in the midst of a very rich farming district, abounding in pure water and good pastures, and admits of every advantage useful to the farmer and his dairy interests.

"The factory dairy numbers 300 cows, which are principally owned by practical farmers of means and enterprise. The breeds of cows which this large dairy embraces are Ayrshires, Durhams, Alderneys, Holsteins, Devons, and Jerseys, with a large per cent. in the first three classes. The best dairies of our factory are mostly of good-blooded stock, from one-half to full-bloods, and will compare well with the dairies of our county.

"The breed of cows producing the largest amount of milk per head is the Durham, this dairy being mostly full-bloods, while the dairy producing the least amount of milk per head is the Devons and a general mixture.

"The ordinary dairy cow of our section weighs from 800 to 1,000 lbs., and the ages are from three to twelve years. Our dairies are milked about nine and one-half months in the year, coming to milk in the months of March and April.

"The mode of feeding the dairy, which is our next class, and is to embrace the three test months of August, September, and October, is the common way amongst most farming districts, namely, by grazing day and night in separate pastures. The kind of fodder used at this season of the year is sowed corn, bran, and millet. Sowed corn is the most common with our dairymen, while bran and millet are used to quite an extent. The method of feeding sowed corn, bran, and millet is now mostly confined to the barn at milking time; but in some cases, for convenience, it is fed in the pasture. The time of feeding these substitutes for this year is: millet for the month of August, sowed corn for the last of August and September, while bran is used from the first of September to the last of the season.

"The number of bran-fed cows in our factory will exceed 250 this year, and nearly all have been fed on some substitute. Fall feed is mostly used with us very early in September and October, pastures being used after frosts.

"We now come to the method of milking, straining, cooling and delivering of milk at the factory. This part of our industry, which seems small in its detail, and especially so to our patrons, is a point we have not neglected, but one we have heeded; and I can safely say, to teach this lesson well, one needs a great amount of manly effort and persistence, together with a microscopic eye, and a little good sunlight, to point out the fact to our patrons—that which we thought they could not learn. The lesson, I confess, can be easier described than brought into practical use, for of all things to get at, and to have known by the patrons, this is the inevitable—we do persist in having pure, clean milk delivered at our factory—and require tin to be used in handling our milk throughout, while cloth strainers are used to quite an extent.

"The milking of the dairies is very regular, and so far as practicable, at the same hour morning and night. The cooling of the night's milk with us is a special feature; and, as we receive only one-fourth of the night's milk at the factory, the remainder has to be cared for by our patrons. As our location is blessed with plenty of good running water, our patrons have adopted the sure method of cooling milk by having milk pools for their cans; and all not having running water are required to cool their night's milk 25 degrees below animal heat. In hot weather —as this year, for example—we require the morning's milk to be cooled to some extent before delivery. The night's milk received at the factory is cooled to 75°, and running water left on the vat over night; next morning the cream is run through the strainer and thoroughly mixed in the milk.

"The morning delivery is very prompt, and by 7·30 we have the milk in the factory ready for use. The milk, after delivery at the factory, receives a thorough straining with cloth, and the milk is kept well mixed till the vat is full. This completed, we proceed with the mixing and heating of the vat till the temperature of the milk is 84°; then the heat is shut off and the coloring mixed in, stirring two or three minutes, after which it is left for five minutes, or until the temperature is 86°; then the rennet is mixed in and stirred for five minutes only. The quantity of rennet is from 5 to 8 ozs. to each 1,000 lbs. of milk, or a sufficient amount to bring it to a proper consistency in thirty minutes, ready for the first cutting. When the curd is firm enough we apply the curd-knife, cutting the vat both ways in as quick a time as possible. After this the curd is left thirty minutes to harden and mature; this time having passed, and the curd being ready to develop, we put on the heat, and with one arm break up the curd from the bottom, in a careful way, and then proceed with the last cutting, the temperature of the vat being about 90°, cutting the short way of the vat, in a triangular way from one side to the other. This done, we begin stirring with both hands, being careful to keep raising the temperature, scalding to 100°. When the temperature is 98° we shut off the heat and apply the curd-rake, stirring from ten to fifteen minutes, according to the curd and its tenacious qualities.

"After completing this the curd is left to ripen and develop for about an hour and a half, or until the curd is ready to cool and work up. In cases where the curd is to be hurried to some extent, it is stirred up every half hour, and not allowed to pack to any great extent. When the curd has sufficient acid to admit of handling and making ready for the press, the water is turned on the vat and we commence breaking up the curd, mixing through for five or six minutes; then draw out about two-thirds of the whey, or until the curd is exposed to the air partially, then stop the whey, and stir the curd over two or three times, exposing it to the air for cooling and mixing, after which the whey is drawn out and the vat tipped up to drain; this completed, we proceed to dipping it into the curd sink for salting and further reducing.

"Here I will answer the questions:—When do we start the whey, and when do we dip the curds? Here, I confess, we are the object of circumstances; but, be that as it may, we rely upon sense of feeling, tasting, and smelling as our guide in determining the acid of a curd, always taking into consideration the temperature and moisture of the day, starting the whey when we think the acid shall have developed sufficiently for dipping by the time the whey is out of the vat. The dipping of the curds is the principal feature of our method; and, as we claim to make an even acid cheese, we must know when to dip out our curds. This we claim to know by experience, for it is the *all in all point with us*, because in our make of cheese we have to dip with less acid than ordinary shipping goods; so from experience we have learned that the curd sink is a sure relief for this feature of exactness.

"The temperature of the curd when taken from the vat is from 92° to 95° on an average, and when put into the press from 80° to 85°. After the whey has leached out to a good extent, we commence to stir in the salt, stirring it over two or three times in a fast way, taking about 20 minutes in salting and cooling. We use three pounds of salt to each 1,000 pounds of milk, on an average, but varying sometimes with the curds and seasons of the year. We press our curds 18 hours each, special attention being given to the first hours of pressing.

"The cheeses, when taken to the curing-room, are left for one hour or so to dry off, then they are greased with hot whey oil on both sides and left for the day, repeating the next day and whenever they require it; the cheeses are turned every morning for the next 30 days, always keeping the benches in a clean condition, and the mold well rubbed off the cheese each day.

"The temperature of our curing rooms is kept very regular, and special attention is given to the curing of our goods, which is done in a slow way. The average time required in curing our cheese is 35 days; while in the spring we cure them quicker, in the fall more time is allowed, but we always aim to send out goods that are wholesome and free from fermenting gases; and now, before leaving this subject, I wish to add that we have many new and more modern ways, but of them all I have given herewith the most successful for our make of cheese, and, while we might do without the curd sink, we do not choose to, for quick drainage and the fast cooling of our curds is what we aim at; and whether this has anything to do with the keeping qualities of cheese I am not prepared to say, but will leave it to the practical cheesemaker.

"Our milk product for 1886 was 2,915,304 pounds of milk, which made 312,993 pounds of cheese, taking 9·32 pounds of milk to one of cheese, and paid 96 c. per hundred to patrons. For 1885, it was 3,009,288 pounds of milk, which made 322,575 pounds of cheese, taking 9·34 pounds of milk to one of cheese, and netting 82 c. per 100 to the patrons. For 1884, it was 2,810,973 pounds of milk, which made 294,597 pounds of cheese, taking 9·54 pounds of milk to one of cheese, and paid 1 dol. 5 c. per 100 to patrons. It costs the patrons 1 dol. 15 c. per 100 for manufacturing, and six per cent. for selling."

The following are extracts from reports made to the Jefferson County Agricultural Society by successful competitors for prizes for best cheese exhibited:—

"*Statement of B. Dickinson, of South Rutland, to whom were awarded the First Prize for Factory Cheese made in July, and the Second Prize for Factory Cheese made in August.*

"The milk was set at 84°; was from 25 to 30 minutes in coming, then stood 35 minutes before cutting the curd. Run one hour, stopped at 96°; stood three hours in the scald, then the whey run off and salted; two and three-quarter pounds to 100 pounds of curd."

"*Statement of H. C. Evans, of Rutland, to whom were awarded the First Prize for Factory Cheese made in August, and the Second Prize for Factory Cheese made in July.*

"Heat the milk to 84°; put in rennet sufficient to coagulate in 45 minutes; then cut the curd and let the whey rise. Heat to 94° and let it stand 30 minutes; then heat to 100°. I test with a hot iron when the whey is ready to be drawn and curd packed, when it threads about an inch on the iron it is ground and salted with two and three-quarter pounds of factory filled salt to 100 pounds of cheese."

"*Statement of John G. Myers, Cheesemaker of the R. L. Sherman Factory.*

"Most of the night's milk is stirred and cooled by the patrons at home. The night's and morning's milk are mixed and heated to 84°, and rennet added to make it coagulate in 40 minutes. It is then cut, lengthwise of the vat, and left 20 minutes to set (stir to make fine curd) before heating to 98°; test by hot iron and smell. After sufficient acid is formed to make a firm cheese, it is put into the curd-sink to drain, then broken fine and salted, three pounds of salt to 1,000 pounds of milk; put into hoops and pressed 12 to 15 hours, then removed to the curing room, the temperature of which is kept at 70 to 74°."

The best cheese is made in St. Lawrence and Jefferson counties, bordering on the river St. Lawrence, and is chiefly shipped through Montreal, and goes abroad as Canadian cheese.

The following are the methods adopted for making imitation "Gorgonzola" and "Neufchatel" cheeses:—

"*Gorgonzola Cheese.*

"Begin with the night's mess, and it is desirable to set the milk fresh from the cow, and at its normal temperature, or if it has cooled, heat to a temperature of 77 degrees, and add sufficient rennet to coagulate in 15 to 20 minutes. The curd should be allowed to become quite stiff, and is then cut fine and allowed to settle for a few minutes, or until the whey begins to appear. The curd is then gathered into linen strainers and hung up to drain off the whey till morning. The morning's milk is then treated in the same manner, except that it is hung up for two hours only. It is then put into the hoop, first spreading a bandage cloth in the hoop (a hoop 12 by 10, making a cheese of about 30 lbs.), in alternate layers, first of the evening curd and then of the morning curd, till the hoop is filled. The morning curd should still be moderately warm, so as to stick to the cold evening curd.

"After filling, the hoops are left standing for five or six hours, when the cheese is turned upside down, putting in a new bandage cloth; this is repeated again during the day. The next day the cheese is removed from the hoop, the bandage cloth also being removed, and placed in the curing room, where a temperature of about 70°

is maintained. Dry salt is rubbed on the *top* and *sides*, the cheese being turned daily; the tops and bottoms are therefore only salted on alternate days, care being taken to rub off the brine, which has formed on the surface of the cheese, each day before rubbing on the dry salt. This process is repeated for eight or 10 days.

"When the cheese will 'take' no more salt, and the surface is uniformly hardened, the salting is discontinued, and they are left in the curing room 20 to 30 days, at first being turned each day, and later every other day, and occasionally being wiped off and moistened, about three times, with lukewarm whey or brine. The cheese is then removed to a curing cellar, which should be cool and free from draught, and, if possible, with slightly moist atmosphere. Here they are rubbed and turned occasionally, and, if they show signs of cracking, the surface is rubbed with fresh butter or olive oil. No mould should be allowed on the outside, though it forms within the cheese during ripening. The Gorgonzola, when properly made, will keep for a year or more. The product from each 100 lbs. of milk is about 12 lbs. of cured cheese, and is sold at a price ranging from $12\frac{1}{2}$ to 18 c. per lb."

"Neufchatel Cheese.

"Heat the milk to a temperature of 86°, and it is advisable to begin the process of manufacturing as soon as the milk comes from the cow, in which case its normal temperature will be sufficient. Add rennet so as to coagulate in 24 hours; the curd is then suspended in bandage cloth and allowed to drain for 12 hours. In regular factories frames are arranged on which to suspend bandage for this purpose. After draining, the corners of the cloth are drawn together, encasing the curd in a bag, which is subjected to a gentle pressure by placing under a board with weights for 12 hours, being occasionally removed and subjected to heavier pressure under lever, so as to remove all the whey.

"After pressing, the curd is removed and placed on a dry cloth, spread on a table, and worked with the hands until a uniform paste is produced. If too moist, the cloth on the table is changed two or three times, and if too dry, fresh curd is worked in. Experience teaches the proper consistency, and at this stage of the process cream may be worked in to enrich the cheese, if desired; here also it is demonstrated, whether the manipulation has been correct; the paste will not be sufficiently firm if the coagulation has been incomplete and pressed too little, and on the other hand, if pressed too hard and coagulated too quickly, it will be mealy and too dry.

"A tin cup, $2\frac{1}{2}$ to 3 inches long by $2\frac{1}{3}$ inches in diameter, open at both ends, is used to mould the curd into shape; into this the curd is pressed by hand, the surplus being cut from each end with a wooden knife. After removing from the mould, the cheese is salted by holding in the left hand, sprinkling on fine dry salt with the right, in proportion 1 lb. to 100 lbs. of cheese, or by rolling over once in a thin layer of salt sprinkled on the table. The cheese is then allowed to stand for one or two hours for the salt to dissolve, when it is wrapped in paper and tin foil, and packed in boxes ready for market. About 22 to 23 lbs. of Neufchatel cheese are made from each 100 lbs. of milk, the price varying from 5 to 10 c. per lb., according to quality."

Cost of a cheese factory.

The cost of a cheese factory for the handling of the milk of from 250 to 500 cows is about 360*l.* The necessary apparatus for such a factory is:—

NEW YORK.

1 5-H.P. return flue portable boiler.
1 600-gallon steam heating cheese vat. (Add 1 additiona 600-gallon vat for each 200 cows.)
1 Frazer patent gang press.
10 Frazer patent hoops, 14½ by 10. (Add 1 additional press with 10 hoops for each 200 cows.)
1 hanging salt scale.
1 70-gallon weighing can, 3-in. gate.
1 set hoisting crane fixtures.
1 14-blade perpendicular curd knife.
1 6-inch wide horizontal curd knife.
1 milk conductor head, large.
1 flat-sided curd pail.
1 curd scoop.
1 1-gallon dipper.
1 siphon and strainer.
1 rubber mop.
1 thermometer.
1 set milk testing instruments, 4 pieces.
2 dozen test tubes.
1 milk book.
1 set 9 months dates.
1 box paste and brush.

Necessary Furnishings.

10 yards 48-inch heavy press cloth.
½-bale 14½ seamless bandage, 525 yards.
25 lbs. of annatoine.
1 10-gallon keg Hansen's Danish rennet extract.
25 lbs. "B. and W." pure potash.
50 lbs. sal soda.
1 package scale boards.

Cost of combined cheese and butter factory.

The cost of a combined butter and cheese factory, with ice and cold storage warehouse, for from 300 to 600 cows, is about 800*l*. The necessary apparatus for such a factory is:—

2 15-inch Danish-Weston centrifugal machines, or 5 twin refrigerator creamers for ice or cold water, capacity 3,000 lbs. each.
2 600-gallon steam heating cheese vats.
1 2,500-lb. cream vats.
1 8-H.P. return flue horizontal boiler, with 6-H.P. stationary engine, governor, steam gauge, and all fittings complete, with inspirator.
2 Fraser patent gang cheese presses.
30 patent self-bandaging hoops, 13½ by 7.
1 300-gallon revolving box churn.
1 improved power butter worker.
1 hoisting crane, complete.
1 Rapp's automatic butter printer for ½-lb. and 1-lb. prints.
1 Fairbank's 7-beam 1,000-lb. factory scale, with wheels.
1 Fairbank's 240-lb. cheese scale.
1 hanging salt scale.
1 scale for weighing prints.
1 70-gallon receiving can, with 3-inch discharge gate
1 milk conductor head, large.
1 curd scoop, tin.
1 curd scoop, long handle, wood.
1 1-gallon dipper.
1 whey siphon, with gate and valve.
1 whey siphon strainer.
1 set milk testing instruments.
1 graduated glass annatto or rennet measure.
4 dozen 5 by 1¼ heavy test glasses.
½ dozen 10-inch white metal thermometers.
1 14-blade, 20-inch perpendicular curd knife.
1 8-inch wide 20-inch horizontal curd knife.
1 solid steel cheese trier

1 solid steel butter trier, 21-inch.
3 rubber floor scrubs.
3 vat scrub brushes.
2 large butter bowls.
2 large butter ladles.
2 hair sieves.
1 box marking paste and brush.
1 set changeable dates for 12 months.
1 brass name plate.
1 milk account book.
1 secretary's or treasurer's book.
1 power upright plunger pump, if necessary.
50 feet ¾-inch water hose.

Necessary Furnishings.

1 bale seamless bandage, 1,050 yards.
25 lbs. annattoine.
1 cask Hansen's Danish rennet extract, 42 gallons.
1 5-gallon can of Hansen's butter colour.
25 lbs. "B. and W." pure potash.
50 lbs. sal soda.
10 yards 48-inch heavy press cloth.
50 lbs. fly-proof cheese dressing.
200 yards butter cloth for wrapping prints.
5 sacks imported salt.
200 56-lb. ash butter tubs.
1 package scale boards.
Additional churns, gang presses, and hoops, and other apparatus may be added as becomes necessary.

Creameries. Butter factories or creameries are increasing rapidly in number in this State: the butter made in them is of a high grade, and is mostly sold for consumption in this and other cities at above export prices. The method of separating cream from milk by centrifugal force was introduced about ten years ago, and is superseding the setting system; in fact, is universally adopted in the larger "creameries." The separating machine is based upon the difference in the specific gravity of the fat and the rest of the milk; the fat, being the lighter, goes towards the centre, and the remainder, containing the caseine, albuminoids, and salts, and whatever dirt or foreign solid matter is present, is found nearest the walls of the cylinder, the dirt being next to the periphery. The cost of a butter factory or creamery for the handling of the milk of 500 cows is about 400*l*., of which about 170*l*. is the cost of the building complete. The necessary apparatus for such a creamery is:—

1 8-H.P. return flue horizontal boiler, with 6-H.P. stationary engine, governor steam gauge, and all fitting and connections complete, with inspirator.
2 15-inch Danish-Weston centrifugal machines.
1 hoisting crane, complete.
1 milk receiving vat.
1 2,500-lb. cream vat.
1 300-gallon revolving box churn.
1 improved power butter worker.
1 Rapp's automatic butter printer for ½-lb. and 1-lb. prints.
1 Fairbank's 7-beam 1,000-lb. factory scale, with wheels, or 1 600-lb. platform scale.
1 hanging salt scale.
1 scale for weighing prints.
1 70-gallon receiving can with 3-in. discharge gate.
1 milk conductor head, large.
1 1-gallon dipper.
3 rubber floor scrubs.

1 set milk testing instruments, comprising 2 graduated 1-pint jars, 1 graduated ½-pint jar, and a lactometer.
4 dozen 5 by 1¼ heavy test glasses.
1 graduated measuring glass.
½ dozen 10-inch nickel plate thermometers.
1 solid steel butter trier, 21-inch.
3 vat scrub brushes.
2 large butter bowls.
2 large butter ladles.
2 hair sieves.
1 box marking paste and brush.
1 power upright plunger pump, if necessary.
50 ft. ¾-inch rubber water hose.

Necessary Furnishings.

200 yds. butter cloth for wrapping prints.
5 sacks imported salt.
200 56-lb. ash butter tubs or Bradley butter boxes.
1 10-gallon can of Hansen's Danish butter colour.
Additional churns and other apparatus may be added as becomes necessary.

Milk is purchased of the farmers in some cases, but more frequently it is received from them under a co-operative system; in this case there is a charge of 3 to 3½ c. (1½d. to 1¾d.) packing and selling the butter when the creamery is not owned by the farmers who supply the milk: when the creamery is owned by a community of farmers the stock is generally held in the proportion of the number of cows each farmer has; a fixed price, say 3 c. per pound, is charged for making and selling the butter, and the profits are then divided according to the interest of each in the "creamery." When the butter is purchased of farmers by the proprietors of the creameries, the price is usually based on the highest price for dairy butter in New York as given in the leading commercial papers; for example, if the highest market price of butter is 25 c., deduct 3 c. for making and selling, which would give 22 c. for 26 or 27 pounds of milk, which are estimated to be required for the manufacture of a pound of butter, but this estimate is based upon butter made on a farm. With the use of the separating machine a pound of butter can be made from 22 to 23 pounds of milk from an ordinary herd of stock. The average return to the farmer in 1887 was about 90 c. per 100 pounds of milk. When the centrifugal system is used, the skim milk which is separated immediately is returned to the farmer at once, and then used for feeding to stock, the farmer paying for it when the milk is purchased 10 to 15 c. per 100 pounds. Under the co-operative system the skim milk is returned to the farmer free. At one of the condensing factories in Orange county the price paid during the year for milk from high-grade cows was 1 dol. (4s. 2d.) per 100 pounds for four months, 1 dol. 35 c. for four months, and 1 dol. 70 c. for the remaining four months.

The following is an extract from a report made by a large dairy farmer to the State Dairymen's Association:—

"Method of Butter-making.

"The first few years of my farming I spent in raising my dairy. I first bought a registered thoroughbred male and bred from the best cows in my vicinity.

"The past season I made an average of one pound of butter from 19·67 pounds of milk for the month of June, 17·43 pounds of milk in July, 17·56 in August, 17·80 in September, 18·43 in October, and 19·48 pounds for November.

Butter-making.

"My dairy now consists of 100 cows, high grade and thoroughbred Jerseys, aged from two to 10 years. The average weight of the herd is about 750 pounds. I try to have my cows come in milk in the fall and early winter. In summer the cows are pastured during the day and kept in the yard at night.

"In the early part of the season I give a feed of corn ensilage and bran or malt sprouts night and morning. About the 1st of July I commence feeding with green clover in place of ensilage, and continue that until about the 1st of August. The past season I fed hay for a couple of weeks in August. About the middle of August I commenced feeding with planted corn, well-eared without grain. The rations were two hills to each cow night and morning. I continued that feed until I commenced feeding from the silo.

"My cows have been kept in yard and stable since the 1st of October, and their daily rations are about 40 pounds each of corn ensilage, with about eight pounds of bran or malt sprouts, and two pounds of corn meal. In pleasant weather the cows are let out in the yard and watered from the well. In stormy or cold weather they are kept in and watered in the stable. They are interviewed once or twice daily with comb and brush. I bed with saw-dust, and use 12 to 15 tons of plaster in the stables during the winter. My cows are fed regularly, ensilage and grain at half past seven, morning and evening, and a grain ration after watering at noon. In summer we commence milking at six, night and morning; in winter at six in the morning and half-past five in the evening.

"I raise the cream by the Cooley process. The milk is set as soon after milking as possible, and iced thoroughly. The milk remains in the creamer about 22 hours after skimming. The cream is warmed to a temperature of about 62° in summer and 65° in winter. The cream skimmed one day is ripened so as to churn the next; during the process of ripening, the cream is stirred often and thoroughly, as it is when the second skimming is added. I aim to keep the temperature uniform until the cream is ripe for the churn.

"In summer I churn at a temperature of 62° to 64°, and in winter 64° to 67°. My experience is that cream raised in cold submerged setting has to be churned at a higher temperature than when raised in the open pans. I use the revolving box churn, and the average time of churning for the year is about 40 minutes. As soon as the butter begins to separate in granules, the churn is stopped and the buttermilk is drawn off. I rinse the butter with a weak brine until the water comes off clear. The butter then stands a few minutes to drain, when it is taken from the churn, weighed, salted, and put into shape for market.

"The real question for the dairyman is that of profits. I find that on my farm if I depend upon hay for the principal ration the balance is against me. I cannot raise to exceed an average of one ton per acre, and it takes at least the product of two acres to keep the cow through seven winter months. It costs 37 dols. to keep a milch cow seven months. The past season my ensilage, to take the place of hay, has cost me 4 dols. 70 c., including the interest on land; the cost of grain, 21 dols., added to that makes the cost of wintering the cow seven months, 25 dols. 70 c.

"A dairy of fresh cows fed on the above rations should produce three-fourths of a pound of butter per day or 160 pounds for the winter, making the cost of butter with the hay aud grain 23·12 c., and with ensilage and grain 16·06 c., leaving a balance in favour of the ensilage system of 7·06 c., or a difference for the winter of 11 dols. 29½ c. per cow.

"If the dairyman can get a living under the old system, he can get a better one under the new."

The total product of butter in the State was estimated last year at 120,000,000 lbs.

Seeding of meadow and pasture lands.

The dairy farmers pay a great deal more attention than they formerly did to the seeding of their meadow and pasture lands. It was found scarcely possible to make a permanent meadow with timothy only, yet with the exception of clover it was almost the only seed used until, with the information acquired from the State and local agricultural societies, the farmers were able to select, intelligently, the seeds best adapted to the soil and climate. In many parts of the State there are meadows yielding from over three tons of hay to the acre, which, under timothy barley produced one ton, with little or no aftermath for autumn. Experiments have shown that the mixing with timothy a variety of good, hardy, succulent grasses that will ripen, or nearly so, with it, is the best method of insuring a good crop and a permanent meadow, while under timothy alone there is the change of upheaval by frost or destruction by heat to such an extent as to require an annual re-seeding. A well-known agriculturist writes in this connection:—
"Almost all distinguished writers on grasses in this country follow the lead of the English authorities, and recommend in their meadow mixtures of grasses and forage plants, some of which will not ripen, uniformly with our staple grass, timothy, while others will not stand the winters of central New York. In meadow mixtures, even our highest authorities recommend the famous ray grass, or what is known as English perennial rye grass ('lolium perenne') which is to British agriculture what timothy is to the American farmer, the staple grass. There are many bales of the seed of this grass imported every year into this country, and the seed is extensively and indiscriminately used in meadow mixtures all over the country. Until better instructed, I must say that English perennial rye grass is good for nothing in northern and central New York. Almost all writers on the grasses in this country conclude their essays or books with a formula of meadow grasses for the whole Northern States, regardless of the differences of climate. Some writers advocate a score or more of grasses to grow with timothy, conspicuous among which are the two large, valuable, and very early varieties, the orchard grass ('dactylis glomerata') and the meadow-oat grass, which are altogether too early to grow with timothy; but when these two, the oat grass and the orchard grass, constitute a meadow in about equal proportions, no combination of grasses can be more profitable to the dairy farmer, either for early hay, and afterwards for soiling or late pasturing. I am reluctantly led to the conclusion that there are but few grasses adapted to our meadows. I mean by this that there are but few that will stand the climate and ripen evenly together, making a good uniform sward with our timothy. I name such as my own observation and actual test, on bleak uplands and in intervals, have shown to be by their time of ripening, hardiness, structure, and average altitude adapted to our soils and to grow with timothy and clover: rough stalk, foul meadow, yellow oat, Italian rye, tall fescue, meadow fescue, and red top. If the meadow is moist then fescue or bromus grass and alsike may be introduced. The grasses above-named are most of them good, not only for meadow but for pasture after one or two mowings.

"I will now name separate mixtures for meadow and also for pasture, such as I know have been productive of the very best results. For an average meadow, per acre: a mixture consisting of 12 lbs. of timothy, 5 lbs. of Italian rye grass, 5 lbs. of meadow fescue or tall fescue, 4 lbs. red top, 3 lbs. rough stalked meadow grass, 6 lbs. medium clover; as before stated, if the meadow is moist, bromus or alsike may be introduced, the red top increased and the fescue and clover lessened. For a permanent pasture, per acre: 5 lbs. Kentucky blue grass, 5 lbs. meadow oat grass, 5 lbs. orchard grass, 5 lbs. meadow fescue, 5 lbs. red top, 2 lbs. sweet vernal, 2 lbs. Pacy's dwarf rye grass, and, if not natural to the land, 2 lbs. white clover."

Number of farms in State, and number cultivated by owners.

Rental of farms, cash and by shares.

The Commissioner of Agriculture reports that there are in this State 241,058 farms, of which 201,186 are cultivated by the owners; that, for the farms cultivated by tenants, 18,124 dol., is paid as a cash rental, and 21,748 dol., as a share rental. The Commissioner states that in the Eastern States the preferable mode is to take the farm as the "halves," the tenant having house-rent, firewood from the woodland, keeping the fences in condition, and dividing equally such products of the farm as are not used on it. It is usually required that hay and coarse fodder shall be fed upon the farm, as the barn-yard manure is the only resource for maintaining fertility. In some cases the owner pays for half the seed, and the tenant pays half the taxes, though required to work out the road tax. In New York one-half is usually obtained by tenants, or one-third with a minimum of provision or responsibility beyond mere labour. In some instances the taxes or the threshing bill may be divided between the farmer and the tenant, or interest may be charged for use of stock and tools. The size of the farms is given in the following Table:—

Size of farms.

	Number.
Under 3 acres	370
3 to 10 acres	14,543
10 to 20 "	17,229
20 to 50 "	40,386
50 to 100 "	70,661
100 to 500 "	96,273
500 to 1,000 "	1,315
Over 1,000 "	281

The total area of land in farms is 23,780,754 acres, of which 17,717,862 are improved.

Wages for agricultural labour.

The wages paid for agricultural labour by the year are, in this State, 24 dols. 13 c. per month without board, and 16 dols. 30 c. with board. The average daily wages in harvest time are 1 dol. 80 c. without board, 1 dol. 37 c. with board.

New Jersey.

The product of the cereals, &c., of New Jersey in 1886 and 1887 is given in the following table:—

		1886.			1887.		
		No. of Acres in each Crop.	Quantities Produced.	Average Yield per Acre.	No. of Acres in each Crop.	Quantities Produced.	Average yield per Acre.
Wheat	Bushels	144,528	2,260,000	15·6	143,083	1,459,000	...
Indian corn	"	346,866	9,418,000	27·1	346,785	10,406,000	...
Rye	"	103,518	1,232,000	11·9	No statistics available.		
Oats	"	137,455	3,734,000	27·2	138,830	3,221,000	...
Buckwheat	"	35,376	453,000	12·8	} No statistics available.		
Potatoes	"	40,098	3,208,000	80·0			
Hay	Tons	503,664	517,943	1·0			

NEW YORK.

There are 2,096,297 acres of improved land, in 34,307 farms. There are 178,114 milch cows in the State, and the product of the dairy averages about 15,500,000 gallons of milk, 10,000,000 lbs. of butter, and 575,000 lbs. of cheese. There are few creameries or cheese factories in the State. Of the 34,307 farms, 25,869 are cultivated by the owners, and the remainder are let in about equal proportions for a cash rental and on shares. One-half the product is the rule in share contracts, with variable conditions, and labour receives one-fourth to one-third. The item of fertilisers is important, and the quantity required affects the terms of the contract. The tenant is usually required to furnish implements, teams, and seed. In some cases the tenant is allowed two-thirds of the grain and one-half of the hay. The average size of the farms is 85 acres.

Quantity of land improved. Number of milch cows. Product of dairy. Number of farms cultivated by owners.

In 1880 an Act was passed founding an agricultural experiment station, defining its duties to be the promotion of scientific and practical agriculture, as well as the development of unimproved lands. The result has been the equipment of a laboratory, in which analyses of fertilisers, fodders, and feeds could be made, and data thereby secured for properly answering questions relative to the quality and use of those products. The State laws regulating the sale of fertilisers recognise only the question of delivering a product of guaranteed quality, and provide penalties for failure to keep such guarantees. The station has published and circulated widely the guaranteed analyses of every brand of complete fertilisers which it has been able to secure in the State. It has also published its own analyses of these brands side by side with the manufacturers' guarantees, giving consumers every opportunity to see for themselves which dealers make good their promises. In 1880, 24 samples only of complete fertilisers were secured, 47 in 1882, 76 in 1884, and 148 in 1886.

CONNECTICUT.

The product of the cereals, &c., of Connecticut in 1886 and 1887 is given in the following table:—

		1886.			1887.		
		No. of Acres in each Crop.	Quantities Produced.	Average Yield per Acre.	No. of Acres in each Crop.	Quantities Produced.	Average Yield per Acre.
Wheat	Bushels	2,193	36,000	16·4	2,171	37,000	17·0
Indian corn	,,	58,140	1,992,000	34·3	58,140	1,977,000	34·0
Barley	,,	632	14,000	22·2	No statistics available.		
Oats	,,	39,027	1,123,000	28·8	30,417	7,088,000	23·3
Rye	,,	20,981	390,000	13·0			
Buckwheat	,,	10,865	147,000	13·5			
Tobacco	Lbs.	7,292	11,667,000	1600·0	No statistics available.		
Potatoes	Bushels	31,541	2,208,000	70·0			
Hay	Tons	574,650	540,400	·94			

The first agricultural experiment station in the United States was established 12 years ago in Connecticut, and it has proved a very useful institution. The State cannot be described as a good agricultural one; the land is much broken up and soil generally poor. Indian corn and oats are the only cereals which can be grown to advantage, and these only in favoured localities. The planting of

Experiment station. Quality of land.

Tobacco growing.

Fruit and garden crops.

Milch cows.

Number of acres of improved land, and number of farms.

Land cultivated on share system.

tobacco is increasing yearly, and the quality of some of it is excellent. The value of the crop in 1886 was 1,633,380 dols. (336,480*l.*). Fruit and garden crops have taken the place in many localities of grain growing, and the products of both orchards and gardens have done a great deal to increase the value of agricultural interests. There are in the State 127,153 milch cows. The State has 1,642,188 acres of improved land, in 30,598 farms, of which 27,472 are cultivated by the owners. The land cultivated by tenants is generally on the share system. In Connecticut the tenant, getting half the product, sometimes pays a share of the taxes and of the fertilisers if any are used beyond the resources of the farm. Where only labour is furnished, the farm being fully equipped by the owner, and work animals fed, the labourer gets one-third, or, if the land is in a high state of cultivation, one-fourth. The average size of the farms is 80 acres.

The law is very strict in the State in regard to the sale of fertilisers; every seller of a commercial fertiliser of a retail value of 10 dols., or over, per ton must affix conspicuously to every package thereof a plainly printed statement, clearly and truly certifying the number of net pounds of fertiliser in the package, the name, brand, or trade mark under which the fertiliser is sold, the name and address of the manufacturer, the place of manufacture, and the chemical composition of the fertiliser, expressed in the terms and manner approved and currently employed by the State Agricultural Experiment Station. If any such fertiliser be sold in bulk, such printed statement shall accompany every lot and parcel sold. The fine for violating the law is 100 dols. for the first offence, and 200 dols. for each subsequent violation.

Delaware.

The product of the cereals, &c., in Delaware in 1886 and 1887 is given in the following table:—

		1886.			1887.		
		No. of Acres in each Crop.	Quantities Produced.	Average Yield per Acre.	No. of Acres in each Crop.	Quantities Produced.	Average Yield per Acre.
Wheat	Bushels	94,790	1,177,000	12·4	94,790	929,000	9·9
Indian corn	,,	216,595	3,590,000	16·6	216,595	4,332,000	20·0
Oats	,,	21,409	492,000	23·0	21,623	458,000	21·2
Rye	,,	857	6,000	7·0			
Buckwheat	,,	437	6,000	13·7	No statistics available.		
Potatoes	,,	4,182	272,000	65·0			
Hay	Tons	50,621	50,025	·99			

Number of acres improved land.

Products of State.

Rented farms.

Average size of farms.

Delaware has 746,958 acres improved land, in 8,749 farms. The principal products of the State are Indian corn and wheat. There are few farms in which dairying is carried on to any extent. There are more farms cultivated by tenants than in any other Northern State. The tenant gets from one-half to one-quarter of the produce, according to his limitation of responsibility and personal expense beyond labour. The average size of farms is 125 acres.

Rhode Island.

The product of the cereals, &c., of Rhode Island in 1886 and 1887 is given in the following table:—

		1886.			1887.		
		No. of Acres in each Crop.	Quantities Produced.	Average Yield per Acre.	No. of Acres in each Crop.	Quantities Produced.	Average Yield per Acre.
Indian corn	Bushels	12,946	408,000	31·5	12,946	414,000	31·9
Oats	,,	6,353	184,000	29·0	6,353	165,000	25·9
Rye	,,	1,372	19,000	13·8			
Barley	,,	824	21,000	25·5			
Buckwheat	,,	127	2,000	15·7	No statistics available.		
Potatoes	,,	6,493	649,000	100·0			
Hay	Tons	95,778	78,016	·81			

Rhode Island has only 298,486 acres improved land in 6,216 farms. There are 4,980 farms cultivated by owners. Tenants generally pay a cash rental.

Number of acres improved land, &c.

LONDON:
Printed for Her Majesty's Stationery Office,
By HARRISON AND SONS,
Printers in Ordinary to Her Majesty.
(1125   10 | 88—H & S   538)

WITHDRAWN